W9-CAS-498

Psychology
Explorations in Behavior and Experience

SARNOFF A. MEDNICK
NEW SCHOOL FOR SOCIAL RESEARCH

JERRY HIGGINS
UNIVERSITY OF CALIFORNIA, SANTA BARBARA

JACK KIRSCHENBAUM
FULLERTON COLLEGE

JOHN WILEY & SONS, INC.
NEW YORK LONDON SYDNEY TORONTO

Dedicated to
Birgitte, Beth, and Adrienne

Library of Congress Cataloging in Publication Data:

Mednick, Sarnoff A
Psychology: explorations in behavior and experience.

Bibliography: p.
Includes index.
1. Psychology. I. Higgins, Jerry, 1937-   joint
author. II. Kirschenbaum, Jack, 1933-
III. Title. [DNLM: 1. Behavior. 2. Psychology.
BF121 M491p]
BF121.M43   150   74-22239
ISBN 0-471-59017-7

Printed in the United States of America

10 9 8 7 6 5 4 3

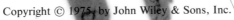

Preface

What does psychology mean for me, for society, and for humanity? What are the problems psychologists are interested in? How do they go about solving them? These are questions that frequently prompt people to take an introductory course, and these are the questions to which this book is addressed. We want to introduce the reader to the kinds of problems psychologists are struggling with, to the strategies and techniques they have developed to cope with these problems, and to the implications that their efforts have for every individual in daily life and for the survival and well-being of society.

This book is not a compendium, an exhaustive review of all psychology. Rather, it is a selective introduction to exciting and representative topics — topics that we feel have significance for life in a changing society. Psychology, like all science, is an adventure, an exploration of the unknown, an excursion to the frontiers of knowledge. Like other scientists, psychologists are constantly making discoveries that have dramatic impact on the general conception of human "nature" and human potential. In recent years, psychologists have made notable advances in studying how behavior can be controlled by the implantation of electrodes in the brain, by the manipulation of rewards and punishments, and by drugs; how bodily functions can be influenced by meditation and feedback; and how opinions and attitudes can be shaped by persuasive communication and the mass media. Students today want to learn about hypnotism, dreaming, and abnormal behavior. They are interested in the genetic transmission of intelligence, the fostering of creativity, and the reduction of international tension. We intend not only to satisfy their curiosity in these and other areas, but also to provide a clear idea of how psychologists undertake their investigations. With this background the student can better understand and evaluate psychological research as it relates to the needs of the individual and of society. We want to do more than expose the reader to psychology; we want to help the reader gain a grasp of it, a real sense of what it's all about.

In order to achieve these objectives, we have organized the book in a distinctive way and we have incorporated a variety of instructional aids. All the major topics of modern psychology are introduced. But as noted, rather than cover each with encyclopedic breadth and brevity, we concentrate on a number of pivotal, representative, high-interest aspects that we discuss in depth. In our presentation we aim to give the student an insight into the practice of psychological research, analysis, and explanation without unnecessary involvement with technical jargon. The text is divided into chapters (plus a chapter-length appendix). Each chapter is broken into several major subsections, each of which constitutes a "chunk" of material that can be mastered in a short study session. Every new technical term is placed in bold face type the first time it is presented and it is immediately discussed and explained in context. (The index also contains a glossary of major terms.) Within each chapter there are short discussions called "Focuses"; these provide either a technical, intensive exploration of the methods and issues covered in the main text, an interesting side light, or enrichment of the main topics discussed. Each chapter has a summary to facilitate study and review. The book has been written with an eye on high human interest and readability (and we have endeavored in our writing to find our way around the inherent sex bias of our language and culture). To stimulate interest and motivate the reader, we begin chapters and subsections with a vivid account of a major research study, a case history, or an activity involving the reader. The first chapter, in particular, has been designed to engage the reader's interest while simultaneously providing an overview of the scope of psychology.

We would like to acknowledge the help and encouragement of several people: June Reinisch of Teachers College, Columbia University, for providing material on the biological determinants of sex identity; Kenneth Hunter for assistance in researching and drafting materials; L. Joseph Stone and Joseph Church for material on the birth process adapted from *Childhood and Adolescence,* 3rd ed. (New York: Random House, 1972); Nancy Mann for diligent typing of successive drafts of the manuscript. We are deeply indebted to the patience, persistence, and perceptiveness—and sheer hard work—of Jack Burton, our sponsoring editor, and Ron Nelson, our managing editor.

We would also like to acknowledge the assistance and advice of those who reviewed the manuscript, in whole or in part: Gerald C. Davison, State University of New York, Stony Brook; David Elkind, University of Rochester; Elliott T. Entin, Ohio University; Barry Gillen, Old Dominion University; I. I. Gottesman, University of Minnesota; Alan E. Gross, University of Missouri, St. Louis; Edward E. Jones, Duke University; Daniel Katz, University of Michigan; William Kessen, Yale University; Kenneth MacCorquodale, University of Minnesota; Brendan Maher, Harvard University; George Mandler, University of California, San Diego; Robert M. Pasen, William Rainey Harper College; Lawrence A. Pervin, Rutgers University; James H. Roll, William Rainey Harper College; H. Richard Schiffman, Rutgers University; William C. Stebbins, University of Michigan; Brian Sutton-Smith, Teachers College, Columbia University; Benton J. Underwood, Northwestern University.

Contents

Section Three
Sensing, Conscious Being 135

Chapter Five
Sensation, Perception, and Consciousness 136

Section Five
Thinking, Knowing Being 259

**Section
Seven
Social
Being 405**

Chapter One
Panorama
of
Psychology

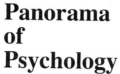

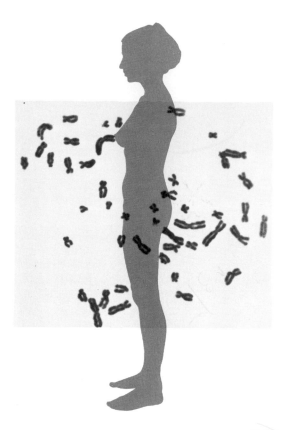

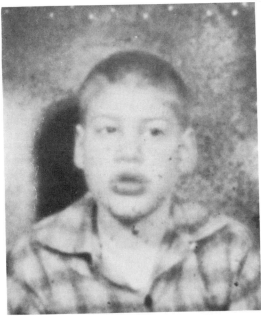

A. PROBLEMS, SITUATIONS, AND CASE STUDIES

BIOLOGICAL BEING

The Case of Julie. When Julie was 18 she visited her physician because she had never menstruated. She was engaged to be married and she wanted to be sure she could bear children. She was five feet, six inches tall, had well-developed breasts and hips, and was conventionally feminine in dress and behavior. Yet as her physician discovered, Julie had "male" chromosomes. But because of a genetic defect, as a fetus she could not develop as a male. Her external sex organs were female, but her internal female organs were incomplete, and there were partially developed male organs.

The Case of Steven. In size, at least, Steven looked very much like many other early adolescent boys. His intelligence, however, was at the level of a six-year-old; his speech was hard to understand and often incoherent; and he had difficulty relating to other children in the institutional ward where he lived. Steven's problem was traced to a genetic defect called phenylketonuria, or simply P.K.U. Had Steven's problem been diagnosed during infancy and had he received proper treatment, he could have developed normally.

Julie's and Steven's behavior and experience were shaped by a complex interaction of nature and nurture. **Nature** *refers to the hereditary, or genetic, qualities passed on by parents.* **Nurture** *refers to the effects of learning and of the social and physical opportunities provided by environments.* Each of these cases raises many provocative questions about the relationship between nature and nurture.

Julie's condition brings up these questions: How much of our identity and behavior as men and women is determined by biology and how much is shaped by society? What can go wrong in development to produce a female when the chromosomes would seem to indicate a male? Are the mannerisms and behaviors associated with masculinity and femininity innate or learned?

Steven's plight leads to the following sorts of questions. What are the genetic mechanisms that transmit behavioral characteristics from one generation to another? How can we overcome or prevent behav-

ioral defects that are traced to genetic abnormalities?

In Chapter Two, *Nature and Nurture,* we will look into the basis of genetic inheritance and the interplay of nature and nurture that shapes the development of behavior, including sex identity.

Electrical Brain Implants. Armed only with a small radio transmitter, Yale University researcher José M. R. Delgado stood in a bullring before a charging bull.

Just before the enraged bull reached him, he transmitted a pulse to a receiver strapped to the bull's back; the receiver sent a small electrical current surging into the bull's brain through a thin wire electrode. The bull stopped in its tracks. Delgado and other researchers have found that electrical stimulation of various parts of the brain in animals and humans can produce pleasure and pain, control the movements of limbs, elicit or turn off violent rage, and reduce the pain suffered by a terminal cancer patient.

Max: A Case of Epilepsy. Max, a 48-year-old war veteran, suffered from epilepsy. His periodic seizures were quite violent. They began with a cry and a gasp as he fell unconscious to the floor. His body became stiff as a board for a few moments, then he twitched and flailed his limbs wildly for a few seconds. His breathing became labored and gasping, and his face turned blue from lack of oxygen. Although drugs help most epileptics to control their seizures and live almost normal lives, they didn't help Max at all. An electroencephalogram (EEG), which plots the electrical activity of the brain, enabled his medical advisor to identify the focus of the epilepsy on one side of his brain. In a daring surgical procedure, the nerves connecting the left and right sides of his brain were cut to isolate the focus of the epilepsy. The surgery worked and Max was relieved of his epileptic attacks. Subsequent psychological study, however, revealed some unusual side effects. These indicated that each hemisphere, or side, of the brain has its own unique functions and states of consciousness.

How much of our behavior, thoughts, and feelings are determined by the design of our nervous system? What effects do various drugs have on brain functions and be-

havior? How do the functions and malfunctions of the nervous system affect behavior and experience? How do our various life experiences, in turn, alter our nervous systems? How much of our behavior can be controlled by manipulation of the brain by electrode implants, drugs, and surgery? These questions and others will be explored in Chapter Three, *Brain and Behavior*.

ENERGIZED BEING

Fat Rats and Obese People.   When a section of a rat's brain located in a region called the hypothalamus is destroyed, the animal overeats and rapidly gains weight. Eventually the rat becomes a big, furry ball of fat. The fat rat will consume enormous quantities of sweet food. If a small amount of bitter quinine is placed in the food for the next meal, however, the rat refuses to eat. A normal lean rat under the same feeding conditions will eat the same amount of sweet and bitter food at each meal.

In a research study, when overweight humans were given tasty ice cream to eat, they stuffed themselves. Later, when these obese people were given ice cream that had been spiked with a little bitter quinine, they refused to eat it. Lean people under the same conditions ate the same amount of ice cream for each meal.

A Test of Motivation.

EXPERIMENTER: Make yourself comfortable. All right, now take a look at this picture. I want you to make up a story about the picture. Tell me what is happening, what led up to the event, and what will happen.

SUBJECT: O.K. This looks like a picture of a guy who is hard at work. He wants to please the boss and show him that he can do the work. He is quite intelligent and wants to make something of himself. He will be successful. He is probably a college student and is working part time to earn his room and board.

When people are asked to tell stories to pictures such as the one in the photograph, they reveal something about their motiva-

tion. These stories can even be reliably scored to assess certain aspects of motivation, such as the need to achieve.

The study of motivation is concerned with such questions as these: What are the sources of the energy and stimuli that impel various behaviors? What factors determine when a behavior like eating will start and stop? What determines the direction and goals of behavior? To what degree are behaviors determined by the biological conditions of an organism (such as hunger, thirst, sex, and pain) and to what degree by social and environmental conditions (such as the behavior of others and child-rearing practices)? What constitutes emotional experiences such as joy and anger? How can a person's motivation be measured? How can the motivation of a society as a whole be assessed, and how does this motivation relate to the society's economic growth, political climate, and social change? We will explore the answers to questions such as these in Chapter Four, *Motivation and Emotion.*

SENSING, CONSCIOUS BEING

When the Blind Are Given Sight. Sam, age 52, had been blind since infancy. Now, as a result of a new surgical procedure, he would be able to see. After the operation the surgeon darkened the room and slowly removed the bandages from his eyes. What would Sam see? Would he see color, shapes? Would he recognize objects by sight that he had been touching for years?

Can You Feel a Bee Wing on Your Cheek? Could you smell one drop of perfume diffused in a three-room apartment? Would you feel the wing of a bee on your cheek if it fell from a two-and-one-half-inch height? Could you see a candle flame 30 miles away on a clear, dark night? Can you accurately

name the cards before they are dealt? Can you read the thoughts another thinks?

Babies at the Cliff Edge. A mother sits at the edge of a large table covered with glass and tries to encourage her six-month-old baby at the other end of the table to cross over to her. The baby looks at the mother, then at the table top. The half of the table on the mother's side looks as if it drops off to the floor like a cliff. However, it is covered with a strong glass plate and is quite safe. Will the baby cross the cliff?

What You Value Determines What You See. A group of students were given a set of questions that enabled them to express their values in six areas: religious, social, economic, aesthetic, political, and theoretical. The students were then visually presented words related to each value for very brief intervals. As each word was flashed, the students had to discover or guess what the word was. The students more quickly and accurately recognized the words that related to their values than those that did not. For example, students with religious values were more likely to recognize words like "priest" and "minister" than words like "bonds," "price," or "cost."

How much of what we see is based on learning and experience? What are the limits of the sensitivity of our senses? Is the perception of depth and perspective inborn? How much of what we see is influenced by what we believe or want to see? How can a person be objective if motives and beliefs influence what is perceived? To what degree can early deprivation of sensory stimulation (as in blindness) be overcome by later training? Can extrasensory perception be studied scientifically? In Chapter Five, *Sensation, Perception, and Consciousness,* we will take up these issues; we will describe how physical stimuli are received, encoded, organized, and given meaning by our sense organs and brain. We will also examine how drugs, hypnosis, meditation, motivation, and learning affect various states of consciousness such as paying attention, seeing, sleeping, dreaming, and thinking.

LEARNING, REMEMBERING BEING

Learning How To Starve.   Mary, age 37, weight 47 pounds, height five feet, four inches, was admitted to the hospital because she was dying of starvation. When she married at age 18, she weighed 120 pounds. Her physician warned her that she was sexually undeveloped and that marriage might or might not have a beneficial effect on her. Adjusting to marriage was very difficult for her. She was faced with a crowded apartment with no facilities for cooking, sexual difficulties, and homesickness. After a few months of marriage she

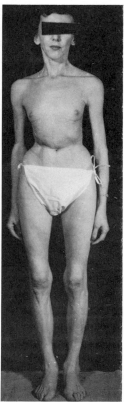

lost interest in eating and began to lose weight rapidly. She returned home and was cared for by her parents. Despite appetizing food and constant coaxing, she continued to lose weight over the years. Medical doctors feared that when her weight fell to 47 pounds she was at death's door, but they could find no physical reason for her refusal to eat. Her condition is called anorexia nervosa, which is Latin for "nervous non-eating."

The psychologists who planned treatment for Mary had an idea that her noneating behavior was learned and was now being maintained by very powerful social rewards. By paying attention to her noneating and by coaxing her to eat, her parents and friends were unknowingly rewarding and strengthening her noneating behavior. The psychologists reasoned that if she were rewarded only for eating and ignored for noneating, her behavior could be modified. Mary's psychologists were eventually able to teach her to eat and start a new life.

The Educated Heart.

PSYCHOLOGIST: Your medical advisor has sent you here because your blood pressure is danger-ously high. Just relax as you recline in the easy chair. I want you to watch these red, green, and yellow signals. They are like traffic signals, except these will indicate your heart rate. When you see a red signal, I want you to lower your heart rate. When you see a green light, I want you to raise your heart rate. When you have reached the desired rate, a yellow light will turn on. The meter on the right indicates the percentage of time your rate is at the desired level.

PATIENT: That's impossible. I can't learn to lower my heart rate.

PSYCHOLOGIST: Relax and try.

Test-Cramming Blues.

STUDENT: I wonder why I did so poorly on your exam?

INSTRUCTOR: Did you study?

STUDENT: I sure did. I spent three solid hours the night before. When I put the book down, I felt I knew it all. I'm a good reader, I understand everything . . . but . . .

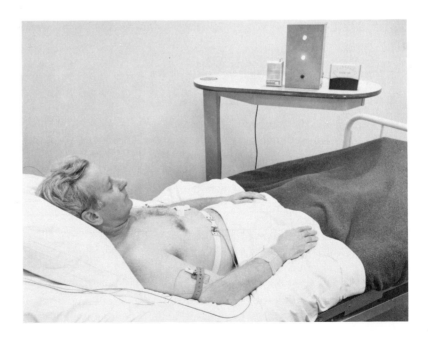

INSTRUCTOR: But . . .

STUDENT: Well, when I took the exam, I recognized the material, but I couldn't remember enough to get answers right. It's a problem I have with most tests. Is there something wrong with my memory? I swear to you I knew it the night before.

Each of these situations poses a number of questions that will be examined in Chapter Six, *Learning Principles,* and in Chapter Seven, *Verbal Learning, Memory, and Forgetting.* How flexible is human behavior? Can behavior be shaped to any form by those who would control rewards and punishments? What are the biological and hereditary limits, if any, to what one person can make of another through learning? Is it possible that parents who are ignorant of the learning principles they apply each day can inadvertently cripple a child's emotional and intellectual growth? To what degree can we attribute human "evils" to faulty learning? Can a person develop control over blood pressure and other internal body functions? Can a person really learn to control his or her own brain waves? What happens in the brain when memory is stored? Why do people forget? Can a person's memory power be increased? Do some study methods produce more lasting retention than others?

THINKING, KNOWING BEING

Intelligence, Creativity, and Problem-Solving. Attempt to answer each of these questions and problems:

1. What would be the results if everyone suddenly lost the sense of balance and was unable to stand in an upright position for more than a few moments?
2. How many uses can you think of for a brick?
3. How many English words of four or more letters (excluding proper names or places) can you form from the word *generation?*
4. In what way are the following word pairs alike?
    dog and cat
    saw and hammer
    truth and wisdom
5. Define the following words:
    sluice
    border

slander
sterile

6. Answer the following questions:
   Why should people wear seatbelts?
   Why is it necessary for every citizen to pay a fair share of taxes?
7. Draw four continuous lines, without lifting the pencil from the page, that will connect all nine dots.

8. You will need six matchsticks (or toothpicks, if they are more convenient). Arrange the six matchsticks in such a way that they form four triangles, all the sides of which are the same length as that of the sticks.

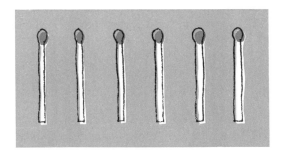

The first three items are similar to the kinds of questions and tasks psychologists have used to assess creativity. Items four to six are similar to those from an intelligence test. The last two items are used to study problem-solving strategies. You will have an opportunity to learn the answers to these questions in Chapter Eight, *Intelligence,*

and in Chapter Nine, *Creativity, Problem-Solving, and Language.* In these chapters we will discuss how intelligence tests are constructed and interpreted, used and abused. We will take a look at theories and tests of creativity and explore the factors that influence human creative behavior and problem-solving activities.

The Case of Mark. Mark was a six-year-old black child who lived in the crowded, poverty-stricken center of a large city. Despite his participation in a special federally funded Head Start educational program, Mark's intelligence test score was no better than that of his classmates who had not participated in the program. Even after a year of school, the average intelligence

rating of Mark and his classmates would be far below that of the white children from middle-class communities across town.

Mark's situation goes to the heart of the complex, stormy issues involving race, intelligence, and social conditions. How much of our intelligence is inborn? Are the differences in intelligence test scores among races due to genetic or environmental factors? To what degree do genetic and environmental factors place limits on the developmental potential of a human being? These questions will also be explored in Chapter Eight.

Talking to the Apes. Lucy is eight years old. She was adopted by a young couple when she was just two days old. Since Lucy can't speak, her foster parents taught her the American Sign Language (ASL). ASL is a system of communication taught to deaf people. It consists of a set of hand gestures that correspond to individual words. For example, the word "drink" is indicated by making a fist with an extended thumb touching the mouth. Lucy now has a vocabulary of over 80 words and in sign language she can name things in her environment, tell you how she feels, and carry out simple conversations. Lucy is a chimpanzee. Several psychologists around the country who are studying apes and languages have taught chimps to "talk."

If asked, most people will tell you that the human being is the only creature that can talk. Recent findings that chimpanzees can be taught how to use sign language raise a number of questions about the nature and role of language in humans and animals; these questions will also receive attention in Chapter Nine.

INDIVIDUAL, ADAPTIVE BEING

Case 1: "Why Nylons, Autos, and Cancer."

Why nylons, autos, men city people more cancer—because more polluted meat and drinks not one single connection with cigs—never jitters from narcotics or disorganization of nervous system—"I-am-ity" Megalomania—why Napoleon had to conquer world—Hitler and Mussolini and Me Too so now that I have conquered all mystery diseases (asthma and rheumatism too/experiment any dementia case) I am going to conquer the Russians. . . . *(From Kisler, 1964.)*

Why would a person write a letter like this?

Case 2: "My Brain is Being Eaten Away."

DOCTOR: Good Morning, Mr. H., how are you today?

PATIENT: (Long pause—looks up and then head drops back down and stares at floor.)

DOCTOR: I said good morning, Mr. H. Wouldn't you like to tell me how you feel today?

PATIENT: (Pause—looks up again) . . . I feel . . . terrible . . . simply terrible.

DOCTOR: What seems to be your trouble?

PATIENT: . . . There's just no way out of it . . . nothing but blind alleys . . . I have no appetite . . . nothing matters any more . . . it's hopeless . . . everything is hopeless.

DOCTOR: Can you tell me how your trouble started?

PATIENT: I don't know . . . it seems like I have a lead weight in my stomach . . . I feel different . . . I am not like other people . . . my health is ruined . . . I wish I were dead.

DOCTOR: Your health is ruined?

PATIENT: . . . Yes, my brain is being eaten away. *(From Coleman, 1964.)*

What is this institutionalized patient's problem? What are the causes of mental illness? Can mental illness be treated? Can mental illness be prevented?

Case 3: "My Legs Are Paralyzed."

Mildred A. was the daughter of a Rocky Mountain ranchman whose means and education were extremely limited. She was in her early adolescence when she lost the use of both her legs. At the time there was an alarming epidemic of paralysis among ranch animals and it was generally assumed that Mildred was a human victim of the epidemic. This explanation was welcomed by the girl's parents although they knew originally that it was not true. . . . Whenever attempts were made to get her up, she seemed frightened, her legs buckled under her, and she could not stand unsupported. The family physician correctly ascribed her reaction to fright, but he unwisely recommended that she stay in bed until her legs grew strong again. [Mildred didn't walk for ten years but remained bedridden despite all efforts of her family to get her to walk.] *(From Cameron, 1963.)*

What kind of emotional crisis led to Mildred's paralysis? How can emotional stress produce paralysis? What kinds of therapeutic methods are used to help people with such emotional and behavioral problems?

Case 4: Scared of Girls.

Wally wanted to go out on dates but couldn't get enough courage to ask a girl. While the thought of girls excited him, the thought of asking a girl for a date scared him. His well-meaning friends tried everything they could think of to get him to date, but it only made matters worse.

How can people resolve the frustration and conflicts that life presents? How can they overcome their own internal inhibitions and anxieties? Chapter Ten, *Personality,* and Chapter Eleven, *Psychopathology and Treatment,* will be directed to answering the questions that followed these case studies and others like them. In addition, these chapters will detail the ways psychologists assess and study the development of personality and how each of us adapts to the pressures and emotional stresses of daily life.

SOCIAL BEING

The Case of Freddy. Freddy is 15 but he looks and acts like a 12-year-old. He is shorter than his classmates and has not yet reached sexual maturity. His classmates make fun of him and he, in return, has become the class clown. Freddy is physiologically normal, but his condition raises questions. What is the course of normal development? What are the typical ages and stages for the appearance of various physical, social, and sexual characteristics? How wide a range of developmental deviation can be considered "normal"? What impact do pre- and postnatal infant care have on the development of a person?

Self-Esteem. Which child-rearing procedures and which parent and child characteristics in List B below are most likely to be associated with people having the degrees of self-esteem described in List A?

Monkey Mother Love. How important is a mother's love for the normal development of infants? To get some answers to this question, psychologist Harry Harlow of the University of Wisconsin isolated infant monkeys from their mothers after birth and placed them in a cage with wire "mothers." Some wire mothers were equipped with a bottle for feeding; some were covered with terry cloth for clinging. Can monkey infants survive without mothering? If they do survive, will they, as adults, be able to bear and care for their own infants? How will they get along with other monkeys? How

LIST A

HIGH SELF-ESTEEM	LOW SELF-ESTEEM
Realistic self-appraisal, positive self-attitude, self-reliant, self-assertive and confident, socially and academically optimistic, few personal problems or conflicts.	Negative self-appraisal, easily discouraged, socially withdrawn and unassertive, self-conscious, sensitive to criticism, preoccupied with personal problems and conflicts.

LIST B

1. "Good" behavior amply rewarded by parents.
2. Parents remain emotionally distant.
3. Parental punishment consists of isolation and withdrawal of affection.
4. Parents have high social status and income.
5. Parents have high self-esteem.
6. Parents are inconsistent in giving rewards and punishments.
7. Parents hold high hopes for child's achievement.
8. Physical attractiveness of child.
9. Parents are extremely permissive with regard to rules and standards of behavior.
10. Child is successful in achieving goals.

much of the findings from monkey studies can be applied to human beings?

Are You a Moral Philosopher? The following questions are similar to those used in a recent research survey. There are no "right" or "wrong" answers—simply *your* answers.
1. Under what conditions would stealing be morally justified? Specify reasons.
2. A young married student with a wife and two children held down two jobs as well as a full load of courses at college. When studying became difficult, he cheated on exams. Is the student's cheating justified? Why or why not?

Can a person's moral development be objectively measured? Are there moral stages of development through which all children must pass on the way to adulthood? How do differences in stages of moral development affect judgment and behavior?

The questions pertaining to these situations and to others will be explored in Chapter Twelve, *Development and Socialization.*

Changing Attitudes Toward Smoking. Subjects were first assessed for their attitudes toward smoking. Then they were asked to read a so-called "scientific digest prepared by members of the faculty of a prominent university" arguing that smoking causes lung cancer. In reality, two such "digests" had been prepared. One, given to half the subjects, was designed to elicit *mild fear* concerning smoking. For example:

Since cancer of the lungs is more likely to develop from moderate smoking than cancer of the lips, some experts have advised all smokers to take account of the symptoms . . . of lung cancer. In contrast to cancer of the lips, cancer of the lungs is described . . . as highly malignant . . . and extremely difficult to diagnose . . .

The second report, received by the other half of the subjects, was designed to evoke *strong fear.* For example:

Anywhere along the respiratory tract a single cancerous cell can start the growth of a malignant tumor that eventually may kill. Such a tumor can prove fatal either by causing suffocation or by sending deadly cells into other parts of the body . . .

Which statement, the mild or the strong, produced the greater change in attitude toward smoking?

Polling Racial Attitudes. Thomas Pettigrew of Harvard University conducted a poll of the white population of four small Northern and four small Southern towns. The poll contained such antiblack statements as: "Most Negroes would become officious, overbearing, and disagreeable if not kept in their place." "Laws which would force equal employment opportunities for both Negroes and whites would not be fair to white employers." "Seldom, if ever, is a Negro superior to most whites intellectually." How many Americans agree with such statements?

The two studies are samples of research reviewed in Chapter Thirteen, *Attitudes and Prejudice,* which is addressed to such questions as: What are the relationships between a person's beliefs and attitudes and behavior? How are attitudes formed? What effects do various emotional appeals, such as fear, have on changing attitudes? What role do personality factors play in determining prejudices? How do social factors, such as family background and region of residence, influence prejudices? What part does a person's social status, religious beliefs, and occupation play in determining prejudice? What psychological effects does prejudice have on its victims? How can prejudice be combated?

My Lai in the Laboratory. "Am I late?" the middle-aged gentleman asked as he hurried into the laboratory. "No, you're just in time," said the experimenter. "The person who will be your partner just arrived, too. In this experiment we will be studying the effects of punishment on learning. Draw lots now to determine which one will be the 'teacher' and which one the 'learner'." The man who drew the role of the learner was then led away and strapped to a chair out of sight behind a room partition. The experimenter then turned to the remaining man and said, "You will be the teacher and be able to talk to him later over the intercom. You will be going to teach him to memorize this list of words. Every time he makes a mistake, I want you to punish him with a shock. Look at the 30 switches on the control panel in front of you. Each switch delivers a shock to the learner from a mild 15 volts to the highest, 450 volts, which is a very dangerous, severe shock. Let me connect the electrodes to you and show you what 45 volts feels like. You can use it

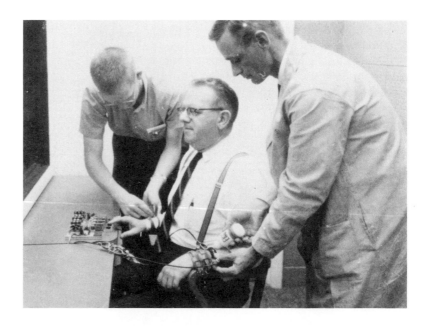

as a reference point in delivering shocks."

After the instructions were given and the experiment had progressed for a few minutes, the experimenter said, "Your student is not learning the list too well. You will have to shock him with more than the 60 volts you have been using." The subject then gradually raised the shock to 150 volts, at which time the learner was heard over the intercom to grunt and shout out to stop. Even at 150 volts the learner's performance didn't improve and the experimenter urged the subject playing the role of the teacher to increase the voltage. As the experiment progressed, the teacher was constantly urged to increase the shock level.

The above briefly paraphrases some of the experimental procedures used as part of a study on human conformity by Stanley Milgram, then at Yale University. If you had been a subject in the study, would you have increased the shock level as instructed? How high would you have gone? The subjects in the study represented all walks of life, from student to laborer to professional. What percentage of these people do you think obeyed the experimenter's commands and delivered the maximum of 450 volts to the learner? How much of our behavior in daily life is a response to the social pressures and expectancies of people around us? Under what conditions are people vulnerable to social pressures? Under what conditions will they resist?

Where Are the Good Samaritans? Catherine Genovese, walking home from her night job in the early morning hours, in a very middle-class, apartment-house section of New York City, was accosted by a man who inexplicably drew a knife and stabbed her. She screamed and he ran off. She screamed loudly and repeatedly, appealing to the windows of the surrounding apartment houses for help; the man returned again and again and continued to stab her for a horribly extended period of time. *New York Times* reporters interviewed 38 residents of this "nice" neighborhood who admitted to having seen some part of this macabre murder. No one went to her aid; no one even called the police. She died screaming to drawn curtains in an empty street. That day the whole nation asked itself why no one had intervened, why no one even telephoned for help.

Under what conditions will people intervene and help others who are facing a crisis? Is there safety in numbers? Are people in groups apathetic to the plight of victims? The questions raised in the last two situations will be discussed in Chapter Fourteen, *Conformity and Involvement.*

Group Structure. Compare the kind of interpersonal relationships and communication patterns that develop in a large lecture class with a small discussion group that sits in a circle. Which group would be more efficient?

Group Atmosphere. Think of the most domineering, dictatorial group leader you have known and compare the atmosphere of his or her group with the most democratic group leader you have known. Which group is more productive?

Group Decision. Blips appear on the radar screen. They may be enemy missiles approaching; they may be a flight of geese. A group of experts is hastily assembled to decide what to do. What do you think the group will decide to do? What would you do?

Chapter Fifteen, *Groups,* will be addressed to the questions posed in the three preceding paragraphs. In addition, we will examine group cohesiveness as well as the role and development of group leaders, followers, and deviants.

Destruction or Détente? You are president of a rich and powerful country called Enuk on planet Tera. Your country has the greatest industrial power and the largest armed force with the smallest population on the planet. Your planet has enjoyed an unstable peace for the past ten years. Your biggest competitor, Amra, is close behind your nation in industrial power and military forces and is rapidly catching up to you. Over the past five years Amra has outstripped your nation in world trade and influence. One day you receive a communiqué from Amra which states:

Amra demands Enuk's renunciation of nuclear weapon development or face military steps.

You call your five-man cabinet together to determine your new policy toward Amra. What will it be?

This situation is part of a game that was designed to study how human decision-making is affected by crisis. "Gaming" is one of many methods used to study the psychological factors underlying group relations.

In Chapter Sixteen, *International Conflict,* we will be posing such questions as the following: How much can we learn about political behavior and world conflict from subjects playing games in psychological laboratories? What psychological factors contribute to international tension? Is war inevitable? Does the doctrine of balance of power work? How may international tensions and hostilites be reduced and international trust and cooperation be increased?

The problems, situations, and research studies presented in this panorama are samples selected from this book to provide you with an overview of the topics that concern psychologists. Now let's look at the field of psychology as a whole and its relationships with other social and behavioral sciences.

B. THE SCIENTIFIC EXPLORATION OF BEHAVIOR AND EXPERIENCE

Psychology *is usually defined as the scientific study of behavior and experience.* The goals of psychology as a science are the description, explanation, prediction, and control of behavior and experience. A scientific study can be likened to an exploration, a search to discover and investigate the unknown. For the explorers of old the unknown consisted of lands beyond the seas. For the astronaut the unknown includes the moon and the planets. For the biologist the objects of exploration are the structure and function of living organisms. For the psychologist the regions of exploration span the biological, environmental, and social events that determine the behavior and experience of animals and human beings. Scientific study is distinctive for it follows a number of basic rules and methods to obtain its findings. The rules and methods of psychology will be discussed in detail in The Appendix, *The Scientific Basis of Psychology.*

Psychologists are concerned with exploring questions about many matters including thoughts, feelings, motivations, perception, learning, and normal and abnormal behavior. The situations, case studies, problems, and experiments you have just read about are samples of the wide variety of behaviors and experiences that interest psychologists. **Behavior** *refers to bodily movements and the internal and external responses people make to environmental events. These movements and responses include walking, talking, secreting from glands, answering test questions, fixing a car, and writing a poem—in short, the full range of human actions.* **Experience** *refers to those aspects of behavior that involve* *personal private feelings, thoughts, dreams, hopes, and fears, as well as the awareness of things we do and the things that happen to us, that we can keep to ourselves or share with others.*

PSYCHOLOGY AS A BIOLOGICAL, BEHAVIORAL, AND SOCIAL SCIENCE

When beginning students examine the panorama of topics, methods, findings, and issues that are covered by the field of psychology, they are often surprised at the variety of subjects pulled under one disciplinary roof. The students are not alone. Psychologists often have the same feelings when looking at the field. No one has yet been able to put it all together in a way that meets the approval of all our colleagues. There are many theories and points of view but none "big" enough to handle all that has been discovered. We take no comfort from the fact that many allied sciences have similar problems. In this text we have organized the study of behavior and experience so as to provide you with a broad framework from which to view psychology. This organization can be best explained as we try to answer the question, "What is humanity?"

What Is Humanity?

The answer to this question is as varied as the people who attempt to answer it. For example, an anthropologist, a sociologist, a psychologist, and someone on the street would each give a different answer. Whether we focus on the human being as an individual or on humanity as a whole, the question covers a vast domain of phenomena that is beyond the comprehension of any one person or scientific discipline. In fact, the domain of human behavior is so complex that it has necessarily been broken down

into several behavioral and social sciences.

Each science has also been further broken down into subfields and specialties. This results in a scientific division of labor. Each science and each scientist specializes in a relatively narrow area of study (within the capacity of one person or a group of persons to handle). This division of labor and specialization makes the study of nature's most complex events possible. Anthropologists study and compare human behavior across different cultures; sociologists look at group and institutional behavior within a given culture; psychologists focus on the biological, environmental, and social factors that influence the behavior and experiences of individuals alone or in groups. In their attempts to answer questions about human nature, scientists and laymen are very much like the blind men in the parable of The Blind Men and the Elephant. Each, from the special vantage point of unique life experiences or scientific knowledge, can answer the question about human nature. But each answer would, like those of the blind men, contain only part of the "truth."

THE BLIND MEN AND THE ELEPHANT by John Godfrey Saxe

It was six men of Indostan
   To learning much inclined,
Who went to see the Elephant
   (Though all of them were blind),
That each by observation
   Might satisfy his mind.
The First approached the Elephant,
   And happening to fall
Against his broad and sturdy side
   At once began to bawl:
"God bless me! but the Elephant
   Is very like a wall!"

The Second, feeling of the tusk
  Cried, "Ho! what have we here
So very round and smooth and sharp?
  To me 'tis very clear
This wonder of an Elephant
  Is very like a spear!"
The Third approached the animal
  And, happening to take
The squirming trunk within his hands
  Thus boldly up he spake:
"I see," quoth he, "the Elephant
  Is very like a snake!"
The Fourth reached out an eager hand,
  And felt about the knee:
"What most this wondrous beast is like
  Is very plain," quoth he:
'Tis clear enough the Elephant
  Is very like a tree!"
The Fifth, who chanced to touch the ear,
  Said: "E'en the blindest man
Can tell what this resembles most:
  Deny the fact who can

This marvel of an Elephant
  Is very like a fan!"
The Sixth no sooner had begun
  About the beast to grope
Than, seizing on the swinging tail
  That fell within his scope.
"I see," quoth he, "the Elephant
  Is very like a rope!"
And so these men of Indostan
  Disputed loud and long,
Each in his own opinion
  Exceeding stiff and strong.
Though each was partly in the right,
  They all were in the wrong.

Consider the approaches of anthropologists, sociologists, and psychologists to the study of sexual behavior.

Anthropologists focus on the effects of culture on sexual behavior and the variations between societies. Sociologists are interested in those social institutions, such as marriage, that govern sexual behavior, as well as sexual mores in subgroups within society. Psychologists have a variety of possible viewpoints. Looking at the biological being, they focus on how the nervous system and hormones in the body affect sexual moods, feelings, and expression. Looking at the learning individual, they focus on how a person from infancy to adulthood develops a sex identity and learns to think, feel, and behave as a male or female. Looking at the social being, they focus on how personal moral values, attitudes, and feelings about sexual behavior affect and are affected by social pressures and interpersonal relationships. Notice again that psychology as a science explores the biological, environmental, and social factors that influence behavior and experience.

Like the blind men and the elephant, each specialist views humanity from a different vantage point; as a result certain factors are overemphasized and others ignored or diminished. Each specialty, however, has a contribution to make to our total understanding of humanity. The occasional contradictions between the views of the specialists are inevitable, given the complexity of the task and the diverse vantage points. It is the task of a maturing science to try to minimize the contradictions and synthesize the separate findings into explanatory and predictive theories. Seen in this light, the diverse viewpoints and their contradictions serve as a challenge to stimulate scientific creativity.

Seven Levels of Analysis and the Organization of This Book

Psychology, like other sciences, is composed of subfields, each of which explores its own region of emphasis. This book has been organized in a way we think will help you grasp the scope of psychology. Following this panorama, which is an orientation to psychology as a field of study, you will find seven sections devoted to each of seven interrelated levels of analysis. Table 1.1 gives a schematic view of the panorama of psychology as it is organized in this book. The seven groupings of case studies, problems, and situations in the opening sections of this chapter illustrate the seven levels of analysis. The final chapter of the book is devoted to the scientific basis of psychology.

TABLE 1.1 **Conceptual organization of the textbook**

SECTION	LEVEL OF ANALYSIS	CHAPTER
		1. Panorama of Psychology
One	Biological Being	2. Nature and Nurture 3. Brain and Behavior
Two	Energized Being	4. Motivation and Emotion
Three	Sensing, Conscious Being	5. Sensation, Perception, and Consciousness

Four	Learning, Remembering Being	6. Learning Principles 7. Verbal Learning, Memory, and Forgetting
Five	Thinking, Knowing Being	8. Intelligence 9. Creativity, Problem Solving, and Language
Six	Individual, Adaptive Being	10. Personality 11. Psychopathology and Treatment
Seven	Social Being	12. Development and Socialization 13. Attitudes and Prejudice 14. Conformity and Involvement 15. Groups 16. International Conflict
		Appendix: The Scientific Basis of Psychology

PSYCHOLOGY AS A PROFESSION

Psychologists as professional men and women apply the methods and findings of psychology in seeking out answers to questions about human behavior. These questions are often of great practical as well as theoretical relevance to each of us in our daily lives.

The professional efforts of psychologists range from "pure" research to "applied" science. "Pure" and "applied" science are labels for activities that lie at the ends of a continuum. **"Pure" research** *refers to an exploration of questions at the frontiers of human knowledge that may have no immediate or obvious practical application.*

"Applied" science *includes research that has a current problem-solving orientation as well as the employment of "pure" scientific findings in the daily affairs of humanity.* Very often the distinction between "pure" and "applied" research breaks down, for many of the discoveries of pure research have unforeseen applications, and many practical problems and experiences are the basis for asking questions that are at the borders of knowledge. Schematically,

Table 1.2 summarizes the professional activities of psychologists and identifies their typical work-settings. Psychologists are employed in a variety of public and private organizations, and they are engaged in diverse activities, such as teaching, testing, research, and treatment of emotional disorders.

TABLE 1–2 Psychology as a professional occupation

OCCUPATIONAL ENVIRONMENT	OCCUPATIONAL TITLE	RESPONSIBILITIES
Schools, Colleges, Universities (51%)	Counseling Psychologist Clinical Psychologist School Psychologist	Administer and interpret intelligence tests, aptitude tests, achievement tests for student placement and guidance. Educational guidance. Career planning. Group, individual therapy.
	Instructor, Professor	Teach courses on psychological topics at colleges and universities.
	Experimental Psychologist	Plan, carry out, interpret, and report on surveys, observations, case studies, and experimental studies of behavior and experience.
Industry, Business, Government, Military Service (30%)	Industrial Psychologist	Develop and administer on-the-job training programs. Study and modify work environment to reduce fatigue, tension, and accidents and increase productivity. Develop programs to foster employee morale.
	Personnel Psychologist	Administer and interpret job aptitude and skills tests. Personnel selection and placement. Counseling guidance.
	Consumer Research	Conduct surveys, interviews, experiments to determine product acceptance and consumer needs.
	Survey Researcher	Design and administer public opinion polls and interviews.
Schools, Hospitals, Private Practice (12%)	Clinical Psychologist	Diagnose and treat nonphysical-based behavioral and emotional disorders. Give and interpret psychological tests.
Community Action, Nonprofit Organizations (9%)	Many jobs in social, clinical, industrial, and academic settings	Carry out many functions to help communities in areas of ecology, mental health, crisis clinics, halfway houses, drug rehabilitation centers, child guidance centers, etc.

Figures are percentage of employment. Total is greater than 100% because of rounding off. (Based on statistical data from S. Ross and R. F. Lockman, 1965, *A Career in Psychology,* Washington, D.C., American Psychological Association.)

SUMMARY

1. **Psychology** is defined as the scientific study of **behavior** and **experience** (page 18). The panorama of problems, situations, and concerns of psychologists covers the biological, environmental, and social factors that affect behavior and experience.

2. As a science, the goals of psychology are the description, prediction, explanation, and control of behavior and experience.

3. As a profession, psychology requires the men and women who pursue it to apply the methods of science to seek out answers to questions that involve **pure** and **applied research** (page 22).

4. As a field of study, psychology has many specialized subfields. Psychologists carry out research in such topics as learning, perception, personality, social behavior, and intelligence testing—in short, all topics involving behavior and experience.

5. Psychologists are employed in industry, government, and schools, colleges, universities, and are found in private practice.

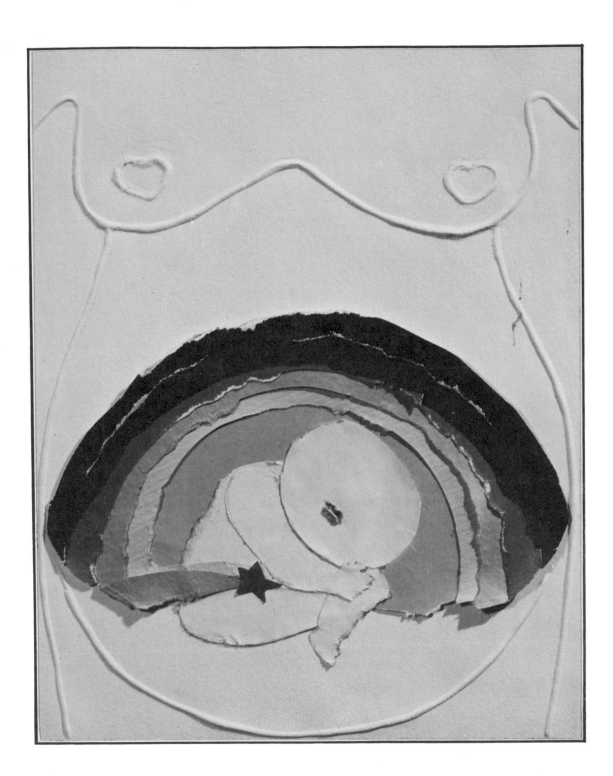

Section
One
Biological
Being

How much of behavior and experience is based on inherited biological factors and how much is determined by learning and the social and physical opportunities provided by the environment? As you read this section you will realize that there is no easy answer to this question. Behavior and experience are shaped by a complex interaction of both nature and nurture.

At the biological level of analysis psychologists are concerned with the mechanisms of heredity and the structure and function of the nervous and glandular systems. In our discussion of humans as biological beings we will take a close look at case studies and research on the biological basis of sexual development, genetic abnormalities, brain surgery, electrical stimulation of the brain, and the effects of drugs on behavior and experience.

Chapter Two
Nature and Nurture

A. THE BIOLOGICAL DETERMINANTS OF SEX IDENTITY*

We briefly described Julie, a case reported by John Money of Johns Hopkins. She visited her physician when she was 18 and had never menstruated. Her breasts and hips had developed normally in early adolescence. Now, engaged to be married, she wanted a pill that would start her menstruation and thus ensure her child-bearing capacity. The physician's preliminary examination aroused his suspicions. Her uterus could not be found; her vagina ended blindly with no cervix. A blood and urine analysis also showed a surprising anomaly. Despite her prominent secondary female sexual characteristics, Julie's specimens showed very large supplies of male sex hormone (androgen). Examination of Julie's cells revealed genetic elements that are found in males. When her sex organs were carefully examined, incompletely developed male testes were found. In order to explain how Julie came to be a female in appearance and behavior we will explore both the biological and environmental bases underlying sexual development. While we will emphasize the biological, this exploration will reveal some of the complex interplay between biological and environmental factors that shape behavior and experience.

THE GENETICS OF SEX DETERMINATION

The fastest woman in the world in the 100-meter dash would not even have been given a place with the first 100 male competitors in that event at the 1972 Olympics. Earlier, because of such evidence of sex differences, when certain remarkably unfeminine types began regularly winning events in the

* Dr. June Reinisch prepared material for this section.

women's Olympic competition, some women athletes began to demand careful, independent testing of the gender of their competitors. When such testing was announced in advance of the 1964 Olympic Games in Tokyo, several former "women's" champions failed to appear. The question facing the Olympic Committee was what test for gender to employ. The test had to be objective and minimally embarrassing. They decided on a *karyotype,* or a photo of the chromosomes. **Chromosomes** *are structures that contain hereditary information and are found in the nucleus of every cell.* The body cells of normal human beings contain 46 chromosomes arranged in 23 pairs. One of the 23 pairs of chromosomes determines sex. Two kinds of sex chromosomes, called X and Y, have been identified. If the sex chromosomes are both X, then the individual can be classified as a female; if the sex chromosomes are X and Y, then the individual is a male. (See Figure 2.1.) Whether a fetus has an XX or XY configuration is determined by the type of sperm that fertilized the mother's egg. The mother always contributes an X chromosome. If the father's fertilizing sperm is X, then the fetus will have a female chromosome pattern (XX). If the father's fertilizing sperm carries a Y chromosome, then the fetus will have a male chromosome pattern (XY).

Sex determination is but one of a vast number of areas of study that falls under the topic of genetics. **Genetics** *is the study of the transfer of inherited characteristics from one generation to another.* Later in this chapter we will explore the mechanisms of genetics more fully and examine how different physical and behavioral characteristics are inherited and modified by the environment.

The decision of the Olympic Committee to employ chromosome karyotyping for sex

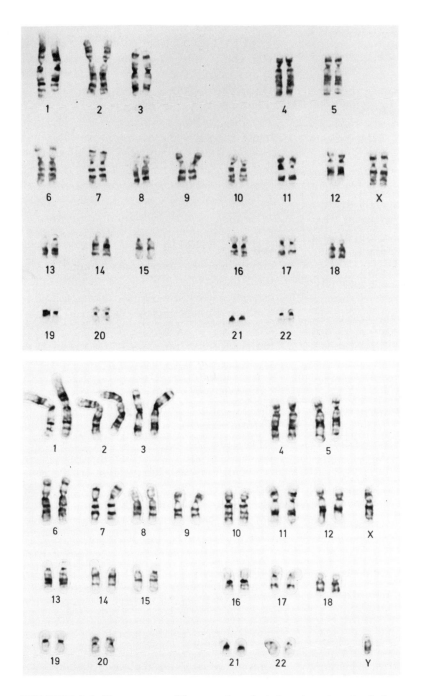

FIGURE 2.1 *Karyotypes of human female (above) and male (below)*
chromosomes. Note the pair of X chromosomes in the female array,
the X and Y chronosomes in male karyotype.

determination was a wise one, but it has some risks. Almost all individuals who appear female have **XX** chromosomes; almost all males have **XY** chromosomes. But the chromosome pattern laid down at conception is not an absolute determinant. It is more like a blueprint for a building. There are many points in the construction process where the original blueprint can be bypassed or overridden by constraints, internal or external, to the developing organism. In Julie's case, the male genetic blueprint was overridden by other genetic instructions starting in the sixth week of fetal development when male hormones began to be secreted, but Julie's cells were not responsive to them.

SEX HORMONES AND FETAL SEX DEVELOPMENT

For the first month and a half of fetal life there are no structural differences between a male and female other than the chromosome pattern. The fetus has two sex glands (gonads) but they are identical for males and females at this point. At about six weeks, the chromosomes begin to exert their influence. Out of the core of the six-week-old gonads the XY's testes will develop; out of the rind of the gonads the XX's ovaries will develop. When these gonads become large enough they begin to secrete sex hormones; it is these hormones that direct further sexual development. **Hormones** *are chemical secretions of certain glands that play an important role in regulating growth and bodily processes* (see page 68). Two of them determine whether a fetus will develop male or female sex organs. For example, all normal fetuses have two embryonic duct systems, the Wolffian (male) and the Mullerian (female). (See Figure 2.2.) The secretions of the gonads determine which will become

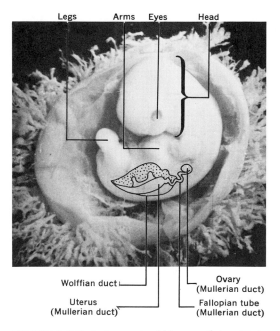

Legs   Arms   Eyes   Head

Wolffian duct — Uterus (Mullerian duct)   Ovary (Mullerian duct) — Fallopian tube (Mullerian duct)

FIGURE 2.2 A six-week-old human fetus. Note that the fetus has both male (Wolffian) and female (Mullerian) embryonic duct systems. The amount of male hormone secretions at this critical period will determine the sexual identity of the fetus.

dominant and which will atrophy. Male gonads (testes) normally secrete two substances:

1. *Androgen.* This is the crucial male sex hormone. Androgen promotes the growth of the internal male sexual apparatus from the embryonic Wolffian ducts.

2. *Mullerian-inhibiting substance (MIS).* This substance inhibits the growth of the female Mullerian ducts. Male fetuses need both androgen and MIS for normal development.

Surgeons have operated on male babies for an apparently ordinary hernia only to find that the infants actually had a good beginning toward a full set of internal female sexual equipment, including fallopian tubes and a fully differentiated uterus. In these males, Mullerian-inhibiting substance was not secreted during the fetal stage by the testes so that the growth of the Mullerian ducts was not inhibited. Therefore, these structures went blithely on developing into the fallopian tubes and uterine tissues. Sexually these men function normally.

The Critical Period

What is decisive in sexual differentiation is the presence of sufficient male sex hormones during the critical period starting in the sixth week of fetal development. **Critical period** *refers to a particular stage in the development of an organism in which a physical or chemical change or experience has the most effect on later development.* The female gonads, ovaries, are not active in the critical period. If *no* male sex hormones are secreted, the fetus forms female sexual organs. For the development of a normal male, the testes must secrete both androgen and MIS at this critical time of fetal growth (sixth week). The same story can be told concerning the external sexual organs. If sufficient quantities of androgen are present and *effective,* the fetus (no matter what its chromosome pattern) will develop male sexual structures. If insufficient androgen is available, female sexual organs will result (no matter what the chromosome pattern).

Genetic Error

There is another possibility in a fetus with normal male (XY) chromosomes. These chromosomes direct the embryonic sex glands to develop into testicles, and the testicles produce copious amounts of androgen. But sometimes, because of a genetic quirk, the fetus is not sensitive to the andro-

gen, and its cells behave as though there were no androgen present at all. The Wolffian ducts fail to differentiate. Effectively, there is no androgen, so the body reacts as though the fetus were female and develops a normal vagina, a clitoris, and labia majora and minora. When the baby is born, there is usually no reason for the obstetrician to suspect that a problem exists. The parents are congratulated on their new baby girl. The child, though endowed with a set of testicles hidden in the body cavity, is raised as a girl.

Testicles produce not only the male sex hormone, androgen, but also quantities of estrogen (the female sex hormone). The amount of estrogen is about the same as that produced by the normal female during the lowest estrogen-producing period of her menstrual cycle. At puberty, this amount of estrogen in the androgen-insensitive individual is quite enough to promote the growth of entirely normal secondary female sexual characteristics. And so the androgen-insensitive "male," raised as a girl, now develops the breasts and broad hips characteristic of the normal female.

What Happened to Julie? Clearly, we have just described the reason for Julie's difficulty. What finally happened to Julie? Well, her ineffective testicles were removed, since in such cases they often develop cancers. She is maintained on regular doses of estrogen. She married, adopted two children, and is leading a very happy life as a housewife and mother. What is especially fascinating about Julie is that she is exceptionally "feminine" in her personality and psychological behavior. Part of this femininity may, perhaps, be ascribed to the influence of her unusual hormonal situation on the development of her brain and behavior. Julie's femininity may also be attributed to the effects of her social environment. She was treated as a female and was taught how to act and feel feminine. We will explore both factors further, but first we need to describe how the brain and hormones normally interact and influence behavior.

HORMONES, BRAIN, AND BEHAVIOR

When the fetal testes begin to secrete sex hormones, the effects are not restricted to promoting the growth of the sex organs. The hormones circulate throughout the entire body, with crucial influence on the formation of certain brain structures. In response to androgen the *hypothalamus* (a part of the brain with vital regulatory functions) develops the potential to regulate the production of testicle-stimulating substances at a *constant* rate with the onset of puberty. In the female fetus, in contrast, no sex hormones are present. In the absence of androgen during fetal development, the hypothalamus develops the potential to begin regulating, at puberty, the *monthly* secretion of substances, establishing the menstrual cycle. That is, these substances, at and after puberty, will be released by the hypothalamus in a set pattern of carefully regulated amounts during the month, resulting in ovulation and menstruation. All of these intricate processes are prepared during the fetal stage.

Fetal Androgen and Adult Sexual Behavior

The presence or absence of ample quantities of androgen during a critical period of fetal brain development has crucial consequences for later sex-related behavior. The precise time in fetal development in which the critical period falls varies from animal to animal. Whenever it occurs, if androgen is present at the critical time, later sex-related behavior will tend to be masculine. If androgen is not present, later behavior will be feminine. As we saw in the case of Julie, the chromosome (XX or XY) pattern is, *at that point,* not relevant. Let us now look at several animal studies that offer some insight into these mechanisms.

Sex and the Maturing Rat. When normal adult rats engage in coitus, the female assumes the inviting position, called lordosis, and the male mounts her as in Figure 2.3. If you castrate the adult male rat he will still mount during coitus. But if you chemically castrate him during his fetal development so that he has no effective androgen circulating, he will, in adulthood, very likely assume the lordosis position in coitus. The female, remember, does not have sex hormones circulating during the fetal period. Consequently, if a rat has no androgens present in the critical period, brain development goes in a feminine direction.

FIGURE 2.3 Normal coital position for rats. The sexual behavior of both males and females is influenced by hormone secretions at a critical period of fetal development.

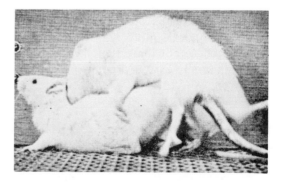

But if androgens are given to a pregnant rat during this critical period, her female pups will, in adulthood, tend to mount during coitus. Frequently such females completely lose the ability to assume the lordosis position and are incapable of mating.

The explanation is that brain structures related to later coital behavior do not differentiate in a masculine or feminine direction until the critical period is reached, and the direction then depends on the presence or absence of androgen. These brain structures help to determine later behavioral tendencies.

At least this is so in rats. The distance between the sexual behavior of rats and that of humans is a big one, however. To bridge part of this gap, William C. Young, Robert Goy, and C. H. Phoenix manipulated fetal androgen levels during the critical period in rhesus monkeys and then observed the resulting sex-typed behavior. These studies are significant because rhesus monkeys more closely resemble human beings than do rats in length of gestation time, in the time it takes to reach sexual maturity, and in behavior. Nevertheless, social-developmental influences are without doubt a far more important factor in determining sex-typed behavior in humans than in laboratory-reared rhesus monkeys. Conversely, biological factors such as fetal androgen level probably play a relatively more important part in a monkey's sexual development than in a human's. Even so, if the fetal androgens do influence the sex-typed behavior of monkeys, we would be encouraged to conclude that they also influence human sex-typed behavior, though less strongly.

Monkey Sex Life. Rhesus monkeys are rather common laboratory animals. Their sex-typed behavior has been very well doc-

umented. Just as with humans, the male rhesus, far more than the female, engages in threatening behavior and rough-and-tumble play, with the males chasing one another around the cage. Young, Goy, and Phoenix decided to see what effect fetal androgens have on this sex-typed threatening and play behavior.

Having decided on the sex-typed behavior they would study, the investigators then proceeded to plan their fetal androgen work. The point of the research was to see if, when males were deprived of androgen or when females were given androgen during the critical fetal period, their later sex-typed behavior would be reversed. For example, if female fetuses were given androgen they would be expected to behave like a male, exhibiting rough-and-tumble play, threatening behavior, and sexual aggressiveness (see Figure 2.4).

To deprive a rhesus male fetus of androgen they would have to surgically open the mother and do a fantastically delicate operation on the tiny fetus in order to remove the testes and thus remove the source of androgen. The experimenters chose the less risky route of simply injecting androgen into the pregnant rhesus mother. If the fetus were a male, nothing should happen; if the fetus were a female, then the androgen should direct the structuring of brain tissue so as to make her behave more like a male monkey than a female when she grew up.

The female rhesus monkeys treated with androgen were observed in social interaction with untreated normal females. The question was whether they would behave in a masculine or feminine sex-typed manner, whether their behavior would be affected more by their chromosomes or by the androgen treatment given during pregnancy.

Their behavior left no doubt. They ran

FIGURE 2.4 Dominance and submission behaviors and sexual behavior of rhesus monkeys are affected by the male hormone, androgen. Here a female, treated with androgen as a fetus, mounts another female.

and chased and threatened and initiated play far more than did the normal females. In many ways their social behavior was almost equivalent to that of a normal male rhesus. Their mating behavior was also abnormal for females. They mounted other females at relatively high frequencies. All these marked alterations in behavior resulted from the injections of androgen into their mothers at that time in pregnancy when the relevant brain structures in the hypothalamus were forming. If an injection of androgen is given to a female monkey during childhood or adulthood there will be little effect on her mating or social behavior. To have an effect, androgen must be given during the critical period in pregnancy.

SEX DIFFERENCES IN INFANT BEHAVIOR

How much of a role do sex hormones play in determining behavior differences in human beings? This question is difficult to answer because sociocultural factors are so important in gender-related behavior. An investigator who wished to seek some data to help answer that question might try to observe newborns. Newborns have not had much opportunity to be taught that girls play with dolls and sit quietly while boys play with trucks and are aggressive. Of course, the range of behavior that can be observed in the newborn is quite restricted.

Anneliese Korner at Stanford University has done some careful observation of infants in the first three days of life. There are no important differences in the treatment of these infant boys and girls during these first three days. Differences observed in their behavior must be attributed to prenatal (before birth) influences. In view of the rat and rhesus research results, we must include among these influences fetal androgen level. The 32 infants she observed were 45 to 85 hours old. They were all born after a full-term pregnancy and they were all bottle fed. There were no unusual conditions surrounding pregnancy or delivery. Thus, we can be relatively certain that the infants' behavior was not grossly affected by any factors other than their gender. The infants were observed over a nine-hour period, with one hour out for two feeding sessions. They were observed both before and after feeding and at the mid-time between feedings. Korner made long movie records of the infants' behavior. She found three types of behavior that occurred quite frequently in these 32 children:

Startle reaction: Spontaneously occurring, massive body jerks that involve both the stretching and flexing of the arms and legs.

Rhythmical mouthing or reflex sucks: Bursts of a series of rhythmical, shallow sucks that are separated by periods of no activity.

Reflex smiling: Upward and sideward movement of the muscles of the mouth that looks like later smiling but in the neonate, or newborn, is unrelated to social stimuli.

There were clear and consistent differences between the male and female infants. Boys startled more than girls. On the other hand, girls smiled more and engaged in more frequent bursts of rhythmical mouthing and sucking. The total number of these three acts performed by the boys and girls was about the same. Korner concluded that these observations highlight biological and physiological differences between the sexes, identifiable at birth, that may be developmental precursors of later sex differences.

Other sex differences in response to stimulation have also been identified in infants. For example, newborn females react more than males do to the removal of covering blankets, to airjet stimulation of the abdomen, and to small amounts of electrical stimulation. These sensitivity differences seem to hold up in slightly older infants as well. On the other hand, male infants raise their heads higher than newborn females. These male-female differences would be difficult to attribute to sociocultural factors.

Sex differences in fundamental sensitivity responses are also found in male and female adults. Women are more sensitive to the smell of musk and certain chemicals in urine and are reported to have greater olfactory acuity in general than do men. There is also some evidence to support women's greater acuity in tests of hearing. There is no evidence that these differences are determined by postnatal learning experiences or social and cultural factors. In addition, they parallel the findings in infants.

Do fetal sexual hormones play a part in determining human sex-typed behavior? Is the absence of androgen during pregnancy crucial in determining that a baby girl will prefer to play with dolls and be more passive than her be-testicled, androgenized brother? The hormone effect has been observed with monkeys whose brain and behavior are not too unlike those of humans. In addition, from research on human fetuses, we know that the presence or absence of effective androgen during a human pregnancy will influence the brain structures and will certainly influence the growth of the sex organs. Observation of newborn infants reveals important sex differences in responsiveness to stimuli. From these facts, it is not unreasonable to conclude cautiously that fetal androgen has an effect on human sex-typed behavior similar to that in rhesus monkeys—similar, but probably not the same.

As opposed to lower animals, humans have a very long period of dependency. This characteristic doubtlessly gives sociocultural factors overriding importance in the determination of sex-role behaviors. In an adult, it is impossible to judge what proportion of sex-role behavior is biologically determined and what proportion is socioculturally determined. However, by examining differences in the way boys and girls are brought up and reviewing some anthropological findings, we would be in a better position to draw some tentative conclusions. This important sociocultural exploration will be continued in Chapters 4 and 12.

B. THE MECHANISMS OF HEREDITY

We introduced you to Steven in the introductory panorama. Steven was the 15-year-old mentally retarded boy with the intelligence of a six-year-old. Steven's problem was traced to an inherited defect, called phenylketonuria (P.K.U.). During **metabolism,** *a process by which food is broken down to be used as a source of energy by the body,* certain by-products, or wastes, are produced that are actually poisonous to our bodies. Such by-products are usually broken down chemically by various enzymes. **Enzymes** *are substances that speed up or slow down chemical reactions, but remain unchanged themselves.* Enzymes are essential to the metabolic process, because they render the poisonous by-

products harmless so that they can be eliminated as waste. **P.K.U.,** then, *is a disorder of metabolism that prevents the conversion of phenylalanine* (a protein component of many foods) *into chemicals the body can eliminate.* The result is that infants with P.K.U. tend to accumulate phenylalanine in the blood and in brain tissue. The associated mental retardation is due to damage suffered by growing brain cells. Most of the damage occurs in the first six months of life. Fortunately, P.K.U. can be easily detected at birth and the retardation prevented by proper diet. Since phenylalanine occurs in such foods as milk and vegetables, these must be restricted. Milk substitutes and fruits and food supplements must be started soon after birth. By the age of four or five an afflicted child can begin a normal diet. After this age, high levels of phenylalanine don't seem to cause any problems.

About one out of 15,000 individuals is born with this genetic disorder. A simple urine or blood test for P.K.U. is required by law in many states for newborn infants. One test consists of placing a strip of chemically treated paper on a wet diaper. If a green color results, the child has P.K.U.

Parents of P.K.U. children are normal in mental ability and do not show any P.K.U. symptoms. After fasting, however, they show higher levels of phenylalanine than non-P.K.U. parents. This means that potential P.K.U. parents can be identified and counseled. To understand how P.K.U. is inherited and to explore the role of heredity in behavior, let us now turn to the principles of genetics.

CHROMOSOMES AND GENES

In the mid-nineteenth century, an Augustinian monk, Gregor J. Mendel, conducted

Focus 2.1
DNA: The Genetic Code Book of Life

We have described chromosomes, those threadlike bodies in the nucleus of cells, as the carriers of hereditary traits. Clearly, however, even in complex combinations 46 genetic units would not be enough to lead to the development of a human being. Each chromosome is actually composed of about 2000 of the smaller units called genes. James D. Watson, Francis H. C. Crick, and Maurice H. F. Wilkins were awarded the Nobel Prize in 1962 for discovering the structure of *deoxyribonucleic acid,* or *DNA,* segments of which make up each gene.

DNA *is the chemical substance that contains the hereditary information for a cell's structure and function.* It has the capacity to duplicate itself from chemicals present in each cell. This precise duplication of the arrangement of a DNA molecule is the basis for the exact duplication of chromosomes during cell division. A particular DNA molecule determines the nature of a particular trait by influencing the production of enzymes that guide the development of body cells. The type, size, and number of these cells then result in the actual physical characteristics of the individual.

The chemical arrangement of the DNA molecule is a code that carries all the information needed to direct development from a single cell to a complete, functioning organism. According to Crick and Watson, the DNA molecule is like a spiral staircase. Phosphate and sugar compounds form the twisted rails of the stairs. The steps are made up of pairs of nitrogen compounds, which are joined in the middle. These nitrogen compounds are chemical bases; there are four of them— adenine, thymine, cytosine, and guanine, called A, T, C, and G for short. When these bases pair off, cytosine always joins guanine and adenine always joins thymine. (See Figure 2.5.) However, these stair steps, the paired bases, can be placed in any order in almost endless sequences. The coiled DNA in a human cell contains over six billion steps and, if stretched out, would form a microscopically thin thread three feet long. The sequence of these steps encodes genetic information. This genetic library is microscopic, yet there is enough room to store as much information as several sets of 24-volume encyclopedias.

During mitosis (discussed in the text), the DNA in a cell reproduces itself by a kind of unzipping motion that splits the spiral staircase down the middle of each step. All the A's separate from the T's and the G's from the C's. Each half of the staircase then picks up its complementary base from the cellular material surrounding it and forms a new staircase. Two staircases now stand where there once was one, and each becomes part of a new cell. In this way every cell in the body carries identical genetic information. DNA is so tiny that all the thread-like DNA needed to give rise to the three billion people alive in our world would fit into a one-eighth-inch cube.

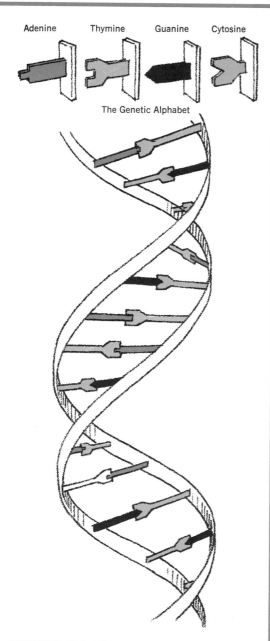

Adenine   Thymine   Guanine   Cytosine

The Genetic Alphabet

FIGURE 2.5 The DNA molecule.

and reported the experiments that provided the basic answer to the problem of how physical traits are inherited. In the garden of his monastery, Mendel, with incredible care, crossbred generations of smooth pea plants and wrinkled pea plants to see what texture the offspring would have. Mendel's work ranks among the exquisite human accomplishments, both for its precision and for its contribution to man's understanding of biological inheritance. Our exploration is based on Mendel's findings as expanded during the last century.

In order to explain the data he collected from his pea plants, Mendel was forced to invent a theoretical genetic unit, a carrier of hereditary traits. He gave this theoretical unit the properties necessary to explain his observations. Scientists of our century have identified Mendel's unit and called it deoxyribonucleic acid (DNA), a chemical substance contained in chromosomes. **Chromosomes** *are rod-shaped structures found in the nucleus of every cell capable of dividing.* (The word means "colored bodies"; they were so named because of their tendency to absorb certain dyes.) Each living cell of a given species of plant or animal has a characteristic number of these rod-like structures; human beings have 46, dogs have 78, fruit flies have 8. Chromosomes are very complex chemicals consisting mainly of proteins and DNA. The chemical structure of DNA combines a variety of compounds into long chains arranged like a twisted ladder. (See Focus 2.1: DNA: The Genetic Code Book of Life.) **Genes** *are the specific locations along the DNA ladder that carry the instructions needed for the development and functioning of the individual.* In animal research specific gene locations have been related to particular physical and behavioral traits. Genes direct cell activities by giving instructions for protein synthesis to a complex chemical called RNA (ribonucleic acid). The RNA then acts like a gang of construction workers moving around the cell assembling proteins and enzymes. A P.K.U. child has a defective gene, so instructions are never given to the RNA to produce the enzyme needed to break down phenylalanine.

CELL DIVISION

Ordinarily, chromosomes are scattered throughout the cell nucleus. During mitosis, *a process whereby cells reproduce themselves to make new cells or to replace worn-out body cells,* they line up in pairs, with corresponding chromosomes forming each pair. Each chromosome then splits in half, so instead of 23 pairs in each human cell there are 46 pairs. Then the elongated single cell splits into two new cells, with 23 pairs of chromosomes moving into each new cell (see Figure 2.6). Meiosis, *a second type of cell division, is the crucial process by which parent organisms produce egg and sperm cells (gametes).* In mitosis, the chromosomes line up in pairs and duplicate themselves. This activity yields two *sets* of pairs of chromosomes, or enough for two normal body cells. In meiosis, however, four cells are produced instead of two, each containing half the usual number of chromosomes. In a male, the process occurs in the testes. Each testicular cell contains 46 chromosomes before meiosis. After the duplication and division of meiosis, there are four sperm cells, each with 23 chromosomes. A similar process occurs in the ovaries of women, producing egg cells with 23 chromosomes (see Figure 2.6).

At conception, when a 23-chromosome sperm and a 23-chromosome egg successfully combine, they form a single unit, called a **zygote,** *with the usual human number of 46 chromosomes.* From the blueprint contained in the 46 chromosomes of this single cell (in interaction with the environment), an adult human is developed. Given an accommodating environment, these 46 chromosomes determine whether this organism has brown rather than blue eyes, whether it has a high or low intellectual potential, whether it is a woman or a man, and they ensure that it is a human being rather than a cockatoo.

DOMINANT AND RECESSIVE GENES

One of the most important concepts of genetics is that some genes are dominant and some are recessive. This concept can be illustrated by the inheritance of P.K.U.

On one of the 23 human chromosome pairs there is a gene controlling the production of the enzyme that breaks down phenylalanine. In P.K.U. victims, as we said, this gene is defective and so the needed enzyme is not produced. We'll symbolize a normal gene for producing that enzyme by a capital N. Since each gene on a chromosome is matched by a gene on the pairing chromosome, a normal gene pair can be symbolized by an NN genotype. (**Genotype** *refers to the actual genetic make-up of a person.*) A person with P.K.U. will have two abnormal genes, symbolized by an aa genotype. A person with one normal and one abnormal gene, Na, will not have P.K.U. because, in this case, the normal gene N is dominant and the abnormal gene a is recessive. (Capital letters are used for dominant genes, lowercase letters for recessive ones.)

A **dominant gene** *determines the phenotype, the actual physical and behavioral characteristics of the offspring.* A dominant gene will almost always prevail over a re-

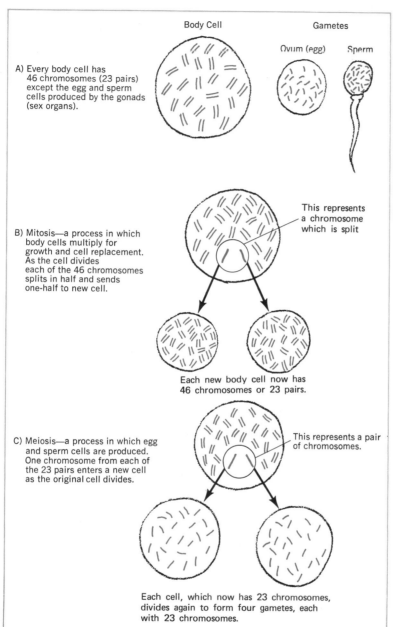

A) Every body cell has 46 chromosomes (23 pairs) except the egg and sperm cells produced by the gonads (sex organs).

Body Cell

Gametes

Ovum (egg)   Sperm

This represents a chromosome which is split

B) Mitosis—a process in which body cells multiply for growth and cell replacement. As the cell divides each of the 46 chromosomes splits in half and sends one-half to new cell.

Each new body cell now has 46 chromosomes or 23 pairs.

This represents a pair of chromosomes.

C) Meiosis—a process in which egg and sperm cells are produced. One chromosome from each of the 23 pairs enters a new cell as the original cell divides.

Each cell, which now has 23 chromosomes, divides again to form four gametes, each with 23 chromosomes.

FIGURE 2.6 A simplified diagram of mitosis and meiosis.

cessive gene. For example, a person with an Na gene combination would not have P.K.U. and would have a normal phenotype. For P.K.U. to appear the person would have to have two recessive genes. *A reces-* *sive gene usually does not affect the phenotype when it is paired with a dominant gene.* When a dominant gene is present, the effect of a recessive gene is inhibited. A recessive gene typically affects the phenotype

Father's gametes (sperm)

Mother's gametes (ova)

	N	N
N	NN	NN
N	NN	NN

Case (a) Both parents are normal and all children will be normal.

	N	a
N	NN	Na
N	NN	Na

Case (b) Both parents appear normal but one parent has Na gene pattern. All children will be normal but half will be P.K.U. carriers.

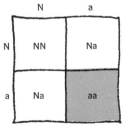

	N	a
N	NN	Na
a	Na	aa

Case (c) Both parents appear normal but both are carriers of P.K.U. which is recessive. If parents have many children, three-fourths of them will appear normal, one-half will be P.K.U. carriers with a recessive P.K.U. gene, and one-fourth of the children will have two recessive genes and P.K.U.

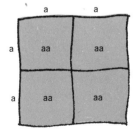

	a	a
a	aa	aa
a	aa	aa

Case (d) Both parents have P.K.U. and all children will have P.K.U.

N = normal gene

a = abnormal P.K.U. gene

only when it is paired with another recessive gene. There are some instances, to be discussed later, when a recessive gene does influence a dominant gene and the phenotype. But this is not the case for P.K.U.

The possible combinations and recombinations of genes in connection with P.K.U. are illustrated in Figure 2.7. Examine Case (c). The parents appear normal and do not have P.K.U., but each parent carries a recessive, abnormal gene for P.K.U. The odds are one in four that any child they bear will have P.K.U.

A number of other genetic defects that produce behavioral abnormalities are described in Focus 2.2: Genetic Mistakes and Their Consequences.

INDEPENDENT ASSORTMENT

The development of **gametes** (*the cells of reproduction: egg and sperm*) during meiosis has been carefully observed by microscopic examination; when the two sets of chromosomes arrange themselves into four groups to form four gametes, they do so completely randomly with respect to which chromosome goes to which gamete. If we consider the chromosomes as they line up in pairs, we can talk of left chromosomes and right chromosomes. If the first left chromosome of a pair goes to the first of the four gametes, we have no hint of the destiny of the second left chromosome. The first gamete may end up with all left chromosomes or any combination of left and right chromosomes or all right chromosomes. An important consequence of this independent assortment of chromosomes is diversity of genetic material in a species. The **law of independent assortment** *states that traits carried on different chromosomes combine and recombine completely independently of one another.*

For an example, see Figure 2.8. An eye

FIGURE 2.8 The independent assortment of curly hair and eye color. The various combinations of parent gametes can produce numerous genotypes and phenotypes. Note the incomplete dominance of a Bb genotype, which results in a light-brown-eyed individual.

Mother's gametes (ova)

	CB	Cb	sb	sB
CB	CC BB Curly hair Brown eyes	CC Bb	Cs Bb	Cs BB Curly hair Brown eyes
Cb	CC Bb	CC bb Curly hair Blue eyes	Cs bb	Cs Bb
sb	Cs Bb Curly hair Light brown eyes	Cs bb	ss bb	ss Bb
sB	Cs BB Curly hair Brown eyes	Cs Bb Curly hair Light brown eyes	ss Bb Straight hair Light brown eyes	ss BB Straight hair Brown eyes

Father's gametes (sperm)

Focus 2.2

Genetic Mistakes and Their Consequences

The discovery of the genetic factors underlying P.K.U. retardation is not an isolated event; the hereditary sources have been found for a number of other conditions, a few of which we will briefly consider.

Down's Syndrome. Nancy ran over to the visitor, a total stranger in her hospital ward, hugged him, and took his hand. The visitor was embarrassed by this unexpected display of affection. Although Nancy was 25, she was as short as a ten-year-old and had the intelligence of a five-year-old. Her thick, protruding tongue gave her speech a halting, hard-to-understand, garbled sound. As Nancy grabbed the visitor's hand, the visitor pulled back in surprise. Nancy's hands were very dry and her fingers unusually stubby. Nancy's face was rather flat and her eyes had an almond-shaped, "oriental" look. Nancy was a victim of a genetic disorder called Down's syndrome. Children with this defect are extremely retarded mentally, with intelligence scores ranging between 20 and 70. As can be seen in Figure 2.9, they have a distinctive appearance — thick protruding tongue, flat face, and short stature. An epicanthic fold in the eyelids of such children gives them what, to Westerners, seems a superficial resemblance to Orientals, hence, the old name Mongolism. From 1887, when J. Langdon Down presented the first systematic description of this abnormality, an intensive effort was made to determine its cause.

In 1959 English and French scientists simultaneously reported the observation of a chromosomal deviation in Down's syndrome victims. Microscopic studies of the victims' cells revealed that in almost all cases they were burdened with extra chromosomal material. Instead of two units of one particular chromosome (number 21), the Down's syndrome patient has three, a condition labeled *trisomy*. In the course of later research, a number of Down's syndrome cases were turned up that seemed to have a "normal" complement of 46 chromosomes. But even in these cases chromosome 21 was still the guilty party; an extra chromosome had attached itself to 21, producing a single extra-long chromosome. This condition is called *translocation*. Phenotypically normal brothers and sisters of an individual with Down's syndrome may also have a translocated chromosome 21; however, they would have a normal complement of 46 chromosomes, and one of the chromosome-21 partners would be missing from its usual position. Both in trisomy and translocation, Down's syndrome seems to stem from the presence of *extra* chromosomal material in the zygote. The likelihood of the birth of such a child increases strikingly with the age of the mother. A woman 45 years old has about 55 times as great a chance of having an afflicted child as a woman 20 years old. The age of the father does not seem to matter at all.

The predisposition for trisomy and translocation is transmitted geneti-

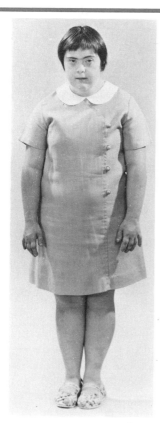

FIGURE 2.9 Female with Down's syndrome.

cally. Prospective parents with a Down's syndrome child in the family can now be given a good estimate of the probability of offspring with this condition. In these cases, microscopic examination of the chromosomes of family members will enable a genetics counselor to state the odds accurately. Frequently individuals must be advised to refrain from having further children; but more often, near-relatives of Down's syndrome victims can be freed of the dread of having an afflicted child.

There is also a medical procedure that can be used to examine the chromosomes of a fetus. A small amount of the fluid in which the fetus floats is extracted during the third or fourth month of pregnancy. Fetal cells in the fluid are analyzed for some of its genetic composition. If genetic abnormalities are found, the parents can decide whether to terminate the pregnancy. This procedure is called amniocentesis.

Procedures like this are only the tip of an iceberg of the developments in genetics that can affect our society. For example, each year over 5000 children with Down's syndrome are born in the United States. It is estimated that over a billion and a half dollars a year are spent on public and private hospital care for them. Amniocentesis can be used to identify the potential Down's syndrome fetus. There are many economic, social, and psychological principles, as well as ethical factors, that Americans must consider in deciding on the public actions to be taken regarding these new methods. The time may well be near when the general public will receive genetic counseling education and service, much as abortion information is now provided.

Turner's Syndrome.   Whenever an entire chromosome is lost, an organism usually dies before it is born. In one startling exception to this rule, females have been born with a missing X chromosome. Instead of a normal XX pair, they have only one X chromosome. The physical and behavioral pattern associated with this condition is called Turner's syndrome. The syndrome includes retardation, abnormal development of the sex organs, and disturbances in vision and intellectual growth.

Extra Chromosomes.   Public interest in genetics was aroused in recent years by reports indicating that male criminals convicted of murder and other violent crimes had extra Y chromosomes. Instead of the usual XY chromosome pairs, these individuals had an XYY arrangement. The data here are still inconclusive and further research is in progress.

Genetic Counseling.   Years ago, before much was known about human genetics, people tended to attribute a genetic cause to abnormal behaviors and physical infirmities that they did not understand. Today, a genetic counselor, a geneticist, or a specially trained physician, armed with recent research findings, can provide reassurance and genetic advice for couples planning to bear children to correct any misconceptions about genetics they may have.

color, say brown, can appear in a curly- or a straight-haired person. The law also means that children can have phenotypes different from their parents'. For example, brown-eyed, curly-haired parents can have blue-eyed, straight-haired children. All this is made clear in Figure 2.8. Curly hair (C) is dominant and straight hair (s) is recessive. Brown eyes (B) are dominant over blue eyes (b). Yet a "BB" genotype is expressed as a dark-brown-eyed phenotype and a "Bb" genotype is expressed as a light-brown-eyed phenotype. It seems that brown is not completely dominant, and that the recessive gene has an effect on color. Blue eyes can only occur with two recessive genes. **Incomplete dominance** *refers to situations where the dominant and recessive genes combine or blend their influences to produce a phenotype.* A curly-hair gene is always completely dominant. Straight hair can only occur if there are two recessive genes.

Now, in Figure 2.8 notice that there is a variety of genotypes and phenotypes that can occur as the traits combine and recombine. A brown-eyed person can have curly or straight hair. Curly-haired, brown-eyed parents (mother Cs, Bb and father Cs, Bb) can have straight-haired, blue-eyed children (ss, bb). Even though a recessive gene for straight hair is associated with a dominant gene for curly hair in the parents, it doesn't lose its capacity to produce straight hair in the next generation when it is combined with another recessive straight-hair gene. The **law of segregation** *states that even though genes may or may not blend their influences to produce a phenotype, combining genes in one generation does not change the code contained in the genes for future generations* (see Figure 2.10). In other words, regardless of past combinations, genes do not change their effects from one generation to the next.

MECHANISMS PROMOTING GENOTYPIC DIVERSITY

The system that governs genetics assures the uniqueness of each individual and so ensures that some members of a species will survive under widely varying and changing competitive conditions. It is estimated that, simply as a result of the independent assortment of human chromosomes, the chances are only one in 73,000,000,000 that a couple will produce two children with identical genotypes (except for identical twins; see Focus 2.3: Twinning). The chance of this duplication occurring with two children from different sets of parents is infinitesimal. It is probably true that (again excluding twins, triplets, etc.) each of the three billion or so people on earth has a unique genotype. It is in some way reassuring in a mass-communication society to know that despite the formidable efforts expended to foster conformity and erase signs of individuality, the genes are always busily at work promoting human diversity.

Other evolutionary mechanisms than independent assortment also tend to diversify the species. Chief among these mechanisms are crossing-over and mutations.

Linkage and Crossing-Over

The law of independent assortment is clearly supported by the observation that parental chromosomes travel to gametes randomly. Contained within each chromosome, however, are about 2000 genes, and these genes travel in groups to the gamete as part of the whole chromosome. This group travel shows up phenotypically as a linkage between certain traits of the organism. If the genes determining hair color and temperament occur on the same chromosome, then these traits will always ap-

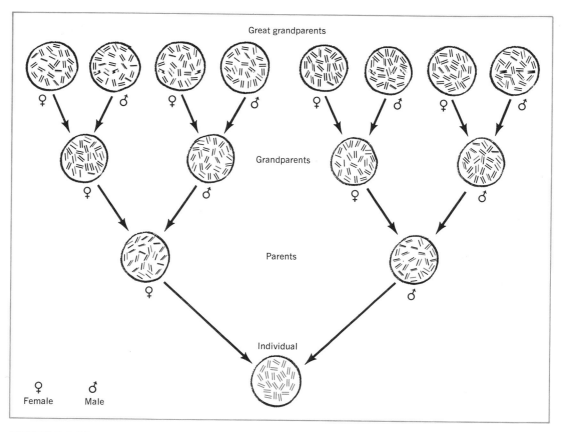

FIGURE 2.10 As a general rule, each individual receives one half of his or her chromosomes from each parent, one quarter from each grandparent, and one eighth from each great grandparent. Regardless of past chromosome and gene combinations, a gene does not change in its effects as it passes from generation to generation.

pear together in succeeding generations. On the other hand, if the genes are located on two different chromosomes, the two traits may or may not appear together in succeeding generations (that is, they sort independently).

In genetic experiments it has been noticed that *linked genes might at some point become "unlinked" or linked with a different set of characteristics; this change in linkage is termed* **crossing-over.** It occurs during cell division when the 46 chromosomes come together to make 23 pairs. When they touch, precisely matching segments sometimes break off each chromosome and transfer to the other. The genes on the broken segment are no longer linked with the genes on the main body of their original chromosome, but become linked with genes on the main body of the partner chromosome (see Figure 2.12). Crossing-over thus increases the diversity of the trait combinations of succeeding generations.

Focus 2.3 Twinning

Once a sperm and an ovum unite to form a zygote, it takes some 50 cycles of mitosis to produce a human infant. After the first cell divides there are two cells, then four, then eight, etc. If, during the first few cell divisions, one cell breaks away from the others and begins to develop on its own, then identical twins will be formed. Since both cells came from the same zygote, their genetic endowment will be identical. Since identical twins come from the same zygote, they are referred to as monozygotic (*mono-* means single or one). When two or more ova are fertilized at the same time, each zygote formed is a separate, genetically distinct individual. Twins in such a case are called dizygotic (*di-* means two) or fraternal. Fraternal twins are no more alike genetically than any nontwin siblings (brothers or sisters).

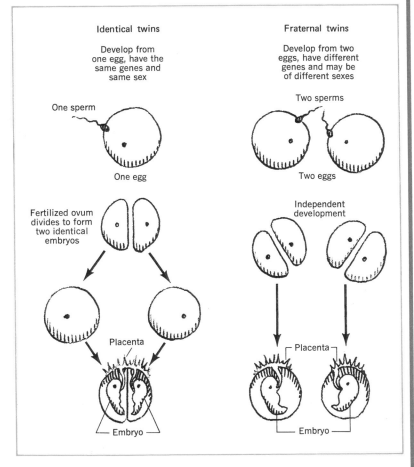

Identical twins

Develop from one egg, have the same genes and same sex

Fraternal twins

Develop from two eggs, have different genes and may be of different sexes

One sperm

One egg

Two sperms

Two eggs

Fertilized ovum divides to form two identical embryos

Independent development

Placenta

Placenta

Embryo

Embryo

FIGURE 2.11 The twinning process for identical (monozygotic) and fraternal (dizygotic) twins.

Stage I   II   III

FIGURE 2.12 Crossing-over. During meiosis a pair of chromosomes exchanges corresponding sections.

Mutations and the Gene Pool

The *gene pool* is an intriguing and humbling concept used by behavior geneticists to represent the total number of genes in a population. The study of the gene pool is called *population genetics*. If we accept the estimate of 100,000 genes in each human, then a town the size of Brockton, Massachusetts, has a gene pool of 7,000,-000,000 packaged in 70,000 individual units called people.

The human gene pool originated with the first "men" and has passed on from generation to generation, expanded or contracted, unchanged in some ways and altered in others, over the millenia of human existence. Each human conception is a drawing in the fantastic, universal genetic lottery; each drawing yields a new combination of genes that determines the heritable characteristics of the new individual. Each of these characteristics is given its opportunity to compete with the products of other existing gene combinations. The combinations that succeed, that is, tend to reproduce, are kept in the onflowing gene pool and are said to be *selected*. Unsuccessful combinations tend not to reproduce and so are dropped.

Factors producing new combinations in the genetic system, such as crossing-over and independent assortment, work over many generations at an agonizingly slow pace before they bring about a noticeable change in the gene pool. There is, however, another source of change and diversity that is outside the system and operates dramatically and abruptly—mutations. **Mutations** *suddenly, permanently, and often radically alter the gene structure an individual can pass on.*

We have noted that each single gene is a complex body containing DNA chains with precise arrangements of sugars, phosphates, and bases. These arrangements are highly stable; on rare occasions, however, an errant oxygen atom or high-energy particle might smash into a relatively sensitive point in the chain causing a rearrangement of the code. As we have seen in the case of P.K.U., a slight alteration of a gene can produce profound effects.

The location of any "slight alteration" is completely random. Since humans are a highly successful species with extremely complex organizations of intricate and precise subsystems, a random change in one or more of those systems is most likely to be a harmful one. (Consider what would happen if you reached into the motor of a well-running car and interchanged a few wire connections.) Indeed, in the human, most mutant zygotes do not even survive conception. Those that do survive are, in most cases, less fit for life, tend not to reproduce, and are likely to drop from the gene pool. Over the millennia, however, mutations have on rare occasions produced advantageous changes that have "improved the breed." Experimental geneticists can now mimic and hasten this evolutionary process in animals and plants by producing mutant changes through radiation and other techniques. By selecting out for breeding that tiny proportion of cases in which advantageous mutant changes have occurred and by discarding the great mass of unsuc-

Focus 2.4
Methods of Genetic Research

To study the mechanisms of heredity, geneticists have developed a variety of methods, which are summarized in this focus.

Pedigree Method. The pedigree method involves studying a trait in every possible member, living or dead, of a family line. The trait's genetic characteristics are inferred from the phenotypic characteristics of family members. This method was used to study the heritability of the ability to taste phenylthiocarbanide (PTC), a recessive trait. All members of a family—brothers, sisters, cousins, uncles, second cousins, etc.—were asked to taste a sample of the chemical and report their sensation. Some reported a bitter taste, others found the sample had no taste. By drawing a family tree and indicating which individual could or could not taste the chemical, inferences about genetic transmission could be made.

Twin Study. Identical (monozygotic) twins, fraternal (dizygotic) twins, and siblings (brothers and sisters) are compared with regard to a trait. Since monozygotic twins have identical genotypes, differences in their phenotypes can be used to infer the relative effects of genetics and environment.

Cytological Studies. In cytology, or the study of cells, cells are commonly examined under a microscope after they have been specially

cessful mutants, researchers can greatly improve strains for chosen characteristics. It was through this process that high-yield penicillin mold was developed, making the manufacture of penicillin an economically feasible undertaking (see Focus 2.4: Methods of Genetic Research).

Until recently mutation-producing, or mutagenic, agents were, relatively speaking, not of grave concern for the human gene pool. Ultraviolet light from the sun, for instance, is mutagenic, but because of its low tissue-penetrating properties has little, if any, effect on human sperm or ova cells. Medical and dental X-rays *can* be mutagenic, but that use is thought to be under reasonable control. As is well known, however, some part of the energy released in nuclear reactions and explosions comes off in the form of high-energy radiation. Some radioactive substances, such as strontium 90, are extremely mutagenic and especially serious since their radiation penetrates human tissue quite easily and thus can reach germ cells. Since World War II the amount of such radiation has increased noticeably as a consequence of atomic bomb testing in the atmosphere (see Figure 2.13). We can all hope that this increase will not continue, but what has happened has unquestionably already had some genetic effects.

INTERACTIONS OF HEREDITY AND ENVIRONMENT

Hybridization

Extensive research with animals leaves little doubt that a complex interaction between genetic factors and the environment plays a key role in the development of prepared to make their structures visible (as by staining with a dye). The discovery of the conditions associated with Down's syndrome was based on this technique.

Breeding Experiments. Some of the most important principles of genetics have been discovered through breeding experiments with plants and animals. Mendel's classical studies of the pea plant involved breeding. If a trait being bred selectively changes in a specific direction from generation to generation, it provides evidence that heredity is a factor. For example, in a now-famous experiment, R. C. Tryon selected the brightest rats in learning to run a maze and bred them together generation by generation. Similarly, he selected and inbred the dullest. After several generations, he had bred "maze-bright" and "maze-dull" strains of rats. Through selective inbreeding, that is, mating animals that are genetically related, pure strains have been developed that have very similar genotypes. By changing the environmental conditions for animals with similar or identical genotypes, the effects of environment on the phenotype can be studied. Obviously, breeding experiments are not possible with humans, so behavior geneticists must use other methods or cautiously generalize their findings in animal-breeding experiments to human beings.

FIGURE 2.13 An atomic bomb test above ground. Debris from the explosion enters the atmosphere and the radioactive fallout is carried long distances from the test site. The radioactive particles eventually enter human bodies, producing genetic damage that may alter human biology and behavior.

physical and behavioral characteristics of organisms. This interaction is effectively demonstrated by an interesting series of studies by Gardner Lindzey and Harvey Winston. In one of these studies they developed separate strains of mice, each of which had been heavily inbred by up to 100 generations of brother-sister matings. The inbred mice were subjected to a trauma, or shocking experience, soon after birth. When they were four days old they were placed on the floor of a 12-gallon washtub that had four loud doorbells mounted on the inside walls. For four days running, the infant mice endured the simultaneous ringing of all the bells continuously for a two-minute period. This is a severely trying experience for a four-day old mouse.

As a check on the effect of this infantile trauma, at the age of three months the mice were tested for their ability to run through a maze to a goal box containing food and for their ability to escape from water. For the latter test, a washtub was filled with water to a depth of three-and-one-half inches. At one end of the washtub a wire-cloth escape ramp was provided. On each trial, the mouse was removed from its cage and lowered into the water by its tail in such a way that its head faced toward the opposite wall from the escape ramp. The experimenter then recorded the time it took each mouse to escape from the water.

When the inbred strains reached mating age, they were interbred to produce new hybrid strains. A **hybrid** *is an offspring of genetically different parents.* The young hybrid mice were now subjected to the same infantile trauma when they reached four days of age and were given the same water escape and maze tests at the age of three months. The point of the experiment was to compare the differential effect of the infantile trauma on the inbred and the hybrid mice. The hybrid mice were faster at escaping from water than were their inbred parents (see Figure 2.14). They also made fewer errors in learning to run the maze. The fascinating result from the findings was the quite different ways the hybrid and inbred mice reacted to the infantile stress. The inbred mice made many more errors in learning to run the maze; the ability of the hybrid mice did not seem at all affected by the infantile trauma. Hybridization appeared to protect them.

The influence of hybrid genetic make-up in cushioning the effects of early infantile stress has been observed with other animals, other stresses, and other tests of behavior (see Focus 2.5: Hybrid Vigor). It represents a clear instance of a gene-environment interaction. A nasty environment acting on a weakened genetic structure produced large effects. There are doubtless areas of behavior where genetics plays a dominant role; there are doubtless areas of behavior where the environment is all-determining. However, both of these kinds of areas are probably few; truly to understand the origins of a human or animal's behavior, both genes and experience must be considered.

FIGURE 2.14 Water-escape times for inbred strains of rats and for hybrid strains.

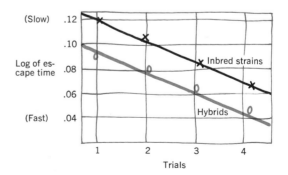

Focus 2.5
Hybrid Vigor

When two different pure-breed populations are crossbred, the resultant *hybrid* generation is superior to either of their inbred parents on many counts. This increase in strength and ability associated with crossbreeding is called *heterosis,* or *hybrid vigor.* The superior strength and resistance to disease of a "mutt" in comparison to the highly inbred, highly sensitive, purebred dog is well known. Crossbred animals show superior strength and size; they have a longer life expectancy and are more resistant to disease. They are more adept at learning and exploratory behavior and are more active. We will leave to speculation the interesting implications of hybrid vigor for human beings in the light of traditional opposition to interracial marriages.

Norm of Reaction and the Polygenic Determination of Traits

Gregor Mendel was a lucky man, for the phenotypes he selected to study in the pea plant had a direct one-to-one relationship with the genotypes under the conditions of his research. Later investigators have found that most phenotypes don't have a simple one-to-one linkage with the genotype and that a specific genotype may produce different phenotypes under varying environmental conditions. *The variety of phenotypes that can be expressed for one genotype under varying environmental conditions is referred to as the* **norm of reaction** *for that genotype.* Experimental geneticists have found that environmental variation in temperature and food supply could produce variations in shape, size, color, behavior and other characteristics of animals with the same genotype. Among human beings, variations in a child's experiences and nourishment can dramatically affect the youngster's intelligence, height, weight, and so on.

Most human traits, such as intelligence, temperament, and height, are a phenotypic expression of a large number of genes acting together. Such *traits involving many genes acting together are called* **polygenic traits.** One of the defining characteristics of almost all single-gene traits is the "yes-no" nature of the phenotype. Either you are brown-eyed or you are not. You have blood type O or you do not. There is a single gene; either you are positive or negative for that characteristic. In contrast, the phenotypic expression of a polygenic trait is distributed on a continuum, like black to white with many shades in between; skin color is, indeed, a good example of a polygenic trait in man.

A mating between white-skinned and black-skinned individuals almost always produces children who are neither "white" nor "black" but of intermediate color. The explanation is that many genes are involved in determining skin color. Some of these genes tend to produce a dark phenotype, some a lighter one. The phenotypical skin color for any individual depends on the mixture of genes inherited.

"Intelligence" (see Chapter Eight) is another good example of a polygenic trait. There are few mentally retarded individuals; there are few geniuses; most individuals fall between these extremes. Many genes create the genetic basis for intellectual development, and for each one of these genes an individual can be either positive or negative. (For purposes of clarity, we have assumed only two possibilities for each gene.) If you are positive for almost all of the "intelligence" genes, you may be a genius. If you are negative for too many, you will be retarded. Most people are positive for a medium number of genes.

For all behavioral traits of human beings, this polygenic foundation provides the likely *upper or lower limit* that a specific trait can reach phenotypically. That is, given a very large number of the "intelligence" genes, an individual will become a highly intelligent person *if* he or she is provided with proper nutrition during the mother's pregnancy and thereafter; *if* the child's birth does not cause too much brain damage; *if* the child is later supplied with adequate education; in short, *if* the environment does its share. If the environment does something less than its share, the genetic potential will not be realized. Once again, we note that the observable phenotype results from the interaction of what the seed contains and what the soil and climate contribute. The behavior geneticist studies this interaction and evaluates the relative weights of the contributing variables.

During the meiotic production of gametes (sperm and ova), as we have explained, the 46 chromosomes in the gonad cells are sorted into gametes with 23 chromosomes each. Any member of a chromosome pair can go into either gamete. Accordingly, one male can produce $2^{23} = 8,388,608$ different combinations of sperm and a female can produce the same number of ova combinations. Theoretically, any two parents can produce any one or more of over 150 trillion different kinds of combinations. In actuality, if you add to their combinations the shifting of genes from one chromosome pair to the other (and there are 2000 or so genes per chromosome), the potential for producing unique individuals on a genetic basis alone is staggering. When you add to this genetic source of diversity the myriad of unique environmental events that can influence a developing person, you have a dramatic reason why there has never been anyone just like you (unless you are an identical twin and even then, subtle environmental and experiential differences will produce differences in you both.)

This brief discussion of the mechanisms of genetics should give you a glimpse into the fantastic complexity of life and into a major factor contributing to the uniqueness of each individual.

SUMMARY

A. The Biological Determinants of Sex Identity

1. The normal sequence of fetal development is genetically determind. If something goes wrong at certain **critical periods** (page 32) of development it will have a dramatic impact on the growing organism. This was illustrated by the case of Julie, who had XY (male) chromosomes but developed into a feminine individual both in behavior and appearance.

2. The sex of the individual is determined by one pair of **chromosomes** (page 29). The XX combination produces a female and the XY combination a male.

3. The sex chromosomes indirectly influence sex development. In the absence of the male hormone androgen, development proceeds in a feminine direction; with sufficient quantities of androgen (and normal androgen sensitivity), development proceeds in a masculine direction.

4. Human sexual development, appearance, and behavior are related to the combined influences of chromosome make-up, hormonal sensitivity, and childhood socialization.

5. Studies of human infants and animals have revealed some basic differences in behavior and sensitivity to environmental stimuli. These differences are probably not as critical for sex identity in humans as in animals because of the influence of learning and social factors.

B.   The Mechanisms of Heredity

6. **Genetics** (page 29) is the study of heredity. The intricate mechanisms of heredity were illustrated by the case of Steven, a child with **P.K.U.** (page 37). P.K.U. is due to faulty **metabolism** (page 37) and usually leads to mental deficiency. The basis of the problem has been traced to a faulty **recessive gene** (page 41). The damaging effects of P.K.U. can be prevented by proper diet if begun early in infancy.

7. **Chromosomes** (page 39), which contain **genes** (page 39), are the basic units of heredity and carry the "blueprint" for each individual.

8. Chromosomes are very complex molecules consisting mainly of proteins and **deoxyribonucleic acid,** or **DNA** (page 38).

9. Some genes are **recessive** (page 41) and others **dominant** (page 40). Recessive genes usually can influence the **phenotype** (page 40) only when the **genotype** (page 40) contains two recessive genes.

10. Chromosomes have the capacity to duplicate themselves when new body cells and **gametes** (page 43) are produced.

11. Each parent contributes half (23) of the 46 chromosomes that are found in each body cell.

12. Through the course of evolution, genotypic diversity has resulted through the mechanisms of **independent assortment** (page 43), **crossing-over** (page 47) and **mutations** (page 49). When these mechanisms produced traits in their carriers that enhanced survival, the trait was passed on to the next generation.

13. Most human traits are **polygenic** (page 53) and their development is complexly determined through an interaction of heredity and environment.

Chapter
Three
Brain
and
Behavior

P. J. Vogel and J. E. Bogen of the California College of Medicine were faced with a 48-year-old war veteran suffering from a very severe epilepsy. We named this veteran Max and described his seizures in the introductory panorama. Most cases of epilepsy can be controlled by drugs. In a few difficult cases like Max's the drugs are not effective; epileptic seizures may become quite violent, spreading from a small focus in one hemisphere (or one half of the brain) to a massive attack that envelops both hemispheres. These violent seizures can result in serious brain damage in both hemispheres, not just in the originally affected one. The new brain damage can, in turn, lead to a greater frequency of seizures. This spiralling of difficulties would eventually completely incapacitate the victim.

Vogel and Bogen knew that, since drugs did not work for Max, they were powerless to treat Max's original focal disturbance. They reasoned that their best strategy lay in saving the unaffected hemisphere from further damage. *The two hemispheres of the brain are connected by a thin strip of nerve tissue called the* **corpus callosum** (see Figure 3.1). When an epileptic seizure spreads from one hemisphere to the other it travels across the corpus callosum. What if this connection were cut? Undoubtedly the spread of the seizures would be stopped. But is the operation safe? What unexpected side effects could occur in a split-brain person? Does each hemisphere of the brain have its own functions?

Exploring answers to questions such as these is, in the field of psychology, the concern of physiological psychologists. In

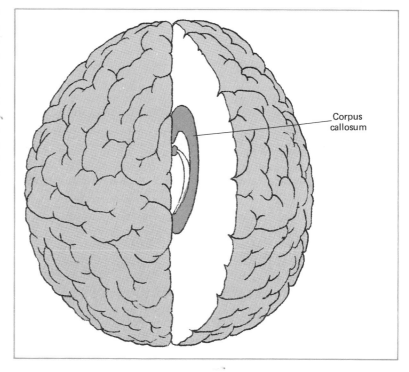

FIGURE 3.1 The two hemispheres of the brain are connected by the corpus callosum. This tissue can be cut, severing the connection between the hemispheres. (Adapted from "The Split Brain in Man" by Michael S. Gazzaniga. Copyright © August 1967 by Scientific American, Inc. All rights reserved.)

Corpus callosum

this chapter we will examine the research findings that help our understanding of how the brain and nervous system operate, how chemicals and drugs affect brain, behavior, and experience, and how the split-brain man helped reveal some of nature's secrets about brain functioning and about consciousness.

A.   THE SPLIT-BRAIN MAN

Happily for Max, some information on the split brain existed in the psychological literature. Ronald E. Myers and Roger W. Sperry of the California Institute of Technology had reported a surprising discovery. When they cut through the corpus callosum of a cat, the two halves of the brain continued to function quite independently. The surgery created problems for the cat in certain specially designed laboratory situations. Otherwise the cat behaved and thrived quite normally. Vogel and Bogen decided that, rather than allow the epileptic process to continue to destroy their patient's brain, they would try the dramatic Myers and Sperry operation. If all went well, they would be able at least to save one hemisphere of the brain. As a matter of fact, things turned out much better than they had hoped. The operation almost completely eliminated the patient's seizures. Ten other patients later successfully underwent the same corpus callosum operation. Afterwards, they were carefully studied for any psychological consequences. The investigators were most impressed that no readily noticeable change in the intelligence, personality, or temperament of the patients seemed to occur. Indeed, it was only by very close observation that the effects of the operation become apparent.

THE EFFECTS OF CUTTING THE CORPUS CALLOSUM

After they had recovered from the corpus callosum operation, Vogel and Bogen's patients were brought into a psychological laboratory for tests. For example, each patient was told to fixate his gaze on the center light in a row of lights. Lights were then briefly flashed on either side of the center. The patient was asked to report when he saw a flash. Strangely, in every case, he reported flashing only for lights to the right of center, never for left-of-center lights. How can we explain this curious fact in terms of the operation that had isolated the two halves of his brain?

As you can see from Figure 3.2, the lights on the right were registering only in the left hemisphere. Since the brain center responsible for speech is also located in the left hemisphere, the patient's left hemisphere could both see a right-of-center light and report it. However, while the right hemisphere could see the left-of-center lights, it could not report them verbally because the right hemisphere has no way of initiating speech. In a normal individual the right hemisphere's perception of the left-of-center light would have been relayed to the left hemisphere via the corpus callosum. But after the operation this transmission was impossible. Hence, the patients could make no verbal report of events perceived only by the right hemisphere. But if they are told to point at the light, then the right hemisphere can indicate that it has perceived one.

Sensory information (touch, pressure, heat, etc.) from the right side of the body goes to the left hemisphere, and vice versa. If an unseen familiar object was placed in a split-brain patient's right hand he could easily name it, since the left side of the brain contains the speech center. As might

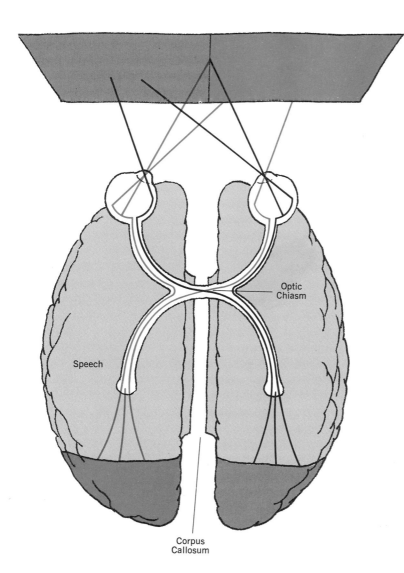

FIGURE 3.2 The right visual field (color) is projected, via the optic chiasm, to the left hemisphere of the brain. The left visual field (black) is registered in the right hemisphere. A patient with a severed corpus callosum cannot describe stimuli in the left visual field because the right hemisphere has been disconnected from the speech center, which is in the left hemisphere. (Adapted from Gazzaniga, op. cit.)

be expected, an unseen object placed in the left hand could not be named; but it could be matched correctly to an identical item among a group of objects.

If a printed word was presented to the right hemisphere via the left visual field, the patient either would not respond to a request to read it or would guess incorrectly (see Figure 3.3). The incorrect guesses apparently come from a completely unin-

formed (but hopeful) left hemisphere. In one interesting experiment, the word HEART was flashed to a patient with the HE to the left of, and the ART to the right of, the visual center. When the patient was later presented with the two words HE and ART and asked to point to the word that had been flashed, the left hand pointed to HE and the right hand to ART! Thus, although the right hemisphere

(Control of the right side of the body is exercised almost completely by the left hemisphere and that of the left side of the body by the right hemisphere.) Thus, although the right hemisphere was not capable of speech, it evidenced reading comprehension. The left hand was also able to obey auditory commands. For example, it would pick oranges or pencils out of a bag solely by touch after instructions to do so.

The experimenters' tests often were disrupted by forms of communication of some sort between the hemispheres. In one experiment, for example, red and green lights were periodically flashed to the right hemisphere; the patient was asked to state what color had been flashed. At first, the patient could only name the color correctly at about a chance level. After all, his left hemisphere (where the speech center is located) was giving the answers and his right hemisphere was seeing the color of the light. Therefore, the left hemisphere, when giving the response, was just making blind guesses. To the experimenters' surprise, however, after a few trials the patient's score began to improve mysteriously. They discovered after some investigation that when by chance the left hemisphere named the correct color the right hemisphere heard the answer and noted that it was correct. When the left hemisphere made a mistake in color naming, however, the right hemisphere would produce a frown and a shaking of the head. The left hemisphere would pick up this hint, called a "cross-cue," and change its answer. By picking up cross-cues, one hemisphere could learn from the other. It was almost as though the experimenter was dealing with two different people housed in the same body.

Although the right hemisphere could understand some language, it was inferior

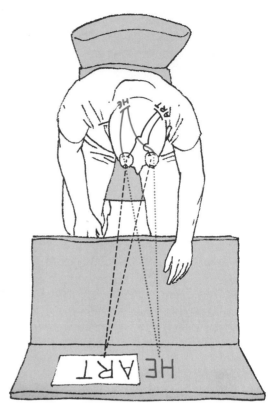

FIGURE 3.3 *The letters HE were presented in the left visual field, the letters ART in the right visual field. They were projected, respectively, in the right and left hemisphere. (Adapted from Gazzaniga, op. cit.)*

to the left hemisphere in this function. It seemed mainly limited to understanding simple, nonabstract nouns. On the other hand, the right hemisphere seemed superior to the left in tasks involving spatial relations. Study Figure 3.4 to see how much better the left hands of these patients could copy three-dimensional drawings.

IMPLICATIONS OF SPLIT-BRAIN RESEARCH

These cases offer several important lessons about the functioning of the brain. First,

EXAMPLE   LEFT HAND   RIGHT HAND

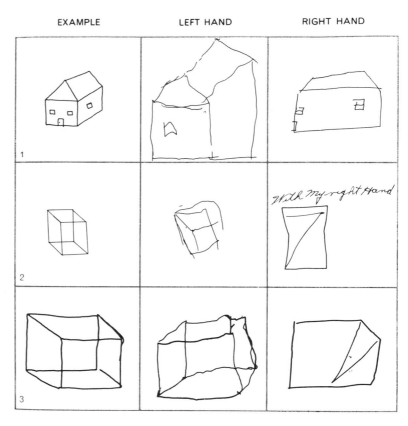

FIGURE 3.4 The right hemisphere (controlling the left hand) is superior in tasks involving manual copying of visual stimuli. These drawings were done by a right-handed patient with a severed corpus callosum. (Gazzaniga, op. cit.)

they make evident the workings of the corpus callosum in transferring information from hemisphere to hemisphere. Second, and perhaps most important for overall understanding of brain functioning, they contribute to knowledge of the location of various functional centers in the brain, such as a center for speech, a center for understanding spatial relations, and centers for voluntary motor control. Third, they show how control by the brain is "contralateral," that is, the left hemisphere controls the right side of the body and vice versa. We must, however, note that although the understanding of speech and language is localized in the left side of the brain, the function also exists, to some extent, in the right hemisphere. The split-

brain person also teaches us a fourth lesson, that is, the human being's remarkable ability to learn to adapt and to overcome major damage to the nervous system.

Now we will explore the structure and functions of nerve cells and the brain in greater detail.

B. THE BUILDING BLOCKS AND STRUCTURE OF THE NERVOUS SYSTEM

In Bologna, Italy, in the late 1700s, the windows of butcher shops were festooned with a special delicacy, frogs' legs. To the average Bolognese it was neither remarkable nor interesting that the muscles of some of these disembodied frogs' legs would frequently twitch in the most lively manner. But Luigi Galvani, a professor of anatomy at the University of Bologna, became curious about the muscle-twitching. Walking home one evening in 1786, he went into a shop and noticed that the frogs' legs were hung on copper hooks that were attached to iron nails. The legs that twitched were those that were touching an iron nail. Galvani (for whom the galvanometer was named) knew that, if two different metals are in physical contact, a small current passes between them. He reasoned that the frogs' legs, connecting the iron and copper, produced a current, which, in turn, was stimulating the muscles and producing the twitching. It was this chance observation by Galvani that first suggested the electrical basis of nerve-impulse transmission.

In this section we will explore some of the basic physiological facts about the nerve impulse and the nerve cells that are the basic building blocks of the nervous system. We will then show how these basic building blocks are put together to form the central nervous system.

THE NEURON

A **nerve cell,** *or* **neuron** (see Figure 3.5) *has the highly specialized function of receiving impulses from neurons or sense receptors and transmitting them to other neurons. At the receiving end of each neuron are* **dendrites** (in some nerve cells these make up a tree-like dendritic formation). A nerve impulse enters the neuron via the dendrites and passes as a wave through the cell body and into the axon. *From the* **axon** *the impulse is passed on to the dendrites of the next neuron.* A neuron has many dendrites, often several thousand in

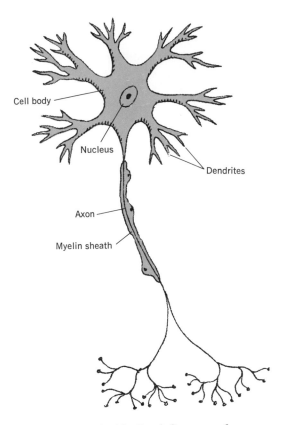

FIGURE 3.5 An idealized diagram of a nerve cell. Dendrite stimulation fires the nerve impulses, which travel along the axon to the dendrites of the next nerve cell. The myelin sheath is a fat-like covering that protects the axon of many but not all nerve cells.

the case of a sensory neuron, but it has only one axon, although this sometimes has branches.

Neural Transmission

As Galvani discovered, the nerve impulse is transferred along the neural pathways in the form of electrical discharges. We now know that this electrical activity involves electrochemical changes along the nerve fiber. The details of this electrochemical activity have been carefully studied. The basic facts can be stated quite briefly. The inside of a neuron at rest has a greater negative electrical charge than the outside. This difference in electrical charge is equal to about 80 millivolts (less than one tenth of a volt). This charge is maintained by the resistance of the "skin" of the neuron, the cell membrane. Basically, the cell membrane is impermeable to electrically negative particles inside the cell (see Figure 3.6). The negative particles inside the cell can't pass outside through the membrane. But the membrane will allow positive particles outside to permeate the cell under certain conditions. When the cell dendrites are stimulated by, say, the axon of another cell, the cell membrane at that point becomes more permeable and permits positively charged particles to pass into the cell. Now the outside of the cell is more negative than the inside. Through a sequence of alternating charges on either side of the cell membrane, from the point of stimulation the nerve impulse continues to pass along the cell in a wave that sweeps the length of the cell to the tip of the axon. This wave of positive charges crossing the membrane is what we mean when we say that a nerve cell *fires*. This electrochemical firing of nerve cells is the basis of transmission of messages in the nervous system.

Excitation at a dendrite must reach a certain level, or **threshold,** *before a cell fires; if that level is reached, the cell fires.* If many axons fire onto the dendrites of a single neuron, resulting in very strong excitation, the target neuron can only fire in its accustomed way. It will not fire at a greater intensity. The intensity of a message is transmitted by other means, such as the number of neurons that are excited or the frequency at which a neuron fires. The firing of a neuron at a single consistent

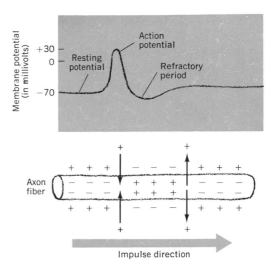

FIGURE 3.6 The electrochemical basis of the nerve impulse. Nerve transmission consists of a wave of interchanging charged particles passing through the nerve membrane. The action potential is a voltage charge that travels down the axon.

intensity is summarized by the **all-or-none law;** *a neuron either fires at its fixed intensity or it does not fire at all.* This standard neuronal impulse forms the basic unit of all nervous activity.

One further fact about neurons: *after a neuron has fired, it takes some time to recover its electrical balance before it will fire again; this recovery time is called the* **refractory phase.** No matter how strong the stimulation, during the refractory phase the neuron will not fire. The refractory phase varies among different nerve fibers and, for the fastest recovering fibers, lasts about one millisecond. Thus, a neuron can carry from a few hundred to a thousand impulses a second.

To visualize the action of a nerve fiber, think of it as a string with a burning match at one end. If the match is not hot enough or close enough the string will not catch fire, much like a neuron that will not fire if the excitation is below its threshold. If the heat is great enough, however, the end of the string catches fire and each section of string ignites the next section, on down to the end, in a continuous motion. This process is analogous to the electrochemical discharges in a nerve fiber. If at the end of the burning string there is another string (that is, nerve fiber) and if that other string gets hot enough (reaches a threshold), it too will catch fire (be triggered to fire). The burned-out string can't be re-ignited any more than a nerve in its refractory phase can be fired. Unlike the string, however, the living nerve cell is restored. The electrochemicals along the nerve fiber return it to its initial charge state and the nerve can transmit again. Again, unlike the slow-burning string, nerve cells can conduct an impulse at relatively high speeds, varying from a few hundred feet to over 200 miles per hour. The energy for the string to burn is provided by the chemical components of the string and not the match that began the fire. Similarly, the electrochemical charge stored in the nerve provides the energy for the nerve impulses, not the instigating stimulus.

The Junction of Neurons: The Synapse

The original stimulant to a neural impulse can be a mechanical force (such as pressure or sound vibrations) or an electrochemical input from a sense organ or from another nerve. Once begun, the impulse transmission proceeds from neuron to neuron by a combination of electrical and chemical means. *At the junction point between two neurons the axon of one cell meets the dendrites of the next cell. This junction is called a* **synapse** *(see Figure 3.7). The synapse is actually a gap between the two nerve cells.* When the wave

of positive charges in a firing neuron reaches the end of its axon, it arrives at the synapse; there it releases certain chemical substances called transmitters. *These* **neurotransmitters,** *which are stored in tiny globular synaptic vesicles* (see Figure 3.7), *pass through the cell membrane into the gap forming the synapse and then into the dendrite of the next cell.* In this way messages are carried from place to place in the nervous system. It takes about one thousandth of a second for an impulse to traverse the synapse. When an impulse crosses over a synapse it can only go in one direction, from axon to dendrite.

Drugs and Synaptic Transmission. The chemical basis of neural transmission across the synapse has some very useful implications relating to the chemical control of behavior as well as to the actions of certain poisons and drugs affecting the nervous system. Among the several chemical transmitters that have been identified, one is called *acetylcholine* (ACh). When ACh action is blocked, a nerve impulse cannot be transmitted and fatal paralysis can occur. A variety of substances can block the release or action of ACh. Curare (a poison used on arrows by South American Indians) prevents the ACh released by an axon from stimulating the dendrites of the next nerve fiber. Botulism toxin, which is found in spoiled or improperly canned foods, blocks the release of ACh from the synaptic vesicles. Botulism is very toxic and can produce a fatal respiratory collapse due to paralysis. Fortunately, antitoxins are available.

Noradrenalin is another neurotransmitter found in many brain cells. A number of tranquilizers, such as chlorpromazine, block the release of noradrenalin, thus diminishing the rate of neural transmission.

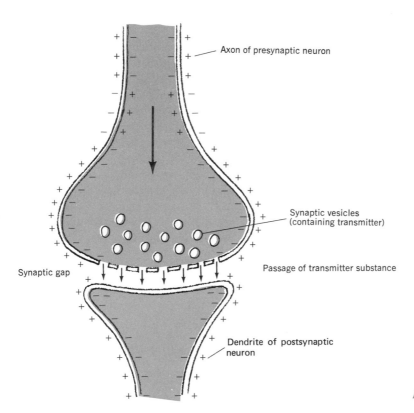

Axon of presynaptic neuron

Synaptic vesicles
(containing transmitter)

Synaptic gap

Passage of transmitter substance

Dendrite of postsynaptic
neuron

FIGURE 3.7 A synapse.

Chlorpromazine is highly effective in reducing the anxiety and agitation of people with emotional and behavioral disorders.

Some clues to how LSD produces its effects are provided by recent neurotransmitter findings. LSD has a chemical structure very similar to that of *serotonin,* which is a neurotransmitter in many brain centers. Evidence based on animal studies indicates that LSD accumulates in certain brain centers and may overstimulate neural transmission. In effect, the drug seems to interrupt the normally regulated conduction at the synapses and "makes" the brain go "wild" by turning on too many neural transmissions. This effect would, in part, account for the collage of vividly colored images, sensations, and emotions reported by the drug's users.

THE NERVOUS AND ENDOCRINE SYSTEMS

From a biological point of view our behavior and experience depend on an integration of the biological processes within our bodies. Nature has delegated the responsibility for this integration to two systems: the nervous system and the endocrine (hormone) system. The brain and the spinal cord make up the central nervous system. Nerves and their networks that branch out of the brain and spinal cord are called the peripheral nervous system. The peripheral nervous system plays an important role in motivation and emotion and will be discussed in the next chapter. The endocrine system consists of a number of glands, located in various parts of the body, that secrete hormones directly into the blood.

Focus 3.1

The Evolution of the Vertebrate Brain

Through the long process of evolution the more highly developed organisms arose from their simpler predecessors. This process is strikingly illustrated in the evolution of the brain (see Figure 3.8). The brain's three major sections are the hindbrain, midbrain, and forebrain. The hindbrain, the most primitive, was probably the first to evolve. It contains structures that are essential for survival, such as the medulla (which controls circulation, respiration, digestion), the cerebellum (balance and muscular coordination), and the pons (interconnection fibers). The midbrain, which is relatively small in humans but large in primitive animals, controls auditory and visual functions. The forebrain, which is largest in humans, is the center of intellectual processes, of thought, of memory, and of motor and sensory integration, which are centered in the cerebrum. The hypothalamus and thalamus are also in the forebrain.

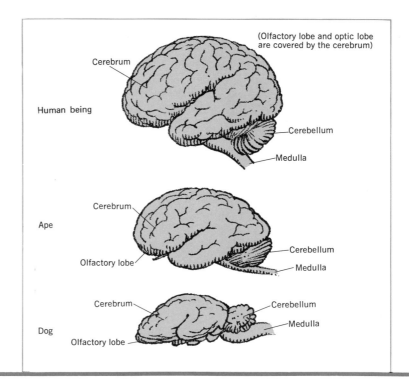

Size alone is not the critical factor in evolutionary development. The more elaborate the forebrain relative to the rest of the brain, the higher the evolutionary development of the organism. For example, the elephant's brain is more than ten times the size of a chimpanzee's, yet the chimp displays greater thinking ability and can be taught to use language (see Chapter 9D).

The relative size and complexity of various sections of the brain often reflect an organism's adaptation to the environment. For example, the olfactory (sense of smell) lobes are largest in animals such as dogs, reptiles, and fish that depend on smell as a major source of environmental information. (As those animals evolved, a more developed olfactory lobe proved adaptively advantageous.) In humans, the olfactory lobes are quite small, but the forebrain, particularly the cerebrum, is enlarged; it is small in dogs and very small in reptiles and fish.

FIGURE 3.8 Evolution of the vertebrate brain.

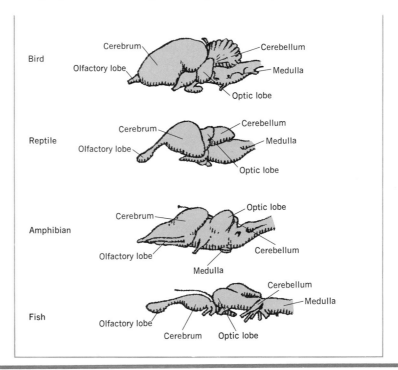

The Structure and Function of the Central Nervous System. The human nervous system is a complex organization of billions of cells that has evolved over millions of years (see Focus 3.1). It controls the muscles involved in physical action, the heart beat, and respiration, as well as every other biological system needed for life. In addition, the brain enables human beings to carry out complex adaptive behavior, learn and solve problems, and store experiences as memories. Figure 3.9 and Table 3.1 summarize the major anatomical components and functions of the central nervous system.

Chemical Regulators of the Body: The Structure and Functions of the Endocrine System. The seven endocrine glands secrete **hormones** (from a Greek root meaning to excite or stimulate). *These chemical substances have a wide range of regulatory functions in the body, including energy expenditure, growth rate, responsiveness to stress, and sexual development.* **Endocrine** (meaning ductless) *glands secrete hormones directly into the bloodstream.* Figure 3.10 and Table 3.2 (see pages 70–71) summarize the wide range of hormones and their regulatory effects on body functions and behavior.

TABLE 3.1 **The central nervous system**

STRUCTURE	FUNCTION
1. The Brain	
Cerebrum	Sense perception, control of voluntary movements, learning, memory, thinking, consciousness
Corpus Callosum	Connecting left and right cerebral hemispheres
Thalamus	A relay station for impulses to cerebral cortex
Hypothalamus	Control of or influence on such functions as endocrine balance, temperature regulation, appetite, metabolism, emotions
Cerebellum	Coordination of voluntary movements, body balance, muscle tone
2. The Brain Stem (The upper portion of the spinal cord)	
Reticular formation	Activating cerebral cortex; its impulses play an important role in consciousness, awareness, sleep
Pons	Connecting the two hemispheres of the cerebellum
Medulla	Via 12 cranial nerves, extending brain control over breathing, swallowing, heart beat, digestion, etc.
3. Spinal Cord	Carrying brain impulses to body and impulses from body to brain, controlling many reflexes

FIGURE 3.9 The central nervous system.

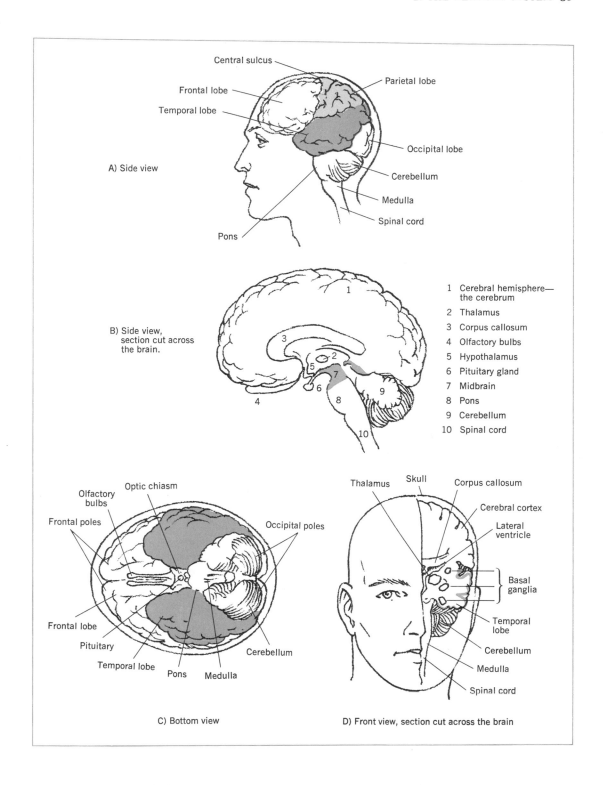

A) Side view

Central sulcus
Frontal lobe
Temporal lobe
Parietal lobe
Occipital lobe
Cerebellum
Medulla
Spinal cord
Pons

B) Side view,
section cut across
the brain.

1 Cerebral hemisphere—
   the cerebrum
2 Thalamus
3 Corpus callosum
4 Olfactory bulbs
5 Hypothalamus
6 Pituitary gland
7 Midbrain
8 Pons
9 Cerebellum
10 Spinal cord

C) Bottom view

Olfactory
bulbs
Optic chiasm
Frontal poles
Occipital poles
Frontal lobe
Pituitary
Temporal lobe
Pons
Medulla
Cerebellum

D) Front view, section cut across the brain

Thalamus
Skull
Corpus callosum
Cerebral cortex
Lateral
ventricle
Basal
ganglia
Temporal
lobe
Cerebellum
Medulla
Spinal cord

TABLE 3.2 **Endocrine glands and their function**

ENDOCRINE GLAND	HORMONE	FUNCTION AND INFLUENCE ON BEHAVIOR AND EXPERIENCE
1. Pituitary		The master gland: pituitary hormones control the secretion of other glands
Anterior Pituitary	Growth Hormone	Growth of skeleton and body
	Corticotropin (ACTH)	Adrenal gland stimulation, influences emotional behavior
Posterior Pituitary	Vasopressin	Blood pressure, water regulation and secretion
2. Thyroid	Thyroxin	Metabolic rate, body weight, level of physical activity, intellectual development, irritability to stimuli
3. Thymus	Thymus Hormone	Development of body's immunity reactions
4. Parathyroid	Parathyroid Hormone	Calcium metabolism; maintaining normal reactivity of nervous system
5. Pancreas	Insulin	Sugar metabolism
6. Adrenal		
Adrenal Cortex	Cortisone	Salt and carbohydrate metabolism; secondary sex characteristics (voice, hair, etc.)
Adrenal Medulla	Noradrenalin (or Norepinephrine) Adrenalin (or Epinephrine)	During emotional stress releasing blood sugar, increasing blood pressure, heartbeat, feelings of tension and anxiety
7. Gonads (testes, male) (ovaries, female)	Androgen Estrogen Progestin	Primary and secondary sex characteristics are linked to all three hormones Menstruation, pregnancy, and emotional irritability are linked to estrogen and progestin

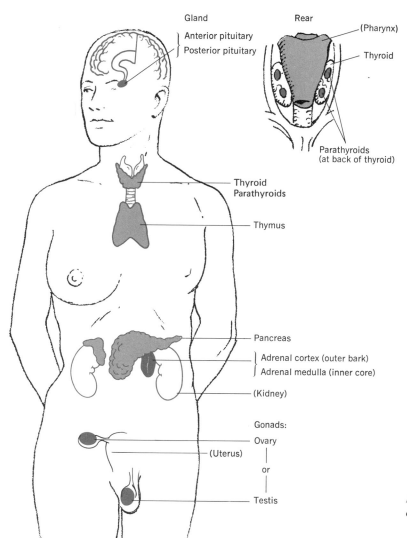

Gland

Anterior pituitary
Posterior pituitary

Rear

(Pharynx)

Thyroid

Parathyroids
(at back of thyroid)

Thyroid
Parathyroids

Thymus

Pancreas

Adrenal cortex (outer bark)
Adrenal medulla (inner core)

(Kidney)

Gonads:

Ovary

(Uterus)

or

Testis

FIGURE 3.10 **The endo-crine glands.**

C. THE LOCALIZATION OF BRAIN FUNCTIONS

Before the middle of the nineteenth century it was generally believed, not surprisingly, that the brain functions as a unit. To the naked eye the human brain has the appearance of a bowl of thin, cold, white mush. Others have described it as a bowl of grey gelatin. In any case, because of its unprepossessing appearance, it

is understandable that a discovery in the middle of the nineteenth century by Paul Broca, a surgeon, created quite a sensation. His great discovery came when he removed a specific area in the left hemisphere of a patient's brain and found that the patient was suddenly unable to talk. As you might expect from results in patients with a severed corpus callosum, Broca's patient was still able to understand language. In other words, Broca had dis-

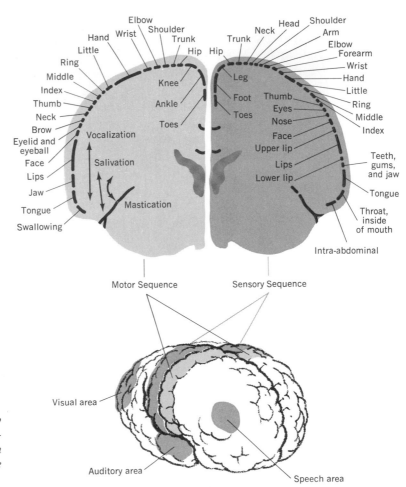

FIGURE 3.11 (Top) Map
of the functions of the cortex. (Bottom) Projection
areas. Broca's area is the
speech area.

covered that the function of producing speech was located in this specific area of the brain, now called Broca's area (see Figure 3.11).

METHODS OF STUDYING THE BRAIN

Encouraged by Broca's discovery, other scientists began to explore the surface of the brain by another method. First, they exposed the brain of an animal by removing a portion of its skull. Then they applied a tiny current of electricity through a needle to stimulate portions of the cortex (that is, the outside layer of the brain). They located motor centers where stimulation would reliably produce specific body movements. These early observations were followed by a century of mapping of the functions of the cortex. (Figure 3.11 shows some of the results of this mapping.)

The methods illustrated by Broca's discovery and the discoveries of the motor areas illustrate two important methods of brain research. In one case, damage is inflicted on areas of the brain of an animal and the effects of the resulting *lesions* are observed in the creature's behavior. In the other case, electrical stimulation of parts of the brain is correlated with observations of the subsequent behavior. During the exciting days of mapping the cortex, most of the important sensory and motor systems were rapidly located.

When scientists began looking for a neurological understanding of learning, emotion, and other experience, the quest took them into deeper areas of the brain. This work progressed a bit more slowly for two reasons. First, it was difficult to get into the deeper structures of the brain without causing gross damage to the cortex of the brain. Therefore, it was impossible to judge whether observed effects were the result of lesions or electrical stimulation to the deeper areas of the brain or whether the effect observed was simply the result of the gross damage done to the cortex. Second, it was difficult to measure complex learned responses. It was easy to test to see whether an animal would respond with the twitch of a muscle. But how could one determine whether the animal was learning, experiencing pleasure, or feeling annoyance?

BRAIN-RESEARCH INSTRUMENTATION

The first of these problems, the question of access to the deeper areas of the brain, was solved by a Swiss physiologist, W. R. Hess. Hess developed a technique for permanently implanting **electrodes** *(consisting of long, thin, insulated wires through which a current can be passed)* into the brain. These are usually called *chronic implantations*. Through a hole bored in the skull, an electrode is sunk into a specific portion of the brain and affixed to the skull. The electrodes are so minute that they

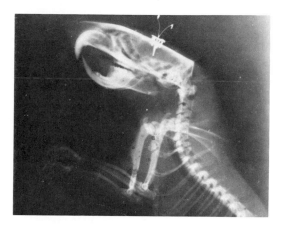

FIGURE 3.12 X-ray photo of implanted electrode in brain of a rat. The electrode, held by a plastic cap attached to the skull, can be used to record electrical impulses or stimulate the brain.

avoid the problem of damaging the cortex of the brain while reaching down into the deeper structures. The animal does not appear to suffer ill effects from this operation; after a period of recovery the animal's brain functioning can be studied, via the electrode, while the animal continues its normal activities (see Figure 3.12). In addition to the problem of avoiding injury to the cortex while studying the deeper areas of the brain, the investigator is interested in placing the tip of the electrode with extreme accuracy. The area of study might be extremely minute. Two physiologists, Horsley and Clarke, devised a *stereotaxic instrument* that can be used to place electrodes into the brains of rats or other animals accurately. The rat's head is placed in the instrument and is positioned by use of a fixed point near the eardrums. A clamp is attached either to the animal's snout or in such a way that the incisor teeth lock on to it. The purpose is to hold the animal's head rigidly in a known, fixed position (see Figure 3.13).

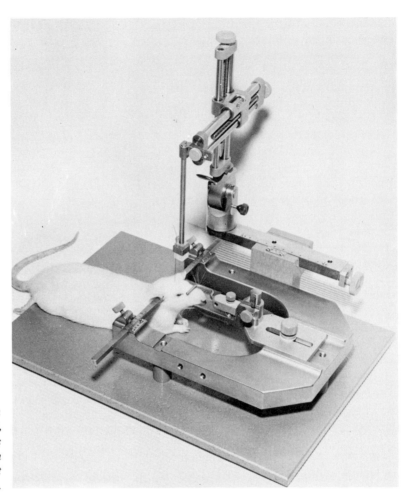

FIGURE 3.13 Rat in a stereotaxic instrument, which holds the animal's head in a fixed position to simplify the placement of electrodes in the brain.

Such electrode implants in deep structures of the brain permit us to study the neurological processes underlying complex functions such as emotions and learning. An overview of the major methods of studying the brain is presented in Focus 3.2: How To Study the Brain.

BEHAVIOR RESEARCH AND CONTROL THROUGH ESB

Laboratory albino rats have had much of the wild rat's meanness and lustiness bred out of them, but they still exhibit some instinctual behavior. For example, when first placed in an open, well-lit area, a laboratory rat can be counted on to hug the walls and avoid open areas. One historic rat that James F. Olds and Peter Milner were studying just would *not* behave this way. Olds and Milner were observing the effects of *direct electrical stimulation* of rat's brains (ESB), via electrodes that were surgically implanted in various locations. The electrodes are held in place by a plastic carrier screwed to the skull (see Figure 3.12). What Olds and Milner didn't know was that in this par-

Focus 3.2

How To Study the Brain

Several ingenious methods have been developed to find out how the brain operates. The methods and procedures are summarized below.

1. Study of Brain through Injury or Disease. Brain tumors, gunshot wounds, and other disease or accidental injury to specific brain areas produce a variety of symptoms. By noting the symptoms and identifying the site of the injury, it is often possible to infer the role of various brain locations.

2. Ablation. Rather than wait for disease or injury, surgery on an animal can be conducted and a section of the brain removed or cut (ablated) and its effects on behavior observed.

3. Electrical Stimulation of the Brain (ESB). When portions of the skull are removed, the surface of the brain can be stimulated with an electrode and its effects on behavior observed. Electrodes can also be implanted deep in various brain locations to study their behavioral effects. Electrical implants can even be used to record electrical activities of a single cell.

4. Electroencephalograph. Slight electrical currents occur in all brain activity. By attaching electrodes to the scalp and amplifying these currents electronically, they can be recorded on a moving strip of paper traced by a pen. The machine that does this is the electroencephalograph (EEG). The record of brain activity it makes is shown in Figure 3.14. By relating behavior and environmental stimulation to brain-wave patterns, inferences about brain activity can be made.

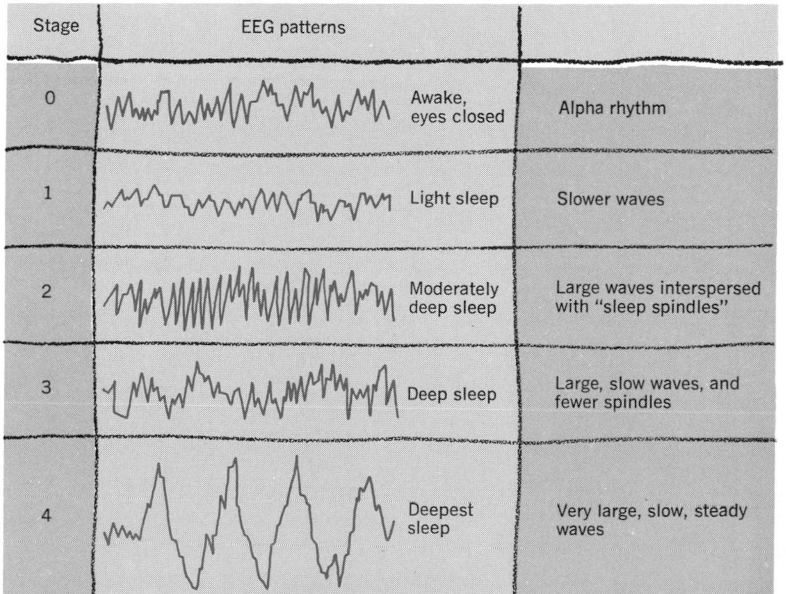

FIGURE 3.14 Electrical activity of the brain recorded during various stages of wakefulness and sleep.

Stage	EEG patterns		
0		Awake, eyes closed	Alpha rhythm
1		Light sleep	Slower waves
2		Moderately deep sleep	Large waves interspersed with "sleep spindles"
3		Deep sleep	Large, slow waves, and fewer spindles
4		Deepest sleep	Very large, slow, steady waves

ticular rat the electrode was implanted into a brain location, called the septum, which was a bit off the section they were aiming for. As a consequence, they found that the rat completely disregarded its usual tendency to hug the wall and returned repeatedly to the spot on the floor where it had been standing when it had last been electrically stimulated. The more brain stimulation it received at that spot, the more time it spent there. The rat seemed to "like" it! Moreover, Olds and Milner found that the rat would do almost anything they could think of, as you will see below, if its behavior was rewarded by brain stimulation. The septum, then, can be considered a pleasure center of the rat's brain.

One of the simplest and most effective ways of measuring the response of a rat to stimulation is to see whether it begins to respond more quickly or more slowly or just stops responding altogether. One of the best environments for observing changes in a rat's responses is a device called the Skinner box, named after its inventor, Harvard professor B. F. Skinner (see Figure 3.15). A hungry rat is placed in a box that contains a lever. Typically, in the course of the rat's explorations of the box it will happen to press the lever. (This event can be hastened by placing a little wet food on the lever.) If nothing happens as a result of its action, then lever-pressing is not likely to occur again. If, on the other hand, the animal receives a pellet of food, then it will soon learn to press the lever with increased frequency. The apparatus thus fulfills the need for a method to measure responses more complex than muscle twitches and is commonly used in physiological-behavioral research.

Olds and Milner used a Skinner box to train rats in their research program to do the most improbable things simply by

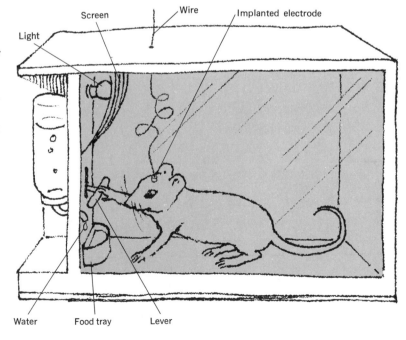

FIGURE 3.15 Rat in a Skinner box. Ordinarily rats are trained into certain behavior patterns of pressing the lever with food as the reward. Olds and Milner found they could use electrical stimulation of the brain as a reward.

Light

Screen

Wire

Implanted electrode

Water   Food tray   Lever

rewarding them with electrical stimulation of the septum. Every time a rat placed its paw on the treadle in the Skinner box it could electrically stimulate its septum. Some rats stimulated themselves for 24 hours without rest and as often as 5000 times an hour. Rats would stimulate themselves in preference to eating available food to such an extent that they would die of hunger. Rats would even run across a charged electrified grid in order to obtain brain stimulation by pressing a lever on the other side of the grid.

This pioneering discovery by Olds and Milner is part of an exciting series of findings based on the effects of direct electrical stimulation of the brain. Areas have been charted where stimulation will produce rage, calm, penile or clitoral erection, and orgasm. Olds' and Milner's first experiments required complex and awkward overhead trolley wires to get a tiny electric current to the brain of the free-moving rat. Now, however, the current can be delivered easily and conveniently via radio transmitter. In the introductory chapter we described the work of Yale researcher José M. R. Delgado. Armed only with his little radio transmitter, he stood in a bull ring before an electrode-implanted charging bull. Just before the enraged bull reached him he transmitted a pulse into the bull's brain that turned off the bull's rage and stopped the charge.

Such direct electrical stimulation of the brain has been carried out in human beings. Prison volunteers or individuals undergoing brain surgery are the usual human subjects. Stimulation of certain areas can produce personal memories so vivid that an individual seems to be reliving the experiences (see Focus 3.3: The Brain as a Tape Recorder). One experiment revealed a remarkable evolutionary carry-over. Stimu-lation of a highly specific point in the visual area of the brain of the Macaque monkey led to unmistakable, quick, fly-catching hand movements. A human epileptic patient undergoing surgical procedures, stimulated in precisely the same visual area, performed *identical* fly-catching movements. When asked what he was doing, the patient said that he was trying to catch "that butterfly!"

A rat or monkey or cat with properly located electrodes implanted in its brain is just about completely under the control of an experimenter with a button. There are few researchers working in this area who are not convinced that human beings would be equally controllable. A person could be made hungry, or sexually aroused, or calm, or murderous, or simply have behavior completely arrested. ESB has been used to control epilepsy and reduce the pain of terminal cancer patients. Within some practical limits an individual could be made to say things at the will of the experimenter with the button.

There is, however, another, less Machiavellian, context in which to view implanted electrodes. In lighter moments of conversation, direct-stimulation investigators have been known to express mixtures of curiosity and envy concerning their pleasure-center-implanted rats. How would it be to be completely wired but be the only one who could press the buttons? We have all found ourselves in situations demanding that we be a bit more aggressive, a bit more alert, a bit more sexually aroused. Some have suggested that it might also be fun to dip the platinum needle at random into the grey matter and see what state of consciousness, what remote memory, or what forgotten image might be fished out—especially if whatever came up could be dismissed with the press of a button.

Focus 3.3

The Brain as a Tape Recorder

Wilder Penfield, head of Montreal's Neurological Institute, has conducted brain surgery on numerous epileptic patients. His usual procedure involves injecting local anesthesia into the scalp before opening the skull. The patient remains fully awake during the operation, since the brain itself is so insensitive to pain that the patient is not aware of any surgical activity. With the brain exposed, Penfield has explored the cortex surface with an electrode (see Figure 3.16). When he stimulates the motor area, patients move limbs even when they attempt to inhibit the movements. If the appropriate brain site is stimulated while a patient tries to move the area of the body linked to that brain site, the movement is inhibited. Most exciting was the discovery that when the temporal lobes are stimulated, old, long-forgotten memories are elicited. Stimulation at some points is so vivid that patients report that they feel they are reliving an experience rather than merely remembering it.

FIGURE 3.16 Penfield exposes the brain and drops numbered labels on the surface to mark the location of areas he stimulates with his electrode. The patient's behavior and reported experience are recorded.

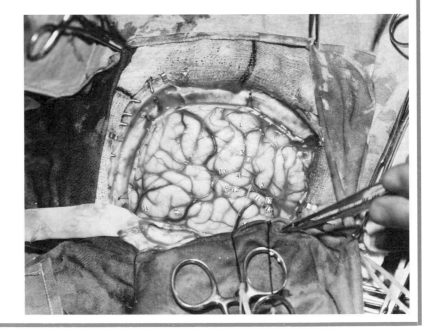

D. DRUGS AND BRAIN FUNCTIONING

The drug *amphetamine sulphate* (known in certain circles as "speed") is a remarkably effective stimulant; some people take it to improve physical performance and to keep awake or alert. The drug also has the property of markedly reducing appetite, so it is sometimes prescribed by physicians for dieting. It can also temporarily produce a happy euphoric feeling. Scientists reason that if it acts on appetite it must do so via the hypothalamus. This reasoning is based

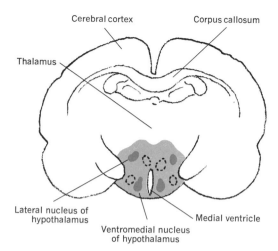

Cerebral cortex · Corpus callosum · Thalamus · Lateral nucleus of hypothalamus · Ventromedial nucleus of hypothalamus · Medial ventricle

FIGURE 3.17 Cross section of a rat's brain, looking from the front, showing the hypothalamus. Lesions of the lateral and ventromedial nucleus cause dramatic changes in the organism's eating behavior

on the following facts. *The* **hypothalamus** (see Figure 3.17) *plays an important role in initiating and integrating many physiological functions, including hunger and eating.* Electrical stimulation of the hypothalamus or damage to it from tumors can result in excessive overeating and weight gain. Indeed, when amphetamine is injected into a cat, a great increase in electrical activity is noted in a section of the hypothalamus called the *ventromedial nucleus.* Destruction of the ventromedial nucleus causes rats, cats, and monkeys to overeat, and stimulating the nucleus causes hungry animals to stop eating. Electrical stimulation of the *lateral hypothalamus,* an area near the ventromedial nucleus, causes satiated animals to eat. Researchers have concluded from these discoveries that hunger and eating behavior are controlled by a balance of excitation and inhibition of these hypothalamic areas.

STIMULANTS

Amphetamine, as we said, is a stimulant, yet it functions as an appetite depressant through its effect on the hypothalamus. This is one example of the complexity of the effects of drug action on the brain and behavior. Drugs that affect one area of the brain in one manner have no effect at all in another area and, in a third area, have an opposite effect. Also, drugs that affect one person one way may affect another person in a quite different way. For example, amphetamine can (in large dosage) send an adult into a high-flying mental disorder, but it has a very calming effect on some hyperactive children. Common prescription of amphetamine for appetite control has placed large quantities of this drug within the grasp of the teenage children of overweight parents. It is called "speed" or "uppers" in popular parlance because of its ability to violently stimulate and accelerate brain function. With continued use a person develops a tolerance; that is, increasing amounts of the drug will be needed to produce the same effect. Increased dosages are accompanied by numerous side effects, such as difficulty in paying attention and concentrating thoughts, unjustified suspiciousness of others and hallucinations (seeing or hearing things that are not there). These side effects are the symptoms of serious mental illness that are frequent consequences of amphetamine abuse.

THE HALLUCINOGENS

In Central and South America, in India, and in other areas of the world, the tired and hungry, as well as mystics, would gather to seek supernatural or divine experiences. As part of their search, they would eat certain plants and mushrooms (see Figure 3.18) containing powerful chemicals that can alter brain functioning.

FIGURE 3.18 Natural sources of hallucinogens. Psilocybin comes from mushrooms: Stropharia cubensis *(top left) and* Psilocybe mexicana *(top right). LSD is derived from a fungus (ergot) that grows on cereal grains. An infested seed head is shown bottom left, the ergot fungus bottom center. Mescaline comes from the peyote cactus (bottom right). (Adapted from "The Hallucinogenic Drugs," by Frank Barron, Murray E. Jarvik, and Sterling Bunnell, Jr. Copyright © April 1964 by Scientific American Inc. All rights reserved.)*

The Aztecs, for instance, ate peyote, a cactus, to aid them in their religious experience. This practice was common among their priests and medicine men. Today several American Indian tribes still use peyote as part of their religious ritual.

At the end of the nineteenth century, chemists, fascinated by the effects of peyote, managed to detect the active chemical substance, *mescaline,* that produced the mind-changing effect. When mescaline was given to normal subjects, it produced in them hallucinations and strange thoughts that, in some ways, resembled the derangement accompanying serious mental illness. In addition, mescaline and other **hallucinogens** *(drugs that produce hallucinations)* such as LSD and psilocybin are chemically similar to synaptic neurotransmitters that occur naturally in the brain. The symptoms produced by high dosage of these drugs and their similarity to neurotransmitters suggest that some forms of mental illness may be the result of chemical disturbances in the brain.

The discovery in 1943 of LSD (d-lysergic acid diethylamide) has contributed to this line of theoretical thinking, since it closely resembles *serotonin,* a substance that some investigators feel plays a role in one type of mental illness, schizophrenia. Interest in these chemical theories of mental illness is still very high, as is evidenced, for example, by the very frequent appearance of articles in popular newspapers and magazines that "conclusively" reveal the fundamental problem in schizophrenia and describe the cure. Unfortunately, by the time these reports find their way to scientific journals (if they ever do) their tone is somewhat softened and the investigators themselves have often contradicted their own findings. Research in this area is quite difficult; consider the research described in Focus 3.4: Hippuric Acid and Schizophrenia. One must read articles in the popular media reporting scientific findings with caution.

LSD

The three major hallucinogens being scientifically studied or privately enjoyed today are mescaline, psilocybin, and LSD. The most common and potent of these drugs is

---

Focus 3.4

Hippuric Acid and Schizophrenia: the Importance of Experimental Controls

Hippuric acid is excreted in human urine; anxiety states seem to increase the amount of the acid excreted. It was of great interest, therefore, when abnormal levels of hippuric acid were found in the urine of hospitalized schizophrenic patients. Since schizophrenics suffer long-term hospitalization, the first question asked by investigators was whether the abnormal hippuric acid levels were due simply to the hospitalization or were something essential to the nature of schizophrenia. They tested this question by housing a group of normal volunteers and a group of schizophrenics in separate-but-identical wards and feeding them both "a similar and planned hospital diet" from the same kitchen. All were allowed unlimited "access to a variety of beverages including coffee and tea." As you can see in Table 3.3, in spite of this identical environment and diet, the hippuric acid levels were far greater in the schizophrenics than in the normals. Can we conclude that there is a relationship between hippuric acid and schizophrenia?

TABLE 3.3   **Relative hippuric acid scores of 12 subjects**

SCHIZOPHRENICS		NORMALS
245		69
201		59
102		44
84		15
41		8
8		1
113.5	Average	32.17

(From Dastur, D. K., Mann, J. D., and Pollin, W., Hippuric acid secretion, coffee and schizophrenia. *Arch. Gen. Psychiat.*, 1963.)

But the story was still not complete. The alert investigators had noted that, while the two groups had been given the same diet, the schizophrenics were rather heavy coffee drinkers whereas the normals were not. When the same data from the 12 subjects in Table 3.3 were reassembled as in Table 3.4, it became clear that the major factor increasing hippuric acid secretion was coffee intake. (Later research showed that coffee intake does influence the amount of hippuric acid secretion in urine.) Hippuric acid could be dismissed as a factor causing schizophrenia.

TABLE 3.4   **Relative hippuric acid scores**

COFFEE DRINKERS		NOT COFFEE DRINKERS
245 (schiz.)		69 (normal)
201 (schiz.)		59 (normal)
102 (schiz.)		15 (normal)
84 (schiz.)		8 (schiz.)
44 (normal)		8 (normal)
41 (schiz.)		1 (normal)
119.5	Average	26.7

(From Dastur, Mann, and Pollin.)

Note in this case the problem of the researchers. They had to be sure that the only difference between the schizophrenic and the normal was diagnostic. They housed and fed the subjects the same way to the best of their ability, but an extra difference in the form of coffee drinking crept into the results. Had they been less alert, they might have followed up the false lead suggested in Table 3.3. This case illustrates how careful a researcher must be in evaluating research results.

LSD. The effects of LSD taken orally make themselves felt in less than an hour; some of the effects last eight or nine hours. LSD tends to bring sleeplessness for up to 16 hours. With LSD the risk of serious psychological breakdown is present. In a systematic survey, however, only ten instances of psychoses lasting more than 48 hours occurred among 5000 cases.

The subjective effects of LSD have been studied by Harris Isbell of the University of Kentucky. The kinds of experiences that his subjects reported after taking LSD are reported in Figure 3.19. The most common effect is a feeling of dizziness and sense of unreality (as if in a dream). Many of the subjects report visual and auditory abnormalities. Colors seem more vivid and alive. If the subjects are listening to music they report more precise perception of each note in chords. Things look and sound more "real." With the eyes closed, a riot of images and colors present themselves. Widespread use of LSD began to diminish amid reports that its use led to chromosome damage; however, these reports have not

FIGURE 3.19 Positive responses to six items in a questionnaire on physiological and perceptual effects of LSD. Solid color lines: subjects given between 100 and 225 micrograms; light color lines; subjects given between 25 and 75 micrograms; black lines: subjects given an inactive substance. (Barron et al., op. cit.)

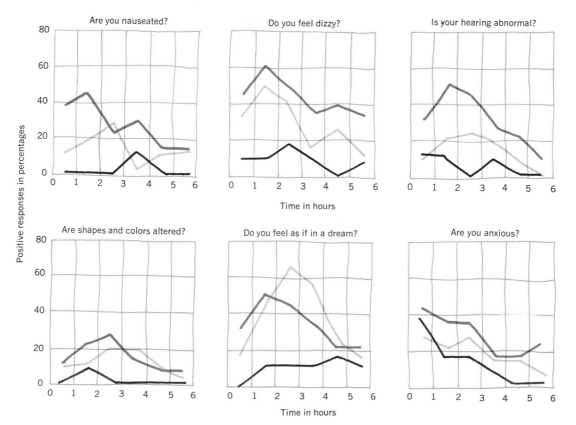

been confirmed. The major danger of LSD probably remains that of a psychotic break with reality precipitated by a "psychedelic" experience the person cannot handle.

MARIJUANA

An advertisement similar to the following was placed in a college newspaper by Andrew Weil, Norman Zinberg, and Judith Nelsen for a research study at the Boston University School of Medicine:

Male volunteers, at least 21 years old, for psychological experiment. Apply Room 402, University Medical Center, March 10 to 14, between 1 and 3 P.M.

After a careful screening process that included a psychiatric examination and elimination of people who couldn't inhale smoke, nine men who had never smoked marijuana (the naive subjects) and eight men who had regularly smoked marijuana several times a week (chronic users) were selected. And so, in the spring of 1969, the first rigorous experimental study of the effects of marijuana began.

The purpose of the study was to determine and compare the behavioral and physiological effects of marijuana smoking on chronic users and naive smokers. Past research studies were not conducted under controlled experimental settings and were open to varying interpretations. Weil and his colleagues conducted this study using the following careful procedures.

1. The marijuana used was of Mexican origin supplied by the Federal Bureau of Narcotics. Experienced users rated the material as "good, average" marijuana in terms of quality and strength. Chemical studies were made of the material used to be certain that the active ingredients were known. The material contained THC (tetrahydrocannabinol), the active ingredi-

ent in marijuana. Care was taken in hand-rolling the cigarettes so all cigarettes had the same amount of THC.

2. The length to which each cigarette was to be smoked was marked with an ink line.

3. Scented aerosols were used to mask the marijuana odor in the laboratory.

4. Each subject was allowed 8 to 12 minutes to smoke and was required to inhale long deep puffs and hold them for 20 seconds. These activities were all timed with a stopwatch.

5. The subjects were asked to refrain from eating or drinking during the four hours preceding each session.

6. Chronic users were tested with no practice session. The naive subjects came for four sessions. The first three sessions were held to teach them how to smoke the marijuana properly.

The actual experimental sequence of procedures in the test session is summarized in the following timetable:

TIME	PROCEDURE
0.00	Physiological measures (baseline): blood sample, blood sugar test, pupil size, heart rate, respiration rate
0.05	Psychological test battery 1 (baseline): attention task, digit coding, self-rating of mood, eye-hand coordination
0.35	Verbal sample 1 – "Describe a dramatic experience in your life into tape recorder." After 5 min. subjects were stopped and asked to estimate how long they were talking.
0.40	Cigarette smoking
1.00	Rest

1.15	Draw blood sample
1.20	Psychological test battery 2 (repeat of battery 1)
1.50	Verbal sample 2 (repeat of sample 1)
1.55	Rest and meal
2.30	Physiological measurements (repeat of sample 1)
2.35	Psychological test battery 3 (repeat of 1)
3.05	End of testing

Here is what Weil, Zinberg, and Nelsen found.

Behavioral Findings. In the neutral setting of the university facilities, naive subjects do not have strong subjective experiences after smoking marijuana. They reported little euphoria, no distortions of visual or auditory perception; however they did report that "things seemed to take longer." Chronic users reported feeling quite "high," in marked contrast to the naive subjects. This puzzling finding has several possible explanations. As use increases, the amount of smoking needed to produce a high decreases. This is the reverse of most drugs that, like amphetamine, require an increase with usage to maintain the same effects. This suggests that increased use of marijuana increases the physiological sensitivity of the user to the drug. An alternate explanation suggests that to experience a marijuana high requires a period of learning and takes practice. It is well known that marijuana users actually "teach" their naive friends to notice the subtle effects of the drug. It

seems quite plausible that both explanations are correct, but more research evidence is needed. The naive subjects showed impaired performance on simple mental tasks and eye-hand coordination as the drug took effect. To the surprise of the experimenters and the subjects as well, the chronic users' performance was not impaired.

Physiological Effects. Marijuana was found to increase heart rate and produce bloodshot eyes. The drug did not produce any increase in the size of the pupil or any change in breathing rate or blood sugar. In the neutral setting of the laboratory, an inhaled dose of marijuana reached its maximum effects in half an hour and was completely dissipated by three hours. The most important physiological finding was that no subject showed any adverse marijuana reaction.

Marijuana Use and Effects. While this study put to rest some of the unsupported horror stories about marijuana, the authors caution against hasty final conclusions until further research is carried out to repeat and expand on their findings. Unanswered are questions concerning the effects of larger doses of marijuana and the long-range effects of the drug on various body organs, the nervous system, and behavior.

Research with hallucinogenic and psychedelic drugs is extremely limited because of the legal difficulties in obtaining them even for experimental purposes. Until further research is undertaken, the full extent of their benefits or dangers will remain unknown. However, based on research studies as well as the reports of users, it becomes very clear that the effects of marijuana are dependent on a variety of factors in addi-

TABLE 3.5 Facts about drugs

NAME	SLANG NAME	CHEMICAL OR TRADE NAME	SOURCE	CLASSIFICATION	MEDICAL USE	HOW TAKEN
Heroin	H, Horse, Scat, Junk, Smack, Scag, Stuff, Harry	Diacetylmorphine	Semi-synthetic (from morphine)	Narcotic	Pain relief	Injected or sniffed
Morphine	White Stuff, M	Morphine Sulphate	Natural (from opium)	Narcotic	Pain relief	Swallowed or injected
Codeine	Schoolboy	Methylmorphine	Natural (from opium), semi-synthetic (from morphine)	Narcotic	Ease pain and coughing	Swallowed
Methadone	Dolly	Dolophine Amidone	Synthetic	Narcotic	Pain relief	Swallowed or injected
Cocaine	Corrine, Gold Dust, Coke, Bernice, Flake, Star Dust, Snow	Methylester of Benzoylecgonine	Natural (from coca, NOT cacao)	Stimulant, local anesthesia	Local anesthesia	Sniffed, injected, or swallowed
Marijuana	Pot, Grass, Hashish, Tea, Gage, Reefers	Cannabis sativa	Natural	Relaxant, euphoriant; in high doses, hallucinogen	None in U.S.	Smoked, swallowed, or sniffed
Barbiturates	Barbs, Blue Devils, Candy, Yellow Jackets, Phennies, Peanuts, Blue Heavens	Phenobarbital Nembutal, Seconal, Amytal	Synthetic	Sedative-hypnotic	Sedation, relief of high blood pressure, epilepsy, hyperthyroidism	Swallowed or injected
Amphetamines	Bennies, Dexies, Speed, Wake-Ups, Lid Proppers, Hearts, Pep Pills	Benzedrine, Dexedrine, Desoxyn, Meth-amphetamine, Methedrine	Synthetic	Sympatho-mimetic	Relief of mild depression, control of appetite and narcolepsy	Swallowed or injected
LSD	Acid, Sugar, Big D, Cubes, Trips	D-lysergic Acid Diethylamide	Semi-synthetic (from ergot alkaloids)	Hallucinogen	Experimental study of mental function, alcoholism	Swallowed
DMT	AMT, Business-man's High	Dimethyl-triptamine	Synthetic	Hallucinogen	None	Injected
Mescaline	Mesc.	3,4,5-trimethoxy-phenethylamine	Natural (from peyote)	Hallucinogen	None	Swallowed
Psilocybin		3 (2-dimethyl-amino) ethylin-dol-4-oldihydro-gen phosphate	Natural (from psilocybe)	Hallucinogen	None	Swallowed
Alcohol	Booze, Juice, etc.	Ethanol Ethyl alcohol	Natural (from grapes, grains, etc. via fermentation)	Sedative-hypnotic	Solvent, antiseptic	Swallowed
Tobacco	Fag, Coffin Nail, etc.	Nicotiana Tabacum	Natural	Stimulant-sedative	Sedative, emetic (nicotine)	Smoked, sniffed, chewed

(From *Resource Book for Drug Abuse Education.* Developed as a part of the Drug Abuse Education Project of the American Association for Health, Physical Education, and Recreation and the National Science Teachers Association (NEA). 1969.)

USUAL DOSE	DURATION OF EFFECT	EFFECTS SOUGHT	LONG-TERM SYMPTOMS	PHYSICAL DEPENDENCE POTENTIAL	MENTAL DEPENDENCE POTENTIAL	ORGANIC DAMAGE POTENTIAL
Varies	4 hrs.	Euphoria, prevent withdrawal discomfort	Addiction, constipation, loss of appetite	Yes	Yes	No*
15 Milligrams	6 hrs.	Euphoria, prevent withdrawal discomfort	Addiction, constipation, loss of appetite	Yes	Yes	No*
30 Milligrams	4 hrs.	Euphoria, prevent withdrawal discomfort	Addiction, constipation, loss of appetite	Yes	Yes	No
10 Milligrams	4–6 hrs.	Prevent withdrawal discomfort	Addiction, constipation, loss of appetite	Yes	Yes	No
Varies	Varied, brief periods	Excitation, talkativeness	Depression, convulsions	No	Yes	Yes?
1–2 Cigarettes	4 hrs.	Relaxation; increased euphoria, perceptions, sociability	Usually none	No	Yes?	No
50–100 Milligrams	4 hrs.	Anxiety reduction, euphoria	Addiction with severe withdrawal symptoms, possible convulsions, toxic psychosis	Yes	Yes	Yes
2.5–5 Milligrams	4 hrs.	Alertness, activeness	Loss of appetite, delusions, hallucinations, toxic psychosis	No?	Yes	Yes?
100–500 Micrograms	10 hrs.	Insightful experiences, exhilaration, distortion of senses	May intensify existing psychosis, panic reactions	No	No?	No?
1–3 Milligrams	Less than 1 hr.	Insightful experiences, exhilaration, distortion of senses	?	No	No?	No?
350 Micrograms	12 hrs.	Insightful experiences, exhilaration, distortion of senses	?	No	No?	No?
25 Milligrams	6–8 hrs.	Insightful experiences, exhilaration, distortion of senses	?	No	No?	No?
Varies	1–4 hrs.	Sense alteration, anxiety reduction, sociability	Cirrhosis, toxic psychosis, neurologic damage, addiction	Yes	Yes	Yes
Varies	Varies	Calmness, sociability	Emphysema, lung cancer, mouth and throat cancer, cardiovascular damage, loss of appetite	Yes?	Yes	Yes

Question marks indicate conflict of opinion. It should be noted that illicit drugs are frequently adulterated and thus pose unknown hazards to the user.

* Persons who inject drugs under nonsterile conditions run a high risk of contracting hepatitis, abscesses, or circulatory disorders.

tion to the potency of the drug used. The experience and expectancies of the user, as well as the environmental setting, play a key role in the kind of "high" experienced. Although no exact figures are available, it is estimated that up to 10 percent of those who have tried marijuana have had "bad" reactions. Experienced users often report occasional "bad" reactions when they smoked marijuana to escape a feeling of depression, anger, or anxiety. This suggests that marijuana may accentuate one's mood at the time of using it.

Recently a national commission studied marijuana use and concluded that there was a great deal of misinformation about the dangers of the drug and recommended that the private use of the drug should not be a crime. Proponents of this view point out that marijuana is less dangerous than alcohol.

Table 3.5 summarizes and compares many common drugs used as stimulants, tranquilizers, and hallucinogens.

SUMMARY

A. The Split-Brain Man

1. Research on humans and animals has revealed much of the biological basis of behavior and experience. The study of epileptics who have had the **corpus callosum** (page 57) cut indicates that each hemisphere of the brain has parallel as well as specialized functions.
2. The main function of the corpus callosum is to transfer information from one hemisphere to the other.
3. Sensory information (e.g., touch, pressure, vision, audition) from the right side of the body goes to the left hemisphere and vice versa. Control of the right side of the body is exercised by the left hemisphere and vice versa.
4. The left hemisphere initiates and dominates speech. While the right hemisphere can understand language, it is inferior to the left hemisphere. The right hemisphere is superior to the left in tasks involving spatial relations.
5. Despite major surgery or damage, the brain has the remarkable capacity to recover and compensate.

B. The Building Blocks and Structure of the Nervous System

6. The **neuron,** or nerve cell (page 62), is the basic unit of the nervous system, which consists of complex interconnections of these cells.
7. The nerve impulse is transferred along the nerve fiber in the form of an electrochemical discharge; this process is known as "firing." Transmission of the nerve impulse occurs across the **synapse** (page 64), a gap between the **axon** (page 62) of one nerve cell, and the **dendrites** (page 62) of another.
8. For a nerve cell to fire, the excitation must be at a certain **threshold** (page 63). Once at threshold, each neuron fires at a consistent inten-

sity; this is known as the **all-or-none law** (page 63). After firing, a neuron recovers during the **refractory phase** (page 63).

9. For most neurons the impulse across the synaptic gap is transferred by a release of chemical **neurotransmitters** (page 64).

10. Various drugs such as LSD and amphetamines have their effects by facilitating or interfering with neurotransmitters at the synapse.

11. The central nervous system (Figure 3.9 and Table 3.1) consists of the brain (Figure 3.11) and spinal cord and is responsible for the neural coordination of the organism. Each of the many structural components of the central nervous system has a variety of specialized functions.

12. The **endocrine** (page 68) system (Figure 3.10 and Table 3.2) consists of ductless glands that secrete **hormones** (page 68) directly into the bloodstream. Hormones chemically regulate growth, metabolism, and other body functions.

C. The Localization of Brain Functions

13. A variety of methods has been developed to study the functions of the brain, including electrical brain stimulation with **electrodes** (page 73), ablation, and study of brain injury (Focus 3.2). These methods have revealed much about the localization of functions.

14. The surface areas of the brain have been mapped to reveal centers for such functions as motor and sensory control and control of speech and vision.

15. Deeper areas of the brain have been explored with electrical brain implants. By direct stimulation of various centers in the brain, control can be exerted on the individual's behavior and feelings, including pleasure, pain, sexual arousal, and muscle activity.

Drugs and Brain Functioning

16. Drugs can affect behavior and experience in a variety of ways via the brain and nervous system.

17. Amphetamines exert an appetite-suppressive effect on nerve centers located in the **hypothalamus** (page 79; Figure 3.9, Table 3.1).

18. The effect of drugs like LSD, marijuana, and amphetamines on behavior and experience varies depending on the experience and mood of the user, the setting in which the drug is taken, and the potency of the drug.

19. Research on **hallucinogens** (page 81) and psychedelic drugs such as LSD and marijuana is limited, so the full extent of their benefits and/or dangers is still not completely known.

Section
Two
Energized
Being

The rhythm of life involves recurring cycles of behavior directed toward satisfying biological needs such as hunger and social needs such as the striving to achieve success. The study of motivation is concerned with the expenditure of energy as it is directed toward pursuing and attaining goals. The study of emotion, a closely allied topic, is concerned with body changes that accompany behavior and the subjective awareness of them.

In our discussion of energized being we will look closely at some of the biological bases of obesity, the social basis of human strivings for achievement, the biological and social bases for feelings and emotion, the role of emotions in producing physical illness, and the biological and social bases of sex behavior.

Chapter Four
Motivation and Emotion

Froelich's syndrome consists of an un-appetizing group of symptoms including extreme obesity, atrophy of the sex organs, and reduced or absent sex urges. This syndrome is, fortunately, quite rare. It is caused by a tumor of the pituitary gland. The pituitary is a master gland that controls (among other things) the sex glands. The atrophy of the sex organs and the lack of sex urges are, therefore, reasonable symptoms of a tumorous pituitary gland. But gross obesity does not fit the picture, since the pituitary gland does not control feeding and weight. (If you remove a rat's pituitary gland, for instance, the animal continues to feed normally.) There is a clue to the solution of this puzzle, however, in the fact that tumorous organs tend to occupy more room than normal ones. They press against and often damage the organs around them. Just above the pituitary sits the hypothalamus (see Figure 3.8). If an enlarged pituitary pressed on the hypothalamus, what would be the effect?

Animal experiments provide us with some answers. If you damage a rat's hypothalamus just above the pituitary (the area called the ventromedial nucleus of the hypothalamus), that rat will start eating furiously and will develop an obesity to challenge any Froelich's syndrome (see Figure 4.1). The amount of obesity will correlate with the amount of the ventromedial nucleus that you damage. The obesity of Froelich's syndrome, then, is clearly the result of pressure from the pituitary tumor causing damage to the neighboring section of the hypothalamus. A lesion to the ventromedial nucleus inevitably produces overeating and consequent obesity. This has been uniformly observed in monkeys, rats, cats, dogs, mice, chickens, and human beings.

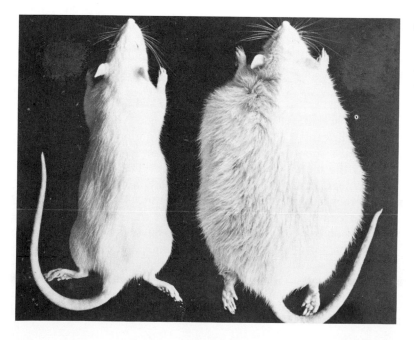

FIGURE 4.1 Destruction of specific centers in the hypothalmus can lead to overeating and obesity, as in the rat at right.

These observations have implications for behavior other than eating and lead to some important questions. What factors are responsible for initiating behaviors like eating and drinking? Since such behaviors are not continuous, what stops them after they start? How are specific behavioral goals selected? Are behaviors like human striving for success and achievement based on mechanisms that are different from the mechanisms underlying hunger and thirst?

Each of these questions is concerned with the motivation of behavior. Psychologists define motivation in many different ways to express different viewpoints. However, the **motivation concept** *generally refers to the biological, social, and learned factors that initiate, sustain, and stop goal-directed behavior.* In this chapter we will explore motivation and a closely related topic, emotion.

A.   THE BIOLOGICAL BASIS OF MOTIVATION

Only a minute portion of the hypothalamus is involved in controlling appetite. After the ventromedial nucleus has been damaged, a rat will eat at a fantastically increased rate, perhaps two or three times as much as a normal rat. It will do so until it reaches about three times its weight before the operation. The rat reaches this great weight in just a few weeks, then reduces its intake and maintains the high weight. The ventromedial nucleus seems to work like a thermostat or any other such stabilizing device. If a thermostat controlling the temperature of a room is suddenly set higher, the heating system strains for a period of time, consuming more fuel until this higher level is reached; then the system levels off and maintains itself at this level.

Overeating rats (called hyperphagic) eat the same number of meals as normal rats, but each meal is much larger. If a hungry animal is eating and the ventromedial nucleus is stimulated, it will stop eating immediately and will only resume eating when the stimulation ceases. Clearly, the ventromedial nucleus serves as a "stop-mechanism" in the eating process. When a certain level has been reached, the eating is shut off. The hypothalamus when undisturbed controls eating so that a relatively normal weight is maintained. But if the ventromedial nucleus is damaged, this control function is effectively weakened. A higher level is set. The rat must indulge in some intensive eating until it reaches this higher level. At this point the animal tapers off and eats enough to maintain the new level.

It has been found for many behaviors that if a "stop-mechanism" is situated in the brain, a "go-mechanism" will be located alongside. This holds true for the hypothalamus. This "go-mechanism" is found in the lateral hypothalamus. If you damage the lateral hypothalamus extensively, a rat simply will not eat; it will actually starve to death while surrounded by food. If (with an implanted electrode) you stimulate the lateral hypothalamus of a rat that has just been permitted to gorge itself thoroughly, the rat will immediately begin eating again. It will not stop eating until the stimulation is shut off. So the lateral hypothalamus precipitates eating. The ventromedial nucleus directly inhibits the activity of the lateral hypothalamus. Stimulate the lateral hypothalamus and the rat eats. Stimulate the ventromedial nucleus and it inhibits the lateral hypothalamus and eating stops.

How is the hypothalamus itself regulated? The lateral hypothalamus is always ready to start the eating process. Eating, in fact, will take place if the ventromedial nucleus is not exerting an inhibitory influence. In a sense, then, the control rests with the ventromedial nucleus. The ventromedial nucleus, in turn, is responsive to variations in level of blood sugar. If an animal has eaten a full meal, the level of blood sugar will be high. This will stimulate the ventromedial nucleus, which will then inhibit the lateral hypothalamus and suppress eating. When the level of blood sugar drops, the activity of the ventromedial nucleus drops (activity is measured by rate of firing of the neurons that make up the hypothalamus as detected by an implanted electrode). This frees the lateral hypothalamus from the inhibitory influence of the ventromedial nucleus. If food is available, the animal will begin to feed.

The hyperphagic rats' problem is more complex than just not knowing when to "push themselves away from the dinner table." These rats will eat enormous quantities of sweet foods, but if researchers make the foods harmlessly bitter with quinine, these animals will eat less than their cousins that are neurally intact. Furthermore, such a rat becomes "lazy": if required to "work" for food by pressing a lever, it will eat less than normal rats. Neither will it suffer as much electric shock to get to food. It seems that rats with this brain lesion become less sensitive to internal signals to eat and more sensitive to external cues. In a phrase, if eating is sweet and easy, a hyperphagic rat is more than happy to do more than its share; otherwise, it's not interested. Are human beings any different?

THE STIMULUS CONTROL OF HUNGER AND EATING

Experiments by Stanley Schachter at Columbia University show that the behavior patterns of the rats are also found in severely overweight people. For instance, Schachter asked groups of obese and normal people to rate two types of ice cream and to feel free to take as much ice cream as they needed to make a fair rating. One of the two bowls contained regular ice cream. The contents of the other bowl were mildly flavored with quinine. Schachter found that lean people would take about the same amount of ice cream from both bowls, whereas the fat subjects took large quantities of the sweet ice cream and almost none of the bitter. Like the hyperphagic rats, the obese people seemed to be more sensitive to external factors, in this case, sweetness.

Using a trick clock that could be speeded up or slowed down, Schachter demonstrated another external cue to which the obese were unusually sensitive: indicated time. When offered food, the overweight ate more when the clock read 6:00 than when it read 5:15. On the other hand, the lean people observed seemed to be unaffected by the changing clock readings, apparently scheduling their eating by internal "clocks." In another experiment, students were left alone in a room after being told they might dine on sandwiches left on a platter and in a refrigerator. The obese subjects proved to be "good boys and girls" in the sense of eating everything set before them and *only* what was set before them. The number of sandwiches placed on the platter was intentionally varied by the researchers. If many sandwiches were left out, the normal subjects would usually leave some untouched; if few sandwiches were left out, the "normals" would go to the refrigerator to get more of them. But whether few or many sandwiches were placed on the platter, the obese subjects ate the sandwiches on the platter but did *not* go to the refrigerator. Again, the behavior of the obese paralleled the hyperphagic rats in "laziness." For both hyperphagic rats and corpulent people, external cues to eat seem to be very effective, internal stimuli are of little consequence.

The established oversensitivity to external eating cues on the part of the obese can guide the design of weight-reduction programs. Alerted to the danger of external stimuli, the overweight can deliberately control the environment that is controlling them. How well can people learn how to regulate their eating by controlling external cues? This question was answered by Richard B. Stuart of the University of Michigan who developed a program for weight reduction in which each of the participants learned how to control the eating cues in their environments. Not only did the eight women in his study lose from 26 to 47 pounds, but they were also able to keep fat off by using the same stimulus-control methods. Several follow-up studies have supported Stuart's findings. This is a remarkable accomplishment, for most studies of weight control report that while various methods for weight reduction are successful in *taking* pounds off, they are not successful in *keeping* pounds off. The basic idea underlying self-control is to intercept or eliminate those cues in the environment that elicit the undesired behavior and then associate desirable behavior to the cues. For example, if the refrigerator is a cue for eating, you stay out of the kitchen if weight is to be lost. If you can't stay out of the kitchen, then substitute acceptable behavior to the cue such as filling the refrigerator with low-calorie foods. (See Focus 4.1: Weight Control.)

HOMEOSTASIS

Homeostasis is a term coined by Walter Cannon, a physiologist, in 1929. *It is de-rived from Greek words meaning "steady state." The word refers to the tendency of organisms to maintain a steady state in their internal conditions despite changing conditions in the environment.* Homeostasis helps to explain how the absence of something, such as food, or an excess of something, such as temperature, can instigate behavior. The self-regulatory relationship between the "go" lateral hypothalamus and the "stop" ventromedial nucleus is an example of homeostasis. The body is comfortable and at ease when a certain amount of nutrients is present in the blood, as detected by the hypothalamic centers. When this level falls below limits of tolerance, the organism becomes agitated, energized, and active until the situation is corrected and the homeostasis level restored (see Figure 4.2).

Evolutionary theory offers an explanation for the presence of homeostatic mechanisms in living organisms: natural selection. Not all organisms that ever lived had such internal regulators. An organism without a sense of hunger, for instance, would not last long, certainly not long enough to reproduce and genetically duplicate its deficiency. Of course, by the time any creature resembling human beings appeared, such defects had been weeded out. Natural selection might be considered a research and development program that worked to the advantage of a surviving species such as human beings. We are at the end (so far) of a long line of winners in the evolutionary struggle, the inheritors of a sensitive, although not completely foolproof, homeostatic system. The difficulties many of us have in keeping a trim waistline attest to the imperfections in nature's equilibrium mechanism.

The study of hunger begins to provide some answers about the biological basis of the initiation and termination of eating but

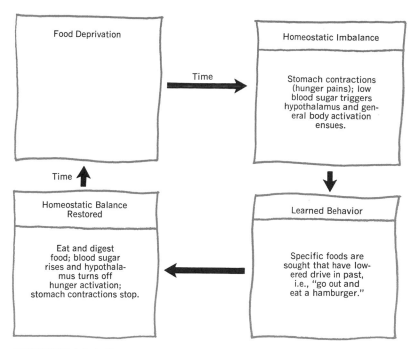

FIGURE 4.2 A diagrammatic representation of the homeostatic mechanism underlying hunger.

doesn't answer the question about specific behavioral goals. Why, for instance, does one hungry person seek out steak and another lobster? (We'll return to this question under Theories of Motivation at the end of the next section.) Why does one person choose to become a doctor and another a lawyer? These questions involve the study of how organisms learn and are influenced by society. We will begin exploring the answers to such questions in the next section and return to them from other points of view in later chapters.

Another question concerns those behaviors that do not have any obvious homeostatic basis, such as novelty-seeking, thrill-seeking, and curiosity. This issue is discussed in Focus 4.2: Curiosity and Exploratory Behavior, page 100.

B. THE SOCIAL BASIS OF MOTIVATION

Look at Figure 4.3 and make up a story about what is going on, what led up to the situation depicted, and what will happen next.

When people are asked to tell imaginative stories to pictures such as the one illustrated, they reveal something about themselves that can be reliably scored to assess certain aspects of their motivation. Compare these two stories given to Figure 4.3, page 100.

Story One.
A young fellow is sitting in a plaid shirt and resting his head on one hand. He appears to

Focus 4.1
Weight Control

Michael Mahoney of Pennsylvania State University and Carl Thoresen of Stanford University have summarized the stimulus-control techniques that have proven effective in weight control. The principles have been successfully applied to self-control, study habits, and many other behaviors. These techniques are:

"1. *Limit the cues you associate with eating.* Eat in one specific room and preferably at one place in that room. This means that eating should become a "pure experience"—that is, it must be separated from other other activities that might gain stimulus control over it and/or reinforce it. When you eat, eat—but avoid other simultaneous activities (such as television viewing, phone conversations, pleasure reading, and studying). This means that an ongoing activity (for example, watching a football game) must be interrupted while you eat.

2. *Do not eat to avoid waste.* Childhood training and the desire not to waste money have resulted in countless extra calories for people who can't stand seeing food thrown out. A woman who consumes her children's unfinished meals is one example. Another is the individual who stuffs himself at a restaurant in order to consume everything that has been included in an entree. Get in the habit of leaving small portions of food on your plate so that the cue for meal termination will not be an empty bowl or a clean plate.

3. *Restrict your food intake ahead of time.* Bountiful bowls of food on the table are powerful cues for eating (and *over*eating). Prepare your plate ahead of time, put the foods away (or leave them in another room), and then sit down to your meal. Arrange food portions so that they look larger by spreading them out over a plate or by using small or shallow dishes. When you are eating at a restaurant, restrict tempting cues ahead of time. For example, request that the potato or bread be omitted from your plate.

4. *Make fattening foods less available and nonfattening foods more available.* You are much more likely to eat fattening snacks if they are stored in your own kitchen instead of at the local store. Don't buy high-calorie snacks. It's easier to avoid them if you *always shop for groceries after a full meal* (*never* on an empty stomach). If you must keep sweets in the house (for example, for children's lunches), buy brands that you dislike, store them in an inconspicuous place (the back

of a cabinet rather than the cookie jar), and instruct your children to get them for themselves. Keep a large supply of safe snacks on hand at all times (for example, unbuttered popcorn, raw vegetables, diet soda).

5. *Alter the eating process.* Eating slowly reduces the quantity of food consumed. Swallow one bite of food before putting the next bite on your fork. (This may entail actually putting the fork down between bites.) Toward the end of a meal, get in the habit of interrupting your eating for two to five minutes to gain control over the behavior (and to dissociate it from such stimuli as a clean plate or an empty bowl).

6. *Modify the physiological cues for eating.* Many people eat in response to internal sensations of "emptiness" or "hunger pangs." Eat high-bulk, low-calorie foods (such as celery, carrot sticks, and popcorn) or drink a large amount of liquid before or during the meal to produce a sensation of "fullness." Moreover, to maintain an appropriate blood-sugar level and to avoid cravings for sweets, eat high-protein foods (particularly early in the day) and use sugar substitutes extensively (not only in coffee but also in baking and meal preparation). Reduce intake of nutrients that produce large blood-sugar swings (for example, caffeine, processed sugar, white bread, and noodle products).

7. *Arrange social cues that encourage appropriate eating.* Many people find the presence of certain other people a cue for more moderate and adaptive eating patterns. If this is the case, arrange to eat only in the presence of those people. On the other hand, if some persons model inappropriate eating habits, arrange to eat separately from them.

8. *Develop nonfattening responses to emotional upset.* Many people report very strong eating temptations when they are anxious, frustrated, or depressed. The association between these emotions and eating has two possible bases: (1) many children grow up learning that foods (particularly sweets) are used to soothe them and to lift their spirits, and (2) emotional upsets actually represent mild physiological arousal that under certain conditions may lead to low blood sugar and cravings for food. To modify the association between emotions and food, develop alternative reactions that are incompatible with eating. For example, you can learn to relax in emotion-provoking situations by engaging in certain breathing and muscle exercises." (Mahoney and Thoresen, 1974.)

Focus 4.2
Curiosity and Exploratory Behavior

A Martian examining the human cultures of Planet Earth would likely note that the common heroes, as ancient as Ulysses or Sinbad the Sailor or as modern as the most recent TV series cop, are not necessarily those who advanced the culture by developing methods of dealing with practical problems but those who seem to have engaged in adventures for little more motivation than the "thrill" of it. Psychological research indicates that many organisms, including humans, actively seek out novel stimuli; boredom seems to be innately aversive. The most obvious manifestation of this inferred need for novelty is common "curiosity."

Researchers B. T. Leckart and K. S. Bennett of Ohio State University demonstrated the reinforcing power of novel stimulation for rats. Hungry rats were placed in a T-shaped maze apparatus. When they left the box in the center arm of the T, they had the choice of going to the right or the left. The boxes at the ends of the corridors were either empty or contained food pellets or novel stimuli in the form of changing colors and textures. The rats were divided into three groups: one group had the choice of a food box or an empty box; one had the choice of a novel stimulus or an empty box; and the third group had the choice of novel stimulus or food. The first group rapidly developed a preference for the side they knew led to food. The second group showed a preference for the novel stimulus. Most interesting was the behavior of the group offered a choice between novelty and food: the rats, although deprived of food, would seek novelty as often as they sought food. Evidently there is a real "hunger" for novelty just as there is for food.

Another experiment, done at Purdue University by C. D. Smock and B. G. Holt, involved first-grade pupils. The investigators allowed the

FIGURE 4.3 *A picture similar to those used to elicit stories to be scored for need for achievement.*

be thinking of something. His eyes appear a little sad. He may have been involved in something that he is very sorry for. The boy is thinking over what he has done. By the look in his eyes we can tell that he is very sad about it. I believe that the boy will break down any minute if he continues in the manner in which he is now going.

Story Two.
The boy is a thinker, bored with his schoolwork he is attempting to do. His mind wanders. He thinks of his future. The boy has

children to watch a mock TV set that showed film strips displaying either familiar objects; novel objects defined in terms of incongruity, such as birds with four feet and a horse with wings; or vague, undefined drawings, such as line abstractions. The slides were displayed for a quarter of a second before the screen dimmed. A child could repeat the same slide by pushing a button or change the picture by pulling a lever: the frequency with which each slide was displayed gave the experimenters an indication of the children's preference. Results showed that novel pictures were preferred over familiar ones. Furthermore, novel pictures were preferred to *vague* ones; apparently unusual or surprising perceptions provoke more curiosity than merely vague ones.

There are limits to the hunger for novelty. *Many perceptions of change in the environment elicit what is called the* **orienting response.** *A sudden noise, expecially when unexpected, will bring an immediate physiological and psychological response, increasing the amount of "information" available and raising the level of physiological arousal as though in preparation for any response that should be necessary if the change is perceived as a threat.* This orienting response is adaptive, but a high level of arousal or arousal maintained over long duration is fatiguing. Maintained long enough, arousal will even result in exhaustion.

In brief, many organisms, including humans, have not only a hunger for food, water, sex, and other necessities but also a very definite motivation for seeking novel stimulation that is expressed in curiosity and exploratory behavior. Witness the child requesting to be tossed in the air, the crowds at the amusement park lining up to ride the roller coaster, the artist starving in a garret but determined to paint a masterpiece, and the scientist pursuing a problem despite all sorts of tissue deprivation.

completed all but the last of his high school career. The boy is *eager to graduate.* He has *faith in his capabilities* and *wants to get started* on the job he has lined up, *dreaming of advancements.* The boy *will graduate* ranking near the middle of his class. *He will do all right* on the outside.

It is obvious that, unlike the first story, the second story reflects a rather strong *need to achieve,* as indicated by the number of words and phrases that relate to achievement. The number of achievement-related words and phrases are, essentially, counted and yield a need achievement score. People who use a large number of achievement-related words in such stories have been found, for instance, to be successful businessmen who are always trying to improve themselves — to find a shorter route to the office, a faster way to read their mail, or a method for boosting their company's production. They love taking personal responsibility to solve problems and achieve moderate goals that involve calculated risks, but not a gamble. They are challenged by tasks that involve their skills and personal effort. The need to achieve is a social motive that has been found to play a role in the educational and economic success of individuals as well as the economic rise and fall of nations.

In this section we will explore the development of **social motivation;** *motivations that are learned in the process of growing up and living in a society.* Although there are many different motivations that can be learned, such as needs for affiliation, power, or domination, we will focus on one motive in some detail, the need for achievement.

THE NEED
FOR ACHIEVEMENT

David McClelland and his associates at Harvard University have extensively studied the **need for achievement** or "n Ach" as it has come to be known. *(Achievement was taken to be performance in terms of a standard of excellence or a desire to be successful.)* They developed the ingenious way of measuring n Ach that introduced this section. The method consists of presenting an individual with several ambiguous pictures of the kind illustrated in Figure 4.3 and asking the subject to make up imaginative stories. (The pictures are ambiguous in that it is not clear what is "going on.") In doing so, the individual projects his or her motives into the story. The stories are then analyzed for evidence of n Ach. The procedure is so objective that a computer has been programmed to score the stories by counting words and phrases that match a list of n Ach words and phrases stored in its memory.

Occupational Choice and Ring-Toss Games. What is the relationship between need for achievement and occupational choice? A reasonable prediction would be that the higher the person's need to achieve, the higher would be the level of occupational aspiration.

A simple laboratory experiment gives a good idea of how need for achievement affects level of aspiration. The task in question is a "ring-toss" game; a player attempts to toss a rope ring over a peg placed on the floor. The players in this experiment were grade school children. They were permitted to choose the distance from which they tossed the ring. A revealing thing happened. Those children who had previously been assessed as being high in n Ach chose "moderate" distances—the distances were far enough from the peg to provide a real challenge, yet not so far as to be impossible. These children set difficult, but realistic, levels of aspiration for themselves. Their behavior actually makes sense: people with a high need to achieve, as measured by McClelland's test, indeed have high aspirations, but not so high as to be unattainable—if they were unattainable, the person would be thwarting the need to achieve. (These children are reminiscent of the high n Ach businessmen who adopt moderate goals that involve calculated risks, but that are not sheer gambles.) And what of the children who were low in need for achievement? They chose either very close distances to the peg (which virtually guaranteed success) or very great distances (which all but guaranteed failure). These children were either playing it "safe" or setting themselves such impossible goals that no one (including themselves) could possibly blame them for failing. In short, they were apparently afraid to try, afraid of the subjective experience of failure.

These results have been replicated with college students in games of ring-toss and shuffleboard. But, of course, it is not such games, as illustrative as they may be, that concern us. The problem is need for achievement and occupational choice. Occupations, too, may be ranked in terms of level of aspiration, ranging roughly from "Supreme Court Justice" to "unskilled laborer." What happens when people with high and low n Ach are presented with occupational choices? The results paralleled those of the ring-toss game. People with high need for achievement choose moderately difficult occupations relative to their abilities; people with low need for achievement choose very easy or very difficult occupations relative to their abilities. Thus, the need to achieve influences both a person's choice of occupation and the probability of success in that occupation.

The occupations selected by individuals of high n Ach are most often in the business realm, occupations in which responsibility and opportunity for rewards are closely linked. The small businessman is a prime example of the entrepreneur who makes decisions, takes calculated risks, and personally feels the losses or gains that result. The "opposite type" to the entrepreneur would be a bureaucrat in a large corporation or a government agency. The task of such a person primarily consists of following well-defined instructions, and personal promotion is fixed and automatic, having little or no relation to performance or production.

Oddly enough, the desire for wealth *per se* or for social acknowledgement does not seem to mark individuals with high n Ach. Experiments in which money and prizes were offered for high performance in various tasks showed that these factors did not bait people in the high n Ach group into higher performance; instead, they seem to work to satisfy an internal standard of excellence. More than those with low n Ach, they not only crave to know when they have successfully completed a task, but also prefer situations where feedback — positive or negative — comes quickly, apparently to improve their performance. Strongly oriented toward the achievement of their internal standards of excellence, those with high n Ach will even choose skilled partners over friends in laboratory game situations. Traits like these make people with high n Ach the most likely "winners" in the roles they often select; the desire to experience achievement and to receive quick feedback seems to guide them into the entrepreneurial fields. In contrast, research scientists who spend years working on avenues of investigation with no guarantee that they are not tracking down dead ends are not necessarily high in the need for achievement.

Once the major characteristics of high need achievers had been identified, McClelland and his colleagues began to look for the sources of the motive in child development and parent-child relationships.

The Development of n Ach

What determines an individual's level of n Ach? Why do some children develop an ample hunger for achievement while others never do? Birth order in a family is a significant factor in the development of n Ach; the first-born characteristically score high (see Focus 4.3: Birth Order). Furthermore, in general, the nurture of a child appears either to discourage or encourage the independence in seeking internal goals that characterize high n Ach people. Parents who are relatively demanding in terms of the independence they expect of their children at various ages are likely to develop strong n Ach in their offspring. One survey by Marian Winterbottom, under McClelland's direction, showed that children with high measures of n Ach had mothers

Focus 4.3
Birth Order

Philip Very and Joseph Zannini entered 60 Rhode Island beauty salons and asked beauticians their ages and the ages of their brothers and sisters (if you are concerned with the all-too-human tendency of people to falsify their age, Very and Zannini also obtained a simple ranking of order of birth of all siblings in the family). When the final tally was in, it was discovered that second-born children were disproportionately overrepresented among the beauticians. Why should this be so?

In order to answer this question we have to venture into the labyrinth of child-rearing practices, specifically the differential treatment given to first-born (and only) children and to later-borns. The first-born (or only) child presents a real problem to new parents; they have to learn to deal with children. They are understandably somewhat unsure of themselves in this new role, they don't know quite what to do or how to relate to the new arrival (note the way in which a first-time father holds an infant as contrasted to the savoir-faire of the "veteran"). Thus relatively rigid rules are established for rearing and disciplining the first-born. These rules tend to be strictly enforced, including strict training in what is "right" and what is "wrong." The result is a high level of conscience development in the child, heavy dependence on adult norms, and great expectations of achievement. These tendencies are strengthened by the twin facts that the first-born child has exclusive access to the parents (at least for a while) and that children model themselves after their parents. And these tendencies—a large conscience, a reverence for sanctioned norms, and the need to achieve—are the characteristics treasured by the educational system. The first-born thus meets with success in school and rapidly gains the teachers' approval, which further reinforces these very characteristics.

But what of the second-born? By now the parents are "child-wise." They are much more relaxed with their second child, and, perhaps as a consequence, more affectionate. Their expectations are also more realistic; they are less demanding, less coercive, more casual in their discipline, in short, more permissive. And, as adults, second-born children tend to be *(on the average)* affectionate, easygoing, open, harmonious. Now do you understand why more beauticians are second-born? Among the traits emphasized as vital by the instructors and managers of beauty salons are "courtesy" and "cooperativeness," both second-born characteristics.

But back to the first-born. William Altus of the University of California has given intensive study to the effects of birth order. He has compiled some rather striking facts concerning birth order and achievement. For example, first-borns are overrepresented among eminent scientists, writers, poets, historians, and even professors; among members of *Who's Who,* Rhodes scholars, and National Merit Scholarship finalists.

There are proportionally more first-borns among university and college students, at both undergraduate and graduate levels; this ratio increases as the schools become more selective. All of the early Mercury and Gemini astronauts were first-born sons (which could have occurred by chance only once in 268,435,456 times), as are 90 percent of all American astronauts to make space flights.

The birth-order difference can be found in other countries as well. Lillian Belmont and Francis A. Marolla of the New York State Department of Mental Hygiene analyzed data on tests of intellectual performance of nearly 400,000 19-year-old men in the Netherlands — the entire male population born in a three-year period. They found a clear and consistent decrease in performance as birth-order position increased. First-borns, *on the average,* scored higher than second-borns, who scored higher than third-borns, and so on. There is no known genetic explanation. Again, the first-born comes out first.

According to Altus: "In our Western European complex of cultures there seems to be a definite linkage of birth order to eminence, however it is defined, and apparently, in all fields. . . ."

"[The] dependency of the first-born on adult approval and later on the approval of the group he admires serves him in good stead in our present ant-hill society. It makes the first-born better able to survive in our world which is increasingly becoming more group-oriented, so far as our jobs, our recreations, and our general living space is concerned. But his ambition for position, his pliability, his need for approval do not appear to make him an especially likable person. He survives; he gets the power; he owns the bank; he governs the state; he preaches the sermon; and he knows many, many people but few of them probably have any enduring affection for him."

The implication couched in Altus' conclusions is clear: the occupational dice are loaded in favor of the first-born, at least with respect to the likelihood of attaining the upper rungs of the occupational power hierarchy in our society. And to the extent that this is true, the values and dispositions of first-borns have a disproportionate effect upon all of us. The full impact of this prospect comes home in the words of the Chief Psychiatrist of the Navy's Aerospace Medical Institute, who reports that 76 percent of top jet pilots are first-born. After offering the opinion that they are "very nearly the nation's ideal men," he goes on to describe them as "trim and steely-eyed, self-assured, but modest and solidly in control of their emotions." And he concludes that "The first-born will likely continue to be the forerunner of the evolution of mankind." But what may sound "ideal" to some may not be equally ideal to others. Some sort of environmental compensatory measures must be taken to repeal the cultural law of primogeniture.

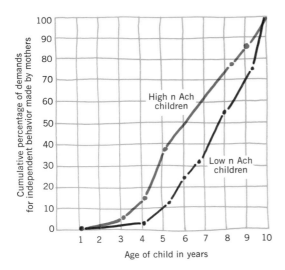

FIGURE 4.4 The relationship between independence training and need for achievement. Mothers of high n Ach children reported that they expected and demanded independent behavior at an earlier age than mothers of low n Ach children.

who expected them to have mastered such skills as crossing streets with the light, being alone, and spending pocket money at an earlier age than did mothers of low n Ach children (see Figure 4.4). The mothers of high n Ach children also rewarded independent behavior with physical affection. Thus, people who develop high need for achievement are those whose childhood achievements and independence are encouraged and rewarded by parents, especially mothers. McClelland reasoned that, since the motivation and efforts of a society's business people play a key role in economic growth, an assessment of n Ach for a society might be predictive of that society's economic rise and fall.

Culture and n Ach

McClelland and his associates have compared the need for achievement in differ-

ent cultures. They collected fourth-grade readers from different countries all over the world, taking at random 21 stories from each country's readers. They scored these stories as if they were answers to the test for n Ach. Strong relationships were found in the countries studied between the n Ach scores from the fourth-grade readers and the countries' economic growth over a 20-year period. The n Ach scores gave a highly accurate prediction of the "winners" and the "losers."

David Berlew, a student of McClelland's, even found a relationship between the amount of achievement imagery in ancient Greek literature and the growth of economic and political power in Classical Greece. With the decline of n Ach in literature, the economic power of the merchant Greeks waned (see Figure 4.5). McClelland explains the decline this way: prior to affluence, children were reared to be independent, as befitted the children of sea traders. As affluence grew, however,

FIGURE 4.5 The relationship between achievement motivation and areas of trade in ancient Greece. Need for achievement measured in terms of achievement themes in Greek literature anticipated in time the rise and fall of ancient Athenian trade.

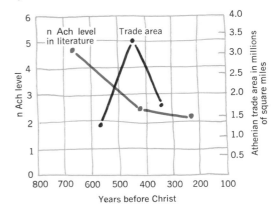

slaves took over the chore of child-rearing and independence in the children of the successful traders was no longer encouraged. N Ach declined and, with it, entrepreneurial vigor and economic activity.

In another study, Evan Davis read the strength of n Ach from the designs of Cretan pottery as if they were "doodles" that reflected personality. He found a decline in the achievement motive in the Minoan culture that preceded the sudden disappearance of Cretan power from the Mediterranean limelight in 1400 B.C., an event that still puzzles historians.

Researchers Richard de Charms and Gerald Moeller attempted to detect trends in the achievement motive level in American history. To do so they rated children's readers in the United States back to 1810 for achievement imagery. The achievement images declined from 1810 until 1830, then rose until 1890. Since then, the n Ach rating has been falling at about the same rate it rose. Interestingly enough, the curve that represents the number of patents issued by the U.S. Patent Office for every million people in the population follows by a few years the curve of rising and falling n Ach imagery.

Is it possible that the economic trends of the United States as well as other nations may reflect the motivational characteristics of their citizens? If the n Ach scores are an accurate predictor of our economic future, Americans may be well advised to look closely at the results of psychological research for strategies to ward off economic decline. There are methods that have been developed to teach people to raise their n Ach level.

n Ach Training

Is it possible to raise the n Ach level of business people who are low in this mo-

tive? If n Ach is raised, would their business success increase?

Through prior research McClelland had discovered that n Ach for small businessmen in India was on the average lower than for their American counterparts. He and his colleagues developed a training program for the businessmen based on the following assumptions: Part of any learned motivation is a network of associations, images, and fantasies that are, in effect, "symbolic rehearsals of the sort that facilitate actual performance." If a person can be taught to think and fantasize n Ach, it should, in time, lead to n Ach behavior. Students in the training program were taught to score stories for n Ach. Then they were asked to write and rewrite their stories until they scored high in n Ach. They then participated in business games that emphasized setting their own moderate goals, taking responsibility for solving problems at moderate risk, and getting rapid feedback. Notice that the game emphasized and taught each participant to think and act in ways that are characteristic of businessmen with high n Ach.

Two years later the veterans of the training groups were compared with a group of businessmen with similar backgrounds who had not been trained: the veterans had started four times as many new businesses, invested twice as much new capital, and created more than two times as many jobs as had their untrained compatriots. Clearly, the development of motives that takes place during childhood is not irrevocably determined by parental influence, since they can be altered by later education. The implications of this research are still being explored, but it seems reasonable to expect that future development of such training programs for shaping adult motivations may produce methods that can bring about changes in societies.

Focus 4.4
A Hierarchy of Motives

Some theorists, such as the late Abraham Maslow of Brandeis University, believe that all motives are organized in a hierarchical manner, which can be graphically depicted as a pyramid (see Figure 4.6). At the base of the hierarchy are physiological needs, such as for food, water, and elimination. The increasingly "human" needs operate in the upper levels, such motives as compassion and creativity being near the top. According to Maslow, instigation of "higher" motives is unlikely unless "lower," more basic motives have been satisfied; a person who never has quite enough to eat is not likely to display compassion or creativity.

Evidence supporting this idea is provided by an experiment conducted with conscientious objectors during World War II; they were placed on a semistarvation diet for 24 weeks, resulting in a 25 percent average weight loss. According to observers, all voluntary activities were reduced. Humor, sociability, and courtesy all but disappeared, and surliness became common in interpersonal relationships. Personal grooming became sloppy. Romances suffered and engagements were broken. Food became a common obsession. When a normal diet was restored, these symptoms disappeared. It would seem that when energy is scarce, it will be channeled to the more basic needs of the body; achievement, affiliation, and other "higher" motives must wait their turn.

FIGURE 4.6 Maslow's hierarchy of motives.

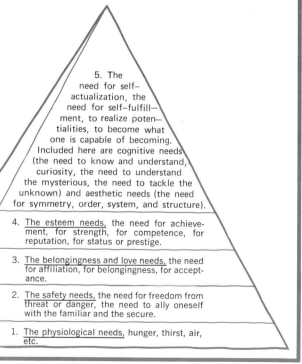

5. The need for self-actualization, the need for self-fulfillment, to realize potentialities, to become what one is capable of becoming. Included here are cognitive needs (the need to know and understand, curiosity, the need to understand the mysterious, the need to tackle the unknown) and aesthetic needs (the need for symmetry, order, system, and structure).

4. The esteem needs, the need for achievement, for strength, for competence, for reputation, for status or prestige.

3. The belongingness and love needs, the need for affiliation, for belongingness, for acceptance.

2. The safety needs, the need for freedom from threat or danger, the need to ally oneself with the familiar and the secure.

1. The physiological needs, hunger, thirst, air, etc.

THEORIES
OF MOTIVATION

A variety of theories of motivation has been proposed over the years. Each of these theories has been useful in explaining certain kinds of behavior and, consequently, has enjoyed great popularity among psychologists. It has also often happened, however, that each theory of motivation was challenged when behaviors were identified that were difficult or impossible to explain with the theory. When such a crisis occurs, the theory is scrapped or altered in significant ways and a new or "improved" theory takes its place. Then the new theory enjoys popularity until it, too, runs into crucial problems with which it cannot deal.

An example of this kind of change was seen in *drive theory,* which was stated in its original form by Yale's Clark Hull more than three decades ago. Hull's explanation of motivation was closely linked to biology and the concept of homeostasis. *Hull proposed that behavior changes occur only when the organism is energized into action by a tension that it is impelled to reduce or to eliminate. The energizing state produced is called* **drive.** Drives could be produced by deprivations such as hunger and thirst or by excesses such as pain. *Since hunger, thirst, and pain drives are tissue needs essential for survival and must be dealt with before other drives, they are called* **primary drives.** Hull suggested that any behavior that reduced drive was strengthened and, therefore, was likely to recur in future instances of the same drive. *Any object such as food or water that could reduce a drive is called a* **primary reinforcement** (see Chapter 6B). Hull further proposed that *any object or event that is associated with primary drive reduction gains the power to act as a reinforcement and is called a* **secondary reinforcement.** For example, a mother's smile or voice gains the

capacity to serve as a reinforcement because of its frequent association with the reduction of the feeding infant's hunger drive. Money becomes a powerful secondary reinforcer as a result of its association with the primary drive reducers for which it can be exchanged.

Hull's theory worked very well in explaining some behaviors, such as the observation that giving food-deprived rats a food pellet after they press a lever will increase their lever-pressing activity whenever they're hungry. But critics could cite circumstances the theory could not explain. How could drive reduction explain behavior that was not related to any sort of biological deprivation or excess, behaviors such as the curiosity of a well-fed human or animal, the commonly observed tendency of the creature to explore its surroundings or of the human to seek adventure? To explain the occurrence of such behaviors, which often take place even at the cost of pain and frustration, seemed beyond drive theory as Hull stated it.

Hull's students tried to meet these criticisms by redefining the concept of drive. Instead of explaining drive as a result of biological deprivation or excess, Neal Miller proposed that *any strong stimulus could serve as a* **drive.** The experience of hunger or thirst is "driving," suggested Miller, because it produces very *intense stimulation;* reducing the level of this stimulation or eliminating it is reinforcing. Breaking away from the strictly biological notion of drive in many ways made Miller's drive theory more versatile than Hull's had been. Uncertainty, unfamiliarity with one's surroundings, or boredom could conceivably result in intense stimulation, a *drive,* to be reduced by exploratory behavior. However, many psychologists noted that there are instances of behavior that cannot be explained as reducing the intensity of stimulation. For instance, sexual behavior involves *increasing* sensory stimulation to extremely high levels before orgasm occurs, and sex is certainly experienced by most people as reinforcing. And to a person lost in the dark, the sight of a flashlight in the distance—an *increase* in stimulation—is a welcome experience. On the other hand, as the flashlight becomes dim on a dark night, drive might actually increase. So there are types of behavior for which drive reduction is not a convincing explanation.

To explain many behaviors, it is the *context* of the stimulus as well as the nature and intensity of the stimulus that must be considered. And often, the relevant context is social rather than physical or biological; there is nothing *optically* intense about a loved one's smile. In many cases, it is the *significance* of the stimulus—a purely cognitive event, the individual's interpretation of the stimulus, rather than the physical stimulus alone—that often plays the key role in the individual's response. **Cognitive** *approaches to motivation stress significance of a stimulus to an individual within a specific context.* The significance of many such stimuli are learned and vary from individual to individual. For a person with high need to achieve business success, a situation requiring him to constantly make decisions and accept responsibility for the consequences would be exciting and pleasurable. For a person with low need to achieve business success, however, the same situation would be overwhelming and aversive. The difference is not in the physical events or stimuli in the situations, but in cognitive factors, the interpretation and meaning of the stimulus to the individual.

Hull's theory would explain the choice of steak or lobster in a restaurant in terms of the prior reinforcement history of the person. The food that has had the greatest number of reinforcements, primary or secondary, will be selected. Miller's theory encompasses Hull's explanation and adds the idea that people might also choose lobster because it promises to reduce the intense stimulation of boredom associated with eating frequent steaks or hamburgers. Theorists concerned with concepts of novelty and stimulus change would predict that the choice would be the food promising the greatest taste novelty, provided that the person never or rarely ate lobster and has no aversion to it. Theorists with a more cognitive approach would look for the meaning behind each choice. For example, a person might choose lobster in order to impress a companion with his "gourmet" taste or wealth, in which case hunger, or seeking escape from boredom, or novelty plays a small role or none.

Each theory is successful in explaining certain behaviors and in generating predictions that are confirmed, yet no one theory is currently adequate to explain and predict all of behavior. Each theory contains some element of the "truth" that must be identified and combined into more effective new theories. As in the parable of the Blind Men and the Elephant, when different perspectives are assembled, a more realistic picture of the investigated event or object is likely to emerge.

C. EMOTIONS

A concept closely linked to motivation is that of emotion. Whereas the study of motivation focuses on the activation or energizing of goal-directed behavior, the study of emotion, the next topic to be considered, is concerned with the person's subjective awareness, the feelings, and the physiological changes that accompany motivated behaviors.

Two male college students are sitting in the comfortable chairs of a private room in a university. One of the students picks up a sheet of newspaper from a nearby table and meticulously folds it into a paper airplane which he then pitches into the center of the room. As the plane finds its way into the lap of the other student, the paper-plane aviator falls into peals of laughter. The other student glares at the joker with the disapproval generally reserved for bad jokes, but suddenly he joins in the laughter and frivolity. His reactions are being observed and recorded by psychologists through a one-way mirror, because he is unknowingly participating in an experiment designed to determine factors that influence emotional expression and experience. Now we will explore some of those factors.

THE DETERMINANTS OF EMOTION

The "aviator" was a stooge, a person planted to help carry out an experiment on the nature of human emotions. Two psychologists, Stanley Schachter and Jerome Singer of Columbia University, arranged to have a group of male college students injected with what the students were told was a "vitamin complex" for the alleged purpose of testing the effects of the vitamins on vision. What the students were actually injected with was either a harmless saline (salt) solution or *adrenalin.* Adrenalin, a hormone secreted by the adrenal glands, has the effect of speeding up heartbeat, increasing blood pressure, and even causing trembling. Physiologists have demonstrated, however, that all of the physical effects associated with strong emotion, such as rapid heartbeat, perspiration, dry mouth, "butterflies" in the

stomach, could be produced by adrenalin injections without any *reported* "emotional" experience.

The college students in the Schachter-Singer experiment were divided into three categories: 1) "informed" students who were told the "vitamins" would produce adrenalin-like side-effects; 2) "misinformed" students who were told to expect "numbness, itching, and headaches" as side-effects; and 3) "ignorant" students who were told nothing about expected side-effects. All the students who received saline-solution injections were treated as "ignorant" subjects. The various treatments in this experiment are summarized in the left-hand side of Table 4.1.

The students in each group were asked to wait for the full effects of the "vitamins" in a separate room. Stooges were then sent to each room and were instructed either to behave in a playful manner (like the "aviator") or to act irritated and angry (the "irritated, angry" stooges took a questionnaire that was given to them by the experimenter and ripped it to pieces.) The reactions of each naive subject to the stooge's behavior were observed, and questions were later asked of them about their emotional state.

The behavior patterns observed and the responses to the questions revealed the following: The students who most often reported "catching the stooge's mood" were the "misinformed" students exposed to the playful, euphoric-acting stooge. Those least affected by the same stooge were those who had been correctly informed of the effect of the drug. The degree of responsiveness of the other groups lay somewhere in between; the "ignorant" were less responsive than the "misinformed" but more responsive than the "informed" (see Figure 4.7 and Table 4.1). The same pattern held for students exposed

TABLE 4.1   **Schachter and Singer's experimental design and general findings**

SUBJECTS		RESPONSES TO:	
		EUPHORIC, PLAYFUL STOOGE	ANGRY STOOGE
Injected with Adrenalin	Correctly Informed	Least susceptible to stooge's mood	Least susceptible to stooge's mood
	Misinformed	Highly susceptible to stooge's mood	This condition was not included in study
	Ignorant	Moderately susceptible to stooge's mood	Moderately susceptible to stooge's mood
Injected with Saline Solution	Ignorant	Slightly susceptible to stooge's mood	Slightly susceptible to stooge's mood

(Adapted from Schachter and Singer, 1962.)

to the angry stooge, although there was less influence. Nonetheless, the effects of the hormone injection were variously interpreted as both euphoria and anger. Both these feelings are recognizably emotional reactions. But what *is* an emotion?

A Definition of Emotion.   In our daily lives we each recognize in ourselves and others emotional reactions that we have learned to label as love, hate, fear, jealousy, delight, depression, and so on. Most psychologists agree that the term **emotion** *refers to a subjective awareness of the accompanying physiological changes in behavior.* Schachter's and Singer's subjects displayed all of the characteristics of emotion. They reported feelings of anger or euphoria. Physiological changes accompanying the adrenalin injection, such as speeding up of the heartbeat, occurred,

and these changes were interpreted as different emotions depending on what the subjects had been told. To explain these findings, Schachter and Singer proposed a theory.

Cognitive-Appraisal Theory.   Their interpretation of these observations was as follows. Faced with a state of physiological arousal (beating heart, trembling, etc.) and no adequate explanation for it, the "misinformed" group scans the environment for clues and attributes their arousal to the behavior of the stooge. They then label the emotional feelings they experience as either "anger" or "euphoria" depending on the environmental cues. On the other hand, the "informed" students already *had* an explanation for the aroused state they experienced and so had no need to identify some external cause. Those in the "igno-

FIGURE 4.7 *The emotions experienced by the subjects in Schachter's study were determined by each individual's explanation for an aroused physiological state.*

rant'' group were only slightly susceptible to the stooge, possibly, Schachter speculates, because, without any information provided by the experimenter, they formed their own appraisal.

The theory of human emotion that resulted from this research is called the **cognitive-appraisal theory.** *The theory states that experienced (or at least reported) emotion is the result of an individual's explanation for an aroused physiological state.* Our evaluation of a situation and our feelings, which can be influenced by people around us, powerfully determine the emotion we experience.

THEORIES OF EMOTION

This proposal is, of course, only one of a variety of theories to explain emotion that have been proposed over the years. Each theory was based on a limited set of findings which the theorist generalized to explain all emotions. Research stimulated by each theory often led to findings that either contradicted the theory or that couldn't be explained by it. Each new theory that was proposed improved over its predecessors by more effectively encompassing and explaining findings.

James-Lange Theory

William James of Harvard University proposed his theory in 1884. Carl Lange, a Danish scientist, proposed a similar theory about the same time. The theory asserts that an emotional response precedes the emotional experience. For example, the theory predicts that if someone points a gun at you, your body would respond by trembling, your stomach would begin to "churn up," your knees begin to weaken. (Today we know that the sympathetic branch of the autonomic nervous system to be discussed below and the hormone adrenalin are involved in this physiological arousal.) When you become aware of these bodily changes, you then experience the emotion. This is just the opposite of the common sense notion that places awareness of the emotion first, followed by bodily reactions.

Cannon-Bard Theory

If the James-Lange theory were correct, then each emotion would have a discriminably different set of physiological cues. Walter Cannon, an American physiologist, found evidence not only that visceral changes are too slow to be used as a source of cues for rapidly changing emotions, but also that different emotions are accompanied by the *same* visceral responses. (Compare Schachter and Singer's subjects who variously experienced euphoria or anger following an adrenalin injection.) This criticism was made in 1929 and has been supported by later research. In the ensuing years, it has been found that, although physiological patterns for anger and fear are different, *no* differences have been found for most other emotions. Cannon and P. Bard proposed that the conscious emotions we experience come from a discharge of the thalamus portion of the brain into the cortex. While this part of the theory didn't hold up, their contention that emotion served as an emergency energizer preparing the organism for action anticipated modern activation theory. According to Cannon and Bard, we see the gun and, *simultaneously,* we are aware of the emotion and our body makes an emotional response.

Activation Theory

Donald Lindsley of UCLA coined the term "activation theory." He proposes that the **reticular system,** which consists of a network of special neurons in the brain stem, must be activated before emotions can occur. The reticular system serves as a general energizer. Its activity level influences arousal and wakefulness. If the reticular system is destroyed, the organism doesn't awaken and dies in its sleep. Lindsley showed that emotional arousal is accompanied by changing patterns in the electroencephalogram (EEG). However, it is presently not possible to discriminate between different emotions by an EEG. The theory is important because it points out the role of general activation or excitement that is an essential part of emotion, and the role of the reticular system.

Cognitive-Appraisal Theory

The cognitive-appraisal theory, as we explained, proposes that emotional states are a function of both physiological arousal and of a cognition (idea, thought, appraisal) of the arousal. A physiologically aroused person without an explanation for the arousal will label the arousal in terms of the cognitions available. The cognition a person selects can be influenced by the situation as well as the behavior, moods, and cognitions of other people. This means that the same state of physiological arousal could be labeled as "joy" or "fury" or "jealousy" or any other emotional label depending on the cognitions generated or available. This theory, which is supported by the experiments we described, nicely integrates and accounts for the findings used to support older, competing theories of emotion.

THE AUTONOMIC NERVOUS SYSTEM

Essential aspects of the physiological changes that accompany or produce emotions are a function of the autonomic nervous system. The nervous system (as we have seen in Chapter 3) is composed of two main branches; the central nervous system (CNS), consisting of the brain and spinal cord, and the peripheral nervous system, consisting of the somatic nerves and the autonomic nervous system. **Somatic nerves** *carry information from the sense organs to the CNS, and the CNS issues commands that control body movements via somatic nerves.* **The autonomic nervous system** (ANS) *influences the action of the heart, stomach, and glands (collectively referred to as the viscera) and plays a key role in emotions and preparing the body to deal with stress as well as relaxation and rest.* (The term *autonomic* means self-governing or independent.)

The autonomic system is composed of two subsystems, *the sympathetic* and *the parasympathetic.* The sympathetic system was so called by early anatomists, who thought the system acted in "sympathy" with the central nervous system; it is indeed linked to the CNS, but it has its own major functions. The parasympathetic ("next to the sympathetic") is so called because its fibers originate in the brain stem and sacral (lower back) region of the spinal cord, *next to* the sympathetic fibers that exit the spinal cord between the brain stem and sacral region. *The* **sympathetic system** *is excitatory, putting out great amounts of energy in times of stress, while the* **parasympathetic system** *is essentially inhibitory and generally is more active during times of relaxation and restfulness.* The sympathetic and parasympathetic systems often work in opposition—the energizing and speeding up of vital processes alternates with inhibiting and slowing down of the actions of various organs that is essential if exhaustion and death are not to result (see Focus 4.5: The General Adaptation Syndrome, p. 118).

The anatomy and functions of the auto-

nomic system as well as its effects on emotions are summarized in Figure 4.8, pages 116-117. (See Focus 4.6, page 118, for a discussion of the effects of motivation and emotion on performance.)

EMOTIONS AND PHYSICAL DISORDERS

The relationship of physiological arousal and emotion is reciprocal. As we have seen, bodily processes, along with cognitive appraisal of these processes, play a role in determining emotions. But the emotions also play a role in the control of physiological functions, often to the detriment of the well-being of the person involved. *The term* **psychosomatic disorder** *is given to physical disorders that are in part due to emotions and psychological stress.* Psychosomatic disorders come in many varieties including colon and stomach ulcers, skin eruptions, asthma, muscular pains, and headaches.

A psychosomatic ailment commonly connected with psychological stress is peptic ulcer, which has been studied by Joseph Brady. In the hope of understanding the effect of stress on people, Brady looked into the effect on monkeys of decisions under stress. Brady strapped two monkeys into "restraining chairs" that permitted free movement of head and limbs but held the body in place (see Figure 4.10, page 120). The monkeys were given a harmless, but presumably painful, electric shock every 20 seconds. A lever was within reach of each monkey. One of the levers was a dummy, having no effect, but the other monkey's lever was so wired that it could prevent the shocks. If this monkey, called the "executive" monkey, pressed the lever at least once every 20 seconds, neither of the monkeys received a shock. The "executive" monkey quickly learned its task. The other monkey also quickly

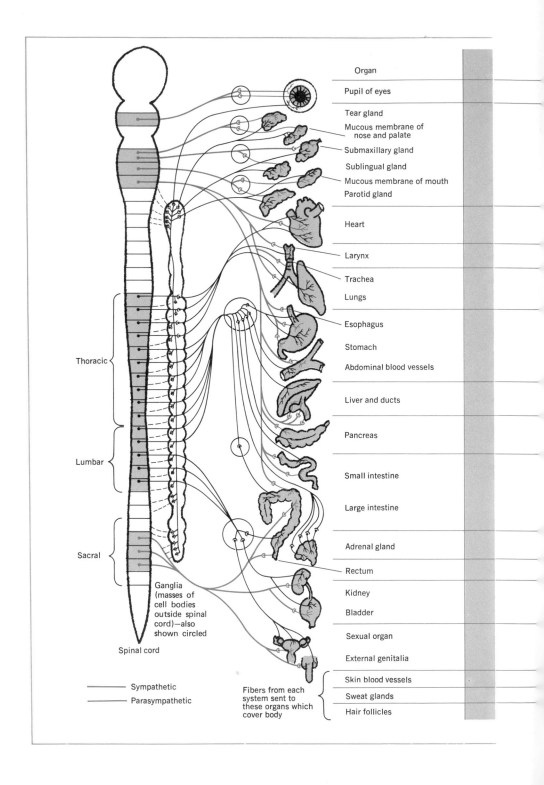

Organ

Pupil of eyes

Tear gland

Mucous membrane of
nose and palate

Submaxillary gland

Sublingual gland

Mucous membrane of mouth

Parotid gland

Heart

Larynx

Trachea

Lungs

Esophagus

Stomach

Abdominal blood vessels

Liver and ducts

Pancreas

Small intestine

Large intestine

Adrenal gland

Rectum

Kidney

Bladder

Sexual organ

External genitalia

Skin blood vessels

Sweat glands

Hair follicles

Thoracic

Lumbar

Sacral

Ganglia
(masses of
cell bodies
outside spinal
cord)—also
shown circled

Spinal cord

Sympathetic
Parasympathetic

Fibers from each
system sent to
these organs which
cover body

Parasympathetic system		Sympathetic system	
Function	Experience	Function	Experience
Constriction	Diminished light	Dilation	Increased light
Stimulates secretion		Inhibits secretion	Dryness in nasal passage, mouth, and throat
Deceleration, constriction of blood vessel		Acceleration, dilation of blood vessels	Increased blood pressure, heart pounding
	Relaxed throat, lower pitch		Tense throat, higher pitch
Constrict bronchi	Relaxed breathing	Dilate bronchi	Rapid breathing
Stimulates secretions and peristalsis		Inhibits secretions, peristalsis, and blood flow	Butterflies in stomach, heavy, tense feeling, indigestion
Liberates bile	Light, "free," relaxed internal feeling	Inhibition	
		Releases blood sugar	Excited, energetic feeling
Stimulates secretion		Inhibits secretion	Butterflies in stomach, heavy, tense feeling, indigestion
		Inhibits secretion	
Excitation	Expulsion of feces	Inhibition	Retention of feces
Excitation	Expulsion of urine	Inhibition	Retention of urine
Erection during early arousal	Excitation	Ejaculation during later arousal	Orgasm
Dilation	Skin and body feel relaxed and calm	Constriction	Skin feels cold and clammy, hairs stand on end, perspiration increases
Inhibition		Secretion	
Relaxation		Erection	

FIGURE 4.8 *The structures and typical functions of the autonomic system. Under extreme stress the functions may differ.*

Focus 4.5
The General Adaptation Syndrome

Hans Selye of McGill University has contributed to our understanding of the adaptive behavior of organisms under stress. He identified a mechanism he calls the **general adaptation syndrome** (GAS). *The GAS is a sequence of adaptive responses to both physiological and psychological stress.* There are three stages: alarm, resistance, and exhaustion.

The *alarm* reaction is the "battle cry" of the organism, the behavioral indication that stress has been perceived. Regardless of the exact nature of the stressor, all mammals, including humans, show similar complex physiological responses of alarm. These responses appear to be triggered by the pituitary-adrenal system; they include the secretion of adrenalin into the bloodstream, the speeding up of the heart, a diminishing of the blood supply to the outer body regions (sometimes observed as "blanching" or "going white"), and an increase of blood to the central internal organs. This stage is also accompanied by extreme emotional responses such as anger, fearfulness, tension, and agitation. Gradually, these symptoms disappear and the alarm stage is replaced by the *resistance* stage; during this the organism's resources are used

Focus 4.6
Motivation, Emotion, and Performance

Nearly everyone has felt at some time or another a sudden awkwardness when wanting intensely to impress someone or the "freezing" that sometimes occurs when under intense pressure to perform. Sometimes examinations that seem important are the occasions of "freezing" or "blanking out"; you feel sure that if the pressure were absent, the exam would be much easier. Sometimes this sort of explanation may be nothing more than an excuse for poor performance, but there is evidence that extremely high motivation and the associated emotional excitement do at times harm performance.

Motivation and emotional excitement always affect performance, but not necessarily in simple ways. Up to a certain optimal point, increasing motivation results in increased effectiveness of performance, but beyond that point increasing motivation results in decreasing effectiveness and poorer performance. This principle is known as the Yerkes-Dodson Law. Different activities also have different optimal levels of motivation. In general, the greater the complexity or difficulty of the task, such as solving mathematical problems or playing an instrument, the lower is the optimal motivation level. Tasks that are simply and easily done, such as running a football or digging a ditch, can withstand high levels of motivation before performance suffers. With more complex tasks, such as taking psychology or math examinations, too much pressure tends to interfere with performance. The changing shape of the motivation-performance relationship is shown in Figure 4.9.

in defense against the stress. These defenses again are triggered by the pituitary-adrenal system. Often "neurotic defenses" (discussed in Chapter 11B) are a part of this phase, especially if the stressor is social or symbolic in nature. After the resistance efforts of the organism have come into play, then the *exhaustion* phase sets in. If the stress is severe enough, death will ensue when the bodily resources are no longer able to sustain the increased rates of activity. If the organism is permitted to rest and recuperate, new stress can be handled.

An important aspect of the general adaptation concept is that these adaptive stress responses are not specific to either physiological or psychological stress. This concept helps to make psychosomatic disorders more intelligible. Selye has designated a whole host of psychosomatic ailments as "diseases of adaptation" because they appear to result from prolonged resistance to stress as the organism attempts to adapt to its environment. Like all good conceptual schemes, this one allows apparently diverse phenomena to be tied together in meaningful ways.

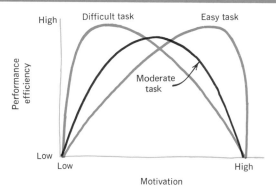

FIGURE 4.9 *The relationship between motivation levels and task performance.*

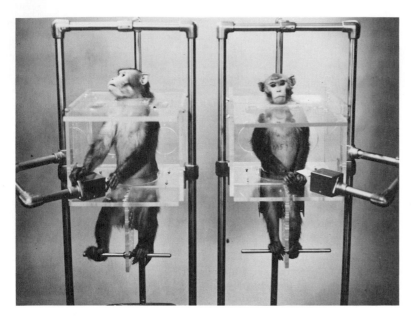

FIGURE 4.10 These monkeys were periodically subjected to harmless, but painful electric shocks. The monkey on the left learned to prevent the shocks by operating a lever. The task was stressful to the monkey and contributed to the development of an ulcer. The monkey on the right learned that its lever was inoperative, so it endured the shocks passively and did not develop an ulcer.

learned that nothing it could do would prevent shocks. Both monkeys were put on a schedule that alternated six hours of shocking with six hours of rest. This schedule was continued for 23 days until the executive monkey, who until this time had appeared to be in good health, collapsed and died. Under autopsy, it was observed that a severe ulceration had perforated the lining of the small intestine near its juncture with the monkey's stomach, a common location for ulcers in human executives. The other monkey was sacrificed and examined. No damage was found. Although ulceration was the immediate cause of the "executive's" death, it could accurately be said that stress contributed to its death since its partner shared all elements of the situation *except* the stress of the "executive" decision—whether or not to press the lever.

In humans, psychosomatic effects are common to the digestive tract, the cardiovascular system, the respiratory system, the endocrine system, and many other or-gans. Sexual impotence and frigidity have often been traced to emotional stress. Ulcers occur most often in those who must continually make decisions where the consequences are (or *seem* to be) important; the executive is the classic example. The fact that more men than women have ulcers may reflect sociological conditions. As women assume a larger portion of positions of responsibility, ulcers may be more equitably distributed. Although it would be tempting to say simply that ailments such as ulcers are caused by tension and let it go at that, the situation is not quite that simple. Some executives never get ulcers. Other people in positions of no great responsibility do develop them. So how do we explain these incongruities?

Two-Factor Theory. A group of psychologists under the leadership of Jeanne Block at the University of California at Berkeley examined the interplay of physical susceptibility and emotional stress in children with bronchial asthma. The experimenters tested each asthmatic child for *physical suscepti- bility* to asthma by reactions to **allergens** (an **allergen** *is any substance which pro- duces a rash or body reaction when intro- duced to the skin or blood stream*). The experimenters also rated the amount of *emotionally stressful* conditions to which each of the asthmatic children had been exposed, such as divorce of parents or emotional instability in the mother. The data clearly showed that the asthmatic children who had shown the least poten- tial for allergy—that is, low physical susceptibility scores—were those who had

been exposed to the greatest amount of stressful environmental influences. In con- trast, children who showed great potential for allergy came from environments with a wide range of stress. From the evidence, it would seem that many of the low-allergy- potential children would most likely *not* have developed asthma if emotional stress had not played its part. In others, however, a predisposition toward the malady would most likely result in asthma *regardless* of emotional stress or its absence. Thus, the **"two-factor"** theory *ascribes psychosomatic ailments to an interplay of physical pre- disposition and emotional stress.*

Focus 4.7

Emotions and the Lie Detector

FIGURE 4.11 A poly- graph consists of a series of different physi- ological measuring de- vices linked to a device to record the changes. Moving pens record physiological changes on a strip of moving paper. The cuff on the subject's right arm senses blood pressure changes; the tubes around the chest pick up respiration rate, and the sensors on the sub- ject's left hand pick up changes in skin resis- tance (GSR).

Seated at a large table in a well-lit laboratory room, a gangly-limbed, thin young man about 23 is connected to a machine called a polygraph —or more commonly, a lie detector (see Figure 4.11). A tube to measure breathing rate circles under his arms and around his chest. Two of the fingers of his left hand have electrical terminals pasted to them to meas-

ure skin resistance, and a cuff around his right arm measures blood pressure. The young man is seated facing a police detective who is asking him various questions about incidentals such as his name, address, phone number, and age. A police technician is attending to the various dials and graphs of the suitcase-sized polygraph, which records the measurements being made. The investigator is interrogating the young man in the hope of determining whether he is the murderer of a 19-year-old girl.

After the initial neutral questions, such as, "What's your name," "How old are you," the investigator begins to show photographs of different people to the suspect. At first, the photos are mixed samples of men and women, young and old. Occasionally, the investigator pauses to allow the technician to determine the "normal" level of arousal for this particular suspect. The detective then shows the suspect a series of photos of young women without eliciting a strong response. But as he uncovers a photo of the dead girl, the dials on the polygraph jump wildly. During this time the detective has asked no questions. Having seen this initial response, the detective then shows photos of various locations in the city, including the site of the crime. Again the polygraph reports an immediate arousal reaction. The detective informs the suspect that they know about his reactions and that he is now strongly suspected of the crime. Overwhelmed by the transparency of his reactions, the young man submits to questioning and confesses.

The polygraph consists of a series of different physiological measuring devices linked to a device that records changes. The term "polygraph" simply means "recording" (graph) "many things" (poly). The polygraph has been mislabeled the "lie detector." It is not lies that the polygraph detects; rather, it records the reactions that are under the control of the autonomic nervous system. These include heart rate, blood pressure, breathing rate, and the galvanic skin response (GSR) in which the skin's electrical resistance varies with minute amounts of perspiration. The use of this device as a "lie detector" is based on the theory that a person who is lying will experience some degree of stress, some variations in GSR, blood pressure, or respiratory response that are so slight they are often not apparent to an unaided observer but are readily apparent in the polygraph, which amplifies and makes a visible record of bodily responses.

Although the polygraph can be a very effective instrument in the hands of a qualified specialist, it can lead to erroneous conclusions on occasion. Burke Smith of the University of Virginia School of Medicine cites the case of a bank manager who, when routinely examined with a polygraph, showed a violent, emotional response to the question, "Have you ever stolen any money from the bank or its customers?" Although he claimed not to remember the theft, the young bank manager was convinced of the machine's infallibility, so he confessed to the crime and described the manner in which he thought he must have committed it. Another crime-fighting victory for the "lie detector," right?

Wrong! The bank's auditors found no missing sums. When examined by a psychiatrist, it was discovered that the young manager had unconscious guilt feelings about financial dealings he had had with his wife and his mother, dealings involving large sums of money. Apparently the key to his response was the question's phrasing, ". . . from the bank or its customers"; both his wife and mother happened to be customers of the bank.

It is clear that any words with strongly emotional associations can elicit responses that may easily be misinterpreted as "lying." For a particular individual, four-letter words or perfectly normal, everyday words may set off even *unconscious* associations with strong memories of childhood experiences or parental prohibitions. These associations may yield emotional responses in the subject and lead to false conclusions by the polygraph examiner. Burke Smith reminds us that there are, in fact, no patterns of response that invariably indicate lying; there are only nonspecific patterns of emotional arousal that vary from individual to individual. There are no hard and fast lines that distinguish a "normal" from an "abnormal" emotional state. For example, one individual may show extreme emotional sensitivity in GSR readings but little or no simultaneous variation in the blood pressure or breathing rate; for another individual, these sensitivities may be reversed. All polygraph operators must by necessity employ a large helping of "intuition" when they interpret the readings for any individual. It is possible that the same readings might be interpreted in contradictory ways by two different examiners.

Although the polygraph gives a better-than-chance determination of the truthfulness of the subject's statements, we certainly are a long way from electronic "mind reading." For these reasons, the courts are very reluctant to make use of the lie detector. Lie detectors are extremely useful instruments *when their limits are understood.* Courts usually do not allow their findings as evidence, but the devices are often useful to the police in eliminating suspects or determining the likelihood of a suspect's guilt. As in the example given earlier, the polygraph findings may even induce a confession from a suspect who sees that the police are nearly certain of his culpability and will inevitably prove it. They are also used by private companies and public agencies for security clearance or personnel qualification: thieves or spies can often be weeded out in this manner. Most importantly for the psychologist, they demonstrate the physiological aspect of stress and emotion.

D. THE SOCIALIZATION OF SEX

Is sex all in your "mind"? A yes answer is suggested by researcher Frank Beach of the University of California at Berkeley, a veteran in the study of hormones and their effect on sexual behavior. Beach reports an interesting shift in the nature of sexuality as we climb the phylogenetic scale from lower mammals such as rats and dogs to our own species. In all mammals the differential production of hormones controls the development of secondary sexual characteristics and, in the females, cyclical changes in hormones determine the periods of *estrus,* or fertility. In most mammals, including rats, the period of fertility is also the only time the female is sexually receptive. There is a close linkage of fertility and mating in most animal species until we arrive at the human level, where sex activity occurs without reference to the female's fertility. Beach sees this as a reflection of the shift in control over sex behavior from hormonal influences to the cortical regions of the brain, areas which are associated with memory, learning, and, by implication, cultural influences. While this shift "liberates" the higher mammals, including ourselves, from the domination of hormonal schedules, it places heavy stress on the role of society in sexual behavior.

In this section we will explore how both biological and social factors interact to produce the behaviors, feelings, and emotions that are linked to human sexuality.

THE BIOLOGY OF SEX BEHAVIOR

There is no doubt that culture plays a strong role in determining sexual behavior, at least in humans. But in all sexual behavior there is, of course, a biological aspect. In all mammals gender seems to be in many respects determined by chromosomal structures. Mature sexual characteristics wait on the production of hormones in differential amounts. We have examined the critical role of hormones in sex determination during embryonic development in Chapter 2.

After birth and until puberty, boys and girls will both produce about the same amounts of androgen and estrogen, the "male" and "female" hormones. Only at puberty do males begin to secrete large amounts of androgen from the testes and females large amounts of estrogen from the ovaries, producing the common secondary sexual differences between male and female: deep voice, facial hair, and heavier body in the male, breasts and hip development and the onset of menstruation in the female (see Focus 4.8: Learning Menstrual Depression), pubic hair in both sexes, and, most significantly, the capacity of reproduction. In the female, the amount of estrogen secreted varies in cycles and determines periodic occasions of fertility and menstruation.

Only recently has the physiology of human sexual activity been carefully observed in a laboratory setting by William Masters and Virginia Johnson of the Reproductive Biology Research Foundation. They reported their findings in the book *Human Sexual Response.*

The studies of Masters and Johnson are psychophysiological in focus. They record the initial vasocongestion (congestion of blood vessels) in genitals and secondary sexual regions and the increased heartbeat and blood pressure. With increased sexual arousal, the breathing rate and perspiration increase, the heartbeat rate rises as high as 100 beats a minute, blood pressure elevates, and the body develops a general flush. Perhaps the most important

Focus 4.8

Learning Menstrual Depression

The human female has no clearly identifiable estrus period in which hormonal variation increases sexual receptivity. The menstrual period has often been associated with a *cessation* of sexual intercourse, but a recent study by Karen Paige of the University of California at Davis indicates that neither sexual receptivity nor the emotional anxiety often associated with menstruation is the clear-cut result of hormonal changes.

Paige studied the emotional responses of 52 women who were taking birth-control pills that minimized their hormonal fluctuations. Some women respond to such birth-control pills with decreased menstrual flows, while other women experience no change in their menstrual flow. Paige kept track of the amount of bleeding each woman experienced during menstruation, both by the personal report of the individuals and the number of sanitary napkins and tampons they used daily. Also, she employed a psychological test to keep track of the level of anxiety and hostility each woman experienced during different times of the month.

Even with similar hormonal levels maintained by the birth-control pills, it was evident that different women experienced different levels of anxiety during menstruation and that the level of anxiety correlated with the amount of bleeding. Women with reduced bleeding not only felt less anxiety, but were less likely to avoid sex during their menstrual period. Paige further compared the different levels of menstrual anxiety with the religious upbringing of each woman and discovered that the women brought up in Catholic or Jewish households were more anxious during menstruation and more reluctant to engage in sex during that period than were Protestants. Paige concluded that this reflected the different attitudes of the religious traditions toward the "uncleanliness" of the woman and her menstrual flow; both Jewish and Catholic faiths have strong sanctions against intercourse with a menstruating woman or any contact with the menstrual flow, while Protestantism for the most part ignores the question.

So, unlike the lower mammals, the significant changes in the receptiveness or the general emotional state of the female during specific stages of the fertility cycle seem to owe very little to hormonal changes. Instead, they appear to be socially conditioned responses to the visible effects of the hormonal change—the bleeding during menstruation—rather than direct effects of the changes. If we exclude the role of these socially conditioned responses, human males and females are both able and apparently willing to engage in sexual activity without reference to hormonal level. Page's findings provide additional support for the view that learning plays an important role in human sexual behavior.

contribution of Masters and Johnson has been to dispel the myth that sex is essentially different for men and women. The researchers emphasize that, although average rates of increase in any of the physiological factors may differ for men and women, the reactions show much more striking similarities than differences; apparently, sex is sex for both men and women, at least at a physiological level.

LEARNING REPRODUCTIVE BEHAVIOR

In an experiment with rhesus monkeys, Harry F. Harlow of the University of Wisconsin showed that males raised in isolation were attracted to and aroused by sexually responsive females but could not successfully mount the females; they apparently did not know how (see Figure 4.12). Similar experiments have demonstrated the role of experience in rats and dogs. As we go up the phylogenetic scale the relative size of the cortical region and its control over sexual behavior increases, but apparently it does not increase at the same rate for both sexes. When cortical areas of the brain are surgically removed from *female* rats and dogs they become sexually clumsy but can still copulate. If the same operation is performed on *male* rats and dogs, however, they immediately cease sexual activity. Needless to say, this experiment has never been tried with human subjects, but theorists suspect that there may be subtle differences in the cortical organization of sexuality in men and women. The greater incidence of sexual fantasies in males while masturbating (89 per cent in males as opposed to only 64 percent in females, according to Kinsey Foundation surveys) might well reflect the difference, since fantasizing is a behavior associated with cortical region.

FIGURE 4.12 *Male monkeys who were raised in isolation were attracted to and aroused by sexually responsive females but did not know how to mount the females. This disability demonstrates the importance of experience and learning in the sexual behavior of monkeys.*

Sexual Stimuli. The strong control exercised by the cortex over sexual behavior is probably the source of the extreme diversity of sexual stimuli to which we respond as well as the variety of and variations in our sex behaviors.

If by "mind" we mean the cortical center of *learned* rather than biologically determined behavior, then we might well agree with Beach and say that sex as humans know it is in the "mind." The control of sexual activities in higher mammals, and especially in humans, shifts from hormonal influences to the cortex—a region that occupies a greater percentage of brain volume as we ascend the evolutionary ladder. In human beings, the emancipation is complete to the point that hormones play a diminished role once the necessary physiological changes are accomplished. Studies of men who have been castrated (their testes removed) show that their sexual activities are little if any less frequent than before castration, provided they were mature when the mutilation occurred. Castration of a rat will virtually eliminate signs of sexual desire and activity.

The "cues" that instigate sexual behavior can be almost anything from nudity to body smell to intimate clothing of the opposite sex depending on previous learning and experience. Of course, this does not deny that some cues are universally popular. For instance, there is little doubt that the most common cue for sexual behavior in the male is a female, especially in surroundings that do not effectively preclude intimate behavior. But people have reported sexual responses instigated by contact with anything from panty hose to high-powered rifles.

SEX ROLES
AND CULTURE

Left momentarily to his devices in a room filled with toys of various kinds and in various conditions of newness and repair, a small boy of kindergarten age looks about at them. He kneels to pick up a dilapidated cowboy gun and holster. He pulls the pistol from the holster, fires a few tentative shots at an imaginary enemy, then sets the gun aside. He walks over to a new, shiningly painted and very intricate doll's-house and for the moment appears absorbed in it. The door knob clicks as an adult, the child's mother, enters the room and sits quietly on a chair in one corner. But before he has even cast a backward glance to ascertain the identity of the entering person, the little boy stands up and abruptly deserts the doll's house for his discarded, dilapidated cowboy's pistols and further showdowns with his imaginary foe.

Sex-Role Development. This is a reconstructed scene from an experiment conducted by Japanese researchers Kobisa-

FIGURE 4.13 An individual's conception of his or her sex role is learned early in life and is reflected in and influenced by toys and play behavior.

gawa, Arakaki, and Awiguni, who attempted to detect gender-associated play preferences in male kindergarten pupils. Individual boys were allowed free play among toys classified as being "masculine," "feminine," or "neutral." The feminine" toys were new and attractive, but the other toys were older and less intrinsically attractive. As illustrated in the case above, the boys were more likely to choose to play with toys appropriate to their gender, *even though the toys were less attractive.* The presence of an adult increased the likelihood of the choice of "masculine" toys. By observing groups of boys, rather than individuals, the researchers found that seeing another boy playing with a "feminine" toy increased the likelihood of a child's choosing to play with an attractive "feminine" toy. Strong preferences for toys and pastimes suitable to their sex roles were obvious in this study of five- and six-year-olds. Similar studies done in the United States indicate that even in four-year-old boys and girls strongly defined role behavior is observable. It is clear that sex-role behavior is determined early in life.

In the 1970s sex roles are established (we are forced to assume) in much the same way they have always been. They are learned principally from parents, as well as from siblings and, as a child grows older, from peer groups and through exposure to books, television, movies, and other mass media. This learning seems to take place through imitation of the parent of the same sex and parental approval for sex-appropriate behavior.

Sex Roles in Three Primitive Societies. That sex roles are learned and culturally determined is evident in anthropologist Margaret Mead's observations of three

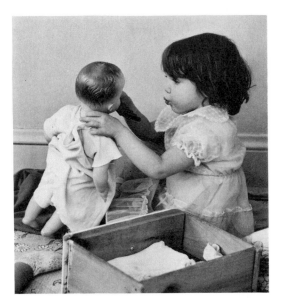

FIGURE 4.14 Children learn their sex roles by using their parents as models, and, beginning at a very young age, they practice the roles in their play behavior.

New Guinea cultures, each with different definitions and expectations of male and female behavior. Among the *Arapesh,* who are hillside dwellers, the women are "motherly" in our own culture's terms, being gentle and loving and cooperative — but so are the men. Both sexes would be described as "feminine" from our point of view, in the sense of being passive and gentle and of treating power over others as undesirable. Leadership responsibilities are only reluctantly assumed duties, gladly relinquished when completed. Members of both sexes enjoy "mothering" their children.

By contrast, the *Mundugumor* culture, until recently situated on a river bank in New Guinea, boasts men who are self-assertive, arrogant, individualistic, fierce warriors and women who are just as arrogant, assertive, and fierce. Domestic life is a continual quarrel for the Mundugumor; not only between a fierce husband and his equally fierce wife, but extending even to children, who are taught early to taunt their parents. This taunting is a lesson provided by Mundugumor mothers, who otherwise have as little as possible to do with their offspring. In brief, both male and female Mundugumors have traits we would define as "masculine" in our society.

In a third group, lake dwellers called the *Tchambuli,* the roles we associate with men and women seem reversed in contrast with our concept of the traditional male and female roles. Women take care of commerce and food-gathering because they believe that men are emotional creatures, sentimental, thin-skinned, and easily hurt, who will only bungle any responsibility that requires serious decision-making. Instead, the men gather daily in groups to gossip and produce the Tchambuli's artistic output, their drama, music, and painting.

Observations such as Mead's rule out any argument that sex roles are "natural" in the sense of being completely biologically predetermined. (See Focus 4.9: Homosexuality, page 130.) Clearly, sex roles differ from one culture to another, and different child-rearing practices result in different definitions of male and female roles within a society.

Sex Roles and Need for Achievement. As might be noted from our own experience and from Mead's description of the New Guinea cultures, sex roles are generally more than a matter of appearance. Behavior, too, is a part of the role. In America and Europe, men are generally driven to demonstrate that they are strong, powerful, and competent. The need-for-achievement motive is consistently higher in males than in females. Women have traditionally felt obliged to demonstrate that they are passive, even submissive, emotional creatures who desire, not to achieve, only to please.

Even in our currently liberalizing culture, the achieving woman often faces anxiety when she feels her professional or intellectual prowess disqualifies her from being feminine or desirable. Matina Horner asked subjects to complete stories offered without endings; from the results she discovered evidence of what she terms the "need to avoid achievement" in intelligent female college students. Even when females do possess a high need and capacity for achievement, in our society they are strongly inclined to feel anxiety about their sexual role precisely *because* of that capability. On the other hand, in men a "fear of achievement" that centers around its appropriateness for the male sex role is unknown. Even in the 1970s such is the abiding power of the traditional sex roles.

Focus 4.9:

Homo-sexuality

In many American states sexual intimacy between freely consenting adults of the same sex is punishable by imprisonment. In such states homosexuals make up 15 percent of all imprisoned "sex offenders." Presently, however, some states are repealing legislation against homosexuals, notably Illinois and Connecticut. Even so, many homosexuals still live in danger of imprisonment, although attitudes toward them seem generally to be liberalizing. In the mental health professions this liberalizing trend is also apparent. In 1973 the American Psychiatric Association issued a statement that "homosexuality" would no longer be catalogued as a "personality disorder" but a "personality dysfunction" on the same level as impotence or frigidity.

There are different answers to basic questions about homosexuals: Should a homosexual be considered a criminal? Is he or she "sick?" Are homosexuals dangerous to society? The way responsible members of our society answer these questions will affect the lives of millions of people.

The history of homosexuality is long and the social attitudes toward it have varied widely. Among the ancient Jews it was sufficient cause for death, while the Greeks regarded it as at least as respectable as conjugal affection. In one of the Platonic dialogues, Alcibiades boasts of his attempts to seduce Socrates. Western puritanical culture forced homosexuality underground, and it was only after World War II, in Kinsey's studies of sexual behavior in the United States, that an accurate picture of homosexuality in America began to emerge. According to the study, 18 percent of American male adults reported primarily homosexual activities. But 35 to 40 percent of adult males have experienced orgasm at some time from contact with another male. Figures are generally lower for females: only between 10 and 15 percent of adult women have experienced orgasm resulting from contact with other women. Although the percentages may change among different groups, it is evident that homosexuality is a regularly occurring event in human relationships.

Several theories for the origin of homosexuality have been suggested. Some psychologists, for instance, simply explain homosexuality in terms of early experience, asserting that it is likely to result from a pleasurably experienced seduction in childhood or adolescence. But there is no widely accepted understanding of homosexuality. Many psychologists and psychiatrists have regarded homosexuality as an emotional illness or as a symptom of an underlying mental illness. San Francisco therapist Martin Hoffman has attributed this idea to a combination of moral attitudes and the "clinical fallacy" of judging an entire segment of the population from those who are seen for treatment. Disturbed homosexuals who seek the aid of a therapist would, of course, give the impression that all homosexuals are emotionally disturbed. To investigate this bias, UCLA psychologist Evelyn Hooker administered a battery of psychological tests to 30 homosexuals who were *not* in treatment and to 30 "straight" males. Both groups were matched in terms of age, IQ, and educational background. She then had psychologists analyze the results of these tests without telling them which tests were completed by homosexuals. The clinicians were unable to distinguish between the two groups, and Hooker herself found no significant differences in the overall psychological makeup of the homosexuals. Apparently homosexuality is neither a "mental illness" nor is it indicative of emotional problems.

A certain emotional shallowness has often been reported in the homosexual relationships between males in modern society. This impersonal and anonymous sexuality is evident in the "cruising" behavior of males who make pickups in bars and public toilets for associations of brief duration. An educational psychologist, Paul Goodman (himself a bisexual), regards this "shallowness" as the result of the homosexual's acceptance of society's characterization of himself and his partners as "dirty" and "subhuman"; he does not expect to like himself or what he is doing or the person he is doing it with. Lesbians do not usually suffer the same degree of legal and social persecution as their male counterparts; this latter difference perhaps explains why their relationships appear generally to be of longer duration and greater emotional involvement. This might tend to confirm the thesis that social pressures are responsible for the "shallowness" of male relationships and other stereotypical characteristics. Certainly relationships between men in Classical Greece were not thought to be lacking in emotional depth. The ancient Roman writer Plutarch even felt it necessary to defend the possibility that a man might love a woman as deeply and sincerely as another man. It may well be that changing social attitudes will not only increase acceptance of homosexuals by society, but also increase the self-understanding of homosexuals, thus changing the entire face of this phenomenon.

SUMMARY

A. The Biological Basis of Motivation

1. The concept of **motivation** (page 94) generally refers to the biological, social, and learned factors that initiate, sustain, and stop goal-directed behaviors.
2. The hunger drive is regulated by a "stop-mechanism" and a "go-mechanism" in the hypothalamus region of the brain that is sensitive to the blood sugar level.
3. Rats whose hypothalamus is damaged become very obese. Their eating is based on external factors, such as taste and availability, rather than internal factors, such as metabolic requirements. Research with obese humans indicates that this "externality" in eating behavior is also a characteristic.
4. The concept of **homeostasis** (page 96) refers to the tendency of organisms to maintain a steady state in their internal conditions despite changing conditions in the environment.
5. Curiosity and exploratory behavior are examples of behaviors that have reinforcing value for humans and many animals despite the fact that, unlike food and water, these often have no obvious homeostatic basis.

B. The Social Basis of Motivation

6. Many behaviors cannot be explained in terms of biological factors. Human beings have many complex motivations, such as strivings for achievement or affiliation; such **social motivations** (page 102) must be explained in terms of social influences.
7. Researchers such as David McClelland have identified and studied a particular motive known as **need for achievement** (page 102). Individuals with high levels of n Ach tend to select goals and occupations that are moderately difficult for their capabilities, whereas those low in n Ach tend to select goals that are either very easy or very difficult for their capabilities. Those high in n Ach seem to work to match internal standards of excellence rather than for the external rewards that may result from their achievements.
8. High n Ach children generally have parents who require independence and competence from their children at an early age. Often affection is made contingent upon achievement for these children.
9. Birth order has a distinct effect on achievement. First-born children are proportionally overrepresented among high achievers; this is the result of differences in parents' child-rearing practices between first-borns and later-borns.
10. Theorist Abraham Maslow has asserted that motives are arranged

hierarchically in terms of their urgency, with the biological motives first and the social and self-expressive motives contingent on
the satisfaction of the biological motives.

11. There have been many attempts to develop a theory of motivation.
Clark Hull proposed that **drives** (page 109), or tensions that require
relief and energize action, are the source of motivation. Neal Miller
modified the concept of **drive** (page 109) to mean intense stimulation.
Cognitive theories (page 110) stress the individual's interpretation of
stimuli.

C. **Emotions**

12. The term **emotion** (page 112) refers to a subjective awareness of
physiological and observable changes in behavior.

13. The **cognitive appraisal theory** (page 113) of emotion states that experienced (or at least reported) emotion is the result of an individual's
explanation for an aroused physiological state.

14. The **autonomic nervous system** (ANS) (page 115) plays an important
role in emotion. The ANS is composed of the **sympathetic** and the
parasympathetic systems (page 115), which generally function in
opposition.

15. The term **psychosomatic disorder** (page 115) is given to physical
disorders that are, in part, according to the **two-factor theory** (page
121), due to emotions and psychological stress.

D. **The Socialization of Sex**

16. While sexual behaviors are dependent on biological mechanisms,
in humans they are largely influenced in their specific expression
by social factors.

17. The role of sex hormones in humans is largely developmental.
Once secondary sex characteristics are developed, the role of
hormones is greatly diminished.

18. The physiological aspects of the sexual response are controlled by
the autonomic nervous system. These responses include heart rate,
blood pressure, respiration rate, and vasocongestion in certain
body areas. These responses are similar in both sexes.

19. In the higher mammals and humans, appropriate stimuli and sexual
behaviors are the result of learning and social experience. Likewise, sex roles vary widely according to cultural influences.

20. Sex roles develop early in the child, as expressed in preferred
behaviors and play.

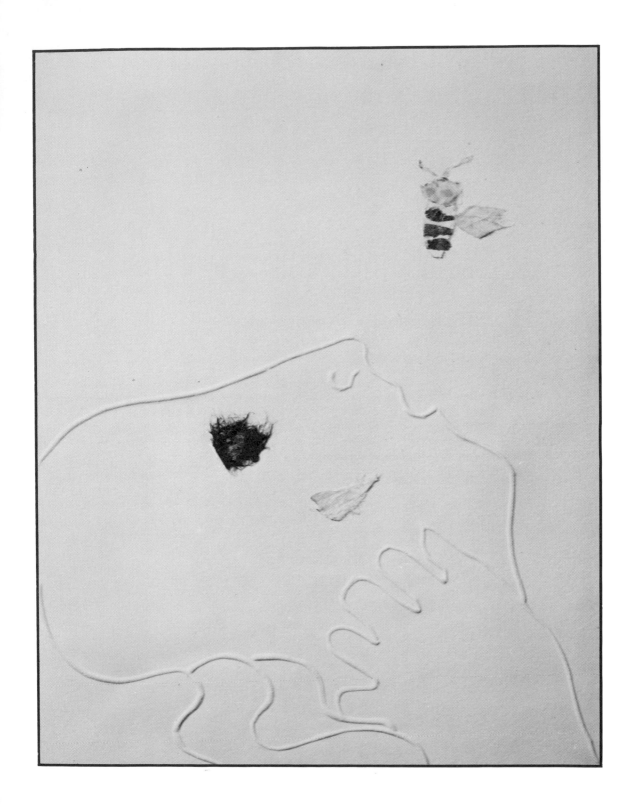

Section Three
Sensing, Conscious Being

Adaptation and survival in a constantly changing environment require information. The world that surrounds us abounds with information in the form of energy changes that excite our sense organs and give rise to sights, sounds, pressures, and smells that can delight or frighten, attract or repel. In this section, which focuses on the sensing, conscious aspect of being, we will study the physiological basis of sensation, examine how visual stimuli are processed to give rise to visual experience, consider the roles of nature and nurture in perception, and explore such altered states of consciousness as hypnosis, dreaming, and extrasensory perception. We will examine the case history of a man who after a lifetime of blindness regained his sight; we will look at research studies in which subjects sleep and dream in laboratories while their brain waves are recorded; and we will give you an opportunity to participate in numerous perception demonstrations.

Chapter Five
Sensation, Perception, and Consciousness

If on a perfectly clear, pitch-black night someone on a mountaintop 30 miles away lit a match, your eye could register it. If on a quiet day a slight sound occurred that produced a movement of your eardrum no larger than the diameter of a hydrogen atom, your ear could detect it. If you watch a friend walk away from you, his perceived size will remain constant while the image he casts on your retina will get smaller. Such experiences are the province of psychologists who explore sensation and perception.

The study of **sensation** *is concerned with the relationship between physical stimuli such as light and sound waves and their effects on sense organs such as eyes and ears.* Research in visual sensation is concerned with such questions as: How is light energy converted into neural impulses? How does the light that strikes the eye give rise to images and figures? Why do objects that appear in full color in daylight turn into shades of gray as night falls?

The study of **perception** *focuses on the process that selects, organizes, and interprets sensory input.* A perceptual researcher is interested in such questions as: Although the image an object casts on the retina changes with distance, why does the object's perceived size remain constant? Why is a series of disconnected dots perceived as a "row"? How much of the way the world appears to us is attributable to experience and how much to innate mechanisms?

In the past, a sharp distinction was made between sensation and perception. Today, that distinction is not appropriate because what we experience has been found to be a product of sensory input, innate perceptual mechanisms, and experience. As long as you keep this in mind, it is still convenient to focus on the sensory and perceptual aspects separately in order to simplify studying the whole complex process.

A. SENSATION

Each sense (vision, hearing, touch, balance, smell, etc.) has developed incredibly specialized means of informing the brain of the changes in our inner and outer world. Light waves strike the retina of the eye, sound waves enter the ear, a hand is placed on an arm; in every case the result is an electrochemical impulse to the central nervous system. Sound waves striking the eye or light shined in the ear produce no effect. The stimulus-receptor relationships are unique. The information they report begins in the form of energy changes (e.g., a light goes on). These energy changes stimulate a specialized receptor (the retina in the eye). This receptor contains units (in the retina, rod and cone cells) that convert the energy into the electrochemical impulses of nervous transmission. The impulses pass through neural way stations and finally relay the messages on to a portion of the central nervous system (such as the visual cortex; see Chapter 3C) specialized to receive this information of the senses (see Figure 5.1). Since there are certain basic similarities in the functioning of all the senses, we will concentrate our exploration on sight and hearing.

VISION

The Eye

For centuries philosophers and scientists have conjectured about the mechanism by which light striking the eye can be translated into visual experience. The first steps have long been understood; some of the

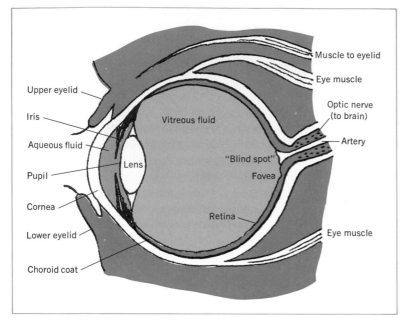

FIGURE 5.1 **The structure of the eye and its relationship to the brain.**

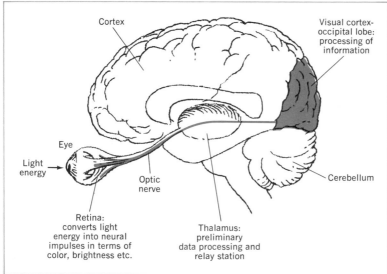

later stages are only now yielding to research. When light strikes the eye, the pupil controls the amount entering the eye, and the lens focuses the light onto the retina. Sense receptors in the retina convert light energy into electrochemical impulses by means of photosensitive chemicals. The sense receptors are called, because of their distinctive shapes, rods and cones. This electrochemical reaction initiates a nervous impulse in a dendrite. The impulse is transmitted (as described in Chapter 2) from the rods and cones to a complex network of nerve cells (see Figure 5.2). These nerve fibers leave the eye in the cable-like *optic nerve* (we experience this as the *blind spot*).

In the brain, the impulses pass through a number of processing and relay stations. Ultimately, after passing through the thalamus, they reach the **visual cortex.** *There, the visual neurons are "projected" in an astonishingly precise representation of the retina.*

Over 6,000,000 cones and over 120,000,-000 rods are distributed throughout the human retina. The two types of receptor have very different functions. The **cones** are *specialized for acuity of vision.* They are concentrated in the central portion of the retina, where they are a majority in contrast to rods. The *fovea,* in the very center of the retina, is composed only of densely packed cones; it is the point of greatest acuity of vision. *The* **cones** *are sensitive to differences in the wavelength of light energy that we experience as color.* Cones are active in daylight vision. If you are reading this page under high to mod-

erate light conditions, you are using your cones to do most of the work. **Rods** *come into play at night and under poor lighting conditions. They give rise only to sensations of black, white, and shades of grey.* Rods are concentrated on the periphery of the retina where cones are in a minority. The rods respond to very low levels of light energy that are too weak to stimulate the cones. This difference in the two receptors explains why objects that appear in full color by daylight become a shade of grey as night closes in.

Cones generally connect with only one optic nerve fiber; this is always true of foveal cones. The rods, in contrast, are connected in groups to *bipolar cells* (see Figure 5.2). In effect, they are capable of cooperative action. This difference relates to the different functions of cones and rods. Each cone transmits a separate impulse to the brain, thus producing a high degree of

FIGURE 5.2 This drawing displays, in simplified form, the human retinal components and their interconnections (bipolar and ganglion cells). The six million cones in the retina are active during daylight and give rise to color vision. The 120 million rods are active at night and give rise to black-white-grey vision. The arrangement of retinal components is the reverse of what one might expect. Before light reaches the sensitive parts of the rods and cones, it must pass through several nerve layers, which are, fortunately, transparent.

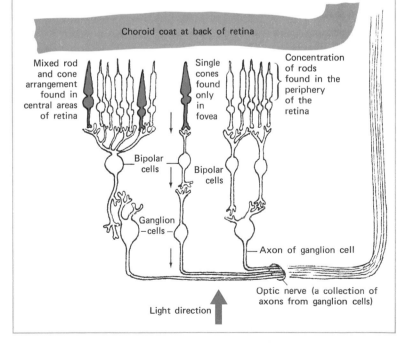

precision, or acuity, though a low level of sensitivity. The rods, by combining impulses, can send a strong message from very low light levels, thus producing a high degree of sensitivity, but not much acuity. (For a discussion of the sensitivity of the senses, see Focus 5.1: How Sensitive Are We: The Story of Psychophysics.)

When stimulated by light, photosensitive receptors in the retina lose their sensitivity to subsequent stimulation, but in the absence of light they recover it. This is the basis of adaptation. **Light adaptation,** *the transition from the rod vision of night to the cone vision of day,* is gradual and takes a few minutes. You have probably experienced the shock to your eyes when coming out of a dark movie theater into full daylight. **Dark adaptation,** *the transition from cone vision to rod vision,* also is gradual (see Figure 5.3). You have probably experienced the difficulty of finding your way in a dark theater when coming in from the bright outdoors. These transi-

Focus 5.1

How Sensitive Are We? The Story of Psychophysics

The dimmest light you can see would be a candle flame at a distance of 30 miles on a dark, clear night. The smallest sound you could hear would be the tick of a watch 20 feet away in a quiet room. The most dilute sugar solution you could taste would consist of one teaspoon of sugar dissolved in two gallons of water. The lightest touch you could feel would the the wing of a bee falling on your cheek from a two-and-one-half inch height. The faintest smell you could sense would be a drop of perfume diffused in a three-room apartment.

The weakest stimulus that we can detect by any sense is called the **absolute threshold.** The opening paragraph of this Focus lists some sample absolute thresholds. These thresholds reveal how remarkably sensitive the human senses are to the world of events that surrounds us. *The determination of sensory thresholds and the study of the relationships between physical stimuli and human sensation is called* **psychophysics.**

If a stimulus is too weak (below the threshold), then it will not be sensed; if strong enough, it will be sensed and reported. In an investigation of psychophysics in a laboratory, subjects are presented with stimuli from a large range of physical values, from those that are not strong enough to be sensed to those that are strong enough. By convention, the stimulus intensity that is detected in 50 percent of the trials is called the absolute threshold. Most psychophysicists think of the threshold as a zone or region that surrounds the 50 percent value, as shown in Figure 5.4.

Ernst Weber, a German physiologist of the last century, discovered a relationship between a stimulus magnitude and the amount of stimulus change needed for a person to detect the change. He called this the difference threshold. Here is an example. If you were in a large room with 60 burning candles, you would notice the addition of one more

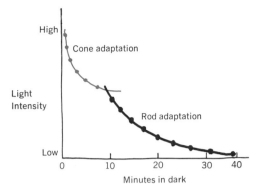

High

Cone adaptation

Light Intensity

Rod adaptation

Low

0   10   20   30   40

Minutes in dark

FIGURE 5.3 In a laboratory setting, a subject views a bright light until he is adapted to it. Then the subject is placed in a dark room. As the subject becomes dark-adapted, test lights are flashed. The curves show that a subject becomes sensitive and responds to lower levels of light intensity as dark-adaptation progresses. The color dots indicate that the subject reports seeing color. The black dots indicate that the subject does not report seeing any color.

candle. However, if there were 120 candles burning, you would not notice one more. It would take the addition of two more burning candles before you would notice the change in illumination. It would take the addition of five candles to notice a change among 300 burning candles. Thus, Weber's Law, as it is now called, can be expressed by a simple formula:

$$\frac{\Delta I}{I} = K$$

In plain English, this equation tells us that the smallest detectable change in the intensity of a stimulus (ΔI) is a constant proportion (K) of the intensity of the reference stimulus (I). In the case of the candles, $K = 1/60 = 2/120 = 5/300$. Weber's Law holds up quite well in the middle range of stimulus intensity but it breaks down at very low or very high intensities. The constant, K, varies among sensory dimensions. For example, for tone, $K = 1/10$, for skin pressure, $K = 1/7$, for salty water, $K = 1/5$, and for lifted weights, $K = 1/50$.

FIGURE 5.4 The absolute threshold is defined as the level of intensity at which a subject can detect a stimulus 50 percent of the time.

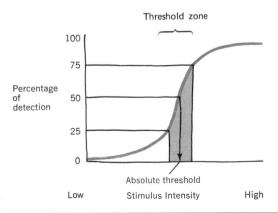

Threshold zone

100

75

Percentage of detection

50

25

0

Absolute threshold

Low   Stimulus Intensity   High

tions require a chemical change in the rods and cones. At dusk, both rods and cones operate at low levels of effectiveness. During the shift from cone to rod vision at this time, great caution is needed when driving until the rods have had a chance to come up to full operational efficiency.

Vitamin A deficiency in the diet prevents the photochemical in the rods from operating properly, leading to what is called *night blindness*. Proper diet, however, helps keep rods properly functioning.

The Visual Cortex

But how is all this activity translated into visual experience? We seem to be a bit closer to an answer today. David H. Hubel and Torsten N. Wiesel at Harvard University conducted a series of intricate and painstaking studies on the vision of cats. They first anesthetized a cat and faced it, with eyes open, toward a wide screen onto which images and shapes could be projected. Next they sank microelectrodes (only 4/10,000 of an inch wide) into the visual cortex (see Figure 3.11) of the brain so that they could record the firing of individual neurons in response to the patterns of light on the screen. Then they flashed varying patterns on the screen to see which patterns striking the retina of the cat's eye evoked responses from which of these single visual cortex cells (see Figure 5.5).

The cat's retina is composed of millions of receptors. Any single cortical cell is

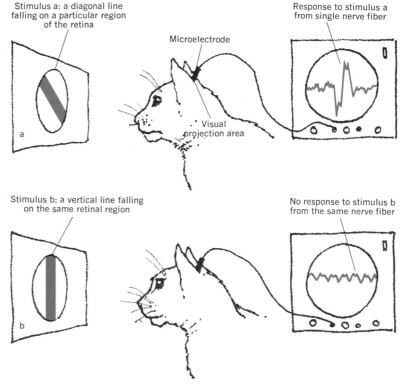

FIGURE 5.5 This figure shows a microelectrode implanted in a cell located in the visual cortex of a cat. The cell is sensitive to diagonal lines (a) and shows a response on the oscilloscope. The same cell shows no response when the retina is stimulated with a vertical line (b). (An oscilloscope is an instrument that converts the electric impulses of the nerve into a picture on a television-like screen.)

Stimulus a: a diagonal line falling on a particular region of the retina

Microelectrode

Visual projection area

Response to stimulus a from single nerve fiber

Stimulus b: a vertical line falling on the same retinal region

No response to stimulus b from the same nerve fiber

connected to only a small number of these retinal cells. It is not surprising, therefore, that Hubel and Wiesel often spent many hours trying different patterns and movements of light striking different areas of the retina before they hit on the combination that would fire the specific cortical cells under investigation. Working in this way, Hubel and Wiesel examined literally *hundreds* of such visual cortex cells to discover what type of light patterns would stimulate them. This achievement sounds and *is* impressive, until you consider that the visual cortex is composed of millions of such cells. This work is only beginning; the results are already astonishing.

The essence of Hubel and Wiesel's discovery is the extreme specialization of each of the visual cortex cells. It is clear why they might take hours to elicit a response from a single cell. The cells probed respond only to lines of light or dark at a specific angle of orientation. That is, if you shine a line of light at a particular spot on the retina, the cortical cell connected to that area still will not respond unless the line of light is oriented at a specific angle. If the cell responds only to vertical lines and you project a horizontal line, you will elicit no response from that cell. (Of course, somewhere in the cortex some unknown cell that responds only to horizontal lines and that also connects with that specific spot on the retina will be firing furiously.) A stimulus not only has to hit the retinal area that is connected to a given cortical cell, but it also has to be of the *correct shape* and at the *correct angle*. Cortical cells that respond to lines of light are dubbed *simple* cells. Other cells, called *complex* cells, respond vigorously only if a properly oriented line of light moves in a specific direction. For instance, a specific complex cell will respond only to a horizontal bar and will show sustained firing only when the bar is moved downward. As Hubel and Wiesel put it,

. . . for each stimulus, each area of the retina stimulated, each type of line . . . and each orientation of stimulus there is a particular set of simple cortical cells that will respond; changing

---

Focus 5.2
Electronic Eyes for the Blind?

Giles S. Brindley and Walpole S. Lewin of the University of London have been able to give a totally blind woman visual experience using a very clever electronic device. What they did was to implant a series of electrodes into the visual cortex of her brain. When patterns of stimulation were fed into the electrodes, the woman was able to identify them. When an electrode was stimulated, the woman reported a glowing spot. When a series of electrodes was stimulated, the woman reported a pattern similar to what we would see in a sign made up of light bulbs. The woman was able to identify many letters and numbers with this apparatus. The simulated visual resolution of the brain was very gross since each electrode probably stimulated hundreds of cells at one time. It is hoped that with future research the resolution of the visual cortex can be improved by stimulating one or a few cells at a time. Although artificial eyes for the blind are still a long way off, this research will help expand our knowledge of the visual process.

any of the stimulus arrangements will cause a whole new population of cells to respond. The number of populations responding successively as the eye watches a slowly rotating propeller is scarcely imaginable.

If you stare at a white clothesline against a dark background, a horizontal strip of retinal cells will fire. In your visual cortex a smaller number of simple cells responsible for successive, overlapping portions of this strip of retinal cells will each fire. This activity is enough to transmit to your brain the basic message that a white line exists "out there." If the wind blows, the tree limb bends and the clothesline moves down. Then complex cortical cells, which are sensitive to downward movement, will fire. This informs your brain that the white line "out there" is moving down. All of this does not quite explain how we arrive at the conscious experience of a "white clothesline whipping up and down in the wind" . . . not yet, but because of research like this, we are getting closer.

HEARING

The ear transmits electrical impulses that carry information on the pitch and the loudness of sound waves. The outer ear is fashioned so as to collect sound waves and funnel them down to the eardrum, which transmits them to the middle ear. There, a series of small bones, functioning like mechanical levers, carries the sound down into the deeper structures of the inner ear and amplifies it on the way (see Figure 5.6). These small bones are called the hammer, anvil, and stirrup. Special structures in the inner ear in an organ called the cochlea transform the sound into neural impulses and send them to the brain. We will examine each of these organs after we have taken a look at the physical basis of loudness and pitch.

Loudness and Pitch

When a drumstick strikes the head of a drum, it pushes the tightly stretched, flexible membrane out of shape. When the membrane snaps back it compresses the air in front of it and rarefies the air behind it. The compressed air then expands and in turn compresses the air around it. In this manner waves of compression and rarefaction spread in all directions from the drum membrane. When these waves strike a comparable tightly stretched, flexible membrane in the human ear (the eardrum), the membrane begins vibrating and we hear a sound. Sound must have a medium in which to travel such as air, water, or a solid. If a bell "rings" in a vacuum it cannot be heard.

The harder a drum is hit, the more the membrane is displaced and the greater the compression and rarefaction of the air around it. *The difference between the amount of compression and rarefaction is an exact measure of* **sound intensity.** *Intensity is experienced as* **loudness.** In general, the more physically intense a sound, the *louder* it seems to us psychologically. The human ear is a good apparatus for picking up sound intensity; it records everything from a pin dropping to the roar of a jet engine. Sound intensity is usually measured in units called *decibels* (dB) (see Figure 5.7, page 146).

The **pitch** of the drum *is determined by the* **frequency** *of vibration,* that is, the number of times or cycles per second that the drum head snaps back and forth and in turn compresses and rarefies the air (see Figure 5.8, page 147). One *cycle* is a single complete compression and rarefaction. If you thump a big bass drum, the drum head may vibrate at the rate of 200 to 300 times per second; if you pluck a taut violin string it may set off vibrations of 15,000 cycles per second. The human ear can detect a frequency as low as 15 cycles per second and as high as 20,000 cycles per second. In general, the more cycles per second (higher frequency) the higher the psychologically judged pitch of a sound. The human ability to register high-frequency (or high-pitched) sounds is rela-

tively limited and grows more limited with age. (Thus, it may be foolish for a middle-aged person to pay a premium for a home sound system because it reproduces frequencies above 15,000 cycles per second.)

The bat, in contrast, can detect frequencies up 120,000 cycles per second;

FIGURE 5.6 (A) The structure of the ear. (B) Schematic presentation of the passage of sound waves through the ear. The cochlea is shown as if uncoiled.

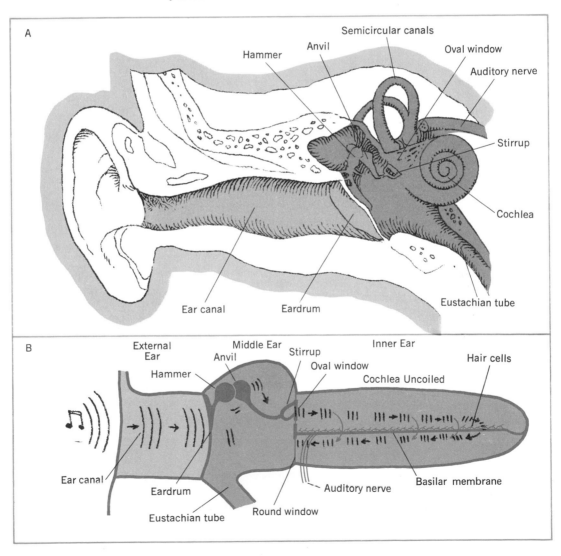

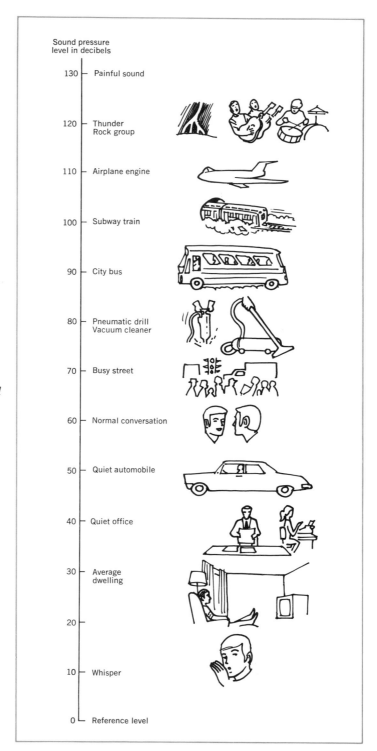

FIGURE 5.7 The decibel level of familiar sounds.

the porpoise is sensitive to frequencies up to 150,000 cycles per second. Both the bat and porpoise use their extraordinary sensitivity to find food and avoid obstacles. They emit high-intensity beeps and from the echoes of these beeps detect objects around them.

Vibrations to Nerve Impulses

The inner ear contains the structures that convert compressions and rarefactions (sound waves) into nerve impulses. The crucial part is contained in the cochlea. *The* **cochlea** *is a coiled tube* (shaped rather like a snail's shell) *filled with fluid and sealed at one end by a membrane.* This membrane, like the tight skin of a drum, is stretched across the mouth of the coch-

lea. It picks up sound wave vibrations from the middle ear bones and transfers them via the fluid into a small duct (cochlear duct). This duct contains the basilar membrane, which is lined with special "hair cells," so called because they contain hair-like structures. When these hair-like structures move with vibrations of the cochlear fluid, they cause the hair cell to "fire" the auditory nerve to which these are connected (see Figure 5.6).

Since different pitches cause maximal vibrations at different locations of the basilar membrane, the brain can detect which pitch has entered the ear according to the location of the hair cells stimulated. High-pitched (high-frequency) tones produce maximal vibrations at the mouth of the cochlea. Low-pitched (low-frequency) tones produce maximal vibrations at the

FIGURE 5.8 The loudness and pitch of the sounds we hear are related to the amplitude and frequency of the sound waves that strike the ear. The greater the amplitude, in general the louder the sound: the sounds become successively louder in examples d through a. The greater the frequency (the more cycles per second), the higher the pitch. The pitch becomes successively higher in examples a through d.

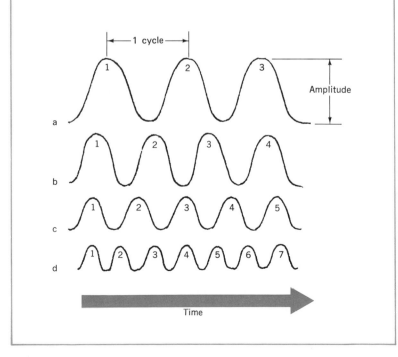

Focus 5.3

The Electronic "Ear"

Thomas F. House, a professor of surgery at the University of Southern California Medical School, is a man who brings a new hope to many deaf people who thought themselves doomed to a silent existence. House specializes in the study of nerve deafness, a form of hearing loss untreatable by normal hearing aids. Until recently, people diagnosed as nerve-deaf were thought to be totally hopeless because of the "deadness" of the auditory nerve leading from the ear to the brain. Subsequent research, though, has established that more than two-thirds of people so diagnosed still have operative auditory nerves. In these cases, the problem is actually loss of the fine, responsive hair cells in the cochlea that stimulate the auditory nerve. Some people with this problem are born without the hairs; others lose use of the hairs through the aging process, drugs (such as the antibiotic streptomycin), or damage caused by loud noises.

House's solution to the problem is an electronic "ear" (shown in Figure 5.9) that replaces the function of the ineffective cochlea. Basically, electrical impulses stimulate the nerve as it would normally be stimulated by the agitation of the cochlear hairs. The impulses are controlled by wires leading to an induction coil that is surgically implanted in the mastoid bone directly behind the ear and is wired to a microphone that can be carried in a shirt pocket with a miniature, transistorized amplifier. Thus, the system replaces the entire function of the ear, turning sound into electrical impulses that directly stimulate the auditory nerve.

The hearing that results is at best a poor substitute for natural hearing. So far the quality of electronic hearing allows patients to recognize environmental sounds but does not permit recognition of words reliably

upper end of the cochlear duct. This intricate process was described by Georg von Békésy, who, in 1956, was awarded the Nobel Prize for his discovery.

The auditory nerve, which takes messages from the basilar membrane, consists of some 30,000 fibers. To fire any one of these nerve cells it is necessary for the sound stimulus to reach sufficient intensity, that is, to exceed the threshold of the cells. At any one moment, this sufficient-intensity threshold of a cell will vary from cell to cell because of refractory, or resting, phases and individual characteristics of

the nerve cells. An intense sound will produce two effects that will inform the brain of its loudness. First, a relatively large number of cells in the auditory nerve will be fired by an intense sound. Second, when each cell returns to normal threshold after the refractory phase, an intense sound causes it to fire immediately. Thus, for an intense sound a large number of individual cells will be going through the fire-refractory-fire cycle repeatedly and rapidly. This relays to the brain the fact that an intense sound has impinged upon the ear. All of these functions take place in the cochlea.

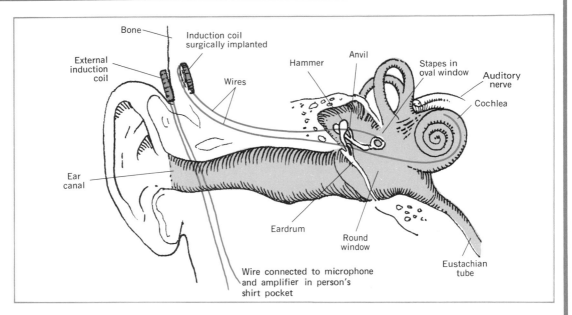

FIGURE 5.9 The electronic ear consists of a microphone and an amplifier in the subject's shirt pocket that sends current to an induction coil behind the ear.

enough to permit conversation. House himself says that the electronic "ear" is to a natural ear what a wooden leg is to a real limb. However, the electronic "ear" is in its early stages of development and improvements are expected. In the meantime, even the limited perception provided by the "ear" can provide a welcome reprieve from silence.

We have dealt at some length with vision and hearing. But as we pointed out earlier, there are certain similarities in sensory-perceptual systems. The faculties of smell, taste, balance, touch, temperature, pain, movement, as well as hearing and sight are compared in Table 5.1, p. 150.

B. PERCEPTION OF THE VISUAL WORLD

Here are some demonstrations of perceptual phenomena.

Demonstration 1. Which colored circle is larger, the left one or the right one? You will probably find the right one looks larger, yet both have the same diameter.

TABLE 5.1   **The sensory-perceptual systems**

SYSTEM	MODE OF ATTENTION	RECEPTIVE UNITS	SENSE	STIMULI	INFOR-MATION OBTAINED
Visual	Looking	Rods and cones	Vision	Light	Information about the shape and size of objects, motion, pattern, color
Auditory	Listening	Basilar membrane in cochlea	Audition	Sound (air vibrations)	Frequency, pitch, location of objects
Haptic	Touching	A variety of specialized receptors embedded in the skin	Touch	Skin contact with objects	Information about shape and texture
	Touching (or passive registration)	A variety of specialized receptors in the skin	Temperature	Temperature changes	Air or object temperature
	Locomotion or body movement	Specialized receptors in deep muscles and joints	Kinesthetic sense (body and limb movement)	Muscles stretching, joint movement, skin pressure	Location and movement of body and limbs
	Passive registration	Free nerve endings	Pain	Intense stimuli, pressure, breaks in skin	Degree of injury or damage to body
Chemical Senses	Smelling	Odor receptors in nasal passages	Smell	Chemicals in air	Odor
	Tasting	Taste buds on tongue	Taste	Chemicals in solution	Taste, chemical value of material
Equilibrium	Body balance	Semicircular canals in inner ear	Vestibular sense (body balance)	Body and head movement	Direction of motion, balance of body

Demonstration 2. A tall man standing among tall women appears to be shorter than when he is standing among tall men. Why?

Demonstration 3. Take two identical patches of grey cloth or construction paper and place one on a white background and one on a black background. You will notice that the grey patch against the white background looks darker than the grey patch against the black background.

Demonstration 4. Place your left hand in very cold water and your right hand in very warm water for about two minutes, then plunge them both into room-temperature water. The right hand will experience the

room-temperature water as cool and the left hand will experience it as warm.

Demonstration 5. Assemble three books, a very heavy dictionary, a moderate-weight text, and a very light notebook. Hold the heavy book up for one minute, then lift the text. You'll note that the text seems quite light in weight. Now hold up the light notebook for a minute with the same hand, then lift the text. You will notice that the text seems heavy.

PERCEPTUAL CONTRAST

You have just explored a series of experiences in which the perception of the same stimulus is influenced by its surroundings or context. The context can be either simultaneous or successive. Demonstrations 1, 2, and 3 involved simultaneous contrast (both stimuli occurred at the same time). Demonstrations 4 and 5 showed successive contrast (a time delay between the first and second stimulus). In either case, **perceptual contrast** *is based on a difference in context.* Contrast is one of many factors that influence our experience of the world. In this section we will examine various demonstrations of perception and explore the mechanisms that help explain them. We will confine most of our explorations to the visual world because the demonstrations can easily be presented on the printed page. You should be aware, however, that the basic principles of visual perception can often be generalized to other senses.

A major problem of perception research is to determine how the brain "reads" reality from the sense organs. This is a very big problem, for the sensory image is often quite different from the objects and the world we perceive. The perception of distance, shape, size, and color can be distorted by illusions. In general, perception is dependent on context, past experience, and innate neural organizing mechanisms. All these complex interacting mechanisms serve to keep the world we perceive consistent and orderly despite the wide range of varying stimulation that excites our sense receptors.

PERCEPTUAL CONSTANCY

Demonstration 6.

Demonstration 7.

Demonstration 8. See color plates after page 178.

Demonstration 9. See photos at right.

In Demonstrations 6 to 9 you perceive different stimuli in the same way. The door in Demonstration 6 still appears rectangular even though it is drawn as a trapezoid. The cup rim remains circular to your brain despite its elliptical shape on the page. As daylight fades, the car in Demonstration 8 is perceived as the same color even though it becomes pink with

sunset and shades into grey with dusk. The girl in Demonstration 9 doesn't grow taller as she approaches the camera although the absolute size of the image on your retina does get larger. These demonstrations show that we *tend to perceive objects as stable and enduring even though the patterns of physical energy that strike our sense organs are constantly changing; this is known as* **perceptual constancy.** What we see, our *percept*, corresponds more closely to the actual object than to the stimulation impinging on our sense organ.

Size Constancy:
A Case of Perceptual Constancy

Figure 5.10 illustrates the geometric relationships between an object's distance and its projected size on the retina. Notice that as the distance of the object increases, its retinal image decreases in size. Obviously, since the object is perceived to be the same size regardless of its distance, other factors must be operating along with the retinal image to determine what we see. Most important of these factors is our knowledge of the actual size of the object based on our past experience. Thus, *what we see is a compromise between retinal image and prior experiences. This phenomenon is known as* **size constancy.**

Infants have some degree of size constancy for objects up to nine feet away

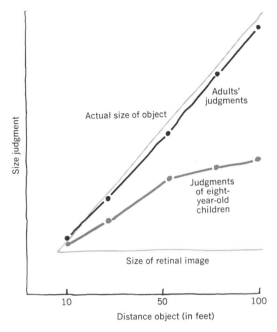

FIGURE 5.11 *The relationship between size perception and age. Both eight-year-olds and adults make accurate size judgments up to ten feet. Beyond ten feet the children's judgments decline in accuracy. This indicates that their judgments are more strongly influenced by retinal size than distance cues.*

but not beyond. As a child grows older, size constancy improves. Figure 5.11 shows that at age eight children have almost perfect size constancy at ten feet but, as distance increases, their accuracy falls off and becomes more and more in-

FIGURE 5.10 *The relationship between object size, distance, and the retinal image. Notice that* **the closer an object is to the eye, the larger its retinal image.**

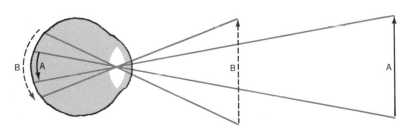

fluenced by retinal size; adults' judgments remain accurate. As children grow up, their size-constancy skills gradually reach the adult level.

The influence of experience on the development of size constancy is dramatically illustrated by the anthropologist Colin Turnbull's report of his experience with the Ba Mbuti pygmies. These people live in a dense African forest. They rarely venture outside and therefore have little or no experience in observing objects at a distance. When Turnbull took one of his pygmy friends out of the forest for the first time, they spotted a herd of buffalo grazing in a field a half-mile away. The pygmy asked what kind of "insects" they were. He refused to accept that they were buffalo. He kept insisting that they were some kind of beetle. When they finally approached the animals, the pygmy was shocked and upset by their growth in size, suspecting that he was a victim of witchcraft. Throughout his trip beyond the forest, he made size errors that one would expect from a child. These errors were due to his lack of experience in observing objects at a distance.

What we learn to help us determine the size of an object are distance cues. Edwin G. Boring demonstrated how important distance cues are in maintaining size constancy. He had his subjects judge the size of objects placed at various distances in a long hallway. He eliminated distance cues by dimming the lights and requiring the subjects to look through small peepholes. For example, the peepholes and dim light eliminated the depth cues provided by the surface texture of the walls, floor, and ceiling. Surface texture is composed of an array of similar elements, such as the individual blades of grass on a lawn or the waves on an ocean or the irregularities of a painted wall or the details of a wallpaper

pattern. The farther away the observer is from a location on a surface, the more closely packed or dense the individual elements appear (see Figure 5.12, page 157). When an object moves away from us, its retinal size diminishes and the density of the surface texture near it increases. Both distance cues, such as surface texture, and the size of the retinal image are needed to accurately judge the size of an object. Therefore, as distance cues are diminished (see page 156), size constancy should be impaired. Sure enough, Boring found that as distance cues were diminished, the subjects lost their accuracy in judging the size of the objects as distance increased.

The brain mechanisms underlying the integration of depth cues and the size of retinal image to produce size constancy are not known. However, since children do increase in their accuracy of judging the size of distant objects, we can assume that learning probably plays an important role in the process. Let us now examine some of the cues our binocular vision and the environment provide us to infer depth, which plays such an important role in size constancy.

DEPTH PERCEPTION

Binocular Disparity

Demonstration 10. Instructions: Place this book on a flat surface. Then take a piece of cardboard or a Manila folder about a foot long and place it vertically between A and B along the dotted line in the figure on the top of the next page. Place your nose on the upper edge of the cardboard so your left eye sees A and your right eye sees B. Now, stare "through" the figures as if you were looking at an object several feet away until the two figures fuse and a pyramid appears.

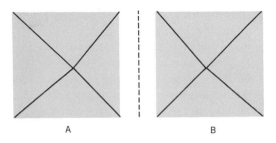

A   B

Demonstration 11. Instructions: Follow the same instructions used above for the "random dot patterns" below. These dot patterns will also produce a three-dimensional effect, but it takes more time than with the pyramid. Be patient.

How can the two-dimensional stimulation on your retina give rise to the three dimensions of spatial experience? As you examine Demonstration 10, you will notice that each figure is drawn so that each eye will receive a slightly different image. The visual system uses these two views to produce depth perception. *As you look at an object in daily life with both eyes open, each eye also receives a slightly different image because each eye is viewing the object from a slightly different position, that is, from different sides of the nose. This is called* **binocular disparity.** It promotes three-dimensional, or depth, perception. Binocular cues are essential for very fine eye-hand coordination, such as threading a needle.

Binocular disparity is also achieved in the dot patterns of Demonstration 11. The pattern is first generated using black and white squares arranged randomly so there is no observable pattern. The original dot pattern becomes side A. Side B is produced by duplicating side A and shifting several sections in it horizontally; together the two sides yield the effect of binocular disparity. Until recently it was assumed that binocular depth perception was dependent on first learning to perceive form. If form were not perceived, then depth perception would not be possible. Yet no form is recognized in the dot pattern before depth is perceived. It is now assumed that binocular depth perception need not be dependent on form perception or prior experience and can occur as an automatic function of neural mechanisms in the brain. However,

A   B

for most visual experience in life, prior experience does play a key role. This is also illustrated in the case of one-eye, or monocular, cues, to be discussed next.

Monocular
Depth Perception

Demonstration 12. Examine the drawing below. Notice that the artist was able to achieve a sense of depth by a variety of techniques. Can you identify them?

Artists have discovered and use a variety of techniques to give the illusion of depth in a two-dimensional picture. These cues for depth are not dependent on binocular vision; they can be experienced with monocular vision as well. The cues of monocular depth perception are learned. The artists' techniques are based on the following facts, illustrated in Figure 5.12.

1. Distant objects produce a smaller retinal image than near objects.
2. The number of details that can be seen diminishes as distance increases.
3. Near objects obscure or cover distant objects (interposition).
4. Parallel lines converge as they approach the horizon.
5. Objects further away appear to be higher on the visual plane.

6. The texture of surfaces becomes finer with distance (texture gradient).

For most distance perception, monocular cues predominate. This is why people who have lost an eye have little or no difficulty in such depth-perception-dependent tasks as driving a car. Indeed, for years the top receiver in professional football was a one-eyed end. And when these learned cues are removed (as in Boring's experiment), our experience of depth all but disappears. For example, with dusk all distance cues except retinal image are diminished. This is why it is illegal to drive in the dark with just parking lights on. If parking lights are mistaken for headlights, a car will be seen as being farther away than it actually is.

Motion Parallax

Demonstration 13. Seat yourself comfortably and close one eye. Hold up a pencil in front of you and keep its position fixed. Now, move your head and notice where the pencil's position is, relative to the room. Even though the pencil didn't move, your head movements produced a change in its location relative to the rest of the room.

Demonstration 13 illustrates *motion parallax,* a cue for depth that can't be used in a painting. As your head moves because of walking, riding, or turning, the objects near to you move rapidly in your visual field, while distant objects tend to remain stationary. Hence the feeling that trees and lamp posts whiz by in the other direction as you speed down the road while the countryside passes by much more slowly. The relative speed of moving objects in your visual field provides a very compelling cue for distance.

In sum, knowledge of an object's distance enables us to interpret its retinal size to yield accurate judgment of its true size.

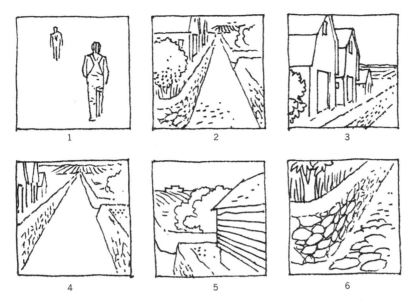

FIGURE 5.12 *Artists have discovered and use a variety of techniques to achieve a sense of depth. See text for description.*

PERCEPTUAL ORGANIZATION

Demonstration 14. Eight identical X's form different patterns depending on how close together they are placed.

X X X X X X X X

X X X X X X X X

X X X X X X X X

Demonstration 15. Do you see three vertical columns of X's and two vertical columns of O's? Or five horizontal rows of mixed X's and O's?

X O X O X
X O X O X
X O X O X
X O X O X
X O X O X

Demonstration 16. Do you see a group of dots or do you see a circle?

Do you see a set of blotches or a man on a horse?

Gestalt Principles

Human beings have a strong tendency to organize experience. In the above demonstrations, you probably found vertical columns of X's and O's more compelling than horizontal rows of mixed X's and O's and the figure of a circle or of a man on a horse more compelling than a collection of dots or blotches. To explain these experiences, a group of psychologists, known as the Gestalt school, held that there is a strong tendency to organize experiences into whole, complete patterns. They identified several perceptual principles or laws. The following relate to the demonstrations presented above:

1. **Proximity**—*separate elements making up a perceived object will be organized into wholes according to their nearness (proximity)* (Demonstration 14).
2. **Similarity**—*separate elements in a percept will be organized into wholes according to similarity among them* (Demonstration 15).
3. **Closure**—*figures with gaps in them will tend to be filled in and perceived as a whole* (Demonstration 16).

Figure-Ground

Demonstration 17. What do you see, two faces or a vase?

The Gestalt psychologists uncovered another very important characteristic of perceptual experience, figure-ground relationships. As you look at the demonstration and focus on the faces (figure), the white space (ground) becomes the background. If you focus on the vase, it becomes the figure and the dark faces become the background. Any scene you look at can be analyzed in terms of figure-ground relationships. Perception of the figure-ground relationship is probably innate. People who have gained their sight after a lifetime of blindness are able to see objects against a background even if they don't recognize what it is they are seeing (see page 168).

We can also identify figure-ground relationships with our sense of hearing. You can hear a friend calling your name against the background sounds of a cocktail party conversation and you can hear the vocalist's song against the orchestra's background accompaniment. These facts seem so obvious that they seem hardly worth mentioning—but so is gravitational attraction, the study of which has been very useful. (See Focus 5.4: Mach Bands and Figure-Ground, page 160.)

ILLUSIONS

Demonstration 18. Study this figure. Is the tinted side in the front or at the rear of the cube?

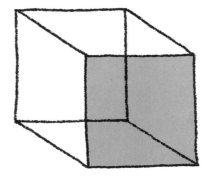

Demonstration 19. Which line is longer, X or Y?

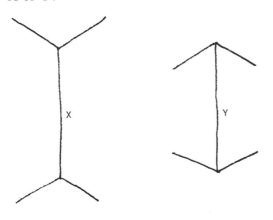

Demonstration 20. Which log is larger, X or Y?

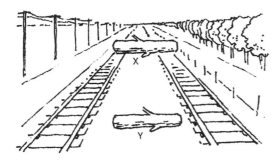

Demonstration 21.

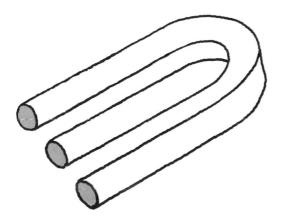

Demonstration 22.

In 1832 a Swiss naturalist, L. A. Necker, noticed that a transparent cube drawn on paper spontaneously reverses in depth (see Demonstration 18). Since that time, many people have tried to formulate theories to explain this illusion. As you study Demonstration 18, you will probably find that the tinted surface jumps back and forth between the front and back of the figure without any effort on your part. The fact is, you will not be able to keep the tinted side standing still.

Necker's reversible cube and the other illusions, as well as the previous demonstrations, illustrate that our perceptions are not identical to the visual stimuli. What we perceive involves more than what is contained in the visual image on the retina. Richard L. Gregory of the University of Edinburgh proposes that any perceived object is a hypothesis based on the sensory stimuli. The two-dimensional representation of three-dimensional objects with ambiguous or absent cues creates competing perceptual hypotheses. The Necker cube illusion is produced by such a conflict, for it contains no clue about

Focus 5.4

Mach Bands an Figure Ground

Ernst Mach was a nineteenth-century physicist who noticed one day that a distinct line or band appeared at places in a stimulus array where there was an abrupt change in light intensity. In Figure 5.13, you will probably notice that the borders of the black circle seem a bit darker than the center and the white borders touching the black a bit whiter than the rest of the background. Whenever objects of contrasting shadings come into contact the borders are sharpened. Since every effort has been made to keep the black circle and white paper uniform in intensity, the appearance of the bands must be the result of events in your retina or brain.

Floyd Ratliff and Haldan Hartline uncovered a neural mechanism within the retina that explains these Mach bands. They used the horseshoe crab, *Limulus,* which has very large retinal cells that, because of their size, facilitate research studies. A line of these cells was implanted with electrodes, which were then connected to an oscilloscope. When a stimulus, similar to Figure 5.13, was presented to the crab's eye, the cells fired and their electrical discharges (see page 142) were picked up on the oscilloscope. The oscilloscope, which displayed the cells' discharging on a television-like screen, revealed a line of neural activity as shown in Figure 5.14. Notice that the rate of neural discharge is greater for the light than for the dark stimuli. Also note that at the border (XY) between stimuli the cells on the light side are more active and the cells on the dark side of the borders are depressed.

Intensive study of retinal anatomy and physiology has revealed a complex interconnection of nerve fibers (see page 139). Under certain conditions, some cells will either inhibit or excite the discharge of other cells. It is reasonable to assume that our experiences with the enhanced

which of two hypotheses on the location of the tinted side is correct. Our neural circuits cannot find the answer, so they alternate between the two perceptions. Hypothesis-testing of this kind occurs in all vision, according to Gregory. In most common visual situations, however, only one hypothesis arises. When we see the cube in three dimensions, the additional depth cues end the illusion and only one hypothesis is available.

In 1879 Franz Müller-Lyer presented the world with a most compelling illusion that now bears his name; it is illustrated in Demonstration 19. If, by chance, you haven't seen this illusion before, measure and compare the X and Y lines. Measurement reveals that Y is the same as X, but Y *looks* smaller than X. Gregory proposes that the figures are unconsciously interpreted as three-dimensional skeleton structures resembling either an inside corner of a building or an outside corner of a building. An innate perceptual mechanism is assumed to shrink the outside corners and enlarge the inside corners. But this innate mechanism, if it exists, is not the only factor that plays a role in this illusion, since the degree to which a person is susceptible to it varies with culture. The role of learn-

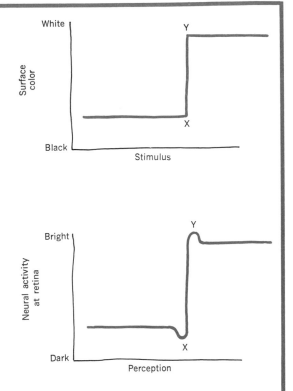

FIGURE 5.13 (Above) Do the borders of the circle seem darker than the central portions of the figure?

FIGURE 5.14 (At right) The lower curve shows 'the oscilloscope image reflecting the neural firing of a crab's retina when a black stimulus framed against a white background (upper curve) was presented to the crab's eye.

borders of objects are due to some facilitating, inhibiting mechanisms in our retinas, which, in this way, are similar to the crab's. It is also very possible that the figure-ground phenomenon is based on similar neural mechanisms in the retina or within the brain.

ing in perception is dramatically supported by a cross-cultural comparison of susceptibility to illusions by M. H. Segal, D. T. Campbell, and M. J. Herskovits. They found that African Bushmen who live in environments in which rectangular objects are virtually nonexistent are not as susceptible to the Müller-Lyer illusion as Americans who live in an environment filled with rectangular shapes. This and other findings by the Segal group indicate that susceptibility to illusions depends both on the type of illusory figure and the perceiver's environment. More importantly, however, they point out that our percep-

tual hypotheses about what sensory stimuli "mean," what is "out there," are largely determined by learning and experience.

The two rectangles superimposed on the railroad tracks in Demonstration 20 are exactly the same size and have equal retinal projections. Past experience tells us that railroad ties are equal in size. The picture gives the effect of distance by presenting us with several learned distance cues such as converging parallel lines, the changes in surface texture, and the reduction of an object's apparent size as distance increases. Given these depth cues, our perceptual hypotheses tell us that the upper

Focus 5.5

Some Aspects of Color Vision

Visible light is one small segment of the full array of wavelengths in the spectrum of electromagnetic radiation (see Figure 5.15; the figures for this Focus all appear in the color plates after page 178). Very short waves include X rays, very long waves include those used in the transmission of radio and television. The normal human visual sensory system is receptive only to wavelengths in an extremely narrow band, from about 400 to 700 nanometers (a nanometer is one billionth of a meter). But from that small range we gain an enormous amount of information about objects in the world, for our varied experience of color is a function of the wavelengths in that narrow band. For example, the range from 460 to 470 gives rise to the experience of blue, the range from 570 to 580 to yellow. The light from the sun—white light—is composed of *all* wavelengths in the visible range. If white light is passed through a prism, it is scattered, or broken up into its constituents; that is, the light passes through the prism differentially according to wavelength, in a sequence from short to long waves, producing the familiar spectrum of visible light (see Figure 5.16).

In everyday experience we seldom see single wavelengths; what we see is composed of mixtures of wavelengths. These mixtures produce the experience of color (or hue, as it is called technically). Of course, we do not ordinarily see light; we see light reflected off the surfaces of objects. The pigments in surfaces absorb some wavelengths and reflect others. A red wall, for instance, absorbs most wavelengths except those at the red end of the spectrum, which it reflects. All colors can be produced by a mixture of just three primary wavelengths—a red-yellow, a green, and a blue-violet. These primaries of colored light should not be confused with the more familiar primaries of pigments—red, yellow, and blue. There are in fact two types of color mixture: Mixing lights and mixing pigments (see Figure 5.17). Mixing lights is an additive process; the wavelengths are added together in stimulating the eye. When all wavelengths are added together the result is white. With pigments, the mixing is subtractive; these, when mixed, produce other colors through the subtraction of absorbed wavelengths. All pigments put together yield black, since all wavelengths are absorbed.

There are many curious and interesting phenomena associated with color vision. Complementary colors provide a particularly vivid experience. (Two hues that yield grey when mixed are called complementary; in effect, they cancel each other out.) If you stare at a field of color for a time and then turn your gaze to a neutral (grey or white) surface, you will experience the color that is the complement of the original (see Figure 5.18 for a three-color demonstration of this.) The effect you see, such as the ghostly green grass in place of the red on the page, is called a *negative afterimage*.

Another intriguing phenomenon is color blindness. The most common form of color blindness (which affects 7 per cent of men and 1 per cent of women) is a severe impairment in the ability to distinguish between red and green. More rarely, people are unable to distinguish between yellow and blue. Most rarely, an individual perceives no colors at all. There are also forms of color weakness, in which extraordinarily high intensities of light are needed for color recognition. It is difficult for people with normal vision to conceive of what the world looks like to someone with defective color perception. In Figure 5.19, we see the depiction of the world by a painter with defective color vision. In one painting he selected the pigments; in the other his wife, with normal color vision, made the selection. As the painter described it:

"The colors in those two paintings do not look to me like neutral greys . . . Neither do the two paintings look exactly alike. . . . They both look 'equally realistic,' but the one my wife helped me with by kibitzing appears as though one was looking north about 10 A.M. (incidentally this was the first one painted) and the one I painted with colors I knew were wrong but looked OK to me—appears to me as though one was looking south about 4–5 P.M. The Alizarin Crimson sky looks blue—the chartreuse clouds look yellow—the orange on the sunny trees on the hillside to the left as well as the same trees in the first picture look 'yellowish.' The *evergreens* in the two pictures do not look the same. I would probably call them different shades of brown rather than grey."

The facts of color mixture, along with such phenomena as complementary colors and defective color vision, have been the main inspiration for, and the main problems in, theories of color vision.

Since all colors can be reproduced by three primaries, it was proposed that there are three receptors that are sensitive to red, green, and violet. The experience of color was presumed to result from differential stimulation of these receptors. The theory was first proposed by Thomas Young early in the nineteenth century and developed by Hermann von Helmholtz. In this century it has been possible to confirm the existence of three kinds of cones in the retina, each sensitive to a different range of wavelengths and each with a different peak sensitivity. On the basis of these peak sensitivities, the three receptors can be called "red," "green," and "blue" cones. This *three-component theory* could account for much of color vision, but it appeared to ignore the basic psychological experience of yellow (yellow ended up as red-green) and it could not satisfactorily explain the common defects of color vision. A four-color theory was proposed, first by Ewald Hering in the nineteenth century and developed in this century by Leo Hurvich and Dorothea Jameson. This theory assumes opponent processes, not in the retina but in the neural structures farther along the optical pathway to the brain. It is proposed that there are two pairs of neurons, a red-green pair and a yellow-blue pair. One set of fibers is excitatory for red, inhibitory for green (+R–G); the opponent is excitatory for green and inhibitory for red (+G–R). Similarly there is a +B–Y and +Y–B pair. (There is also a black-white pair which relates to brightness.) When light hits the cones in the retina, the resulting impulses either excite or inhibit the opponent neurons in the brain. The neurons are activated by different combinations of stimulation of the receptors. If one member of a pair is stimulated more than the other, its hue will be the one experienced. If they are stimulated equally the result will be gray (they cancel each other out). Colors other than the four primaries are the result of combinations of stimulation. The opponent-color pairs, unlike the three-component theory, can be related to defective color vision, which occurs in pairs (red-green and blue-yellow), and also to negative afterimages. Currently the two theories seem to have come together. Receptors consist of three components (three differentially sensitive cones), but neural responses farther along the optical pathway to the brain are four-component in nature (opponent pairs).

rectangle has been "shrunk" down because of distance just like the railroad ties. Our perceptual mechanism compensates for the expected shrinkage of the upper rectangle (even though there is no shrinkage to compensate for), and we see it as larger than the lower rectangle.

Demonstrations 21 (an impossible figure) and 22 (*Relativity,* by M. C. Escher) present some fascinating illusions that can be produced when presenting three-dimensional figures on two-dimensional surfaces. The incompatible information produces competing hypotheses that our brains cannot decisively interpret.

The importance of these and other illusions is that they reveal the active, hypothesis-making nature of perception. This quality is normally so automatic that it escapes detection. Illusions and the other phenomena discussed in this section indicate that what we perceive is based on a complex interaction of three factors — physical sensations, neural mechanisms, and past experiences.

C. PERCEPTION AND THE NATURE-NURTURE ISSUE

A large amount of the research on the functioning of the sensory and perceptual systems is done with animals. The results of this research can tell us a great deal about human systems. Since there are important differences, however, many functions can be studied only with human beings. Here are two visual examples that illustrate the differences.

Consider the frog. The frog's visual system is beautifully tailor-made to the requirements of the frog. The eyes are adequate for locating small insects flying across the field of vision. Such a stimulus elicits an uncannily accurate tongue-flicking response. The frog has an enviable quality lacking in human beings; if you sever its optic nerve, the nerve will promptly regenerate and the frog will soon be back fly-catching as usual. Roger Sperry of the California Institute of Technology severed not only the optic nerve of a frog but also the eye's connecting muscles. Then he rotated the eyeball 20 degrees and sat back and waited while the optic nerve, muscles, and connecting tissues regenerated. As might be expected, when the frog had recovered completely, it lashed out its tongue as usual at a fly crossing its field of vision. But unfortunately as a result of the eyeball rotation, its tongue waved in the air just 20 degrees from the fly, which proceeded unharmed. The result was not surprising. What was revealing, however, was that the frog apparently could not *ever* learn to adjust to the rotation of its eye. Left to its own devices the frog would have starved to death.

In contrast, consider the world of psychologist G. M. Stratton who, one morning in 1895 at Stanford University, donned a pair of special goggles that inverted his field of vision. At first, like the frog, Stratton had a rather bumpy, difficult time of it. But after several days Stratton found himself adjusting quite well to his new world. In fact, when he finally removed the goggles and returned up to up and down to down, he had a surprising amount of trouble adjusting again to what had been his lifelong visual orientation.

The perceptual apparatus of the frog depends less on experience than is true for the human being. The frog's complex bug-catching facility seems to be largely wired-in, requiring little or no training for its development. In fact, training seems relatively powerless to change it. Stratton's experience demonstrates that the human perceptual system is much more adaptable and is more influenced by training.

The question of what part of our perceptual ability is wired-in at birth and what part is learned from experience has intrigued scholars for centuries. Data needed to resolve the issues are beginning to take some shape; we will explore the evidence in this section. Like the frog, the human infant is born with some basic perceptual abilities; unlike the frog, experience has a lot to do with whether these abilities will develop optimally. The question is not easy to study. It takes some ingenuity to find out if a baby is perceiving forms or can see three dimensionally. Some researchers, however, have demonstrated such ingenuity.

DOES THE INFANT PERCEIVE DEPTH?

Eleanor Gibson and Robert Walk questioned whether the ability to perceive depth was a function of training or simply developed as a result of maturation. They studied the behavior of six-month-old crawling infants on a table top, half of which (the "safe" side) was painted in a checkerboard pattern. The other half (the "unsafe" side) was a clear sheet of glass through which a checkerboard floor could be seen several feet below. The infants were placed on a slightly raised platform between the two sides and allowed to crawl. Their mothers stood on the unsafe side and called to them. If they drew back from the "visual cliff" when they came to the clear glass, their behavior would be clear evidence that they had depth perception. If they did not react to the apparent drop, it could be assumed that they perceived the checkerboard pattern below as an uninterrupted continuation of the pattern on the safe side (see Figure 5.20).

Twenty-seven of the tested children moved off the central platform to the "safe side" and three crept over to the "unsafe side." Some of the children cried when their mothers called but were unwilling to cross the "unsafe side." A few patted the glass on the "unsafe side" but still crawled away.

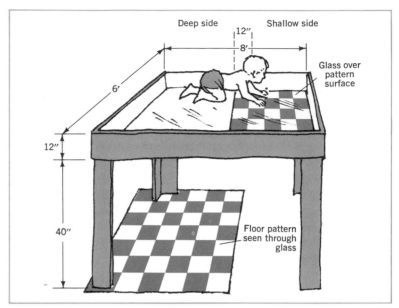

FIGURE 5.20 A baby avoids the "unsafe side" of the visual cliff apparatus.

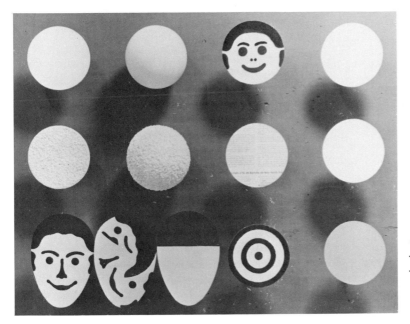

FIGURE 5.21 Stimulus patterns used to study infant form perception. Infants prefer to look at the "normal" face rather than the scrambled face or other patterns.

Clearly, at six months infants can detect the drop and, hence, have depth perception. Since babies have had limited opportunity to learn depth perception, the investigators interpret their results as indicating that depth perception is built in. However, the limited opportunity the babies had in the crib and crawling on the floor may have been enough experience for learning depth perception. The experiment would have been more convincing if the infants had been younger.

(While not relevant to the purposes of the experiment, it is perhaps useful for present or potential parents to know that an infant's appreciation of danger at the cliff does not always prove effective in preventing behavior that would send the child tumbling off a real cliff. Babies usually neglect to consider carefully enough where their legs will end up when they withdraw from the cliff's edge. They swing their heads around but may end up with their lower half "in thin air" on the clear glass.)

FORM PERCEPTION

William James described the perceptual world of the infant as "a blooming, buzzing confusion." Until recently, it has been difficult to test the accuracy of his description; infants make poor witnesses. Robert L. Fantz has devised a brilliant method for determining if James was right. His work suggests that the world of babies is not completely chaotic.

Fantz places pairs of objects or patterns in their visual field. He then films their eye movements in order to determine which of the objects or patterns they tend to look at. If babies could not make anything out of the patterns, they would tend to look at them equally often. But, as a matter of fact, they tend to spend more time looking at certain kinds of patterns. When tested with the many patterns in Figure 5.21 they prefer to look at the normal face pattern rather than the scrambled face or the geometric or shaded figures. Although it is possible that this preference is partly due to the infant's experience with the mother's face, a Swiss pediatrician, F. Stirnimann, has noted the same preference for facial patterns in infants as young as one day. It seems most likely that this preference is largely due to built-in visual structures. Some degree of form perception and preference seems to be innate in human beings, and the preference for human faces may be relevant to survival. To be successful at melting parents' hearts by smiling at them, a baby must first be capable of attending to their faces.

Just what can a newborn infant see and what must the baby learn to see? The question is not new. The seventeenth-century English philosopher John Locke received the following letter from a friend:

Let us imagine a man born blind, and now adult, taught by his touch to distinguish between a cube and a sphere of the same metal. Suppose then the cube and the sphere were placed on a table and the blind man made to see: query; whether by his sight, before he touched them, could he distingish and tell which was the globe and which the cube? . . . The acute and judicious proposer answers: not.

Locke agreed; he reasoned that the previously blind man would have to learn to *see* the sphere and cube as different. Neither of these gentlemen of the seventeenth century imagined that this miracle could occur so that they could test their prediction. But since that time a number of people, blind since birth, have been given their sight by operations on their lenses or their corneas. In the latter operation, an opaque (or nontransparent) cornea is removed and replaced by a healthy cornea.

Blind since Birth: The Case of Mr. S. B.
Such a case has been vividly described by Richard L. Gregory and J. G. Wallace.

S. B. was fifty-two years old when he first could see. When the bandages were first removed from his eyes so that he was no longer blind, he heard the voice of the surgeon. He turned to the voice, and saw nothing but a blur. He realized that this must be a face, because of the voice, but he could not see it. He did not suddenly see the world of objects.

Within a few days, however, Mr. S. B. became quite good at using his eyes. He could tell time from a wall clock; it seems he had once learned to tell time by feeling the hands of a pocket watch. He navigated the corridors of the hospital with no help. In this first week he was completely delighted by his rapid progress.

Mr. S. B.'s progress, while quite heartening, was also quite variable. His ability to see and recognize objects seemed to be very heavily dependent on his having once learned to deal with these objects by touch. For example, it was found that he very quickly began to recognize block capital letters and numbers by sight. This was a great surprise. But Mr. S. B. explained that at the school for the blind he had been taught to read block capital letters by touch. He had never been taught to read lower case letters. It was a painful process to teach them to him. Actually, he never learned to read by sight; he simply continued to read by braille as he had originally learned. When he was first presented with a machine lathe, he very quickly moved his hands over the entire surface with his eyes closed. Then he stepped back, opened his eyes and said, "Now that I have felt it, I can see it." In Figure 5.22 we can see Mr. S. B.'s progress in drawing a London bus during his first year of vision. It is clear that he could better identify parts of the bus that he had experienced by his senses of movement and touch.

Personally, the case of Mr. S. B. ended in tragedy. Before his eye operation he had

FIGURE 5.22 *Drawing of a London bus made by Mr. S.B., a 52-year-old man who had gained his sight after a lifetime of blindness. The figures were drawn 48 days, six months, and one year after sight was regained. Notice the increasing accuracy and detail, which gives evidence of perceptual learning.*

been extremely active. He would ride bicycles and would often venture out alone into the street with his white cane. He very aggressively crossed streets in the thick of London traffic. After he could see, he was terrified by traffic and almost had to be dragged across the street. Before the operation he was active socially, but after the operation he would spend hours sitting by himself in a completely dark room. He was very disturbed by the drabness and the peeling paint that he saw in the city of London. He became quite upset by the realization of the opportunities his blindness had caused him to miss in life. He very gradually gave up active living, kept to himself, and died three years after the operation. Depression soon after this kind of operation is not unusual. However, with proper psychological counseling the patient can usually recover from the depression and live a relatively "normal" life.

Cases such as Mr. S. B. are of some special interest because they provide an opportunity to find out how much of our perception is innate and how visual perception develops. In Mr. S. B. we have an articulate, intelligent adult who suddenly

began the development of visual perception at the age of 52. In some ways, he was like a newborn infant who could explain in detail how he was experiencing each phase in the development of his vision. However, Mr. S. B. was not an infant. He had the benefit of his earlier movement and tactile experience and language. So we must be cautious in drawing conclusions about visual development in the newborn from the pattern of development of adults who, like Mr. S. B., have regained their sight.

Von Senden, a physician in Germany, collected data on cases like S. B.'s. He found that, following their operations, the patients were immediately able to see differences in color and the location of objects; however, they could not identify objects. Each patient needed many visual exposures to objects in order to learn to name them. Even then, a slight change in the context of an object produced confusion. For example, a patient could learn to identify a spoon on a table but, when it was placed on the floor, could not identify it. The patients learned to distinguish between circles and triangles but had difficulty in discriminating between triangles and squares. Years after the operation, they could only identify a few of the faces of those friends closest to them. Also, many continued to experience great difficulty in judging distances. For example, when one patient looked out a window, he reported that he could see cars moving in the street below but had no idea how far down they were.

The evidence clearly suggests that while certain aspects of perception are innate and "automatic" a great deal of learning is needed for the normal perceptual experience we so easily take for granted. It also indicates that visual development may have critical periods. If a person is deprived of childhood visual experience, the loss is never made up when sight is regained in later life.

MOVEMENT AND TOUCH IN VISUAL DEVELOPMENT

One significant aspect of the case of Mr. S. B. and others like him is the key role that movement and touch played in the full development of visual perception. Richard Held of the Massachusetts Institute of Technology took the next reasonable step. He tested the hypothesis that the normal development of the sense of vision in infants depends on the development of the sense of movement and touch. In an ingenious study, Held arranged an experiment in which pairs of 10-week-old kittens experienced visual stimuli together. One kitten of the pair saw the same stimuli passively while being towed by its companion who saw the stimuli actively. In Figure 5.23 you can see the contraption that Held built for this study. Every time the active kitten moved about in this space the passive kitten was moved an equivalent amount. What they saw was the same.

The difference between them was this: for the active kitten visual experience was accompanied by concomitant, coordinated, active movements; for the passive kitten visual experience was not coordinated with any movements. Except for their experience in the apparatus, the kittens were reared in total darkness. How would the kittens respond to various tests of visual development after this experimental treatment? The passive kitten did not behave normally. When a fast-moving object was made to approach its eyes, the passive kitten did not demonstrate a normal blinking response; the active kitten did. The passive kitten walked unconcernedly across the "visual cliff," while the active kitten demonstrated that it had mastered three-dimensional vision. When the active kitten was gently carried down an incline toward a wall, it put out its forepaws to avoid a collision; the passive kitten did not.

Held also has shown that this finding for kittens is applicable to humans. He had adults learn a task which required the subjects, while seated, to judge the direction of a target (a small light) that was flashed in different locations in a small room. He then had them wear goggles that distorted their vision (such as those worn by Stratton). Some walked down a garden path for an hour, others were pushed in wheelchairs. Held reasoned that if the walkers adapted well to the distorting goggles, then their performance on the fine-visual-adjustment task would be distorted when the goggles were removed. That is, if they were adapted to the goggles, which displaced their vision about ten degrees, when they went back to the fine-visual-adjustment task they would show errors of about ten degrees. His prediction was confirmed. The walkers made such errors. But the subjects who were pushed evidenced no errors, indicating that there had been no adaptation

FIGURE 5.23 As the active kitten moved about the apparatus its movements were transferred to the passive kitten in the gondola. The active kitten developed normal sensory-motor coordination. However, the passive kitten did not develop normally until it was freed for several days. (Adapted from "Plasticity in Sensory-Motor Systems," by Richard Held. Copyright © 1965 by Scientific American, Inc. All rights reserved.)

to the goggles. It seems clear that visual adaptation in human beings requires coordination between visual and motor behavior.

THE NATURE-NURTURE ISSUE

We can now return to the question we raised at the beginning of this section. How much of human perceptual ability depends on learning? How much depends on wired-in programs? Well, it certainly seems clear that adult humans can adapt and relearn their way of perceiving in very remarkable and radically altered situations. This ability does not prove conclusively that they followed this same pattern in their development as babies. But a strong bet can be made that for human infants, learning is crucial in visual development.

It is likely, however, that normal visual functioning in humans depends on the concomitant exercise of movement, touch, and vision early in life. So, the answer to the nature-nurture question is, as usual, not a simple one. Yes, visual functioning is primarily learned, but it is associated with such nonvisual factors as age and locomotion.

D. ALTERNATE STATES OF CONSCIOUSNESS AND PERCEPTION

Psychologists study many topics that contain more questions than answers. Such topics—hypnosis, sleeping, dreaming, and extrasensory perception—will be explored

Focus 5.6
Motivation and Perception

Many people have difficulty estimating the true size of coins. In one experiment, Jerome Bruner and his students at Harvard University projected a circle of light, the size of which could be easily controlled by the subject. Half of Bruner's subjects, who were ten- and eleven-year-old boys, came from wealthy families; the other half came from backgrounds of poverty. When asked to project circles the size of a penny, a nickel, a dime, and a quarter, all of the boys tended to overestimate, making circles larger than the actual size of the coins. However, the children from poor families tended to overestimate the size of the coins much more than their well-off peers. The conclusion investigators have drawn from such experiments with children and adults is that differences in motivation and values can affect perceptions.

Motivation can also affect the readiness of the individual to perceive certain kinds of stimuli. Employing a *tachistoscope,* an instrument that projects words or images on a screen for controlled, very brief periods of time, David McClelland and his associates at Harvard projected a list of words one at a time to a group of college students. Some of the words were positively related to the need for achievement (such as "success" or "profit"); others were negatively related to the need for achievement (such as "failure" or "loss"); still other words were not related to need for achievement (such as "vacation" or "friendship"). One group of subjects was selected for their high n Ach, the other for low n Ach. McClelland found that those with high n Ach recognized the achievement words significantly faster than did the subjects with low n Ach. On the other hand, the low n Ach subjects were faster at recognizing the words that were negatively related to achievement. In similar experiments, it has been found that when "taboo" words, such as obscenities, are projected, a "blocking" occurs and much longer exposures are needed to recognize the word. Still other studies have found that when people are deprived of food, they tend to see food when presented with ambiguous stimuli. What we see is often determined by our needs, values, and motives.

Albert Hatstorf and Hadley Cantril filmed a football game of the 1951 season between Dartmouth and Princeton in which charges of foul play were made against both teams. The film was shown at both schools to undergraduates who were asked to count the number of foul plays made by each team. Princeton students counted twice as many Dartmouth fouls than Princeton fouls. Dartmouth students counted the same number of fouls for both teams but only found half as many fouls as the Princeton students, even though both saw the same film replay. In this situation each student's perception was influenced by school loyalty and peer pressure. In a tense situation how many students could maintain their objectivity? What we see can be influenced by social pressure as well as personal bias.

in this section. These are often referred to as alternate states of consciousness. By **consciousness** we mean *the awareness a person has of the surrounding world and of internal feelings and thoughts.* We have already explored the role of sensation and perception in our organization of the world around us. Now let's explore certain phenomena that are altered states of perception.

HYPNOSIS

In a large introductory psychology class, the lecturer has called for volunteers in a demonstration of hypnosis. Numerous students — though by no means all — volunteer. A student is selected and asked to relax and get comfortable in a large, cushioned chair at the front of the room. The curtains are drawn to dim the midday light. The lecturer asks for silence. He then begins the hypnotic induction in a slow, calm, clear voice:

You are slowly becoming more and more completely relaxed. Your body is slowly becoming heavier and heavier and sinking deeper and deeper into the soft cushions of your chair. *Feel* the pressure of your body on the chair. And as you become more and more relaxed, your breathing is becoming deeper and smoother. All of your body is breathing so that with each full breath, you feel your whole body from head to toe rising and falling, expanding and shrinking with the rhythm of each full breath. I will now count backwards from twenty, and as I do, you will become more and more deeply relaxed and your conscious mind will sleep deeply and ever more deeply. Twenty . . . nineteen . . . eighteen . . . . . . three . . . two . . . one. Now everything inside of you is totally relaxed, your mind is asleep as you imagine yourself far away on a green hillside. It is a sunny day and there is just a hint of breeze touching your face and bringing to you the smell of wild flowers. As

you continue to become more and more deeply relaxed, this scene will rest you deeply, leaving you with a refreshed sense of being completely at peace with the world. You will continue to remain on the hillside and enjoy this deep, deep relaxation. You will be aware only of this hillside scene and the sound of my voice.

When the subject appears to be sleeping peacefully and oblivious to the surroundings, the lecturer says:

Your right hand is becoming lighter and lighter, as though it were filling with helium. As it becomes lighter and lighter, it will float into the air all by itself, without any effort on your part.

Promptly the hands floats from the resting position on the arm of the chair, rising with an uncanny steadiness, as though floating rather than being moved by effort. Then new instructions are given:

Extend your right arm straight out palm up. Your arm is encased in a band of steel, making it absolutely impossible for either you or anyone else to bend your arm. I repeat, it is absolutely impossible for anyone to bend your arm!

Then, two students are given an opportunity to try their muscles against those of the hypnotized student. One places his shoulder under the extended forearm and both place their hands over the volunteer's elbow; they apply their full strength to the task of bending the arm, but the expenditure of all their efforts merely leaves them frustrated and the extended arm still extended.

**Hypnotic Induction
and Trance**

Hypnotic induction, the process of hypnotizing a person, generally follows the outlines of the procedure described above. Extraneous stimuli such as light and sound are reduced. Instructions to relax or to sleep are repeated. Sometimes suggestions are given to focus on imaginary sensory stimuli of a concrete sort, such as the hillside scene in the example above. It should be noted that, in general, only a *willing* subject can be hypnotized: the reluctant person "dominated" by the power of a hypnotist is a myth. When successfully achieved, hypnosis is characterized by behaviors such as the floating hand or the immovable arm when these responses are suggested by the hypnotist; on the other hand, if left alone, the subjects will simply remain peacefully in a very relaxed state or fall asleep, eventually awakening of their own accord.

In research, the "hypnotic trance" is rated for "depth" by the sorts of behaviors that can be elicited by suggestion. Will the hand rise "involuntarily" upon suggestion? Will the subject hallucinate with closed eyes? With open eyes? A scale of rating the trance depth according to behaviors was developed by Ernest Hilgard of Stanford University (see Table 5.2). People show differing capacities to attain deep states of hypnosis, for reasons that are not well understood.

**Preconceptions
about Hypnosis**

Almost everyone has some sort of an image of the hypnotic state, including the sleep-like behavior and the willingness to accept suggestions or to play roles very different from normal everyday behavior. But many researchers have disputed the essential characteristics of the hypnotic state; skeptics believe that preconceptions about what hypnosis is "supposed to be like" play as much of a role in producing the hypnotic behavior as does the hypnotic state. To separate the effects of these influences is a difficult if not impossible task. To demonstrate the power of a subject's preconceptions about hypnosis over his behavior

when hypnotized, Martin Orne of the University of Pennsylvania arranged to *add* an unusual preconception about hypnosis to the experience of college students; he then observed its effect on their own hypnotic experience.

To do this, Orne conducted demonstrations very much like the one described above. During introductory psychology course demonstrations at a number of universities, Orne and his collaborators placed two "volunteers" in a hypnotic trance. These volunteers had been hypnotized previously and given the posthypnotic suggestion that in future hypnotic experiences they would develop a catalepsy (rigid immobility of a limb or the body) in their dominant hand and *not* in their recessive hand: one of the pair was right-handed and one left-handed, to show that the catalepsy was associated with dominance of the hand. In these "rigged" demonstrations, this catalepsy of the dominant hand was specifically pointed out as a "normal" characteristic of the hypnotic trance. Later, volunteers who had observed the rigged demonstration and students who had seen an unrigged demonstration were hypnotized; they were observed by an experimenter who knew neither which demonstration they had seen nor who was right- or left-handed. There was an obvious and overwhelming tendency for those subjects who had been led to believe that dominant-hand catalepsy was "normal" in hypnosis to show it spontaneously when hypnotized.

By questionnaire, Orne found that *all* of his subjects had rather clear ideas from literature or films or other sources about what hypnosis is "supposed to be like." But how many of the "normal" features of hypnosis are the result of these preconceptions rather than of the hypnotic state? Neither Orne nor any other researcher has peeled the onion of hypnosis down to its

Table 5–2   Sample items from the Stanford Hypnotic Susceptibility Scale, Form C

ITEM	SUGGESTED BEHAVIOR	CRITERION FOR PASSING
1. Arm Lowering	Right arm is held out and subject is told that arm will become heavy and drop.	Arm is lowered at least six inches in 10 seconds.
2. Moving Hands Apart	With hands extended and close together, subject is asked to imagine a force acting to push them apart.	Hands are six or more inches apart in 10 seconds.
3. Mosquito Hallucination	It is suggested that a mosquito buzzing nearby alights on the subject.	Any grimacing movement or acknowledgement of mosquito occurs.
4. Taste Hallucination (Sweet, Sour)	The subject is told to imagine that something sweet and then something sour is in the mouth, the taste growing stronger.	Both tastes are experienced and accompanied by overt signs or verbal report.
5. Arm Rigidity	Right arm is extended; subject is told that arm is growing stiffer.	Less than two inches of arm bent in 10 seconds.
6. Arm Immobilization	Subject is told that left arm will get heavier and be difficult to lift.	Arm rises less than one inch in 10 seconds.
7. Ammonia Test	Suggestion is made that subject will be unable to smell the odor when given a bottle of ammonia.	Odor is denied and overt signs are absent.
8. Hallucinated Voice	Subject is told that a person in the room will ask about age, residence etc.; however, no questions are asked.	Subject answers realistically at least once.
9. Negative Visual Hallucination	Three boxes are placed on table. The subject is told there are only two boxes and is asked if anything else is seen.	Subject sees only two objects.
10. Posthypnotic Amnesia	Subject is awakened and asked to recall above items.	Three or fewer items are recalled before subject is told, "Now you can remember everything."

(Adapted from Weitzenhoffer and Hilgard, 1962.)

essential character as yet, but they have demonstrated that preconceptions can play a powerful role in hypnotic behavior.

Are Hypnotized Subjects Stronger? In another experiment, Orne challenged the idea that the hypnotic subject is abnormally strong, manifesting strength impossible in an unhypnotized state. Students in a deep trance were told to hold a kilogram weight at arm's length with the suggestion that the weight and their arm were resting on the top of an imaginary table so that they could not possibly drop it. Of course, holding up a real weight uses up real energy, imaginary tables notwithstanding, and the arms eventually dropped under the strain. The length of time which the subject maintained the weight's position was recorded. Meanwhile, nonhypnotized subjects were invited to play a game in which the object was to hold the weight at arm's length as long as possible. Small sums of money were awarded for each successive period of time the subject endured the trial, and subjects were asked to give 30-seconds notice before dropping the weight. The results showed that the non-hypnotized game players not only matched but exceeded the average scores of the hypnotized subjects. While this experiment does not show what actually caused the high scores of the hypnotized subjects, it does demonstrate that motivation can account for endurance scores. Of course, if increased motivation is the key to the high scores of the hypnotized subjects, then a genuine characteristic of the hypnotic state may be that it exaggerates the motivation to comply with suggestions. It is evident, however, that hypnosis does not result in any superhuman strength by itself.

Actually, the phenomenon of the "immovable arm" as described in the initial part of this chapter is not unknown even outside the hypnotic state: practitioners of the Japanese martial arts, such as Aikido (eye-kee-doe), routinely demonstrate this unusual strength. And most of us have heard accounts of small men or women who in emergencies perform incredible feats of strength such as lifting cars to release trapped accident victims. It might be suggested that all of these cases are examples of "spontaneous hypnosis." But to employ the term "hypnosis" to describe too many different kinds of situations is to risk making the word meaningless. For our purposes, we restrict the term hypnosis to situations which follow a conventional hypnotic induction procedure and in which the kinds of hypnotic behavior in Hilgard's depth-of-trance scale are observed.

Trance Logic. Many researchers, including Orne, believe that although much "hypnotic behavior" is at least partially the result of other processes, such as preconception and motivation, nonetheless, there is an essential hypnotic state, one that is admittedly a subjective and elusive phenomenon. The subjective essence of hypnosis shows up in the peculiar "trance logic" of those in deep trances. To demonstrate this, Orne arranged to have some student subjects (picked at random and with the choice unknown to him) attempt to fake the hypnotic state well enough to fool him. Many of the hypnotic phenomena were demonstrated both by the genuinely hypnotized students and the fakes, but the subjective difference showed up in the way that suggested hallucinations (seeing or hearing things that are not there) were handled by the two groups. While sitting in a chair in such a way that they could see an experimenter standing before them, the subjects were instructed to close their eyes.

When subjects had complied, the experimenter quietly got up and walked around behind them. The subjects were told that when they opened their eyes, they would continue to see the absent investigator as standing before them. When they opened their eyes, "fakes" and "genuines" alike reported that they saw the experimenter as they had been instructed. They were then instructed to turn around so that the real experimenter would be in full view and asked to describe what they saw. Here was the crucial difference: the "fakes" refused to acknowledge the contradiction. Instead, they stated that they saw someone other than the experimenter or that they saw nothing there at all. On the other hand, the genuinely hypnotized subjects would say something such as, "Hmmm, this is rather strange . . . I see so-and-so in front of me *and* in back of me," but they would attempt no explanation for the contradiction.

This tolerance for the contradiction between normal sensory data and the suggestions received from the hypnotist, Orne believes, is an essential part of the hypnotic state. In hypnosis, hallucination and perception are allowed to coexist peacefully. Other researchers have suggested other characteristics they believe to be intrinsic to hypnosis, including the readiness to enact unusual roles, and the frequency of posthypnotic amnesia (the condition in which a subject cannot recall being hypnotized).

Until quite recently hypnosis was almost a taboo topic for scientific study. This attitude was probably an accident of history, because hypnosis had become associated with charlatanism and quackery. In recent years, researchers like Orne have brought hypnosis into the laboratory. Orne's findings are accepted; his explanations, however, are debated.

SLEEPING AND DREAMING

Sleeping peacefully in a bed in a dark room, a young man is busily engaged in a nocturnal life known to all of us, though strange and only in part understood by any of us; he is dreaming. He is one of 16 subjects in a study conducted by William Dement and Edward A. Wolpert of Stanford University; his slumber is not typical since he is wired to an electroencephalograph (EEG) (see Figure 5.24). Along with other factors, such as eye movement, body movement, and the role of different stimuli, his neurological activity is under study for its possible relationship to sleeping and dreaming.

Sleep and Dream Research

Previously, investigators Eugene Aserinsky and Nathaniel Kleitman at the University of Chicago had made a significant discovery about subjects who were awakened immediately after periods when *rapid eye movements (REM's)* were observed under their closed eyelids: they were regularly able to report dreams. Apparently, dreams only occur during periods of REM sleep. Dement and Wolpert documented a similar relationship between neurological activity and REM's and dreaming. During the course of sleep, four different kinds of EEG patterns are observed to occur in a regular cyclical progression (see Figure 5.25); these patterns accompany four phases of sleep. REM's and dreaming seem to occur only during the Phase I periods. This phase is the first to occur upon falling asleep. However, dreaming occurs only during the *later* appearances of Phase I.

The rapid eye movements of the dreamer seem to be related to the dream in various ways. For instance, larger eye movements

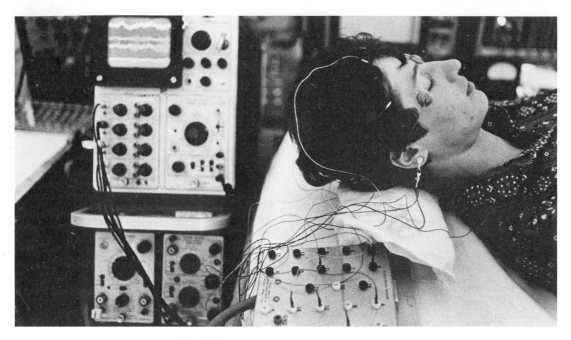

FIGURE 5.24 Electrodes placed in the scalp of the subjects pick up electrical activity of the brain, which is amplified by the electroencephalograph (EEG) and recorded by pen on a moving strip of paper as a wave-like tracing.

and more active REM's appear to be characteristic of "active" dreams in which the individual imagines being an active participant rather than a passive viewer. As well as size and activity, the direction of the eye movements appears to be meaningful. Immediately after a session of REM's, subjects were awakened and asked to recount their dreams. In 74 percent of the cases their final eye movement (as observed by an experimenter)—up, down, right, left, or none at all—corresponded with the direction they reported looking in the final scene of the dream, such as looking down from a high building or up at a flash in the sky.

Dream Stimuli. Do dreams reflect stimuli from outside or inside the dreamer? Are

dreams a method of protecting sleep, ways that the sleeping individual "explains" stimuli so as to make awakening unnecessary? To test this hypothesis, Dement and Wolpert subjected their sleepers to the sound of a steady tone, to a doorbell, to a flash of light, and to a spray of water. If these stimuli occurred during an REM dreaming sequence, they *were* incorporated into the dream as roaring sounds, telephones, flashes of lightning, rainfall, or other plausible "explanations." However, if these same stimuli were applied during non-REM periods, no dreams occurred. This suggests that, although they may be incorporated into an ongoing dream, external stimuli are not sufficient to "trigger" or initiate a dream.

To see if *internal* stimuli, such as thirst,

Demonstration 8.

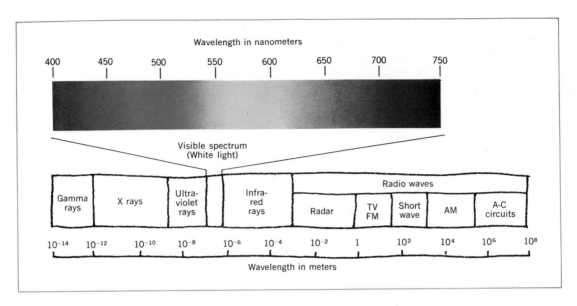

Visible spectrum
(White light)

FIGURE 5.15 (top) The position of visible light in the spectrum of electromagnetic radiation.

FIGURE 5.16 (bottom) White light passed through a prism is differentially scattered into its constituent wavelengths.

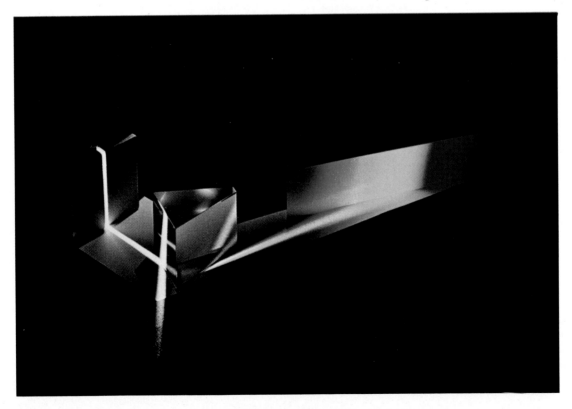

B

FIGURE 5.17 Color mixture. (A) Additive mixture of lights; the total produces white. (B) Subtractive mixture of pigments; the total produces black.

A

FIGURE 5.18 To develop the negative afterimage effect, stare at the drawing for about a minute and then shift your gaze to a blank sheet of white paper or a blank wall.

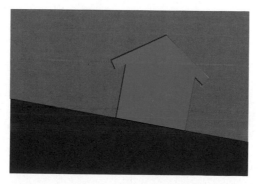

(A)

(B)

FIGURE 5.19 Paintings by Dr. Henry Crawford, a man with defective color vision. In (A) he selected the pigments; in (B) his wife, with normal color vision, picked the paints.

affected dream content, subjects were asked to go without water for 24 hours prior to one of the sleep sessions. If thirst were effective in determining dream content, then the thirst experienced by the subjects should show up in the dreams they reported in fairly obvious ways. But transcripts of the dreams showed no awareness of thirst and no incidents when the dreamer drank anything. Since most of dream content is not completely controlled by immediate internal or external stimuli, what factors determine the content of dreams? We will now examine some representative answers to this question that have been offered from ancient times to the present.

Dream Interpretation and Content

The purpose and significance of dreams has been subject to a variety of interpretations. The ancients believed that gods and demons influenced dreams and that dream events were often omens of good or ill fortune. The Egyptians believed that dreams represented communication from the gods and actively sought dream interpretation and guidance from their high priests. Dreams and visions occupy important places in many religious traditions.

The beginning of modern dream interpretation is usually credited to Sigmund Freud (who is discussed in another context in Chapter 10A). Freud considered dreams

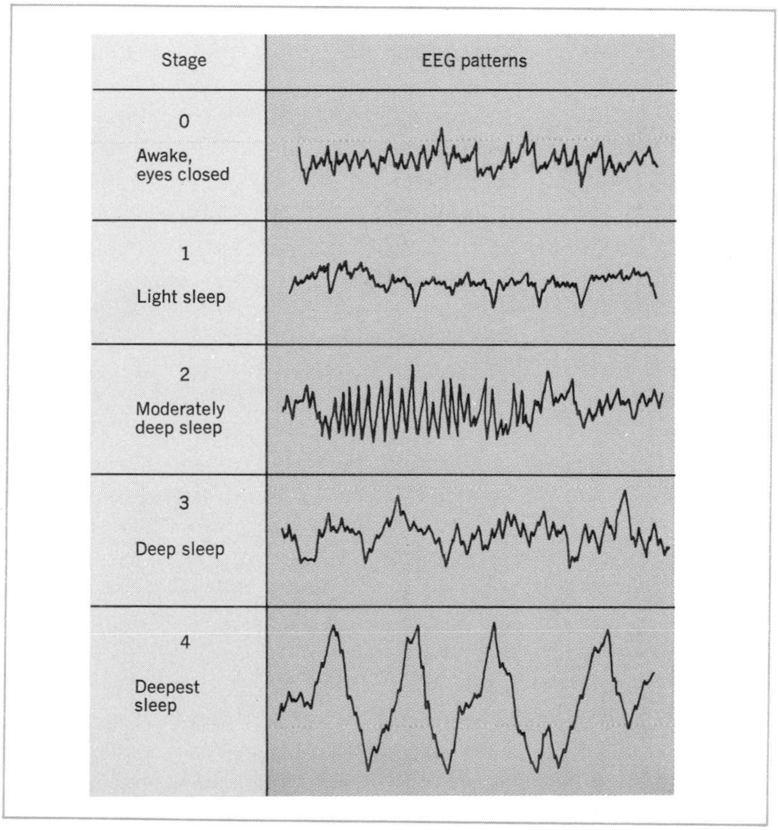

FIGURE 5.25 Electroencephalograph patterns indicating various stages of sleep.

to be a communication from the unconscious, a storehouse of thoughts, feelings, and desires that are unacceptable to the conscious mind. In Freudian theory, the content of dreams has a twofold nature. *The* **manifest content** *consists of the action and events of the dream which we remember and report. The* **latent content** *consists of symbolic messages from the unconscious hidden in the manifest content.* Freud thought that the manifest content of the dream served to disguise the unacceptable feelings and desires that were expressed in the latent content, the recognition of which would damage the serenity and self-image of the dreamer. Freud saw dreams as important sources of information about the self not normally available to an individual —he called dreams "The Royal Road to the Unconscious."

Freud also proposed the hypothesis that dreams act as guardians of sleep by providing reasonable explanations for stimuli and preventing awakening. But as Dement and Wolpert have shown, unusual stimuli do not initiate a dreaming sequence, although they may be integrated into a dream already in progress. Today, researchers believe that the roles are just the opposite of what Freud suggested, that sleep is the "guardian of dreams." Indeed, people show agitation and irritability when they are deprived, not of sleep in general, but specifically of REM dreaming sleep. One of sleep's primary functions, apparently, is to help fulfill a "need to dream."

Sex Differences in Dream Content. The contrasting content of dreams reported by men and women has been recorded by Calvin Hall and Robert L. Van de Castle. Their study is based on the reports of 550 female dreams and an equal number of male dreams from college students and 450 dreams from children. Men's dreams tend to be adventurous; they contain many outdoor activities, little friendliness, and frequent aggression. Twice as many of the characters in men's dreams are male as compared to the characters in women's dreams. The females in men's dreams are usually sex objects; indeed, they appear frequently enough that sexual content in general is high in comparison to women's dreams.

Women's dreams contain less overt sexual activity and about equal numbers of male and female characters. The people in female dreams tend to be more friendly than in male dreams. Pregnancy and menstrual cycle changes figure heavily in women's dreams. Menstrual cycle changes usually make themselves felt in dreams by significant changes in the amount of the colors red and pink that occur in the dreams.

Children often dream of animals, the frequency decreasing with maturation. The appearance of animals apparently occurs without respect to sex differences.

Dreams and ESP. A rather unusual factor in the content of some dreams may be extrasensory perception (see Focus 5.7: Parapsychology and ESP). In an investigation performed by Montague Ullmann and Stanley Krippner of the Maimonides Medical Center Dream Laboratory, agents in separate rooms attempted to transmit images of different paintings to sleeping subjects who were in Phase I, REM-type sleep. After each dreaming sequence, a subject was awakened and asked to give his impression of the dream imagery. During one session, a subject named Erwin consistently reported images of a restaurant or some sort of eating place, seafood, and a dozen or so fishermen. After each dreaming

FIGURE 5.26 The Sacrament of the Last Supper *by Salvador Dali was used in an ESP study described in the text.*

session, Erwin reported the imagery:

... an ocean ... fishing boats ... a dozen or so men ... a Christmas catalogue ... Christmas season ... restaurant ... place to eat ... food of different sorts ...

When asked to describe his dream images the next morning, Erwin reported that

... the fisherman dream makes me think of the Mediterranean area, perhaps even some sort of Biblical time. Right now my associations are of the fish and the loaf, or even the feeding of the multitudes ... Once again I think of Christmas.

What was the picture "transmitted" to Erwin? It was *The Sacrament of the Last Supper,* by Salvador Dali, shown in Figure 5.26. The accuracy of Erwin's imagery can be seen by looking at the painting, showing a picture of Christ serving the wine and bread to his disciples against a backdrop of the Mediterranean Sea and fishing boats. Do extrasensory stimuli play a role in dream content? Although more research is needed to confirm results like Krippner and Ullmann's, this case is certainly suggestive. However, research in the area of extrasensory perception is rife with studies that have not stood up to rigorous standards of scientific research.

While our knowledge about the nature of dreams is limited, it has been rapidly growing in recent years. Researchers like Dement and Wolpert have correlated the occurrence of dreams with rapid eye movement and with specific electroencephalograms. REM's have been demonstrated to be imaginary observations during dreaming. The effect of external stimuli and internal physiological stimuli is evidently limited. The significance of the dream content and the reason for its manifestation is less clearly understood. Theories concerning the significance of dreams are not lacking, but we have no basis for declaring one — or none — of these theories the "correct" explanation of dreaming. Each theory poses additional questions waiting for answers.

Focus 5.7
Para-psychology and ESP

Reports of magic, miracles, and witchcraft attest to the perennial fascination the paranormal—whatever cannot be explained scientifically—holds for most of us. In the late nineteenth century, such giants of psychology as William James became interested in the "psychic." Societies for Psychical Research were founded in Britain, the U.S., and many other countries. Their methods were mostly *anecdotal:* they compiled accounts of strange, unexplained occurrences with critical consideration of these alleged events. But it remained for Joseph Banks Rhine to introduce emphasis on laboratory experimentation and statistical analysis of numerous trials into the study of the paranormal. In 1934, Rhine, with a few colleagues, established the Parapsychology Laboratory at Duke University. Since then, the laboratory has been succeeded by the Foundation for Research on the Nature of Man. From the Duke investigations have come vast amounts of data on psychic phenomena; these data have been critically challenged by many research psychologists.

Rhine reclassified the field. To separate the phenomena he intended to study from alleged "supernatural" events, *he coined the term* **"parapsychology"** *to indicate that he was concerned with what were assumed to be natural functions of the human mind which simply are not understood at present.* He divided the field of parapsychology into two major subdivisions. One was **psychokinesis** *(PK), the influence of mind over physical events.* The other division included all **extrasensory perception** *(ESP), including* **telepathy** *(the perception of other's thoughts),* **clairvoyance** *(perception of objective events at a distance by means other than sensory perception), and* **precognition** *(perception of events prior to their occurrence).*

Rhine spent his initial efforts investigating the evidence for the existence (as opposed to the mechanisms) of parapsychological phenomena. For example, to test for clairvoyance subjects are asked to attempt to "call" the proper order of a series of cards (see Figure 5.27) at a distance or from behind barriers. For PK, the gambler's nemesis—a set of common dice—is used: subjects attempt to influence their fall repeatedly. Rhine generally employs numerous trials for his experiment. Unusual events are not the criteria for the presence of ESP or PK; *series* of events that differ significantly from chance are what count. As far as Rhine and some others are concerned, the results are considered supportive of ESP and PK, but the causal mechanism or the basis of transmission is unknown.

On the other hand, most psychologists are skeptical about Rhine's work. Some of the objections can be explained as simple general skepticism about any alleged events or processes that do not fit neatly into a materialistic world view. Other criticisms are based on the inade-

FIGURE 5.27 *Cards used in ESP research to test for clairvoyance. Subjects are asked to attempt to "call" the proper order of a series of cards at a distance or from behind barriers.*

quacy of the statistical methods used by Rhine and other ESP researchers. Other criticisms are more pointed: improved experimental techniques in parapsychology have usually resulted in fewer confirming observations, so it is reasonable to suspect that many of the positive results reported are in part due to experimental errors. However, another explanation for the disappointing results of "improved" experimental techniques to detect ESP or PK is suggested by Gardner Murphy's assertion that it is too early for rigorous experimentation because we have not yet created any plausible theories of the paranormal that might tell us "where to look" for its occurrence.

Court is still out on this frontier of investigation, but interest in the paranormal remains strong.

SUMMARY

A. Sensation

1. The study of **sensation** (page 137) is concerned with the relationship between physical stimuli, such as light and sound waves, and the responsiveness of sense organs, such as eyes and ears. The study of **perception** (page 137) focuses on the processes that select, organize, and interpret sensory input.

2. The sensory receptors in organs (such as eyes, ears, skin surfaces, etc.) change environmental stimuli (such as light or sound waves) into electrochemical responses that are transmitted to specialized areas of the central nervous system by neurons.

3. The sense receptors of the eye are **rods** and **cones** (p. 138). The rods are sensitive to low levels of light (night vision); the cones are specialized for color vision and acuity (day vision).

4. The research of Hubel and Wiesel demonstrates that individual cells in the **visual cortex** (page 139) are highly specialized in their responsiveness to stimuli. For a specific stimulus, only a specific set of cells will respond.

5. The term **absolute threshold** (page 140) refers to the weakest stimulus that we can detect. The determination of sensory thresholds and the relationships between physical stimuli and human sensation is called **psychophysics** (page 140).

6. The ear translates the **intensity** and **frequency** of sound waves into information on **loudness** and **pitch** (page 144). The sense receptors are located in the **cochlea** (page 147) of the inner ear.

B. Perception of the Visual World

7. We emphasized that there is no hard-and-fast distinction between the realms of sensation and perception; the two overlap. But for the sake of convenience, we separately consider the processes that give us information about the physical changes in the world.

8. The term **perceptual contrast** (page 151) refers to phenomena in which the perception of the same stimulus is significantly affected by its surroundings or context.

9. The term **perceptual constancy** (page 153) refers to the tendency to perceive objects as stable and enduring even though the patterns of physical energy that strike our sense organs are constantly changing; an example is **size constancy** (page 153).

10. **Binocular disparity** (page 153) refers to the slight difference between the images perceived by the two eyes; the disparity is interpreted by the brain as depth. But most depth perception depends on learned monocular cues, such as difference in retinal image size for near and far objects, interposition, and texture gradient.

11. Gestalt theorists maintain that there is a tendency to organize experiences into whole, complete patterns. Several principles of perceptual organization, such as **proximity, similarity,** and **closure,** have been identified (page 158).

C. **Perception and the Nature-Nurture Issue**

12. To what degree is perception determined by innate factors and to what degree is it determined by environmental influences? In general, the evidence indicates that visual perception in humans primarily involves learning, but it is also dependent on nonvisual factors, such as early stimulation, movement, and touch. Research with people, blind since birth, who have had their sight restored supports this view.

13. There is some evidence that infants have innate depth perception. Similarly, some degree of form perception (including preference for human faces) seems to be innate.

14. What is perceived can be influenced by needs, values, motives, and expectancies.

D. **Alternate States of Consciousness and Perception**

15. The so-called "hypnotic state" is an altered state of consciousness in which suggestibility is enhanced to the point where hallucination can be induced; individuals show a striking tolerance for contradictions between their hallucinations and their perceptions.

16. Many of the so-called hypnotic phenomena have been demonstrated to be "artifacts" of processes that are observed in everyday states of consciousness, such as heightened motivation, role-playing, and the effect of preconceptions about the state of hypnosis.

17. One of the primary functions of sleep seems to be to fulfill a need to dream. Research has established definite relationships between physiological events during sleep—such as rapid eye movements and EEG records—and dreams (page 177). Sleep occurs in four phases, as gauged by EEG patterns. REM's and dreaming occur during Phase I sleep. The role of REM's as imaginary "glances" in the dream plot has also been demonstrated.

18. There are several different schools of thought that explain and interpret the content of dreams (page 179). Freud, in his pioneering work, distinguished between the **manifest** (literal) and **latent** (symbolic) **content** (page 180) of dreams. Research has revealed differences in the typical dream content of men, women, and children.

19. Research on **parapsychology** (page 182)—**extrasensory perception** and **psychokinesis**—is still regarded as inconclusive by most psychologists.

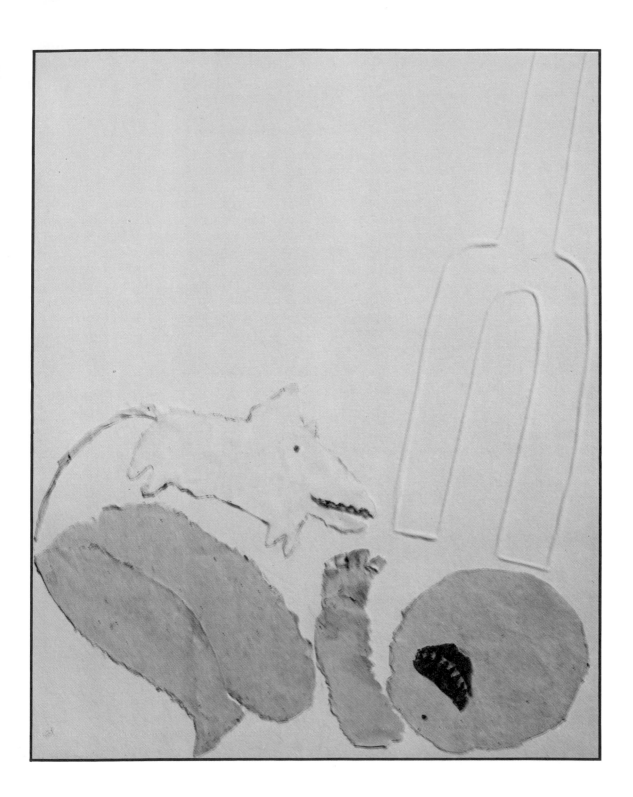

Section Four
Learning, Remembering Being

Lower forms of animals can rely on instincts to guide behavior needed for survival. Human beings cannot rely on instincts but must learn almost every behavior needed for survival. How are adaptive behaviors acquired? How are behaviors that are no longer useful extinguished? How are learned behaviors stored and retrieved when needed? What are the basic mechanisms underlying learning and memory?

These questions, explored in this section, relate to the nurture side of the nature-nurture issue introduced earlier. In our discussion we will consider how rewards and punishment influence learning and then, through a case study of a "spoiled brat," examine how social environment shapes behavior. We will explore the exciting new field of biological feedback control which applies the principles of learning and biology to teach people how to control internal biological functions from heart rate to headache. We will present case histories of one man who could not forget what he learned and another man who could not remember what he learned. At the end of the section we will take a look at ways that memory can be improved.

Chapter Six
Learning Principles

Ivan Pavlov, a Russian physiologist, had won a Nobel Prize in 1904 and world fame for his study of the digestive process in dogs. Several years after he had won the prize, he noticed that every time the assistant who ordinarily fed the dogs came into the lab the dog in the lab would begin to salivate just as if it had been given some food. Pavlov called this a *psychic secretion* and decided to study it. His friends and colleagues in physiology advised him to forget it because they believed that "psychic secretions" sounded very unscientific and probably had nothing to do with physiology. After some very careful thought, Pavlov embarked on a 30-year study that provided the basis for our understanding of some basic principles of learning. In this chapter we will explore the principles of learning that Pavlov and others have studied and examine how they apply to understanding behavior.

A. CLASSICAL CONDITIONING

Classical conditioning (sometimes referred to as *respondent conditioning*) and the name Pavlov have been popularly associated with control of people's minds and actions. The villain of a recent film thriller supposedly had his mind programmed at a "Pavlov Institute" to kill an American presidential candidate. Pavlov's techniques have also been associated in the popular media with "brainwashing" (see Focus 13.2: Brainwashing). In the book and film *A Clockwork Orange,* the hero is conditioned to feel revulsion for violence and sex.

All of this reflects a growing concern with the capabilities of learning psychology both for good and for evil.

CLASSICAL CONDITIONING PROCEDURES

Pavlov was born in Czarist Russia in 1849; he died in 1936, a leading physiologist of the Soviet Union. In the course of his work with dogs he noted a rather common event that impressed his informed intelligence. When the dogs were fed, they salivated. This is a **reflex response** (*a simple, automatic, unlearned response to a stimulus*) that Pavlov understood. What he did not understand was the fact that the dogs also salivated when they simply

FIGURE 6.1 Ivan Pavlov (center figure) shown in his laboratory with his assistants.

heard the footsteps of their keeper at meal times. As he later discovered, the innate response of salivation had been brought under the control of a new stimulus, the sound of footsteps, after the sound had been repeatedly paired with the original stimulus, meat. Pavlov wondered whether training could also cause this response to be elicited by a completely neutral stimulus, such as a tuning fork. Is this type of relationship the basis of all learning? In this section we will explore the answers to these questions.

Pavlov assembled the apparatus shown in Figure 6.2. The dog was restrained by straps. One crucial aspect of the experiment was the measurement of the amount of the dog's salivation. Pavlov, by surgery, exposed a duct of the dog's saliva gland. As a result, the saliva dripped out and could be collected and measured by weight or by number of drops. Instead of ordinary food, he used dry powdered meat, which produced profuse salivation and was easy to store and handle.

Pavlov wished to see if he could, by training, induce the dog to salivate at the sound of a tuning fork. He began by pre-senting the dog with the tuning fork alone in order to be sure that the tuning fork itself would not produce salivation in the dog before training. It didn't; the dog simply turned its head and cocked its ears. Then he began to sound the tuning fork and at the same time blow meat powder into the dog's mouth. The sequence— tuning fork/meat powder/saliva—was repeated several times. Then the crucial test was run. The tuning fork was sounded and no meat powder was delivered. Would the dog now salivate to this sound that previously had brought only an attention response?

Not only did the dog salivate, but also, Pavlov noted, the more times the sound had been presented along with the meat powder, the more salivation was produced. In Table 6.1 you can see the relationship between the number of drops of saliva produced and the number of times that the tuning fork was paired with the meat powder. Pavlov, as we noted, called this response a psychic secretion, a term that he later abandoned. He found he had to develop a whole new vocabulary to refer to the various parts of the experiment.

FIGURE 6.2 Apparatus used in Pavlov's classical conditioning studies.

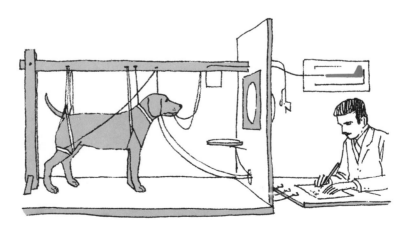

TABLE 6.1   **Pavlov's dog conditioned to salivate to a tuning fork**

NUMBER OF PAIRINGS OF TUNING FORK AND MEAT POWDER	NUMBER OF DROPS OF SALIVA WITHIN 30 SECONDS AFTER TUNING FORK SOUNDED
1	0
9	18
15	30
31	65
51	69

Classical Conditioning

Terminology

Pavlov called the stimulus-response (S-R) relationships learned through this procedure the conditional reflex. He was trying to indicate by this term that the S-R connection was acquired and not innate, that is, the former reflex response was conditional upon the training. When Pavlov's major book was rendered into English the term "conditional" was improperly translated as "conditioned"; this term stuck. *The S-R connection based on this training is called the conditioned reflex or the* **conditioned response, CR.** The salivation of the dog when the meat powder was blown into its mouth was a reflex response not based on previous training. For this Pavlov used the term the unconditional response. The meat powder itself was called the unconditional stimulus. It is a stimulus that can automatically elicit the unconditional response. The translation error produced the terms **unconditioned stimulus (UCS)** and **unconditioned response (UCR).** Pavlov called the tuning fork the conditional stimulus, which we now more commonly call the **conditioned stimulus (CS).** The total procedure is diagrammed in Table 6.2. Before the conditioning begins, the tuning fork (CS) elicits attention responses but does not elicit salivation. The UCS (meat powder), without training, elicits copious salivation (UCR). When the CS is paired with the UCS for a number of trials, it then achieves the power to elicit salivation when presented alone (CR).

Classical conditioning *can be described as learning through stimulus substitution so that the functions of the original unconditioned stimulus (UCS) are acquired by the new, conditioned stimulus (CS) by repeated associations.* It should be clear that in this learning process the organism has no control over the occurrence of either the UCS or CS; both occur regardless of its behavior. For human beings a wide variety of physical stimuli, words, and other symbols can become conditioned stimuli. Figure 6.3 presents some common symbols that have become associated with some very strong emotional responses. Here is a list of conditioned stimuli that evoke strong emotion in most people when they occur: a flashing red light and the siren of a police car signaling your car to pull over, the angry flush on the face of your employer, the sight of a drill in the dentist's office. Most of our emotional responses to environmental stimuli are ac-

TABLE 6.2 **The sequence of steps in classical conditioning**

STEP 1: PRETRAINING TEST
        CS (Tuning Fork)   ⟶ Attention Response
STEP 2: CONDITIONING (TRIALS REPEATED MANY TIMES)
        CS (Tuning Fork)
        UCS (Meat Powder) ⟶ UCR (Salivation)
STEP 3: TEST FOR CONDITIONING
        CS (Tuning Fork)   ⟶ CR (Salivation)

The tuning fork is the conditioned stimulus (CS). It serves as a signal for the meat powder which, in turn, is the unconditioned stimulus (UCS).

The unconditioned stimulus, without training, can elicit the reflex response, salivation, which is termed the unconditioned response (UCR).

As a result of the pairing of the CS and UCS, the unconditioned response becomes attached to the conditioned stimulus and is then called the conditioned response (CR).

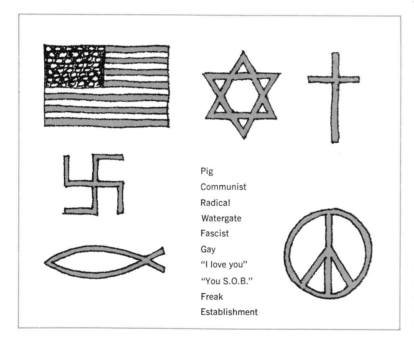

Pig
Communist
Radical
Watergate
Fascist
Gay
"I love you"
"You S.O.B."
Freak
Establishment

FIGURE 6.3 Through classical conditioning a wide variety of words and other symbols can gain the capacity to evoke emotional responses.

quired by way of classical conditioning.

A great deal of research in classical conditioning consists basically of trying to answer the following questions:

1. What happens to the CR when we stop pairing it with the UCS and repeatedly present the CS?

2. After a response is conditioned to one CS, will it also be elicited by stimuli similar to the CS?

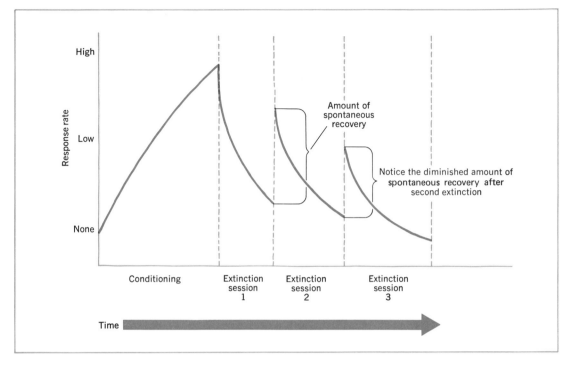

FIGURE 6.4 The life history of a conditioned response. The four curves show the course of conditioning and extinction of a classically conditioned response. During the conditioning phase the response rate or strength gradually rises as the CS and UCS are repeatedly paired. When the UCS is withdrawn, extinction occurs gradually. After time delay, the CR spontaneously recurs when the CS is presented. However, without the UCS, extinction occurs again. This cycle can be repeated until the CR is completely extinguished.

3. In most research the CS precedes the UCS. What is the optimal CS-UCS interval for conditioning?

The answers to these and other questions will be presented as we introduce and discuss the basic concepts of extinction, generalization, and discrimination.

Extinction

As long as the meat powder is given to the dog fairly regularly, it will continue to salivate to the CS. If you stop the UCS for a series of trials, the CR begins slowly to wane and finally will stop altogether. **Extinction** *is the process of eliminating a response by omitting the UCS.* The CR is not permanently lost, however. If you wait a day and test again with the CS, the CR will return at almost its pre-extinction strength. *The return of a response after extinction trials to almost full strength without further reinforcement Pavlov called* **spontaneous recovery.** If you repeat this extinction-spontaneous recovery process many times, the spontaneous recovery becomes ever smaller. Eventually, the response does not recur at all. Figure 6.4 pictures this entire extinction process. Note that within each extinction session, the CS (not accompanied by the UCS) loses its power to elicit the CR. After a 24-hour rest, the response shows spontaneous recovery. The spontaneous recovery is never quite up to the initial level of strength of the previous day's session. Eventually, the CS will be powerless to evoke the CR, even after rest. Even then, however, the CR is not completely lost. If the experimenter begins training again, it will be noted that the CR will reach full strength considerably more quickly than it did originally.

Stimulus Generalization

Pavlov found that once a dog had been conditioned to salivate to the sound of a specific bell (CS), it would also salivate to the sound of a different bell. The more similar the sound of another bell to the CS, the greater the amount of saliva that was secreted. This phenomenon is called **stimulus generalization,** *which means that once an organism learns to respond to a specific stimulus it will also emit the response to similar stimuli.* Psychologists have carefully studied the manner in which variations in similarity of stimulus produce variations in response. The stimulus variations have been explored along a number of dimensions. Loudness and pitch have been varied for sound stimuli. For light stimuli, brightness and color have been investigated. For example, if an animal is conditioned to respond to a green CS, an investigator might test for amount of response to a chartreuse or yellow stimulus. Typically, the closer the test stimulus to the CS, the larger the generalization response.

Pavlov also studied generalization using the spatial dimension. His CS was a vibration to the shoulder of the dog; the UCS

was meat powder blown into the dog's mouth. He found the spatial generalization pattern shown in Table 6.3. The CS (shoulder vibration) elicits the largest number of drops of saliva. As we move the test stimulus farther and farther from the location of the CS, the generalization response decreases.

A study by Marjorie Bass and Clark Hull repeated this experiment of Pavlov's with male college students. In the place of salivation as a CR, Bass and Hull studied the galvanic skin response (GSR). The GSR is a measure that reflects a state of emotionality, tension, or excitement. If you trickle a very tiny current through a person's hand (so tiny that it cannot be felt), you can measure the resistance of the person's hand to the passage of the current. If you excite the person by a kiss or by an electric shock, the sympathetic nervous system will stimulate the person's sweat glands to secrete. The salty sweat will reduce the electrical resistance of the skin. This reduction in electrical resistance can be measured by appropriately arranged electrical meters called galvanometers. The GSR is very sensitive to stimulation, and techniques for its measurement are highly advanced (see Focus 4.7). Consequently, it is a commonly used response in psychological research. But let us return to Bass and Hull, who wished to repeat Pavlov's spatial generalization study using college students rather than dogs.

Just as Pavlov arranged it, the CS in the Bass and Hull experiment was a vibration to the left shoulder. This was immediately followed by an electric shock (UCS) to the right wrist; the CR was a GSR measured in the left hand.

| Vibration to left shoulder (CS) | → | Shock to right wrist (UCS) | → | GSR in left hand (CR) |

TABLE 6.3   **Spatial pattern of stimulus generalization in dogs**

PLACE STIMULATED	NUMBER OF DROPS OF SALIVA IN 30 SECONDS
Front Paw	6
Shoulder (CS)	8
Side near Shoulder	7
Side near Thigh	3
Thigh	0
Hind Paw	0

(From I. P. Pavlov, *Conditioned Reflexes* (translated by G. V. Anrep), London: Oxford University Press, 1927.)

After conditioning, a vibration to the left shoulder was followed reliably by a GSR in the left hand. Bass and Hull then tested for GSR's at points 16, 32, and 48 inches downstream (small of back, left thigh, left calf) from the shoulder. The amount of GSR to each of these points is graphed in Figure 6.5. This type of curve is called a **gradient of stimulus generalization** *and displays the decline in response strength as the differences between the conditioned stimulus and test stimulus increase.*

Many stimuli associated with objects and events in our environment vary from time to time. For example, the sound of a police siren varies from vehicle to vehicle and from town to town, yet you can readily recognize variant forms of the sound when you hear them for the first time. The symbols presented in Figure 6.3 may be presented in many variations, yet once we have learned to respond to one, we also respond to its variants. Stimulus generalization simplifies our learning to respond to signs and signals in our environment. Without this mechanism we would be overwhelmed with the task of learning to respond anew to each variant of the objects and events that surround us.

Secondary Generalization. Gradients of primary generalization are defined by *physical* characteristics, such as color, sound, size, and spatial location. If we trained a GSR response to the word "brown," we would expect a primary generalization response to the word "town." But would we

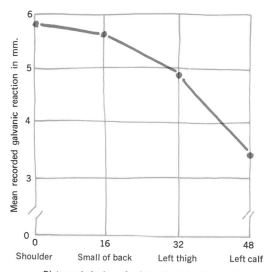

FIGURE 6.5 A stimulus generalization gradient obtained by Bass and Hull.

Distance in inches of points stimulated from left shoulder (CS)

also expect a generalization response to the word "tan"? This word has no physical similarity to "brown," but it is similar in terms of learned meaning.

Gregory Razran at Queens College in New York City conducted a study of the secondary generalization of a conditioned salivary response in college students. The subjects were sat at a table and fed salty snacks while they attended to words being flashed on a screen. When they ate the salty snacks, they salivated. The salty snacks were systematically paired with the presentation of certain words, for example, "brown." Razran assumed, then, that the salty snacks would act as a UCS to elicit salivation (the UCR) and the words would be the CS. His problem was to measure the amount of salivation (CR) to the CS and generalization stimuli. Pavlov had operated on his subjects so as to expose a salivary gland duct. This was not the method of choice in this case. Razran ingeniously inserted dental cotton wads into the students' mouths for a specific number of seconds while he exposed the training word or CS ("brown") and synonyms or generalization stimuli — words like "tan" and "beige." After each stimulus exposure, he removed the dental cotton and noted the precise increase in its weight. He compared the increase in weight of the dental cotton in response to the CS, to synonyms, and to neutral stimuli, words that were semantically unrelated to the CS. The dental cottons used for the CS and synonyms showed evidence of considerably more salivation than the dental cottons corresponding to the neutral words. It was clear that *generalization based on learned similarity* (synonyms) *does occur.* Psychologists have termed this phenomenon **secondary generalization.**

There is a limit, however, to the adaptive value of stimulus generalization. For Pav-

lov's dog, not all tones were followed by meat powder. For humans, not all sirens belong to police cars and the same symbols may not always be associated with the same unconditioned stimulus. *The term* **overgeneralization** *refers to inappropriately responding in the same way to similar stimuli.* There are times when it becomes necessary to learn to respond differently to variations of the same stimuli.

Discrimination

In Pavlov's experiments dogs could learn to salivate to a wide variety of CS's, even a metronome ticking at a specific speed, say 100 beats per minute. Because of stimulus generalization, a dog would also salivate to the metronome at 80 beats per minute. But if Pavlov persisted in providing the meat powder UCS only for the 100-beats-per-minute rhythm and omitted the UCS for the 80-beats-per-minute rhythm, the dog became able to **discriminate.** *That is, it responded* (salivated) *only to the rewarded stimulus,* 100 beats per minute. At this point, Pavlov found that he could push the dog to finer and finer discriminations. He continued to use the 100-beats-per-minute stimulus as his CS but pushed the 80 beats per minute stimulus up to 85 . . . then 90. The upper limit seemed to be 96. The dog was able to discriminate very well between 96 and 100 metronome beats per minute. Pavlov's findings have been duplicated with many animals and human beings for a wide variety of stimuli.

The adaptive significance of discrimination becomes apparent when you realize that variations of many stimuli are associated with different objects and events. If we responded *indiscriminately* to these variations, such as wandering into the wrong (but somewhat similar) house or

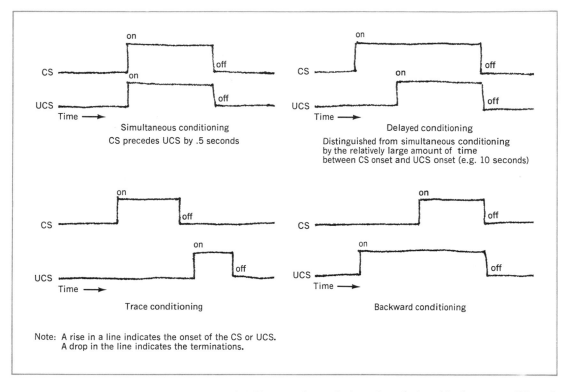

FIGURE 6.6 *Four main variations in relationship between CS and UCS.*

embracing the wrong (but somewhat similar) sexual partner, our problems would be serious indeed.

Time Relations

In a conditioning experiment the researcher has control of two facets of the experiment, the CS and the UCS. Experimenters have reacted to this predictably enough by varying the CS and UCS in every conceivable way. The most important ways are pictured in Figure 6.6. Should the CS or should the UCS come first for most efficient conditioning? How much first? The answer has been very clear. Experiments by Helen M. Wolfle, A. Spooner, and W. M. Kellogg have definitely indicated that

conditioning proceeds most quickly if the CS precedes the UCS by one-half second. Figure 6.7 is a composite giving the average results of three different studies. As you can see, backward conditioning and delayed conditioning are rather inefficient methods. Using these methods, conditioning takes many more trials, but it does occur. When the CS precedes the UCS by one-half second, conditioning proceeds most rapidly. This intriguing fact is quite reliable but, as yet, has evaded explanation.

CLASSICALLY CONDITIONED EMOTIONAL RESPONSES

John B. Watson, a prominent psychologist during the early part of this century, was

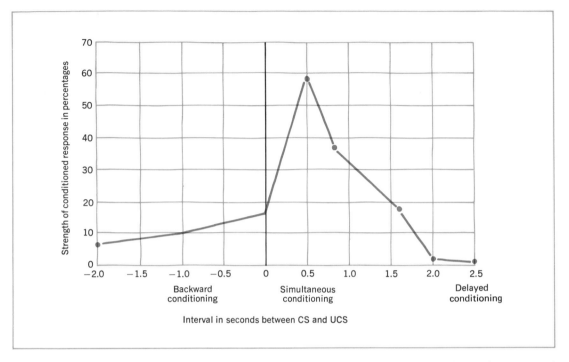

FIGURE 6.7 The interval between the conditioned stimulus (CS) and the unconditioned stimulus (UCS) influences the strength of the conditioned response (CR). A delay of about .5 second seems optimal for conditioning to take place.

quite optimistic about the ability of conditioning psychology to remake man and his world. His own work almost completely denied any influence of genetics on behavior. Conditioning would explain everything. Much of his research consisted of attempts to show how conditioning was at the basis of behavior. In a rather well-known demonstration, Watson (in collaboration with Rosalie Rayner) attempted to show how children learn fear.

Albert, a nine-month-old infant, was allowed to examine a tame white rat. The peaceful rat excited the child's curiosity. When the white rat (CS) was again presented to Albert, its appearance was accompanied by the alarming sound of ham-

mering on a large steel bar (UCS). Of course, the child was frightened at the sudden noise and began to cry (UCR). The rat and noise made five more joint appearances. By then the conditioning had become effective. Just the presence of the white rat was enough to cause Albert to cry and move away (CR). Albert had been conditioned to fear a harmless animal that, before conditioning, only aroused his curiosity. Watson and Rayner, and many psychologists since then, suggest that such classical conditioning is a model of the origin of many learned fears and other emotions in humans.

Watson and Rayner discovered that the white rat was not the only stimulus that provoked fear in Albert. Similar objects, such as a ball of white cotton, a rabbit, or a white mask, also could frighten him. This spread of the conditioned response (fear, in this case) from the original conditioned stimulus (white rat) to similar stimuli (e.g., a ball of cotton) is a good example of *stimulus generalization* of an emotional response. Little Albert was taken home from the hospital in which these studies were conducted so no follow-up studies could be made.

Incompatible Responses. Extinction is not the only way to eliminate a conditioned response. It is also possible to simply train another response to the same CS. The new response must be one that makes the old response unlikely or impossible. Thus, if you wish to get a dog to stop flexing its right front paw to a tuning fork, simply train the left front paw to flex to the same tuning fork. The dog, in simultaneously attempting both responses to the tuning fork, would be very likely to fall on its nose. The responses are incompatible.

The training of an incompatible response could have been used to cure Albert of his fear of the white rat. At least it worked on Peter, who showed up in the laboratory of psychologist Mary Cover Jones. Peter had a fear of white rats that generalized to rabbits, fur coats, and so on, very much like Albert's. The method that rid Peter of his fear was to teach him an incompatible response in the presence of a rabbit. The incompatible response to fear was eating ice cream. While Peter sat gobbling the ice cream, a rabbit in a cage was brought into the room. It was kept at a safe distance so that Peter could comfortably continue enjoying his ice cream while warily keeping a check on the whereabouts of the menacing rabbit. This encounter was re-

peated, the rabbit being brought closer and closer to Peter with each session. Peter could not cry and run away while continuing to eat his ice cream. Jones could not simply have brought the rabbit close to Peter in the first ice-cream-eating session. She would have risked having him learn to fear ice cream. An incompatible response (CR) (happy contentment) gradually had to be built up in the presence of the rabbit (CS) by pairing it with a new UCS (ice cream).

Experimental Neurosis. When Pavlov tried to push for discriminations between stimuli that were very similar, his dogs suffered a canine nervous breakdown, which Pavlov called *experimental neurosis*. In one famous case, he trained a dog to salivate to a circle. He then taught the dog to discriminate this circle from an ellipse which was twice as wide as it was high. As in the metronome-discrimination experiment, he brought the ellipse ever closer in shape to the circle by making the vertical and horizontal diameters more nearly equal. He began at a 2:1 ratio; when he reached 9:8, the dog could no longer discriminate the ellipse from the circle. The dog whined and fought against its restraints in the apparatus. It stopped responding "rationally" to circles or ellipses. Its behavior became disturbed and disorganized. Experimental neurosis has also been elicited in cats and sheep. In some studies, some of the symptoms have persisted over many years.

Many of the characteristics of the experimental neurosis of animals seem similar to those of human neurosis (see Chapter 11). In both cases the neurotic behavior 1) occurs when the organism is exposed to prolonged stress and insoluble problems; 2) involves behaviors that deviate from the organism's usual or normal behavior; 3) persists for many years without extinction; 4) involves fear and anxiety. Several modern therapeutic procedures for dealing with neurotic behavior are based on the principles of extinction, incompatible responses, and other learning principles (see Chapter 11).

ADAPTIVE SIGNIFICANCE OF CLASSICAL CONDITIONING

Survival in our world requires at least two basic kinds of information. First, we must know how events in our environment are related to one another, and secondly, we must know what consequences our own behaviors have on the behaviors of others and on the environment. The first kind of information can be acquired through classical conditioning. Classical conditioning can be seen as the means by which we learn about what stimuli in our environment are associated with neutral, pleasant, or painful events. Since most neutral or pleasant events generally are associated with safety and painful events with damage, classical conditioning provides us with a signal, the conditioned stimulus, that can help us predict events and prepare us for what may be coming. Of course, there may be times when the signal is in error, as in the case of overgeneralization or failure to discriminate. On the whole, however, the mechanism has a high survival value in life. The second kind of learning is called **operant conditioning.** *With operant conditioning we learn what consequences our behaviors have on the environment: which behaviors will yield pleasant consequences and which behaviors will let us avoid unpleasant consequences.*

B. OPERANT CONDITIONING

An elaborate research laboratory was built in the basement of a large Massachusetts mental hospital. The plan was to study the possibilities of positive modification of the behavior of the mentally ill through operant conditioning techniques. The investigators were dealing with extremely disturbed patients and often found it impossible to bring them down to the laboratory from the wards. An undergraduate from a nearby university made use of an operant conditioning technique called shaping to bring a particularly ill patient to the experimental rooms. In **shaping,** *the experimenter rewards responses that more and more closely approximate the desired behavior until the desired behavior occurs.* It is a type of "hot and cold" game in which the experimenter uses a reinforcement or reward instead of saying "hot."

The patient that the student chose to work with had little control over urination and defecation. He did not speak. He would occasionally bite people who came too close to him. The student first determined that the patient would accept little candies. Then, the student waited for the patient to turn his head toward the door leading to the stairway to the basement laboratory. When he did, the student was quickly there with a bit of candy. The candy acted as a reward for head-turning and increased its probability of occurring. The young researcher continued to reward door-oriented head-turning. When this response was established, the candy reward was withheld until the patient turned his body toward the door. This act was rewarded until the patient simply stood facing the door. Now the student, with reinforcement ready, waited for a first step toward the door. In small stages, with repeated disappointments and difficulties, the student brought the patient through the doorway to the stairway, down the stairs, and into the basement laboratory. The patient, who had not behaved in such an organized manner in some years, has been re-educated through operant conditioning.

The use of operant conditioning as a therapeutic technique is discussed in Section C of this chapter and in Chapter 11E. It is also illustrated in the opening panorama in the case of the woman with anorexia nervosa who stopped eating. In this section we will explore the general principles of operant conditioning and its applications.

OPERANT CONDITIONING WITH POSITIVE REINFORCEMENT

The behavior change described above illustrates the crucial aspect of operant conditioning, namely, the effectiveness of systematic reward. Here is another example, one you can try out. Ask a friend to call out a word every ten seconds. Without telling your subject, decide on some category of words (say, two-syllable words) to reward. Each time your subject calls out a word in that category of words, you immediately respond, "Good." Have another friend record the number of "goods" per one minute block of time. Typically, the subject's *rate of emission* of two-syllable words will increase during the session. Your friend need not figure out the category or may decide that the category is actually something quite different. But if the person decides that the category is boys' names, the responses will tend to be "Edward, Harry, Joseph, Robert, Jerry, Willy, Amos, Monty . . .", all boys' names with two syllables.

Operant Analysis of Behavior. Let us analyze this situation. We must have a response (two-syllable words) that the subject can give. Then, we need a stimulus ("good") that is capable of increasing the probability of that response. The response is called an **operant;** *it operates on the environment to bring on the reinforcer* ("good"). *A* **positive reinforcement** *may be any object or event that, when presented, can increase the probability of a response that precedes it.* Food, praise, and money are examples of common positive reinforcements.

The term operant conditioning was coined by Burrhus F. Skinner, now at Harvard University, who has conducted extensive research on the process. The term is often used synonymously with the term *instrumental conditioning.* For his work with animals, Skinner designed the apparatus we have already mentioned in Chapter 3, the Skinner box, shown in Figure 6.8. The Skinner box contains a small lever and a device for the delivery of food-pellet reinforcers. Typically, the lever is wired electronically to a recording pen. This recording pen rides on a moving strip of paper. The mechanical device, including recording pen and moving paper, is called a *cumulative recorder.* When there is no response, the pen on the moving strip writes a horizontal line. Each response displaces the pen up one notch and produces a curve, such as the one you can see in Figure 6.8. (The different types of reinforcement schedules shown in the figure are explained on pages 207–209.)

From a recorder curve, we can get a picture of the rate of responding by connecting any two consecutive response points. The faster the rate of responding, the steeper the slope of the connecting line. For example, in Figure 6.8B Animal

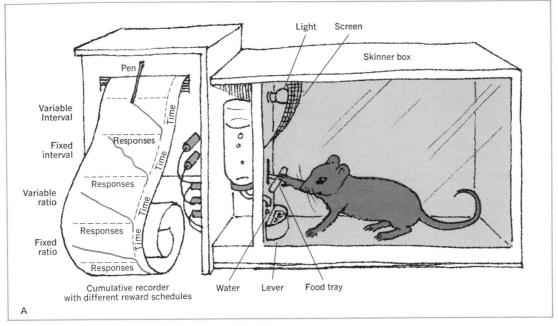

Variable Interval

Fixed interval

Variable ratio

Fixed ratio

Pen

Responses

Responses

Responses

Responses

Time

Time

Time

Time

Time

Cumulative recorder with different reward schedules

Light   Screen

Skinner box

Water   Lever   Food tray

A

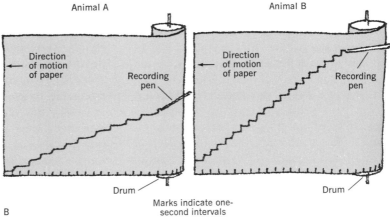

Animal A

Direction of motion of paper →

Recording pen

Drum

Animal B

Direction of motion of paper →

Recording pen

Drum

Marks indicate one-second intervals

B

FIGURE 6.8 *(A) The Skinner box. When the rat presses the bar it may receive a food pellet in the food tray below. The animal's response rate can be studied by examination of the response data recorded on the cumulative recorder. If the reward schedule is varied, the animal's response rate can be controlled. In some laboratories the box and its controls are connected to a computer to regulate the delivery of the reward and collect and analyze the data automatically. (B) Cumulative records of two different animals.*

Focus 6.1

Eight Ways To Elicit a Response

The process of controlling behavior has an outstanding characteristic: when it's effective you can't tell who is controlling whom. — Anonymous

After listening to a lecturer enthusiastically describe the effectiveness of behavior control by operant conditioning methods, a perplexed parent said, "I don't doubt the power of this method, but how can we reinforce behaviors that just *aren't there at all?*" Of course, the simplest answer to the puzzled parent is: you can't. Since operant behavior must occur before it can be reinforced, it's necessary for a parent, trainer, or teacher to modify his or her own behavior first—at least enough to employ a bag of tricks recommended by specialists in operant conditioning to elicit those absolutely essential operant behaviors which in the beginning (as the parent put it) "just aren't there at all."

1. Structuring the Environment. One trick is to change the environment so that opportunities to emit the desired behavior are more easily available, more prominent. For instance, a parent who wants to reshape the eating behavior of an obese child would do well to keep in the house only dietary foods, and toss out the ice cream and the potato chips. Then when the youngster does eat the "right" kinds of food, they should see that secondary reinforcement, such as a pat on the back, is quickly forthcoming.

2. Imitation. This technique may really require self-modification of the trainer or parent since it takes consistent demonstration of the desired behavior for the student. Studies carried out by Albert Bandura of Stanford University show that there is a natural tendency for children to spontaneously imitate the behavior that they see on TV and in those around them. For example, studies show that the likelihood of a person's being a smoker is strongly related to the number of adult smokers who surrounded the person as a child.

3. Verbal Instruction. This method is of little use in housebreaking Rover, but with humans it is often much faster and simpler just to tell a child to clean a room (and, of course, to give a reward after the room is cleaned).

4. Trial and Error. This "you're on your own, kid" method is very similar to many life circumstances in which no instructions are available. A student is given every opportunity to try out all kinds of behavior until the one that leads to a reward or problem solution is found. The disadvantage of this approach is that sometimes the desired behaviors may not show up and frustration will be the principal harvest. The advantage is that when it is successful the subjective satisfaction derived by the learner in solving a problem is its own very powerful reinforcer.

5. Shaping. Rather than wait for the behavior desired, a teacher or parent may reward any behavior that is *even close* to the desired response. By a series of rewarded, successive approximations, a student learns the desired response. This method is described in the opening of this section.

6. Forcing or Guidance. The execution of a desired response can be physically assisted. However, the assistance need not and should not be brutal. This technique is very useful for behaviors that are difficult to describe, such as good penmanship, judo throws, and ballroom dancing.

7. Increasing Motivation. Essentially, this involves threats or promises, either verbal or nonverbal. The promise of Heaven and the threat of Hell have often been used to increase the motivation for "virtuous" behavior. A drawback to this method is that the response may be "mercenary." For example, a child who achieves high grades for promises of money may never learn to enjoy learning for its own sake. This technique is often very effective in getting a behavior started. Once the desired behavior is started, other more appropriate reinforcers can be used.

8. Lowering Restraints. If environmental influences or prior conditioning are inhibiting the response, removing the restraint may bring forth the operant behavior. For instance, a woman who is frightened of men might more likely make social contact with men if given a hypnotic suggestion that would lower her fear reaction.

The successful application of these procedures requires ingenuity on the part of the parent or teacher as well as sensitivity to the needs of the learner. Bear in mind that before you can alter the behavior of any other creature, your own behavior must to some degree be altered.

B is responding at a faster rate than Animal A (the line's slope would be steeper). Perhaps Animal B has been deprived of food for a long time or is receiving a larger quantity of food as a reinforcement.

What Is Reinforcing?

The following five categories provide an overview of the kinds of objects and events that the concept of reinforcement covers: primary reinforcements, secondary reinforcements, responses, feedback, chemical and electrical reinforcement.

Primary Reinforcements. Food, water, or sex-object for an appropriately deprived organism or escape from a painful stimulus can serve as very powerful reinforcers. These kinds of reinforcers help maintain homeostatic needs and enhance survival. **Primary reinforcements** *refer to such things as food, water, or pain avoidance, which can strengthen a response the first time they are used since they are not dependent on prior experience.* Reinforcement can be classified as positive or negative. A positive reinforcement, as we have defined it above, refers to any event that, when presented, strengthens a response that precedes it. *A* **negative reinforcement** *refers to any object or event that, by its removal or termination, strengthens the response that precedes it.* The termination of the pain upon removing the hand from a hot stove reinforces the hand-withdrawal response. We will have more to say about the important distinction between negative reinforcers and the concept of punishment in the next section of this chapter.

Secondary Reinforcements. Money, trophies, gold stars, medals, and pats on the back are all used to exert control over our behavior. The effectiveness of these reinforcers depends on a classical conditioning process. *Any time a neutral stimulus is associated with a primary reinforcer, it acquires the "power" to reinforce behavior. Such learned reinforcers are called* **secondary** *or* **conditioned reinforcers.** The effectiveness of secondary reinforcers, such as money, praise, grades on an exam, are not dependent on biological processes as are primary reinforcers. It is necessary to note that secondary reinforcers can be positive or negative. Almost any stimulus object or event can become a reinforcement through classical conditioning. All that is necessary is the regular association of an event with a primary reinforcer, such as the repeated pairing of a mother's voice with food — the mother's voice then acquires reinforcing properties of its own. Most of the reinforcements that shape and mold us and that we use to influence others fall in this category. The mentally ill patient described in the study that introduced this section of the chapter was rewarded with candy. As the patient began to respond to his environment, words like "good" and "fine," as well as the smiles of the young researcher, all of which were associated with the candy, became secondary reinforcers and could be used in place of the candy.

In some treatment procedures the patients are given tokens as a reward for washing before lunch, cleaning up their rooms, dressing neatly or any other behavior the hospital personnel wanted to condition. These tokens, secondary reinforcers, could then be traded in for primary reinforcers such as candy, food or special privileges, such as watching television. Token economies, as they are called, have produced dramatic behavior changes among mental hospital patients.

The starving woman with anorexia nervosa described in the introductory chapter was also brought back to health by using social reinforcements to reshape her eating behavior.

Responses as Reinforcements. David Premack of the University of California at Santa Barbara carried out some interesting research and stated a principle that now bears his name. Premack gave his animals an opportunity to play and respond without manipulations and pressure while he carefully observed them. Rats would run on their exercise wheels, climb the walls of the cage, eat a little, drink a little, run a little. From observing them, he hit on a very powerful concept. *Any response that has a high frequency or a high probability of occurring could be used to reinforce a low-frequency response.* His studies showed that well-exercised but thirsty rats would learn to run on an exercise wheel to get water, and exercise-deprived rats would learn to drink water to get a chance at the exercise wheel. Some people call this "Grandma's Law" after the countless grandmothers who for ages have been applying this principle to control their grandchildren. When Grandma says, "As soon as you clean up your room you can go out to play, kids," she is applying the Premack Principle. Parents and teachers often use a frequent, preferred activity as a reward for an infrequent, low-preference one.

Feedback. A person who is learning to play the piano must learn the consequences of his hand and finger movements in order to learn how to play. The sound informs the student how well the piece is being mastered. Information about the consequence of a response *(feedback)* can affect the future occurrence of the response and, as such, act as reinforcement. Telling people they are right or wrong is one kind of feedback commonly used to shape behavior.

Chemical and Electrical Reinforcement. As we saw in Chapter 3, the application of electrical stimulation to certain brain centers can act as a reinforcement and can be used to alter responses. The effects of drugs on behavior that we discussed earlier can now be interpreted in terms of reinforcement. Drugs such as LSD, tobacco, marijuana, and heroin reinforce the acquisition behavior that precedes their use.

Extinction, Generalization, and Discrimination

The principles of classical conditioning such as extinction, generalization, discrimination, and spontaneous recovery also apply to operant conditioning.

Extinction. Recall that in classical conditioning, when the unconditioned stimulus (UCS) is withdrawn, the conditioned response (CR) diminishes in strength and finally ceases. Extinction of an operant response will also occur if it is no longer followed by a reinforcement.

Parents are often advised by pediatricians and child psychologists to use extinction procedures to get rid of what they consider to be undesirable behavior in their children. Some children learn that some forms of disruptive operant behavior, such as temper tantrums, nagging, or crying, can get such reinforcements as parental attention, extra desserts, toys, or permission to stay up late. By withdrawing attention and any other reinforcement from these behaviors, they can be extinguished. Elementary school teachers also find that by ignoring many of the disruptive behaviors of their students and paying attention to and rewarding "desirable" behavior, undesirable behavior can be extinguished and desirable behavior strengthened.

Stimulus Generalization and Discrimination. Once an operant response is conditioned to a specific stimulus, it will generalize to similar stimuli. For example, pigeons were conditioned in a Skinner box to peck at a disk with a specific color for their reinforcement. After several training trials, the pigeons were tested on colors that were systematically varied from the training stimuli (see Figure 6.9). The greater the similarity between the test and training stimuli, the stronger the response. By reinforcing the pigeon only for the specific training stimulus, the animal's generalized responses to other stimuli were extinguished and discrimination could be said to have occurred.

Operant discrimination learning takes place when the organism's operant behavior is reinforced only in the presence of a specific stimulus, called the positive discriminative stimulus and symbolized by an S^D. When negative discriminative stimuli

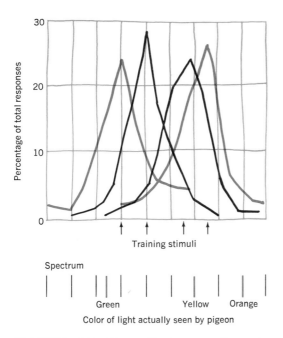

FIGURE 6.9 Generalization gradients in pigeons for four differently colored stimuli (shown by arrows).

are presented, symbolized by an S$^\Delta$, no reinforcement is given. Over a period of time the organism responds only to the S^D and not to the S$^\Delta$.

The adaptive value of generalization becomes clear if you will imagine for a moment the difficulties life would present if many of the skills we have developed to specific stimuli and situations did not generalize. We would have to relearn our driving skills for every new car we drove, relearn typing skills for every new typewriter we used, and relearn our social skills every time there is a variation of our social situation. On the other hand, there may be changes and differences between automobiles, typewriters, and social situations that require us to discriminate and learn new skills. Both mechanisms, generalization and discrimination, are

needed to adapt to constancies as well as changes in our environment.

SCHEDULES OF REINFORCEMENT

Continuous reinforcement *is a term used to refer to situations in which a reinforcement is given for every correct response.* **Partial,** *or* **intermittent, reinforcement** *is a term used to refer to situations in which reinforcement is not given for every correct response.* A reinforcement schedule can be based on time between reinforcements or on the number of responses the organism must make before a reinforcement is given. The reinforcement may also be administered on a fixed basis or on a variable basis. These dimensions yield four schedules, as illustrated in Table 6.4.

Fixed-Interval Schedule (FI). In **fixed-interval schedules** *the reinforcement is administered after a fixed interval of time regardless of the organism's response rate, as long as at least one correct response is made.* For example, an organism may be rewarded once every minute, regardless of its response rate. This schedule produces a distinctive "scalloping" effect on the cumulative response record (see Figure 6.10). The scalloping reflects the immediate drop in response rate after each reinforcement and the gradual buildup just before the next reinforcement.

People who receive their wages at the end of each week or month are on a fixed-interval schedule. Note the "salary spurt" of professional baseball teams toward the end of each season. Many students receive their grades at fixed intervals called semesters. As a student, you can attest to the frantic study and cramming that takes place just before an exam or the end of

TABLE 6.4 **Schedules of reinforcement**

	INTERVAL	RATIO
	Reinforcement is based on time interval.	Reinforcement is based on the number of responses made.
FIXED The reinforcement is regular.	The time interval between reinforcements is constant. (Weekly paycheck, mid-term and final grades)	The number of responses required for a reinforcement is constant. (Piecework and salesmen on commission)
VARIABLE The reinforcement is irregular.	The time interval between reinforcements changes periodically. (Scores on a surprise quiz)	The number of responses required for a reinforcement changes periodically. (Slot machine)

a semester and the slacking off after an exam. Behavior of this sort is quite characteristic of a fixed-interval reinforcement schedule.

Variable-Interval Schedule (VI). **Variable-interval schedules** *provide reinforcements after an irregular or variable interval of time regardless of the organism's response rate, provided that at least one correct response has been made.* For example, a reinforcement may be given 30 seconds after one reinforcement, then 15 seconds later, then after 50 seconds and so on. Such a schedule can be identified in terms of the average time interval between reinforcements (see Figure 6.10).

The grades on surprise quizzes consti-

tute a variable-interval schedule. This schedule produces a more evenly distributed study rate than fixed-interval test schedules.

Fixed-Ratio Schedule (FR). *If the reinforcement is tied to the number of responses (for example, it occurs precisely at every fifth or tenth or even fiftieth response), the schedule is called a* **fixed-ratio reinforcement.** Farm workers paid by the box of fruit picked or seamstresses paid for the number of seams stitched are working on a fixed-ratio schedule. The salesman who works for a percentage of his sales is also on a fixed-ratio reinforcement schedule.

The fixed-ratio schedule produces a

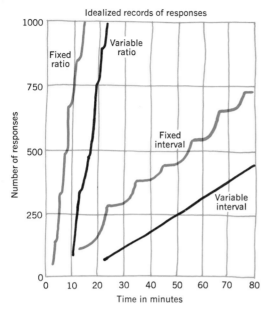

FIGURE 6.10 *Typical response curves for various reinforcement schedules. Each reinforcement schedule generates a characteristic response curve, which is presented in an idealized form. Notice that the ratio schedules produce a more rapid rate of responding than the interval schedules and that the steeper the slope of the curve, the more rapid the rate of responding. The fixed-interval schedule produces a very distinctive "scalloped" curve. This indicates that the organism stops responding after each reinforcement and waits until the next reinforcement is about to occur before responding. All of these schedules lead to greater resistance to extinction than continuous-reinforcement schedules.*

steady, high rate of responding (see Figure 6.10). Pigeons have been kept on a fixed-ratio schedule in which the total number of food pellets used as a reinforcer could barely sustain life. The higher the ratio, the higher the response rate.

Variable-Ratio Schedule (VR). *Under a* **variable-ratio schedule** *the number of re-*

sponses required before a reinforcement is received varies. For example, reinforcement may occur after five responses, then after 17 responses, then after eight responses and so on. Variable ratio schedules are identified by the average ratio of nonreinforced to reinforced responses (see Figure 6.10).

Variable-ratio schedules produce very high and steady rates of responding. Gambling involves a variable-ratio schedule. Slot machines, for example, pay off on a variable-ratio schedule.

Mixed Schedules. Clearly, we live in a world that exposes us to a variety of schedules of reinforcement. Many life experiences involve a mix of schedules. For example, the very important reinforcers of love and affection that family members and friends receive from one another vary from day to day. Often they depend on a person's meeting certain performance standards as well as on the mood of the family members. Each specific reinforcement schedule we are exposed to has a different impact on our behavior.

**Reinforcement Schedules
and Extinction**

The effects of partial reinforcement are very different during and after training. When you are first training a response, partial reinforcement is uneconomical; it is quicker to train a subject with 100 percent reinforcement. But if you have trained under partial reinforcement, the response will continue longer after the reinforcement stops. In other words, partially reinforced responses take a longer time to extinguish.

For an example of how this works, consider the study by Donald J. Lewis and

Carl P. Duncan. They managed to wrest a condemned slot machine from the grasp of a crusading Cook County, Illinois, sheriff and converted it for research purposes. It was a quarter machine, so subjects were provided with a large supply of quarter-size discs and allowed to play the slot machine as long as they pleased. Every quarter slug the subjects won could later be cashed in for a nickel. Lewis and Duncan varied the percentage of reinforcement during the playing period by giving a payoff for one of every three trials for one group, two of every three trials for a second group, and 100 percent of the time for a third group. After the training periods were completed, the payoffs (reinforcements) ceased completely. The subjects were allowed to continue to respond (play the slot machine) until they voluntarily quit. Figure 6.11 presents the number of times the lever was pulled after the conclusion of training for each of the three reinforcement groups, 1/3, 2/3, 3/3. The higher the percentage of reinforcement during training, the quicker the subjects stopped responding when the reinforcement was removed.

The explanation for this is probably related to our earlier discussion of stimulus generalization. The similarity of the test situation to the training situation will determine the probability of response in the test situation. For the partial-reinforcement groups, it is no new thing to have a response with no reinforcement. For the 100-percent-reinforcement group, however, it is a great change. This is one possible explanation for the partial reinforcement group's continuous responding when reinforcement is discontinued.

It is useful to know these facts when training children, adults, or animals. For example, when training a child, heavy, consistent reinforcement is the order of

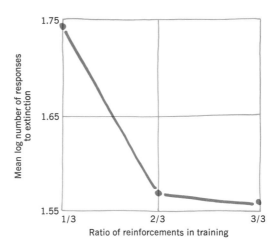

FIGURE 6.11 Number of "slot machine" responses after payoffs (rewards) were terminated in the Lewis and Duncan study.

the day at the beginning. When the child has mastered an act, the ratio of reinforcement is reduced gradually so as to assure the act a long life, even when the parents are not nearby or are fresh out of candy. Gradual reduction of the ratio is important. If the ratio is changed too rapidly, the child, or any other organism, may stop responding. This condition is called *ratio strain*.

Superstitious Behavior

Have you ever carefully watched a baseball pitcher? You may have noticed a number of mannerisms displayed before every pitch that obviously had nothing to do with his performance, such as pulling an ear or twisting or stretching before the windup. If you asked the pitcher about these movements, he would probably tell you that they bring good luck. Analysis of this behavior in terms of operant conditioning explains it this way. Reinforced responses are strengthened. Sometimes responses are reinforced accidentally. That is, the reinforcement just happened to have occurred when the response was emitted but they were unrelated. The pitcher's mannerism may have occurred just before he struck out several batters during a game. Once the mannerism started to be used, it was strengthened by a partial reinforcement schedule of success with successive batters. *Behavior that develops as a consequence of accidental reinforcements is called* **superstitious behavior** — that is, behavior that continues even though it has no effect on reinforcement. Many people have superstitious behavior that arises in this way, such as a gambler's lucky number, a habit of crossing fingers for luck, as well as various facial expressions and body postures. Behaviors of this sort will persist if they are maintained by a partial reinforcement schedule.

C. AVOIDANCE LEARNING, ESCAPE, AND PUNISHMENT

Jeff was an eight-and-one-half-year-old spoiled brat. He was an expert at throwing frequent temper tantrums at the slightest provocation. He had no hesitancy about physically attacking his mother, his teacher, or other children. His parents tried to discipline him by spanking and by withdrawing privileges, but without any success. He was a habitual bed-wetter. He told his mother where to sit and what to do. When he spoke he sounded as if he were reciting lines from memory in an exaggerated, mechanical manner. Jeff also had a number of nervous mannerisms, including a constant rocking motion and head-nodding that gave a very bizarre impression. Because the local public school refused to

accept him, he was enrolled in a private school where he bullied and tattled on the other children. Needless to say, he had no friends, no playmates at school or in his home neighborhood. Jeff was a problem to his parents and his teachers as well as to himself.

Jeff's problems were so severe that his distraught mother was finally persuaded by school authorities to seek psychological and psychiatric help. Jeff was taken to the UCLA Psychiatric Clinic where a treatment program was carried out by Martha E. Bernal and her colleagues.

AVOIDANCE AND ESCAPE CONDITIONING

Initial Interview. Most of the data presented thus far were based on interviews of both parents when the case was accepted by the clinic. In order to gain additional data as well as follow the course of treatment effects, both parents agreed to permit audiotape recordings of home life and videotape recordings of all activities in the clinic. In addition, the mother was asked to keep very careful notes and records of what happened at home with Jeff — what was said, how conflicts ended, and how soon. Since the father was about to make a temporary move to another city, only Jeff and his mother were included in the treatment.

Throughout Jeff's life his parents had had marital difficulties and at the time of referral were on the verge of separation. The audio- and videotape recordings, as well as the mother's very complete diary of her daily interactions with Jeff, provided the basis for analyzing the factors that maintained Jeff's and her behavior. She responded to Jeff in a meek, soft monotone even when trying to discipline him. If she refused to give him what he wanted, he would scream and say, "If you don't, I'll scream," or, "I'll hit you," or, "I'll have an asthma attack." She usually gave in. If she didn't, Jeff would carry out his threats. Jeff controlled his mother absolutely and completely. He was a tyrant and she his meek slave.

Avoidance Conditioning and Negative Reinforcement

The mother's behavior falls in the class of operant avoidance and escape reactions. **Avoidance conditioning** *takes place when an organism's response prevents an aversive, unpleasant event from occurring.* Every time the mother gave into Jeff's demands, she prevented or avoided a very unpleasant scene. Every time this happened, her avoidance behavior was strengthened. The cessation of Jeff's tantrums and screams was a *negative reinforcement.* As defined earlier, any object or event that strengthens a response when it is prevented or terminated by the response is called a negative reinforcement. (The differences between negative reinforcement and punishment will be discussed later.) Any object or event that produces pain or anxiety or is associated with unpleasant consequences can operate as a negative reinforcement.

Escape Conditioning

Escape conditioning *occurs when an organism is already undergoing a painful, aversive experience that is terminated by a response.* For example, when Jeff began to scream, stage a tantrum, or start to wheeze and make the choking sounds of an asthma attack, his mother learned to escape these painful events by giving in to his demands.

Both avoidance and escape conditioning are similar in the sense that they both involve negative reinforcements. The difference between them is this—escape conditioning requires learning a response that terminates the aversive stimuli whereas avoidance conditioning requires learning a response that prevents the aversive stimulus from occurring. The reinforced behaviors are strengthened and tend to become stereotyped and inflexible. Jeff's mother's behavior in response to her son's demands was expressed with very little variation, if any, from day to day. She was stuck in the same self-defeating behavior and she could not change without help. Every time Jeff's mother gave into Jeff, she reduced the fear and anxiety she experienced in anticipating his tantrums and abuses. In this sense, her responses to Jeff were self-reinforcing. Every time she refrained from disciplining Jeff, she avoided an unpleasant situation and her anxiety was reduced. This is why avoidance responses are self-perpetuating. Mechanisms of this kind are the bases of many kinds of maladaptive behavior that will be discussed in Chapter 11.

Treatment Strategy

You no doubt have noticed that in a social interaction, learning is a two-sided affair. While Jeff's behavior and response to his mother shaped her responses, her behavior toward him shaped his behavior. During these interactions, Jeff was having his spoiled-brat behavior strengthened. Every time his mother gave in to his demands with an extra candy bar or toy, his demanding behavior, an operant behavior, was positively reinforced and strengthened. Bernal and her colleagues decided that by coaching Jeff's mother and teaching her to employ the principles of aversive and escape conditioning, she could turn the tables on Jeff and win back control. With that control, she could then extinguish Jeff's spoiled-brat behavior and shape him into a "good boy." In effect, these procedures amount to a kind of social engineering or behavior reprogramming. *The application of learning principles to therapy and control of behavior is called* **behavior modification.**

The first step in training Jeff's mother was to teach her to reduce her verbal output and selectively ignore all of Jeff's sulking, threats, screaming, and abusive activities. These procedures were intended to extinguish Jeff's behavior. The assumption was that her responses to Jeff's abuses reinforced them and that ignoring them would extinguish them.

The second step was to help her set up maternal behaviors that could serve as cues for negative reinforcement. She was to frown, warn, and express anger and associate these with vigorous spanking if his abuse did not stop. It was hoped that the anger, tone of voice, and warnings (discriminative stimuli) would take on the properties of a conditioned (or secondary) negative reinforcer by virtue of their repeated pairings with the primary negative reinforcer of spanking. In a manner analogous to secondary positive reinforcement (see previous section), any neutral cue can attain reinforcement properties by association with a primary (in this case, a primary negative) reinforcer. A painful spanking for a child associated with angry tone of voice, warnings, and frowns can make these cues very effective secondary negative reinforcers.

If you feel hostile to Jeff by now, you probably are thinking that he deserved it. But be careful not to jump to conclusions about punishment. We will have more to say about this later. The conditioned nega-

tive reinforcers, once developed, could then be used to control and shape Jeff's behavior. Jeff could learn to *escape* or *avoid* the negative reinforcers his mother presented any time she disapproved of his actions. You might ask why spanking hadn't worked in the past? Those spankings usually occurred in moments of extreme anger and frustration. They were unpredictable events and had not been consistently associated with cues that Jeff could distinguish as discriminative stimuli. In addition, in the past the mother often threatened Jeff with spankings that were never delivered. Only when spanking is reliably and consistently associated with a warning or recognizable anger does it have any useful control function as a negative reinforcement.

The third step was to train the mother to identify and positively reinforce Jeff's acceptable behavior. In the past, she rarely expressed her love or warmth toward Jeff. In fact, she said she did not like him and was terrified of him. It was hoped that ultimately she could gain and maintain control by the use of positive reinforcements while minimizing the use of negative reinforcements.

Treatment Procedure and Results. Martha Bernal and her associates divided the treatment steps into lessons that they called interventions; taken together, these interventions constituted the treatment. Each intervention took place in a room at the clinic and was videotaped. Before each session, the mother was instructed in what she was to do. During the session, a series of tone signals reminded her to carry out her previous instructions. Following each session, the therapist would warmly praise her for the adequate aspects of her performance. The videotapes were used to

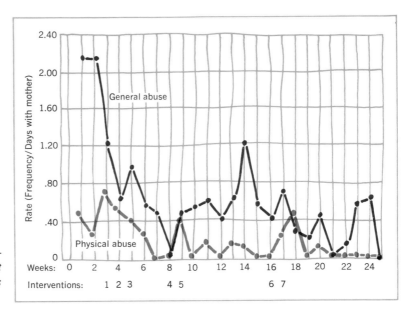

FIGURE 6.12 The pattern of Jeff's abuse at home based on records kept by his mother.

help her identify inadequate performances and demonstrate where new control behavior could be incorporated.

The behaviors of each session were scored by trained observers. You can get an overview of what went on by examining Table 6.5 and Figure 6.12 which summarize the data and indicate the nature of the mother's instructions. The pre-treatment sessions serve to provide a baseline or reference point to compare with later behavior and evaluate the effects of the treatments. You'll notice the dramatic changes in the frequency of Jeff's abuse and the increase in the mother's control and expression of affection. During Intervention I, when she was instructed to ignore Jeff's abuse, she was severely abused, including being bitten on her hand, but she stuck to her instructions. By Intervention 5, the mother had learned to express anger by words and by facial expression. Jeff indicated that he appreciated her anger after his third spanking, which occurred when he refused to sit down on her

command. "Are you angry?" he asked as he sat.

The treatment continued for 25 weeks and there was a gradual improvement in their relationship. The mother showed increasing control, self-esteem, and confidence and Jeff indulged in less spoiled-brat behavior. Changes in Jeff's general and physical abuse of his mother are illustrated in Figure 6.12. This is based on the careful home records kept by the mother. Careful record-keeping was important for two reasons. It served to document events and it reinforced the mother by showing the success her new behaviors produced. As therapy progressed, she lost her fear of the boy and gradually grew to like him. The change in behavior is illustrated by the following excerpts from the mother's diary.

After 14 weeks of therapy:

On the freeway, I started to sing to myself. Jeff told me to stop, as he always has, and to turn off the radio. I realized I was being ordered by

TABLE 6.5 **Jeff's behavior during treatment (the first three interventions)**

SESSION AND INSTRUCTION	JEFF ABUSES	MOTHER IGNORES ABUSE	PERCENTAGE OF ABUSES IGNORED	PERCENTAGE OF SESSION MOTHER IGNORES ABUSES	NUMBER OF COMMANDS JEFF OBEYS	PERCENTAGE OF SESSION MOTHER AFFECTIONATE
Pretreatment						
No Instruction	9	1	11	3	0 of 4	0
Intervention 1						
Ignore Abuse	13	13	100	73	–	0
Intervention 2						
Spank if He Hits You	13	11	85	72	–	0
Intervention 3						
Differentiate Positive and Negative Response	13	13	100	43	1 of 2	7
Posttreatment						
No Instruction	2	2	100	7	2 of 2	20

(From Bernal et al., *J. clin. Psychol.*, 32, 1968)

my child, so I told him, loudly, firmly, and without misunderstanding that I would sing anytime I felt like it. Instant tantrum. I ignored him and continued humming. He begged me to stop, and finally asked, "Why can't you stop when I tell you?" I said because I was the boss and if I felt like doing something, I would. No argument, he calmed down and asked for donuts at the drive-in. I stopped and we got a different order from the last time. He questioned the selection, but didn't argue or pout. "Okay, mother, whatever you feel like," he said. I very nearly choked.

After 18 weeks of therapy:

He asked to talk to me. He asked if he could take piano lessons. I told him he had a bigger project first—learning to get along with others, including children—and in a few years perhaps he could take lessons. As I went out the door he said, "I love you." I replied the same and told him how pleased I was with him. After the door was closed I heard him say to himself, "She's swell! I feel great!" (From Bernal, et al., 1968.)

The treatment program was considered successful from the point of view of the mother's control and the affection growing between parent and child. Unfortunately, the authors were not able to determine how effective the treatment was in changing Jeff's behavior at school. However, other research studies using such methods in school classrooms have found them just as effective. These methods have been successfully applied to a wide variety of people with behavior problems—juvenile delinquents, the mentally retarded in hospitals, and problem children in home settings (like Jeff).

PUNISHMENT

Negative reinforcement should not be confused with punishment. In negative reinforcement, an organism's response avoids or terminates an aversive stimulus and the response thereby gains in strength. *In* **punishment,** *the organism's response actually initiates an aversive stimulus and the response is thereby suppressed for a while.* Table 6.6 contrasts and compares negative and positive reinforcement and punishment. The distinctions among them are important for each has a different consequence.

TABLE 6.6   **Comparison of types of reinforcement of operant responses**

POSITIVE REINFORCEMENT OF OPERANT RESPONSE
Response ──────────────→ Positive Reinforcement ──────→ Response Strengthening
NEGATIVE REINFORCEMENT
   Escape:
Aversive Stimuli ──────────→ Response ────────────────→ Escape from Aversive Stimuli
   Avoidance:
Discriminative Stimuli ──────→ Response ────────────────→ Avoidance of Aversive Stimuli
(Cues for Aversive
Event)
PUNISHMENT
Response ──────────────→ Aversive Stimulus ──────────→ Response Suppression

**Five Principles
of Effective
Punishment**

When carefully used, punishment provides a very effective method of controlling behavior. Let's examine the list of punishment principles developed by Nathan Azrin and William Holz. These are based on their own experiments as well as their extensive review of the research literature.

Immediacy. The sooner an organism is punished, the more effective the punishment. Delay of a punishment, as is the case with positive or negative reinforcement, tends to diminish its effectiveness. Jeff's mother was instructed to spank him as soon as he deviated from her command.

Intensity. One of the most important effects of punishment is that it suppresses the behavior that precedes it. The greater the severity or intensity of the punishment, the greater its suppressive effects. In a study involving pigeons, George Reynolds found that the greater the intensity of the punishment, the greater the suppression of

the response (see Figure 6.13), but the response still returned when the punishment was removed.

There is a point, however, when the punishment intensity is great enough to completely eliminate the response. Jules Masserman, for example, found that when hungry cats were air-blasted in the face as they approached their food dish, they stopped responding. Many of the cats starved rather than approach the dish again. What probably occurred was that the cats developed a fear reaction classically conditioned to the food dish. This shows a very severe risk involved in using punishment. Whenever punishment is effective, it may produce side effects that can be as "bad" as the behavior it was supposed to eliminate. Children may react by avoiding or attacking their punisher.

In the case of Jeff, his mother was instructed to spank him just hard enough to suppress abusiveness and show that she was serious. With practice she was able to determine just how much of a spanking was needed: intense enough to suppress, but not enough to bring on undesirable side effects. The suppressive effect of punishment provides an opportunity to teach

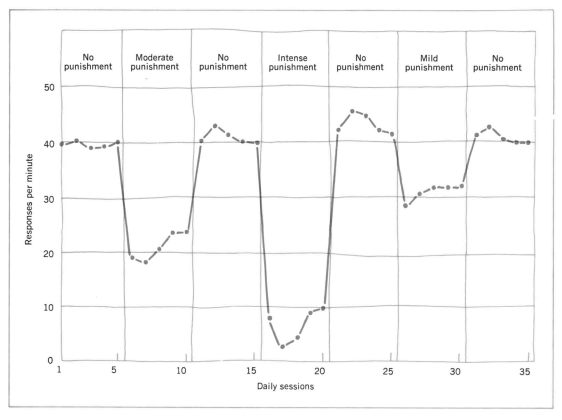

FIGURE 6.13 The effect of varying degrees of punishment on response rate. Notice that when punishment is removed the response rate returns to its prepunishment rate.

an organism more appropriate responses. For example, after Jeff learned to obey his mother to avoid spanking, his mother was instructed to reward Jeff for good behavior.

Consistency. During the early shaping of any response, continuous reinforcement, positive or negative, is more effective in building response strength than intermittent schedules. This holds true for punishment, too. If the incorrect response is punished every time it occurs, the effectiveness of the punishment is increased.

Suddenness. Punishment is most effective when it is presented at the maximum intended level on the first and succeeding trials. Punishment loses its effectiveness if its intensity begins at a low level and is escalated for each succeeding trial. Slow escalation gives an organism time to adapt and the punishment loses its effectiveness. It was essential that Jeff's spanking hurt him enough on the first trial for him to realize that his mother's warnings and commands were to be taken seriously thereafter.

Brevity. Punishments must be delivered during a very brief time period. When the time for delivery is prolonged, the organism can adapt and recover from its effects. Recovery is particularly likely at lower levels of intensity.

A Word of Caution

As indicated above, punishment can be a very effective behavior-control method, but it must be handled with intelligence to prevent the undesirable side effects of fear or hostility. Positive reinforcement methods should probably be tried first and, when they are exhausted, the use of punishment can be explored. Unfortunately, in daily life, parents use punishment under the most inappropriate conditions: when they are tired, frustrated, or angry, and without any prior planning. Under such conditions, the principle of systematic use of reinforcements is violated, with unfortunate consequences for both parents and children.

For a discussion of one point of view regarding the implications of behavior control for individuals and for society, see Focus 6.2: Moving Beyond Freedom and Dignity.

D. BIOLOGICAL FEEDBACK CONTROL

LEARNING TO CONTROL "INVOLUNTARY" FUNCTIONS

South American Indians discovered that if they dipped their arrow points in a blackish, resinlike substance called *curare,* victims impaled by these arrows died quickly of respiratory failure. Curare is alarmingly effective in blocking nerve impulses to muscles; consequently, the muscles of victims' bodies (including those muscles involved in breathing) become *totally* paralyzed. Other bodily functions continue more or less as usual. For example, human beings who have been brave enough to undergo experimental injections and artificial respiration for research purposes, report continued clear consciousness. If an animal such as a rat is artificially respirated, it will recover completely from three milligrams of curare in about three to four hours.

This potent drug has proved to be very useful in research on learning. Leo DiCara and Neal Miller at Rockefeller University used it to paralyze a rat so as to do away with the rat's muscle movements. Having thus quieted the rat, and maintaining it with artificial respiration, they attached highly sensitive photoelectric cells to the rat's ears. A photoelectric cell converts light into electrical energy that can easily be measured. Light passing through the tissues of the rat's ear struck these cells. If the blood vessels of the rat's ear were relaxed (dilated), the amount of light coming through the ears was increased. When the blood vessels of the ear were constricted, the amount of light was reduced. Thus DiCara and Miller had arranged things so that they could instantly measure, for both ears, vasoconstriction and vasodilation (*vas* is Latin for vessel).

They prepared this peculiar ensemble of animate and inanimate materials in order to attempt what at first may seem a rather foolish and specialized task: *to train the blood vessels in the rat's left ear to dilate while those in the right ear did not!*

The Operant Control of Blood Vessel Dilation

In this operant conditioning experiment, then, the sensitive photoelectric cells on the rat's ears were arranged so that they

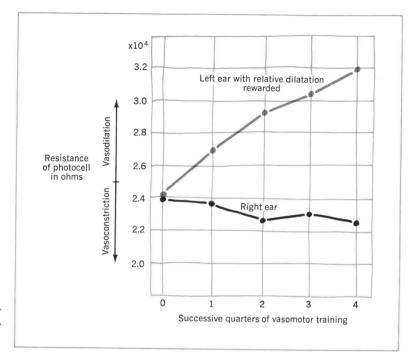

FIGURE 6.14 Operant conditioning of dilation of blood vessels in the ears of curarized rats.

could register the response under study: very tiny changes in the vasodilation of the blood vessels. Because the researchers wanted to increase the probability of this response, each time the left cells registered a dilation relative to those in the right ear, they needed to have a reward that was automatically given to the rat. As can be imagined, it was hard to find a reward for this totally paralyzed animal; obviously food and drink were out. The experimenters hit on an ideal solution. When the left photoelectric cell registered dilation, a pulse of electrical stimulation was directly delivered to the pleasure center of the brain (as with the Olds and Milner rat, Chapter 3C). In other words, the rat was being rewarded for the response of dilating blood vessels in its lcft car. As conditioning continued and the number of dilation-reward sequences mounted, the blood vessels of the rat's left ear actually became more and more

dilated. (See Figure 6.14.) The rat *learned* this minutely specific response of the left ear. Meanwhile, as you can see from Figure 6.14, the right ear was learning nothing. These results were not by-products of overall changes in heart rate or blood pressure because these would affect both ears equally.

Using similar conditioning techniques, Miller and his associates were able to train the rats' heart-beat rate to increase or decrease depending on the light level of their surroundings. They also trained rats to avoid electric shocks to their tails by increasing or decreasing their heart rates. Miller and Banuazizi measured rats' intestinal contractions "with a little balloon filled with water thrust approximately four centimeters beyond the anal sphincter." By rewarding with direct brain stimulation, they found they could train either increased or decreased agitation of this portion of

Focus 6.2

Moving Beyond Freedom and Dignity

No mere text on behavioral principles would have been likely to cause the stir that followed the 1971 publication of B. F. Skinner's *Beyond Freedom and Dignity*. With this book a leading American research psychologist stepped out of academia onto the center stage of current political and social affairs. This excursion was not the first for the Harvard professor; in his famous 1948 novel, *Walden Two*, he had fictionally portrayed his version of a Utopia, which was based on the principle of operant behavior control. In 1971 Skinner made explicit what *Walden Two* had strongly suggested: that the assumptions underlying contemporary Western culture not only are unscientific but also must be discarded if the culture is to flourish or even to survive. The controversy was aroused because, besides criticizing current society and the traditional concepts of freedom and dignity, Skinner offered an alternative to modern society based on the results of his findings. For Skinner, the solution to current social problems requires the systematic application of the principles of operant conditioning. Whatever we are as individuals is a function of our reinforcement history. Changing the behavior of an individual or of the individuals making up a society requires the systematic social control of the rewards and the conditions of reinforcement.

Skinner believes that even now the principles of operant conditioning and reinforcement control the behavior of us all, but that people in our current society unwittingly apply conditioning principles in ways that are haphazard or even destructive to our chances of survival as a culture. Skinner singles out "freedom" and "dignity". as reflecting two major ways in which society is "killing" itself by unscientific notions that some events, such as our personal creative behaviors, are unlike all other events in that they have no causes or are uncontrolled. He believes that this notion arose in the "literature of freedom" in past ages. This was designed to promote rebellion against authorities, whether civil or religious or intellectual, who employed primarily aversive reinforcements or punishment to promote and control the behaviors they wanted. Although this literature of freedom served well enough to get men's backs out from under the slavedriver's lash, it has outlived its usefulness. Now it has become a block to personally and socially useful controls over positive reinforcement. To Skinner, "true freedom" is a myth; an individual may be free from pain or fear or other aversive stimuli, but to be free in the sense of being truly uncontrolled is a kind of chaos that cannot exist in an orderly universe.

What keeps this fictitious "freedom" alive is the social reinforcement of "dignity," the appearance of self-control in the behavior of an individual. "Any evidence that a person's behavior may be attributed to external circumstances seems to threaten his dignity or worth." We offer little credit for achievements that are not due to "personal control" and, conversely, a disturbed "state of mind" is valid legal grounds for an acquittal or a minimal sentence. The emphasis is on personal, autonomous responsibility, with behavior arising from within the individual and not from the environment. To Skinner, an extreme environmentalist, this is an unrealistic distinction. He feels that nearly all of human behavior is learned and shaped by its consequences. A criminal, a secretary, a congresswoman, and an unskilled laborer all learn their behaviors according to the same principles of operant conditioning. For each of them, all of the reward contingencies originated primarily in the environment. Therefore, while we may judge some behaviors to be desirable and others undesirable, personal autonomy has no place in the picture. It is simply that behaviors that effectively conceal their environmental source, such as a poet's lyrics or an artist's painting or a hero's sacrifice, are more socially admired and, therefore, reinforced. But such "autonomy" can be likened to a scout who covers his tracks; although he has spent considerable effort in hiding his path, we may be confident that he walked to his current location like anyone else. The rewarding of apparent "autonomy" not only promotes wasteful, energy-consuming efforts, but it also results in practices that are inhumane. An example of this is the punishment given criminals for being "bad people." In Skinner's world, such punishment entirely misses the point: "the problem is to induce people not to be good but to behave well." Society, he feels, must modify and shape behavior into more acceptable forms and not classify people as "good" or "bad" and give them their "just desserts." Society produces the criminal and the saint, the hero and the coward, through the application of the same learning principles. Skinner believes that, until we recognize this fact and begin to apply the principles of learning to shape our society, we will continue to be faced with the social problems that truly demean all humans and threaten our survival.

Skinner's critics have asked who will control the controller under his system? Who will decide on the social behavior to be selectively shaped and reinforced? In response to these questions Skinner asks another: who controls them now and with what consequences?

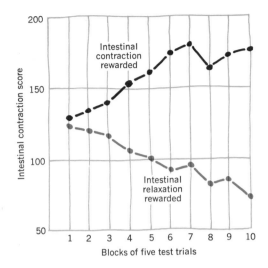

FIGURE 6.15 *Operant conditioning of intestinal response of rats.*

the rat's gut (see Figure 6.15). The number of stomach contractions, blood pressure, and brain wave activity are other "involuntary" responses in rats that Miller and his associates have brought under the control of learning techniques. The implications of this study (part of a large-scale program of research) are that many specific disturbed and diseased functions of the body may become amenable to effective treatment and control by learning techniques.

Can humans indeed also have their involuntary emotional and physiological responses controlled in this manner? Miller thinks so: "I believe," he said, "that in this respect they are as smart as rats." In this section we will relate the research and application of the principles of learning to an exciting field called biological feedback control. **Biological feedback control** *consists of providing an organism with information about a bodily response (heart-rate, skin temperature, blood pressure) by*

some mechanical or electronic means so the organism can learn to adjust or change that response.

Operant Control of Autonomic Responses

The possibility of using operant conditioning techniques to train involuntary responses controlled by the autonomic nervous system has provocative medical applications. Consider the ulcer patient who might learn to inhibit the secretion of acid into his tender stomach or the patient with dangerously high blood pressure who might be trained to lower his blood pressure at will. All of this could be accomplished without drugs and their irritating, if not dangerous, side effects. Clearly the study of the operant conditioning of these functions could potentially reap practical as well as theoretical benefits. Experimenters around the world began to attempt to determine the conditions that would make possible the control of these involuntary functions. But the problem was not an easy one to solve, as we shall see next.

The Mediation of Autonomic Control. A Russian, Lisina, reported in 1961 that via operant techniques she had trained the dilation of blood vessels. She was careful to point out, however, that this training might actually be the result of an indirect effect. Without knowing it, she may have actually trained a relaxing muscular response or a breathing response, which may in turn have resulted in dilation of blood vessels. In other words, it was highly possible that the operant conditioning was only affecting voluntary muscular responses. These may have brought on the involuntary responses as side effects. This type of indirect effect, besides being theoretically unsatisfying, is rather inefficient from a practical viewpoint since it produces only small changes. The search took on new dimensions. Not only did experimenters have to produce reliable changes in involuntary functions by operant techniques, they also had to guard against the possibility that they were only getting a side effect resulting from voluntary functions.

Figure 6.16 summarizes how operant conditioning could produce autonomic nervous system changes. Figure 6.16A shows *direct* heart-rate conditioning of the autonomic nervous system. Figure 6.16B shows indirect changes whereby reinforcement of muscle activity produces heart rate changes. In order to demonstrate a direct learning effect, it is necessary to eliminate the skeletomuscular activity.

Jay Trowill and Neal Miller decided to attempt to train animals that were heavily dosed with curare, because it is impossible for the muscular responses in such animals to cause heart rate increases indirectly. While an animal is under curare, only the voluntary muscles are blocked. The autonomic nervous system functions normally and is available for learning. Trowill and Miller decided to train some rats to increase and some to decrease their heart rates using electrical stimulation of the "pleasure center" of the brain as their reward (see Figure 6.17, page 224).

The Heart Can Learn. While at rest, human hearts operate at an average of 80 beats per minute. A rat's heart beats at about five times that rate. If Trowill and Miller were going to reinforce a faster rate, they had the difficult task of monitoring these rapid little heartbeats (about seven per second), registering when a single interval between beats varied from a sev-

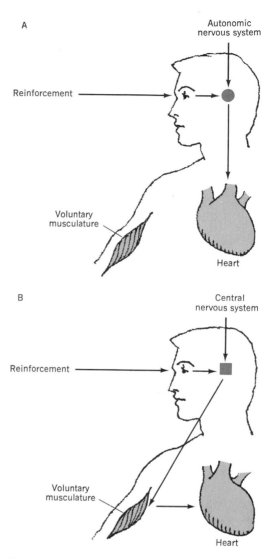

FIGURE 6.16 *A comparison of the (A) direct and (B) indirect bases of biological feedback control.*

enth of a second, and delivering a reinforcement to the rat before the next heartbeat took place one seventh of a second later. This feat was accomplished by feeding the heart beat signal into a computer. The machine was programmed to note the inter-

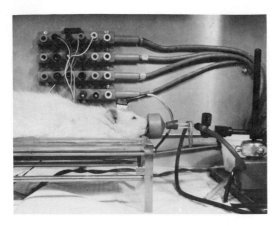

FIGURE 6.17 After a rat is paralyzed with curare, a respirator keeps it breathing while electrode implants to the pleasure center of its brain are used to reinforce change in heart rate.

beat interval and instantly to deliver a reward for a certain slow interval (for one group of rats) or for a certain fast interval (for another group of rats). The results were consistent. Of the 19 rats rewarded for speeding up their heart rate, 15 responded appropriately. Of the 17 rats rewarded for slowing their heart rate, 15 responded appropriately. The possibility that operant conditioning could affect autonomic nervous system functioning was now tentatively established. What was most important was that the beginnings of a good technique had been developed.

Leo DiCara and Neal Miller wondered if the amount of change could be increased by improved conditioning techniques. Trowill and Miller could only achieve about a five percent increase or decrease. DiCara and Miller changed the procedure by instituting shaping (the same technique the graduate student used to bring the mental patient down to the basement laboratory). Rather than simply reward a rat every time its heart rate reached a given level, they rewarded minute changes in the desired direction and then required further changes before giving further reinforcement. The computer was programmed so that (for one group) it delivered a reinforcement if an interbeat interval was two percent faster than the resting level. When this new level (rest + two percent) was established, it was considered the baseline and the computer waited for a further two percent increase before delivering a further reinforcement. The same procedure was used to train a decreasing heart rate. The results are graphed in Figure 6.18. The changes are quite remarkable. Could such changes have practical significance? Well, for some of the rats put through this type of procedure, the consequences have been rather significant. Miller reports that "while none of the 40 rats that we have rewarded for speeding up their heart rates died during the experiment, 7 of the 40 rats that we have

FIGURE 6.18 Operant conditioning of the heart rate increase and decrease of curarized rats.

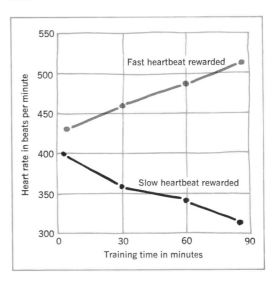

rewarded for slowing down their heart rates had their hearts stop and died."

Because curare was used, it seemed clear that voluntary muscle responses were not mediating the responses of the autonomic nervous system. It was also clear that the changes brought about by operant conditioning (under curare) could be quite dramatic and might be used therapeutically with humans.

Neal Miller and his group at Rockefeller University are puzzling through the problems of applying these methods to treat individuals with disturbances in heart functions. One difficulty is that the effects with human subjects have not been as great as they have been with the curarized rats. However, when the experiments have been run on rats without curare, the effects are also not great. They are at the level of the effects with humans. It is not that humans lack the rats' cleverness in their autonomic nervous system; the curare is the crucial difference. The normal animal (human or otherwise) has a multitude of muscular stimuli interfering with the learning of autonomic changes. Curarized animals are completely free of such interference. They cannot move their eyes or their heads. Their musculature is completely and utterly relaxed. Neal Miller has compared their condition with the trance state of yogis who have genuine control over some of their internal functions. Other laboratories and clinics throughout the country are also experimenting with biological feedback control. Let's turn now to a brief summary of some of the exciting applications of this method.

Heartbeat Control. Premature ventricular contractions (PVC's) are irregularities in the heartbeat that can lead to sudden death if not brought under control. Bernard Engle and his associate, Theodore Weiss, teach their patients to control their heartbeat using biological feedback. Electrodes taped onto the patient's chest pick up the electrical activities of the heart, these are amplified and sent to a computer. The computer analyzes the heartbeat and turns on a red light when it is too fast, a green light when it is too slow and a yellow light when it is just right. The patient is told to follow the "traffic signals" and drive his own heart: speed up when green, slow down when red, and hold steady when yellow. The patients could not describe how they did it, but, after many days of training, they could control their heartbeat even when they were sent home.

Migraine Headache Treatment. A doctor at the Menninger Clinic led his patient into the treatment room. The patient, who had been suffering from very painful migraine headaches for years, was asked to seat himself comfortably before an electronic thermal-feedback instrument. Migraine headaches are caused by increased blood pressure in the scalp's vessels. The temperature of the scalp is increased by blood flow through these vessels. The lower the temperature, the lower the blood flow. Electrodes that picked up temperature changes were placed on the patient's finger and forehead. The patient was instructed to concentrate on the instrument and try to get the temperature reading of his forehead to be less than that of his finger. In other words, he was to cool his forehead and warm up his finger. Successful patients were able to produce temperature differences of from three to 15 degrees after several hours of training. The most exciting finding was that 74 percent of the 28 patients studied thus far reported a significant decline in headache symptoms and severity even when they were disconnected from the equipment.

OTHER APPLICATIONS AND IMPLICATIONS OF FEEDBACK
Alpha Waves and Meditation

The **alpha rhythm,** *a slow, even EEG wave,* has been known since the 1920s and *is generally associated with a state of relaxed, alert awareness.* In the late 1960s, the principle of biofeedback was applied by Joseph Kamiya of the Langley Porter Neuropsychiatric Institute of San Francisco to teach subjects to control voluntarily and "turn on" their own alpha rhythms. In 1971 Akira Kasamatsu and Tomio Hirai of the University of Tokyo reported that the Zen monks they had tested displayed large and consistent amounts of alpha rhythm during meditation. In view of the fact that Zen discipline requires years of effort, whereas biofeedback training often resulted in the successful control of alpha rhythms in 30 minutes or less, it seemed that Americans had discovered a streamlined method of attaining "enlightenment."

The claims of "instant enlightenment" quickly became embarrassing to serious investigators. Biofeedback machines quickly became standard equipment for self-help schools that had formerly specialized in the "power of positive thinking." Commercial, so-called "mind control institutes" freely employ the term "alpha-wave," implying that it can be used for any purpose from relaxation to the development of a flawless memory to "cosmic consciousness." Perhaps the worst part of the irresponsible publicity is that serious researchers are not at all sure yet of the potential of biofeedback control of brain waves, and exaggerated claims can only hinder their research efforts.

Subvocalization

One of the many factors that may contribute to poor reading ability is subvocalization. **Subvocalization** *is the habit of mouthing words silently while reading.* This habit seriously limits reading speed to about 150 words per minute and quickly produces reader fatigue. Curtis D. Hardyck, Lewis F. Petrinovich, and Delbert W. Ellsworth have developed a relatively simple way to eliminate this habit. The student is seated in a comfortable chair, and small, metallic electrodes are placed on each side of the Adam's apple. The electrodes are hooked up to an **electromyogram (EMG),** *a device that amplifies the electrical activity of muscles,* in this case the throat muscles involved in speech. To demonstrate the EMG, the student is asked to whisper. The muscle movement is immediately detected, amplified, and turns on a tone. As soon as the student can turn the tone on and off easily, the training begins. The student is asked to read while keeping the tone off as much as possible. At first, this task is difficult, but as treatment progresses, the student finds the tone can be kept off and the subvocalization problem is solved. Most people who subvocalize are unaware of it, and even if told about it, subvocalizers cannot control (or eliminate) it without feedback training.

The Implications of Biological Feedback Control

Since stomach contractions, blood pressure, and the other twitches, wheezes, and gushes of our internal organs can be affected so remarkably and specifically by conditioning, it seems highly probable that psychosomatic bodily ailments are learned (see Chapter 4C). If they are learned, perhaps they can be unlearned; or, more correctly, perhaps a new, more functional response can be learned to replace the ailment. Indeed, there is no need to restrict the field to ailments that may have been learned. Certain heart and stomach conditions, for example, are very likely candidates for this therapy. Cardiac arrythmias (a heartbeat irregularity) and aspects of epilepsy have already been treated by this method with some success. In work with humans, instead of the somewhat dangerous curare, hypnosis may be used to reduce interfering stimuli and responses. People may be able to learn how to control at will what are now called the "involuntary" responses of the inner body. They may be able to learn how to direct states of consciousness without drugs. They may be able to learn to inhibit nonproductive gastrointestinal upset and muscular tension.

In a modest way, we are entering an age that may usher in a psychobiological revolution.

SUMMARY

A. **Classical Conditioning**

1. **Classical conditioning** (page 191) can be described as learning through stimulus substitution whereby the functions of the original unconditioned stimulus (UCS) are acquired by the new, conditioned stimulus (CS) through repeated associations.

2. The **unconditioned stimulus (UCS)** is any object or event that originally produces the **unconditioned response (UCR)**. In Pavlov's experiment, the UCS was meat powder and the UCR was the dog's salivation. The **conditioned stimulus (CS)** is any stimulus that, through association with the UCS, has come to have the "power" to produce the response; when the response can be produced by the CS, it is referred to as the **conditioned response (CR)** (see page 191 for all terms).

3. Many emotional responses to neutral stimuli are the result of everyday instances of classical conditioning.

4. **Extinction** (page 193) is the process of stopping a conditioned response by omitting the UCS.

5. **Spontaneous recovery** (page 193) consists of the return of a response after extinction trials without further reinforcement.

6. **Stimulus generalization** (page 194) means that once an organism learns to respond to a specific stimulus, it will also respond with that response to similar stimuli. If the similarity between stimuli is *learned,* the term used is **secondary generalization** (page 196).

7. The **gradient of stimulus generalization** (page 195) is a graphed line that displays the decline in response strength as the difference between the conditioned stimulus and the test stimulus increases.

8. Inappropriate responses to similar stimuli are the result of **over-generalization** (page 196). This is a failure in learning to **discriminate** (page 196) between stimuli.

(B) Operant Conditioning

9. In **operant conditioning** (page 200), obtaining a reinforcement is dependent on the behavior of the organism. By controlling the type and frequency of the reinforcement, behaviors can be increased or decreased or shaped.

10. **Shaping** (page 200) is a process in which the experimenter rewards responses that more and more closely approximate the desired behavior until the desired behavior occurs.

11. A **positive reinforcement** (page 201) may be any object or event that when presented can increase the probability of a response, or **operant** (page 201), that precedes it.

12. A **negative reinforcement** (page 205) refers to any object or event that strengthens the response that precedes it by its removal or termination.

13. The term **primary reinforcement** (page 204) refers to such things as food, water, and pain avoidance, which can strengthen a response the first time they are used. Their reinforcing value is not the result of prior experiences.

14. **Secondary** or **conditioned reinforcers** (page 205) are originally neutral stimuli that, by association with primary reinforcers, have acquired the "power" to reinforce behavior.

15. Various schedules of reinforcement have been shown to affect response rate and resistance to extinction. Schedules of reinforcement are based on varying the time interval—**fixed-interval** (page 207) and **variable-interval schedules** (page 208)—or the number of responses required—**fixed-ratio** (page 208) or **variable-ratio schedules** (page 209)—before the reinforcement is delivered.

16. Accidental reinforcements can produce **superstitious behavior** (page 211).

C. Avoidance Learning, Escape, and Punishment

The case of Jeff was used to illustrate the principles of avoidance, escape, and punishment.

17. **Avoidance conditioning** (page 212) takes place when an organism's response prevents an aversive, unpleasant event from occurring.

18. **Escape conditioning** (page 212) takes place when an organism is already undergoing a painful, aversive experience that is terminated by a response.

19. **Punishment** (page 215) is an effective means of diminishing unde-

sired behavior when it is immediate, intense, consistent, sudden, and brief in duration. However, positive reinforcement methods should be used when possible to avoid the side effects of fear or hostility that often result from aversive conditioning.

D. Biological Feedback Control

20. Recent research has indicated that the responses of the autonomic nervous system can be modified by operant conditioning.
21. **Biological feedback control** (page 222) consists of providing an organism with information about a bodily response (heart rate, skin temperature, blood pressure) by some mechanical or electronic means so that the organism can adjust or change that response.

Chapter
Seven
Verbal
Learning,
Memory,
and
Forgetting

There have been many cases in the history of science in which the accident, illness, or abnormality of an individual has provided an insight into normal functioning. We have already mentioned several such instances: the individuals who had the corpus callosum severed and Mr. S. B., the blind man who recovered his sight. We will now introduce you to two more cases, those of Mr. R. and of Mr. S.

Mr. R. was a 27-year-old skilled worker who gradually found himself being cut off from his job and social life because of his frequent and severe epileptic seizures. Drug therapy was not effective in helping him. Because of his desperate condition a final-resort operation was decided on. From clinical and EEG examinations it was determined that his condition was in part due to a disturbance in the temporal lobe of his brain (see Figure 3.8). On the first of September in 1953 disruptive sections of the temporal lobe were removed from both hemispheres. The operation was highly successful; his epileptic seizures were relieved. Unexpectedly a new complication occurred. He had apparently lost the ability to record new experiences in his memory. Brenda Milner, at McGill University, studied him 20 months later and reported that:

He gave the date as March, 1953 (it was of course May, 1955) and his age as 27. He knew that he had had a brain operation, but I think only because the possibility had been entertained for so many years before the operation was actually performed. He kept saying, "It is as though I am just waking up from a dream; it seems as though it had just happened."

As far as we can tell, this man has retained little, if anything of events subsequent to operation, although his IQ rating is actually slightly higher than before. Ten months before I examined him, his family had moved from their old house to one a few blocks away on the same

street. He still has not learned the new address though remembering the old one perfectly, nor can he be trusted to find his way home alone. He does not know where objects constantly in use are kept; for example, his mother still has to tell him where to find the lawn-mower even though he may have been using it only the day before. She also states that he will do the same jigsaw puzzle day after day without showing any practice effect and that he will read the same magazines over and over again without finding their contents familiar. It is only with great effort that he can remember a number or a phrase which has just been read to him. If the slightest distraction occurs he loses the memory of the number or phrase. If he is introduced to someone and then encounters the person one hour later, he behaves as though they had never met. (From Milner, 1959.)

Milner has studied other patients who have had the same operation and evidenced the same deficit in short-term memory. One patient said, "My brain feels like a sieve; I forget everything."

Mr. R and others like him suggest that there may be at least two separate memory storages, one for long-term memory and another for short-term, immediate experiences. If so, Mr. R.'s long-term memory for events prior to the surgery is intact while his short-term memory is impaired. Most important, he has a severe deficit in the ability to transfer information from short-term memory to long-term memory.

Each morning the editor of a leading Soviet newspaper would distribute assignments to his reporters. These intricate assignments consisted of people to interview, events to cover, leads to chase down, and investigations to be made. While all the rest of the staff sat attentively making careful notes of their assignments, one reporter, Mr. S., typically sat staring out the window. The editor noted and endured Mr. S.'s strange behavior until one day when

FIGURE 7.1: "They say he's gifted with total recall." (Drawing by Stan Hunt; © 1973 The New Yorker Magazine, Inc.)

he lost his temper. Following the distribution of staff assignments, he asked Mr. S. to stay. He upbraided Mr. S. for his inattentiveness and for his disrespectful conduct. He asked him whether he had any idea of what his assignment was to be that day. Mr. S., in surprise, turned to him and repeated word for word the assignment the editor had given him. He then showed himself able to repeat, word for word, the assignments that the editor had given all the other staff members. He then astounded the editor by picking a day in the previous week and rattling off with no hesitation his complete personal assignment. He even turned to an assignment he had had one year and nine months earlier and recalled, "It was a rainy Tuesday; you wanted me to speak to three patients and two doctors at the Budenko Neurological Hospital in Moscow at 4 P.M." Luckily, the editor was acquainted with Alexander Luria, a leading Soviet psychologist; he immediately sent Mr. S. to be studied by Luria.

Upon testing, Luria discovered that, indeed, Mr. S. had what we commonly call a photographic memory. Although the average individual can immediately recall a list of seven words, Mr. S. was able to recall perfectly lists of words, letters, and/or numbers running up to 70 items. He could also produce this list on demand in reverse order (you will realize the difficulty of this achievement if you just attempt to repeat the alphabet backwards).

To Luria's amazement, Mr. S.'s photographic memory was less a blessing than a burden. Mr. S. could not read anything very comfortably because every single image called forth by the reading brought to his attention highly detailed memories that interfered. In addition, his understanding of the meaning of words was extremely concrete. If a passage in a book called an individual a baby on one page and a child on another, it was very difficult for him to understand that the references were to the same individual. Consequently, it was almost impossible for Mr. S. to understand the overall meaning of material that he was reading.

Mr. S.'s "total recall" memory must be considered a disorder of memory just as much as Mr. R.'s condition. One possible interpretation of Mr. S.'s difficulty is that his memory storage is normal but that he has a defect in his ability to *inhibit* recall of this storage. This would be the interpretation of psychologists who feel that almost all experiences are recorded somewhere in the nervous system. Mr. S.'s experience also tells us that humans *need* the ability to forget. If we were always conscious of all of our memories we would be totally disabled. It would be impossible for us to fix our attention on any ongoing activity. Some forgetting is obviously necessary. Mr. R., on the other hand, forgot all too well, so much so that he could not benefit from experience or learn. Memory is a crucial part of learning. Without memory, there would be no improvement as a result of our efforts to learn.

These cases raise a number of questions that we will examine in this chapter, such as: What role does short-term memory play in long-term retention? What are the differences between the functions and operations of these two memory storages? What are the consequences of these differences for our behavior and experience? How are memory and forgetting measured? What factors cause forgetting to occur? By what methods can retention be improved?

A. SENSORY, SHORT-TERM, AND LONG-TERM MEMORY

There is good evidence that we have not one but three distinct, yet interconnected memories. The case studies presented above provide some information pointing to a short-term memory (STM) and a long-term memory (LTM), but there also seems to be a very fleeting sensory memory. In this section we will consider the evidence for each of these memories.

SENSORY STORE

Has this ever happened to you? While you were watching television, a telephone number was flashed on the screen that you didn't expect but wanted to retain. You recognized every number, but by the time you got a pencil to write it down, it had faded from memory. If you tried to remember the first digits, you forgot the last and vice versa. George Sperling at Bell Telephone Laboratories developed an ingenious method to study retention immediately after a visual presentation. He used a device called a *tachistoscope* to flash a 3 x 3 block of letters on a screen for 0.05 second (see Figure 7.2). Subjects reported that they could recognize the letters at that speed but couldn't retain very much of what they saw. A tone of high, medium, or low pitch signaled the subjects which row to recall and report. If the signal was given immediately after the visual presentation, the row identified by the tone was reported with about 75 percent accuracy. If the signal was delayed, however, accuracy was impaired. The longer the delay, the less the accuracy. At one-second delay the subjects were no better than when no signal was given. The accuracy of the subjects' recall with the aid of an immediate tone signal indicates that for a fleeting moment they did retain some sort of memory of all the letters. Studies of this kind have led to the concept of a sensory-storage memory. **Sensory store** *is assumed to be a large-capacity storage that receives information when it is first presented; the information is held in sensory store very briefly, and it is lost very rapidly unless it is transferred into short-term memory.*

SHORT-TERM MEMORY

A vivid example of short-term memory (STM) is provided by the experience of

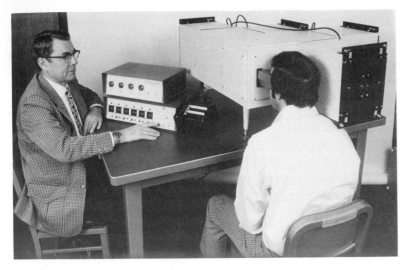

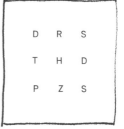

FIGURE 7.2 The tachistoscope is used to present visual stimuli such as words and letters to a subject for short periods of time. Modern electronics enables researchers to control the exposure time precisely. The letters shown are typical stimuli for Sperling's study.

looking up a telephone number. After you find the number in the phone book, you can keep it in mind as long as it is needed by repeating it to yourself silently or aloud. However, if you are distracted before you dial the number, you tend to forget it, and most likely the number is completely forgotten after the phone call.

What is the Capacity of STM? As early as 1850 short-term memory was being studied, under the names "span of apprehension" and "span of immediate memory." The basic procedure then was to present a subject with progressively longer strings of numbers or letters. The memory span was the length of the longest string that could be immediately recalled. More recently, George A. Miller of Rockefeller University has extensively studied the memory span and has concluded that it tends to

average seven items, plus or minus two. The number seven stands for seven "chunks" of information. For example, the word *triskaidekaphobia* (fear of the number 13) contains 17 letters. As such, it could be considered to exceed our memory span. Once we know the word, however, we can use it as a single chunk. Our **short-term memory** *span can contain approximately seven chunks or units at a time regardless of the number of physical elements within these units.* "Plus or minus two" simply means that *most often* we can remember seven items. Sometimes this figure will drop as low as five, sometimes it will go as high as nine; the average will be seven. Another example of chunking is provided by an apprentice telegraph operator who first hears "dits" and "dahs" separately. With practice, he learns to organize the "dits" and "dahs" into sound patterns that correspond to letters, then words and then whole phrases. As learning progresses, he forms larger and larger chunks that enable him to handle and retain more information. Chunking, then, is an active process in which information is organized into meaningful units that are more easily remembered.

Burton H. Cohen of Lafayette College offered rather convincing evidence for Miller's chunk theory of the acquisition of memory. In one of his experiments, Cohen presented two lists of words to his subjects. One list contained 20 unrelated words. The other list contained 70 words, all of which belonged to one or another of 20 categories. For example, four of the 70 words were: spring, summer, winter, fall. He hypothesized that the number of chunks of information in the list containing 20 categories should be the same as in the list of 20 unrelated words. And indeed, the 70-word list was remembered as well as the 20-word list. This study indicates that categories can be considered "chunks" in Miller's sense. By categorizing what we must retain, we can increase our retention.

The next question is, how long can short-term memory retain these chunks?

Duration of Short-Term Memory. Research on short-term memory has turned up some rather surprising facts. You would think, for example, that if you were presented with a three-consonant syllable such as "btr," you would be able to recall it 18 seconds later. As a matter of fact, this is not very likely. In an experiment by Lloyd and Margaret Jean Petersen at Indiana University, an unusual method was used for analyzing short-term memory. The experimenters presented their subjects with trigrams (three-consonant nonsense syllables such as "btr"). Now, if the subjects were simply permitted to wait

18 seconds and then recall these three letters, most of them would probably spend the interval rehearsing the three letters (repeating them silently to themselves). Petersen and Petersen decided to try to work out a method to prevent such rehearsal. Immediately after the subjects saw a trigram, they were asked to begin counting backwards from 363 by 3's. After a few seconds of backward counting, the subjects were asked to recall the trigram. In Figure 7.3 we see the results of this experiment. After 18 seconds, less than 10 percent of the subjects could recall the trigram correctly. Looking at it another way, over 90 percent of them had forgotten the trigram after only 18 seconds.

IS THERE A DIFFERENCE BETWEEN SHORT-TERM MEMORY AND LONG-TERM MEMORY?

Long-term memory (LTM) can also be illustrated by experience with telephone numbers: you can recall your own tele-

FIGURE 7.3 When subjects are not allowed to rehearse nonsense syllables their retention is impaired. If rehearsal is prevented for 18 seconds, most subjects will forget the syllable.

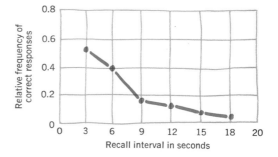

phone number and those of friends anytime they are needed. In this section we will explore the similarities and differences between these two memories and examine their implications for daily life. Psychologists have come upon evidence suggesting how the two operate differently.

Some interesting research by Reuben Conrad of the Medical Research Council's Applied Psychology Research Unit, Cambridge, revealed a unique characteristic of short-term memory. He visually presented a series of 10 *letters* (e.g., BCPTVFM-NSX) to subjects, one letter every three-fourths of a second. After the presentation, subjects were asked to recall the letters. The errors they made were revealing. Even though the letters were presented *visually,* the subjects tended to confuse letters that *sounded* somewhat alike (B, C, P, T, and V).

In a supporting experiment, Alan Baddeley of the University of Sterling tested to see whether short-term memory would be confused by *words* (as opposed to letters) that sound alike. He had two types of word lists. One consisted of similar-sounding words such as "cap, cad, can, cat, cab." The other contained words that were distinctively different in sound. The subjects recalled only 9.6 percent of the similar words, whereas they recalled 82.1 percent of the dissimilar words. It seems clear that in some way short-term memory is coded in terms of auditory characteristics. When a subject tries to retrieve the memory, words that have similar auditory patterns tend to interfere with one another. (This relationship between short-term memory and auditory characteristics is thought-provoking. Recall that Mr. R. lost his short-term memory after removal of part of his temporal lobes. The auditory center of the brain resides in the temporal lobes.)

Baddeley also tested to see whether similarity in *meaning* would cause inter-

ference in short-term memory. It did not. Subjects recalled lists of words highly similar in meaning (big, large, great, high, long) as well as lists composed of words disparate in meaning. Short-term memory, then, is not affected by meaning similarity. In another experiment, however, Baddeley showed that *long-term* memory is *not* very much confused by auditory similarity but *is* heavily affected by meaning similarity.

Donald O. Hebb of McGill University provides evidence that both STM and LTM operate at the same time. He had his subjects listen to 17 nine-digit strings, over 124 trials. One of the strings was repeated every third trial. A subject was asked to recite the digits after each trial. Hebb compared the rate of improved retention for the repeated digit string and the 16 nonrepeated digit strings. As Figure 7.4 reveals, there was no improvement for the nonrepeated digits but a gradual improvement for the repeated digit string. This is taken as evidence that LTM operates for the repeated digits, whereas the results for the nonrepeated digits reflect STM.

What if Hebb's study were carried out using subjects with the brain damage of

FIGURE 7.4 *These curves illustrate the Hebb repetition effect, which provides evidence that repetition improves retention in LTM but has no effect on STM.*

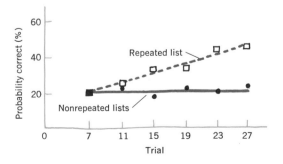

Mr. R., who had difficulty transferring information between STM and LTM? It has been done, and no difference was found between the repeated and the nonrepeated items. The clinical, neurological, and experimental evidence, therefore, indicates that two types of memory, STM and LTM, represent two related, but relatively independent, processes.

A THREE-PROCESS THEORY OF MEMORY

Richard C. Atkinson of Stanford University and Richard M. Shiffrin of Indiana University have proposed a three-stage theory that can explain a great many of the facts about memory we have presented (see Figure 7.5). Information enters sensory store, which holds the input for fractions of a second. If attention is paid to some aspect of the sensory input, some of the information is transferred to short-term memory. Short-term memory contains a buffer storage that can hold some seven chunks of information. STM has a rapid decay, or forgetting, rate of a few seconds. However, if a person rehearses the contents of STM's buffer storage, it is preserved momentarily. **Rehearsal** *refers to the silent or out-loud repetition of the material to be remembered.* The word

FIGURE 7.5 The three-stage theory of memory process and the basic characteristics of each stage.

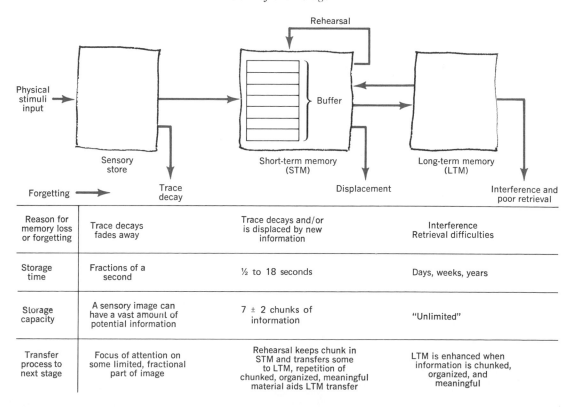

	Sensory store	Short-term memory (STM)	Long-term memory (LTM)
Reason for memory loss or forgetting	Trace decays fades away	Trace decays and/or is displaced by new information	Interference Retrieval difficulties
Storage time	Fractions of a second	½ to 18 seconds	Days, weeks, years
Storage capacity	A sensory image can have a vast amount of potential information	7 ± 2 chunks of information	"Unlimited"
Transfer process to next stage	Focus of attention on some limited, fractional part of image	Rehearsal keeps chunk in STM and transfers some to LTM, repetition of chunked, organized, meaningful material aids LTM transfer	LTM is enhanced when information is chunked, organized, and meaningful

"buffer" means "protected," so the term buffer storage is an apt one. It's the rehearsal that keeps the information alive until it is displaced by new information, or the person decides to transfer it to long-term memory by some coding, organizing, or study activity. If the buffer contents are not transferred to LTM, the item is displaced by new information or it fades from memory and is forgotten. LTM, which stores things for days or years, may fail because of inadequate coding or improper cues at the time of recall needed to locate the information desired. It is also possible that a search of LTM comes up with nothing because the information is not there; it wasn't transferred from STM to LTM in the first place.

Have you ever taken an exam in which you couldn't remember a thing? Yet you crammed for it the night before and "knew it backwards and forwards"? In such a situation, you may not have rehearsed enough to keep the memory in the buffer, so it was displaced by each new fact you read. Or you may not have taken the time to code it or categorize it in some meaningful way so that it could be stored in LTM for easy recall. There are a number of ways long-term retention of information can be enhanced. These will be pointed out in the next section on long-term retention and forgetting. Beforehand, it would be useful to read Focus 7.1: When Nonsense Makes Sense, which discusses some of the methods used to measure retention.

B. LONG-TERM RETENTION AND FORGETTING

Memory is an exasperating and delightful feature of our existence. It is delightful when, touched off by some trivial event, it can replay some lovely moments of the past. It is exasperating when, despite considerable struggle, it fails to come forth with the name of an approaching acquaintance who must be introduced to a companion. But despite occasional slips, memory performs prodigious tasks. *Perhaps the most impressive part of the memory process is not that vast amounts of experience can be stored, but that the information can be retrieved, somehow fished out of storage. This process is known as* **retrieval.** Consider how quickly you can retrieve certain facts. Who was the first U.S. President? What is your favorite flavor of ice cream? Where is the Yucatán? Name a small country beginning with "D." Sometimes the retrieval is not so quick. In this section we will explore some of the factors that facilitate recall and account for forgetting in long-term memory.

RETRIEVAL DIFFICULTIES

Some psychologists are working with the hypothesis that difficulties in remembering are not the result of any loss of the memory. The memory, they claim, is just quietly lying somewhere "in there." (See Focus 3.3: The Brain as a Tape Recorder.) We simply must set the stage for retrieving it. A simple but direct demonstration was provided in an experiment at the University of Toronto by Endel Tulving and Zena Pearlstone. They asked subjects to memorize a list of words organized into labeled categories. For example, crimes: theft, arson; animals: cow, dog. Subjects were instructed to remember the names of the items but not to bother with the category names. When they tested for recall, the experimenters divided the subjects into two groups. One group wrote what they recalled on a blank sheet of paper without any hints. The other group was given the category names as a hint. The group

Focus 7.1
When Nonsense Makes Sense: The Measurement of Retention

Nonsense Syllables. Hermann Ebbinghaus was a brilliant, patient, and persistent man. Just before the close of the last century he developed a method of studying learning and memory that was a major scientific breakthrough. Prior to Ebbinghaus, many scholars claimed that memory could not be precisely measured, therefore its scientific study was not possible. Ebbinghaus developed a unit of measurement for memory that opened up a whole new branch of psychological research. His unit was the **nonsense syllable,** *formed by putting a vowel between two consonants,* as in KUL, NOV, GEK. He selected nonsense syllables because he believed that they were essentially free of the influences of past experiences and the emotional factors associated with prose, poetry, or common words. Ebbinghaus made up hundreds of lists of these syllables and memorized them himself, using the same procedure throughout his studies. He first memorized a list, recording exactly how long it took him. Then he set the list aside for a predetermined time interval. When the interval was over, he relearned the same list again, keeping careful records. *The difference between the original learning and* **relearning** *time provided a measure of retention.* Figure 7.6 illustrates a typical finding by Ebbinghaus that has stood the test of time. Notice that the rate of forgetting is greatest during the first hours after learning, then the rate diminishes. Much of our forgetting follows a similar course. For example, if you were asked to recite the contents of a lecture immediately after class, you could probably give a complete account. In a few hours, however, you would have forgotten most details, and after a day or two you would find it difficult to give more than a brief outline.

All learning does not follow this forgetting course. Material that is overlearned (constantly repeated after it has been mastered), or that is very important to an individual, may be retained over a lifetime, such as names of people and language skills.

FIGURE 7.6 Ebbinghaus's findings relating to amount of retention over time has been confirmed in numerous research studies.

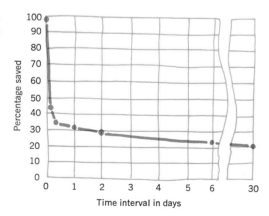

Since Ebbinghaus's day psychologists have explored memory with a variety of materials including prose, poetry, and lists of meaningful words. However, whenever the influence of past associations and meaning is to be minimized, nonsense syllables may still be used for memory research. Here are the principal methods used by psychologists to study memory.

Recall. *A psychologist typically measures* **recall** *by asking a subject to recite or to write down all the items from a list of words or nonsense syllables to which the subject has previously been exposed. The recall score is the number of correct answers.* The distinctive feature of the recall method is that no hint or help is given to the subject's memory. The subject must dredge up and reproduce material that was previously learned. The material can be reproduced either in its original order (as with a list of words, syllables, or numbers) or in any order that the subject can remember. In the classroom the essay examination is a typical example of a recall test.

Recognition. For **recognition** *a subject is asked to pick, from a number of items, the one example that was previously learned.* Multiple choice tests are an example of this type of measurement. In a typical learning experiment using the method of recognition, a subject memorizes a list of items and then is asked to select those items learned from a longer list containing distracting items.

Relearning. Harold E. Burtt was a psychologist to the core. When his little son reached 15 months of age, Burtt began to supplement his daily reading-time diet of nursery rhymes and Winnie-the-Pooh with selections from Sophocles. He was methodical, reading three selections a day and reading these same three selections for three months. He shifted to three other selections every three months until a year was up. Each selection was composed of 20 lines of Greek.

The son seems to have survived this regimen since he was available five years later when Burtt wanted to see if the boy had any memories of the Greek passages. His son, now seven years of age, was asked to memorize some Greek selections. Half of these selections were ones that Burtt had read five years earlier. Half were new. Burtt reasoned that if the boy learned more quickly the Greek materials to which he had already been exposed, this would be the evidence that the boy's memory retained some trace of the exposure. Indeed, his son *relearned* the original Greek selections in 317 repetitions whereas he needed 435 repetitions to master the equivalent new selections. Apparently, because of his early experience, he was able to learn the original material at a faster rate. If the boy had been asked to recall or to recognize the original Greek selections, he probably would have failed to do so. Thus, we can see that *relearning,* the method originally devised by Ebbinghaus, is a rather sensitive measure.

The various measures of memory vary distinctively in their sensitivity. In Figure 7.7 you can see a typical example of the sensitivities of the three major methods of measuring memory. Recognition shows the highest percentage of retention; however, you should be aware that this effect can be varied greatly by changing the distracters in the list in which the items to be recognized are embedded. If the items are embedded in strikingly similar material, the recognition score will suffer. Since recall demands an exact reproduction of the material presented, it will almost inevitably have the lowest score. It should be obvious that the strength of the memory is not greater when we measure it through relearning or recognition. It is just easier to detect the persistence of memory when we use a more sensitive measure.

FIGURE 7.7 Measures of memory vary in their sensitivity, as indicated by the percentage of retention.

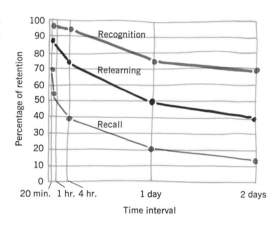

given the category names as a hint did considerably better than the unaided group. When the blank-paper group was given the category names, their performance improved by about 40 percent.

This experiment indicates that when an item cannot be recalled, it has not necessarily been lost. Given the proper retrieval cue, the memory can frequently be fished out quite easily. The tip-of-the-tongue phenomenon (see Focus 7.2) also sheds some light on memory storage and retrieval.

Gordon Bower of Stanford University

has conducted a study that sheds light on the role of hierarchical categorization of information in recall. Bower used a list of 112 words that could be organized into four hierarchies. Table 7.1 illustrates one of his lists. The subjects in one group were first taught how to organize the list of words in terms of the first three levels of the hierarchy; then they were given Level 4 words to memorize. Another group was given Level 4 words to memorize but knew nothing about the potential hierarchical categorization of the words. Figure 7.8 shows the average number of words each

Focus 7.2
The Tip-of-the-Tongue Phenomenon

Have you ever been asked a question to which you are sure you know the answer but are unable to recall immediately? You try to dredge up the answer, but each attempt, as close as it comes, is just not right. This tip-of-the-tongue phenomenon (TOT), as it is called, can be quite frustrating.

Roger W. Brown of Harvard University and David McNeill of the University of Chicago devised a very clever way to produce the TOT experience in the laboratory for study. They read to their subjects (college students) the definitions of words that occur infrequently in the English language. The subjects were asked to state the word being defined. If they couldn't recall the word, they were asked a number of questions about what they were thinking in their attempt to find the word. Play the role of a subject and try to state the target word defined by each of the following:

A. A waxy substance secreted by whales which is used to make perfumes.
B. A common cavity into which intestinal and urinary passages open in birds, reptiles, and fishes.
C. A small boat in the Far East with a roof made of bamboo mats that is propelled by a single oar.

If you have the TOT experience with these definitions, write down the words you have in mind as you search for the target word. How many syllables does the target word have? What is the first letter of the target word?

When Brown and McNeill's subjects had a TOT experience with a definition, they were able to answer each of these questions accurately, as well as produce words similar in meaning or sound to the target word. For example, definition C describes a sampan. The subjects would produce such similar-sounding words as scram, Saipan, Cheyenne, or "sympoon," and such similar-meaning words as junk, barge, or rowboat. This study indicates that storage and retrieval is not a simple all-or-none process. Although we may forget some characteristics of a word, we may retain others. The study also indicates that memory retrieval may also be a reconstructive process. Each item in memory may consist of a bundle of information related to the definition, such as sounds, letters, and meanings, that are loosely tied together. When we try to remember, we search for elements of these bundles and, when enough are retrieved, can recite the word.

(Definition A is for ambergris and definition B is for cloaca.)

TABLE 7.1   **Bower's hierarchy of minerals for recall study**

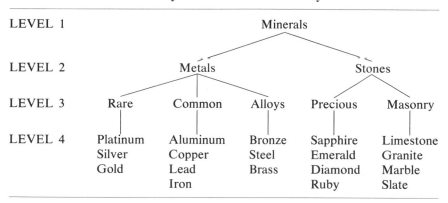

LEVEL 1		Minerals		
LEVEL 2	Metals		Stones	
LEVEL 3	Rare	Common	Alloys	Precious	Masonry
LEVEL 4	Platinum	Aluminum	Bronze	Sapphire	Limestone
	Silver	Copper	Steel	Emerald	Granite
	Gold	Lead	Brass	Diamond	Marble
		Iron		Ruby	Slate

group was able to recall over four trials. It is clear that when material to be memorized is organized and structured in some meaningful way, retention is enhanced.

One source of memory failure, then, is the lack of a proper cue for retrieval, such as category labels, sounds, and word meanings that are important memory aids. Research in this area is just beginning. The basic task is to determine the organization of memory storage. It's a bit like a large library filing system; once you understand the reason why the librarian stores a book at a specific position on a certain shelf in a definite stack on the third floor, it is no mystery that the book can be almost instantly retrieved 15 years later. So the psychologists in this area are trying to determine the Dewey Decimal System of the mind.

CHANGES IN THE MEMORY TRACE

Another approach to understanding failures of memory takes a more neurophysiological turn. This approach is built mainly on research on how perceptions change over time. The basic principle in this explana-

tion of memory failure is that the neurophysiological memory trace changes automatically over time because of certain (unspecified) brain processes. A **memory trace** *is assumed to be a change produced by learning in the chemistry or the neurological circuitry of the brain that is responsible for a memory.* There is some in-

FIGURE 7.8 The average number of words recalled from word lists is enhanced when subjects are trained to organize a list in terms of hierarchical categories.

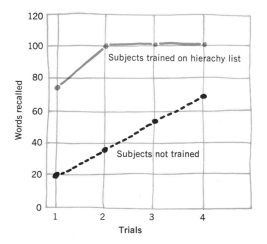

direct evidence to support this hypothesis.

Leonard Carmichael, H. P. Hogan, and A. A. Walters presented subjects with the group of somewhat ambiguous figures drawn in the center column of Figure 7.9. After all the figures had been presented, the subjects were instructed to draw the figures from memory. Just before a figure was exposed, one group of subjects was told that the ambiguous figure looked like a familiar object, which was named. Another group of subjects received the same instructions, but a different name was used. When the subjects attempted to reproduce the figures, their drawings tended to change the shapes according to the names used in the instructions. Changes are illustrated in the outer columns of Figure 7.9.

Our memory does change over time. How we label and categorize during learning will, then, play an important role in what we recall as well as the accuracy of our recall.

Trace Decay

There was a time when it was thought that the mind was more or less like a muscle. For example, students were forced to learn Latin not because they had any conceivable use for Latin, but because the logic of the language would exercise their minds properly, and as a result their logic functions and their memory functions would be improved. A corollary of this position was that if a person were to neglect the use of any facet of the mind or any bit of his memory, the memory would slowly decay. Until this century it was a general belief that memories would fade away from disuse.

There actually may be some physiological process that corresponds to the "law" of disuse. However, it does not seem to be terribly important in failures of memory. A fascinating experiment by J. G. Jenkins and Karl Dallenbach was of great help in laying to rest the principle of dis-

FIGURE 7.9 *Recall of ambiguous figures is influenced by the way they are labeled.*

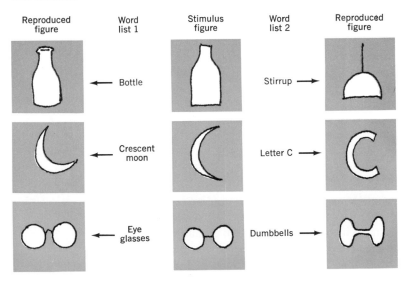

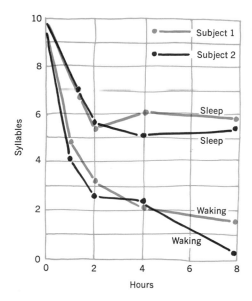

FIGURE 7.10 *The student who went to sleep after studying nonsense syllables had better retention than the one who continued his daily activities. These data support the interference theory of forgetting.*

use. Jenkins and Dallenbach wished to find out if time alone, with no intervening activity, would suffice to reduce an individual's memory. They asked two students to learn a list of nonsense syllables. One student continued his usual daily activities while the other simply went to sleep. After retention intervals of 1, 2, 4, and 8 hours, the experimenters asked the students to recall the nonsense syllable lists. The sleeping student had one retention interval tested per night.

The results portrayed in Figure 7.10 clearly show that the sleeping student remembered more of the list of nonsense syllables than did the waking student. Of the material that the sleeping student forgot, 46 percent was lost during the first two hours of his sleep period. Much of this loss may have occurred during the

time he lay awake before falling asleep. It is interesting that from the second to the eighth hour of sleep there was no real increase in forgetting. The awake subject, on the other hand, showed a progressive increase in forgetting as a consequence of performing regular daytime activities. As Jenkins and Dallenbach concluded: "Forgetting is not so much a matter of decay (due to disuse) as it is a matter of interference, inhibition, or obliteration of the old by the new." What is the nature of this interference?

INTERFERENCE

The **interference hypothesis** *states that the difficulty we have in recalling a specific item is due to the interference or competition of other memories. The source of interference can be items learned after the desired memory* (**retroactive interference**) *or items learned before the desired memory* (**proactive interference**). To clarify the distinction between retro- and proactive, keep in mind that retro means backward and pro means forward. In retroactive interference, current memories "move back" and interfere with what you have memorized in the past. In proactive interference, past memories "move forward" and interfere with recently memorized material.

Retroactive Interference

Let us attempt to analyze retroactive interference, as shown in Table 7.2, in terms of interference theory. In Step 1 the subject has learned to respond with response B to Stimulus A. Let us assume that he must respond to "elephant" with the word "table." In Step 2 the subject must learn to respond to the stimulus "elephant" with the new word "egg." The word "elephant" now tends to produce both "table" and

Focus 7.3 Brain Chemistry and Memory

One of the pioneer investigators to maintain that experience is at least in part imprinted in the brain in the form of chemical changes is James McConnell of the University of Michigan. McConnell raised a storm of controversy with his research on the planarian, a primitive flatworm that may be found in good supply on the underside of rocks in mildly stagnant, polluted water. In many ways the planarian, only three-quarters of an inch long, is an outstanding creature. From the point of view of evolutionary development, however, it must be confessed that it has not come very far. But the planarian has certain unique characteristics that fit McConnell's research needs perfectly. The planarian has a bilaterally symmetrical nervous system with synapses. It can learn simple responses to simple stimuli. Further, if you slice one in half the parts simply regenerate a new head and tail or become two planaria. In addition, and crucial to our story, planaria are cannibalistic.

In Figure 7.11 you can see why the regenerative powers of the planarian are important. If you take a planarian and cut it in half and allow the head and tail to regenerate, both of the resulting planaria retain the benefit of training, not just the "head." McConnell pondered this fact. If the traces of training were not centered in the planarian's head but were also present in the tail, then perhaps these traces were not composed of nerve-to-nerve connections in the head but, rather, of some chemical code that was distributed throughout the three-fourths-of-an-inch body. How to test this? The planarian's cannibalism came to the researcher's rescue. McConnell reasoned that if he trained a planarian to contract in response to a light, then that trained planarian's body would contain the hypothesized coded chemical. If he could get this chemical into an untrained planarian then, because of this chemical, the untrained planarian should show signs of having "learned" the training response. And that is where the cannibalism proved useful. The untrained planarian could acquire the "coded chemical" by simply eating a ground-up

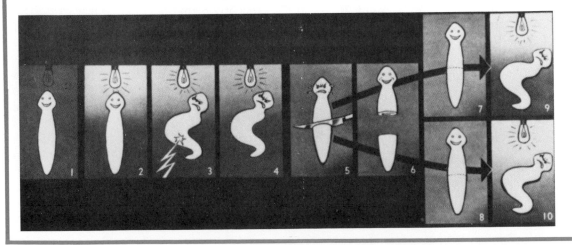

trained planarian. After this meal, it could be tested to see if it had "learned" anything. As a comparison, McConnell could have untrained planaria eat other untrained planaria. McConnell wrote an article entitled "Memory Transfer through Cannibalism in Planarians" in which he demonstrated that in learning the contraction-to-light response, the planaria that ate trained planaria had a great advantage over others that ate untrained ones. As might be expected, this article raised much interest and much heated controversy. Some scientists called his findings "sheer unmitigated rot" and "chimerical and absurd."

Georges Ungar of Baylor University used rats and mice as subjects, rather than planaria, but his research design follows and supports the McConnell pattern. He trained rats to avoid a dark box by shocking them if they entered it. He then chopped off their heads and homogenized their brains, making a chemical preparation that he injected into untrained mice. Other mice had chemical preparations injected from untrained rats. All mice were then placed in a compartment between a dark box and a lighted box; they had access to both for 180 seconds. Mice ordinarily prefer dark boxes. The question was, "How many of those 180 seconds would the mouse spend in the dark box?" Before injection, they spent an average of 130 of the 180 seconds in the dark box. After injection of the trained-rats' brain extract, they spent an average of only 52 of the 180 seconds in the dark box. The mice injected with brain extract of untrained rats spent an average of 120 seconds in the dark box. This work was a massive effort; almost 4500 rats were trained and processed to produce these results.

But for Ungar this was just a beginning. For him the crucial question was the exact identity of the chemical substance that could induce a mouse to avoid the dark. By conducting chemical analyses of trained and untrained brains, and by making some educated guesses concerning the general nature of the chemical substance, Ungar, D. M. Desiderio, and Wolfgang Parr identified it and named it "scotophobin" (Greek for "fear of the dark"). Once the substance was identified, Parr was then handed the task of duplicating scotophobin synthetically. When he succeeded, it was injected into untrained mice. When these mice were tested they showed avoidance of the dark box! Ungar predicts that scotophobin is the first in what promises to be a large series of chemicals likely to be identified by the various laboratories of the world working in this area.

FIGURE 7.11 (1–4) By pairing a light and an electric shock, it is possible to train a planarian to respond to a light with a body contraction. (5–8) If the planarian is cut in two, each half will regenerate a complete organism. (9–10) Each of the new planaria retains the contraction-to-light response.

With further research and the resolution of the controversies they have unleashed, the significance of these discoveries will become clearer. Will we have "pills for French"? Will these substances be useful in helping the mentally retarded? Will the transmission of acquired characteristics be possible through "brain transplants" that are chemically injected?

TABLE 7.2 **Experimental designs for studying pro- and retroactive interference**

RETROACTIVE INTERFERENCE

CONDITION	STEP 1	STEP 2	STEP 3
EXPERI-MENTAL GROUP	Learn List 1 A B Elephant-Table	Learn List 2 A B Elephant-Egg (Interpolated Task)	Relearn or Recall List 1 A B Elephant-Table
CONTROL (CONTRAST-ING) GROUP	Learn List 1 A B Elephant-Table	Rest or Non-interfering Task	Relearn or Recall List 1 A B Elephant-Table

PROACTIVE INTERFERENCE

CONDITION	STEP 1	STEP 2	STEP 3
EXPERI-MENTAL GROUP	Learn List 1 A B Elephant-Table	Learn List 2 A B Elephant-Egg	Relearn or Recall List 2 A B Elephant-Egg
CONTROL (CONTRAST-ING) GROUP	Rest or Non-interfering Task	Learn List 2 A B Elephant-Egg	Relearn or Recall List 2 A B Elephant-Egg

"egg." The response "egg" then interferes with the response "table" in Step 3 when the "elephant-table" pair must be relearned. The response "table" is forgotten because the response "egg" is interfering.

Using a similar analysis, Arthur Melton and J. McQ. Irwin had five groups of subjects learn a list of nonsense syllables. This step was original learning (Step 1). One of these groups then rested for a period of time before being asked to recall the original list. The other four groups were asked to learn a second list for 5, 10, 20, and 40 trials, respectively. Learning this second list constituted interpolated learning (Step

2). At the end of interpolated learning, all five groups were asked to recall the original list (Step 3).

As might be predicted from interference theory, the groups that learned interpolated lists tended to have more difficulty recalling or relearning the original list. The more the interpolated practice, the more the interference.

In the Melton and Irwin experiment there was no special definition of the kinds of material that subjects learned in Step 2. What was varied was only the amount of material. However, it also makes a difference what *kind* of material is interpolated in Step 2. John McGeoch and William McDonald did an experiment that showed fairly conclusively that the similarity of the material learned in Step 2 to the material learned in Step 1 would be very important in predicting the interference effects in Step 3. The more similar the interpolated material, the more the interference noted at Step 3. These findings have important implications for any learning or test situation. It is clear, for instance, that before an exam you should not study or read material similar to whatever will be called for in the exam.

Proactive Interference

The Melton and Irwin experiment makes it clear that one source of forgetting is experience between learning something and trying to remember it. But isn't there another possible source of interference in memory? What of all the experiences that precede what we have called original learning? In fact, they produce proactive interference. Indeed, many psychologists maintain that the chief cause of forgetting in adults is the interference of old habits. Such interference is also one of the reasons why it is difficult to "teach old dogs new tricks." Table 7.2 summarizes the experimental setup for proactive interference.

The way one psychologist tracked down the pervasive effects of proactive interference on memory reads like a piece of master detective work. Benton J. Underwood of Northwestern University noticed that in some laboratories subjects seemed to be able to recall as much as 80 percent of the material they had learned, whereas in other laboratories subjects were only able to recall about 10 percent. Ebbinghaus (see Focus 7.1), who certainly had ample practice in recalling nonsense syllables, evidenced recall of only about 35 percent

of the material he had learned. Could it be that a subject in an experiment who had learned only one list could remember nonsense syllables better than a "professional memorizer" who had learned literally hundreds of different lists? It seemed incredible. Underwood began his investigation by examining a number of preliminary questions:

1. Were there differences in the material used in the different laboratories? Perhaps some laboratories were using more difficult lists. By and large the answer was no.
2. Did procedures vary from laboratory to laboratory? Again the answer was generally no.
3. Did the subjects vary? Not in any way related to their intelligence or education. But careful sleuthing did reveal one difference. The subjects in the studies varied markedly in terms of the amount of experience they had had in verbal learning experiments.

Underwood sensed a clue. Accordingly, he went back to all the published experiments and carefully compared the treatment of experimental subjects. After extensive sorting of evidence, Underwood discovered the key to the puzzle. Students in one experiment who had learned 16 different lists before the time they were asked to recall the last list, recalled only about 20 percent of that final list. In a study in Underwood's laboratory, when each subject learned and recalled only one list, the recall rate was as high as 75 percent. After examining the reports of results in 14 different experiments from different laboratories, Underwood concluded that the percentage of material subjects recall is clearly related to the number of previous lists they had learned.

What this means is that interference in recall is in large measure due to the interfering effects of previously learned habits and information. Proactive interference, in the form of already existing habits, is probably the major cause of forgetting. The phenomenal ability of children to recall details of events long forgotten by their parents is doubtless due in part to their shorter lives and consequent lesser degree of proactive interference.

This continual interference and "struggle for ascendency" in our memory might be expected to result in a continuous jumble of thoughts. We are saved from this disaster, however, by continually practicing important acts, such as dressing, finding our way to work, and conversing as well as categorizing and organizing what we learn. Responses that are not practiced in this manner are likely to be replaced or, in short, forgotten. Interference and the other sources of memory failure we have discussed are consequences of thinking and being. But there are other sources of memory failures that are more tied to our emotional and nonrational life.

EMOTIONAL INFLUENCE— REPRESSION

Sigmund Freud noted that many of his patients found it impossible to recall events related to their symptoms. From study of these patients he concluded that these lapses in memory were actually methods the patients were unconsciously using to defend themselves against painful or emotionally disturbing memories. *By forgetting a disturbing thought or event, the patient himself could defend against the anxiety that such memories would otherwise produce. This type of motivated forgetting is called* **repression**. Because this process goes on automatically and unconsciously, a person is not aware of it. A classic illustration is the case of a soldier who develops amnesia for the events surrounding the death of a buddy who was killed in a nearby foxhole during the previous night's bombardment.

Repression has been observed repeatedly in daily life and clinical practice, but it has been difficult to study in the laboratory. First a researcher must show that the material being repressed has been learned. Then the material must be associated with some event that is psychologically or physically painful or embarrassing. Finally, a test must show evidence of forgetting of the specific material. Some investigators have also attempted to show that when the pain or embarrassment is removed, the memory returns.

Andrew Zeller conducted a systematic laboratory investigation of repression. He told college freshmen that the material with which he was testing them was excellent in predicting college success. Part of the material involved memorizing nonsense syllables. One subgroup of the subjects was then told that they had done terribly on the tests. (The tests were rigged so that the student actually did "experience" failure.) When they returned for the next session, Zeller tested their ability to recall the nonsense syllables. Sure enough, the subgroup that experienced failure did relatively poorly. They had repressed the aspects of experience related to the painful failure.

After the test, Zeller conducted a "therapeutic" interview with the subjects, explaining that they hadn't done poorly at all and describing the rationale of the experiment. When he next tested this subgroup, their memory of nonsense syllables had returned to normal (that is, the level that was achieved by "nonfailure" groups). Zeller thus succeeded not only in demonstrating repression but also in eliminating its effects.

C. METHODS THAT IMPROVE RETENTION AND RECALL

There was a Greek poet named Simonides whose experiences with memory were reported by Cicero. The methods developed by Simonides for improving memory are still being followed today in the memory courses advertised in many popular magazines.

It is said that Simonides first came upon this method following a disaster at a banquet given by a nobleman of Thessaly. Simonides was reading his poetry when he was abruptly called away from the banquet. Minutes after he left the banquet hall, the entire roof fell in upon the guests and everyone was crushed to death in the ruins. The bodies were so mangled that almost none of the victims could be identified. It was considered important in Greek religion that families properly bury their relatives; otherwise the souls of their loved ones would haunt the earth, seeking a final resting place. Simonides, as the only survivor of the banquet, was asked to try to recall who was seated where. By visualizing the banquet seating arrangement and who sat at each position, Simonides found that he could identify each of the bodies. What was essential here was that there was a spatial structure to which he could associate the names of each of the guests at the banquet. If, on the other hand, Simonides had simply tried to list those individuals who had been at the banquet, he probably could not have done as well. Simonides used this experience to develop ways of improving memory. If things to be remembered could be assigned fixed positions and visualized, then memory would be helped. The basic advantage of the Simonides technique lies in associating material to be learned with fixed positions, which are easy to remember.

VISUAL IMAGERY AND ORGANIZATION

Simonides' method can be easily applied to remembering any list of things, such as a shopping list. Suppose you were sent to the supermarket to purchase apples, carrots, milk, and bread. Visualize a room in your house, such as your bedroom, and locate each item against a familiar object. For example, imagine the apples in bed, the carrots sitting at a desk, the milk on the night table, and the bread on the window sill (see Figure 7.12). To recall the items, all you need do is visualize the room and look at each spot to see what has been placed there. Schemes like this are the basis for the methods used by professional memory experts who dazzle audiences with their skills.

Why Imagery Is Effective. Some psychologists hold that the coding of memory is composed of two processes — a nonverbal process consisting mainly of images and a symbolic process consisting mainly of words and numbers. When we are working with pictures or objects, the imagery section of the memory process becomes activated. In addition, the verbal process is also activated because of our verbal associations to or labels for the pictures or objects. Consequently, when we work with pictures or objects, both imagery and verbal processes are at work and both kinds of memory trace will be established. Words, especially abstract words such as "justice" and "honor," are less likely to evoke vivid visual images, and only verbal memory traces will be established.

To overcome problems with memory, if a series of items is to be memorized, associate each item with a very familiar series of objects that can be visualized. The apples in your bed and the carrots on your

FIGURE 7.12 Visual imagery of a familiar room can be used as a memory aid to retain a group of items, such as a shopping list.

desk chair are examples. If, on the other hand, the material is verbal and abstract, then it would be best to try visualizing it. For example, "justice" can be visualized as a blindfolded lady holding a balance, "peace" can be visualized as a dove. In this way both processes—imagery and word symbols—are brought to bear on preserving the memory.

PRACTICE AND STUDY METHODS

Overlearning as an Aid in Memory. Once you have learned a list of materials perfectly, does it pay to go back over it and spend more time studying it? Research by W. C. F. Krueger at the University of Chicago certainly supports the point of view that studying material is of great use in aiding memory. Krueger had students learn lists of words. After they had learned them once perfectly, he had them continue to study them for varying amounts of time. The more they worked at studying the list, the better they recalled the list—up to a month later. All of the groups that continued to study after they had learned the

list perfectly showed improvement (see Figure 7.13). But there is a point of diminishing returns. The greatest return *for effort spent* came in the group that only put in a moderate amount of extra study. (In the Krueger research, a moderate amount of extra study meant 50 percent more time than they took to learn the list to one perfect trial originally.) This research clearly suggests that a moderate amount of "overstudying" is useful for memory, especially with regard to retention for periods of over two weeks.

Improving Retention by Recitation. An experiment by Arthur Gates demonstrates the value of recitation as a study method. He had five groups of subjects spend *equal time* memorizing short biographies and lists of 16 nonsense syllables. The difference among the groups was the percentage of time spent in recitation—reciting, repeating, and self-quizzing. The group that spent zero percent of the time in recitation simply read the nonsense syllables and the short biographies during the entire period allowed for studying. One group had 80

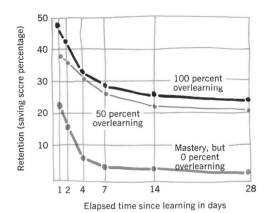

FIGURE 7.13 The relationship between over-learning and retention.

percent of the time devoted to recitation and only 20 percent to reading. The other groups had time distributions that fell between these extremes. The results of these varying amounts of recitation are given in Figure 7.14. The subjects performed best when they spent only 20 percent of their time reading syllables and 80 percent of their time in recitation. The results for the nonsense syllables and biographies were the same as the results for other experiments working with French vocabulary, spelling, and arithmetic. The possible mechanisms underlying the effectiveness of recitation have been presented in our earlier discussion of short- and long-term memory.

Distribution of Study Time and Effective Retention. Parents and educators have not had the luxury of waiting for tidy research results before deciding on educational or rearing practices. For want of empirical evidence, choices in teaching procedures have frequently depended on experience and reasonable guesses. The choices have sometimes also tended to have a moralistic flavor. For example: "The student *should* distribute his hours for studying according to a regular study schedule rather than indulge in a 24-hour marathon of cramming just before exam time."

In this case, the research evidence agrees with the moralistic choice. Study hours that are distributed relatively evenly are more effective for retention than the final-exam blitz. For example, if you have two weeks to study for an exam and decide to spend six hours studying, then distributing your six hours over the two weeks—an hour one day, half an hour another day, two hours another day, etc.—would produce longer-lasting retention and higher exam scores than cramming for six hours the day before the exam. Indeed, **distribution of practice,** *that is, study sessions that are separated by rest periods,* in most learning situations produces superior retention than does the **massing of practice,** that is, *studying without any rest periods.* This effect holds true for rats running a maze or for people recalling a variety of tasks.

FIGURE 7.14 Recitation can significantly increase retention as indicated in the data summarized in this bar graph.

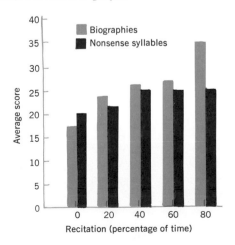

Focus 7.4

Transfer of Training

Latin is a dead language. Other than in classrooms, religious ceremonies, and medical prescriptions, it has not been used as a means of communication for centuries. The grammar is very complex, logical, and intricate. This rigid logic and regularity recommended Latin to educators as a topic that would strengthen students' powers of reasoning and intellect. This idea that the training in one topic would transfer its effect to other fields is referred to as the theory of *formal discipline.*

Research did not support this theory. Those students who were superb in Latin did indeed tend to be superior in other subjects. But they were superior before they began Latin. Partly because of these research findings, Latin has gradually dropped out as a high school requirement. But in the process of conducting their studies, the researchers discovered that *if the effects of training are to transfer from one subject to another* (**transfer of training**), *there has to be some specific similarity between the tasks.* Thus, Latin was a help in learning French or Italian. Tasks that were completely dissimilar did not affect each other very much. They also discovered that the transfer effect of the similarity depended markedly on whether the task *stimuli* or the task *responses* were similar. For example, if you learn to drive on a manual-shift Ford, this training will transfer very well to learning to drive a manual-shift Plymouth. The stimuli are similar and the responses are just about identical. But if you turn from the manual-shift Ford to a Ford with automatic transmission you will find yourself groping around for the gearshift handle and pounding the floorboards with your left foot in search of the clutch. Here the stimuli are similar but the responses are quite different. The two cases provide examples of very general psychological principles of transfer of training.

Positive Transfer. *In learning two tasks one after the other, if the responses are identical* (manual shift) *and the stimuli are similar* (Ford and Plymouth), *the transfer will always be* **positive.** That is, the effect of learning the first task will be beneficial to the second task. The amount of benefit will vary directly with the similarity of the stimuli in the two tasks.

Negative Transfer. *If the stimuli are similar but the responses change* (Ford manual shift to Ford automatic transmission), *the transfer will almost always be* **negative.** Negative transfer does not mean that first learning is not carried over. Quite the contrary: the responses are carrying over into the second task and hampering the new learning. The negative carry-over, or transfer effect, mainly results because these old responses are evoked by the similar stimuli and appear where the new responses should be. A distinction between proactive interference and negative transfer must be made. Proactive interference refers to interference with what has already been memorized; negative transfer affects the process of learning new materials or skills.

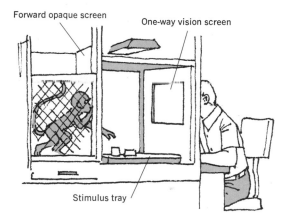

FIGURE 7.15 The apparatus Harlow used to present monkeys with stimuli for the learning-set research.

Learning How to Learn. Harry Harlow at the University of Wisconsin has conducted a series of studies with monkeys involving **learning sets,** *or an increase in the ability to learn a task that involves discrimination with increased practice in that type of task.* Harlow presented his monkey subjects with a series of discrimination problems in a specially built apparatus (see Figure 7.15). Each problem requires an animal to select one of two objects, for example, a triangular or a circular wooden block. If the correct object is selected, the animal is reinforced with a banana chip. The positions of the objects are varied from trial to trial so that the item to be selected is sometimes on the left and sometimes on the right. The monkey must learn to ignore the position cue and select the object by shape cue alone. When the monkey has mastered a problem, it is given a new problem with new shapes. In the course of the experiment, the animals work on hundreds of problems. Sample learning curves for problems are presented in Figure 7.16.

Since there are only two choices in each problem, the guessing monkey will be correct at least half the time by chance alone. This is why the curve starts at 50 percent correct. Notice the gradual improvement of the animal in problems 1 to 8. By problems 17 to 24, 80 percent of the choices are correct by the fourth trial. As an animal gains experience with the problems, it begins to solve the problems in fewer trials and the learning curve becomes steeper. By problem 312, the animal is able to solve the task with one trial. The monkeys have learned that if the object picked on the first trial is rewarded, they should stick to it on later trials, regardless of position. If the object picked on the first trial is not rewarded, then they pick the other object.

The monkeys have *learned how to learn,* or to put it in Harlow's terms, they have developed a learning set for these types of problems. Once the learning set has developed, a monkey can continue on the basis of "insight" rather than trial and error.

FIGURE 7.16 The curves for the learning-set studies show that a monkey's performance gradually improves over learning trials.

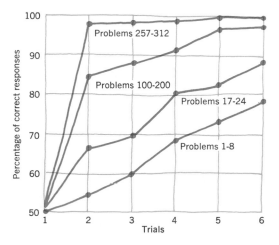

Harlow and his students have replicated their findings with a variety of creatures, including humans, and have uncovered some interesting facts about the learning set phenomenon. Learning set development requires a gradual increase in complexity; simple problems must be mastered before more complex ones are presented. During the process of learning how to learn, an organism may be learning many different things, such as what cues to ignore or pay attention to, a principle rather than a specific response, and how to relax and pay attention to the problems presented.

In practical terms, the effort you spend in developing skills in memorizing a wide variety of subjects, using reference books, interpreting tables, writing term papers, and so on, will have a big payoff as you develop a learning set and can transfer skills to other courses or your vocation.

SUMMARY

A. Sensory, Short-term, and Long-term Memory

1. Research supports the hypothesis that there are three kinds of memory—long-term and short-term memories and sensory store.

2. **Sensory store** (page 233) is assumed to be a large-capacity storage that receives sensory information but loses it very rapidly unless transferred into short-term memory.

3. **Short-term memory** (page 234) seems to be limited to a capacity of about seven "chunks" of information.

4. Experiments by different investigators indicate that one-half to 18 seconds is the limit of retention for short-term memory unless **rehearsal** (page 237) of the material takes place.

5. Short-term memories are apparently coded on the basis of auditory characteristics (such as the sound of words or names of items); in contrast, in the coding of long-term memories the *meaning* of the material is the most significant characteristic.

6. Ebbinghaus developed the first scientific measure of retention. He measured the time required to learn a list of three-letter **nonsense syllables** (page 239); then after a specified period of time he measured the length of time required for **relearning** (page 239) the same list. The difference between the two required learning times is used as a measure of retention.

7. **Recall, recognition** (page 240), and relearning are the most common methods of measuring retention.

B. Long-term Memory and Retention

8. Every one of us carries an enormous catalog of long-term memories that serve us in every aspect of our lives; the inability to recall desired information has been a problem to all of us.

9. Experiments such as those with the *tip-of-the-tongue phenomenon* (page 242) have led some researchers to assert that inability to recall long-term memories is usually a result of **retrieval** (page 238) problems rather than a loss of the "stored" memory.

10. Meaningful organization of material and meaningful clues—such as category labels—enhance the process of retention and make retrieval more efficient.

11. A **memory trace** (page 243) is assumed to be a change produced by learning in the chemistry or neurological circuitry of the brain that is responsible for memory.

12. The **interference hypothesis** (page 245) asserts that forgetting is primarily the result of interference or competition with the memory in question by other memories that may have been learned either before—**proactive interference**—or after—**retroactive interference**—the memory in question.

13. Forgetting because of **repression** (page 250) prevents recalling painful or disturbing material.

C. Methods That Improve Memory Recall

14. One aid to memory is visual organization, the association of items with a position in a spatial pattern or with objects in fixed positions that are familiar, such as the furniture of a familiar room, or the rooms of a house, etc.

15. Vivid imagery association with words or abstract ideas is a useful device, perhaps because both the verbal and nonverbal memory functions are involved.

16. Overlearning past the point of perfect recall increases retention up to a certain point, but after a moderate amount of extra study the increased retention for study time expended begins to diminish.

17. Recitation, or self-quizzing, of studied material is an effective use of a portion of study time, yielding better retention than the same amount of study without a portion of it devoted to recitation.

18. For most learning tasks distributing practice over a period of time enhances retention more than massed practice.

19. **Transfer of training** (page 254) refers to the effects of learned material and skills on learning new material and skills. If prior learning aids subsequent learning it is called **positive transfer.** If prior learning interferes with new learning, it is called **negative transfer.**

20. Humans (and some animals) develop **learning sets** (page 255), which consist of strategies that enable them to assess relevant information quickly in new situations similar to ones they have previously confronted.

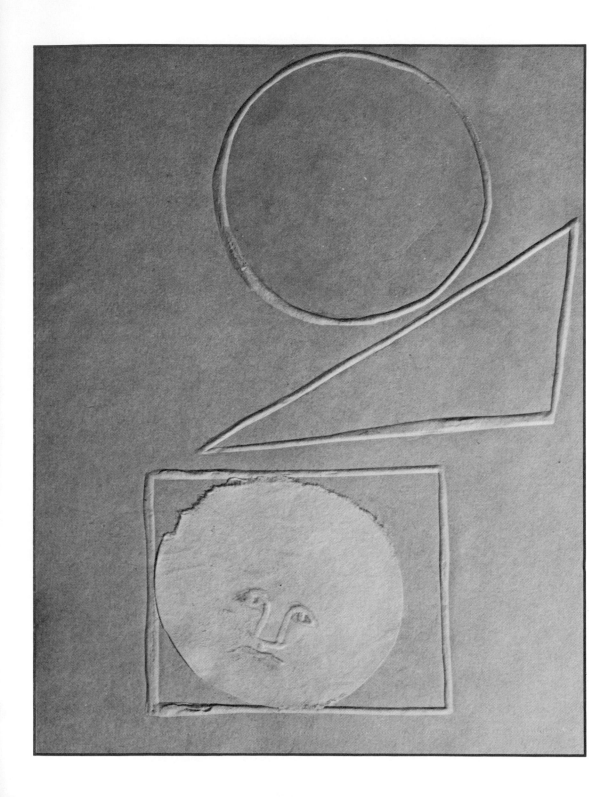

Section
Five
Thinking,
Knowing
Being

No two human beings are exactly alike. Individuals differ in a multitude of ways including intelligence, language abilities, and problem-solving skills. The assessment of these dimensions of differences and the exploration of the nature and nurture factors that produce these differences is the concern of this section, which focuses on the thinking and knowing aspect of our being. We will explore the answers to such questions as these: How are intelligence and creativity assessed? What role do nature and nurture play in the development of intelligence and creativity? What factors influence human language development and problem-solving behavior? What role does language play in problem-solving?

In our exploration of thinking and knowing we will take a close look at the way intelligence tests are used to assess individual differences. We will examine the issues underlying the current controversy over the role of race, nature, and nurture in determining intelligence. You will have an opportunity to try out sample questions and problems selected from creativity and problem-solving tests. And you will find out how chimpanzees have been taught to use language.

Chapter
Eight
Intelligence

FIGURE 8.1 Alfred Binet.

In 1904 the French Minister of Public Instruction presented Alfred Binet with a problem that was to make him—already a physiologist, hypnotist, lawyer, and playwright—a psychologist as well. The problem was to devise a means for identifying retarded children in the Paris school system so that they could be provided with special education. Binet's task, then, was to invent the world's first intelligence test. His solution to this problem, like most great solutions, was both brilliant and simple.

Binet reasoned that a child with average, or "normal," intelligence should be able to perform the same kinds of intellectual activities as other children the same age. If brighter than average, however, the child should not only be able to solve problems that age-mates can solve but should also be able to go beyond them, solving problems that ordinarily only older children are capable of solving. In other words, for this child **mental age** would be somewhat greater than **chronological age,** *or age in years.* On the other hand, if duller than average, the child would not be able to cope with material that age-mates find manageable but would function at a level characteristic of younger children—that is, mental age would be less than chronological age.

Once this line of reasoning concerning the relationship between mental (or intellectual) development and chronological age had been set forth, the construction of the actual intelligence test followed quite logically.

Binet gave large numbers of different kinds of problems to large numbers of children of different ages. If most (75 percent) of the children at a given age were able to solve a given problem, Binet included that problem in his test as representing characteristic performance at that age. The test that Binet eventually developed proved to be highly useful. Indeed, the **Stanford-Binet Intelligence Scale** (so named because of its revisions by Lewis Terman and Maud Merrill of Stanford University) remains to this day the most popular means of assessing the intelligence of children.

In this chapter we will describe some widely used tests that have been developed to measure intelligence and then turn to some of the ways intelligence tests can be misused. We will consider the development of intelligence and the characteristics of intelligent people. Next we will consider the question of the determinants of intelligence: what is responsible for intelligence—heredity or environment? Finally, we will look at the determinants of intelligence in the context of race.

A. INTELLIGENCE AND ITS ASSESSMENT

Before we continue we must ask the question: "What *is* intelligence?" This is far from an easy question to answer, and various psychologists have proposed different definitions. One thing they have all agreed on, however, is what intelligence is *not:* intelligence is not an entity, a "thing." You cannot open a skull, look in, and see "an intelligence." Intelligence is, rather, inferred from behavior in a variety of situations; it is a shorthand term for describing the quality or level of that behavior. Indeed, intelligence tests attempt to sample bits of behavior over a wide range of little problem-solving situations. In a sense, then, intelligence is what an intelligence test tests.

But this is a somewhat less-than-satisfying answer to our initial question. So we will offer you a definition that seems reasonable to us. This definition is provided by David Wechsler, who developed the most extensively used test of adult intelligence (which we will describe shortly). According to Wechsler:

Intelligence *is the aggregate or global capacity of the individual to act purposefully, to think rationally, and to deal effectively with his environment.*

Now let's survey some of the ways psychologists have devised to measure intelligence, starting with the Stanford-Binet.

THE STANFORD-BINET INTELLIGENCE SCALE

As we mentioned, this test has undergone several revisions but retains the same structure devised by Binet. Like Wechsler, Binet conceived of intelligence as a general, global capacity that finds expression in a number of ways. Consequently, he included a number of tests for each age, each tapping a different ability. Thus, there are six different subtests, or items, at each age level. For example, here is what the average two-year-old is expected to do on the Stanford-Binet.

The child is first presented with a form board containing blocks of different shapes — square, triangle, and circle. The examiner removes the blocks from their holes in the board and then says, "Now put them back into their holes." This is a test of spatial perception and analysis. For the next subtest, the child is shown three boxes and a small toy cat. The child is told, "Look, I'm going to hide the kitty, and then see if you can find it again" while the examiner puts the cat under one of the boxes. The examiner then screens the boxes from the child's view, counts off ten seconds, and tells the child to "find the kitty." This delightful game is designed to assess the child's attention and memory span.

Next, to assess awareness and comprehension, the child is shown a doll and asked to "show me the dolly's hair . . . mouth . . . feet . . . ear . . . nose . . . hands . . . eyes." Then a dozen one-inch blocks are scattered on the table, and the examiner constructs a tower four blocks high. Leaving the tower standing as a model, the examiner tells the child to "make one like this." Not only must the child be capable of the necessary eye-hand coordination but also, more importantly, the child must be capable of constructing the tower in response to the examiner's request; that is, the child must be capable of purposive behavior.

Next the two-year-old is shown cards with drawings of familiar objects, such as those in Figure 8.2, and asked "What's this? What do you call it?" Here the child is being tested for language development. Finally, the child's spontaneous speech dur-

FIGURE 8.2 Simulated items of the type used in the Stanford-Binet picture vocabulary subtest.

ing the testing session is monitored by the examiner for combinations of words, such as "Mama bye bye," "All gone," "See man," which represent rudimentary concept-formation.

Rationale for Tests. Although these tests seem to be almost embarrassingly simple in conception and construction, they involve many complex intellectual functions. The items, particularly at the lower age levels, are designed to engage and hold the frequently elusive interest of young children—hence their game-like quality. But the items have been retained not merely because they happen to appeal to children, but because they have survived a stringent screening process involving decades of work and thousands of subjects. The Stanford-Binet works, and works very well. For instance, it is a good predictor of school performance—astonishingly good when you consider the unreliability of grading procedures. The Stanford-Binet is also used in a variety of other settings, such as child clinics and special education programs. However, the tone of the Stanford-Binet makes it less appropriate for use with adults. At the adult level the **Wechsler Adult Intelligence Scale,** or **WAIS,** has emerged as the preferred instrument.

THE WECHSLER ADULT INTELLIGENCE SCALE

The WAIS consists of eleven subtests, six tests stressing verbal abilities and five involving perceptual-motor skills. Thus, a "verbal" and a "performance" score can be derived independently, as well as a full-scale, or "total," score. Perhaps the best way to describe the WAIS is to present you with some items from the different subtests together with the functions measured by the subtests.

FIGURE 8.3 *David Wechsler.*

Verbal Subtests

Let's start with the verbal subtests, in the order in which they are presented to the examinee. Examples are given in Figure 8.4. (The items are simulations of test items in order to preserve the integrity of the actual test.) All the verbal subtests are given orally.

Performance Subtests

The first performance subtest is Digit Symbol, which requires the examinee to substitute symbols for digits according to a key such as the one that appears in Figure 8.5A. As many substitutions as possible must be made within 90 seconds (unlike most of the verbal subtests, all the performance subtests have time limits). The Digit Symbol subtest measures perceptual-motor coordination and rote learning ability. The Picture Completion subtest taps visual analytic abilities and awareness of relevant detail; it requires the examinee to identify a missing component or part in a picture, as in the drawing of the animal (a simulation of the test) in Figure 8.5B. In Block Design, the next subtest, the subject is given a number of red-and-white blocks

SUBTEST NAME	SAMPLE ITEM	FUNCTION MEASURED
Information	What is a kumquat? What is a subpoena? What is a windjammer?	Long-term memory; openness to environment
Comprehension	What is the advantage of keeping money in a bank? Why is copper often used in making electrical wires? Why should a contract be honored?	Abstraction and generalization; awareness of social norms
Arithmetic	If two apples cost 15 cents, what will be the cost of three dozen apples? (20-second time limit) If a tree grows 50 percent of its height each year, and is eight feet tall when planted, how tall will it be after three years? (20-second time limit)	Concentration; computational skills
Similarities	In what way are an hour and a week alike? In what way are a circle and a triangle alike? In what way are mercy and courage alike?	Verbal abstraction
Digit span	I am going to say some numbers. Listen carefully, and when I am through say them right after me: "8-1-3-7-4-9-2-6-5" [numbers are presented at the rate of one per second].	Attention; short-term memory
Vocabulary	I want you to tell me the meanings of some words. What does "apathetic" mean? "induce"? "obfuscate"? "reify"?	Language development; long-term memory

FIGURE 8.4 Simulated items of the kind used in the WAIS verbal subtests. (The first two items under Comprehension and Similarities provided by the Psychological Corporation.)

and asked to construct designs such as the one shown in Figure 8.5C. This is a test of visual abstraction. The Picture Arrangement subtest has the examinee arrange a set of pictures (for example, see the simulation in Figure 8.5D) "so that they make the most sensible story." Performance here indicates the examinee's awareness of and appropriateness of response to situational cues. Finally, Object Assembly requires the examinee to solve a number of puzzles; the scattered pieces of a simulated one may be seen in Figure 8.5E. The Object Assembly subtest depends on the ability to perceive part-whole relationships, as well as on concentration.

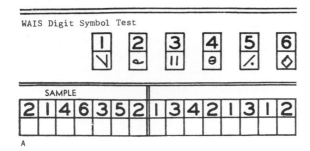

WAIS Digit Symbol Test

A

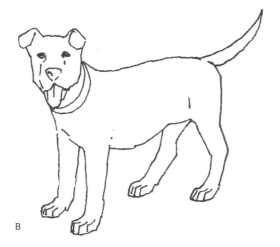

B

C

Profiles

Scores on the various subtests of the WAIS yield a picture or "profile" of intellectual abilities, showing relative strengths and weaknesses. For example, the profile in Figure 8.6 represents the WAIS performance of a 22-year-old, single, male college senior who was applying for a sales job. The unusual feature of this profile is the singularly high score that he obtained on the Picture Arrangement subtest, suggesting a heightened sensitivity to social nuances and situational cues.

The WAIS, like the Stanford-Binet, has undergone extensive and painstaking revision. The sample used to develop the test consisted of 1700 people chosen to be representative of the population of the United States with respect to age, sex, geographic region, urban or rural residence, race, occupation, and education. Two dozen testing centers were set up throughout the country, and from these, trained examiners spread out to cover the local area. For example, an examiner in the South would be required to find and test a male who was white, between 45 and 54 years old, who was a craftsman, who lived in an urban center, and who had no more than eight years of education. It is largely owing to such procedures that the WAIS has been so widely accepted.

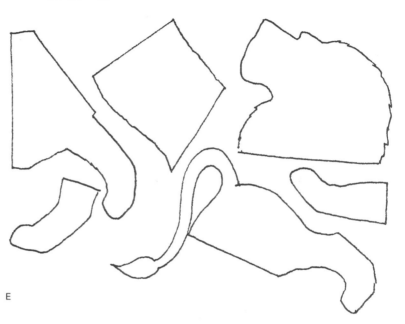

FIGURE 8.5 (A) Simulated Digit Symbol subtest of the WAIS (Courtesy The Psychological Corporation). (B) Simulated Picture Completion subtest of the WAIS. (C) Example of Block Design subtest (photo, Courtesy The Psychological Corporation). (D) Simulated Picture Arrangement subtest of the WAIS. (Drawing by CEM; © 1974 The New Yorker Magazine, Inc. The drawing, jumbled here, can be seen in its correct order on page 288.) (E) Simulated Object Assembly subtest of the WAIS.

E

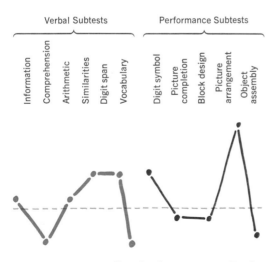

FIGURE 8.6 Profile of subtest scores. Broken line shows examinee's average performance.

GROUP TESTS OF INTELLIGENCE

Both the Stanford-Binet and the WAIS are administered to a single examinee at a time and so are time-consuming (and expensive, in terms of the examiner's time). Such individually administered tests are preferable in some settings—such as schools, clinics, and hospitals. But in many situations a gross measure of intelligence, obtained in a rapid, cheap, and efficient way, can prove useful as an initial screening device. In the armed services, for example, large numbers of people must be evaluated and processed. It was in response to this need that the Army General Classification Test (AGCT) was developed. This test makes use of multiple-choice items and can be machine-scored (Figure 8.7). While lacking the flexibility and richness of individual tests, group tests are better than no tests at all. For example, the AGCT can predict success in Officer Candidate School.

Now that you have seen some of the techniques used to measure intelligence, we can move on to consider such questions as these: How are intelligence tests abused? How can this abuse be prevented? How do an individual's test-taking attitude and motivation influence the test results?

B. ABUSES OF INTELLIGENCE TESTS

You are a fledgling **psychometrician** (*a specialist in giving and interpreting psychological tests*), and it's your first day on the job at a ghetto school. You are somewhat apprehensive, not only because you are new on the job but also because, having been reared in a middle-class environment, you are not quite sure what to expect or how to react in your new surroundings. As you are arranging your testing materials, the door opens and your first examinee of the day is ushered in by a person who hands you a slip of paper on which there is the cryptic message: "Slow reader. Cannot pay attention. Disturbs other children. Suspected mental deficiency." After admonishing the examinee to sit still and mind you, the messenger turns and walks out, leaving the two of you together in the strained silence of the small, drab, and windowless testing room. The examinee who sits with downcast eyes across the table from you is a thin, poorly clothed, and poorly fed nine-year-old boy. His nose is running profusely from what must be a

severe cold, and his left eye is badly bruised, perhaps the result of a morning beating. As you attempt to ease the situation by making a few friendly remarks, it is obvious that he is both frightened and hostile. It also becomes rapidly apparent that he has no idea why he is there or what you are going to "do" to him. As you explain the nature of the test, he merely nods; there is no real way to determine whether he understands or not, or even if he is listening. Indeed, he is almost mute, speaking only when spoken to, and then in monosyllables. As you begin the test, he responds only in the most perfunctory manner. He exerts just enough effort to comply with your demands but is unwilling to go further. It is an effort to pull each answer from him. He seems to brighten slightly when working on performance tests, but he lapses back into sullen apathy as soon as verbal materials are reintroduced. Although you have been working with him for over an hour, it is obvious that he trusts or likes you no more than he did at the beginning. Now, just as you are in the middle of a test which you feel is at last challenging his potential, the bell rings, doors slam, and pandemonium breaks loose in the hall outside.

Are Your Results Valid? How valid do you think the results of your intelligence test will be? Herein lies the greatest source of the misuse of intelligence tests, the belief that performance on an intelligence test reflects anything more than one's *present level* of functioning. In other words, intelligence tests reflect ability (what one is currently doing) not capacity (what one could do under optimal conditions). Intelligence tests can only provide a reasonable index of intellectual capacity or potential when they are administered under optimal

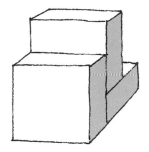

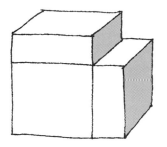

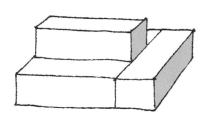

To CHEER means most nearly   (U) unite (V) mail (W) fear (X) shout

To PERMIT is to........ (Y) demand   (Z) thank   (A) allow   (B) charge

CALM means................ (G) loud   (H) cross   (I) quiet   (J) thin

PROFIT is................. (K) crop   (L) attempt   (M) help   (N) gain

Tom spends 15 cents a day for carfare, and Jim spends 10 cents a day for carfare. How much do Tom and Jim spend together for carfare in 5 days?   (M) $1.75   (N) 85¢   (O) $1.00   (P) $1.25

A square lot has two hundred feet of fence around it. How many feet of fence are there on one side of the lot?   (Q) 20   (R) 50   (S) 100   (T) 75

FIGURE 8.7 Sample items from the Army General Classification Test. How many blocks are in each group?

conditions. And there are many conditions, some obvious and some subtle, that can and do lower performance on intelligence tests. These conditions *must* be taken into account in evaluating any individual's performance on any test. The problem is, they are often overlooked. There seems to be a public predisposition to treat intelligence tests as magic and their scores as sacred. There are few things that have the ring of immutable, unalterable truth as does the **IQ score,** *the quantitative summarization of an individual's performance on an intelligence test.* The real truth is, however, that there are few things that are as meaningless *in and of themselves* as IQ scores. IQ scores can be affected by a host of factors, and the competent examiner is alert to these factors and evaluates their impact on the examinee's performance. Let's look at some of them.

INFLUENCES ON TEST RESULTS

Long-term Factors. First, there are longstanding factors, such as chronic physical or mental illness. If you are chronically run down or sick you are not going to do well on anything, let alone a test. Similarly, emotional disturbance disrupts all aspects of functioning, and intellectual

Focus 8.1
Why Test?

CUSTOMER (to shoe salesman): How did you happen to get into this?

SHOE SALESMAN: Well, it's not the kind of thing you start out hoping you'll be. I began as a stockboy and just kept getting raises and promotions until, now, I'm the store manager. If I changed jobs, I'd have to take such a cut in wages that I couldn't afford it.

CUSTOMER: Do you like it?

SHOE SALESMAN: Honestly? No.

Why give psychological tests? The answer is: Either to help psychologists make decisions about people, or to help people make decisions about themselves. As an example of the former case, personality tests (Chapter 10) are used to establish diagnoses and indicate treatment procedures for mental illness, as discussed in Chapter 11. As an example of the latter, let's return to the little vignette with which we introduced this focus—vocational choice. The most recent Dictionary of Occupational Titles published by the Department of Labor lists 21,741 distinct occupations ranging from "abalone diver" to "zylomounter" (one who mounts lenses in zyloplastic eyeglass frames). How is one to choose intelligently among such an array of alternatives?

In the absence of relevant information, people tend to find themselves with vocational "plans" similar to those of 1600 eighth-graders surveyed in Cincinnati. If these students actually wound up in the occupations of their choice, Cincinnati would be a fascinating place to live in ten years hence. For instance, the health of the inhabitants would be amply protected, since there would be five doctors and four nurses for every person. (However, health services would be prohibitively expensive, since few people could afford to support five doctors and four nurses.) And it might well be that all these doctors and nurses would be needed in a city with no water supply and no sanitation sys-

functioning is no exception. And then there's poverty. Many children come to school with no more than a cup of coffee for breakfast (if that), and they have no money for lunch. They can hardly be expected to exhibit their optimal performance. Cultural differences are also important. Although attempts have been made to develop "culture-fair" tests, these have not met with great success, and most intelligence tests in use today were developed by white middle-class psychologists (and, in some cases, standardized on white, middle-class samples). The content and

material of the tests reflects this bias, and prejudices the performance of other cultural groups. For example, an item from the Stanford-Binet reads: "Donald went walking in the woods. He saw a pretty little animal that he tried to take home for a pet. It got away from him, but when he got home, his family immediately burned all his clothes. Why?" How many ghetto children have seen a skunk? These children tend to be more familiar with other forms of animal life; for example, many ghetto children identify a picture of a Teddy bear as a "rat." (Sometimes, if tem, since no one chose to enter these fields. But it might prove difficult to call a doctor in a city which had only three telephone operators and no telephone linemen to make repairs. Indeed, simply getting enough to eat would present a problem, since the lines would be long in front of the three grocery stores. Long hair would be fashionable even among the Establishment, since the one barber could hardly be expected to handle the rush, although he could refer some of his customers to the 28 beauticians. The city plumber would probably have his hands full, too. If people got tired of waiting for the two bus drivers and three taxi drivers, they could always avail themselves of the services of the 67 airline pilots. Even so, it might still be difficult getting to the stadium to watch the 40 baseball players.

Psychologists have developed aptitude, interest, and value tests to assist people in making choices about their future. These tests serve a number of purposes. First, such psychological tests attempt to maximize the likelihood that individuals will be both productive and happy in positions commensurate with their talents and predilections, in which they will find intrinsic gratification and a sense of self-fulfillment. Second, such psychological tests attempt to minimize the often tragic frustration, disillusionment, and alienation of people seeking positions on bases other than their aptitudes and interests. As Abraham Maslow of Brandeis University put it: ". . . the ultimate and perfect ideal would run something like this: This person is the best one in the whole world for this particular job, and this particular job is the best job in the whole world for this particular person and his talents, capacities, and tastes. He was meant for it, and it was meant for him."

Finally, psychological tests are not substitutes for judgment; rather, they provide the individual with objective information that he or she can employ in making an intelligent and informed decision.

rarely, the bias works the other way, as, for example, when children from economically deprived urban areas do better on an item that involves the principle of the siphon.)

Test-taking Attitudes. Perhaps even more important than the actual content of the test are the values and attitudes surrounding the very notion of "taking a test." From birth on, most middle-class children are expected to achieve in school and do well on "tests." They are imbued with the notion that one should always try as hard as one can on tests (even if one doesn't understand the reason for the test), and that doing well on a test is its own intrinsic reward (along with such extrinsic rewards as gold stars and grades). In short, middle-class children are both test-oriented and test-wise. Unfortunately (or perhaps fortunately) the whole world does not share these values. Some reject such values consciously, but many more do so by circumstance. For example, what of the child who is raised in poor and crowded conditions where the father is absent and the mother has all she can do simply to keep the family together? Life is a day-to-day struggle, and long-term goals, such as a college education, are really irrelevant. The children are left pretty much to fend for themselves, and at least they are quiet as long as they are watching television. There are no books in the home. Books, too, are irrelevant, and even if there were books, the mother wouldn't have time (or energy) to read them with the child. But the problem is deeper than this: it's the poverty and despair that makes what goes on in school so meaningless, so divorced from everyday reality. And this is the perspective from which many lower-class children view tests, including intelligence tests. As the test reports often put it, the child's "motivation is suspect."

Short-term Factors. There are also more transitory, or situational, factors which may adversely affect intelligence test scores. One factor that is frequently ignored, but that can have an overriding effect on test performance, is the examinee's perception of the purpose of the test. Examiners would often be astounded if they asked the examinee what he or she thought was the reason for the test. The examiner may view the test as a means of helping the examinee. The examinee, on the other hand, may view the test as an attempt at entrapment. The examinee may be a juvenile who has been ordered by the court to be tested. What is he or she *supposed* to think of the test under such conditions? Consequently, the examinee may attempt to be guarded in responses, to "play dumb." In any event, the examinee's views of the purpose of the test have a bearing on behavior and performance in the test situation and should be explored. Perhaps the cardinal sin is not to explain

anything, leaving the examinee free to imagine all kinds of explanations, such as "Is this to find out if I'm crazy?"

Other simple, but frequently overlooked, factors include transitory illness and anxiety. The examinee may have awakened with a headache or upset stomach that morning but fails to mention it so as not to inconvenience the examiner. The examinee may be anxious about the test. Many, if not most, people are somewhat anxious about being tested; if not allayed, this anxiety may be enough to disrupt performance. This problem leads us to one final consideration, that of rapport. Rapport refers to the quality, or tone, of the relationship between examiner and examinee. It is up to the examiner to establish "good" rapport, that is, to put the examinee at ease and engage the person's interest and cooperation. Unless good rapport has been achieved, the results of an intelligence test are open to question.

PREVENTING ABUSE

Most abuses of intelligence tests stem from a failure to take such factors into account. Please note, however, that criticism is not an indictment of intelligence tests but of the unsophisticated (and occasionally irresponsible) manner in which they are sometimes used. The key to preventing the abuse of intelligence tests lies in ensuring that they are administered and interpreted by skilled and sensitive people who are aware of the limitations as well as the advantages of the tests. As Alfred Binet found in his early work, even a relatively crude intelligence test is far more useful than subjective judgments of intelligence. When used by competent personnel, intelligence tests are among psychology's most valuable contributions to society.

C. DEVELOPMENT OF INTELLIGENCE

How does intelligence normally develop? For the answer to this formidable question, we turn to the genius of the Swiss psychologist Jean Piaget. For over half a century Piaget, often using his own children as subjects, has been devising ingenious little experiments that not only permit us to see the world through a child's eyes (rather than a psychologist's) but have also led to a theory of intellectual development.

Sensorimotor Period

According to Piaget's theory, *the first stage of development (the* **sensorimotor period***) occurs roughly during the first two years of life. The child learns to integrate sensory information from different sense modalities* (e.g., to look at what is being listened to) *and to coordinate motor reactions with this sensory input.* The child also learns that objects in the real world (including people) have an existence of their own independent of the child's perception of them; this awareness is not present in the beginning of this stage. For example, Piaget describes the following experiment with his eight-month-old daughter, Jacqueline:

Jacqueline takes possession of my watch which I offer her while holding the chain in my hand. She examines the watch with great interest, feels it, turns it over, says "apff," etc. . . . If, before her eyes, I hide the watch behind my hand, behind the quilt, etc., she does not react and forgets everything immediately.

And, at nine months:

Jacqueline is seated and I place on her lap a rubber eraser which she has just held in her hand. Just as she is about to grasp it again I put my hand between her eyes and the eraser; she immediately gives up, as though the object no longer existed. . . . Same attempts with a marble, a pencil, etc., and same reactions. My hand does not interest her at all; therefore it

FIGURE 8.8 Jean Piaget working with children.

is not a shift in interest that causes forgetfulness; it is simply because the image of my hand abolishes that of the object beneath it. . . . (Piaget, 1954)

Out of sight, out of mind. At the end of the sensorimotor period, however, Jacqueline has become quite sophisticated in finding hidden objects; she has learned that *objects continue to exist even when they can't be seen.* That is, she has developed the concept of **object constancy.**

Preoperational Period

The second stage in the development of intelligence (the **preoperational period***) runs from about two to seven years of age, and it is now that the child begins to use symbols, or representations of objects and events.* For instance, the child plays games of pretend, in which rocking chairs become ponies or dolls become babies. Now, too, the child begins to employ language in a truly symbolic sense, becoming able to talk about things that are not physically present. For example, the youngster can talk about lions and tigers without actually viewing the animals. Still, the preoperational child's thinking is full of inconsistencies and paradoxes that are not resolved until the next stage, as the following experiment illustrates. A seven-year-old child is given a ball of clay and asked to make another of the same size and shape. After the child does so, the experiment begins:

EXPERIMENTER: You see these two little balls here. Is there just as much dough in this one as in this one?

CHILD: Yes.

EXPERIMENTER: Now watch (and the experimenter rolls one of the balls into a sausage).

CHILD: The sausage has more dough.

EXPERIMENTER: And if I roll it up into a ball again?

CHILD: Then I think there will be the same amount. (The clay is rolled into a ball again, and the other ball is flattened into a disc.)

EXPERIMENTER: There's still as much dough?

CHILD: There is more dough in the ball. (Flavell, 1963)

Other examples of preoperational-period paradoxes may be seen in Focus 8.2: The Concept of Conservation, page 276.

Concrete Operation Period

In the third stage (the **concrete operation period** *— seven to eleven years) the child acquires basic notions of time, space, and number.* Now, too, the child begins to deal logically with concrete problems. For example, an experimenter builds a tower of blocks on a table. The child is given some blocks and told to build a tower the same height as the experimenter's on another table. The problem lies in the fact that the child's table is lower than the experimenter's table. There are a number of sticks of different lengths at the child's disposal, although the experimenter provides no clues to their possible use. The younger child compares the towers by eye only in an attempt to equalize the floor-to-top heights rather than the table-to-top heights (that is, the heights of the towers only). Children in the third stage, however, make use of one of the sticks as a measuring unit to determine "how many sticks long" the examiner's tower is (see Figure 8.9).

Formal Operations Period

While the child in the third stage of intellectual development can solve such concrete problems, he or she cannot as yet think in abstract, hypothetical, "what if?" terms. The concrete-operational child can-

FIGURE 8.9 Children between the ages of seven and eleven, like the girl, are able to use measuring units to build towers of equal height, but younger children, like the boy, are unable to do so.

Focus 8.2

The Concept of Conservation

During the preoperational period, the child has not yet learned how to intellectually "conserve." For example, if four marbles that were arranged like this

○ ○ ○ ○

are, right before the child's eyes, rearranged like this

○   ○   ○   ○

the child will steadfastly maintain that the rearrangement contains more marbles. The child is struck by the visual-spatial evidence at that moment rather than by knowledge that these are the same four marbles in new positions. The child cannot maintain the conception of the *number* of marbles in the face of the fact that they now occupy a larger space. Piaget terms this a lack of ability to "conserve" the idea of number. The child also has difficulty conserving other qualities of stimuli, such as volume, mass, or speed if the immediate senses hint at changes (e.g., a row of marbles grown wider) having taken place. The ability to conserve will not come until the concrete operation period, the next stage of intellectual development.

A very prominent psychologist was discussing Piaget with a young developmental psychologist who stated that even very intelligent children of five years of age usually did not have the ability to conserve. The eminent psychologist scoffed at this. His little boy of five could read, write, and had an IQ approaching the boiling point of water. Surely he would be able to conserve! The test was arranged.

The developmental psychologist brought with him the equipment in Figure 8.10A. The high-IQ boy and his eminent father watched him fill two identical glasses with water. The boy admitted that both glasses had equal amounts of water. As the boy and father watched, the developmental psychologist poured the water from one of the glasses into a tall, narrow, glass cylinder (Figure 8.10B). The boy was then presented with glass containers X and Y in Figure 8.10C. Both had equal amounts of water. One was in its original glass; the other was now in a taller and narrower container. "Is the amount of water the same in both containers?" the boy was asked. He unhesitatingly pointed to the taller container and said, "This one has more water." The developmental psychologist looked triumphantly at the father. The father, flustered, turned to the boy and repeated the problem using different phrasings and emphasizing that the boy had just seen the water poured into the container. But the boy steadfastly maintained what he thought his senses told him. The water level was higher in the narrow container. He trusted this concrete evidence above everything. Despite his intelligence, he had not matured enough to take into account simultaneously the two factors of area and height. If the water had been poured into

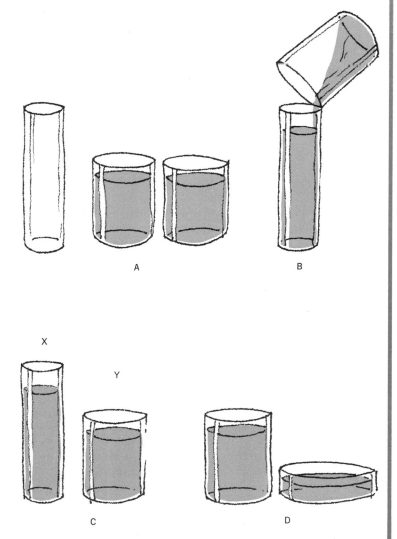

FIGURE 8.10 The conservation concept illustrated with volume of water (see text).

a wide, shallow container as in Figure 8.10D, he would probably have claimed that the shallow container had *less* water. The overwhelming majority of children at this stage of development will agree.

The ability to conserve is critical for later intellectual development. It appears to be determined in part by the growth and development of neurological networks, and in part by the environment giving the child the opportunity to practice the relevant experiences. If a child is not maturationally ready for this stage of intellectual activity, training will only be a frustration. If a child has had restricted experience, maturation is not enough.

Focus 8.3

Piaget and Intelligence Tests

A child is shown pictures of cylinders illustrating the conservation task (see Focus 8.2). By answering such questions as, "Which cylinder has the most water?" or "Which cylinders have the same amount of water?" the child reveals significant information about his or her intellectual development. By selecting a picture similar to those in Figure 8.10, the child helps to place himself into one of Jean Piaget's categories of intellectual development. Originally used in studies of the *development* of intelligence, problems like these are being used in a unique intelligence test under development by Adrian Pinard of the University of Montreal.

To Pinard, the use of Piaget's questions in an intelligence test seems a natural step. Intelligence tests, he believes, should be based on a coherent theory of the nature of intelligence. Most standard test procedures consist of asking children (or adults) to perform a series of tasks and comparing the number of such tasks successfully accomplished to the average performance of the individual's peers. Certainly, the score thus attained reflects an individual's ability to perform the required tasks, but whether or not the performance of the tasks directly reflects the cognitive development that is characteristic of the human being—"intelligence"—is uncertain. We need some notion of what we are seeking to insure that our test measures it.

For an understanding of intelligence, Pinard turned to the work of Jean Piaget and his theory of intellectual development.

Focus 8.4

Characteristics of Intelligent People

What are bright people like? A number of psychological studies of gifted people have shown that the highly intelligent are generally taller, heavier, physically healthier, and (perhaps) mentally healthier than those of average intelligence. These are rather general traits, however, and a more refined, differentiated picture of the highly intelligent individual would be desirable. Jonathan Warren and Paul Heist of the University of California undertook to provide such a picture. Their first step was to select a sample of highly intelligent people. They accomplished this goal by contacting all National Merit Scholarship winners in a given year—over 900 people—whose average level of intelligence exceeded that of 98 percent of the population. Warren and Heist then proceeded to administer various personality tests (which we will discuss in Chapter 10 on personality) to this highly selected group. They compared their responses to those gathered earlier from average college students (who are themselves brighter than the general population). A number of differences that emerged between these groups distinguish the highly intelligent.

In Piaget's research and in Pinard's pilot version of the intelligence test, a problem or puzzle, such as the conservation task, is presented and a verbatim record is made of the child's reasoning. The child's reasoning record is made because the child's justification for the reply —whether the reply is correct or incorrect—is as significant as the selected solution itself. For instance, in one puzzle the child is shown a nail and a container of water and asked if the nail placed in the water will float or sink and *why* it will do so. One child may reply correctly that the nail will sink, but when asked why it will do so will reply, "Because it likes getting wet," showing a *preoperational* level justification. Another child may predict that the nail will float, explaining that the nail "isn't very heavy for its size, so the water will hold it up." Although this reply is incorrect, it displays a process of reasoning from principle that is characteristic of the *formal operational* level, an advanced development compared to the other child who got the "right answer."

Pinard's initial work was a pilot study for the development of a precise instrument for the measurement of intelligence. Although the complete analysis of his results and the completion of the test are still underway, his work has already yielded certain results. In general, his study of Montreal children confirmed Piaget's assertion that the order in which each stage of thinking appears is fixed.

The characteristic that most sharply differentiates the highly intelligent person is an interest in intellectual activities. He or she *likes* to engage in abstract and reflective thought, is interested in ideas and concepts, and approaches the world in a rational and cognitive manner. Another major (and somewhat more surprising) characteristic of the highly intelligent is a strong esthetic orientation. The very bright person prefers artistic rather than utilitarian aspects of the environment and is more concerned with harmony and form in experience. In addition, the highly intelligent person appears somewhat more independent, confident, flexible, and, in the case of men, socially extroverted. Finally, the very bright person exhibits an interesting dichotomy between the intellectual and the emotional life. While intellectually very expressive, and even rebellious, when it comes to emotional expression the gifted individual is more reserved and controlled than the average person. It seems as if highly intelligent people have a life style that is colored by their exceptional intellect, including the hue that is given to their modes of emotional expression.

not, for example, conduct "experiments" in the mind.

This remarkable ability is attained only in a *fourth and final stage (the* **formal operations period***), which occurs between 11 and 15 years of age. The individual has now reached the pinnacle of intellectual development and can formulate and test hypotheses in the head.* The formal-operational person's thinking is no longer constrained by the "givens" of the immediate situation but can work in probability and possibility. The person can now consider the implications of such questions as: "What would happen if pollution of the atmosphere significantly decreased the amount of sunlight striking the earth's surface?"

Are the Stages Invariant?

Although Piaget admits to wide individual variability in attaining these stages, he maintains that their sequence is invariant: later stages depend on and incorporate the functions of earlier stages. This last point — the invariant order of the stages — is in considerable dispute. Many psychologists — most notably, Jerome Bruner of Harvard — claim that children can actually achieve the functions that Piaget assigns to his later stages much earlier in life. This controversy is by no means settled, however, and Piaget's theory remains the most comprehensive account of intellectual development yet proposed.

Although it is not yet fully clear how intelligence develops, it is evident that some people are extremely intelligent. Focus 8.4, on the preceding pages, discussed the physiological and psychological characteristics of intelligent people.

D. THE DETERMINANTS OF INTELLIGENCE

What determines a person's level of intelligence — nature or nurture? The answer, as always seems to be the case with such questions, is: both. Heredity sets the upper limits of intelligence, and environment determines the degree to which those limits are approached. In other words, genes determine an individual's intellectual potential, and experience determines the extent to which that potential is fulfilled.

HEREDITY

The case for heredity draws its strongest support from the study of identical (monozygotic) twins. Since identical twins share the same genes, they have the same hereditary endowment. (See Focus 2.3: Twinning.) Now suppose that we have two pairs of identical twins. One pair has been raised together in the same home but, for some reason, the members of the other pair were separated early in life and raised in different homes, or environments. What happens if we test the intelligence of these two pairs of identical twins in adulthood? It follows logically that the degree to which the reared-apart twins are as similar in intelligence as the reared-together twins is determined by heredity. And, conversely, the degree to which the reared-apart twins differ in intelligence as compared to the reared-together twins may be ascribed to the effects of environment. But what constitutes a "similarity" or a "difference"? To evaluate the size of a difference between any two objects, we need some kind of standard or benchmark. In this case, the ideal benchmark is a pair of fraternal (dizygotic) twins, who are, of course, born together, but who share no more genetic material than do any other sets of siblings.

The Strategy Employed. The strategy we have just outlined was that followed by James Shields of the Institute of Psychiatry in London. Identical twins are a rare occurrence, and identical twins who have been separated early in life and reared apart are rarer still. Nevertheless, through an appeal over BBC television, Shields was able to locate and test 44 pairs of identical twins who had been reared apart; he matched them with 44 pairs who had been raised together. With somewhat greater ease he also collected a sample of fraternal twins. The average *difference* in intelligence between pair members in each of these groups —identical twins reared together, identical twins reared apart, and fraternal twins—is shown in Figure 8.11. The similarity in intelligence of identical twins who were raised apart is far more like that of identical twins who were raised together than that of fraternal twins. This evidence is strong support for the role of heredity in determining intelligence.

The difference in adult intelligence found between the two groups of identical twins suggests that environment (in this case, different rearing experiences) also plays a role. Nevertheless, the striking aspect of Shields's results is that, even after a lifetime of different experiences, heredity is strong enough to exert a powerful and pervasive influence on intellectual functioning in adulthood. This is not to say, as we shall presently see, that environment *cannot* have important effects on intelligence. The experiences of the twins reared apart, while disparate, were probably not dramatically so. Most were raised in Great Britain and, as Shields notes, "wide cultural differences between the homes were

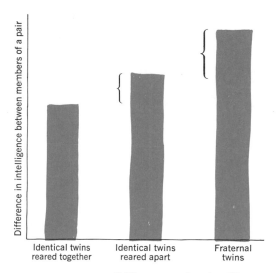

FIGURE 8.11 Differences in intelligence among pairs of twins.

exceptional." But it is to say that, under "normal" conditions, heredity counts, and counts heavily.

ENVIRONMENT

In twins, nature has presented psychologists with a nicely controlled experiment, in that the hereditary makeup of the subjects is known, just as surely as if the experimenter had carefully manipulated it. When it comes to studying environmental determinants of intelligence, however, we are in a less fortunate position. For obvious reasons, it is not possible to take groups of children, submit them to different environments, and then assess the effect of these different "treatments" on their intellectual functioning. When psychologists run up against this sort of impasse, they often turn to the study of other organisms, and this has been the case in the study of environmental influences on intelligence. The impact of the environment on

Focus 8.5
Mental Retardation

Since the early 1960s there has been an enormous increase in public concern for the mentally retarded, a handicapped minority that constitutes three percent of our total population. This concern was partly the result of attention given to the welfare of the mentally retarded by the Kennedy administration and partly a response to the striking success achieved in early detection and prevention techniques. Once a swamp of ignorance and hopelessness, mental retardation is rapidly being opened up to understanding. As one consequence, our capacity to prevent and possibly to cure is also growing.

Mental retardation *refers to mental impairment occurring sometime between conception and 16 years of age that places the individual far below the average in intelligence and in ability to adapt to the natural and social demands of the environment.* Currently, the mentally retarded are classified according to their educational capacities. Those in the *Borderline Mentally Retarded* category (IQ between 68 and 85), by far the majority of retardates, can learn standard school material up to about the fifth or sixth grade level. They usually can learn to be self-supporting members of society. The *Mildly Mentally Retarded* (IQ between 52 and 67) generally will not learn to read or handle symbols with any facility, but they may be able to hold a useful job with some special supervision. They do not usually achieve the ability to live independently. In the relatively rare cases of *Moderate to Severe Retardation* (IQ below 51), close care will be necessary throughout life. The most severely retarded (IQ below 20) may be unable to master even such simple skills as personal hygiene, and they are totally unable to function outside an institution or home.

Retardation has been traced to a variety of causes. Viruses to which the expectant mother is exposed, such as rubella, may impair fetal development and lead to later retardation of the yet unborn infant. Any disorder that limits the supply of oxygen to the unborn or to the child at birth may produce brain damage and possible retardation. Some diseases, such as meningitis and encephalitis, and some poisons, such as lead, may produce retardation in a child born with normal intelligence. Certain forms of retardation that are the result of genetic factors were discussed in Chapter 2 — Down's syndrome and P.K.U.

Not all retardation is the result of physiological defects or damage, however. Retardation can be the result of a deprived environment where language skills and learning opportunities are not sufficient for full development, leaving the child with an enormous disadvantage. A disproportionately large number of retardates come from lower-income, less educated segments of society. Whitney Young, director of the National Urban League, sums up the situation by stating, "There is now ample evidence to show that poverty — and the physical, intellectual, and emotional deprivations that go with it — can be a direct cause of mental retardation."

an organism's life falls into two major periods: prenatal and postnatal. Let's look at prenatal influences first.

Protein-poor Diets. In a laboratory at the University of California's Los Angeles campus, Stephen Zamenhof, Edith van Marthens, and Frank Margolis placed female rats, one month before they became pregnant, on a diet that contained only one-third of their normal protein requirement; the diet was continued throughout pregnancy. Another group of rats received an adequate protein diet. It should be emphasized that the first group of rats was not "starved"; both groups received the same number of calories, the first group receiving enough starch to make up for lost protein calories. In short, they were protein-deprived. When the mothers gave birth, their pups were sacrificed and their brains examined for number and quality of neurons. (Neurons, as we saw in Chapter 3, are the brain cells involved in information transmission; they are fixed in number at birth—you don't get any more.) The brains of the pups born to protein-deprived mothers, compared to the normal-diet group, contained significantly fewer neurons; furthermore, the neurons contained less protein, which is vital to neuronal functioning.

The World Health Organization estimates that half of the world's three-billion-plus (and growing) population suffers from an inadequate food supply; "inadequate" usually means "protein-deficient." In the United States alone, one of every ten people—over 25 million persons—live below the poverty line established by the federal government. Although it is always difficult (and risky) to generalize from animal research to human behavior, a number of field studies have suggested that protein deficiency before birth results in brain de-

ficiency in human infants. In such observational studies of human groups, however, it is impossible to determine whether other factors are not at least partly responsible, such as postbirth malnutrition, infection, or inadequate social and emotional environments. For an experimental answer to this question we must travel to the Berkeley campus of the University of California, where research into postnatal environmental influences on mental capacity has been conducted by Mark Rosenzwieg, David Krech, Edward Bennett, and Marian Diamond.

Stimulus-poor Environments. Again, the organism under study is the ubiquitous rat. After weaning (about one month of age) the young rat pups are taken from their mother and placed in one of two very different environments. In the "enriched" environment, the pup is housed in a large cage with about a dozen other pups. The cage is equipped with a number of "toys" such as ladders, wheels, boxes, and platforms that are varied from day to day (Figure 8.12). Each day the pup, in the company of a half-dozen of its cage-mates, is permitted to explore a three-foot-square area with a pattern of barriers that is also varied daily. In the "impoverished" environment, the pup lives in isolation in an individual cage suspended in a fiber glass box that is, in turn, placed in a sound-insulated room.

The following differences appear between the two groups of rats. The enriched environment produces animals with bigger brains (especially cerebral cortex) and more of the chemical responsible for the transmission of neural messages, acetylcholine. The impoverished environment has just the opposite effect: smaller brains and less chemical. And when the rats are

FIGURE 8.12 Rats reared in enriched environments develop larger brains than rats reared in isolated and impoverished environments.

tested on a discrimination-learning task, the impoverished animals do more poorly. Again, the implications for human intelligence are clear: impoverished environments, sterile and unstimulating, may produce intellectual deficits, just as enriched, stimulating environments may produce gains.

Whether such deficits are reversible or not is unknown. One encouraging report comes from Harvard's Jerome Kagan, who recently studied children born in the backcountry of Guatemala. During the first year of their lives, because of the parents' fear of disease, these children are kept locked indoors; the parents rarely play with them or even talk to them. At two years of age their intellectual development is, indeed, retarded. By the time they are 11, however, their intellectual functioning is perfectly normal. Thus, the disappointing results of such programs as Head Start may not be an indication of any basic inadequacy in the notion of remedial education — it may just be a matter of too little, rather than too late.

The determinants of intelligence we have discussed in this section will be considered next in the context of the issues involving the relationship of race and intelligence.

E. RACE, GENETICS, AND INTELLIGENCE

You met Mark, a six-year-old black child, in the introductory chapter. Mark lived in the poverty-stricken center of a large city. Despite his participation in a federally funded Head Start education program for preschool children, his intelligence-test score (IQ) was no better than those of his classmates who had not participated in the program. After a year of school, the IQ of Mark and his classmates averaged out far below that of middle-class white children across town. Is Mark's problem due to genetics or environment? Can his problem be traced to inadequate schooling? In this section of the chapter we will continue to explore the interaction of genetic and environmental factors involved in intellectual development.

Behavioral genetics occupied a critical place in public decision-making when the issue of schooling for blacks became nationally prominent in 1954 because of a Supreme Court case, *Brown* vs. *Board of Education*. Segregation forces held that blacks are inferior to whites in intelligence. They suggested that school integration would reduce the level of education for white children. Integrationists argued that, although blacks' performance on intelligence tests was generally poorer than that of whites, research indicated the inferior schooling black children had experienced as the cause. They pointed out that when Southern black children moved North and attended Northern schools their intelligence-test scores rose. The Supreme Court responded favorably to these and other arguments of the integrationists in handing down a decision in the case. Except for occasional minor sniping by segregationists and retorts by liberals, the issue seemed to rest with the Court's decision outlawing segregated school systems.

In the winter of 1969, the *Harvard Educational Review* published a 117-page article by Arthur Jensen, an educational psychologist at the University of California at Berkeley. The title: "How Much Can We Boost IQ and Scholastic Achievement?" The message: The evidence is clear that blacks are inferior in tested intelligence, especially in abstract reasoning, and should receive special training emphasizing rote learning. The basis of this inferiority was alleged to be genetic. Jensen stated, "There is an increasing realization among students of the psychology of the disadvantaged that the discrepancy in their average performance cannot be completely or directly attributed to discrimination or inequalities in education. It seems not unreasonable, in view of the fact that intelligence variation has a large genetic component, to hypothesize that genetic factors may play a part in this picture."

When the article appeared, a furor arose in educational, political, and psychological circles. Jensen and his family were threatened; some of his colleagues refused to talk with him; he was accused of being a racist.

If Jensen were a known racist or a noncontributor to the scientific literature, his article might have gone unnoticed. But Jensen is a respectable scholar. Also, Jensen raised this issue in the midst of a strong political controversy over the busing of school children. He took an unpopular position on a matter that is highly crucial to millions.

Let us critically examine the pros and cons of Jensen's evidence and argument. In the process you should improve your understanding of some of the interactions between nature and nurture that determine complex, polygenetic human traits such as intelligence.

THE JENSEN POSITION

Jensen states that IQ is in large part genetically determined. If blacks consistently get low scores on intelligence tests, the explanation must, in part, be that they have genetically inferior intelligence. Consequently, attempts to increase their intelligence through a general improvement in their school conditions are doomed to failure. Jensen concludes that an intensive study is required of the intellectual strengths and weaknesses of blacks, as well as all other racial groups in our society, and specially tailored educational programs can be designed to capitalize on their strengths.

The issues raised by this proposal are profound. Decisions in this area could tear apart or strengthen the fabric of this country. What are the facts of the matter?

Tested Intelligence of Blacks

Fact 1. On Army intelligence tests some groups of Northern blacks achieved higher scores than some Southern whites, yet within the same region white recruits consistently obtained higher intelligence test scores than did black recruits. Aptitude and achievement tests of school children yield similar findings.

Fact 2. According to numerous research studies, the average intelligence score of Northern black children is 90, that of white children is 100.

Fact 3. The situation grows even worse in the Southeastern states (Florida, Georgia, Alabama, Tennessee, and South Carolina). White children maintain their average IQ score of 100, but the black children achieve an even lower average of 80.7 points.

Fact 4. Only two percent of white children have IQ's that fall below 70; 18.4 percent of Southeastern black children have IQ's below 70.

Fact 5. For Southeastern black children, the average IQ of six-year-olds is 84. By age 13 the average has dropped to 65 points.

Fact 6. Despite the massive effort of the federally funded project Head Start to prepare minority preschool children for school, the program had little to no effect on raising intelligence test scores.

How are these facts to be interpreted? Can they be explained in terms of genetics or environmental factors or both?

The Degree to Which Genetics Determines Intelligence

Lois Erlenmeyer-Kimling and Lissy Jarvik scoured the scientific literature for evidence relating to intelligence level and genetics. In all, they found 52 reasonable, reliable studies between 1900 and 1960 that related to the question: "Are IQ test scores for close family members more similar to each other than are IQ test scores for distant family members or unrelated people?" In other words, as the genetic relationship, or similarities of genotypes, between family members increases, does the agreement in their IQ test scores increase? For example, are the IQ scores of identical twins closer than those of cousins or siblings? If so, then this pattern would be considered positive evidence of the role of genetics. The researchers also tried to find studies of the IQ resemblance of blood relations who had been reared apart, including pairs of identical twins (such as those reported in the Shields study discussed earlier).

A definite pattern emerged from the studies they examined. As the number of genes that people have in common increases, the similarity of their IQ test scores increases, regardless of whether or not they were reared in similar environments. There is an almost perfect correspondence between increases in gene commonality and increases in similarity of IQ test results.

If we could only report data on relatives

who had been reared in the same house-holds, it would be reasonably argued that these data do not prove a strictly genetic relationship. After all, the closer the genetic relationship the greater the amount of shared environment. The environment of brothers is more similar than is the environment of cousins. And the environment of identical twins is more similar than is the environment of brothers. Consequently, the similarity in IQ with increasing gene similarity could be as easily explained by increasing environmental similarity. But the researchers have been careful to include studies of blood relations who, by some accident of nature, have not been reared together. When family members have been reared apart, the similarity of their IQ's increases along with the similarity of their genes in much the same manner as in the case of family members reared together. For family members reared apart, much of the similarity in the level of intelligence must be attributed to their common genes inasmuch as their environments were to some extent different.

Within the context of these studies the effect of genetics on level of intelligence is certainly quite impressive. The question that still presents itself is the degree to which environment is also effective in influencing intelligence-test scores. Or, to put it another way, what percentage of phenotypic intelligence is determined by genes and what percentage by environment? According to statistical analysis of the research data, genetic factors seem to account for about 75 percent of the variation in intelligence. *The degree to which a trait is inherited within a population (a large group of people with a common characteristic, such as skin color) is called* **heritability.** An important thing to remember about the concept of heritability is that it has meaning only in reference to *popu-*

lations since its calculation is based on population statistics. This means that heritability can account for the spread of scores for a population but can't be used to conclude that Mark has a lower IQ than Tom because of genetic differences. In summary, every time we observe an increase in the degree of blood relationship, we observe a corresponding increase in the similarity of relatives' IQ scores, even when blood relations were raised in different homes.

One aspect of the Erlenmeyer-Kimling and Jarvik studies is critical. The populations studied were all white Euro-Americans and mainly middle class. Whether such findings can be generalized to black Americans is a question we will consider below. However, it is safe to say that the "different environments" of white middle class Euro-Americans reared apart are unlikely to be as different as the environments confronting the average white child and the average black child in the United States.

EVALUATION OF THE JENSEN ARGUMENT

We have presented three key findings: 1) American blacks receive lower scores on IQ tests than do whites, 2) under certain circumstances scores on IQ tests seem to be heavily determined by genetic factors, 3) despite educational enrichment programs, American blacks' IQ scores do not catch up to the whites'.

From these three findings it does not seem at first glance a far jump to Jensen's conclusion that the lower IQ scores of blacks are due to genetic factors. Let us dispassionately evaluate this conclusion. To begin with, we accept the findings as valid as far as they go. However, Jensen has not taken enough factors into account.

Jensen's argument leans very heavily on the great strength of the relationship found between genetic factors and intelligence. If this relationship were much weaker, Jensen would have to attribute greater importance to the obvious socioeconomic disadvantages that blacks suffer. The crucial question we must ask is, can we assume that the strength of the genetics-IQ relationship found in the white Euro-American populations is the same among black Americans? To date there is no evidence to warrant this assumption and, as we shall see later, there is some evidence that questions it.

Black-White Sociocultural Differences. There are other difficulties in accepting Jensen's conclusions of blacks' genetic inferiority. Most obviously the sociocultural differences between blacks and whites can explain the 10-to-20-point difference in IQ. A difference of this magnitude has, in some extreme cases, even been observed between identical twins raised in the very same household. In fact, the *average* difference between identical twins raised in the same family is six IQ points. Such differences must result from environmental influences. A host of variables that are known to be different for blacks and whites are demonstrably effective in producing differences in IQ. These variables include anxiety level, race and warmth of the test examiner, the mother's attitude toward achievement, the migrancy of the family, the cultural benefits of the home, prenatal care, diet, the degree of anoxia (oxygen deprivation) and prematurity at birth, the amount of time mothers can spend in child care and the richness of the infant's experience. Jensen's failure to adequately consider these variables violates an important criterion of science, controlled observation. This criterion would require the test of blacks and whites who have had about the same level of experience with respect to these important variables before any definitive statement about the black and white intelligence "difference" could be made. Since no study has met this criterion to date, no final conclusions can be drawn.

Early Experience. The importance of early experience in determining later intellectual capacities has been documented in a variety of studies. As we have seen, early deprivation of stimulation can severely handicap subsequent development. Blind and deaf children suffer mental retardation in amounts that are comparable to the rates among black children. We reported above that the IQ's of black children in the southeastern section of the United States decreased markedly from their sixth to their thirteenth year. It seems likely that this decrease in IQ test performance is most easily explained by their exposure to an inadequate, unstimulating social and educational environment. After all, their genetic make-up certainly did not change over the course of these years.

FIGURE 8.5D (Drawing by CEM; © 1974 The New Yorker Magazine, Inc.)

Language of the Black Family. Jensen makes the point that black children are most deficient in abstract categorization. When asked to recall a list of 20 objects that could not be easily classified, black children performed at the same level as white children. However, when the list of objects is selected so they can be classified as either animals, furniture, clothing, or foods, the white children's performance improves considerably while the black children's performance does not. The black children seem to be less able to make use of these categories as an aid in recall. Jensen concludes that this lack of ability is an expression of the special genetic deficit of blacks. Recent research, however, has indicated that the language that black mothers use in dealing with their children is specifically very weak in categorization and conceptualization. The black child learning to think and to use language is disadvantaged from birth. Without some outside intervention into this recurring chain of deprived parent, deprived child, a black child has a reduced opportunity to learn to use concepts and categories.

Race, Social Class, and Intelligence. Further insight into these issues was provided by the influential research studies of Sandra Scarr-Salapatek.

Scarr-Salapatek studied twins, both black and white, from upper and lower socioeconomic schools in Philadelphia. While most of her findings are consistent with the black-white IQ gap described above, she also found significant IQ differences between social classes within a racial group. Twins from upper socioeconomic groups had higher average IQ's than twins from a lower socioeconomic group. Her data also indicated that the heritability of IQ was greater for upper-social-class twins than it was for lower-social-class twins.

These last findings are very important. They mean that heritability of a trait is influenced by environmental conditions as well as by population differences. Scarr-Salapatek points out that lower socioeconomic groups generally have limited experiences of the kind that contribute to the development of skills measured by IQ and school achievement tests. Thus, differences in a genotype (genetic pattern) for IQ do not have a full opportunity to be developed and expressed in different IQ phenotypes. Upper-class twins have a more "enriched" environment in regard to school-related skills so that each of the many genotypes for IQ can be expressed as a different IQ score. In other words, unless the environment provides the stimulation needed, a person with many "smart" genes will not develop and show a high IQ but will tend to produce IQ scores like people without "smart" genes. Thus, Scarr-Salapatek's findings mean that the more enriched the environments of all children, regardless of social class and race, the greater the heritability of the IQ trait. Jensen's lack of consideration of this critical role of the environment is one of the major defects of his argument.

The implication of these findings for society are that equality of opportunity for each individual to develop his or her full genotypic potential will increase the average IQ and increase the spread of IQ scores for all populations. This is certainly an admirable goal for a democratic society regardless of any racial or social class differences that may or may not be found by behavioral geneticists. As Scarr-Salapatek pointed out in closing one of her papers, to conclude that racial differences in IQ are genetic is both scientifically unsound and socially dangerous, like yelling "fire" in a crowded theater.

SUMMARY

1. The first intelligence test was developed by Alfred Binet. His basic notion was to compare a child's **mental age** (page 261), as reflected by performance on a series of problems, to the child's actual (or **chronological) age** (page 261), thereby determining whether the child was average, advanced, or retarded.

A. Intelligence and Its Assessment

2. **Intelligence** (page 262) is inferred from behavior in a variety of situations; it is a shorthand term for describing the quality or level of that behavior.
3. Intelligence tests sample bits of behavior over a wide range of problem-solving situations.
4. The **Stanford-Binet Intelligence Scale** (page 261) (used with children) and the **Wechsler Adult Intelligence Scale** (page 264) are the two most widely used individually administered intelligence tests. Less sensitive group-administered intelligence tests, such as the Army General Classification Test, have been developed for screening purposes.

B. Abuses of Intelligence Tests

5. Performance on an intelligence test reflects one's *present level* of functioning. Extraneous conditions that might have adversely affected performance *must* be taken into account.
6. Factors that affect **IQ scores** (page 271) are both long-term (e.g., chronic physical or mental illness, economic and cultural differences, including test-taking attitudes) and short-term (e.g., perception of the reasons for testing, transitory illness, anxiety).
7. The key to preventing the abuse of intelligence tests lies in ensuring that they are administered and interpreted by skilled and sensitive people who are aware of the limitations of the tests.

C. Development of Intelligence

8. Jean Piaget has proposed that intelligence develops in four invariant stages: the **sensorimotor period** (page 273), the **preoperational period** (page 274), the **concrete operation period** (page 274), and the **formal operations period** (page 280).
9. Highly intelligent people are *intellectually* very expressive and even rebellious; when it comes to emotional expression, however, the gifted person is more reserved and controlled than the average person.

D. The Determinants of Intelligence

10. Heredity sets the limits of intelligence, and environment determines the degree to which those limits are approached.
11. Studies of monozygotic twins reared together and reared apart demonstrate that, *under "normal" conditions,* heredity counts heavily.
12. Both the mother's prenatal diet and early environmental stimulation have been shown to affect intellectual functioning — at least in rats.

E. Race, Genetics, and Intelligence

13. Arthur Jensen has argued that the evidence he presented supports the conclusion that races are genetically different with regard to intelligence. We have questioned Jensen's conclusions and have provided evidence that refutes Jensen's argument and requires us to suspend scientific judgment until more data from controlled observation become available. The evidence, however, does strongly support the claim that intelligence is an interactive product of both heredity and environment. Unless any individual receives adequate opportunities for learning and stimulation, his or her intelligence potential will not be actualized regardless of genetic endowment.
14. As the number of genes that people have in common increases, the similarity of their IQ test scores increases.
15. Genetic factors — expressed by **heritability** (page 287) — seem to account for about 75 percent of the variation in intelligence for white Euro-American populations.
16. A host of environmental variables that are known to be different for blacks and whites have been shown to be effective in producing differences in IQ test scores.
17. The degree to which genetic factors account for the variation of a trait such as intelligence is dependent on both the population studied and the environmental conditions. Enriched environments tend to increase trait variability and heritability; impoverished environments tend to decrease trait variability and heritability regardless of race.

Chapter Nine
Creativity, Problem Solving, and Language

The art teacher's most common technique for art instruction was to pass out mimeographed designs and then to have the pupils fill them in according to a dictated or suggested plan. An alternate approach was to stick up on the wall or on the blackboard some of the drawings on a particular subject that had been done in the previous years. . . . These drawings, neat and ordered and very uniform, would be the models for our children. The art lesson, in effect, would be to copy what had been done before, and the neatest and most accurate reproductions of the original drawings would be the ones that would win the highest approval from the teacher." (From Kozol, *Death at an Early Age,* 1970.)

Most people would agree that such a classroom experience would be unlikely to foster creativity. But can creativity be actively fostered and, if so, how? We will discuss this problem in this chapter. On the way we will consider how psychologists measure creativity, what motivates creative behavior, what sorts of people tend to be creative, and what sorts of family environments creative people spring from. Later in this chapter we will examine the creative activity known as problem solving and a powerful problem-solving tool—language. But first we must ask: What is creativity?

A. THE NATURE AND ASSESSMENT OF CREATIVITY

As is often true with pointed questions, it is easier to say what creativity is not than what it is. First, creativity is not intelligence. Certainly a person must have sufficient intelligence to grasp the basic facts and concepts in a given field, and in some areas the degree of intelligence needed is considerable. *Given the necessary level of intelligence,* however, there does not seem to be any relationship between intelligence and creativity. In other words, in any group of equally intelligent people, some members will still be more creative than others. For example, highly creative mathematicians have no higher scores on the Wechsler Adult Intelligence Scale than do mathematicians of average ability.

Second, creativity is not originality. Again, to be sure, originality is an attribute of creativity, but creativity is more than originality. Originality by itself is a pretty cheap commodity. For example, the ramblings of an emotionally disturbed person, as illustrated in Chapter 1, are certainly original—chances are that no one has ever uttered these phrases before. However, such productions would hardly be termed creative. To be creative, an act or thought must not only be original but also satisfy some criterion (such as being meaningful) or serve some purpose. At first this demand may seem like an arbitrary restriction to impose on creativity. But such a restriction is the only way creativity can be identified without appealing to public "opinion" of what is or is not creative.

If creativity, then, is neither sheer intelligence nor mere originality, what is it? Perhaps some clues may be gleaned from the reflections of eminently creative people on the creative process.

SAMUEL TAYLOR COLERIDGE: Facts which sank at intervals out of conscious recollection drew together beneath the surface through the almost chemical affinities of common elements.

ANDRÉ BRETON: [Art is distinguished by a] marvelous capacity to grasp two mutually distant realities without going beyond the field of our experience and to draw a spark from the juxtaposition.

ROBERT FROST: Let's put this straight. The

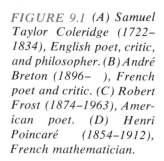

FIGURE 9.1 (A) Samuel Taylor Coleridge (1722–1834), English poet, critic, and philosopher. (B) André Breton (1896–   ), French poet and critic. (C) Robert Frost (1874–1963), American poet. (D) Henri Poincaré (1854–1912), French mathematician.

coupling [of poetic ideas] that moves you, that stirs you, is the association of two things that you did not expect to see associated.

HENRI POINCARÉ: The mathematical facts worthy of being studied are those which reveal to us unsuspected kinship between other facts, long known, but wrongly believed to be strangers to one another. Among chosen combinations the most fertile will often be those formed of elements drawn from domains which are far apart . . . certain among them, very rare, are the most fruitful of all . . . One evening, contrary to my custom, I drank black coffee and could not sleep. Ideas rose in crowds; I felt them collide until pairs interlocked, so to speak, making a stable combination. By the next morning I had established the existence of a class of Fuchsian functions.

A DEFINITION OF CREATIVITY

The common theme of these musings is that creativity consists of pulling together elements that are usually not seen as belonging together to form new combinations. A simple, yet striking, example of this ability to combine "mutually distant realities . . . and to draw a spark from the juxtaposition" appears in Marianne Moore's poetic image of "the lion's ferocious chrysanthemum head." "Ferocious" and "chrysanthemum" do not ordinarily occur together in thought or even in the same context, yet their combination in this instance yields a highly creative product.

But Poincaré reminds us that creativity does not consist solely in making new combinations from known elements: "Any one could do that, but the combinations so made would be infinite in number and most of them absolutely without interest. To create consists precisely in not making useless combinations and in making those which are useful and which are only a small minority." With these provisions in mind, we offer a formal definition of creativity.

Creativity *consists of forming new combinations of old elements. The combinations either meet specified requirements or are in some way useful. The more mutually distant the elements, the more creative is the resulting combination.*

THE ASSESSMENT OF CREATIVITY

Psychologists have developed numerous tests for assessing creativity. It is not our intent to provide you with a catalog, but we would like to give you a sampling of some of the more ingenious measures.

J. P. Guilford of the University of Southern California, one of psychology's pioneers in the field of creativity, is responsible for the first two to be discussed, the *Unusual Uses* test and the *Consequences* test.

Unusual Uses Test. In the Unusual Uses test, an examinee is asked to think of as many uses as possible for some common object. Answers are evaluated in terms of their relative frequency in some appropriate reference group (say, fellow students); the less frequent (but appropriate) answer is taken to be the more creative. For example, how many uses can you think of for a brick? Here are some possibilities:

Make a doorstop
Make a red powder
Make a paperweight
Make a bookcase
Drive a nail
Drown a cat
Throw through a bank window

FIGURE 9.2 *An array of the work of people universally acknowledged to be highly creative in their respective fields. Their activities, personalities, and modes of working are widely divergent, yet they all match our formal definition of creativity. (A) Jackson Pollock painting. (B) George Balanchine choreographing the ballet "Duo Concertant" with dancers Kay Mazzo and Peter Martins. (C) First page of the original manuscript, with the author's alterations, of Walt Whitman's "Song of the Universal." (D) James D. Watson and Francis H. C. Crick with a model of the DNA molecule.*

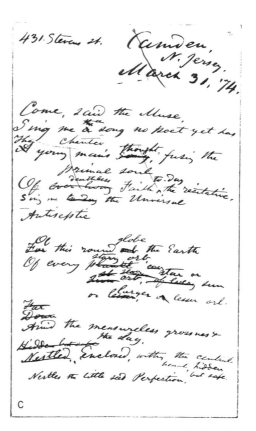

Focus 9.1 Dolphins and Originality Training

The sight of a dolphin playfully leaping out of the water and gracefully arching through the air is a common experience of sailors. The tricks of trained dolphins have become familiar to the public in commercial aquariums in this country. But Hou, a female rough-toothed porpoise *(Stenobredanensis),* is a little different. She may leap out of the water and make her arc through the air *backwards,* or she may fly out of the water in a corkscrew-turning motion, or land on her side, or any of an unlimited number of different responses to the same signal. Unlike other well-trained dolphins, her responses will be unpredictable. She has been trained for originality.

In order to train animals, the principles of learning (see Chapter 6) are commonly employed by trainers. Desired behaviors are reinforced and shaped, often by rewards of food. Fish are fed to dolphins when, after they have been given a signal, such as the sound of a buzzer or whistle, they have successfully executed a desired task. But to attempt to teach originality, Karen Pryor of the Sea Life Park of the Makapukuu Oceanic Center in Hawaii decided to reinforce—with fish—any movement Hou made that was reported by at least two observers and that had not been observed before. Before long, Hou was making the kind of movements described above, movements that never or nearly never are observed in dolphins in their spontaneous activities.

Before Pryor's work with "creative dolphins," Irving Maltzman of UCLA attempted to reinforce originality in human subjects. In the test of Unusual Uses, where subjects attempt to suggest unusual uses for common items, such as a brick (see page 295), the experimenter reinforces originality by saying "good" after every five unusual responses. Maltzman found that his subjects increased their production of unusual uses of common items as a consequence of this reinforcement. There are obvious differences between Maltzman's and Pryor's studies. Reinforcement for the human subjects was verbal and the definition of originality for Maltzman's work was defined as an infrequently given response, a use for an item that had infrequently been suggested by subjects in prior instances of the same test. But the similarities in the effort to reinforce the unusual is clear. The success of both efforts is also clear.

Both experimenters reported what seemed to be a **frustration** *(emotional behavior that accompanies failure to attain a goal or reward)* experienced by the subject before the original-type response was developed. Frustration seems to be an ineradicable side-effect of the quest for originality. Human subjects would often appear to be frustrated and agitated, while Hou would often become agitated in a way that her trainers were tempted to describe as "angry"—she was perhaps feeling anger at her trainers for making a reward so difficult to get!

Consequences Test. In the Consequences test, the examinee is asked to think of as many consequences as possible to certain changes. Again, answers are evaluated in terms of their novelty and appropriateness, usually by a panel of judges. Fifty University of California introductory psychology students, for example, were asked this question:

What would be the results if everyone suddenly lost the sense of balance and were unable to stay in the upright position for more than a moment?

Here are a few of their more creative (and intriguing) predictions:

A sharp decline in the sale of shoes.

Helium balloons would be attached to people's heads.

A spurt in population growth.

No more standing committees in Congress.

The number one hit song would be "You Can't Stand Me Up Any More."

Psychiatrists with couches would be in great demand — except that now they would need one for themselves.

Anagrams Test. Another test that has received wide use (so wide, in fact, that its authorship escapes us) is the Anagrams test. Here the examinee is presented with a word and asked to use the letters of the word to form as many new words as possible; responses are evaluated for creativity in terms of their relative infrequency. To illustrate, the examinee might be given the word GENERATION and told to make from it as many words as possible; the anagrams would have to be English words of four letters or more (excluding proper names and places). Here are some possibilities. Perhaps you can come up with still others.

agar	genie	inner	rang	tanner
agent	genre	integer	range	tare
agree	gent	intern	rant	tarn
anger	gnat	into	rate	tear
anion	goat	iota	ratio	teen
anon	goitcr	iratc	ration	tenor
argon	gone	iron	regain	tern
atone	gore	nation	regent	tier
eager	grain	near	region	tiger
earing	granite	neat	reign	tine
earn	grant	negate	rein	ting
eaten	grate	negation	rent	tinge
eater	gratin	neon	retain	tinner
egret	great	nine	retina	tire
engine	green	nitrogen	rigor	toga
enrage	greet	none	ring	tone
enter	grin	note	riot	tong
ergot	grit	ogre	rite	tonnage
gain	groan	onager	roan	tore
gait	groin	orange	roar	train
gate	ignore	organ	rote	tree
gear	inert	ornate	tang	trio
gene	innate	rain	tangerine	

Remote Associates Test. The final test of creativity we would like to describe is the Remote Associates Test (or RAT) developed by Mednick. This test sprang from the definition of creativity provided earlier in the chapter. To repeat:

Creativity consists of forming new combinations of old elements. The combinations either meet specified requirements or are in some way useful. The more mutually distant the elements, the more creative is the resulting combination.

The RAT provides the person being tested with mutually distant elements and asks the examinee to pull them together by finding a "link" that will combine them. For example, here are three words (elements) that do not ordinarily occur together. The object is to find a fourth word, or link, that relates all three:

RAT   BLUE   COTTAGE

The answer is CHEESE. The words RAT,

BLUE, and COTTAGE all have CHEESE as an association—rat cheese, blue cheese, cottage cheese—but it is not a common association. That is, CHEESE is hardly the first word that comes to mind for most people when they see the words RAT, BLUE, or COTTAGE. Rather, it is an uncommon, or remote, associate of these words. Now that you have the idea, here are some more sample items to try:

COOKIES	SIXTEEN	HEART
POKE	GO	MOLASSES
RAILROAD	GIRL	CLASS
OUT	DOG	CAT

The answers are given on page 301.

The RAT has 30 such items, and the examinee is given ample time to attempt to solve them; the score is simply the number correct. For a person to do well on the RAT, the performance must meet our definition of creativity: the person must form new combinations from mutually distant elements, and these combinations must be meaningful.

THE VALIDITY OF CREATIVITY TESTS

All well and fine, you may say, so we have tests of creativity, some of which have their origins in carefully formulated theories. But do these tests, in fact, measure creativity? This is not an easy question to answer. It is difficult to find a standard against which the worth of a test of creativity can be determined, simply because the presence or absence of creativity is a matter of subjective judgment. This is why psychologists are interested in developing objective tests in the first place.

Creative Groups. There are, however, certain groups in society that, because of the very nature of their activity and their attainments, are presumably creative—such groups as painters, writers, architects, and research scientists. Another group is composed of comic strip authors. Although the daily comics may not be the first of human products to leap to your mind when the word "creativity" is mentioned, nonetheless, a comic strip author must, day in and day out, year after year, somehow provide a fresh little capsule of visual and verbal humor, drama, adventure, or fantasy. As one cartoonist described the challenge of finding a new idea for every day of his 32-year career: "There are days when you think, 'This is it.' But turning an old situation over, you can often get a new angle. I guess I could run out, but so far I haven't." In short, the comic strip author must be creative. How do such people fare on the RAT?

RAT Scores. To find out, the RAT was mailed to comic strip authors appearing in the Santa Barbara, California, *News Press.* As a group, these men answered better than 24 of the 30 items correctly; the lowest score was 15 and the highest 30. (To our knowledge, only one other person has made a perfect score in the thousands of RAT's that have been taken.) Further, the comic strip authors had a higher group average than any other known group tested with the RAT, including research scientists, IBM suggestion winners, and graduate psychology students. Of interest, too, are the brief notes that almost all these author-artists spontaneously included with their tests. Their notes give fleeting glimpses into the minds of these men. Their comments left little doubt that they were interested and involved in taking the test; their enthusiasm seemed to stem from curiosity rather than concern with performance. Sev-

FIGURE 9.3 Comic strip author Charles M. Schulz sketched Snoopy in an expression of his own reaction to the Remote Associates Test. (Copr. © 1958 United Feature Syndicate.)

eral of them indicated real pleasure from problem-solving activities, notwithstanding the attendant frustration.

This was the shortest 40 minutes I've spent in many years . . . Again, many thanks for permitting me to participate.

Education CAN be fun!

I enjoyed the experience even though a few at the end were beyond me.

It was fun (and difficult).

A number also interjected brief notes of humor directed at themselves ("art school drop out," "my damned thick skull") or the test ("the ratty RAT test"). One author sketched one of his strip's characters wearing a befuddled expression (Figure 9.3). In sum, if these comic strip authors are creative, the RAT does a good job of measuring creativity.

B. PERSONALITY AND CREATIVITY

Creativity usually involves considerable effort with little hope of immediate reward. Indeed, the creative person is often exposed to ridicule or censure inasmuch as creativity, almost by definition, involves challenging accepted ways of viewing reality. Why, then, does anyone bother to be creative? Is it possible that creative people have a built-in need to seek novelty in their experience, to embrace the unusual and the incongruous? John Houston at the University of California set out to answer this question in the following way. First he selected two groups of college students, one group that did well on the RAT and one group that did not do well. Then he showed each student in both groups a series of cards; on each card two words had been typed, one a noun (e.g., FATHER), the other an adjective or verb (e.g., BLACK). The student was simply told to call out one of the words on each card, the word that the student preferred, for whatever reason. It turned out that the high-RAT-scorers preferred adjectives or verbs, while the low-RAT-scorers preferred nouns (why this is so is not clear).

Now, Houston reasoned, if creative people have a need for novelty, then it should be possible to get them to do something—to change their behavior—in order to obtain novel experiences (see Focus 4.2: Curiosity and Exploratory Behavior). In other words, novelty should serve as a

HOUSE (outhouse, dog house, house cat)
WORKING (working on the railroad, working girl, working class)
SLOW (slow poke, go slow, slow as molasses)
SWEET (cookies are sweet, sweet sixteen, sweetheart)

The answers to the RAT on page 300 are:

reinforcement with the power to alter behavior. Houston decided to change the creative students' preference (a behavior) for adjectives and verbs over nouns, and this is how he went about it.

Whenever a student called out an adjective or a verb, Houston replied with a very common association to that word; for example, if the student said "black," Houston said "white." However, if the student called out a noun, Houston replied with a novel association; for example, if the student said "father," Houston said "eggbeater."

Figure 9.4 shows what happened to the word preferences of the high-RAT-scorers and low-RAT-scorers over time. The high RAT's started out with a preference for adjectives and verbs but gradually shifted to a preference for nouns. Apparently the "reward" of hearing a novel association was sufficient to change their preference behavior, indicating that novelty is important to them and they will act to obtain it. It is also noteworthy that the low RAT's, when exposed to the unusual associations, showed a decline in their original preference for nouns and moved to adjectives and verbs. The low RAT's may have found the common associations that followed adjective-verb choices to be rewarding— or, possibly, the novel associations following noun choices were aversive. Perhaps these low-RAT-scorers have a need for predictable and "safe" forms of experience. In any case, creative people do crave novelty. But is a need for novelty the only thing that distinguishes a creative person?

THE CREATIVE PERSONALITY

Is there a pattern of specific personality traits that is characteristic of the creative individual? The answer, from several studies, appears to be "No." All kinds of

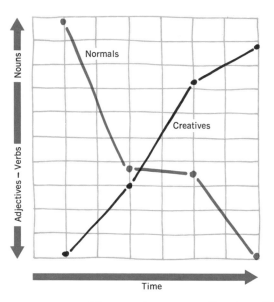

FIGURE 9.4 Noun preference as a function of exposure to novelty.

people can be, and are, creative. There do, however, seem to be certain broad styles of perceiving and thinking that mark the creative person. For a good many years the University of California's Institute of Personality Assessment and Research (IPAR) has been the scene of intensive investigation of highly creative architects, painters, writers, physicians, physicists, biologists, economists, anthropologists, mathematicians, and engineers. The work has been conducted by such men as Donald MacKinnon and Frank Barron. They have identified several general characteristics that distinguish creative people. One is a marked preference for and appreciation of complexity as opposed to simplicity.

Appreciation of Complexity

If creative people are presented with line drawings such as those in Figure 9.5, they

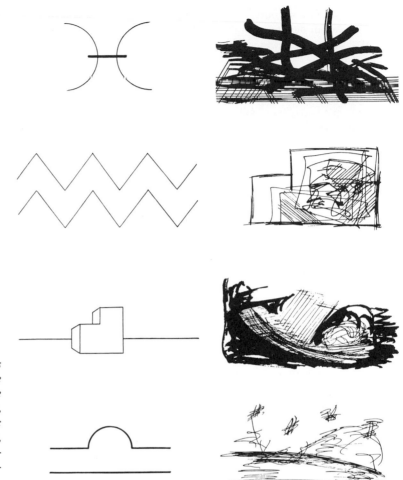

FIGURE 9.5 *Examples from the Welsh Figure Preference Test. Creative people prefer the complex, irregular, almost chaotic drawings on the right, whereas less creative people prefer the simple drawings on the left.*

much prefer the complex, irregular, almost chaotic drawings on the right; normals, however, definitely prefer the simple, orderly, neat figures on the left.

Openness to Experience

Another general characteristic is a greater openness to experience. The way creative people responded to the following choices is indicated by the underlined letters:

If you were asked on a Saturday morning what you were going to do that day, would you

(A) be able to tell pretty well.

(<u>B</u>) have to wait and see.

Is it harder for you to adapt to

(<u>A</u>) routine.

(B) constant change.

Do you like

(A) to arrange your dates and parties some distance ahead.

(<u>B</u>) to be free to do whatever looks like fun at the time.

Are you at your best

(A) when dealing with the unexpected.

(B) when following a carefully worked-out plan.

When you go somewhere for the day, would you rather

(A) plan what you will do and when.

(B) just go.

(Briggs and Myers, 1962)

Intuitiveness

Yet another characteristic of creative persons is their greater inclination to rely on and trust their intuition and nonrational mental processes. Witness their responses to the following choices, again indicated by underlining:

Which word in each pair appeals to you more?

(A) theory	certainty	(B)
(A) build	invent	(B)
(A) statement	concept	(B)
(A) facts	ideas	(B)
(A) concrete	abstract	(B)
(A) foundation	spire	(B)
(A) theory	experience	(B)
(A) literal	figurative	(B)

(Briggs and Myers, 1962)

Independence

Finally, the creative individual is characterized by independence, autonomy, and nonconformity. Let's look at a laboratory situation from which such a conclusion can be drawn, one that was originally developed by Solomon Asch at Swarthmore and refined by Richard Crutchfield at IPAR. In order to understand the rather complicated experimental procedure, put yourself in the shoes of a subject.

The Experimental Setting. You and four other subjects are led into adjacent, but separate, cubicles and seated in front of a panel. You are aware that the four other subjects are seated beside you in their own cubicles, but you can only see your own panel. On the panel there are a set of levers and two sets of lights. The room darkens and two lines of obviously unequal length are projected onto the wall in front of you, in view of all. The experimenter then tells the five of you that your job is to judge which line is shorter. You are to use the levers on your panel to signal your choice. One set of lights records the judgments of each of the subjects as they are made,

FIGURE 9.6 Cubicles used by Crutchfield in his research study on group pressure.

so that each subject knows what the judgment of every other subject was. The second set of lights merely tells you the order in which you are to make your judgment, in other words, whether you are to go first, last, third, and so forth.

Let's say you begin the experiment judging second. As a number of simple judgments go by—differences in length of lines, differences in area of figures, logical completion of number series, and so on—you cannot help but notice, and are not particularly surprised, that your judgments are in perfect agreement with everyone else's. As the experiment progresses, you are signaled to judge third, then fourth, then last. Your judgments have continued to be in agreement with the other subjects', and now you find yourself watching all their judgments appear on your panel prior to making yours. As the next pair of unequal lines is projected, you casually note that the one on the right is considerably shorter than the one on the left, and your gaze wanders down to the panel as you wait to register your judgment. As you sit there waiting your turn, the first subject registers his judgment of the shorter line: Left! You are mildly astonished, and look up to check your judgment; perhaps you were too hasty. No, there's no doubt about it, the shorter line of the pair is on the right. Something must be wrong with the first subject, you are thinking, just as the second subject registers his choice: Left. And so it goes with the third and fourth subjects, until only you remain to register your judgment for all to see. Do you deny your own private judgment and conform, pulling the lever for Left, or do you resist the group and pull Right?

Withstanding Group Pressure. The pressure to conform in this situation is very great, and some subjects not only overtly conform but also report that their subjective judgments actually change, that is, they now actually *see* the left-hand line as shorter than the right-hand line. Actually, what happened, of course, was that the subjects were laboring under the experimenter's deception. Their panels were not hooked together to record their various judgments, but were all completely controlled by the experimenter, who programmed the whole scenario from beginning to end. The IPAR team found that creative people are more likely than others to withstand this apparent group pressure to conform and to adhere to their initial judgment and respond independently.

In summary, then, the creative person takes pleasure in complexity, is receptive and open to experience, is prone to intuition and hunches, and resists pressure to conform.

Mental Health

Finally, what about the mental health of creative people? The possibility of a relationship between creative ability and mental illness has been long and hotly debated. Many obviously creative people—such as Vincent van Gogh and William Blake (see Figure 9.7)—have been just as obviously mentally ill. The IPAR data on this question are revealing. If you were simply to look at the scores of creative people on various psychological tests of adjustment, you would certainly have to classify many of them as mentally ill, and many more as borderline. But, and this is a big "but," it is also clear that these people have stronger-than-average psychological controls. Thus, although a creative person can (and to be creative, must) indulge in all sorts of peculiar thoughts and give free expression to impulses, he or she also possesses the

FIGURE 9.7 (A) "The Ghost of a Flea," by William Blake. (B) "Cypresses," by Vincent van Gogh. Both artists, though mentally ill, were highly creative.

capacity to return to a high degree of rationality and self-criticism, when necessary. As Frank Barron says, "The creative person is both more primitive and more cultured, more destructive and more constructive, crazier and saner, than the average person."

THE NURTURE OF CREATIVITY

What conditions foster the development of the creative individual? What sorts of backgrounds do creative persons tend to come from? Again, we turn to the best available source of data on this subject, the IPAR studies.

The Family

In the family of the creative individual, the parents show an extraordinary respect for the child and confidence in the child's ability to do what is appropriate in most situations. The child is given considerable freedom, even at an early age, to explore the world and make decisions. The parents and child are not particularly close; while the child is certainly not rejected, neither is there a strong emotional bond between parent and child. Also, the child fails to identify firmly with one parent or the other; either an ambiguous identification with both is made or with neither. In the latter case, the child is likely to identify with relatives or other significant people outside the primary family unit. Regardless of degree of identification, both parents present models of effective, resourceful behavior.

Discipline is consistent, predictable, fair, and rarely harsh. Although expected to respect certain standards of conduct, by and large the child is encouraged to develop and maintain personal standards. The parents stress the importance of developing personal ethical codes. Values that are emphasized in the family are concerned with integrity, excellence, intellectual and cultural pursuits, success and ambition, and "doing the right thing."

The Child

The family tends to change residences frequently. Consequently, the child is exposed to a varied and enriched personal and cultural experience. This same mobility also results in some estrangement of the family (and the child) from the immediate neighborhood. The child is frequently alone, shy, and isolated during childhood and adolescence, turning inward and drawing on personal thoughts and fantasies. While the awareness and expression of the child's inner life are encouraged and fostered by one or both parents (who, by the way, are likely to be creative in their own right), the child is not pushed, and interests and talents are permitted to develop at their own pace.

Most of these factors in the family would seem to be fertile soil for the sowing of the seeds of creativity and conducive to the growth of the characteristics of creative individuals.

Although certain early experiences may be more likely to foster creativity than others, is it possible to train people to think creatively? To answer this question we return to the classroom, although a somewhat different classroom from the one portrayed in the beginning of this chapter.

Teaching Creativity

Richard Crutchfield presented a large group of fifth- and sixth-graders with a series of 16 "stories" about two school children, Jim and Lila, and their Uncle John, who is a high school science teacher and amateur detective. Each story presented a little problem-solving episode in which a puzzling or mysterious occurrence confronts the characters—for example, the disappearance of money on a riverboat or strange happenings in a deserted house— and Jim and Lila set out to solve it.

The stories are carefully constructed to encourage creative thinking; each is, indeed, a lesson in creative problem solving.

They [the subjects] are encouraged to generate many ideas and to check these possibilities against the facts. With new facts coming in, they revise their hypotheses. When these fail to solve the problem, Jim and Lila are led to reformulate the problem, to see it in a different way, and thus to generate new ideas. As further incidents occur, they are led closer and closer to a solution, until finally things fall into place, and they achieve the solution. The structure of the lessons is such that the alert reader is very likely to discover the solution for himself, a step ahead of Jim and Lila. This deliberately contrived "discovery experience" is thought to be an . . . important factor in the development and reinforcement of creative thinking skills and attitudes. . . . (Olton and Crutchfield, 1969)

In the first stories Uncle John stimulates and guides Jim and Lila; as the stories progress they (and the reader) are called upon to take a more and more active role in the problem solving. In short, the stories provide the reader with both experience in and strategies for creative problem solving.

The children worked through the stories at their own pace, over a three- to four-week period. Following this exposure they were given a number of tests of creativity, and their performance was compared to that of children who had been exposed to a series of adventure stories on which they were quizzed but not required to solve problems. The results: the children who had read the Jim and Lila stories showed a marked superiority on the creativity tests. When all the youngsters were re-tested for creativity six months later, the trained children were still clearly superior. Thus, it appears that training can promote substantial and persistent enhancement of creativity. It must be remembered, how-ever, that these encouraging results were achieved with ten- and eleven-year-old children. Whether such gains are possible at older ages remains to be seen.

C. PROBLEM SOLVING

To develop the proper mood for this section, let's warm up with some problems (two were shown in Chapter 1.)

Problem 1 concerns the nine dots in the arrangement shown. The task is to connect all nine dots by drawing four continuous lines, without lifting the pencil from the page. These lines may intersect but not overlap. Can you do it?

For Problem 2 you will need six match-sticks (or toothpicks if they are more convenient). The problem is to arrange the six matchsticks in such a way that they form four congruent triangles, all the sides of the triangles being the length of the matchsticks.

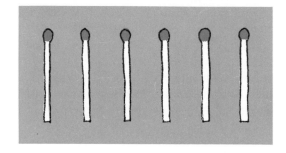

Problem 3 requires you to stand in a room behind the chalk line and place both hoops on the vertical peg. Before you be-gin, you may freely move around the room. You may use anything you see in the room to help you solve the problem.

Each of these problems requires you to be creative—that is, to form new combina-tions of old elements to meet a specific requirement. In this section we will be looking at the expression of creativity in problem solving, which also involves perception and learning.

We are going to look first at some of the phenomena that inhibit problem solving even when all the necessary information or materials are available. Later, we will look at the peculiar processes by which solutions occur and the contexts in which they generally seem to be embedded. We will offer some suggestions for overcoming some of the inhibiting factors and methods that seem to help in producing the "flash of insight" that undoes the knotty problem.

PROBLEM-SOLVING SET

The answer to Problem 1, as shown, is really quite simple—just how complicated can four lines be? What makes the problem difficult for most people is the common assumption that the four lines should not extend beyond the boundaries of the square formed by the outer dots. Of course, this was not part of the instructions. Indeed, most people assume this restriction without even being fully aware that they are doing so.

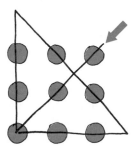

Nobody said that the four triangles in Problem 2 had to lie in the same plane, although most people assume that they must and thereby make the problem insoluble. In fact, the only possible solution is to make a tetrahedron, a geometrical solid figure composed of four triangles.

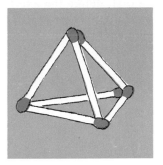

These problems illustrate the obstacle to problem solving posed by set, *a predisposition to respond in a specific way to a problem that may either inhibit or facilitate the novel combinations required for solution.* In such cases, set seems to constitute a kind of mental inertia.

Now that you are acquainted with the effects of set on problem solving, see if you can solve the next set of problems by the simplest, most direct method.

These problems were originated by Abraham S. Luchins of New York University. They involve transferring certain measured amounts of water from one vessel to another. With the use of a little imagination not only can the problems be solved, but also any chance of getting wet can be avoided; the water jars and the water will be imaginary. Here is an example. Suppose that you are provided with two containers, one of them having a capacity of 29 quarts and the other of three quarts. Assuming that you have free access to water and drainage, how can you use the containers to attain a measure of precisely 20 quarts of water? The answer is fairly simple: after filling the larger jar you would use it to fill the three-quart jar three times, thus subtracting nine quarts from the original 29, leaving precisely 20 quarts in the larger jar. Now that you have the idea, here are some practice problems for you to solve before we give you a little problem-solving test. Notice that, unlike the example, all of these problems assume that you are given three jars rather than two.

Practice Problems

CAPACITY OF JARS IN QUARTS			TO GET	ANSWER?
21	127	3	100	Fill 127-qt jar; from it fill 21-qt jar once and 3-qt jar twice: $127 - 21 - 3 - 3 = 100$
14	163	25	99	
18	43	10	5	
20	59	4	31	

With that practice you should be able to do the following test problems.

	CAPACITY OF JARS IN QUARTS			TO GET	ANSWER
Test 1	23	49	3	20	
Test 2	15	39	3	18	

When you have written down your answers, turn to page 318 at the end of this section and compare your answer with ours. Please do this before you begin to read the next paragraph.

Set is a learned strategy: in this case, we took great pains to help you develop a problem-solving set by offering "practice" problems in which the larger jar must be filled first. In Luchins's original experiment one group of students was given the practice problems while the second group was simply shown the initial two-jar example and then asked to try the test problems. Although only 17 percent of the group given the "helpful" practice problems arrived at the simpler answer, *all* of the others discovered the simpler technique. The influence of set is plainly significant. But remember that mental set is by no means entirely disadvantageous. For many activities and problems, learned sets are very effective strategies. For example, driving a car involves a well-learned sequence of behaviors that serve us so well we seldom pay attention to many of the coordinated movements needed. Thus we can solve the problem presented by a new or unfamiliar car very quickly. It is only when novel approaches are required (and real-life problems carry no warning signs marked "Novel Situation") that a formerly successful set becomes an obstacle to success. The development of a set is another example of operant conditioning (Chapter 6B) in which any reinforced behavior becomes strengthened. In the case of set, the behavior refers to covert assumptions and problem-solving strategies that are expressed in the problem-solving behavior.

Functional Fixedness

One specific kind of set is known as **functional fixedness,** *because prior knowledge of an object's function prevents consideration of new uses.* In an experiment performed by Maurice Huling and Martin Scheerer at the University of Kansas, students faced Problem 3, presented above. In a small room individual students were asked to find a way to put two rings on a vertical peg sitting on the floor while standing at a position about six feet from both the rings and the peg. The students could freely move around the room *except* when picking up the rings or placing them on the peg. They were told that they could use anything in the room to solve the problems. Among other objects in the room were two sticks, neither of them separately long enough to retrieve the rings or to place them over the peg but in their combined length a perfect tool for the job. After the experiment, most of the subjects reported that they realized that some sort of cord or string to tie the two sticks

together was needed. Yet, while a string was in the room in plain sight, most of them did not use it. Why not?

To find the answer Huling and Scheerer divided the subjects into several different groups. What distinguished the groups was the conditions under which they worked. In the group that turned out to do well, the string was left dangling from a nail on the wall with no apparent function. In the other experimental conditions, the string was in plain sight but was used to suspend either a mirror, a calendar (look at the figure for Problem 3 again), or a "No Smoking" sign from a nail. "Functional fixedness" in this case meant that the students in the unsuccessful groups usually did not perceive the string as "usable" because it already had a function in the environment; its function was "fixed." Of course, they knew that anything in the room was available to use. In most cases, however, the string was never given even the slight attention required to transform its perceived function as "string as hanger" to its potential function as "string as fastener." Were you a victim of functional fixedness?

The German psychologist, Karl Duncker, who originated the concept of functional fixedness demonstrated it in a clever study. Duncker asked individual students to find a way to mount candles on a *vertical piece of soft wooden board* in such a way that they could burn. He provided the board, three candles, matches, a number of thumbtacks, small cardboard boxes, and a variety of other items. The only difference in experimental conditions was that one group of students got the items with candles, matches, and thumbtacks *inside* the cardboard boxes while the second group received the identical items with the candles, matches, and thumbtacks separate from the cardboard boxes (see Figure 9.8). The second group of students often arrived at

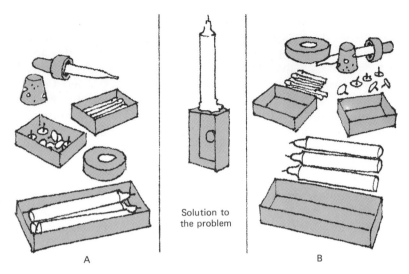

FIGURE 9.8 Materials used in the candle problem. One group of subjects received the candles placed in a box (see A), and the other group received the candles outside of the box (see B). Both groups received a vertical wooden board for mounting.

A

Solution to the problem

B

the correct solution (which was to use the matches to melt the bottoms of the candles, attaching them to the sides of the cardboard boxes, then tacking the boxes to the vertical surface of the board). But, as you might have guessed, the group that received the candles in the boxes rarely arrived at the solution because they only perceived the boxes as "containers" for candles rather than as potential candle mounts.

In a variation of this experiment done at Princeton by Sam Glucksberg and R. W. Weisberg, for one experimental group each item was labeled as "candle," "box," "matches," and so forth. Fewer of these subjects overlooked the possibility that the boxes were "things," items that could be used to solve the problem. They had less of a tendency to perceive the boxes as merely "background."

Overcoming Mental Sets

This experimental variation points up one method for overcoming the inherent drawbacks of sets when fixation prevents novel use of available items. To label or name available items helps to keep them in the foreground where they can be manipulated in imagination. The use of language here illustrates its power as a problem-solving tool. Language can be employed not merely in labeling the "things" involved but also in labeling alternative procedures. Since a set consists of unstated assumptions, stating them verbally makes consideration of alternatives more likely. "These are only containers" is probably not a thought of which Duncker's students were conscious, but many students later acknowledged that this had indeed been their implicit attitude. Had the attitude been verbalized even silently, it might more easily have been recognized as an unjustified assumption. Even verbal instructions to be on guard against such assumptions and sets are effective in increasing problem-solving ability.

Language is not the only means of breaching the inhibiting wall of mental sets. Spatial reorganization, moving items into different positions so as to weaken their associations, such as that between the candles and the cardboard boxes, may permit novel associations to arise. Putting a problem away for a time may also weaken the set. Too high a motivation—whether positive or negative—seems to decrease the efficiency of problem solving. Perhaps this explains why putting a problem aside seems so often to help; the decreased motivational state relaxes the grip of the mental set. All strategies mentioned have in common this goal—relaxing the factors that prevent the solution.

INSIGHT

The students who failed to solve the "string and sticks" problem in the Huling and Scheerer experiment were later shown the string, often simply by its being silently pointed out. Many of them then had a "sudden flash of realization" exclaiming "Oh, no!" or "Of course!" or even slapping their foreheads. Theirs was the familiar **"insight"** or "Aha!" experience: *the sudden reorganization of the elements of a problem whereby the solution becomes self-evident* ("Of course!").

The insight phenomenon was observed by one of the founders of Gestalt psychology, Wolfgang Koehler. During World War I, Koehler was detained on Tenerife, one of the Canary Islands owned by Spain, where he conducted a series of experiments on the problem-solving behavior of apes. One of these experiments, like that of Scheerer and Huling, required the combined use of two sticks for solution. Sultan, Koehler's brightest chimpanzee, was placed in a cage out of reach of a bundle of fruit. A stick long enough to retrieve the fruit lay outside the cage and outside of Sultan's reach. Within the cage was a shorter, "auxiliary" stick capable of reaching the longer one. Initially, Sultan tried to reach the fruit with his hand and then by using

FIGURE 9.9 Sequence of steps in Sultan's insightful problem solving.

the "auxiliary" stick. When he had apparently satisfied himself that the fruit was out of reach by direct means, he settled into a state of apparent inactivity in the opposite corner of his cage. Suddenly, he looked up, walked to the "auxiliary" stick, picked it up, and employed it to rake the longer stick into reach. He then used this long stick to rake the fruit into reach and so enjoyed his dinner. "Insight," the apparently "out-of-the-blue" realization of a relatively complete solution, has also been observed in humans. Consider this verbal report from a subject given problems similar to those described in the opening of this section by Helen Durkin of Columbia University:

Oh, I saw it before I moved it. It came suddenly, upon me as from the outside and I felt absolutely sure. Just like a flash and I knew I was right. Wasn't conscious of it . . . didn't reason about it—it just came to me from the outside.

STAGES OF PROBLEM SOLVING

Two qualifications must be added to the subjective impressions of the "insight" experience. First, although the subject usually feels "absolutely sure" that the insight is the correct answer, insights are no more infallible than any other hypotheses. Second, although the insight often feels as though it appears "out of the blue," numerous observations of the process show that it is almost invariably embedded in a specific context. This process is divided into four stages: preparation, incubation, illumination, and verification.

In the *preparation* stage, the situation is explored and the different objects in the situation are examined, as are the relationships between these items. This exploration is often accomplished through random

"play" or by exhausting the direct and obvious possibilities of a solution, as Sultan did in attempting to reach the fruit by hand and with the available stick. Sultan's period of inactivity after his initial failure is an example of the *incubation* phase. According to subjective reports from human beings, this phase of problem solving does not even entail conscious thought about the problem; thought, apparently, belongs to the preparation stage rather than to incubation. Witness the following statement by the philosopher-mathematician Bertrand Russell:

I have found, for example, that, if I have to write upon some rather difficult topic, the best plan is to think about it with very great intensity—the greatest intensity of which I am capable—for a few hours or days, and at the end of that time give orders, so to speak, that the work is to proceed underground. After some months I return consciously to the topic and find that the work has been done.

Following the incubation phase comes *illumination*, the "flashing bulb" traditionally used in cartoons to represent the "Aha!" experience. The existence of the final stage, *verification*, demonstrates that insight experience is not infallible. It must be tested. The verification may be as simple an act as Sultan's obtaining his dinner or it may be a complex series of experiments putting to the test a scientific theory that was born "in a flash."

Karl Duncker, who supplied us with the concept of functional fixation, also analyzed the approach to the solution of a problem. If the solution is the destination, what kind of route was employed to get there? Duncker asked students to attempt to solve the problem of how to destroy tumors in the body with radiation without damaging the surrounding healthy tissue. He asked his students to "think aloud" while seeking the solution. On the way to a "successful" solution the exemplary student passed through four characteristic phases that earmarked successful solutions.

The first step was the *problem* itself, or rather, a clear statement of it: "treatment of tumors with rays *without* destruction of healthy tissues." From this point the avenues of approach diverged into three *general range* hypotheses, that is, restatements of the problem emphasizing one or another aspect that might be changed to avoid destruction of the healthy tissues (see Figure 9.10). The student considered "desensitizing the healthy tissues," "avoiding contact between rays and healthy tissue," and the possibility of lowering the intensity of the rays while they were in the presence of healthy tissue. Then, *functional solutions* of the form, "If I did _____, then, _____," were considered as ways of implementing each of the general range alternatives. In the third, eventually pro-

ductive, general range, the problem-solver considered either somehow postponing the intensity of the rays until they reached the tumor (an act that is physically difficult or impossible) or keeping the rays weak in intensity while they were in the peripheral area, concentrating them only in the tumor. It was after the formulation of this last functional solution that "illumination" occurred with the characteristic swiftness and surety of insight. Suddenly, the *specific solution* was given as *the* answer, the use of a lens to focus weak rays only on the tumor. As a matter of fact, this "solution" is not quite accurate. Radiation cannot be focused by a lens. In practice, several sources of relatively weak rays converge in the tumor's location. But considering the small amount of background information that was offered to develop a solution, this answer was as good as a bull's eye. Successfully solved problems follow this four-step pattern: problem—general range

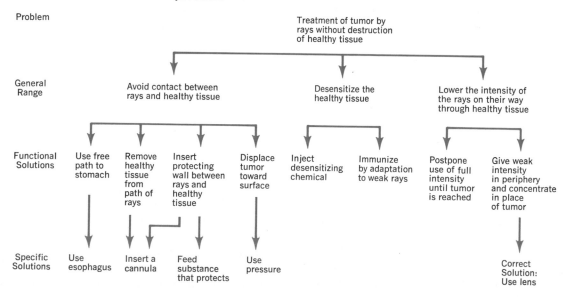

FIGURE 9.10 *One subject's proposed solution to the Duncker cancer problem.*

Focus 9.2

Straight and Stoned Thinking

Earlier in this book we have discussed a variety of orientations to human consciousness. For example, in Chapter 5 we examined hypnosis and dreaming, and in Chapter 3 we considered the effects of drugs on brain functioning. According to Andrew Weil of the National Institute of Mental Health, altered states of consciousness due to drugs, dreaming, hypnosis, or meditation are not merely incidental distortions of the "proper" workings of the human consciousness but are legitimate alternatives to the "normal" conscious state, which Weil refers to as "straight thinking." Weil believes that "stoned thinking" — his term for the state (or *states*) of alternative consciousness — is not only natural but necessary for the mental health of the individual. From his own research on the effects of marijuana (see Chapter 3D), Weil concludes that the human being has an innate capacity for "highs" and, contrary to popular belief among drug users and nonusers alike, the "high" is not somehow "in" the drug, but is "in" the human nervous system and can be induced without drugs.

What is the difference between "straight thinking" and "stoned thinking"? Straight thinking refers to rational and logical thinking processes that abstract principles from sensory experience. According to Weil, straight thinking has five prominent characteristics. 1) In straight thinking, the individual identifies "mind" with the intellect, with the rational cognitive processes that are characteristic of the "straight" consciousness. Nonrational mental processes are, therefore, suspect because to allow them free play is to risk "losing your mind." 2) Second, straight thinking focuses the attention on the input of the five senses. The individual tends to lose touch with the internal feelings and subjective aspects of reality that many people, including Andrew Weil, think are as equally important as the objective realm. 3) The "attachment" to the sensory realm leads to "materialism" — which, for him, means an obsession with possessions, as well as a belief that objects, but not thoughts or feelings, can cause changes in the world. Straight thinking sees stoned thinking as merely the effects of marijuana fumes on the nervous system precisely because in straight thinking such explanations for psychological processes are expected to be found. 4) Straight thinking tends to perceive the differences between things rather than focusing on the underlying unities and continuities of things. It draws the borders between things rather than noticing the qualities that things may have in common; and, perhaps, it takes the differences too seriously. 5) Finally, Weil believes that straight thinking eventually leads to pessimism and despair. Undiluted straight thinking, as mentioned above, tends to see external physical processes as the causes of all changes. Furthermore, the differences between "me" and the "physical world" are strongly emphasized. So, in straight thinking, "I" see "myself" as being at the mercy of physical processes very different from and very alien to myself. The relationship between the individual and the environment comes to be seen as an antagonistic one. Nature is hostile. Other people are the "enemy." Life is a struggle in which defeat (death) is inevitable. His diagnosis is unequivocal: undiluted straight thinking gets you into trouble.

The antidote is stoned thinking. The term stoned thinking does not refer to a clearly defined set of psychological processes, but to all the states of consciousness that are alternatives to straight thinking (see Chapter 5D); hypnosis, drug states, meditation, intuitive thoughts, and dreaming could all be considered examples of stoned thinking. We could begin to describe stoned thinking by contrasting it to straight thinking. Stoned thinking implies an independence from the intellect, an active appreciation of the similarities and the continuities in things, as well as the differences between them. But stoned thinking need not contradict the results of the straight thinking process. For instance, the reliance on intuition is not in opposition to the intellect but might be described as running in parallel to rational thinking, perhaps arriving at the same conclusion but reaching it by an entirely different route.

Many of the greatest scientific discoveries came, not from the plodding efforts of logic, but from leaping intuitions. When asked what experiment or data had suggested to him the theory of relativity, Einstein replied that it had come from no such external source but had been an insight that he attributed to God. Stoned thinking often results in an intimate experience of "infinity," Weil reports, the apprehension in commonplace things not merely of one unexpected meaning but a profundity of meanings that are experienced, not as suddenly injected into the events, but as constantly present meanings whose significance had been ignored until, while stoned thinking was going on, the individual was willing to "listen." Part of stoned thinking is being willing to entertain all of those nonrational "messages" that to the stoned thinker seem to be constantly transmitted to us, but which seem nonexistent or insane to the straight thinker who tunes them out by constantly listening to only one "station"—the intellect.

What Weil argues for is not stoned thinking *instead* of straight thinking, but the recognition of stoned thinking as a natural and important part of human consciousness. It should not be assumed that "stoned thinking" is necessarily connected with the use of drugs. At different times, everyone experiences stoned consciousness, in dreams or in daydreaming, in hypnosis, when intuitively solving a problem, or in meditation, as well as in connection with experiences with drugs. Weil feels that there is a very real danger in employing drugs for the sake of stoned experience. Use of drugs leads to a materialistic attitude, he says, reinforcing the idea that "the experiences . . . came in the joints of marijuana, tabs of acid, or shots of heroin, and they saw no other way of getting them." To be convinced of a dependency on a materialistic (i.e., drug) cause of stoned thinking is, for Weil, the basis of addiction. To learn that alternative kinds of consciousness are the birthright of humanity is to be liberated from the addiction. Weil believes that to fight drugs directly by legal means is futile, serving only to drive their use underground and to cut off communication. He claims that drugs should be accepted as but one contemporary tool of consciousness-altering. Weil feels that "stoned thinking" should be accepted as a common human capacity that is a function, not of drugs, but of the "natural" human mind.

—functional solution—specific solution. In the interplay of logical, gradual methods of limiting alternatives and the "free play" of imagination in the final phase that ends in the flash of illumination, we can glimpse the complexity of the problem-solving task.

Solutions to the water jar problems discussed on pages 309–310. The methods you probably used to solve the practice problems, the *indirect method,* involved filling up the largest jar then subtracting water by pouring into the smaller jars until the large jar has the required amount of water left. However, the test problems, 1 and 2, can be solved by a *direct method.* Test problem 1 can be solved by filling up the 23-quart jar and then removing 3 quarts from it to get 20. You probably solved this problem by filling up the 49-quart jar first, then pouring off into the smaller jars. Test problem 2 can be quickly solved by filling up the 15- and 3-quart jars and pouring them into the 39-quart jar to make 18 quarts. You probably solved this problem by filling up the 39-quart jar first and then pouring off into the smaller jars to get the required amount.

If you worked this way, you have just experienced the effects of a mental set that tends to produce a fixed way of solving a problem. Your set was induced by the practice problems. Abraham Luchins, while at New York University, found that when he gave students the practice problems to produce a mental set for the indirect solution, then on the test problems 81 percent used the indirect solution, 17 percent used the direct solution, and 2 percent

failed to solve them. By way of contrast, when another group of students was simply given the two test problems without the preceding practice problems, 100 percent used the direct solution.

D. LANGUAGE

American Sign Language (ASL) is useful for people who are deaf, because it employs gestures to represent "words," or more exactly, concepts. (There is also an alphabet code used with ASL, in which hand shapes represent letters.) Using ASL sign-words, deaf children can learn language much as hearing children do; the latter obviously learn to speak words long before they are expected to be capable of writing or spelling them. Some of the signs of ASL are illustrated in Figure 9.11.

A particularly significant application of ASL involved Washoe, a female in Nevada who was born without sufficiently developed vocal organs for speaking, although she enjoyed normal hearing. When she was about one year old, Washoe was taken into the household of Allen and Beatrice Gardner of the University of Nevada. She grew up in a house trailer and was accompanied in all her waking hours by the Gardners or one of their associates. They communicated with her

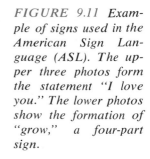

FIGURE 9.11 Example of signs used in the American Sign Language (ASL). The upper three photos form the statement "I love you." The lower photos show the formation of "grow," a four-part sign.

and with each other in the language of the hands, ASL. By age four, she had learned about 160 words, using them spontaneously in combinations that resembled simple sentences. In most children, this would have been very disappointing progress indeed, but the limited success of Washoe was a source of excitement throughout the psychological community. For Washoe is not just an ordinary student. She is perhaps the first nonhuman to have demonstrated the ability to use language in the way that is characteristic of humans. Washoe is a chimpanzee. (For a picture of Washoe in action, see Figure 9.12, page 320.)

Language has traditionally been considered exclusively human. But the Gardners suspected that the "exclusivity" might be the result of specialization of the human vocal apparatus rather than an exclusive human ability to employ symbols. To test

this theory, they raised Washoe with constant exposure to a language in which she might be as potentially successful as any human child, a language of gesture. Not only did she learn 160 words in four years and combine them in ways that she had never been taught, such as "Listen dog," "Hurry give me toothbrush," but she also showed the ability to employ concepts in contexts different from the ones in which she had learned them. For instance, having been taught the sign for "open" in connection with specific doors in the Gardner house, Washoe proceeded to apply it appropriately to faucets, refrigerators, drawers, and containers. Likewise, when taught the sign for "baby," Washoe seemed to form her own concept of the "word"; she applied it not only to infants but also to small-scale replicas such as models of a cat or even photographs.

FIGURE 9.12 Washoe, a chimpanzee, signing the word "sweet."

WHAT IS LANGUAGE?

Among *researchers concerned with the psychological aspects of language, known as* **psycholinguists,** the question of whether Washoe and others of her kind "truly" do employ language is still debated. But in any event, Washoe's extraordinary achievement has provoked a fresh consideration of exactly what characteristics identify language and linguistic behavior. Various linguistic theorists agree on the following identifying characteristics of language. A language-user must:

—Have names for all important environmental objects.

—"Talk" or "gesture" about objects that are not physically present.

—Use signs as *concepts,* not simply in reference to actions or objects or agents.

—Invent combinations of signs in appropriate ways.

—Show a proper *order* of signs when order is crucial to a combination's meaning.

Washoe has already demonstrated that she could meet many of these criteria, while chimps in other research projects have qualified in others. An example is Sarah,

a chimpanzee taught by David Premack of the University of California at Santa Barbara to "read" statements with an "If . . ., then . . ." logical structure, which were written with differently shaped colored symbols. In such statements, the order of the symbols is crucial. (See Focus 9.3: The Education of Sarah, page 322.) Another example is Lana, who has learned a strict computer-controlled artificial language in a program directed by Duane Rumbaugh at the Yerkes Primate Research Center in Atlanta. Lana punches buttons on a computer console, and the computer fulfills her requests for, say, candy or a movie only if the rigid rules of the language are followed precisely. There is no chance for interpretation of meaning by a human, as with ASL. Although not all psycholinguists have accepted the evidence, the verdict seems to be: The human being is no longer the only linguistic creature. Admittedly, though, Washoe's "Gimme tickle" is a far cry from "To be or not to be."

Language Analysis

One of the roadblocks to the discovery of the linguistic potential of other species has been the strong association between language and speech in human beings. We humans have a vocal apparatus that is highly evolved compared to the sound equipment of related species such as the chimpanzee. Because of the priority of the spoken word, in most linguistic analyses the basic units of language are *sounds. These basic units of sound are called* **phonemes** and the set of phonemes for any single language is unique. Table 9.1 shows the phonemes of the English language. Phonemes are merely sounds. At the next level of analysis are **morphemes,** which *are the smallest units in a language that*

TABLE 9–1   **Phonemes and morphemes**

PHONEMES

Examples of some of the 45 phonemes found in the English language.

VOWEL SOUNDS	CONSONANTS
a as in fat	b as in box
a as in car	c as in cat
e as in ten	d as in dog
e as in here	f as in fog
i as in in	g as in goat
i as in bite	h as in hat
o as in go	sh as in ship
oo as in book	th as in this

MORPHEMES

Combinations of two or more phonemes can produce sounds that have meaning; some are words and others are prefixes or suffixes. The 45 English phonemes can produce over 100,000 morphemes. These 100,000 morphemes can in turn be combined to form over 500,000 words.

WORDS	PREFIXES	SUFFIXES
cat	un	able
grow	pre	ed
fun	pro	er
run	co	s (plural, possessive)
paint	dis	itis
ease	re	ing
teach	holo	ly
learn	retro	ous

have meaning. Most commonly they are words, but not necessarily. For instance, the "s" in "words" is a morpheme because it has the meaning of plurality. The *syntactic level* is the next level of analysis. **Syntax** *is concerned with the way morphemes are put together into coherent phrases or sentences.*

In this section we will be examining certain questions about language. How do we understand and remember what is spoken to us? How is it that we produce sentences to express what we wish to say? How do we avoid coming up with nonsense strings of words like, "John squirreled inside the razor?" How are the different forms of sentences, such as a simple expression and its negative counterpart, related to each other? What effect does vocabulary have on thinking?

Making Sentences
by the Rules

The recall and forgetting of simple sentences have enabled Jacqueline S. Sachs at Berkeley to shed light on the way language is handled by human beings. Sachs's subjects at the University of California listened to a simple narrative about the development of the telescope and its early use in astronomy. Unknown to her subjects, Sachs picked different sentences in the narrative to be the "targets" of her recall testing. Either immediately after the target sentence had been heard, or at intervals of 80 or 160 syllables of narrative following the target sentences, a sentence similar to the target was presented. The subjects evaluated the new sentence as either *identical* to the target sentence or as *altered.* Examples of the variations the subjects might be asked to evaluate in comparison to the target sentences are presented in Table 9.2, page 324. Sachs found that after as little as 160 syllables of narrative had followed the original target sentence, the accuracy of the subjects in identifying a similar sentence with a change in form, such as sentence 4, had fallen to 50 percent—no better than chance. And in identifying the passive/active transformation (number 3), the subjects were not much better. After such a brief duration, the *only* variation that was correctly

Focus 9.3
The Education of Sarah

How does one teach language to a chimpanzee? This was the problem facing David Premack of the University of California, Santa Barbara, where he developed his own set of rules for the task of educating Sarah the chimp. First of all, the language must be one that the chimp can use; vocal languages simply will not do because the chimp does not have the necessary physiological equipment for speech. Premack developed a set of "word symbols," variously shaped and colored pieces of plastic with magnetic backings that could be placed on a felt-covered metal "language board." Second, Sarah's education was focused on things she would be interested in "talking" about, such as names and the manipulation of foods and other objects in her environment. The third rule was to *reward* any linguistic efforts Sarah might make, so as to reinforce them.

Initially, Sarah's trainers would place some favorite fruit—an apple, for instance—just outside Sarah's reach, while placing a particular piece of colored plastic that had been selected as the "name" for the type of fruit within Sarah's reach. Sarah would eventually pick up the "word" out of curiosity and the trainer would direct her hand so as to place the "word" on the language board. This sequence immediately earned Sarah a piece of apple. Gradually, Sarah would learn (and be required by her trainers) to pick up the appropriate word and place it on the language board in order to receive the food. Her vocabulary developed quickly, and she soon had words for everything from apricots to peanut butter.

Of course, Premack was after more than just teaching Sarah to name the various items; he hoped that she would be able to learn to produce sentences of considerable complexity. The next step toward this goal was to require Sarah to indicate *agency,* to correctly name the trainer from whom she wanted the food. Plastic names were provided for each of Sarah's trainers. Sarah soon found that it was necessary for her to give the correct name for the particular trainer as well as the particular food and so she soon began producing phrases like "Mary—apple" or "Randy—banana." Premack then gave Sarah a plastic name for herself. Sarah was now required to indicate herself by name when requesting food, to phrase her requests as "Randy—banana—Sarah." It was a simple step after this to add *verbs* to Sarah's developing sentence structure, greatly expanding the possible meanings. Sarah was then able to say things like "Mary—insert—banana—bowl." Once she had grown accustomed to the use of this fairly complete sentence structure, Sarah demonstrated the ability to read and follow instructions contained in complex sentences like "Sarah—insert—apricot—cup—banana—bowl." While it took more time for her to carry out such instructions than simpler sentences, she would eventually place the apricot in the cup and the banana in the bowl.

A real breakthrough in Sarah's education was her learning of the meaning of a *question mark,* that such a symbol required some kind of discriminative symbolic response—the correct answer to a question. Sarah had previously been taught to use comparison symbols: one pair meant "the same as," one meant "not the same as," and another pair meant "yes" and "no." Sarah's trainers would place two identical items, such as the symbols for cups, on the language board with the question symbol and the "same as" symbol between them. Sarah would respond correctly in this case by placing the "yes" symbol after the sequence to indicate her agreement that the two cups were indeed alike. It was found that Sarah could variously manipulate the symbols in such relationships. She could see the symbol for a cup and a banana on the language board with a question mark following them and correctly place the "not the same as" symbol between the two items. She even successfully learned certain concepts such as *color* and *shape.* For example, when the symbol for color was included in a comparison question about a banana and a yellow ball she would correctly reply that they were the same—the same color, that is—in spite of the fact that they were entirely different in terms of shape, smell, and so forth. Sarah had learned to compare things on the basis of specific concepts.

Has Sarah "really" learned language? Without claiming that Sarah can do everything that a human speaker can do, Premack feels that her education has been quite successful, that to equivocate about the status of her accomplishments is pointless. Sarah, he claims, has even learned to talk about "words." When asked a question such as "What is the shape of (apple symbol)?," she will give the answer, "round," which clearly refers to the apple itself and not to the *symbol* for apple, which is *triangular* in shape and blue in color. Premack feels this demonstrates that to Sarah, the little blue plastic triangle means something other than itself, that it is a symbol in the sense that humans use symbols.

TABLE 9.2   **Examples of sentences used in the Sachs language study**

1. He sent a letter about it to Galileo, the great Italian scientist. (The original target sentence.)
2. Galileo, the great Italian scientist, sent him a letter about it. (An alteration in *meaning*.)
3. A letter about it was sent to Galileo, the great Italian scientist. (A change from *active* to *passive* form, but without a change in meaning.)
4. He sent Galileo, the great Italian scientist, a letter about it. (A slight change in *form*, but again no change in meaning.)

identified was the altered sentence where the *meaning* of the sentence was altered, such as sentence 2. From these results, Sachs concluded that what is stored in the long-term memory (see Chapter 7A) is not the sentence *as it is originally heard*, but the *meaning* of the sentence.

Transforming Kernels into Sentences. Sachs's results imply that the process of hearing and remembering a sentence is not a passive, sponge-like soaking up of recognized words but an active effort of *interpreting* its meaning. The form of the sentence is merely a "husk" that is discarded by the memory when the kernel of meaning has been extracted through the interpretive process. When there is no difference in meaning between the target sentence and variations that are merely changes in the form, the memory no longer contains information necessary to discriminate between them. On the other hand, the changed meaning contained in sentence 2 in Table 9.2 is immediately perceived as different from the original—even though the *words* are much the same.

When a person speaks, does this process occur in reverse? Is a "kernel of meaning" retrieved from the long-term memory and *transformed* into one of several sentence forms? If the "kernel of meaning" is all that remains in long-term memory, such a process would seem to be required every time we want to express knowledge. Starting with only this "kernel sentence," the individual produces a sentence that is meaningful to anyone in his culture. How is this done?

Noam Chomsky of the Massachusetts Institute of Technology has developed a theory of transformational grammar that attempts to describe the rules by which an individual changes the kernel into a standard sentence. These rules involve such things as word order, changing tense, altering active to passive, shifting from affirmative to negative, and so on. The kernel must be present before producing a sentence is possible. Further, just as a seed can produce a tree with many distinct branches, so a single linguistic kernel may be the parent of a number of transformations. The inability of Sachs's subjects to discriminate between the different forms of a sentence reflects this *productive* quality of the kernel, that is, the "out of one (kernel), many (sentences)" property. The generation of a specific simple sentence from the kernel at its roots is illustrated in Table 9.3, which shows seven transformations of the original sentence. Clearly, the same information or kernel can be represented in several different specific sentences. But are all of these different forms related in the same way to the kernel? Can differences between the transformations of the sentence be observed?

Sentence Transformations.
KERNEL SENTENCE: John kicked the blue ball.

TABLE 9.3 Kernel sentences and their trans-formations

1. KERNEL SENTENCE: John kicked the blue ball.
2. QUESTION: Did John kick the blue ball?
3. NEGATIVE: John did not kick the blue ball.
4. QUESTION-NEGATIVE: Did John not kick the blue ball?
5. PASSIVE: The blue ball was kicked by John.
6. PASSIVE-NEGATIVE: The blue ball was not kicked by John.
7. PASSIVE-QUESTION: Was the blue ball kicked by John?
8. PASSIVE-QUESTION-NEGATIVE: Was the blue ball not kicked by John?

PASSIVE NEGATIVE: The blue ball was not kicked by John.

Clearly, the second sentence is a transformation of the first. The transformation requires the application of rules involving word order and the formation of the past tense and the negative. After offering examples like this to subjects, George Miller of Harvard University gave them lists similar to those in Table 9.4. They were then required to match sentences on the right with those on the left. He then compared the number of sentences of each type of transformation that were correctly matched in a fixed time interval.

Miller found that different kinds of transformations do indeed require different amounts of time to recognize. In fact, Miller was able to demonstrate *a regular pattern in the time required for each transformation,* a pattern that is illustrated in Figure 9.13. Transformations that are quickly recognized are connected by a single line segment. Transformations requiring intermediate times are connected by two segments. Transformations requiring the longest times are indicated by three line segments. Miller's results indicate that there do seem to be discrete "steps" such as the application of rules in the transformation of a sentence in one form to another of its possible forms, just as Chomsky's theory proposes.

TABLE 9.4 Example of a sentence-matching test

____ The old woman was warned by Joe.	1. The small boy wasn't warned by John.
____ The small boy wasn't liked by Joe.	2. The old woman wasn't warned by Jane.
____ The young man was liked by John.	3. The young man was warned by Jane.
____ The old woman wasn't liked by Joe.	4. The old woman wasn't warned by Joe.
____ The young man wasn't warned by Jane.	5. The old woman was liked by John.
____ The small boy was liked by Jane.	6. The small boy wasn't liked by John.
____ The young man wasn't liked by Jane.	7. The young man wasn't warned by John.
____ The old woman was warned by Jane.	8. The old woman was warned by John.
____ The small boy wasn't warned by Jane.	9. The young man wasn't warned by Joe.
____ The small boy was warned by John.	10. The small boy was warned by Jane.
____ The young man was warned by John.	11. The small boy was warned by Joe.
____ The small boy wasn't warned by Jane.	12. The small boy wasn't liked by Jane.
____ The small boy was liked by John.	13. The young man wasn't liked by John.
____ The young man wasn't liked by Joe.	14. The young man was liked by Jane.
____ The young man was warned by Joe.	15. The old woman was liked by Joe.

This test is designed to study transformations between affirmative-passive and negative-passive sentences. In the blanks put the number of the sentence on the right that is a transformation of each sentence on the left. (Miller, 1962)

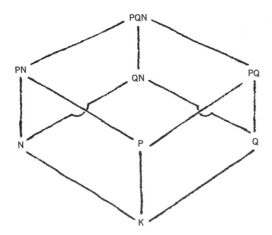

FIGURE 9.13 Different kinds of transformation of a sentence require different amounts of time to recognize (K=kernel sentence, N=negative, Q=question, P=passive, PQ=passive question, QN=negative question, PN=passive negative, PQN=passive negative question).

LEARNING TO MAKE LANGUAGE

The Deep Structure Theory

In Chomsky's **transformational grammar** *theory of syntax, the production of coherent phrases and sentences is assumed to be dependent on certain structures that are innate in the human nervous system. He refers to these as* **deep structures.** Because there are striking similarities in the syntax of all known human languages, Chomsky believes that such deep structures are innate rather than learned. No one ever explicitly states these deep structures, yet they dictate the way people perceive and interpret their world as well as the structure of the language used to express the individual's percepts. To Chomsky, children are born linguists. From the experience of the language being spoken in the child's environment *and* the deep structures, the child's nervous sys-

tem creates a set of rules or theory that dictates the production of language. The rules of transformational grammar are an attempt to describe the theory that almost all people develop and employ in this process of language production. Theoretically, there is a single rule for each of the shortest (one-segment) transformations shown in Figure 9.13. Each of the longer ones is accomplished by a combination of rules and, as Miller's data indicate, takes more time to be carried out. Because Chomsky's theory deals mostly with covert processes that are not directly observable, there are difficulties in testing it; ingenious experimental tactics like those of Miller and Sachs are required.

Washoe's linguistic training was a painstaking, planned effort on the part of the Gardners compared to the seemingly haphazard language instruction of human children. Yet, by the age of five, most children speak their native language fluently. They make original constructions, that is, sentences they have never heard before. In general, they employ the language so well that there will be little change for the rest of their lives, except for expansion of vocabularies. Chomsky's picture of the child as an active "theorist" rather than a "sponge of experience" provides an attractive explanation for the acquirement of language, which is an impressive intellectual feat.

A major alternative to this approach is the associationist theory proposed by Harvard's B. F. Skinner. This theory accounts for the development of language in terms of operant learning (see Chapter 6B).

The Associationist Theory

Skinner stresses that speech responses arise because of the reinforcement people receive for producing them. Speech responses may arise in several ways. Three categories are "mands," "echoic responses," and "tacts." For example, for a child learning to speak, **mands** *reflect needs: "I'm hungry" is an example, or any utterance that is reinforced by an adult's response that is associated with a primary drive.* Crying is perhaps the most primitive mand; it is an undifferentiated indication of distress that becomes associated with relief when a parent relieves the distress. **Echoic responses** *are repetitions of sounds made by the parents or others; they are usually reinforced with attention and perhaps touching.* **Tacts,** *the names for things such as "mama," "doggie," or "chair," are also usually reinforced with attention and approval.* Skinner believes that all mands, echoic responses, and tacts are gradually shaped into the vocabulary of the infant by the same principles involved in operant conditioning, which we have explored in Chapter 6B. By attention, approval, or relief of biological needs, adults reinforce the performance of a speech repertoire. To Skinner, the development of speech is simply determined by the reinforcing behaviors of the parents; if parents were to reinforce other speech behaviors, then other behaviors or languages would be learned—or no language at all. In Skinner's view, compared to Chomsky's, the child is much more influenced by the environment.

Skinner's explanation of sentence-building is the most controversial and difficult aspect of his theory. Supposedly, sentences are associations among words. Some words are primary like "hand" and "food" because they are associated with specific objects and needs. For instance, in "John bit the dog," John, bit, and dog are the primary responses. To Skinner, the sentence is then constructed from those responses plus further responses that have been associated to them. So, in Skinner's theory we have a *binary* process involving some words that are associated to the environment and to need states, and further words that occur because the speaker responds in turn to his or her own speech. *The sentence is the total interaction among the associations between the component words—hence the name* **associationist theory** *that is sometimes applied to Skinner's theory.* Skinner's theoretical framework is probably an accurate description of the role of reinforcement and association in language development, but it is not clear whether the theory can explain the transformations of the kind discussed by Chomsky and illustrated in Miller's experiment. Research stimulated by these theories is still going on. Until more is known, both points of view will compete for supporters. It may even turn out that both points of view have some validity. For example, the activation of "deep structures" may occur as a consequence of the parents' reinforcement of the child's verbal behaviors.

LANGUAGE AND THOUGHT

Sitting at a table in a rural African schoolhouse in Senegal, Patricia Greenfield administered Jean Piaget's now-classic test of the comprehension of conservation (see Chapter 8C) to a young African boy of the Wolof tribe. The boy poured water from a pitcher of one shape into a container of an entirely different form, then answered the researcher's questions in Wolof, his native language. "How much water is there in the second pitcher as compared to the first?" Greenfield asked. "They are the same," the boy immediately replied. "Why do you think so?" The boy stared at Greenfield, obviously not comprehending the question nor the sort of reply he might make. "They *are* the same," he repeated, and shrugged his shoulders as if to indicate, "What more can I say?"

Later, Greenfield performed the same experiment with another Wolof child. This child was *bi*lingual though, having been taught to speak, read, and write French at the schoolhouse. Again, the child was certain that the amount of water had remained the same even if the containers were different. But when Greenfield asked why the boy thought they were equal, he quickly replied in French, "I think it must be the same as it was at the start—after all, it didn't change, did it?"

Language and the Conservation Problem. The two Wolof children illustrate the results of an experiment on the effects of language on thought that Greenfield conducted in collaboration with Jerome S. Bruner of Harvard University. The inability of monolingual Wolof children to comprehend the researcher's question about why they thought the amount of water remained the same indicated what Bruner calls an attitude of "psychological realism." By that he means that the person's beliefs are not distinguished from the events in the physical world to which they refer. By contrast, the Wolof children who had learned French seemed to find the distinction between what they *thought* and what happened in the physical world a natural one. They were prepared to back up their thought by an appeal to a general principle, conservation.

In Wolof there is only one word, *honka,* that is applied to the colors that in English we call "red" and "orange." The French language, like our own, distinguishes between *rouge* and *orange.* Bruner and Greenfield guessed that the Wolof children from the bush who had not gone to school

and knew no French would make more errors in grouping objects by "similarity" of color than the bilingual children. They showed both groups color photographs of bananas, oranges, and round-shaped clocks that were either yellow or red or orange. Then, they asked the youngsters to pick the two pictures that were more alike. The results showed a distinct pattern. The children could have grouped pairs of photos by at least three concepts; by color, shape, or function (use). As predicted, the unschooled monolingual Wolofs were more likely to pair red clocks with orange fruit. The schooled Wolofs made fewer such errors when they grouped by color. However, the errors among the monolingual Wolofs were relatively rare—no more than three errors per 20 children. This error rate decreased as the children got older until no errors were made. This indicates that while language does influence discrimination, reality does overcome some language limitations with age.

Strikingly, the unschooled Wolof children were unable to express a *concept* of grouping when asked why they had paired photos. At best, they would point a finger and say "honka" or simply point a finger and say nothing, as though the grouping were self-evident and no alternatives were conceivable. By contrast, the bilingual Wolofs, when asked the same question, would reply, in French, "They are both the same color." This shows that the bilingual children were clearly making use of what Bruner calls a "superordinate category." This is a concept that includes alternatives so that *types of differences* can be considered abstractly. One example is the superordinate category "color." Objects may be either the same color or a different color. But in either case, the classifying concept is "color." Those bilingual children who could employ the superordinate category of color seemed also to have access to other superordinate categories like "function" and "shape." They were not only more accurate, but more versatile.

Bruner believes that a handicap in the Wolof language is the paucity of words for superordinate categories. There are no words for "color" or for "shape" in Wolof. Without words for the superordinate categories, concepts like color, shape, or function are unlikely to occur to the speaker or to be employed. If the speaker does make such intuitive distinctions, they will very likely be perceived, as the monolingual Wolof boy at the start of this section perceived the water to be the same in either pitcher, in a context of "psychological realism."

(For a comparison of terms for the spectrum in four languages, see Figure 9.14, in the color plate after page 370.)

Concept Formation. **Concept formation** *involves learning to recognize common qualities in different things.* In the Bruner-Greenfield experiment, the pertinent concepts could be "redness," "roundness," or "edible-ness," or some more abstract superordinate concepts. For instance, the superordinate "color" includes both "redness" and all the varieties of "nonredness," that is, other colors. *The process of "pulling out" similarity from objects that are very different in many ways* (such as an orange and a round clock) *is called* **abstraction.** This ability seems to be prerequisite to language, and it is increasingly evident as a species approaches *Homo sapiens* on the evolutionary scale.

An experiment in concept formation using a rat, a chimpanzee, and a child illustrates this. When tested for selecting a triangular form set among other geometrical forms, all three can recognize

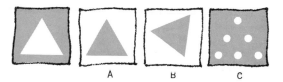

FIGURE 9.15 Rats, chimps, and children can recognize Triangle A; however, rats cannot see triangularity in B, and only the children can see triangularity in C.

(A) in Figure 9.15 as a triangle. With the rotated triangle (B), however, the rat falls by the wayside, leaving the child and the chimp, and *only* the child can see "triangularity" in (C). Of all known species, humans seem to be the champion conceptualizers. But as the Bruner-Greenfield experiment demonstrates, human conceptualizing can be hindered by a language that lacks words for pertinent concepts.

Perhaps the most important conclusion Bruner draws from experiments such as the Wolof research is this: Languages have inherent hierarchical structures in meaning. Although "color" and "red" and "blue" are alike in being *words,* they are distinguished in terms of their hierarchical position in terms of the concept of color. As Bruner puts it, "No matter how rich the vocabulary, it is of limited use as an instrument of thought if it is not organized into a hierarchy that can be activated." Words are initially learned as isolated concepts, perhaps, but are *most completely learned* when they are organized as categories in an increasingly comprehensive, integrated "tree" of concepts (see Figure 9.16, page 330). Although the availability of a superordinate category does not guarantee that a concept will be integrated into an individual's "tree" of knowledge, the lack of the word definitely makes the formation of the concept less likely.

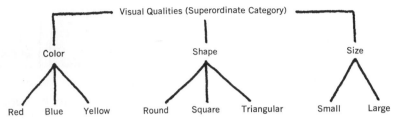

FIGURE 9.16 Many concepts in our language can be organized into a hierarchy.

SUMMARY

A. The Nature and Assessment of Creativity

1. **Creativity** may be defined as the act of forming new combinations of old elements. These combinations either meet specified requirements or are in some way useful. The more mutually distant the elements, the more creative is the resulting combination (page 295).

2. Psychologists have developed a number of tests for measuring creativity, including the Unusual Uses Test, the Consequences Test, the Anagrams Test, and the Remote Associates Test.

B. Personality and Creativity

3. Creative people seem to have a "need for novelty"; they will alter their behavior in order to obtain novel stimuli.

4. The creative person takes pleasure in complexity, is receptive and open to experience, is prone to intuition and hunches, and resists pressure to conform.

5. According to Frank Barron, "The creative person is both more primitive and more cultured, more destructive and more constructive, crazier and saner, than the average person."

6. Creative individuals tend to come from families that are characterized by respect for and confidence in the child, absence of a strong emotional bond between parent and child, and ambiguous identification with the parents by the child. The parents are models of effective, resourceful behavior. Discipline is fair and consistent, and the development of personal codes of conduct is encouraged. The values of integrity, excellence, and "doing the right thing" are emphasized.

7. By providing children with repeated practice in creative problem solving, it has been shown that creativity can be raised and maintained. Studies have also shown that by selectively reinforcing creative behavior in dolphins and humans, creativity can be increased.

C.   **Problem Solving**

8.   A **set** (page 309) is a learned strategy or a hidden assumption about the solution of a problem that may either aid or hinder in solving a problem.

9.   **Functional fixedness** (page 311) is a kind of set in which the prior uses or functions of an object prevent a person from considering new uses that are required for solving a problem.

10.   Mental set can be overcome by such factors as (a) effective labeling of or naming of elements of a problem so they can be manipulated verbally and in imagination, (b) stating problem-solving assumptions so they can be examined, (c) reorganizing the problem conceptually or spatially to see it in a new perspective, (d) maintaining motivation at a moderate level.

11.   **Insight** (page 313) refers to the seemingly sudden solution to a problem based on a reorganization of the elements of the problem whereby the solution becomes self-evident.

12.   Problem solving seems to occur in stages such as preparation, incubation, illumination, and verification.

D.   **Language**

13.   Language has a number of identifying characteristics including names for objects, talk or gestures for objects that are not present, signs used as concepts, and vast combinational organization of the words in meaningful sentences.

14.   Language can be broken up into elementary sounds called **phonemes** and **morphemes** (page 320) as well as into groups of morphemes that must obey the rules of **syntax** (page 321).

15.   According to some theories, such as Chomsky's **transformational grammar** theory (page 326), language usage involves an active process of extracting, storing, and interpreting meaning. Extraction of meaning and forming sentences is based on the application of language processing rules. An organism's capacity to learn and apply rules and process language is assumed to be innate—based on **deep structures** (page 326)—but requiring learning for its development.

16.   **Association theory** (page 327) (Skinner) explains language learning and use in terms of stimulus-response elements based on the principles of operant conditioning.

17.   **Concept formation** (page 329) and problem solving are influenced by the language and categories of hierarchical structures an individual has available to describe and compare objects.

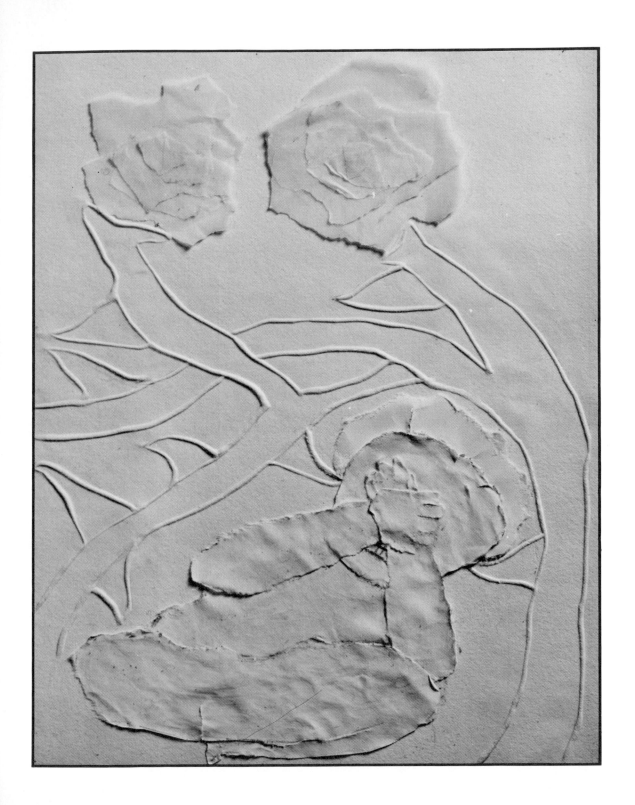

Section
Six
Individual,
Adaptive
Being

Each individual personality is a function of many interacting factors such as genetic structure, biological characteristics, and unique adaptations to the family and cultural environment. The task of integrating these factors into a coherent conceptual framework falls to the personality theorist.

In this section, we will examine several personality theories and methods that psychologists use to assess the development of personality. You will also have an opportunity to study the case histories of people whose behaviors provide insight into normal and abnormal personality functioning.

Occasionally something goes wrong during the process of personality development, leaving an individual with emotional and behavioral problems. In this section we will also deal with such questions as: What factors lead to the development of abnormal behavior? What kinds of therapeutic methods are used to help people with such emotional and behavioral problems? How can people resolve the conflicts and frustrations that life presents?

Chapter Ten Personality

You remember I said before that Ackley was a slob in his personal habits? Well, so was Stradlater, but in a different way. Stradlater was more of a secret slob. He always looked all right, Stradlater, but for instance, you should've seen the razor he shaved himself with. It was always rusty as hell and full of lather and hairs and crap. He never cleaned it or anything. He always looked good when he was finished fixing himself up, but he was a secret slob anyway, if you knew him the way I did. The reason he fixed himself up to look good was because he was madly in love with himself. He thought he was the handsomest guy in the Western Hemisphere. He was pretty handsome, too—I'll admit it. But he was mostly the kind of handsome guy that if your parents saw his picture in your Year Book, they'd right away say, "Who's this boy?" (Salinger, *The Catcher in the Rye*)

How do people come to have such distinctive personalities as the "secret slob"? What sorts of child-rearing practices and past experiences result in different kinds of adults? How do psychologists go about measuring personality characteristics and changes? This chapter will seek to answer these, and other, questions, but first, a basic definition is needed: What is personality?

Personality *is the configuration of characteristics that determines each individual's unique adjustment to the environment, including other people.*

How an individual acquires this "configuration of characteristics" is the concern of psychologists working in the area of personality development. A number of theories of personality development have been proposed: two of the best developed and most influential are the *psychoanalytic* theory of Sigmund Freud and the *social learning* theory of Albert Bandura and Richard Walters. Before we examine these theories, let us take a brief look at the men who were responsible for developing them.

Sigmund Freud was born in what is now Czechoslovakia in 1856, but he lived most of his life in Vienna, fleeing to England upon the Nazi invasion of Austria. Trained as a neurologist at the University of Vienna, Freud never intended to enter private practice but planned to pursue a research career in neurology. However, financial pressures forced him into practice, where his academic background led him to specialize in the treatment of what were then called "nervous disorders." It was largely through his experiences with his patients that Freud gradually evolved a complex and comprehensive theory of personality, including a theory of personality development. Psychoanalytic theory, it should be noted, has had profound and pervasive effects on Western society, influencing the arts, sciences, and humanities, as well as the average person's conception of the fundamental nature of human beings.

Albert Bandura was also trained to work with patients presenting psychological problems: he received his degree in clinical psychology from the University of Iowa. Following a year of postdoctoral clinical training, Bandura moved to Stanford University. There he was joined by Richard Walters, a native of Wales, student at Oxford, and, before going to Stanford, lecturer in philosophy at Auckland University College in New Zealand. After leaving Stanford, Walters joined the Department of Psychology at the University of Toronto and subsequently became chairman of the department at the University of Waterloo. Both Bandura and Walters were influenced by experimental psychology in the field of learning, and over the years they collaborated in a vigorous research program that led to their theory of personality development.

FIGURE 10.1 (At left) Sigmund Freud. (At right) Albert Bandura (top) and Richard Walters (bottom).

A. TWO THEORIES OF PERSONALITY DEVELOPMENT

Perhaps what most differentiates the two theories is their emphasis on events inside the individual as against events outside the individual. Freud's psychoanalytic theory tends to focus on internal forces and pressures, deep-seated and often unconscious, that influence an individual's behavior. Bandura and Walters' social learning theory, as its name implies, stresses the importance of external factors —social factors—in understanding human behavior.

The best way to describe these theories is by examples of their descriptions of the development of three classes of behavior: dependency, aggression, and sex. Most social groups are deeply concerned with regulating these behaviors for they cause most social difficulties. If you see how psychoanalytic and social learning theory handle the development of these areas of behavior, the contrast between the theories will become sharper. After giving these examples, we will look at examples of characteristic research generated by the respective theories, and finally we will attempt to reconcile them.

PSYCHOANALYTIC THEORY

According to psychoanalytic theory, personality development proceeds through a fixed series of stages during the first five years of life. These are decisive for the adult personality. The stages are based on the primacy of "erogenous zones" of the body. *An* **erogenous zone** *is an area of the skin or mucous membrane that, when stimulated, produces pleasurable sensations.*

Stages of Development. In the first year of life the infant's mouth serves as the primary source of pleasure, not only during feeding, but whenever the mouth or lips are stimulated, as in thumbsucking. Thus the mouth is the first erogenous zone and the first developmental stage is referred to as the **oral stage.** Beginning in the second year and running through the third, the anus becomes the chief source of pleasure; stimulation of the lower intestine during elimination provides the erogenous basis for the **anal stage.** During the third or fourth year the child's genitals become dominant, as evidenced by increased masturbatory activity, sexual curiosity, and sexual exploration; the child has entered the **phallic stage.** Although there is some variation between individuals and some overlap between stages, in the orthodox psychoanalytic theory these stages are fixed and inevitable. Although the impact of the environment is not ignored, the emphasis is nevertheless on the internal impulses, demands, and needs of the individual as manifested through the erogenous zones.

Development of Personality Characteristics Dependent, aggressive, and sexual characteristics are developed according to the degree to which erogenous needs are frustrated or gratified. Both frustration and overindulgence at any stage will produce an adult whose personality is colored by the infantile need at that stage. During the oral stage, an infant is completely dependent on the mother for sustenance. If the child is consistently frustrated (starved) or overindulged (stuffed), the whole area of dependency and nurturance will take on exaggerated importance. Later in life, the person's behavior (and thoughts) may be dominated by such "oral" concerns. Sometimes these concerns are expressed quite openly, as in a person who overeats and becomes obese or who is otherwise preoccupied with oral activities such as smoking and drinking. More frequently, however, the person continues to long for

someone to provide care and nurture, someone who can be depended on. Such an individual is incapable of functioning independently in any situation; rather, the person constantly requires reassurance, support, and succor from others in order to function. In other words, relationships with other people are highly dependent.

Aggressive behavior stems from the parents' handling of the child's eliminative functions during the anal stage. This period can be a real contest of wills, since the child can retain feces in defiance of parental wishes or expel them inappropriately. If parental demands in toilet-training are too harsh or their expectations too high, a great deal of rage and resentment may be engendered in the young child. This aggression may be expressed actively in rebellious outbursts of temper, but more frequently will find passive expression in obstinacy or stubbornness. The adult personalities of such people are characterized by passive aggressiveness; they are excessively obstinate and won't "move" or "give." This characteristic is quite pervasive: a person with the trait is arbitrarily negativistic in all sorts of situations and relationships. Such a person also refuses to "give" at any level either materially (as in lending a book) or psychologically (as in expressing feelings). It is just such a person, however, who is prone to fly off the handle at seemingly trivial provocations and to commit highly aggressive acts, thus revealing the underlying reservoir of rage.

During the phallic stage the upsurge in sexual feelings leads to an attraction between the child and the parent of the opposite sex. If the parents react to the child's sexual longings too harshly, or if they fail to establish realistic limits, sexual problems may result. Whether the child meets with parental disapproval and rejection or, what is perhaps even more likely to provoke anxiety, actually succeeds in displacing the parent of the same sex, the net result is the same: sex is viewed as dangerous. This attitude will affect the person's sexual functioning as an adult. The effect may be direct, leading to an incapacity to engage in heterosexual activity. More frequently, however, the effect is indirect, so that the person attempts to overcome fear of heterosexuality. One result is the male who views each heterosexual contact as a "conquest," who is continually trying to "make" women in a driven attempt to prove his masculinity to himself. Another result is the "castrating" female who attempts to "cut men down to size."

Normal Development. So far it would seem that psychoanalytic theory leaves no room for normal development. It must be remembered that the patients Freud worked with presented him with the results of maldevelopment; consequently, abnormal tendencies received emphasis in his theorizing. However, in the Freudian view, if oral, anal, and phallic issues are handled moderately and reasonably by the parents, normal development will ensue: as an adult the person will evince an appropriate degree of dependency in situations that call for it, will be capable of controlled aggression when called for, and will have a gratifying sexual life in the context of a genuine relationship. (See Focuses 10.1 and 10.2 for other aspects of Freudian and neo-Freudian theory.)

SOCIAL LEARNING THEORY

Although the parents play a role in the psychoanalytic view of development, their role is essentially reactive—they react to expressions of internal states in the child. In the social learning analysis of development, in contrast, the presence or absence of dependency, aggression, and sexuality are almost totally dependent on external agents, primarily the parents.

Modeling and Reinforcement. Bandura and Walters propose two mechanisms by which parents are effective in shaping behavior: *modeling* and *reinforcement.* **Modeling** *relates to the tendency of children (and adults) to imitate other people who are "rewarding, prestigeful, or competent, who possess high status, and who have control over rewarding resources...,"* a description that probably fits most parents, at least in the eyes of their children. Modeling can account for a child's acquisition of a behavior. In order to strengthen and maintain it, however, reinforcement is necessary. **Reinforcement** *relates to the consequences of behavior; if the consequences are positive, the child will be likely to repeat the behavior; if they are not, the child will not* (see Chapter 6B). It is the parents who largely have control over consequences, at least during the child's formative years. A good example of how modeling and reinforcement work together to produce aggressive behavior has been provided by Bandura and Walters:

Let us consider a father who devotes some of his time to playing punchball with his young son. He punches the ball himself and then, with or without verbal encouragement, elicits a similar response in the boy. He responds to the boy's punching with approval. The boy punches harder and is again positively reinforced. Indeed, a competition in prowess is likely to develop. In the course of the play, the father both provides the *model* for the hitting response and *reinforces* the response when it is made. (Bandura and Walters, 1963—emphasis added)

Focus 10.1

From Id, Ego, Superego to "I'm O.K. — You're O.K."

Sigmund Freud developed a theory of the human personality that explained behavior in terms of the interactions of three main systems that make up the personality: the id, the ego, and the superego. Each of these systems has its own functions, but it is the interaction of the three that is the most important factor in mental health. If the three interact harmoniously, the individual is happy and well-adjusted; but if conflict among the three is severe, neurosis results. *The most primitive of the three systems is the* **id.** *The id's function is to eliminate tension, to seek immediate pleasure, and to avoid pain.* This effort is what Freud described as the Pleasure Principle, which he believed to be present in all organisms as well as in this primitive part of the human personality. The id attempts to carry out this task in a very short-sighted way, without the capacity to devise long-range strategies or to take into account the consequences of actions. The id might be considered the "spoiled brat" of the personality. But Freud thought that the id can imagine, even though it cannot reason. It produces fantasy images and sensations of those things that are the objects of its desires. In fact, the id cannot distinguish between the fantasies and actual external events.

The portion of the personality responsible for thinking and planning is the **ego,** *the "executive" of the personality.* Freud believed that the ego developed to be the caretaker of the id, able to solve problems that the id alone could not handle. The ego can function as it does because, although it, too, can produce fantasies, the ego alone of the three systems can distinguish fantasy from external reality by observation and reasoning. In charge of all transactions with the external world, the ego may be considered the intermediary between the id and reality.

The **superego** *is the personality's moralist and judge.* This system, Freud thought, was the last of the three to develop and was a response to the need to inhibit the self-serving functions of the id and the ego that could jeopardize the individual's role as a member of society, especially behaviors relating to violence and sex. The result of the individual's assimilation of parental moral standards, the superego is composed of two subsystems, the *conscience* and the *ego-ideal.* The conscience is made up of all the "Thou shalt nots" that the individual learns from parents, all the proscribed actions or thoughts, and the guilt feelings that are associated with them. The ego-ideal is the opposite side of the coin; it is all the approved thoughts and actions and the feelings of security and self-esteem that are associated with them. Notice that we mention *thoughts* as well as actions. Like the id, the superego cannot distinguish between an action and the mere fantasy of the action. As a result, an individual may behave in a completely normal and moral way, but feel strong feelings of guilt because of desires and thoughts that were never acted on.

Over the years Freudian theory has constantly been revised and elaborated by those who accepted some of Freud's ideas and rejected others. Eric Berne, a psychiatrist starting with Freudian theory as a basis, developed his own theory, called "Transactional Analysis." Berne described the three components of personality as being composed of three *ego-states,* the Parent, the Adult, and the Child. Although very comparable to the concepts of id, ego, and superego, there are differences in Berne's concepts. Unlike Freud's biological approach, Berne's theory is largely social; the ego-states are not biological mechanisms so much as they are *social functions* or *roles.* In social transactions one of the ego-states will always be primarily in charge. In Berne's analysis, the Parent and Child are often in charge of social transactions. For example, a sick husband plays Child and says, "I have a headache. Help me." The wife plays Parent and says, "Go to bed. I'll get you an aspirin." As long as both parties receive satisfaction from transactions like these, they do not constitute a problem.

Whereas Freud's personality systems are primarily biological mechanisms for managing physiological problems such as tension, Berne's ego-states are experiences recorded in the brain of the individual at distinct periods in the individual's life and in distinct ways. In the Child, these recordings include not only memories of events, but emotional responses to the events that are inextricably bound in the memories.

The Child consists of the *felt* concept of life, recordings or internal events or feelings that are primarily responses to the parents from the time of birth to the age of five years. The child's primary goal during this period is to please the parents. When the Child ego-state is active in the individual, all the feelings of confused helplessness that are characteristic of the "childhood situation" are replayed. But on the positive side, the Child is also the source of creativity, spontaneity, curiosity, and sensuality.

The Parent ego-state contains the recordings of imposed, unquestioned external events experienced by the child between birth and age five. During this period, the child has not yet developed the intellectual skills necessary to challenge critically the statements and actions of parents, so all of this input is accepted as "Truth," although much of it may be untrue ("Remember, son, you just can't trust women!") and even contradictory ("Do unto others as you would have others do unto you . . ." "You've got to look out for old number one!"). The contents of the Parent are passively accepted by the child, who does not actively "learn" them so much as have them "taught" or *inflicted.*

The Adult is the last of the three ego-states to develop. Unlike the ego, which develops to fulfill the demands of the id, the Adult arises out of the individual's capacity for testing the environment and learning on an experimental basis. The Adult contains the *thought* concept of life, recordings of data which were acquired through exploration, reality-testing, and thinking. The Adult is also capable of editing the dated "instructions" from the Parent and the emotional responses of the Child, although these recordings can never be "erased." But the Adult can choose to play only the recordings it finds to be true or useful, leaving the others dormant as one might leave unwanted books unread on the shelf.

These concepts and others from Transactional Analysis have been popularized by psychiatrist Thomas A. Harris in his book *I'm O.K. – You're O.K.* Harris explains that, because of the experience of helplessness in dealing with the environment in the initial part of life, almost all children make a negative evaluation of themselves; they decide that they are "Not O.K." Just as important in the social transactions of the individual is their evaluation of *other* people: are others O.K. or Not O.K.? The two evaluations are often stable for an entire lifetime and determine to a large extent the individual's personal adjustment. The most common life position is "I'm Not O.K. – You're O.K.": other people are perceived as possessing goodness, competence, beauty, and so forth; here, the goal is to gain others' approval. The opposite life position is "I'm O.K. – You're Not O.K." the typical position of the habitual criminal. "I'm Not O.K. – You're Not O.K." is the position of despair where no one is seen as being worthwhile. The only position that places the responsibility on the Adult and is benevolent in disposition toward others, allowing for the creative solution of personal problems and genuine intimacy is "I'm O.K. – You're O.K." a position that is achieved only by choice.

Focus 10.2

Erikson's Eight Ages of Man

Freud restricted his analysis of human development to five stages of psychosexual development: the oral, anal, phallic, latent, and genital stages, a succession completed in young adulthood. In "normal" lives, according to this scheme, the genital stage covers most of an individual's lifespan, as though later life were anticlimatic. Psychoanalyst Erik H. Erikson of Harvard University has expanded Freud's psychosexual development scheme by describing development in terms of eight stages that encompass the total life span from birth to death. These "eight ages of man" are set out in Table 10.1.

Erikson's psychosocial analysis of development emphasized social factors more than orthodox Freudian theory does. During his lifetime, Freud was adamant about the preeminence of the sexual basis of behavior and development. Erikson's neo-Freudian approach places emphasis on the crucial psychosocial decisions that the individual must

Important (handwritten note)

TABLE 10.1   Erikson's eight ages of man

FREUD'S STAGES OF DEVELOPMENT	ERIKSON'S STAGES OF DEVELOPMENT	POTENTIAL EGO STRENGTH
Oral	Basic Trust vs. Mistrust	*Hope,* a belief in the attainability of desires despite one's own conflicting urges and feelings.
Anal	Autonomy vs. Shame and Doubt	*Will,* the courage to employ one's "free choice" despite the danger of the consequent rejection of others.
Phallic	Initiative vs. Guilt	*Purpose,* the courage to envision and seek goals despite the frustration of infantile desires.
Latent	Industry vs. Inferiority	*Competence,* the exercise of physical and mental skills in spite of frustration and difficulties.
Genital (listed below are the genital substages added by Erikson)		
Puberty and Adolescence	Identity vs. Role Diffusion	*Fidelity,* the ability to sustain loyalties despite conflicts.
Young Adulthood	Intimacy vs. Isolation	*Love,* devotion to others in the face of inevitable conflict.
Adulthood	Generativity vs. Stagnation	*Care,* a deep concern for people as they are, regardless of their past actions or events beyond their control.
Maturity	Ego Integrity vs. Despair	*Wisdom,* the concern with life despite eventual death.

make concerning his relationship with other human beings, at each stage taking a personal stand toward an even larger group of people, from parents to siblings, from extended family to humanity. Although development is in part determined by biological factors, it is "triggered" at each successive stage by social interaction, particularly by social situations that require new adjustments. For instance, during the anal stage, many children seem to "fall in love" with the word "No," with which they arbitrarily respond to parental requests. Erikson explains this as an attempt to assert their separateness from others, their ability to make individual decisions, their *autonomy.* This self-assertion accompanies the growing control the child is developing over voluntary muscles (such as the anal muscles involved in toilet training). If the parents respond punitively to a child's self-assertiveness, then the child may abandon the effort as a result of *shame,* the intense awareness of smallness and helplessness. But if the child's efforts are not thwarted, then the ego-strength of "will" develops (see Table 10.1). Ego-strength involves the skills and attitudes needed to function effectively in decision-making in an increasingly complex social environment. The qualities of the social setting, from mother's arms, through family, to the native culture, can facilitate the successful passage to maturity or can throw obstacles in the path.

As shown in Table 10.1, each stage presents the opportunity for a new *ego-strength* to develop in response to social crisis. In the successful development in any of the psychosocial stages, though, a key element is courage. By courage Erikson means the willingness to change one's basic relationship to others, to develop the new attitude or ego-strength, to become increasingly independent and even creative in an uncertain world. For Erikson it is not enough for the normal human to develop from dependency to autonomy. A person, to develop normally, must grow to the point where he or she *gives,* in terms of love and creative effort. No success can be guaranteed in this climb to maturity, when even the most mature individual is prey to all the accidents possible in an uncertain world. For Erikson normal development demonstrates the courage to love and work together with an ever-widening circle of concern in a world that offers no guarantees of success or happiness, where eventual death is the only certainty.

Deviant Behavior. The dual processes of modeling and reinforcement operate in the establishment of other classes of behavior, such as dependency and sex. A child who has highly dependent parents for models and who is reinforced by these parents for dependency behavior will, in adulthood, encounter adjustment problems in a world that expects a great degree of independence. Similarly, parents who are highly anxious over sexual matters may, as models, react with anxiety to any sexual behavior on the part of the child. Again, the child enters adulthood with anxieties concerning sexual behavior. In extreme situations, modeling and reinforcement can work to produce deviant sexual behavior, as in a case of exhibitionism cited by Bandura and Walters.

A 17-year-old boy was arrested for exhibiting himself in a public park. Apparently this behavior had been going on for a number of years. It turned out that his mother had taken frequent showers with the boy until he was 13 years old. The mother took great pleasure exhibiting herself to the boy, thus serving as a model for exhibitionistic behavior. She also took great pleasure in viewing his body, commenting on his "beautiful masculine endowment," thereby reinforcing exhibitionistic display on the boy's part.

In sum, according to social learning theory, the important influences on personality development originate outside of the child in parental models and reinforcements — not, as psychoanalysts would have it, in needs and demands within the child.

B. RESEARCH IN PERSONALITY

Both psychoanalytic and social learning theory have given rise to a great deal of research, and supporters of both theories can point to impressive arrays of empirical support. To give you an idea of what kinds of evidence the theories rely on, we will present two characteristic research studies, one from each theory. We have abridged these two complex studies in order to highlight the main findings.

PSYCHOANALYTIC RESEARCH

Gerald Blum of the University of California and Daniel Miller of the University of Michigan explored emotional conflicts relating to the oral stage of development. As we mentioned, the theoretical consequences of emotional crises in the oral stage include an unusually strong interest in food and dependency in interpersonal relationships.

Blum and Miller used third-grade children as their subjects of study and their measure of orality was simple and ingenious: nonpurposive mouth movements, that is, oral activity unrelated to eating. Trained observers counted the frequency of such nonpurposive mouth movements as thumb-sucking, lip-sucking, tongue-rolling, and bubbling. Then Blum and Miller set out to test the psychoanalytic hypotheses that those children high in orality (many non-purposive mouth movements) would show extreme interest in food and extreme dependency in their relationships.

Interest in Food. The hypothesis concerning interest in food was tested by two methods: asking the children's teachers, "Which children appear most impatient to eat at lunch time, as if eating were particularly important to them?" and measuring the children's consumption of ice cream. The latter method requires some explanation. In the words of Blum and Miller:

Our measure of consumption of oral supplies was the amount of ice cream eaten after hunger satiation. The children all ate lunch together. The meal, provided by the school, was dietetically planned and ample for all the children. Upon conclusion of a short rest period which followed lunch, they were offered an unlimited supply of vanilla ice cream contained in one-ounce paper cups packaged especially for the study. The carton of ice cream was placed on the table in the center of the room by a female graduate student who supervised the distribution of cups. Each child was allowed to take one whenever he wished. However, only one cup at a time was permitted and that in return for an empty one. No limit was placed on how much a child ate. The carton was kept in the room for the entire forty minutes devoted to arts and crafts, during which period observers recorded the exact number of cups consumed by each child. This procedure was repeated daily over three weeks. From these data averages were computed. The range in any one day's session was quite startling, varying all the way from no cups to thirty-nine for a single child. The absence of any parental complaints concerning illness or lack of appetite was a pleasant surprise in view of the inability of the observers, even at the end of the most frustrating days of the experiment, to eat more than five or six cups without discomfort. (Blum and Miller, 1952)

At the end of the three-week period, Blum and Miller compared the teachers' ratings on eagerness to eat at lunchtime and the number of ice cream cups consumed by each child with the indexes of orality. In both instances, the measures of interest in food were, as predicted, related to orality. The higher the child scored on orality, the more ice cream the child ate and the more eager the child was judged to be at lunch.

Dependency. Next, Blum and Miller turned their attention to dependency. Here they asked the teachers two questions: "Which children do you think are most able to take care of themselves without the help of adults or other children?" "Which children tend to ask the teacher for help most often, even when they know how to do the task?" The teachers' ratings of the children on the first question were, as predicted, related to orality—the higher the orality index, the less able the children were to take care of themselves. However, the second question ("ask the teacher for help") was not related. The explanation may be that the oral person does not have the assertiveness to actively approach someone in authority and request assistance; rather, the oral person's dependency may be passive as in early infancy, when a child, because of helplessness, must simply wait for someone to provide needed care.

In any event, the children high in orality were already suffering in their relationships with their peers. When the students were asked such questions as "Which children in your classroom do you like best?" "Which of the children in your classroom would you most like to invite to a party?" and "Which children in your class are you good friends with?" the youngsters high in orality were chosen far less frequently.

SOCIAL LEARNING RESEARCH

In order to demonstrate the power of modeling, a key concept in social learning theory, Bandura exposed groups of nursery school children to aggressive and nonaggressive adult models; then he observed the extent of the children's aggression in a new situation in the absence of the model.

Modeling. Here is how the experiment went. One group of children witnessed an adult model pummel a Bobo doll for nine minutes. In addition to punching the Bobo doll, the model performed a number of novel aggressive responses:

The model laid Bobo on its side, sat on it and punched it repeatedly in the nose. The model then raised the Bobo doll, picked up [a] mallet and struck the doll on the head. Following the mallet aggression, the model tossed the doll up in the air aggressively and kicked it about the room. This sequence of physically aggressive acts was repeated approximately three times, interspersed with verbally aggressive responses such as "Sock him in the nose . . ." "Hit him down . . ." "Pow . . ." and two nonaggressive comments, "He keeps coming back for more," and "He sure is a tough fella." (Bandura, Ross, and Ross, 1961)

A second group of children was exposed to a nonaggressive adult model who sat near the Bobo doll but ignored it and worked quietly assembling Tinkertoys.

Instigation of Aggression. After being exposed to the model, a child was then taken to another room where anger was aroused in the following fashion. The child was shown a number of attractive toys and encouraged to play with them. No sooner had he or she become involved with the toys, however, than the experimenter inter-

FIGURE 10.2 Children who observed an aggressive model imitated the novel aggressive responses previously performed by the model.

rupted and told the child that these were her very best toys, that she did not let just anyone play with them and that she had decided to reserve these toys for other children. Then the child was ushered into an adjoining room, where there stood a Bobo doll.

What happened? As you can see in Figure 10.2, the children who had observed the aggressive model imitated the novel aggressive responses previously performed by the model. The children who had observed the nonaggressive model rarely made such responses. These results suggest that the mere observation of a social model does, indeed, result in learning. (For other approaches to the study of personality, see Focus 10.3, page 348.)

WHICH THEORY?

Psychoanalytic and social learning theories deal with different domains of data and focus on different issues of development. Different theories offer viewpoints and, as such, complement—rather than contradict—one another. The result is a more valid picture of reality than whatever each theory by itself could offer.

Psychoanalytic theory is primarily concerned with the motivational or energizing forces in personality—what are the dynamics of the system, what makes it go? Thus, the internal drives and demands of a child at various points in development, along with their subsequent influence on the adult personality, are of prime interest. Moreover, in focusing on successively emerging, biologically rooted needs, psychoanalytic theory stresses the similarities among individuals at different periods of development and the differences within a given individual over time.

Social learning theory, in distinct contrast, stresses differences among people at any given age and the relative consistency of an individual over time by virtue of its concern with specific and repeated environmental circumstances. This theory is concerned with the problem of discovering those aspects of the social environment that are involved in shaping behavior.

An Example.   Most situations in life contain elements that relate to both psychoanalytic and social learning theory. For example, in a sexual relationship, each partner makes responses (such as flirting, petting, and other approach activities) that have been learned from models (peers, mass media) and that have been reinforced (met with success) in the past. The intensity and the persistence of these sexual actions are, however, determined largely by the internal needs of the participants. If sexual deprivation has been severe, the sexual responses are likely to be ardent; on the other hand, if sexual gratification has been recent, the sexual responses may be weak or may not even occur at all.

Rapprochement.   In our view, each theory is valuable in shedding light on its own area of interest and emphasis. A reconciliation and eventual merging of personality theories is not only desirable but also inevitable. The situation is not unlike that of the blind men discussed in Chapter 1 who were asked to describe an elephant. One who felt the trunk suggested that an elephant must be very much like

a snake; another who felt the tail thought that an elephant must be very like a rope, and so forth. Only when the different perspectives are assembled does a realistic picture of the object of investigation emerge. So, too, with personality theories.

Now that we have examined some of the forces and factors in the development of personality, we are ready to discuss some of the means that psychologists have developed to assess personality.

C. PERSONALITY ASSESSMENT

Do you agree or disagree with the following statements?

1. When I was younger, I used to tease vegetables.
2. Sometimes I am unable to prevent clean thoughts from entering my mind.
3. I am not unwilling to work for a jackass.
4. I would enjoy the work of a chicken flicker.
5. I think beavers work too hard.
6. It is important to wash your hands before washing your hands.
7. It is hard for me to say the right thing when I find myself in a room full of mice.
8. I use shoe polish to excess.
9. The sight of blood no longer excites me.
10. It makes me furious to see an innocent man escape the chair.
11. As a child, I used to wet the ceiling.
12. I am aroused by persons of the opposite sexes.
13. I believe I smell as good as most people.
14. When I was a child, I was an imaginary playmate. (*Amer. Psychol.,* 1965)

This is an apocryphal personality test. It probably doesn't measure anything, other than, perhaps, your sense of the ridiculous. Psychologists have, in fact, developed a number of instruments that do measure

Focus 10.3 Personality Types and Traits

One of the earliest theories of personality was attributed to the Greek physician Hippocrates, who lived about 400 B.C. His theory asserted that temperament or mood was the result of the relative amounts of four different fluids present in the body of an individual. The four types of personality, each resulting from the predominance of a particular fluid, were the melancholic (sad), the phlegmatic (apathetic), the sanguine (cheerful), and the choleric (irritable). Although Hippocrates' theory is no longer taken seriously, the names of the four "types" of personalities he suggested have remained in the language to this day.

The effort to analyze personality into several basic *types* has its adherents in modern psychology. Type theories of *personality attempt to categorize individuals into a limited number of personality types.* One such effort is the *somatotype* theory of William Sheldon. He classified individuals in terms of three body types, the ectomorphic (or thin), the mesomorphic (or muscular), and the endomorphic (or fat) (see Table 10.2). Observers rated various body segments on a scale for the degree of each type present. No one is likely to be a complete endomorph, ectomorph, or mesomorph, but individuals usually tend towards one of the three body types. Sheldon believed that each of the three types of bodies corresponded to a personality type (see Table 10.2). Sheldon claimed a strong relationship between the ratings of physical types and predicted personality types. But his results were criticized for lack of rigorous scientific control. Critics found that his ratings of personality could have been influenced by the interviewer's knowledge of Sheldon's theory and social stereotypes such as the expectancy that thin people are intellectual while fat people are supposedly jolly. Further, the kind of result produced by Sheldon's research does not tell us whether a personality characteristic is the result of physique or if the physique is the result of physical and eating habits related to personality characteristics. For example, a love of physical activity might well result in a well-muscled, mesomorphic body, rather than vice versa.

TABLE 10.2   Relationship of body and personality types

SOMATOTYPE	PERSONALITY TYPE	CHARACTERISTICS
1. Endomorph (Rounded body contours, soft flabby tissue, undependable muscles)	Visceratonic	Sensuous, slothful, gregarious, and easy-going
2. Mesomorph (Hard, well-muscled, athletic build)	Somatotonic	Aggressive, with a love of physical activity and adventure
3. Ectomorph (Elongated body, thin, fragile, and delicate build)	Cerebrotonic	Intellectual, high-strung, and nervous

One of the basic problems of any "type" approach to personality is that the small number of types forces the researcher to ignore many of the *differences* between people for the sake of fitting them into one of the categories. To create enough "types" to represent these many differences would make the system cumbersome, and, of course, we would never know when to stop devising new "types." Theoretically, each individual human being could be a "type."

Many researchers have responded to this problem by developing more complex systems of *trait* theories. *A* **trait** *is a measurement of a group of behaviors that occur together and are relatively stable over time.* For example, "aggressiveness"—the tendency to behave aggressively in a wide variety of situations and relationships—might be considered to be a trait, with any given individual scoring high, moderate, or low in aggressiveness. To be meaningful a trait must be useful in describing personality and in predicting behavior.

An example of trait analysis is found in the work of Raymond Cattell of the University of Illinois. Cattell has derived what he believes to be 16 important traits or factors in describing personality, as illustrated below. As you will note, the traits are expressed as extremes (even opposites) of certain categories of behavior such as the trait "Reserved to Outgoing." Individuals are rated in the degree to which they approach either extreme of the continuum (on a scale of 10) of a given trait. Cattell believes that he can describe personality meaningfully by plotting the relative strength of each trait. He has found that various groups of people show typical trait patterns. An example of the profiles of airline pilots and creative artists is illustrated below.

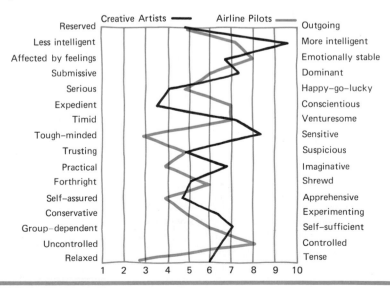

various aspects of personality.

The field of personality assessment has grown from our desire to understand present behavior and predict future behavior on the basis of a relatively small sample of behavior—performance on a test. We will introduce you to three personality tests that have gained wide use and critical acceptance in both research and clinical settings: the Minnesota Multiphasic Personality Inventory, the Thematic Apperception Test, and the Rorschach Test.

THE MINNESOTA MULTIPHASIC PERSONALITY INVENTORY

The Minnesota Multiphasic Personality Inventory—better known simply as the MMPI—presents a number of questions or statements for a person to respond to. (The bogus test presented at the beginning of this section was in inventory form.) The MMPI consists of 550 statements; a testee is asked to respond TRUE, FALSE, or CANNOT SAY as each statement applies personally.

Development of the MMPI

The MMPI is the premier personality inventory and has received substantially more research and clinical use than any other inventory. It was developed by Starke Hathaway and Charnley McKinley at the University of Minnesota; the following account by Hathaway gives a glimpse into its conception.

When I came to the University hospitals in about 1937 and began to work with patients, I started to change from a physiological psychologist toward becoming a clinical psychologist. As we went on grand rounds, I, with my white coat and newly developing sense of role, expected that the medical staff would want the

FIGURE 10.3 Starke Hathaway.

data and insights of a psychologist. I still remember one day when I was thinking this and suddenly asked myself, suppose they *did* turn to me for aid in understanding the patients' psychology; what substantive information did I have that wasn't obvious on the face of the case or that represented psychology rather than what the psychiatrist had already said. I could, perhaps, say that the patient was neurotic or an introvert or other such items suggested from my available tests. I had intelligence tests, . . . and a few other inventories. I didn't have any objective personality data that would go deeper or be more analytically complex than what would suggest general statements, such as that the patient was maladjusted. . . . [As] I then perceived [personality inventories, the] variables and interpretation were not in current jargon nor did they develop suggestions that would be of value to a staff required to make routine diagnostic, prognostic, and treatment decisions.

The real impetus for the MMPI came from reports of results with insulin shock treatment of schizophrenia. The early statistics on treatment outcomes, as is characteristic of new treatment ideas, promised everything from nearly 100% cure to no effect and no value. It occurred to me that the enormous variance in effectiveness as reported from hospital to hospital depended partly upon the unreliability of the validity criterion—the diagnostic statements. If there were some way in which we could pick experimental groups of patients using objective methods, then outcome tests for treatment efficacy should be more uniform and meaningful. I did not have any objective personality instrument that was adaptable to such a design; and, thinking about the needs, I got the idea of an empirically developed inventory that could be extended indefinitely by development of new scales. (Personal communication)

Item Selection. Hathaway and McKinley developed the inventory in the following fashion. First they amassed a large number of statements culled from psychiatry texts, psychiatric examination forms, earlier inventories, and their own clinical experience. Then, they obtained responses to these statements from a group of psychiatric patients in a certain diagnostic category—for example, hypochondriacs (people with an excessive and unrealistic concern with physical health). Next, they gave the statements to a group of "normals," people who were not receiving treatment for any illness. In addition, they gave the statements to a group of psychiatric patients in other diagnostic categories (such as schizophrenics). Thus, three groups of people would receive the pool of statements: known hypochondriacs, miscellaneous psychiatric cases of other diagnoses, and normals. Those statements to which hypochondriacs as a group responded distinctively and consistently differently from either normals as a group or other psychiatric

patients as a group formed the Hypochondriasis Scale of the MMPI. Some of these statements are listed in Figure 10.4. In parentheses are those responses that characterize hypochondriacs.

FIGURE 10.4 Some statements from the Hypochondriasis Scale of the MMPI.

My hands and feet are usually warm enough. (False)
Parts of my body often have feelings like burning, tingling, crawling, or like going to sleep. (True)
I hardly ever feel pain in the back of the neck. (False)
I am troubled by discomfort in the pit of my stomach every few days or oftener. (True)
I have little or no trouble with my muscles twitching or jumping. (False)

Cross Validation. To make sure that the Scale really worked and was not merely the product of chance factors, Hathaway and McKinley gave it to *new* groups of hypochondriacs, other psychiatric cases, and normals, and—in a crucial test—a group of medical patients who were suffering from real (and frequently serious) physical ailments. Again, the Hypochondriasis Scale successfully identified the hypochondriacs as distinct from each of the other groups.

Rationale of the MMPI. We have described this procedure in some detail because it reveals the principle underlying the MMPI. Statements were retained for inclusion, not because Hathaway and McKinley *thought* they measured certain psychological characteristics, but because people with known psychological characteristics *actually responded* to them in a certain way. In other words, statements were retained purely on their proven ability to differentiate psychiatric groups representative of certain personality extremes. Therefore, when tested with the MMPI, a person is tentatively classified as a hypochondriac if he or she responds to the statements in the same way known hypochondriacs respond.

The other MMPI scales—such as the Depression Scale, the Paranoia Scale, and the Schizophrenia Scale—were developed in the same fashion. When scored, the whole MMPI yields a "profile" of scores on all these scales. The profile thus represents the individual's standing on the psychological dimensions represented by the scales (hence the term "Multiphasic,"

meaning multiple dimensions or phases of personality). A profile appears in Figure 10.5. It is the MMPI performance of a 35-year-old woman with low back pain that had proved to be of psychological origin. She scores high on the hypochondriasis, depression, and hysteria dimensions, a pattern that has been referred to as the "neurotic triad." Here is her case history.

A Case History

This woman, who was admitted to the hospital six times, complained of low back pain extending down the right lower extremity and nervousness. The particular pattern of complaints in any one admission varied according

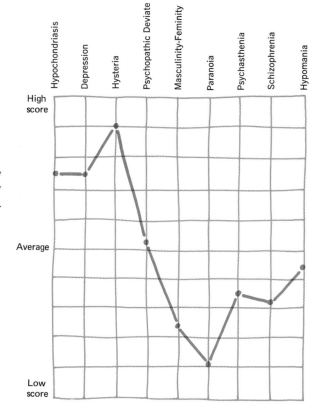

FIGURE 10.5 An MMPI profile of a 35-year-old woman with psychosomatic back pain.

to the date. Besides the six admissions to this hospital, she spent time in other hospitals. An adequate description of the complaints or of the treatment and surgical operations is impossible in a short account. . . . Numerous . . . complicated procedures had been used, and she had at various times worn braces and casts. She had been operated on for "appendicitis" and for a "floating kidney." Apparently fairly well until about the age of 35, in the next years she accumulated one of the thickest records in the hospital.

The patient's personality was described as having been relatively good before the illness and on the whole she always appeared intact even during the worst of her complaints. Of average intelligence, she had worked as a maid and had proved satisfactory in her jobs, but she had never been able to establish social contacts. Her friends included no men. With a poor background, she had been unable to develop social skills. One difficulty was that she spoke brokenly because German was the only language used in her home and in her community. . . . Unassuming and passive, she was without well-developed interests and was almost totally lacking in enthusiasm.

In the hospital the patient appeared, superficially, as a stable person. It was true that she centered conversation and attention almost wholly upon her physical symptoms. Frequently she cried from the severity of pain she said she was experiencing; she would not leave her bed at such times and showed every sign of anguish. Not only was she friendly to the personnel and the other patients, but she submitted readily to any form of treatment recommended. She mentioned daily that she "would do anything to get well," to earn her own living again. It was probable that the superficial appearance of normality, together with the absence of signs of nervousness or instability, explained the fact that so many surgical procedures were carried out in spite of some evidence that the complaints had a neurotic basis.

A long-term psychotherapeutic regime was instituted. Treatment included . . . extensive reassurance and strong urging to become active. She was permitted, as far as possible, to express her feelings of frustration, and she was encouraged to gain insight into what was a problem with her, namely a desire for a husband and a home. Since she was unattractive and without ability to get along socially, it appeared unlikely that she would become acquainted with a suitable man. Cathartic [talking] types of psychotherapy had meager success because the patient was almost inarticulate and spent many minutes completely silent. Occupational therapy and social service, as well as nursing, were all mobilized. In the course of several months she gradually left the bed and improved to the point where she could go to a rest home. While she was at all times carefully checked physically, she was given no opportunity to indulge her physical symptoms. In general, the staff and all who had contact with her spoke casually of these ills and said, if the patient became insistent, she should talk with a specially selected doctor. He did not always examine her but was at all times entirely reassuring, and never indicated that anything was severely wrong. After a year and a half of this intensive regime, the patient had become largely self-supporting again and appeared to have given up the pattern of somatic complaints. (MMPI Atlas, 1951)

This particular story had a happy ending. This woman met a man who worked in a grocery store and they were married. It is probably more than coincidence that following marriage her back pain subsided, and she began doing her own housework. The marriage was apparently a successful, harmonious one, and she and her husband eventually adopted a child.

Although the MMPI was developed in, and continues to be used in clinical settings, the personality characteristics it measures are applicable to normal functioning as well. While the scores of normals tend, of course, to be lower than those of hospitalized patients, the profile or pattern of scores—revealing the relative strength of the dimensions in the person's personality—is equally informative.

PERSONALITY ASSESSMENT BY PROJECTIVE TESTS

Personality inventories have their advantages—they are easy to administer, score, and interpret. However, a psychologist frequently has questions that require richer information than inventories, with their limited number of scales, are able to provide. What are a person's current strategies for coping or problem solving, and in what ways may they be self-defeating? What problems is the person currently trying to solve, and to what extent are these problems responsible for present difficulties? What are the sources of these problems, particularly with respect to current and past relationships? To answer such questions, psychologists employ "projective techniques."

The basic assumption behind all **projective techniques** is that *if you present an ambiguous or unstructured stimulus to a person, the person will interpret it in terms of inner needs and perceptions.* In other words, the basis of the response is within the person rather than in the stimulus. One "projects" oneself into the stimulus and, therefore, responses reveal one's own unique personality characteristics. Since, by the very nature of projective techniques, there are no "right" or "wrong" answers, it is difficult for someone taking a test to give only "socially desirable" responses; further, wishes and needs of which the person is not consciously aware may determine, and be evident in, responses given. The two most frequently employed

FIGURE 10.6 *Henry A. Murray.*

projective techniques are the Thematic Apperception Test and the Rorschach Test.

The Thematic Apperception Test

The Thematic Apperception Test (or TAT) was developed at Harvard University by Henry Murray. The TAT consists of a series of pictures with one or more people in them. An example is shown in Figure 10.7. Although 31 pictures are available, in practice a set of about 10 pictures appropriate to the test-taker's sex, age, and present problems is selected. The pictures are handed, one at a time, to the person who is asked to make up a story based on each picture. Imagination is encouraged: What are the people thinking, feeling, saying, doing? What is going on in the picture? What has led up to the scene in the pic-

FIGURE 10.7 Example of a picture from the Thematic Apperception Test.

ture? What will be the outcome of the situation? The TAT assumes that anyone will interpret, or *apperceive,* the pictures in terms of personal experience: by analyzing the themes of the stories some insight may be gained into the individual's experiential world. In particular, the TAT is considered to be a valuable source of information on the quality of interpersonal relationships—how a person perceives and behaves toward family, friends, authority figures—and on problems in these relationships.

A TAT Story. Here is the story told to a TAT picture that shows a young man, clothed, standing with his back to a bed on which a covered young woman is lying. The storyteller is an 18-year-old male sophomore who came for counseling because he needed "to gain self-confidence and see myself clearly." After being handed the picture, he sat in silence for 42 seconds and then began:

Seeing as how the man, well the man is dressed in modern-day clothes . . . looks like he's just ready to go to class . . . with books in his hand he might be . . . of course the room isn't too lavishly furnished. He's probably in school. In graduate school. Not necessarily although the books are disarranged . . . looks like somebody has been studying there once. And the woman is lying on the bed . . . looks like she's naked under the covers. Man looks like he's . . . he doesn't want to look at her . . . looks like he's ashamed of something. I'm trying to put something together. (Long pause) This might be in the morning. I think, ah, he probably had intercourse with the girl during the night. He's . . . he looks like he's ashamed of what he's done. And . . . she's probably looking like she was dead. Maybe a sex maniac. No can't be. Ah, . . . yah, he's had intercourse with her during the night and he's just gotten dressed himself. He's letting her sleep. She's probably worn out and her arm's dangling. He's getting ready to go to class or to work . . . probably class . . . and he probably knows it's morally and socially wrong. And he just let himself go. And he might not be married to her . . . probably isn't. (Long pause) I think he took advantage of her. She really liked him. And ah (pounds table), and he knew what was right and she really didn't care, and he took advantage of her and now he realizes he shouldn't have . . . and it might be temporary, this feeling of shame, but I don't think so. It's a little too profound. He (long pause). You could imagine he's just getting up and just getting dressed because the light is hurting his eyes. He probably got drunk. Cause there's a white spot on the side of him like the light's coming in from here. Also corresponding shadows on the other side. I like that better. Much better story. He's getting up and . . . (to self: Well you don't rub your eyes like that). I liked the first one better. Mainly because you don't rub your eyes with your entire forearm . . . just your fist. Probably not holding anything in his hand. Also he's wearing his watch on his right hand . . . backwards. Which doesn't mean a hell of a lot. Ah yes, I think he . . . well what I said before . . . He's going with her and that led up to this and ah . . . he's ashamed of what he's done, but he might eventually marry her. And everything comes out in the end.

An Interpretation. There are a number of interesting features about this story. First, let's look at the formal qualities, the structure of the story. Note the long pause before he can even begin responding to the picture—42 seconds. Evidently, the picture is causing him some difficulty. Then, when he does begin his response, he refuses to deal with the human relationship portrayed and carefully skirts the rather blatant sexual aspects of the picture. Instead, he flees into the relatively "safe" procedure of describing the man's dress, his occupation, the room's furnishings, and so on—all really quite irrelevant details. Finally, showing a sign of some psychological resilience, he is able to bring himself to deal with "the woman lying on the bed." Then a lengthy pause while he tries to "put something together." Even after the pause, however, his account is fraught with uncertainty. He can't decide whether the man is the woman's husband, a "sex maniac," a drunk, or all three; "might" and "probably" abound. Again he attempts to extricate himself by describing details rather than dealing with the content of the picture, commenting on such irrelevancies as the direction from which

the light is coming, how one rubs one's eyes, and the position of the man's watch which, as he points out, "doesn't mean a hell of a lot." Clearly, the sexual connotations of the picture produced considerable conflict, to the extent that he was incapable of telling a coherent story. His "story" really has no structure at all, despite his high intellectual level (college) and the time he takes to prepare himself (42 seconds). His response is little more than a fitful series of starts and stops, vacillations, and abortive attempts to come to grips with the material, with an almost magical resolution loosely appended—"everything comes out in the end."

Now let's turn to the content of the story, its theme. The theme seems to be that sex is a potentially harmful and destructive act—the female is perceived as "probably looking like she was dead." As a consequence, sex is something that should be kept under tight control, something that only someone out of control (such as a "maniac" or a "drunk") could permit to happen. Sometimes, however, sexuality is impossible to control ("he just let himself go"), resulting in considerable guilt (". . . it might be temporary, this feeling of shame, but I don't think so. It's a little too profound."). If this story does represent the way in which this young man perceives and deals with sexuality, he may, in fact, be experiencing some difficulty in his heterosexual relationships.

Clinical Interpretation. As mentioned previously, the stimuli used in projective techniques are unstructured or ambiguous. In the scene portrayed in the TAT picture it isn't at all clear "what's going on." Ambiguity permits the person taking the test a wide latitude of response. Although this flexibility is one of the advantages of projective techniques, it also leads to problems in interpretation, since no two responses are ever exactly alike. Thus, in contrast to an inventory where the test results are the same regardless of who scores it, some degree of subjective evaluation inevitably enters into the interpretation of a person's performance on a projective test. The interpretation offered for the story told to the TAT card was given as an example of how an interpretation *might* proceed. Obviously, alternative interpretations are possible, and some may have occurred to you. This problem is perhaps even more acute in the Rorschach Test, where the stimuli are even more ambiguous.

Before we go on to the Rorschach, though, and while we are on the subject of interpretation, this is a good time to point out that a psychologist rarely (if ever) draws conclusions from the results of a single test, let alone a single response. Rather, the psychologist typically administers a series, or "battery," of different tests, each designed to assess the individual's personality from a different perspective. The results of all these tests, together with anything else the clinician may know about the person's past and present circumstances, are considered in making inferences about the person's personality.

The Rorschach Test

The Rorschach is named after Hermann Rorschach, a young Swiss psychiatrist who noted that patients in different psychiatric categories reported seeing different things in inkblots, such as that in Figure 10.8 (see the color plate opposite page 370). According to Rorschach, "The production of such accidental forms is very simple: a few large ink blots are thrown on a piece of paper, the paper folded, and the ink spread between the two halves of the sheet." The construction of the test was not so simple, however, as Rorschach pretested hundreds of different blots before he finally settled on a series of ten symmetrical blots, five with color and five black and white. Cards bearing the blots are handed to the person one at a time and he or she is asked, "What does it look like? What could this be?" The person is told that people see all kinds of different things in the blots and is permitted ample time to exhaust the possibilities the blots bring to mind.

To illustrate, let's look at the responses to the blot in Figure 10.8 as given before and after psychotherapy by an 18-year-old runaway girl with suicidal ideas.

Before Therapy.   Here is her prepsychotherapy response:

It kind of resembles some kind of mass killing when in certain religions in the old days they put them in one of those podiums and got killed off like that. [The people doing the "killing" are the side black figures, the "podium" is the lower black mass, and the victim, as will be seen, are the red areas. When the examiner asks her to expand on her response, she continues:] In the old days like killing Christians to the lions. These are their bodies and they are all red and bloody and . . . some of these bodies are already demolished. Torn apart, just . . . been killed by some kind of monster, or something. Little babies. They're small, it seems like they don't have a chance to enjoy any part of life, they were killed before they even had a chance.

The first thing that strikes one about this response, of course, is its morbid concern with utter, orgiastic destruction, a real bloodbath. What the girl sees in the blot is apparently quite vivid and frighten-

FIGURE 10.9 (Drawing by Al Ross; © 1974 The New Yorker Magazine, Inc.)

ing to her, for she attempts to maintain emotional distance by placing the action "in the old days." Her closing remarks about "little babies," although a trifle histrionic, suggest that she identifies with them and sees herself as a helpless victim at the mercy of powerful forces that threaten to annihilate her totally. These forces may well be within her, threatening to erupt in an act of self-destruction.

After Therapy.   Now let's look at her response to the same card after psychotherapy:

It looks like two head waiters. They're both getting their trays ready. [The examiner requests elaboration.] These are the waiters [side black], the form of the head and the protruding nose, plus you've got on the chest those things coming out and legs, and a dish of whatever they're getting [lower black]. The red spots would be just decorations on the wall. I think so because there's a little bit of light coming through.

This response is clearly much more benign than the previous one. In the first place, the action is innocuous and may even have certain positive connotations associated with food and eating. The choice of "waiters" is interesting. Waiters bring good things to eat, and some psychologists would claim that food is unconsciously equated with love, an association stemming from being held and fed as an infant. Moreover, waiters are paragons of restraint and self-control; they manage to keep their tempers in check under the most provoking circumstances. This aspect is very much in contrast with the earlier theme of unbridled rage and aggression. And these are not just ordinary waiters; they are "head waiters." Does this indicate a rise in the respondent's self-esteem? Possibly. In any event, it's a step up from being a "little baby" who "never had a chance." Finally, note how she resolves the presence of the red; she turns it into "just decorations." A little strained, perhaps, but how much better than torn and bleeding babies! This postpsychotherapy response does seem to indicate improvement.

ARE PERSONALITY TESTS VALID?

When we ask if a test is **valid**, *we are essentially asking, does the test measure what it purports to measure?* The question of validity is the most crucial question that any test must answer. With the MMPI and other inventories the question of validity is relatively easy to answer because, as noted, inventories are scored objectively—they yield the same scores regardless of who does the scoring (indeed, the MMPI is frequently scored by a computer). Although the MMPI is far from a perfect measuring instrument, validity studies indicate that it does a reasonably good job of what it was designed to do, that is, make useful discriminations between people.

When we come to the validity of pro-

jective techniques, however, we are on soggier ground. Objective scoring systems have been devised for a limited number of personality factors (such as needs to achieve, to affiliate, to attain power, to avoid failure), and these have often yielded respectable indexes of validity. However, the tremendous variety and richness of responses generated by the inherent ambiguity of projective tests and the complexity of the questions commonly asked frequently make a human interpreter necessary—at least in our present state of technology. In such circumstances it is impossible to evaluate the technique independently of its user. Largely for this reason, despite hundreds of validity studies, the validity of projective techniques remains equivocal. It is our impression from clinical experience that a projective test in the hands of an experienced, sensitive clinician is a valuable instrument. This is an opinion, however, and not evidence.

Reformulating the Question. When all is said and done, the worth of a personality test lies in its ability to say something about a person's behavior outside of the testing room. Behavior is a function of both the person (personality characteristics) and the demands of a situation. For example, if you and some friends are caught in the midst of a bank holdup and someone has a gun trained on you, even the most intrepid of you is likely to do what you are told. In a more open situation, however, such as a party, personality characteristics are given greater opportunity to determine behavior and, for example, extroverts versus introverts become readily identifiable. Thus, when the question is asked: Are personality tests valid? The counterquestion must also be asked: Valid in what situation?

SUMMARY

Personality (page 335) is the configuration of characteristics that determines each individual's unique adjustment to the environment, including other people.

A. **Two Theories of Personality Development**

1. Sigmund Freud's psychoanalytic theory tends to focus on internal forces and pressures, often unconscious, that influence behavior. Bandura and Walters' social learning theory stresses the importance of external factors in determining behavior.

2. According to psychoanalytic theory, personality development proceeds through a fixed series of stages based on **erogenous zones** (page 336): the **oral, anal,** and **phallic stages** (page 337). The theory also proposes that behavior is a function of the interaction of three systems, the **id, ego,** and **superego** (page 339).

3. Social learning theory proposes two mechanisms by which the environment (such as parents) is effective in molding behavior: **modeling** and **reinforcement** (page 338).

B. **Research in Personality**

4. Orally-fixated children were shown to have an unusually strong interest in food and a dependent orientation in interpersonal relationships.

5. Aggressive adult models were found to be effective in teaching aggressive behavior to children.

6. Psychoanalytic and social learning theories can be reconciled on the grounds that they complement—rather than contradict—one another.

C. **Personality Assessment**

7. Personality assessment has grown from the desire to understand and predict behavior on the basis of a small sample of behavior. Three widely used personality tests were described: The Minnesota Multiphasic Personality Inventory, the Thematic Apperception Test, and the Rorschach Test.

8. The MMPI is objectively interpreted; the person taking the MMPI is placed in a certain personality category if he or she responds to statements in the same way as people known to be in that category.

9. The TAT and the Rorschach are known as **projective techniques** (page 354) because they require the person who is tested to inter-

pret an ambiguous stimulus, thereby "projecting" his or her personality into the responses.

10. Although projective techniques yield richer, more complex information than inventories, their **validity** (page 359) is controversial; this is probably owing to the fact that projectives require subjective interpretation and, hence, are limited by the limitations of the interpreter.

11. Conclusions concerning personality are rarely drawn from the results of a single test; rather, a series of different tests is employed, and the results of these, together with anything else that is known about the individual, are used in the assessment of personality.

Chapter Eleven
Psychopathology and Treatment

To: The football department and its members present and future

The University of New Mexico, Albuquerque, N.M.

I depend on correct, honest supplementation of this card by telepathy as a thing which will make clear the meaning of this card. There exists a Playing of The Great Things, the correct, the constructive, world or universe politics, out-in-the-open telepathy, etc. According to the Great Things this playing is the most feasible thing of all; but it is held from newspaper advertising and correct, honest public world recognition, its next step, by telepathic forces (it seems), physical dangers, and lack of money. Over 10,000 cards and letters on this subject have been sent to prominent groups and persons all over the world. Correct, honest contact with the honest, out-in-the-open world. This line of thought, talk, etc. rule. The plain and frank, Strangers. The Great Things and opposites idea. References: In the telepathic world the correct playings. Please save this card for a history record since it is rare and important for history. (Lewinson, 1940)

This postcard was written by a schizophrenic. Schizophrenia is a serious form of **psychopathology,** *the general term for deviant or aberrant behavior in which psychological factors are thought to play a role.*

Psychopathology is a health problem of staggering proportions. You can get some idea of the immensity of the problem from the statistics on schizophrenia alone. The National Institute of Mental Health estimates that there are currently over 120,000 people hospitalized for schizophrenia—that is roughly equivalent to the population of a city the size of Las Vegas. (See Focus 11.1: The Mental Hospital.) It has also been estimated that about one in 50 people will be hospitalized for schizophrenia at some point in their lives. But hospitalized cases of psychopathology of all kinds are

only the visible tip of the iceberg. Millions of people suffer some impairment of personal and social functioning because of psychopathology, even though their distress may not be so severe as to require hospitalization. The question of what is normal and abnormal is explored in Focus 11.2.

Later in this chapter we will describe and discuss some of the methods used to treat psychopathology. First, however, we would like to present some concrete illustrations of various forms of psychopathology. We will follow the standard classification, which is based on the behaviors exhibited.

A. NEUROTIC DISORDERS

Neurotic disorders *are characterized by a strained or exaggerated reliance on defense mechanisms* (see Focus 11.3: Mechanisms of Adjustment to Stress). A person's functioning is impaired, but not usually to the extent that hospitalization is necessary. Here are some examples of common neurotic disorders.

HYSTERICAL DISORDERS
People suffering from **hysterical disorders** *experience physical symptoms caused by psychological factors.* The symptoms include paralysis, convulsions, skin anesthesia, blindness, deafness, muteness, tics, tremors, impotence, and pseudopregnancy. There is nothing physically wrong with the person; the disorder is entirely psychological in origin.

Consider the case of paralysis brought about and maintained by psychological factors to which you were introduced in Chapter One. We present a fuller discussion of this case on page 368.

Focus 11.1
The Mental Hospital

Our society has chosen to stigmatize and ostracize the mentally ill. Why this is so is not altogether clear, but it is probably rooted in the fear most of us have of that which we cannot readily understand. The result, however, is abundantly clear. Under the guise of treatment and care, tens of thousands of citizens are annually stripped of the barest of human rights and dignity and condemned to indefinite periods of confinement in institutions that, for want of a better term, are euphemistically labeled "mental hospitals." These institutions, while designated as society's agents of rehabilitation and restoration, in effect isolate the individual from any vestige of normal existence. The primary function of the mental hospital is simply custodial—"keep them out of the way where we won't have to look at them and can forget about them."

Who is responsible for this state of affairs? It is always tempting to hunt for scapegoats, and the administrators, staff, and personnel of state hospitals are easy targets. By and large, however, these people are dedicated, overworked, and underpaid professionals. The true culprit is public indifference. Perhaps if it were mandatory for every person to visit the back wards of a mental institution, people would be less complacent. Certainly, few people can make such a visit without being visibly shaken. Recently, and fortunately, there has been a movement away from the concept of the large mental hospital to community mental health centers, where a mentally ill person can obtain help through short-term hospitalization or as an outpatient, at the same time retaining a place in the community.

Until such a time as the community-based mental health clinic becomes a common reality, there is much that you, as a citizen and concerned

Focus 11.2
What Is Normal and Abnormal?

A recent midnight visit by one of us to a low-priced all-night cafeteria on East 42nd Street in New York City yielded an assortment of disturbing cameos: A man of about 50 years of age sitting with his chair facing a blank wall muttering loudly and masturbating energetically; a young girl, about 19 years of age, well dressed, lying on the ground eating a sandwich with one hand and repeatedly gesticulating and chatting to some nonapparent figure somewhere between her and the chandelier; a woman of about 40 years, dressed in rags, grimacing wildly and gesticulating between sips of her tomato soup. Are these people mentally ill?

There is no easy answer to this question. To some extent, mental illness is a matter of social definition, in the sense that when someone steps over the line of environmental tolerance society labels that per-

FIGURE 11.1 A day room in a large mental hospital where patients live socially isolated from one another. Recently there has been a movement away from the concept of the large institution in favor of community mental health centers.

individual, can do to alleviate the problem. For one, you can support your local chapter of the National Association for Mental Health. For another, you can participate in the volunteer programs that exist in most mental hospitals. These programs provide patients with some — frequently their only — contact with the outside world. Whether you take a walk with a patient, leaf through a magazine, or simply sit and chat, you are evidence that they have not been completely abandoned, that someone is concerned. Volunteer programs employing college students have often proved to be remarkably effective in providing help to the afflicted, and they offer a concrete answer to the question: "But what can I do?"

son "sick." Here we are dealing with a somewhat arbitrary set of standards, and it is impossible to draw a sharp line between "normal" and "ill." For example, a few years ago some ex-mental patients were being followed up as part of a mental health survey. One man had an excellent work record, was supporting his family, and reported that he was happy, his family was happy, and things were going well. When asked if he still heard voices, he replied, "Oh, I can still hear them. But I don't pay attention to them any more. The doctors told me not to pay attention to them." Here is a man who is living a full and productive life, but who is suffering auditory hallucinations. Is he mentally ill, or is he not?

Further, we know that different societies, and different groups within society, have different definitions or levels of tolerance for "deviant" behavior. The shaman of an African tribe might well be diagnosed "Acute Schizophrenic Reaction" in this society. Within our society, the lower socioeconomic classes are more tolerant of (or possibly less aware of) mental illness. All you have to do to confirm this observation is to stroll through the local skid road and chat with a few of the inhabitants. You readily find individuals who, were it not for the anonymity and absence of social demands characteristic of the skid road environment, would almost certainly be classified as mentally ill in other strata of society.

Clearly, the line between normalcy and mental illness is a fuzzy one, and the labeling decision is often based on the values, standards, and conventions of a social group. It should be noted, too, that much mental illness is self-defined, in the sense that an individual feels such great psychological distress as to take positive steps to remedy the situation and actively seek professional help. Here too, however, individual standards vary. The man in the street wildly gesticulating and arguing with a lamp post may consider himself perfectly sane.

Merely because the line between normalcy and illness is an admittedly arbitrary one, however, it does not therefore follow that there is no such thing as mental illness. Medicine is faced with an identical problem, but few people question the existence of physical illness. Take tem-

Focus 11.3
Mechanisms of Adjustment to Stress

Any time a person is faced with some threat to self-esteem or physical integrity, the person is said to be under stress.

Three basic types of adjustment reactions to stress can be identified:

1. *Task-oriented* reactions that are directed toward solving the problems or situations producing the stress.
2. *Defense-oriented* reactions that are aimed primarily at reducing the emotional pain accompanying stress by distorting perception and altering behavior.
3. *Neurotic* and *psychotic* reactions that occur when the coping and defense mechanisms do not resolve the stress situation.

The first two types of adjustment reaction will be discussed in this Focus; the third is covered in the body of the chapter.

Task-Oriented versus Defense-Oriented Reactions. The behavior a person shows in a stress situation can be placed on a continuum, or scale, with the labels "Direct Problem-Solving Approach" on one end to "Defensive Responses" on the other end. Behavior that is task-oriented tends to be anchored in reality and focused on solving the problem that produces the stress. The term **defense reaction** (*sometimes called* **ego-defense** **mechanism**) *refers to distortions in behavior, per-*

perature, for instance. Although there might be some question about whether a person with a temperature of 99° or 100° is ill, there is no question at all when temperature registers 105°—that person is sick and needs help. It is also instructive to note that *all* societies recognize some form of mental illness, and, especially in the severe illnesses such as schizophrenia, there is a remarkable similarity in symptoms across societies. Apparently there *is* mental illness in an absolute sense, independent of cultural relativism or social convention.

Let's take the social convention of which side of the road one drives on as an analogy. A person who consistently drives on the right-hand side of the road is at home in North American society. A person who consistently drives on the left-hand side would fit nicely into English or Japanese society. However, a person who is inconsistent, who unpredictably drives on the right one day and on the left the next, couldn't adapt to *any* society. The very notion of a society presupposes *some* set of rules or conventions mutually shared by the members of that society. The point is that some people become so disorganized, so confused, or so depressed that they are a real danger to themselves and quite literally could not survive were they not hospitalized or helped in some fashion. Mental illness is not merely a figment of society's imagination. Mental illness is a real phenomenon, a very real health problem.

ceptions, and thought that are oriented to protect an individual from emotional pain and threat, to preserve self-identity, and to save face.

For example, let us look at a problem faced by the adolescent named Wally, whom we mentioned in Chapter One. Wally would like to go out on dates but is so fearful of being turned down if he asks a girl that he avoids asking. If Wally tries to solve his problem so that he can control his fears, and ask a girl for a date, he would be using a direct, task-oriented, problem-solving approach. This approach might include thinking out a program of action. He might learn to dance and make an effort to talk to girls in his class more often to lower his fear reaction, or he might decide to go for help at the school counseling center. If, on the other hand, he thought up "logical" and "acceptable" reasons to justify and explain his nondating to delude himself and to keep the esteem of his friends, he would be using a defense mechanism. He might say such things as, "I have no time to date this semester; I have to study in order to get good grades," or "The girls at this school are too stuck up to waste time on." The mechanism of using rational thought processes to think up such excuses is called rationalization. **Rationalization** *is a defense mechanism in which the individual* *distorts perception and thought to find rational but false reasons to justify failures or questionable behaviors.* Rationalization is often difficult to identify since there may be an element of truth in what is said. For example, Wally may actually be having a difficult time in college and need time to study (but not *so much* time that he can't take a girl out for coffee). Rationalization can often be spotted when the rationalizer becomes upset when you question the rationalization or when inconsistencies between behavior and rationalization show up (for instance, if Wally constantly goes to the movies alone instead of studying). There is a price each of us must pay for such defense reactions for they prevent us from facing and solving problems.

Sometimes defense reactions are temporary, providing immediate emotional relief until the problem can be solved at a later time. There is always the danger, however, that the mechanism will become a permanent part of the personality and a typical way to handle stress. If the problem gets more severe and stress increases, the individual may be forced to use more distorting and self-defeating mechanisms to defend against stress. If Wally uses rationalization as his immediate face-saving defense with his friends and then goes for counseling help, the total effect will be quite adaptive. If, however, Wally continues to rationalize and adopt other mechanisms of defense over a period of years, it would be very difficult to help him solve his conflicts and sexual frustrations. As we examine each defense mechanism, keep in mind the concept of continuum and remember the role that the situation and the person's background can play in interpreting the meaning of a mechanism.

A Case Study.

Mildred A. was the daughter of a Rocky Mountain ranchman whose means and education were extremely limited. She was in her early adolescence when she lost the use of both her legs. At the time there was an alarming epidemic of paralysis among ranch animals, and it was generally assumed that Mildred was a human victim of the epidemic. This explanation was welcomed by the girl's parents although they knew originally that it was not true.

What actually happened was that Mildred was alone in the ranch house one afternoon when a male relative came in and, after embracing her, attempted to assault her. She screamed for help,

her legs gave way and she slipped to the floor. Here she was found unharmed a few moments later by her mother who had just returned from visiting a neighbor. Mildred could not get up, so she was carried to her bed, and waited upon for several days with unaccustomed devotion. Whenever attempts were made to get her up she seemed frightened, her legs buckled under her, and she could not stand unsupported. The family physician correctly ascribed her reaction to fright, but he unwisely recommended that she stay in bed until her legs grew strong again.

As it became evident that the girl was not recovering, she was allowed to displace her father

Mechanisms of Defense. **Repression** *is the inability to recall thoughts or experiences that are associated with painful emotions or threats to self-esteem* (see Chapter 7B). For example, a war veteran finds that he cannot recall any of the battle experience in which his buddy was killed.

Reaction formation *is an exaggerated expression of behavior that is opposite to underlying "repressed" feelings or motives.* An example would be a mother who feels hostility toward her child but fears rejection by society (and her conscience) if she expresses it; as a result she exaggerates her expression of love and concern for her child.

Projection *is a matter of attributing traits to other people that a person has but cannot accept.* For example, a man who accuses others of being hostile and dishonest but refuses to recognize his own hostility and dishonesty is resorting to projection.

Displacement *refers to a feeling or behavior that is shifted from a threatening person to a substitute person who is available and safe.* For example when a boss scolds a worker, the worker, fearing for his job, says nothing. When the worker arrives at home, he scolds his wife and child.

Regression *is an escape from stress or threat by reverting to behavior and solutions that were appropriate at an earlier stage of life.* For example, when a young child is blocked from a goal it begins to cry or suck a thumb, behaviors that were "appropriate" in infancy.

Fantasy *consists of escaping from threat or painful reality by daydreaming and receiving in imagination gratification that is unavailable in reality.*

in the parental bedroom, which opened into the living room. Here she spent her days in sewing, talking, reading, and napping. Neighbors brought her homemade things to eat or to wear. They discussed her disability over and over. As an invalid and a victim she received the best of food and attention. Her mother continued waiting upon her hand and foot, massaged her legs morning and evening, and slept with her at night. Attempts to get Mildred to stand and walk were finally abandoned because the effort required to encourage her and physically hold her up proved too much for the hard-worked family. She never lost the ability to move her legs in bed or to pull things she needed toward

her with her toes.

Mildred might never have come to the attention of neurologists and psychiatrists had it not been for the intervention of a newcomer in the neighborhood ten years later. The newcomer recognized that the paralysis might be emotional in origin and raised hopes of a miraculous cure among the countryfolk. Money was collected, arrangements were made, and the girl with her parents journeyed several hundred miles to a general hospital. As soon as they arrived it was obvious that the parents expected something to be done immediately to make their daughter well. It was obvious also that she herself resented the whole move and felt that the examinations and the questions asked were really accusations of dishonesty.

After the preliminary examinations, consultations and laboratory work had been completed, and after a recital of her illness, its onset and its course, Mildred came to the end of her willingness to cooperate. She and her parents gave the same story of the epidemic and insisted that her illness was "like infantile paralysis." That was all. Her mother summed up parental feeling when she declared, "It's you and not her that's supposed to do the curing." In the face of Mildred's sullen resentment and noncooperation (and) the parents' secrecy . . . therapy could not succeed. In a month's time the patient left for home unimproved. It was only later, by chance, that the traumatic onset of Mildred's illness, as given above, was disclosed by another member of the family. (Cameron, 1963)

Case Discussion. The give-away that Mildred's paralysis is psychological in origin rather than physical is, of course, her ability to move her legs in order to pull something toward her when she wants it. Note, too, what her illness "does" for her. She is now the center of attention, waited upon hand and foot. Many people, especially those who are deeply passive and dependent, might welcome such an infantile sort of existence. Her parents' complicity in maintaining that the paralysis is physical certainly doesn't help matters. Despite a disability that most of us would find extremely distressing, Mildred seems curiously reluctant to be treated. *This lack of concern* (**belle indifférence**) *over seemingly serious afflictions is quite common in cases of hysteria,* and further suggests that the symptom is serving some sort of psychological purpose. But make no mistake: Mildred is unaware of the function of her symptom and is in no sense malingering or faking; her paralysis is just as real to her as if it were organic.

PSYCHOSOMATIC DISORDERS

We began our discussion of psychosomatic disorders in Chapter 4C and we will continue it here. **Psychosomatic disorders** *are similar to hysterical disorders in that they consist of physical symptoms that are influenced by psychological factors;* the symptoms include high blood pressure, heart disease, ulcers, hemorrhoids, colitis, asthma, dermatitis, allergies, hives, enuresis, constipation, headache, mononucleosis, back pain, and even the common cold. *Unlike hysterical disorders, however, in psychosomatic disorders there is definite and often serious physiological disturbance.* For example, although an ulcer may be caused or made worse by psychological stress, it *is* a real ulcer (a lesion of the lining of the stomach) that must be medically treated. A further difference is that people with psychosomatic disorders are concerned about their symptoms and usually seek help. Here is a case of severe asthma with psychological involvement.

An Example.

When he first consulted Dr. Johnson the patient was 24 years old and single. He had recently graduated from a medical school, but felt himself quite unable to practice because of severe asthmatic attacks. . . . He had a history of asthma since the age of 14. Before this age he had weighed over 200 pounds, but then went on a diet, reduced his weight to 155, and at that time began to develop asthmatic attacks. When he came for treatment the patient was living with his father, a physician, his mother having died when he was 3. Of that event he recalled only the mother's leaving home on a stretcher, fighting with the attendants, and crying as they

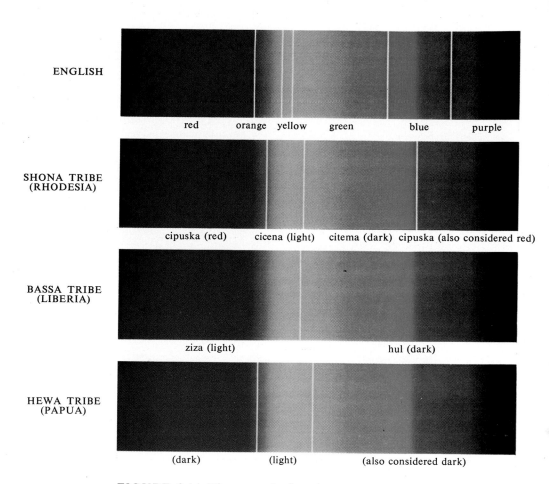

ENGLISH

red   orange yellow   green   blue   purple

SHONA TRIBE
(RHODESIA)

cipuska (red)   cicena (light)   citema (dark) cipuska (also considered red)

BASSA TRIBE
(LIBERIA)

ziza (light)   hul (dark)

HEWA TRIBE
(PAPUA)

(dark)   (light)   (also considered dark)

FIGURE 9.14 The terms in four languages applied to the range of visible wavelengths. Visual sensations are the same for all normal human beings, but the practice of assigning a special word to a very narrow section of the total spectrum is not universal. What this means in terms of perception and cognition is controversial.

FIGURE 10.8 A Rorschach inkblot.

FIGURE 11.5 Paintings of cats by the English artist Louis Wain, who suffered a schizophrenic breakdown, indicate the successive changes in his mental state and the distortions of perception characteristic of schizophrenics.

took her to the hospital, where she died of pneumonia.

After the mother's death the patient and his brother moved next door to live with their father's sister and her husband.

The aunt was very fat and the patient had always told her that he wished to be fat like her. At the time of the treatment, however, he resented her obesity and looked upon her refusal to diet as part of her greediness and infantilism. . . .

When the therapist asked how his aunt accepted his efforts to be more independent, he said she would not stand for it. Any attempt on his part to "talk up" met with a whipping. She thwarted any adventurousness on his part. She "stuffed him with food."

. . . the patient recalled that when he was 9 he realized that his stepmother (his father had by then remarried) was very pretty and nineteen years younger than his father. She encouraged him to fondle her breast and rest his head on her bosom. She would draw him closer and closer until the father, in a rage, would order him off to bed. From the age of 9 to 14, when he was so obese, this seductive situation continued, associated on the patient's part with intense conscious sexual desire for his stepmother. He did not think of her as a mother, and longed to get into bed with her, but feared that she would tell his father. In these years there was extreme fear of his father and of dogs. At 14, when he reduced drastically and felt more attractive physically, all the sexual play with his stepmother ceased and he had no further sexual feeling for her. It was at this time his asthma began to be disturbing. (Alexander 1950).

Case Discussion. It is probably more than coincidence that this young man's asthma attacks date from the time he lost weight—and became more physically at-

tractive to his seductive stepmother. Since he simultaneously lost all conscious sexual desire for his stepmother—which had been quite intense until then—what psychological function did his asthma (and, previously, his obesity) serve? It may have kept him from having to perform in situations that he perceived as threatening.

Mind vs. Body. How the mind can affect the body is often a mystery to students (and others). The "mystery" lies mainly in the way the question is phrased, for it assumes that somehow "mind" and "body" are separate entities. A more productive way of viewing the "mind-body" problem is that they are simply different aspects of the same system, or, by analogy, two sides of the same coin. A hypothetical example, borrowed from Neal Miller, of how psychological factors can produce physical symptoms may clarify the matter.

Suppose a child is anxious about going to school in the morning, perhaps because of failure to prepare for an examination. This anxiety elicits a variety of common physical reactions, such as an upset stomach. If the mother is particularly concerned about gastric distress, she may say "You are sick and must stay home." The child experiences tremendous relief at not having to go to school, anxiety is reduced, and gastrointestinal reaction as a "solution" to problems is heavily reinforced. Multiply this or similar experiences a few hundred times, and you have a well-learned, automatic, and unconscious physical response to psychological stress.

OBSESSIVE-COMPULSIVE DISORDERS

This group of disorders takes its name from the highly repetitive and irresistible nature of the thoughts (**obsessions**) or behaviors (**compulsions**) involved. The **obsessive** *individual has the same thoughts, often of an unpleasant nature, running through the mind over and over and over again, sometimes to the exclusion of everything else.* The person feels that there's no control over these thoughts, that they are alien. The **compulsive** *individual is driven to repeat over and over some seemingly meaningless act or series of actions, often in a ritualistic way.* The person feels compelled to initiate and carry through these actions to completion, as if driven by some outside force. These two sorts of symptoms—obsessions and compulsions—are often found together in the same individual, as is apparent in the following case.

A Case Study.

Ramona M. was the 42-year-old wife of a Minnesota business man and the mother of three children. Her symptoms appeared suddenly. She was serving the family dinner one evening when she dropped a dish on the table and smashed it. The accident appalled her. While clearing up the fragments she was seized with an unreasonable fear that bits of glass might get into her husband's food and kill him. She would not allow the meal to proceed until she had removed everything and reset the table with fresh linen and clean dishes. After this her fears, instead of subsiding, reached out to include intense anxiety over the possibility that she herself and her children might be killed by bits of glass.

The patient's fears and defensive rituals did not stop with this. Ramona developed an irresistible need to examine minutely every piece of glassware that she handled. If anything had the slightest chip on it she threw it away; and she had to carry it to the trash can herself to make

sure that it went out of the house. Then she would hunt for the missing chip which, of course, she could rarely find. She had read somewhere that copper pots and aluminum pots were not safe for certain kinds of cooking. Her worries now included their use. She remembered that her wedding ring had some copper in it as well as gold. First she took it off whenever she cooked or washed dishes; then she lost it.

Meanwhile she heard about other things which raised new fears and touched off further compulsive countermeasures. These included the danger of a spread of virus disease from toilet to kitchen, the dangers of lye and pesticides, and of the chemical and organic fertilizers used on the lawn. Eventually all potential poisons of all kinds had to be isolated from cooking utensils and dishes by storing them in the garage—even the cleaning fluids and scouring powders needed for everyday washing and cleaning.

These endless precautionary rituals drove the family almost frantic. Yet they brought Ramona no lasting peace. Her list of potential dangers kept growing until she simply did not have enough attention to bestow upon them all. If she was not certain that she had or had not done something in a certain way, she would have to rehearse her steps to make sure, or else begin all over again.

One of the hardest things for her to endure was that she could not control what the others did or convince them that her precautions were essential. She tried to make someone stay beside her to help keep track of every move she made; but when they did they proved to be not nearly as meticulous or concerned as she was. She found herself watching her husband and her children furtively for signs of ill health. In the end the whole situation became too much for her and the family to handle. Ramona had to give up housekeeping and seek full time therapeutic help. (Cameron, 1963)

Case Discussion. Obsessive-compulsive persons such as Ramona are usually excessively orderly, neat, clean, and punctual. They are also often frugal and obstinate. Although a certain amount of these traits is appropriate and even adaptive, the *excessiveness* of the obsessive-compulsive's behavior leads to personal and social difficulties. This excessiveness also often belies the obsessive-compulsive's true feelings, which may be unconscious. For instance, Ramona's exaggerated concern over the well-being of her family may say something about her real attitude toward them.

PHOBIAS

Phobias *are intense unrealistic fears, with emphasis on "unrealistic."* There are as many kinds of phobias as there are potential objects or situations to fear, and all you need do to coin your own term is to attach the appropriate Greek or Latin prefix, as in "claustrophobia," which simply means an unrealistic fear of closed places.

While a fear may be unrealistic and even ludicrous to an observer, it is very real indeed to the victim, who is often thrust into a state of terror and panic by a phobic object. Moreover, phobias tend to proliferate; that is, more and more things become feared until nothing is safe, and the person becomes virtually immobilized, afraid to move since the whole environment is now fraught with danger.

A Case Study.

Martha S., a 26-year-old mother of two children was referred by her family physician to a private psychiatrist for the treatment of a phobia which had been extremely disabling at times. A high-school graduate, Martha had been the youthful bride of a junior executive in a large New England shoe concern. They and her elderly parents lived in a large, comfortable home in the suburbs of a middle-sized city.

Martha was born and spent her early years in Chicago. She was the youngest of three daughters and described her childhood as a generally

FIGURE 11.2 Claustro-phobia, the fear of being in enclosed places.

happy one in which she had a very close relationship with her eldest sibling, a sister who was six years older than she. Both girls had an almost sisterly relationship with their mother, who attempted to be as much a companion to her daughters as she could. Martha's father was described in glowing terms, but he actually was a reserved, undemonstrative man whose personality provided a sharp contrast with that of the mother. Martha recalled her early family life as warm and pleasant, with both sets of grandparents as well as uncles, aunts, and cousins taking part in many close family activities. At about the time she began high school, her father, who was an accountant, received an excellent offer from a New England firm, and the family moved there in order to accept it. While in high school Martha met her future husband. He became her steady boyfriend, and they were married three years after she completed her schooling. At the time he was in his last year of business school. Her spouse was described as being quiet, retiring, and understanding, a description very reminiscent of the traits ascribed to Martha's father. Although she felt that their marriage was a good one, Martha admitted that she had never been sexually responsive, finding sexual intercourse painful, and attributing this to the fact that her parents lived with her and she worried that they might overhear her sexual activity or actually intrude during the course of it. Throughout her marriage Martha had chosen to live with or near her parents.

The symptom which brought Martha to a psychiatrist was an almost lifelong fear of small furry animals, especially cats. She had been told that when she was only a few months old she was frightened by a woolly Teddy bear, but her earliest conscious recollection of such a fear dated back to when she was three or four, when she was encouraged to pet a kitten that her father was holding on his lap. At that time she did so and became frightened by the feeling of the fur and the underlying bones. At the time she applied for treatment, Martha was suffering much anxiety when confronted by such small animals and went out of her way to avoid them, particularly when she was alone. For this reason she made every attempt to have someone with her when she went out of her house, even if it was only her two-year-old son. She did not fear that he would be harmed by such an animal, only that she herself might be bitten or have cause to touch it. This fear always placed a limit on her social activities and only the fact that she learned to drive made her somewhat more mobile in more recent years. (Zax and Stricker, 1963)

Case Discussion. Note how utterly unrealistic Martha's fears are: she sees the animals not as harmful to her two-year-old but as a major threat to herself. Many psychologists have speculated that the phobic object — what the person is afraid of — may have a special unconscious or symbolic meaning to the phobic individual. In this respect it is noteworthy that Martha recalls (whether correctly or not) that the first frightening experience with furry animals was petting a kitten that was on her father's lap. In any event, it is interesting that Martha now experiences sexual difficulties with a man who closely resembles her father.

Counterphobias. A phenomenon related to phobias is **counterphobic** *behavior; typically a person seems driven to master or conquer some particularly dangerous challenge.* This behavior is occasionally seen in risky sports or occupations, such as mountain climbing or stunt-flying. The counterphobic almost dies from fright every time but does the fearful thing again and again, each time taking just a little more risk or pushing just a little bit further. As one boat racer put it:

I don't know what it is, but I guess the whole thing about racing is a matter of proving something to yourself. Like when I was starting out in the construction business I had this terrible fear of being buried in dirt, but I went down and shored up sewers when nobody else would. I got buried five times one day, once for an hour and a half. It cut off the circulation in my legs so bad you could see the marks where the dirt clots were. But after every cave-in I went back down. I had to. (Chapin, 1967)

B. PERSONALITY DISORDERS

Personality disorders *are long-standing defects of personality, including sexual deviation, alcoholism and other forms of drug addiction, and the psychopathic personality.* Unlike neurotics, who view their symptoms as inexplicable and alien, those with personality disorders accept their symptoms as part of themselves, and may even flaunt them. As an example of personality disorder, here is a case of psychopathic personality.

PSYCHOPATHIC PERSONALITY

Although the psychopath is usually not hospitalized or treated as a patient, such a person is a social problem. The psychopath is not immoral but *a*moral—the psychopath does not seem to have a conscience, at least with respect to certain areas of life. Such a person shows little concern for, or even awareness of, the needs and rights of others. Relationships with others are superficial and devoid of real warmth, and others are viewed and used as mere means to ends. Often charming, witty, and in good social standing, in

reality a psychopath is vicious, manipulative, and exploitative. The narrator in the following excerpt is the University of Michigan's Elton McNeil:

A Case.

Dan F. was not a patient of mine but he probably told me more about himself and was less defensive than most of the patients I had treated. He was a well-known actor, a "personality" who had appeared on national television a number of times but had never really made it big on what he called the "boob tube." He made a lot of money, had a handsome wife, a big house in an exclusive suburb, drove a beautifully appointed Mercedes, and couldn't care less that there were other people in the world. He was as close as I ever got to what I conceived a psychopath ought to be. . . .

He was urbane, charming, knowledgeable about a variety of subjects, a seeming friend of every nightclub owner and entertainer in the city. Physically, he was commanding—six feet tall, with curly hair and regular features that were enhanced and somewhat glamorized by his personal fastidiousness in dress and grooming. But it was his bearing that added the finishing touch. He wore arrogance and noblesse oblige like a handtailored garment. . . .

He had certain mannerisms that telegraphed some of his feelings, however. Whenever he was going to create a public scene, involving the assertion of "who he was" and "what he had a right to expect," he would tilt his head slightly to one side, tug at his right eyebrow, look piercingly at the person in question, and begin a hostile Socratic dialogue. In a restaurant in which the manager toadied to him and flattered him without restraint, which Dan knew instinctively was a sign of fear and weakness, he carried on one evening about the condition of the Shrimp De Johnge. The dialogue with the waitress went something like this:

Dan F. (in a loud voice.) Is this supposed to be Shrimp De Johnge?

Waitress. (half-smiling.) Certainly, Mr. F., is there something wrong with it?

Dan F. Here, taste it and you tell me.

Waitress. Let me take it back and tell the chef.

Dan F. No! Taste it and tell me if you think this is fit to eat.

Waitress. Well, Mr. F., I really can't tell.

Dan F. You could sure as hell tell about this even if you don't eat here! Send me the manager and make him eat it.

By this time Dan had a nervous audience alerted for the next scene. Enter the bowing, scraping, apologetic manager. When a new plate of Shrimp De Johnge was brought to him, he shoved it rudely aside, refusing to taste it, and ordered London broil commenting in disgust that the chef couldn't do much to ruin that.

The scene he created (I witnessed four such in two years of contact with him) is less relevant to this account than his reaction when he resumed conversation with me. It had obviously been a contrived and calculated act to establish his presence in the restaurant, and no hint of his emotional outburst remained when he resumed discussing the previous subject. He, of course, barely tasted the London broil before pushing it aside disdainfully.

"Dan," I said, "I have a sneaking suspicion that this whole scene came about just because you really weren't hungry."

Dan laughed loudly in agreement and said, "What the hell, they'll be on their toes next time."

"Was that the only reason for this display?" I asked.

"No," he replied, "I wanted to show you how gutless the rest of the world is. If you shove a little they all jump. Next time I come in, they'll be all over me to make sure everything is exactly as I want it. That's the only way they can tell the difference between class and plain ordinary. When I travel I go first class."

"Yes," I responded, "but how do they feel about you as a person—as a fellow human being?"

"Who cares?" he laughed, "If they were on top they would do the same to me. The more you walk on them, the more they like it. It's like royalty in the old days. It makes them nervous if everyone is equal to everyone else. Watch. When we leave I'll put my arm around that waitress, ask her if she still loves me, pat her on the fanny, and she'll be ready to roll over any time I wiggle my little finger."

He was convincing. I believed him. That's exactly what he did on the way out and there was no mistaking the look in her eye. She was ready any time he was, and she thought he was a lot of man. . . . One night, a colleague of Dan's committed suicide. . . . My phone started ringing early the next morning with the inevitable question "Why?" The executives at the station called but Dan F. never did. When I did talk to him, he did not mention the suicide. Later, when I brought it to his attention, all he could say was that it was "the way the ball bounced." At the station, however, he was the one who collected money for the deceased and presented it personally to the new widow. As Dan observed, she was really built and had possibilities.

Dan F. had been married before, a fact he had failed to communicate to his present wife, and, as he described it, was still married only part time. He had established a reasonable basis for frequent nights out since his variety show required that he keep in touch with entertainers in town. He was currently involved sexually with girls ranging from the station manager's secretary (calculated) to the weather girl (incidental, based on a shared interest in Chinese food). . . . Dan F. had charm plus. He always seemed to know when to say the right thing with exactly the proper degree of concern, seriousness, and understanding for the benighted victim of a harsh world. But, he was dead inside. People amused him and he watched them with the kind of interest most of us show when examining a tank of guppies. Once, on a whim, he called each of the burlesque theaters in town and left word with the burlesque queens that he was holding a party beginning at midnight with each of them as an honored guest. He indeed held the party, charging it to the station as a talent search, and spent the evening pouring liquor into the girls. By about 3 A.M. the hotel suite was a shambles, but he thought it was hilarious. He had invited the camera and floor crew from the television station and had carefully constructed a fictional identity for each; one was an independent film producer, another a casting director, a third an influential writer, and still another a talent agent. This giant hoax was easy to get away with since Dan had read correctly and with painful accuracy the not so secret dreams, ambitions, drives, and personal needs of these entertainers. What was staggering was the elaborateness of the cruel joke. He worked incessantly adding a touch here and touch there to make it perfect. The television station crew knew enough about Hollywood to be convincing, and the room hummed with grade-B movie dialogue studded with much name-dropping.

Finally, some of the girls caught on to the gag and spread the word to the others. As they stalked out, with some very vulgar descriptions of Dan's sense of humor, he doubled up on the floor holding his sides in laughter. (McNeil, 1967)

Case Discussion. This sort of unfeeling self-gratification at the expense of others is characteristic of the psychopathic personality. The psychopath does not seem to have the emotional responses to other people that most of us experience; witness Dan's revealing account of an incident in his youth:

I can remember the first time in my life when I began to suspect I was a little different from most people. When I was in high school my best friend got leukemia and died and I went to his funeral. Everybody else was crying and feeling sorry for themselves and as they were praying to get him into heaven I suddenly realized that I wasn't feeling anything at all. He was a nice guy but what the hell. That night I thought about it some more and found out that I wouldn't miss my mother and father if they died and that I wasn't too nuts about my brothers and sisters, for that matter. I figured there wasn't anybody I really cared for but, then, I didn't need any of them anyway so I rolled over and went to sleep. (McNeil, 1967)

C. PSYCHOTIC DISORDERS

Psychotic symptoms are bizarre and, to many, frightening. *A person afflicted with a* **psychotic disorder** *is usually so disorganized, confused, and out of contact with reality that hospitalization is demanded.* Undoubtedly these symptoms are due to some interaction between the environment and genetic factors (see Focus 11.4).

MANIC-DEPRESSIVE DISORDERS

True **manic-depressive disorders,** *wherein a person periodically swings between a hyperactive, euphoric state and a depressed, melancholic state,* are more common in textbooks than in reality, perhaps because of their dramatic appeal. Usually, the depressive component is the dominant, and most often exclusive, mood. The euphoria and excitement of the manic stage, when they do occur, appear to be last-ditch efforts at warding off depression; indeed, suicide is a real danger whenever a severely

Focus 11.4

Genetic and Environmental Factors in Psychopathology

Is psychopathology, or mental illness, inherited? It has long been known that about 16 percent of the children of one schizophrenic parent will be *concordant* for schizophrenia; that is, they will also be schizophrenic. About 68 percent of the children of two schizophrenic parents will be concordant for schizophrenia. Despite the existence of these impressive figures, nothing could be concluded concerning the causative role of genetics because all the children in such studies have been raised by their schizophrenic parents; the results could be ascribed very reasonably to the stress and learning conditions connected with being reared in such a household.

This was the vital, challenging research problem facing Leonard Heston of the University of Minnesota: to separate the genetic from the environmental influence. As is typical of important work, the solution was simple. Heston found 47 individuals who were born to schizophrenic women but had been separated from their mothers during the first two weeks of life. His strategy was to compare these 47 with a group of 50 individuals separated in the first two weeks of life from a normal mother. He set out to find and interview them all some 36 years after their birth. The crucial question was what percentage of the children of schizophrenic women had themselves become mentally ill despite their minimal contact with their mothers. He thus intended to assess the mothers' genetic contribution to mental illness in the children without having to consider the possible environmental influences.

Quietly hidden in Heston's generous acknowledgements to those who helped him is the remarkable tale of his arduous solitary journey to trace these children through nursery homes, Catholic, Jewish, and Protestant charity organizations, state mental hospital files, police and jail files, Veterans Administration records, and Army, Navy, and Air Force records in 14 states and Canada. He interviewed almost all of the 97 individuals. Results: *none* of the children separated from normal mothers had become schizophrenic; 16 percent of the children separated from schizophrenic mothers had become schizophrenic. It was clear that a genetic factor had made its influence felt. The schizophrenic-mother group also contained an unusually large number of other kinds of mentally ill individuals, criminals of an impulsive and violent nature, alcoholics, and mental defectives.

Several other studies of adopted persons, as well as the study of identical (monozygotic) twins reared apart, confirm Heston's findings: heredity contributes to psychopathology. This does *not* mean that schizophrenia, for example, is inherited; what is inherited is a *predisposition* or *vulnerability* to schizophrenia. Although Heston found that 16.6 percent of his sample of children of schizophrenic mothers separated at birth themselves became schizophrenic, it must be remembered that 83.4 percent did not. As we pointed out in Chapter 2, there are probably few, if any, behavior patterns that are not influenced by genetic endowment. Thus, the crucial questions become: What is the nature of the *genotype?* How does the genotype interact with environmental conditions to produce the *phenotype* of psychopathology? What are the environmental conditions responsible for precipitating psychopathology? It is this last question to which we turn next.

"Mrs. Nebb insisted that the twins were geniuses whose activity must not be inhibited by any restrictions . . . She categorically eschewed any discipline, but she was nonetheless extremely controlling and intrusive in other areas, particularly in all matters that threatened her serious phobia concerning contamination. This applied to bowel habits, bathing, food fads, and abhorrence of animals, where any breach in the practices she dictated produced severe rebuff. . . .

"The twins were raised as a unit. They were dressed identically until nine or ten, and they were practically indistinguishable in appearance. Often they were not differentiated by the parents, and both were punished or praised for the deeds of one. Further, Mrs. Nebb had trouble differentiating their needs from her own . . . Often, when she was ill and received medicine, she also gave it to the twins. At one time, the boys could not keep awake in school, and learned that Mrs. Nebb had been placing the sedative she had received for herself in their breakfast food. They were both bowel trained at three months. Suppositories and enemas were liberally used, and enormous amounts of parental affect and energy were concentrated on bowel functions. Later, indeed until late adolescence, mother would give both twins enemas together, often because one was angry with her, which meant to her they were constipated. The enemas were administered according to a ritual in which both boys lay naked on the floor, and mother lubricated their anuses with her finger and inserted the nozzles with water as hot as they could stand. The twin more dilatory in getting into position would have to dash to another floor to the toilet." (Lidz et. al., 1965)

Does this sort of environment produce mental illness? Psychologists have attempted to answer this question by a number of different approaches.

The most common is the study of the *families* of mentally ill people in an attempt to understand the nature of the early social environment. The information is gained either by asking the parents what the home was like during the patient's formative years or by observing the patient's family in the home or a laboratory. In either case, however, there are problems. In the former, people's recall of events several years past is subject to distortion and cannot be relied on. In the latter case, there can be no guarantee that the behavior of the family when observed is anything like what went on years before when the patient was growing up—families, like individuals, change over time.

More objective information can be obtained through records and information compiled early in the patient's development, such as birth records, pediatrician's files, and school tests. Although this approach—the use of *childhood records*—avoids the pitfalls of the family-study approach, it has one glaring weakness: people move. For example, if you select a sample of schizophrenics in Cincinnati, and go back and unearth their second-grade IQ scores, what you have are not the second-grade IQ scores of schizophrenics, but the second-grade IQ scores of schizophrenics *who have been lifelong residents of a given geographical area.* This is hardly a representative sample.

The *longitudinal* approach involves selecting a sample of young subjects (preferably at or near birth), collecting information on them and their families, and following them for the balance of their lives. The purpose is to determine which subjects become ill and which do not. The investigator can look back at the information collected in childhood and determine what early environmental features distinguished those who became ill from those who did not.

This approach solves the problems inherent in the other approaches, yet it has a peculiar problem of its own. Serious mental illness is a *relatively* rare event, and in order to obtain a sample that will eventually

Focus 11.5

Depression as Learned Helplessness

One of the most frequently encountered psychological problems is depression, "the common cold of psychopathology." Depression generally has physical and behavioral symptoms as well as emotional ones. In general, the term depression refers to an overall decrease in responsiveness to physical or emotional stimuli, a "deadening" of the individual's responsiveness. "Learned helplessness" is a similar phenomenon that occurs when an animal or a person is placed in a painful or unpleasant situation from which there is no apparent escape, such as a concentration camp. Individuals *learn* helplessness in the sense that they will not act to avoid or escape from similar subsequent situations, even though avoidance or escape might actually be possible in the subsequent situations. They are passive because they have learned the "lesson" that their actions can make no difference; they are helpless in their *own* eyes. There are striking similarities between depression and learned helplessness. Martin Seligman of the University of Pennsylvania has suggested that the two phenomena are, in fact, identical, at least in what is called *situational depression* (as opposed to *process depression,* where hormonal or other physiological factors are involved).

yield a sizable number of mentally ill members, you would ordinarily have to study hundreds, if not thousands, of people. However, the *"high-risk"* method of longitudinal research offers a solution.

This method involves the selection of a sample that has a high likelihood of developing mental illness, considerably higher than would a sample of children selected at random from the general population. For example, approximately 16 per cent of the children of schizophrenic mothers will themselves become schizophrenic (versus 2 percent for the general population); further, fully 50 percent will become seriously socially deviant (chronic criminals, alcoholics, addicts, etc.). Thus, if an investigator selects a sample from such a population group, it is reasonably certain that a sizable proportion will become mentally ill.

The major problem with longitudinal research is the tremendous investment of time, energy, and money required. Perhaps this drawback explains, in part, the relative rarity of such projects. Currently, though, there is an encouraging trend toward longitudinal high-risk research, as its advantages become more apparent.

As it stands now, however, the evidence for environmental causes of mental illness is of the "back door" variety; that is, since genetics alone cannot account for mental illness, the environment *must* have an effect. But the nature of this effect is unknown.

Or, as Seligman has put it, "Depression is a belief in one's own helplessness."
To understand how helplessness is learned, Seligman and his associates, Steven F. Maier and J. Bruce Overmeier, placed dogs in harnesses so that they could not escape and repeatedly shocked them. Try as they would, the dogs could not escape; their actions were futile. In this situation, they were, indeed, helpless. Then, the shocked dogs and dogs who had not been shocked were placed in a box where a shock was delivered ten seconds after a buzzer sounded, but where avoidance or escape was possible simply by jumping a small barrier. The nonshocked dogs learned in a few trials to escape as soon as the buzzer sounded, avoiding the shock altogether. But the dogs who had experienced helplessness simply sat down and passively whined, accepting shocks of increasing magnitude with apparent resignation. This passivity struck Seligman and his associates as being like the descriptions of depression recorded by many psychiatrists, such as this one: ". . . In severe cases, there often is complete paralysis of the will. The patient has no desire to do anything, even those things that are essential to life. Consequently,

he may be relatively immobile unless prodded or pushed into activity by others. It is sometimes necessary to pull the patient out of bed, wash, dress, and feed him. . . ."

Treatment of learned helplessness required outside intervention. The "helpless" dogs made no attempt to find escape. They could not even be enticed over the barrier with a piece of meat. Only by being dragged with a leash could they be shown that escape was indeed possible. After they had experienced this, the learned helplessness disappeared immediately and permanently.

For humans, too, the strong faith in one's own helplessness becomes an obstacle to testing alternatives that might provide escape from stresses and problems. Several therapeutic approaches currently are used with some success in destroying the patients' faith in their own helplessness. In self-assertion training, the individual rehearses the open expression of feelings, desires, and thoughts, then practices the techniques in everyday situations. By successfully asserting themselves, people undergoing this training learn they really do have a large amount of power over their social encounters. Other therapeutic approaches often include

depressed patient suddenly becomes cheerful and claims to have "never felt better" and to be "on cloud nine."

Everyone experiences depression from time to time, but *deep* **depression** *is characterized by a conviction that one is totally worthless, valueless, and useless.* Also common is guilt of overwhelming proportions, the conviction that one has done "something" forever unpardonable and that one is inherently evil. There may even be feelings that one is so "bad" that one's insides are rotting away, or that one is filled with poisonous substances. Both speech and motor functions are retarded.

A Case Study. To give you a feel for the subjective state of the seriously depressed person, we present the following brief excerpt from an interview with a 47-year-old male depressive.

DR. Good morning, Mr. H., how are you today?

FIGURE 11.3 Depression.

encouraging the patients to assert themselves in new ways, gradually trying more and more difficult tasks. For example, Seligman and his associates started by asking patients to read aloud a short paragraph and graduated them through more and more challenging tasks until each patient gave an extemporaneous speech. Depression lifted considerably as these patients enlarged their conceptions of their own efficacy.

Work has often been ascribed therapeutic qualities because in work individuals demonstrate their ability to accomplish things, to change the environment or things in the environment into desired forms. One approach to work therapy starts by putting depressed patients into bed for a week, then graduating them from light work to heavier and more complex tasks. Success in the task, however, is essential. Failure to successfully complete a job would simply make the problem worse by providing the patients with more evidence for the notion that they are "helpless." Successful cure or prevention of depression is the result of successful mastery of all those skills that allow individuals to experience the power to shape their own lives.

PT. (Long pause—looks up and then head drops back down and stares at floor.)

DR. I said good morning, Mr. H. Wouldn't you like to tell me how you feel today?

PT. (Pause—looks up again) I feel . . . terrible . . . simply terrible.

DR. What seems to be your trouble?

PT. There's just no way out of it . . . nothing but blind alleys . . . I have no appetite . . . nothing matters any more . . . it's hopeless . . . everything is hopeless.

DR. Can you tell me how your trouble started?

PT. I don't know . . . it seems like I have a lead weight in my stomach . . . I feel different . . . I am not like other people . . . my health is ruined . . . I wish I were dead.

DR. Your health is ruined?

PT. Yes, my brain is being eaten away. I shouldn't have done it . . . If I had any will power I would kill myself . . . I don't deserve to live . . . I have ruined everything . . . and it's all my fault.

DR. It's all your fault?

PT. Yes . . . I have been unfaithful to my wife and now I am being punished . . . my health is ruined . . . there's no use going on . . . (sigh) . . . I have ruined everything . . . my family . . . and now myself . . . I bring misfortune to everyone . . . I am a moral leper . . . a serpent in the Garden of Eden . . . why don't I die . . . why don't you give me a pill and end it all before I bring catastrophe on everyone . . .

DR. Don't you think we can help you?

PT. (Pause) No one can help me . . . everybody tries to help me . . . but it is too late . . . (long pause, sigh) it's hopeless . . . I know that . . . its hopeless . . . (Coleman, 1972)

SCHIZOPHRENIC DISORDERS

The hallmark of **schizophrenia** is *thought disorganization,* which is evident in the schizophrenic postcard that opened this chapter. The normal associative sequences deteriorate or become "loosened" to the point where speech becomes tangential, irrelevant, alogical, and sometimes completely nonsensical. In extreme cases such speech is termed "word salad," which is a thoroughly apt description. Somewhat more severe thought disorganization than that in the postcard is evident in the following bit of "schizophrenese":

Why nylons, autos, men city people more cancer—because more polluted meat and drinks not one single connection with cigs—never jitters from narcotics or disorganization of nervous system—"I-am-ity" Megalomania—why Napoleon had to conquer world—Hitler and Mussolini and Me Too so now that I have conquered all mystery diseases (asthma and rheumatism too/experiment any dementia case) I am going to conquer the Russians/It is just a mathematical problem/New York, Cleveland, St. Louis, Detroit, California, Miami/they have control of now pulling in Cincinnati so I won't die of cancer, or the apparent heart attack/but a couple of bullets—so KEEP my name out—Please as I know of one check upon me—mathematics they are watching me see signals in paper. Mathematics if I disappear they have me —please copy and send to Hoover—telegraphers mail men caught in net. (Kisker, 1972)

Other Symptoms. Such disorganized thinking is the central feature of schizophrenia, but other symptoms frequently are present. One of these is **inappropriate affect,** *referring to peculiar emotional responses to situations, such as crying over a joke or laughing uproariously over a tragedy.* In the chronic, or late, stages of the disorder this symptom is usually replaced by **flat affect,** *or a lack of any observable emotional responsiveness to the surroundings.* Flat affect is usually accompanied by **psychological withdrawal;** *the patient becomes inaccessible to others as if existing in a private world. This psycho-*

logical withdrawal, apathy, and lack of interest in the environment is often paralleled by physical withdrawal, with the patient huddled in a corner, crouched over with head in hands for hours on end.

Delusions *(beliefs held in the absence of appropriate evidence)* and **hallucinations** *(perceptions experienced in the absence of appropriate stimuli)* are common and often frightening. For example, the person may firmly believe that the F.B.I. is in pursuit, or may hear or see the Devil commanding the performance of various acts. *The term* **paranoia** *is given to cases characterized by delusions of persecution or grandeur.* Distortions may also be projected into artwork, as shown in the paintings of a schizophrenic in Figure 11.5 (see color plate after page 370).

For a discussion of a childhood form of schizophrenia, autism, see Focus 11.6.

start HERE

D. PSYCHOANALYTIC AND CLIENT-CENTERED THERAPY

There are a number of different approaches to the psychological treatment of psychopathology, but all *share a common goal: the unlearning (extinction) of undesirable responses and the learning (acquisition) of more desirable responses.* These responses can be either overt (behavior) or covert (thoughts and feelings). What distinguishes one treatment approach from another is the techniques employed by clinical psychologists and psychiatrists (see Focus 11.7) to achieve this common goal. In sections D and E we will describe some widely used treatment approaches.

PSYCHOANALYTIC TREATMENT

Psychoanalytic treatment was developed by Sigmund Freud, but the catalytic event

FIGURE 11.4 Schizophrenic patients who exhibit the symptom of flat affect may spend most of their time in a fixed position with little or no movement.

was provided by Joseph Breuer, a prominent Viennese physician and physiologist. Breuer was working with a patient whom he called Anna O. (her real name was Bertha Pappenheim, and she later became Germany's first social worker). Anna O. had a number of symptoms, including paralysis and loss of sensation in three limbs, disturbances of vision and speech, eating difficulties, a nervous cough, and a split, or double, personality, alternating between a rather normal woman and a somewhat mischievous child. Breuer described the historic incident as follows:

It was in the summer during a period of extreme heat, and the patient was suffering from thirst; for, without being able to account for it, she was unable to drink. She would take up the glass of water, but push it away as soon as it touched her lips. . . . This had lasted for six weeks (she had eaten only fruit and melons) when during hypnosis she grumbled about her English lady companion whom she did not like, and went on to describe, with disgust, how she had gone into the lady's room and how her little dog, that horrid animal, had drunk from her glass. . . . After giving further energetic expression of her anger she asked for something to drink, and gulped a large quantity of water without difficulty. . . . thereupon the disturbance disappeared, never to return. A number of extremely obstinate symptoms were similarly removed after she had described the experiences which gave rise to them." (Breuer and Freud, 1936)

Freud heard about this case shortly after it was terminated—to be exact, on Novem-

Focus 11.6
The Autistic Child

Walter incessantly rocks back and forth, pounding his tiny fists against his forehead, his face expressionless, his eyes glazed. Five-year-old Walter is a victim of childhood autism.

Childhood autism is a relatively rare (one in every 2,000 births), but very serious, disorder. The autistic child appears to live in a shell, seemingly devoid of contact with the outside world. As infants, such children typically fail to show the usual cooing, smiling, and social behavior of normal children. The autistic child, however, is not intellectually retarded; while failing to perform the simplest of tasks, such as dressing, the autistic child may be especially attracted to the manipulation of relatively complex apparatus, such as a television set. Indeed, autistic children seem to be drawn to mechanical, at the expense of social, objects.

As might be expected, autistic children have little or no language and are unable (or unwilling) to communicate. Perhaps because they lack, or are cut-off from, external stimulation, they spend much of their time in self-stimulation: head-banging, body-rocking, finger-twirling. Although apparently oblivious to what most of us consider major events in the environment, such as a person entering the room, the autistic child may focus attention intensely on minor details, such as a speck of dust or a crack in the floor.

Focus 11.7
Clinical Psychologists and Psychiatrists

People are often confused about the differences and similarities between clinical psychologists and psychiatrists. The following comparisons should help you clarify the distinction between them.

Clinical psychologists are trained as both research and applied scientists. The Ph.D. (or doctorate in philosophy), plus training in such areas as psychotherapy and psychological testing and a hospital internship in clinical psychology, allows psychologists to diagnose and treat emotional and behavioral disorders. The treatment procedure, called psychotherapy, typically involves helping a troubled patient to talk about guilts, fears, and conflicts and, with the psychologist's help, to learn to see personal problems in a new way or handle and solve those problems more effectively. Most clinical psychologists believe that emotional and behavioral disorders that have no known physical or medical basis are products of faulty learning experience and/or excessive en-

FIGURE 11.6 Ivar Lovaas works with autistic children using various reinforcements.

What causes autism in children? We don't know, yet. However, research efforts are being intensified at such centers as the Institute for Applied Behavioral Science at the Santa Barbara campus of the University of California, under the direction of Elijah Lovejoy. And treatment of childhood autism has progressed; the work was pioneered by Ivar Lovaas of the University of California at Los Angeles. Employing operant conditioning techniques (using M&M's, ice cream, and social praise as reinforcers), Lovaas and his assistants have succeeded in teaching autistic children some social and linguistic skills.

Through the efforts of such dedicated people as Lovejoy and Lovaas, hope is now present where, a decade before, there was none. Researchers believe that the earlier the diagnosis of autism (before 30 months), the better the chance of substantial therapeutic effectiveness.

vironmental stresses that are beyond a person's capacity to cope.

Psychiatrists are first trained as medical doctors. The M.D. (or doctorate in medicine) they earn is an applied science degree. After receiving the M.D. degree, they must enter psychiatric training and residency in a hospital or clinic that treats behavior problems through both medicine and psychotherapy. As a medical doctor, the psychiatrist is qualified to diagnose and treat behavioral and emotional problems that have a medical or physical basis. Psychiatrists are also qualified to use psychotherapy in their treatment.

Compared to the psychiatrist, the psychologist receives a broader training in human behavior, methods of psychotherapy, and scientific research. However, psychologists are not trained or qualified to prescribe drugs or treat behavior disorders medically.

ber 18, 1882. He sought Breuer out and sifted through the details of the case with him over and over again. Although Freud was not present to witness the startling transformation of Anna O., it required his genius to recognize the significance of the event. Psychopathology can be caused by unconscious psychological forces and can be treated by dealing with these forces. As a consequence of this insight the techniques of psychoanalytic treatment were developed to probe the unconscious.

Free Association. Central to psychoanalytic treatment is the technique of free association. *In free association a patient is placed in a quiet, relaxed atmosphere without external distractions—hence the couch for the patient, with the analyst seated out of the patient's field of vision—and instructed to say whatever comes to mind, no matter how seemingly trivial, irrelevant, or unconventional.* Free association actually grew out of unsuccessful attempts at hypnosis. As Freud recalls, "I soon began to tire of issuing commands as: 'You are going to sleep! . . . sleep!' and of hearing the patient say: 'But I am *not* asleep'" (Breuer and Freud, 1936). Freud concluded that a more reliable method for probing the unconscious was necessary; he found that simply urging the patient to concentrate worked. At first Freud would press the patient's forehead with his hand in an effort to "evoke" associations, but when one of his patients, Elizabeth von R., objected to this as distracting, Freud took the hint and association became literally "free."

Free association is much more difficult than it sounds, as anyone who attempts to free associate for a minute or two rapidly discovers. What is important in free association is not what the patient says, but what the patient does not or cannot say. It is not unusual for the patient to "block"; the person cannot think of anything to say, the mind is a blank. The crucial question then becomes: what made the patient block at that precise moment—what was just about to come into consciousness? The very reason that the blocked material could not gain access to consciousness suggests to the psychoanalyst that it may have considerable emotional import for the patient, possibly of a frightening or threatening nature: these unconscious emotional reactions may be responsible for the problems the patient is encountering in everyday existence.

The analyst then proceeds to discover the nature of the patient's difficulty in free associating. The analyst has, of course, some hunches, or working hypotheses. The analyst has taken into account what the patient has related about the illness and early experiences, as well as more recent relationships. But the most important source for each hypothesis comes from the free association procedure itself. The patient, when directed to concentrate on the point of disruption of free association, may be of considerable help. While still unable to produce the blocked material, the patient may nevertheless be able to provide other relevant associations, and, with attention focused on the problem, be able to offer some useful hypotheses.

Transference. Next the analyst attempts to test the working hypotheses by looking for supportive (and nonsupportive) evidence in the patient's behavior during therapy sessions. Does the patient adopt a highly submissive (or domineering) role with respect to the analyst? Does the patient attempt to manipulate the analyst to gain approval (or disapproval)? Does the patient respond with inappropriate hostility (or absence of hostility) given the situation? And so on. *The patient's relationship with the analyst may be largely determined by the patient's redirection of attitudes and feelings concerning significant people in his or her life—such as parents—onto the analyst. This tendency, known as* **transference,** *is also grist for the analyst's mill.*

Interpretation. An integral part of the hypothesis-testing procedure lies in trying out an hypothesis on the patient. The analyst may use one of the hypotheses to interpret to the patient the unconscious meaning of some bit of behavior. Contrary to popular misconception, *the psychoanalyst's interpretations are not directed at "deep," primitive, unconscious forces; they merely restate what is already conscious and then "just a little bit more."* **Psychoanalytic interpretations** *are by design gradual, taking the patient only a little further in self-understanding than the current level.* And for good reason, since the interpretation that is too early or too ambitious runs the risk of not being accepted by the patient even if correct. Worse, it may overwhelm the patient with anxiety evoked by material that he or she is not yet ready to handle.

The patient's response to the interpretation presents the analyst with perhaps the most difficult task: to determine exactly what that response was. Does the patient accept the interpretation as true at some emotionally meaningful level? Or does the person merely go through the motions and verbally accept the interpretation to please the analyst? Or does the patient so vehemently deny the interpretation as to suggest that there may have been a kernel of truth in it; does the patient "protest too much"? In any event, the analyst must decide, on the basis of such cumulative evidence, whether to pursue the hypothesis or to discard it.

Change. For the moment, put yourself in the position of the patient. If the analyst's successive interpretations are correct (and accepted), the net result is that you gradually become more and more aware of yourself, who you are, what your needs are, and what sorts of gratifications you require. This is a long, painstaking, arduous process for both you and the analyst. The analyst must repeatedly point out the unconscious meanings of your behavior in order to make you aware of your real needs. It must be demonstrated to you that these needs pervade a wide variety of situations and relationships—"there, there, there, and there too." And only through slowly recognizing these heretofore unconscious needs can you discover, first, that you have such needs, and second, that you are not punished or reviled or degraded by the analyst for harboring such needs.

Once fears and anxieties concerning your needs are extinguished, you are then free, also with the analyst's help, to develop new and constructive ways of gaining gratification for these needs. You are now in control of your emotions, rather than being tyrannized by unconscious drives that result in maladaptive behavior you neither intend nor understand.

Advantages and Disadvantages. What are the advantages and disadvantages of psychoanalysis? Psychoanalysis has come under considerable criticism for being too long, too expensive, and too selective with respect to patients. It is not at all unusual for analysis to run on for many years, with two or three sessions a week, at considerable cost. Few people can afford to pay for such treatment either in time or money. Further, because psychoanalysis relies heavily on the verbal ability and psychological awareness of the patient, the method seems most suitable to middle- (or upper-middle-) class patients. Finally, since it is so time-consuming, the average analyst can at most successfully treat a relative handful of patients in a lifetime. Even if psychoanalysis were economically feasible for everyone who needed help, there wouldn't be enough analysts to go around, nor would it be possible to train them in sufficient numbers.

On the positive side, psychoanalysis stands alone in the complexity and richness of the behavior with which it deals. It attempts to treat the whole person, to bring about a basic personality change of major proportions, and to promote continued growth long after treatment has terminated. It attempts to free the individual, not just to "get by," but to fulfill his or her potential as a human being. This is no small task.

CLIENT-CENTERED TREATMENT

Client-centered therapy was developed by Carl Rogers, who is currently at the Center for Studies of the Person in La Jolla, California. In part, **client-centered treatment** represents a reaction to psychoanalysis. Rogers felt that psychoanalysis was essentially pessimistic and authoritarian, that it viewed the patient as a sick, dependent individual who had to be shaped and molded by the therapist. Rogers countered this view with the argument that *people are basically* **self-actualizing** *or* **self-fulfilling** *organisms with tremendous potential for growth,* that they have the ability to find solutions to their own problems.

The therapist's job, therefore, is to assist

FIGURE 11.7 Carl Rogers.

the client (note the shift from the term "patient," which implies sickness) in removing distorted perceptions of self and experience so that normal growth and self-fulfillment can proceed. The philosophical orientation of client-centered therapy is thus optimistic and egalitarian, with self-actualization seen as a natural tendency, inherent in all people. This basic premise gives rise to the "client-centered" character of Rogers' approach. The client is given primary responsibility for change. The therapist is relatively unobtrusive, and, in particular, never attempts to "interpret" the client's behavior or in any other way impose opinions or values upon the client.

Unconditional Positive Regard. The therapist in client-centered treatment has two major functions. The first is to establish an atmosphere of **unconditional positive regard,** that is, *complete and total acceptance of anything the client does or says.* This is eloquent testimony to Rogers's faith in human nature; it is also founded on the sound principle that until you feel totally accepted by someone else, you can never totally accept yourself in the sense of recognizing your own fears, needs, and wishes as integral parts of yourself.

Empathy. The second major task of the client-centered therapist is to attempt, insofar as possible, to adopt the client's frame of reference and view the world as the client sees it. This task obviously requires a great deal of **empathy** (*the ability to feel with someone*), but only by this means can the therapist hope to truly understand the client. With such understanding, the therapist is now in the position to assist the client in exploring feelings and perceptions. The therapist does this not by adding or "interpreting" anything, but by "clarifying" what the client has said, either by rephrasing the client's statements or by encouraging the client to explore the implications of those statements further. With these conditions established, normal growth can — and will — proceed.

As he finds someone listening to him with consistent acceptance while he expresses his thoughts and feelings, the client, little by little, becomes increasingly able to listen to communications from within himself, he becomes able to realize that he *is* angry, or that he *is* frightened, or that he *is* experiencing feelings of love. Gradually, he becomes able to listen to feelings within himself which have previously seemed so bizarre, so terrible, or so disorganizing that they have been shut off completely from conscious awareness. As he reveals these hidden and 'awful' aspects of himself, he finds that the therapist's regard for him remains unshaken. And slowly, he moves toward adopting the same attitude toward himself, toward accepting himself as he is, and thus prepares to move forward in the process of becoming. Finally, as the client is able to listen to more of himself, he moves toward greater congruence, toward expressing all of himself more openly.

He is, at last, free to change and grow in the directions which are natural to the maturing human organism. (Rogers, 1967)

Change. Through these procedures, then, the client-centered therapist thrusts the responsibility for change squarely upon the client, while at the same time affirming the client's basic worth and potential for growth. In other words, the process of change is centered on the client rather than the therapist. The following excerpt captures some of the flavor of the relationship between the two parties in client-centered treatment. The client is a young woman struggling with deep feelings of inadequacy and lack of personal worth, who has recently entertained thoughts of suicide.

CLIENT: So I don't see why I should waste your time — coming in twice a week — I'm not worth it — What do you think?

THERAPIST: It's up to you, Gil — it isn't wasting my time — I'd be glad to see you — whenever you come — but it's how you feel about it — if you don't want to come twice a week — or if you do want to come twice a week? — once a week? — It's up to you.

CLIENT: (Long pause) You're not going to suggest that I come in oftener? You're not alarmed and think I ought to come in — every day — until I get out of this?

THERAPIST: I believe you are able to make your own decision. I'll see you whenever you want to come.

CLIENT: I don't believe you are alarmed about — I see — I may be afraid of myself — but you aren't afraid for me.

THERAPIST: You say you may be afraid of yourself — and are wondering why I don't seem to be afraid for you?

CLIENT: You have more confidence in me than I have. I'll see you next week — maybe. (Rogers, 1951)

Advantages and Disadvantages. Just as psychoanalysis is better suited to some types of patients than others, so, too, is client-centered treatment. The burden of responsibility for one's own course of treatment may be more than many patients are able to tolerate. To the patient who enters treatment with the expectation that the therapist will somehow "do" something to make the patient well, the client-centered approach may be overwhelming. For example, it is not unusual for long periods of silence to elapse during client-centered treatment, with the therapist patiently waiting for the client to speak—if and when the client wishes to speak. This can be very unnerving to an anxious, dependent person who, at least at the outset of therapy, needs an active therapist who will step in and, for the moment, assume major responsibility for the interaction. Yet many patients appreciate and respond favorably to the nondirective, nondemanding behavior of the client-centered therapist.

E. BEHAVIORAL AND GROUP THERAPIES

OPERANT CONDITIONING TREATMENT

Operant conditioning treatment *is based on the principle that an organism's behavior can be changed (conditioned) by means of positive and negative reinforcement and other basic techniques of operant conditioning* that have been discussed in Chapter 6. Here we will explore several additional applications of the method as they are used in psychotherapy.

Basic Techniques. First, the rewards used must be *sufficient* to elicit and sustain behavior. Rewards can range from tangible ones, such as food, or M&M's, to more social types such as praise or approval.

Second, the rewards must be made *conditional* upon the desired behavior; they must be given when and only when the desired behavior occurs. The desired behavior is the condition for the reward. Thus, only desired behaviors are reinforced while undesirable behaviors are not reinforced but are extinguished.

Third, the reward should be administered *immediately* upon appearance of the desired behavior. If a period of time were permitted to elapse between the desired behavior and the reward, then other behaviors, possibly undesirable, would be given the opportunity to occur and receive reinforcement. Immediate reinforcement, on the other hand, ensures that the desired behavior, and only the desired behavior, is reinforced.

Fourth, behavior change should proceed in *small steps,* gradually approximating the goals set for the patient by the therapist. By keeping the steps small, the therapist enhances the probability of the correct response and reduces the probability of undesirable behavior, or "errors."

These techniques establish a situation in which the patient is *continually* indulging in *desired* behavior for which gratification is *immediately* received.

Example. These techniques may be seen in the course of treatment conducted with a mute schizophrenic by Wayne Isaacs and his associates. The patient was a 40-year-old man who had not uttered a sound for 19 years, nearly half his life! He regularly attended group therapy sessions (see below) with verbal patients, but remained totally uncommunicative and withdrawn, seemingly unaware of his surroundings.

During one session, however, while the therapist was taking a pack of cigarettes from his pocket, a package of chewing gum accidentally fell out. The therapist noticed the mute patient's eyes move toward the gum and then return to their usual position, staring ahead into space. This minute response to an object in the external world was seized upon by the therapist and used as the foundation for operant conditioning treatment.

The therapist now met with the mute patient three times a week. In the beginning the therapist held a stick of gum in front of the patient's face and waited until his eyes moved toward it. Whenever the patient looked at the gum, the therapist immediately gave it to him; by the end of the second week the patient consistently looked at the gum as soon as it was held up. Now the therapist waited until the patient moved his lips (anticipatory chewing) before he gave him the gum. By the end of the third week the patient regularly responded to the sight of the gum with both eyes and lip movements. The therapist then withheld the gum until the patient made a sound. By the end of the fourth week, holding up the gum elicited eye movement, lip movement, and—a croak. During weeks five and six the therapist held up the gum and said "Say *gum, gum*" and gave the gum only following vocalizations that approximated "gum." During the final sessions of the sixth week the patient, who had not spoken in nearly 20 years, suddenly said, "Gum, please." He had not only acquired the word for which he had been specifically rewarded but had also added one of his own. At this time other vocal responses were reinstated, and the patient began answering questions regarding his name and age. Apparently the gum served as a reinforcement not merely for the specific word which

was rewarded but for verbal responses in general.

After the sixth week the patient responded verbally to questions from the therapist, but to no one else. Accordingly, a nurse was now brought into the room during treatment sessions. At first the patient merely smiled at her, but after a month he began answering her questions, too. Other hospital personnel, who had been accustomed to interpreting and responding to the patient's nonverbal gestures, were now instructed to respond only to explicit verbal requests on the part of the patient. Soon he was vocalizing his requests. For example, at the commissary he said "Ping pong" to the volunteer worker and played a game with her.

Advantages and Disadvantages. The gains effected through operant conditioning treatment are often dramatic, all the more so because this approach seems to hold hope where all other treatments have failed. Whole wards of chronically listless, apathetic, and withdrawn patients have shown striking improvement when privileges and other activities, such as admission to the dining hall, are made contingent upon desirable behavior. However, the goal of moving an individual from self-sufficiency within the relatively structured and non-demanding environment of the hospital into a productive life in the community is far more difficult to attain. Indeed, operant conditioning methods are often combined with other psychotherapeutic methods of treatment as a means of producing improvement in patients (see Focus 11-9).

SYSTEMATIC DESENSITIZATION TREATMENT

Systematic desensitization treatment was developed by Joseph Wolpe of Temple

University; it is based on the principle that an organism cannot simultaneously make two mutually incompatible responses to the same stimulus situation. Perhaps the best way to describe systematic desensitization therapy is by example, and for this purpose we will draw from the work of Peter Lang and David Lazovik in treating snake phobias. Lang and Lazovik worked with University of Pittsburgh undergraduates who had an intense fear of nonpoisonous snakes. For instance, these students avoided going anywhere near a live snake—they would not enter the reptile section of the zoo or walk through an open field. If a snake were shown in a movie or on television they would leave or turn off the set. Even pictures of snakes in magazines or objects such as a snakeskin belt would make them uncomfortable. The subjective experience was described in such terms as "My palms get sweaty; I'm tense," or "I feel sick to my stomach when I see one." Lang and Lazovik's problem was to eliminate the snake phobia, or at least to reduce it to manageable proportions, and the treatment of choice was systematic desensitization.

Hierarchy Building. In the initial phase of systematic desensitization the therapist, with the assistance of the patient, constructs a list of situations or objects to which the patient reacts with increasing degrees of anxiety, ranging from a minimal anxiety to panic. Lang and Lazovik devised a series of 20 situations involving snakes, such as "writing the word 'snake,'" "snakes on display at the zoo," and "stepping on a dead snake accidentally." They then had each phobic student rank these situations from least to most frightening.

Relaxation Training. It is during this initial phase, too, that the patient is taught how to relax deeply. Deep relaxation is not as simple as it sounds, but it is usually achieved in a few sessions by the method of *progressive relaxation:* the patient is taught to relax first one muscle, then another, progressing from one part of the body to other parts. The patient is now ready for the main phase of the treatment.

Treatment. The patient is instructed to relax fully, and at the same time to imagine the situation that was previously rated as least distressing—the smallest "dose" of anxiety. For example, a Lang and Lazovik student would be asked to relax and imagine writing the word "snake," a relatively innocuous situation. The object of this procedure—*simultaneously relaxing and imagining an anxiety-eliciting situation*—is to associate the positive response of relaxation with a situation that had only produced the negative response of anxiety. The basic notion is this: since it is impossible to be both relaxed and anxious at the same time, a person will become desensitized to the threatening situation. For this to occur, of course, the relaxation response must be stronger than the anxiety response, and this is why the patient is started with the least frightening situation. When the patient has managed to relax while imagining one situation, the next situation on the list is presented, and so on—hence the term *systematic* desensitization. The goal is eventually to desensitize the patient to the situation originally ranked as most anxiety-provoking. A new response, relaxation, has become attached to the imagined phobic object.

Returning to Lang and Lazovik's cases, the students who achieved this goal in the treatment session were then confronted with a live five-foot snake. Without exception, all the students were able to approach the snake and touch or hold it.

Advantages and Disadvantages. As with most treatment approaches, it is within its very advantages that the shortcomings of systematic desensitization lie. The procedures are relatively simple and straightforward. Indeed, Lang has designed a machine that administers systematic desensitization automatically by means of prerecorded magnetic tape, with encouraging results. However, it is the very elegance of the procedures that makes systematic desensitization the appropriate treatment for illnesses with relatively specific, encapsulated symptoms (such as phobias and conflicts; see Focus 11.8)—symptoms that can be identified, isolated, and ranked according to amount of distress. But what of the patient who suffers from free-floating anxiety, a feeling of impending doom that cannot be readily ascribed to any situation or event? What of the patient who is chronically depressed but does not know why? What of the patient who is alienated, disillusioned, who sees no purpose in life and feels that the world is falling apart? In such cases the patient's complaints are vague and nebulous, the source of the problem is difficult to pinpoint, and, consequently, systematic desensitization is hard pressed to produce results.

GROUP THERAPY

In **group therapy** *several patients are treated simultaneously.* Beyond this rather simple statement, it is difficult to characterize group therapy, since groups range from those founded on psychoanalytic and client-centered principles to marathon groups and nude encounters. Groups also vary widely in a number of factors other than their commitment to certain therapeutic techniques. Some groups are highly structured, with one or more leaders, while others are "leaderless," the therapist assuming a participant role. Some groups are "closed," with the same membership over time, while others are "open," with constantly changing membership. Some groups focus on specific personal problems, while others emphasize personal "growth" and an increased awareness of one's own experiential world as well as an increased sensitivity to others.

FIGURE 11.8 A group therapy session. Participants in sensitivity or encounter groups often engage in close physical contact; the goal is to remove inhibitions. Group therapy is difficult to characterize, because groups vary widely in purpose, structure, membership, and point of view of the therapist.

Focus 11.8

Approach-Avoidance Conflict

Wally is an adolescent with a conflict problem. When he is with other males of his age, a favorite topic of conversation is females and female attributes, or, more succinctly, sex, complete with vivid accounts of past, present, and future romantic conquests. When Wally is in the same room with the objects of his affection, however, his behavior undergoes a rather dramatic transformation. He becomes a bumbling, blushing incompetent who can't even summon up enough presence of mind to ask for a date. Like many adolescent males in our culture, he is simultaneously attracted to and yet afraid of girls. His conflict in effect blocks his attempts to satisfy an important social need. This paradoxical behavior is an example of *ambivalence*. The term applies to the experience of approach-avoidance conflict when a given person or activity has both positive and negative properties attached to it (that is, is ambi-valent). Ambivalence is, perhaps, the most common type of conflict—and conflict is one of the most common human problems.

Approach-Avoidance Conflict. **Approach-avoidance conflict** *occurs when an individual is faced with two incompatible behavior tendencies — to approach and to avoid the same person or object.* John Dollard and Neal Miller explain conflict behavior by means of a small number of rather straightforward assumptions:

1. The tendency to approach a positive object becomes stronger the nearer one is to that object (the gradient of approach in Figure 11.9A).
2. The tendency to avoid a negative object becomes stronger the nearer one is to that object (the gradient of avoidance).
3. The strength of avoidance increases more rapidly with nearness than does the strength of approach (the gradient of avoidance is steeper than the gradient of approach).

(These assumptions have received strong support from a series of ingenious experiments by Judson S. Brown. He used rats rigged with little harnesses connected to a device that records the strength of pull as they run along an alley toward a goal box in which they have been both fed and shocked.)

Let's apply these principles, then, to the case of the ambivalent young man named Wally. As shown in Figure 11.9A, there are a number of hypothetical steps on the way to Wally's requesting a date with a girl he has seen but does not know. The safest and farthest removed activity is simply fantasizing about the event, alone or with others. Going to a large party where the girl will be is one step closer to the goal. Then, while at the party, introducing himself represents yet another step. The goal, of course, is actually asking for the date. If Wally's approach and avoidance tendencies are as depicted, what will he do? If he is at position A, he will move to position B because there his approach tendencies are stronger than his avoidance tendencies. But then his behavior will become curious. Spotting the girl in a corner of the room he will begin to approach her, only to break into a sweat and discover that his mouth is so dry that

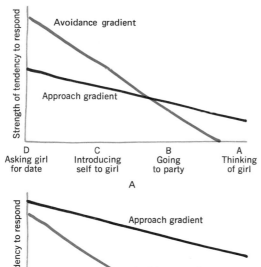

FIGURE 11.9 (A) A diagrammatic representation of approach-avoidance conflict. Note that the avoidance gradient is steeper than the approach gradient. An approach-avoidance conflict can be resolved by (B) raising the approach gradient above the avoidance gradient or (C) lowering the avoidance below the approach gradient.

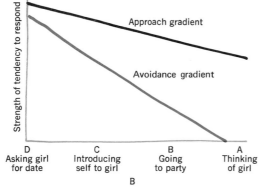

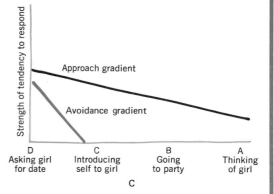

he can scarcely speak; he will slow down, stop, and retreat to pull himself together. After a minute or two, he will try again — and again — and again, never quite attaining the courage to step up and introduce himself, and yet never able to give up and leave the party. Indeed, he may spend the entire evening in this vacillating, indecisive state.

His behavior would seem bizarre to the casual observer but, given Dollard and Miller's principles and the information in Figure 11.9A, it is readily explicable. Between points B and C the gradients of approach and avoidance intersect. At this point of intersection, the tendencies to approach and avoid the girl are of equal strength. If his momentum carries him slightly beyond the intersection point, the avoidance tendency becomes stronger and he beats a hasty retreat. As soon as he has moved away from the girl, back across the intersection point, the approach tendency becomes stronger and he again moves toward her. This crossover of the approach and avoidance tendencies between positions B and C accounts for his vacillating behavior, his inability *either* to approach or avoid. What if a friend, sensing his plight, grabs him by the arm and introduces him to the girl, thereby placing him at position C? Rather than assisting him in reaching the goal, D, this move would have the opposite effect; his avoidance gradient at position C is considerably higher than his approach gradient, causing him to move away from D. This hypothetical example, though simple, does illustrate how relatively complex behavior can be explained by means of a few basic principles.

Resolving Conflict. There are two major ways of resolving approach-avoidance conflict to overcome the vacillation. One is to lower the avoidance gradient so that it is below the approach gradient. The other is to raise the approach gradient so that it is above the avoidance gradient (see Figure 11.9B and C.) For example, a particularly attractive female may be sufficient to raise Wally's approach gradient above his avoidance gradient. Or a number of visits to the punch bowl may substantially lower his avoidance gradient. In Wally's case, as for any human, there are innumerable ways in which conflict resolution can be accomplished. One way is psychotherapy, as discussed in this chapter.

Common Characteristics. There are, however, two factors that are common to all groups: *mutual scrutiny and mutual support. Every group member is open to the scrutiny of every other group member and at the same time is the recipient of every other member's support.* (In this sense groups have a "family" quality, and members often emerge expressing the feeling that they feel closer to and know their fellow group members *better than they have known anyone* throughout their lives). These twin factors—scrutiny combined with support—make the group effective. On the one hand, each member is exposed by the group. This exposure is often relentless (and sometimes harsh) and is difficult to resist in the face of the weight of opinion expressed by one's peers. On the other hand, however, while such exposure may be painful, each member is supported and encouraged by the group in efforts to achieve self-awareness.

At the same time, the group also provides a practice ground for developing interpersonal skills that will serve the member well in outside social situations. The group establishes a relatively "safe" atmosphere for trying out new ways of thinking, perceiving, and behaving, and supports and reinforces the member both for attempts to change and for actual desirable changes. The group, then, serves as a model of group living, with the complexities of interpersonal relationships that are encountered in the real world. To the extent that new responses are acquired within the therapy group, the member is acquiring responses that are transferable to everyday group life with family or friends.

An Excerpt. Here is an excerpt from a group session in which a birthday party given for one member (FF) at the home of another (EF) is under discussion. Note the instances of both intervention and support by the group members:

BM: I am curious why I felt so swell, so friendly and talkative. I was a different guy. I know I can say "it was the alcohol," but usually I get even more glum with drinks.

CM: It couldn't be the alcohol, because you were quite eleated from the very beginning of the party before you had anything to drink.

BM: Touché. I know it. I'd like to know what made me so happy. I wish I could feel that way more often. (Turning to GM) I even felt friendly toward you.

(Group laughter, followed by silence)

THERAPIST (to group): Did you all feel this friendliness and relaxation in BM at the party? (Several patients confirm and elaborate)

HF: What comes to my mind is that you were playing host.

EF: Yes, I asked him to.

BM: Yes, I enjoyed doing that.

THERAPIST: Do you feel the same way about playing host at home?

BM: Oh, God, no! I feel there as if I do not belong.

THERAPIST: In your own home you feel as if you do not belong, but at the party in EF's home you felt differently.

BM: (Laughs) I know there is something screwy.

THERAPIST: Perhaps the group can help BM understand himself more deeply in this situation. Are there any more speculations?

GM: I would go further along HF's line.

HF: I actually did go further myself that very evening when you, BM, were so nice to me. Then I wondered what the hell had happened to you. And I felt, "he has replaced the head of the house." He has taken over the house and EF, the wife. This you loved.

BM: That could be.

THERAPIST: What comes to your mind now?

BM: (Pause) It's silly. My father telling me what to do. (Laughs)

THERAPIST: Can you go on?

BM: Didn't want to mow the lawn. Didn't ever want to do anything the old man demanded because it never was right—never pleased him.

EF: BM, you sure are getting away from the party.

THERAPIST: I feel that his associations here are right on the subject of his feelings about your party, EF.

EF: Oh? How? I don't see it because I am anxious about hearing more.

CM: What do you want to hear more about?

EF: How BM felt when my husband came home. (Long pause)

THERAPIST: I have the feeling that you, EF, and the group, have brought out something helpful to BM. If we try to put the various associations together, what does it say? (Long pause) I have the feeling that something important has been brought out and yet the group does not want me to label or analyze it further. . . . It seems that the associations show that BM is still fighting his father in the form of competing with husbands for a wife's happiness. This fight is stimulating to him, while at home where there is no occasion to work out this interest he is in most low spirits. Also, I felt that EF is recognizing that she is emotionally affected by this competitive interest of BM and really participates in it. How do you all feel about this? (Bach, 1954)

Advantages and Disadvantages. Inasmuch as up to ten or twelve people can be seen at the same time, in group therapy the fee per individual is usually much less than that charged for individual therapy. This fact is partly responsible for the popularity of group therapy; many people who previously wanted but could not afford a therapeutic relationship now find themselves able to do so. In addition, the group may simply provide its members with a feeling of belonging and being cared about, ingredients that are missing from a great many people's lives. Unfortunately, many group therapies border on fads, being so diffuse in their methods and sweeping in their claims that it is all but impossible to evaluate them. Further, the "leaders" of these groups are not infrequently self-ordained, with little or no professional training. This becomes an acute problem when such a leader is unprepared to deal with emotional upheavals precipitated by group experiences that

Focus 11.9

Combining Treatments

Allan Leventhal of the University of Maryland came to an impasse while treating a socially immature female college student by conversation-based psychotherapy.

"Eventually, after struggling for several interviews and for more than 20 minutes of intense concentration in a particular interview, she emitted the word 'sex' as the central feature to her distress. Immediately thereafter she warned the counselor that she could tolerate very little discussion in this area and during the next few sessions related a series of experiences to illustrate her feelings on this subject: mother would permit her to read no book or magazine article with any sexual content and Janet agreed that this was only right; . . . an assigned paperback textbook of readings with a picture on the cover of a Greek male statue could only be read after she had blackened out the 'middle part'; she objected vehemently to topics covered in a Health class because they 'weren't nice'; she had been persuaded by mother that it was unwise to date boys because they were interested 'in only one thing'; . . .

The girl's anxiety over sexuality was so great that she could not even bring herself to name any body part between shoulders and knees! Leventhal used systematic desensitization and operant conditioning to reduce Janet's anxiety over sexual words so that she could use them in a discussion of her fears. Leventhal made up a set of 58 3 x 5 index cards, each with a sex word typed on it—the words were taken from the table of contents of Kinsey's *Sexual Behavior in the Human Female*. He then asked the patient to rate each word according to "how difficult it might be for you to say each word" (that is, to build an anxiety hierarchy). Then, beginning with the least anxiety-provoking word, the patient was required to read each word to herself three times, to write the word three times, to read the word aloud to Leventhal three times, to hear Leventhal read the word three times, to write a sentence using the word, to read the sentence out loud, and to hear the sentence read back to her by Leventhal (desensitization).

When this sequence was completed, Leventhal immediately and forcefully said "Good!", smiled approvingly, and congratulated the patient (operant treatment). The patient systematically worked through the list in this fashion, until all 58 words had been mastered. Once this had been accomplished, conversational therapy could proceed, during which ". . . a good deal of insight and self-confidence were developed. For example, she spontaneously realized that her mother was using her as a replacement for her father and that smiling at a boy did not logically lead to a series of events ending in rape. . . . [W]hile some problems remained, it was clear that Janet felt much more comfortable about herself, was now capable of effective independent living, and would be able to make further progress on her own. (Leventhal, 1968)

Focus 11.10

Does Psychotherapy Work?

The question "Does psychotherapy work?" is comparable to the question "What is normal and abnormal?" Just as there are no hard-and-fast criteria for deciding whether a person is mentally ill, neither are there commonly agreed-upon criteria for evaluating "improvement" following treatment.

What if a *therapist* says a patient has improved? The therapist has a great deal, both professionally and personally, at stake in the success of treatment and can hardly be expected to be a completely unbiased judge.

What if the *patient* reports improvement? The patient, too, has made a large investment in the success of therapy, in time, energy, and not least of all, money. Consequently the patient's testimony on the effectiveness of treatment must be viewed with caution. (This point is nicely illustrated by the "unsolicited testimonials" appearing in popular magazines for patent medicines that have been found to have no medical value.)

What if an *unbiased and objective observer* reports that the patient did (or did not) show improvement? This probably provides the best index of therapeutic effectiveness. But even here there remains the problem of the essentially arbitrary nature of the criteria for improvement. Just what constitutes improvement? Removal of or relief from symptoms? Improved social relationships? A reorganized personality? It is exceedingly difficult to obtain consensus on such questions.

Even if there were objective and universally accepted improvement criteria, there are still several problems that make treatment evaluation a tricky business. We have already suggested that certain treatment methods are better suited for treating certain types of patients or disorders. This fact is not lost on the practitioners of these methods, and consciously or unconsciously therapists select those patients with whom they feel they will have the greatest likelihood of success. This practice is justifiable in that any therapist wishes to focus available resources where they will do the most good. Still, it precludes a representative sampling of mentally ill individuals. A related problem is that it is impossible to separate the therapist from the therapy—just as there are good and bad plumbers, so, too, there are good and not-so-good therapists. Further, it is well documented that certain types of therapists work more effectively with certain types of patients. For example, a warm, supportive, personally involved therapist is more successful with a withdrawn schizophrenic, while a reserved and formal therapist has greater success with the neurotic patient.

The answer to the question "Does treatment work?" is, then, a qualified one: *some* treatments conducted by *some* therapists work with *some* patients *some* of the time. The facts of the matter are that no treatment method is a panacea and that any treatment has its limitations; this reality is far less disappointing once it has been recognized.

have gotten out of hand. Many people have been seriously harmed by such experiences. The point is not that group therapy is ineffective — quite the contrary — but that one should take care when selecting a group, just as one would when selecting an individual therapist.

For the purpose of clarity of presentation, we have described and discussed various treatment methods as if they were completely separate and distinct entities and without considering their effectiveness. In practice, however, psychotherapists often combine treatments as the situation demands. A case report, presented in Focus 11.9, illustrates how treatments can be combined. The question of the effectiveness of treatment is considered in Focus 11.10.

SUMMARY

1. **Psychopathology** (page 363) is a health problem of staggering proportions. Millions of people suffer some impairment of personal and social functioning because of psychopathology. All societies recognize mental illness, and there is a remarkable similarity in symptoms across societies. Large, isolated mental hospitals do not seem to be the answer to this problem; fortunately, community-based mental health centers are becoming more common.

A. Neurotic Disorders

2. **Neurotic disorders** (page 363) are characterized by a strained or exaggerated reliance on **defense mechanisms** (page 366). Such mechanisms include **repression, reaction formation, projection, displacement, regression,** and **fantasy** (page 369). A neurotic's functioning is impaired, but usually not to the extent that hospitalization is necessary.

3. **Hysterical disorders** (page 363) refer to physical symptoms caused by psychological factors. **Psychosomatic disorders** (page 370) involve symptoms that are the product of an interaction between psychological and organic factors. **Obsessive-compulsive disorders** (page 372) involve highly repetitive thoughts and behaviors. **Phobias** (page 373) are unrealistic fears.

B. Personality Disorders

4. **Personality disorders** (page 375) represent long-standing personality defects, including sexual deviation, alcoholism and other forms of drug addiction, and psychopathy. Unlike neurotics, who view their symptoms as inexplicable and alien, those with personality disorders accept their symptoms as part of themselves.

C. **Psychotic Disorders**

5. A **psychotic person** (page 377) is usually out of touch with reality, so that hospitalization is often necessary. Both genetic and environmental factors evidently play a role in psychoses.

6. In **manic-depressive psychosis** (page 377) the victim periodically swings between a euphoric and a melancholic state, although the depressive mood is usually dominant. The symptoms of **schizophrenia** (page 383) include thought disorganization, inappropriate emotional responses, psychological withdrawal, and perceptual distortion.

D. **Psychoanalytic and Client-Centered Therapy**

7. All psychological treatments share a common goal: the unlearning of undesirable responses and the learning of desirable responses. What distinguishes one form of treatment from another is the techniques employed.

8. **Psychoanalytic treatment** (page 384) emphasizes the role of unconscious forces in psychopathology, and, consequently, relies heavily on **free association** (page 388) and **interpretation** of **transference** (page 389).

9. **Client-centered treatment** (page 390) focuses on the self-actualizing potential of human beings; it, therefore, employs **unconditional positive regard** (page 390) and **empathy** (page 391).

E. **Behavioral and Group Therapies**

10. **Operant conditioning treatment** (page 392) is based on the principle that an organism's current behavior can be changed by rewards. In terms of technique, it involves sufficient reward, conditional reward, immediate reward, and continual reward.

11. **Systematic desensitization** (page 393) is based on the principle that an organism cannot make two incompatible responses at the same time. It involves anxiety hierarchy building, training in progressive relaxation, and the pairing of relaxation responses with increasingly anxiety-provoking stimuli.

12. **Group therapy** (page 395) involves the psychological treatment of more than one person at a time — usually six to 12 — by a variety of methods. But all groups share in common two crucial features: mutual scrutiny and mutual support.

13. Psychological treatment methods are most fruitfully used in combination. For example, the combination of conversational and behavioral methods has been shown to yield progress that could not be achieved by either approach alone.

Section
Seven

Social
Being

Unlike lower animals, humans cannot rely on instincts to survive; rather, they must learn to adapt to the environment through a long period of childhood. During this learning process the unique behaviors that characterize human beings are constantly shaped and directed by the social environment.

The chapters in this section explore questions dealing with the social-psychological and developmental dimensions of human life. In earlier chapters we have looked at motivational (Chapter 4), perceptual (5), intellectual (8), creative (9), and personality (10) development. Now we ask: What impact do prenatal and postnatal infant care have on the development of a person? How do child-rearing practices influence the development of self-esteem? What are the stages of moral development through which all children must pass on the way to adulthood? How do attitudes develop and what can be done to change them? What factors produce conformity to group standards? When do bystanders come to the aid of crisis victims? How do leadership and group organization affect group decisions and productivity? Can international tension and conflict be resolved by principles of behavior discovered in the psychologist's research laboratory?

Chapter Twelve

Development and Socialization

A. THE BIOLOGICAL BASIS OF DEVELOPMENT

At the climax of sexual intercourse, a blob of semen is ejaculated into the woman's vagina in the region of the cervix. This blob contains perhaps 375 million sperm cells. Immediately after the launching, they begin to lash their tails furiously and swim like spawning salmon into the uterus and further upstream. Very, very few sperm actually make it to the Fallopian tubes. Those few that do, continue their swimming in "search" of an egg cell (ovum). If they find none, they settle down and wait. They can wait two or three days before they die.

Three or four days before a fertile mating can occur (usually in the middle of a menstrual cycle), a little blister on one of the woman's ovaries bursts; an egg cell appears and starts down one of the Fallopian tubes toward the uterus, drifting at the rate of about 1/16 of an inch every hour-and-a-half. If the ovum drifts near waiting sperm cells, they encircle it. Somehow, one of the infinitesimal sperm cells approaches the ovum and unites with it. This union produces a single cell, 1/175 of an inch in diameter, with 46 chromosomes. The chromosomes with their DNA "code book" of biological instructions will guide that one cell's development so that it will ultimately become a one-hundred-billion-cell man or woman. In this section we will explore the sequence and principles of early development.

FROM EMBRYO TO BIRTH

For the first several weeks after conception, during which the various components of what will later be the major organ systems are taking shape, *the developing individual is called an* **embryo.** After the third month, *when the facial features and limbs are distinct, the term applied is* **fetus.**

Before the first week of development is over, the fertilized egg has divided several times and the resulting group of cells has attached itself to the wall of the uterus and has begun to take nourishment from the mother's blood. The "roots" that this ball of cells sends out into the wall of the uterus develop into the *placenta.* The placenta is the lifeline of the developing organism, taking from the mother all life-giving substances and disgorging waste back to the mother. At the time of birth, the placenta weighs about a pound and measures about seven inches in diameter. It is connected to the fetus by means of a coiled tube, called the *umbilical cord,* that contains an artery and a vein to bring fresh supplies to the fetus and to carry waste products away, respectively.

At two weeks, even though the embryo is now only about 1/12 of an inch long, most of the essential organs and major systems of the body have begun to show themselves. At one month, the embryo already has a visible head, arm buds, and a tail. (The mother by now will have noticed her missed

FIGURE 12.1 A human ovum being approached by sperm.

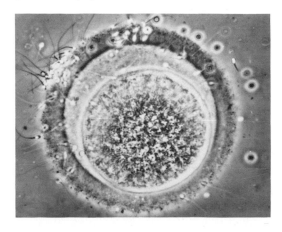

menstrual period, swelling of the nipples, frequent urination, and morning sickness.)

By eight weeks, the embryo is an inch-and-a-quarter long, it has developed an endocrine system, and human-like features have begun to appear. From eight weeks on, all of the primordial structures laid down during the embryonic period begin to develop and grow rapidly. By the fourth month, the fetus is beginning to move spontaneously, although the mother will not as yet be aware of these movements. Various reflexes have begun operating. For example, the fetus can swallow some of the amniotic fluid in which it swims; this is discharged via the placenta. By the fifth month, the fetus's heartbeat is detectable and the mother can begin to feel a mild stirring inside of her (the "quickening"). At this point, the mother is bulging very clearly and she is in the most comfortable period of pregnancy. By the sixth month, the fetus is a foot long, can open and close its eyes, and has even been known to hiccup. Beyond the sixth month, the fetus is, for the most part, elaborating on structures that have already been laid down. It is growing in size and the various vital functions are beginning to operate with some reliability. The last 12 weeks in the uterus prepare the fetus for emerging as an independent being. The fetus is now gaining as much as half a pound a week, filling out rapidly (see Figure 12.2).

The 266-day process, beginning with the sperm cells' siege of the ovum, has produced a full-term infant. The plan for the development of a nervous system, heart, hair, and toes is embedded in the genetic code of the DNA molecule. As a genetic blueprint, however, the DNA code provides an upper limit that the organism can reach. Just how closely the fetus comes to this limit depends very much on the kindness of the uterine environment.

Environmental Influences on the Developing Fetus

There is a curious fact that has appeared repeatedly in psychological literature from locations as far-flung as Baltimore, Maryland, and Stockholm, Sweden. It seems that it is more likely for a schizophrenic (who, as we pointed out in Chapter 11, is characterized by social withdrawal and distortions of thought and behavior) to be born in the late winter than at any other time of the year. An ingenious study by Benjamin Pasamanick in Baltimore revealed at least some part of the reason. It seems that, while the relationship between season of birth and schizophrenia holds true almost every year, it is even more marked in years when the summer is especially hot. This finding suggests some beginning of an interpretation of the curious phenomenon. It is possible that a very hot summer early in pregnancy has a *teratogenic* effect, that is, it causes abnormalities in the development of the new organism. It is also possible that hot weather upsets the diet; specifically, the mother may consume less protein- and vitamin-rich foods than normal and consume more soft drinks and carbohydrates. This change in diet may affect the sensitive early stages of fetal development. This reasearch finding emphasizes the delicacy of the interaction between the developing organism and the environment.

This sensitive relationship is especially true during the very earliest stages of pregnancy. One initial cell multiplies so as eventually to produce billions of cells. One small anomaly at the beginning stages may be reproduced many times in the multiplication of cells so that difficulties in the early environment of the embryo can produce extremely serious deformities. Factors such as abnormal bodily conditions of the mother, gross excesses or

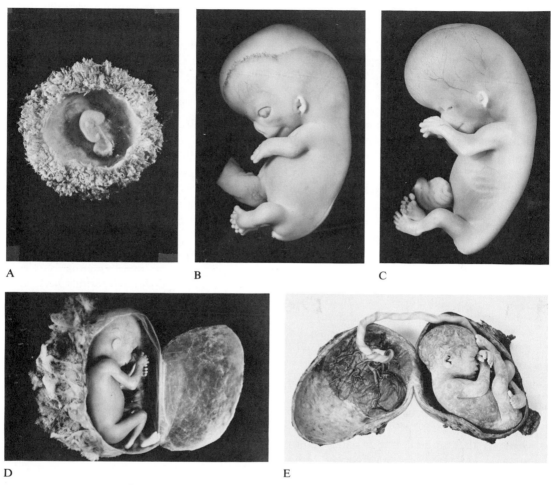

A B C

D E

FIGURE 12.2 Stages of fetal development. (A) 4 weeks. (B) 6½ weeks. (C) 8 weeks. (D) 16 weeks. (E) 28 weeks.

deficiencies of vitamins, lack of oxygen in the mother's blood, poisons, drugs, illnesses of the mother, X-rays, and a variety of sometimes seemingly minor factors can yield extremely unfortunate results in the infant. A highly publicized and tragic example is the phocomelia (seal-flippers instead of arms) produced by the drug thalidomide. This was a tranquilizing drug prescribed to pregnant women for morning sickness.

The type of effect that an environmental disturbance produces on a fetus or embryo depends very much on (when the disturbance appears in its chain of development.) This chain is ordered with precision. During development, almost all phases of the production of the final individual go on at once. At any one given time, however, the development of one specific organ system is dominant: this organ system is growing most rapidly and is absorbing most of the energy being used for developmental purposes. During this *critical period,* a disturbance in the maternal-fetal relationship will maximally affect that particular organ system. An example is found in research with pregnant rats. If the mother is fed huge overdoses of Vitamin A between the eighth and tenth day of pregnancy, the rat puppies are very likely to be born without a brain (anencephaly). If overdosed between the eleventh and seventeenth day, the mother produces rat pups with cleft palates; if between the eighteenth and twentieth day, the rat pups are born with cataracts. It all depends on which organ system has its critical period at the time of the disturbance. Some disturbing agents (teratogens) seem to be dangerous at only one critical period; others will be dangerous at any time during pregnancy. For example, rubella (German measles) in the mother in the first eight weeks can cause brain damage, deafness, blindness, or deformities of the arms and legs, depending on just when the mother contracts this disease.

Disturbances in the fetal environment occurring after the third month of development (that is, after the embryonic period) can cause serious psychological defects, but will not alter the body's structure. For example, emotional stress or mental illnesses in the mother can produce emotionality and anxiety in the offspring. Most of the research in humans in this area is at present in its beginning stages. The great difficulty is the possibility of hidden effects that do not show themselves for many, many years after their origin. Thus, very subtle neurological damage to the developing fetus might not be noticeable in the behavior of the newborn infant or even in the six- to ten-year-old child. At these ages, the environmental demands on children are not excessive. However, the minimal neurological defect may show itself when the individual must face the stress involved in earning a living or competing in college life. To be able to evaluate the influence of such subtle effects requires long-term studies of peoples' lives. There have, as yet, not been enough such longitudinal studies. (See Focus 12.1: Methods of Child Development Research.)

The Birth Process

The fetus floats in amniotic fluid, receiving all its nutrition and oxygen supply through the placenta and umbilical cord. At the end of the 266 days of pregnancy, the fetus turns downward and rests its head in the mother's pelvic basin. At a hormonal signal, the mother's longitudinal uterine muscles begin spontaneous rhythmic contractions, pressing the head of the fetus down into the relaxing and widening circle of the cervix. In order to permit passage of the fetus's head, the bones of the pelvic girdle soften during the weeks prior to

FIGURE 12.3 An infant just moments after birth.

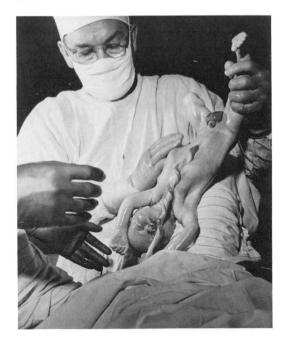

Focus 12.1

Methods of Child Development Research

Developmental psychologists use a variety of methods to study the course of maturation and growth. Each one has its advantages and limitations.

Longitudinal Study. The **longitudinal study** *is based on observation or testing of the same group of children at repeated intervals over several months or years.* For example, to study the course of the development of height, one can measure a group of children every six months starting at birth until the age of 16. Longitudinal studies are valuable since data for each child show the developmental variations due to individual differences; these data are not available with other methods. These data also permit the researcher to determine how early development correlates with later development so that predictions can be made. Valuable as they are, longitudinal studies are expensive and time-consuming and so are rare.

Cross-Sectional Study. With the **cross-sectional** *method, children of different ages are observed simultaneously over a short period of time.* For example, a researcher might study the vocabulary of groups of children at ages six, seven, eight, nine, and ten and infer from his data the course of vocabulary development. Cross-sectional research data can be gathered quickly and cheaply compared to longitudinal methods. Individual differences in growth patterns are obscured, however, since each age level is rerepresented by different children (see Figure 12.4).

Child development researchers also use naturalistic observation, interview surveys, and experimental procedures (see the Appendix).

FIGURE 12.4 A comparison of longitudinal and cross-sectional research studies.

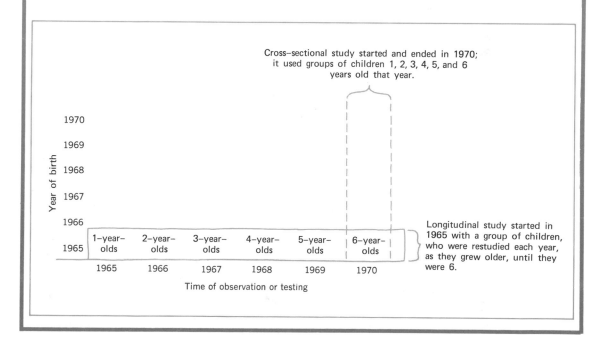

Cross–sectional study started and ended in 1970; it used groups of children 1, 2, 3, 4, 5, and 6 years old that year.

Longitudinal study started in 1965 with a group of children, who were restudied each year, as they grew older, until they were 6.

Year of birth: 1970, 1969, 1968, 1967, 1966, 1965

1-year-olds | 2-year-olds | 3-year-olds | 4-year-olds | 5-year-olds | 6-year-olds

1965 | 1966 | 1967 | 1968 | 1969 | 1970

Time of observation or testing

birth and spread during birth. This first period of labor lasts an average of 14 hours for first-borns and considerably less for subsequent deliveries. In the second stage of labor, the baby passes through the vagina and into the world. During this stage, the mother is urged to speed the process by bearing down with her abdominal muscles, in cooperation with the involuntary uterine contractions. The third and final stage of labor involves the delivery of the placenta and its attached membranes (the afterbirth). Immediately after birth, the mother is frequently injected with a number of hormones—hormones that lower animals usually obtain by licking their young clean of amniotic fluid and/or by eating the placenta. These hormones stimulate the tightening of the uterus and the return of the mother's body to its pre-pregnancy status.

The great danger to a fetus during the birth process is damage to the brain. If the labor is too prolonged, the umbilical cord may be pinched and so not allow oxygen to get through. If the birth canal does not widen sufficiently, the fetus's skull will be subjected to abnormally severe pressures that may pinch off arteries feeding brain areas especially sensitive to lack of oxygen. These pressures may also crush certain brain areas.

The pregnancy and delivery process offers many hazards to the mother and the newborn. Many of the deaths of infants during the first year of life at least indirectly result from disturbances during gestation and birth. The rates of infant mortality in the United States are about the highest among industrialized nations. In the world, the United States ranks 18, just a bit better than Hong Kong. These figures on infant mortality are assuredly only the observable tip of the iceberg. The part of the iceberg not showing includes the far more frequent nonfatal disorders of pregnancy and birth that probably lead to a variety of psychological disorders. This area is only now receiving the attention it deserves. We do not as yet *fully* understand what deplorable health conditions mean for the psychological well-being of the citizens of the United States (and elsewhere). But our state of knowledge does tell us that there is a relationship between, on the one hand, pregnancy and birth disorder and, on the other hand, later mental illness, learning disorders, mental retardation, cerebral palsy, and disorders of reading. It seems reasonable to conjecture that, since the incidence of birth casualty has been increasing in the United States over the past 20 years, as these children grow up, the nation will see a corresponding increase in the above-mentioned behavior disorders.

Forty years ago Denmark's rate of perinatal casualty was at about the same level as in the United States today. By instituting free prenatal and postnatal visiting nurse services, Denmark was able to lower the rate of infant mortality and prematurity by half. The nurses provide nutritional counseling, health checkups, and identification of medical problems that may have led to birth defects or problems. The cost (considering all meanings of the word "cost") of such a visiting nurse service is far less than that of maintaining defective citizens for life in institutions.

INFANT AND CHILD MOTOR DEVELOPMENT

Jimmy and Johnny were appealing fraternal twins who, early in development, were intensively studied and described by M. B. McGraw in a now-famous research report. Johnny was trained, long before Jimmy, in a number of motor skills, such as crawling, walking, and grasping. Weeks or months after Johnny had practiced a skill, Jimmy was trained in it. In activities such as crawling, walking, and grasping, Jimmy caught up to his trained twin, so all the practice Johnny had had gave him no special advantage. Studies like this indicate that *certain behaviors, such as crawling, walking, and talking, emerge at a fixed time in development and are relatively independent of experience and wide variations in the environment. A genetically programmed process of this kind is called* **maturation** (see Focus 12.2: Maturational Trends).

Maturation

The development of the human fetus proceeds according to a relatively fixed schedule of both time and sequence; indeed, it is a good example of the maturation process. Many aspects of child development also follow an orderly sequence of maturational steps (see Figure 12.5), if the environment offers some minimal level of support. For example, as long as Jimmy and Johnny were given love, attention, nourishing food, and opportunities to play in their crib, they would begin to roll over, sit up, stand, and so forth, at approximately the same age regardless of any practice they were given. When their bodies reached a certain stage of development, their genetically programmed behavior would emerge based on internal growth, not on external influence. In general, most children follow the same sequence of maturation. However, the rate at which each sequence occurs or the rate at which each sequence is completed varies from child to child. You can get an idea of the range

FIGURE 12.5 Although development follows a fixed sequence, the age at which each infant reaches a performance stage varies. The vertical line in each bar indicates the age at which 50 percent of infants can perform the stated behavior. Each bar covers the age range in which 85 percent of infants perform the behavior.

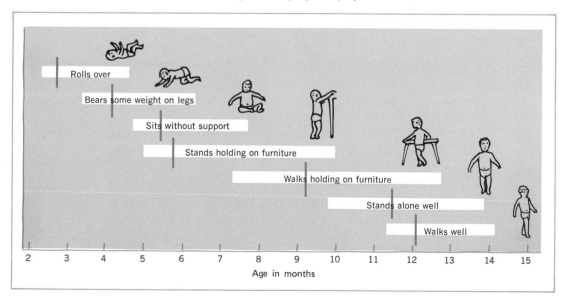

Rolls over

Bears some weight on legs

Sits without support

Stands holding on furniture

Walks holding on furniture

Stands alone well

Walks well

Age in months

Focus 12.2 Maturational Trends

If you were to observe the development of many children carefully over a long period of time, you would discover that there are at least four major maturational trends in development:

1. Cephalocaudal sequence
2. Proximal-distal sequence
3. Differentiation
4. Integration

Cephalocaudal Sequence. Since *cephalo* means head and *caudal* means tail, *the* **cephalocaudal sequence** *refers to the progression of the infant's development from head to foot.* A two-month-old fetus is 57 percent head; at birth an infant is 25 percent head; an adult is 12 percent head. The head is most rapid in growth rate, followed by the trunk, and then by the legs. Behavioral development also follows this course. An infant will be able to lift the head before the shoulders can be raised.

Proximal-Distal Sequence. Proximal refers to the center line of the body, distal to the body's extremities. *The* **proximal-distal sequence** *refers to the progression of growth from the central parts of the body, such as the trunk and shoulders, to the arms and legs, and then to the fingers and toes.* In practical terms, a child must creep before it can crawl and crawl before it can walk. Similarly, a child makes broad arm movements long before it can reach and grasp an object with its fingers.

Differentiation. **Differentiation** *refers to the gradual refinement of behavior as growth progresses.* As you observe a hungry infant, you will notice that its whole body responds with legs and arms thrashing, the little body squirming, the red-faced head twitching, and the tiny mouth screaming. Several months later, the same child will be standing in the crib grasping the rails and focusing all effort on crying for a bottle. The process of differentiation moves in the direction of developing behavior from an all-inclusive body reaction to behavior that is more narrowly focused toward some goal.

Integration. When a baby reaches a certain stage of differentiation, you can begin to notice **integration,** that is, *the many focused responses are pulled together into large behavior patterns.* The hungry baby can sit up, reach for a bottle, grasp it, hold it, put the nipple in its mouth, and suck. The behavior involves an integrated combination of responses.

The concepts of differentiation and integration are not confined to physical growth. They can also be applied to the development of intelligence, emotional control, and social maturation over the full range of the life cycle.

of variation of each developmental step in the maturation sequence from Figure 12.5. Notice that some infants may reach a stage several months before others and some may have completed more steps in a year than others.

There are a number of important implications of the maturation concept for child-rearing practices. For instance, a parent who is aware of the wide variability of children's growth patterns is less likely to get upset if his or her child isn't walking or talking as early as a neighbor's child. An upset parent who feels a child is not developing properly may put too much pressure on the child to perform. Such pressure will not change the maturation rate but may produce emotional problems and damage the parent-child relationship. A damaged parent-child relationship may, in turn, prevent the parent from teaching the child social or other skills that are not so dependent on maturation.

Individual Differences in Development

Fred is 15 but he looks and acts like a 12-year-old. He is shorter than his classmates and has not yet reached sexual maturity. His classmates make fun of him and he, in return, has become the class clown. Clowning around is the only way Fred can get any attention from the other kids. Fred is not physiologically abnormal but he is a late maturer. While everybody follows the genetically determined sequence of maturational steps, we all differ in the rate of maturation. Your own observations will confirm the many individual differences involved in maturation rates for height, physical maturity, sexual maturity, and so on. Individual differences also show up

as early as infancy. Newborn infants differ in temperament, activity level, and responsiveness to their environment. We pointed out the differences in the behavior of male and female neonates in Chapter 2. Regardless of sex differences, some infants cry more than others, some are more sensitive to pain. These differences certainly influence how parents react to a child, how new experiences are approached, and what is learned. A boy who from infancy on is relatively insensitive to pain will respond to and accept rough-and-tumble activity in a very different way from a boy who is very sensitive to pain. A father who wants an athletic son will treat a son who can't take pain or vigorous play and one who can in much different manners. Thus, individual differences in temperament interact with the social environment to add further to the range of individual differences.

B. SOCIALIZATION

Humans and the higher vertebrates begin life in relative helplessness, unable to function without other members of their species. This helplessness is especially evident in human babies. Infant monkeys can usually at least cling to their mothers, whereas the human infant must be carried by the parents like baggage. Birth alone does not ensure the behaviors and skills required for survival. The transformation of this relatively helpless organism into a fully functioning member of its society is a function of maturation and *socialization*. Studies of socialization are especially concerned with such topics as the development of language, aggression and dependency, sex and social roles, and socially influenced perception of the self. In all of these areas, the role of parental practices

Focus 12.3
Deprivation and Development

"Man cannot live by milk alone," declares Harry P. Harlow of the University of Wisconsin—or at least rhesus monkeys cannot. Harlow and his wife, Margaret, were among the first researchers to study experimentally the importance of "love" and the effects of the deprivation of affection on personality and behavioral development. For ethical reasons, these deprivation experiments could not involve human subjects, so the Harlows selected infant rhesus monkeys. The monkeys are relatively inexpensive, small, easily handled, and more similar to humans than are most laboratory animals. What is controversial about the results of Harlow's studies is the degree to which generalization from monkey to human being can justifiably be made. Let's look at the research.

Sigmund Freud (see Chapter 10A) asserted that the most significant relationship in an individual's development occurs between mother and infant. To test the significance of the mother-infant affectional system, the Harlows replaced the monkeys' mothers with surrogate "mothers" made of wire covered with soft terry cloth, with a protruding bottle and nipple (see Figure 12.6). Although these baby monkeys had ample milk and were able to cling and obtain contact comfort from the terry cloth, these infants deprived of a real mother generally showed abnormal behaviors as they matured in play and sexual activities, becoming severely asocial and sullen. Further, if in adulthood they were given infant monkeys, they would ignore, and sometimes attack, the infants.

But another surprising fact was also established. The Harlows discovered that if the mother-deprived infants were permitted to socialize and play with other infant monkeys (as in a natural monkey colony), they grew up without abnormal symptoms. All of the infants with adequate peer play experience developed normal play, sexual, and adult behaviors. But if infants were deprived of peer association between the third and sixth months of life (apparently a critical period), they dis-

is critical, although later in the individual's life the influence of peers and social institutions becomes increasingly important.

ROLES

After first-term finals, Anne finds herself at the top of her medical school class.

If asked to write a completely unrestrained fantasy about Anne's situation, what would be *your* story? Matina Horner of the University of Michigan asked female college students to create stories about Anne and then rated them for negative imagery associated with success. Horner uncovered what she calls the *motive to avoid success*. This need to avoid achievement contrasts sharply with the established n Ach for males in our culture discussed in Chapter 4B.

Horner had no difficulty in finding negative reactions to Anne's success among her female subjects. One of the typical negative-response stories contained this segment:

FIGURE 12.6 *An infant rhesus monkey with its terry cloth surrogate mother.*

played aberrant sex and play behaviors in maturity even if they were later given access to other monkeys. Furthermore, "mother-love" proved to be no substitute for playmates, since infants raised with mothers but without peer association showed severely disturbed patterns of play and sex behavior. Apparently, playmates are more important than mother herself.

The Harlows conclude from their studies that opportunity for peer contact during early development is essential for normal psychological health and development.

Anne is an acne-faced bookworm. She runs to the bulletin board and finds she's at the top. As usual she smarts off. A chorus of groans is the rest of the class' reply. . . . She studies 12 hours a day and lives at home to save money. "Well, it certainly paid off. All the Friday and Saturday nights without dates, fun—I'll be the best woman doctor alive." And yet a twinge of sadness comes thru—she wonders what she really has. . . .

Other stories distorted the fact of the situation as given, as though they *deny* that Anne had really competed successfully with her male classmates. An example of such distortion is:

Anne is really happy she's on top, though *Tom is higher than she is*—though that's as it should be. . . . Anne doesn't mind Tom winning.

Almost two-thirds of the females in the study demonstrated a negative reaction to Anne's success, painting the image of the successful female (or at least the female who was more successful than a male) as unfeminine, lonely, and unmarriageable, physically and socially unattractive. By contrast, in writing about "a top medical student named John," less than 10 percent of males tested indicated any motive to avoid success. The bright woman, according to Horner, is likely to feel as much anxiety about success as about failure—damned if she does and damned if she doesn't.

Sex Roles

The term **role** *refers to a set of attitudes and behaviors expected of a person in a particular social position.* For example, sex roles refer to the attitudes and behaviors that are associated with being male or female in a given society. Learning sex roles, already mentioned in Chapter 4D, is a major part of the socialization process. Specific behaviors are selected by the social environment as "appropriate" for a person's position in society and are positively reinforced. Deviation from behavior that is prescribed for one's sex role is likely to result in social rejection and other negative reinforcements: the prospect of success often does so for women in our culture. Sex roles are established, in part, by the differential reinforcement (varying degrees of reward or punishment) of parents and teachers. For example, when a little girl plays with her doll she is encouraged and complimented, whereas a boy involved in such play would be discouraged and told that it was not appropriate for him. Another important factor is the process of imitating a parent; male children use their fathers, girls use their mothers as models probably, again, because they are reinforced for doing so. When a little boy picks up a hammer after seeing Daddy use it, he is praised; when his sister uses a rolling pin as she has seen Mommy do, she receives affection and attention. (See Chapter 10A.)

The development of sex roles is related to the socialization of aggressive and dependent behaviors. Jerome Kagan and his colleagues at Harvard University performed a longitudinal study of the changes or stability in these behaviors as related to sex. Their subjects were 27 males and 27 females. They were young adults at the time of the study, but there were reliable records of their aggressive and dependent behaviors between the ages of three and ten years. Independent judges interviewed the subjects and rated their level of aggressiveness and dependency as adults. These ratings were then compared with the childhood levels for each characteristic. The comparison revealed a dramatic difference between the sexes. *Dependency* tended to remain stable for female subjects, but not for males, in whom it had markedly declined; conversely, *aggression* remained stable for male subjects but had declined in females by adulthood. The inference was clear. Behaviors that were socially inappropriate for the individual's sex role had been weeded out by socialization sometime between the ages of ten and adulthood, while those that were appropriate were fostered. Socialization may be seen as a process by which a society casts its roles, then supervises their rehearsal and performance.

Role and Birth Order

Roles are assigned on the basis of criteria other than gender, of course. Clear differences in behavior correspond with birth order (see Focus 4.3: Birth Order). One researcher, Hilton, investigated the relationship between birth order and dependency in children. Hilton wanted to find out whether differences in dependency between first-born and later siblings could be correlated with maternal practices. To test this hypothesis, he used 20 first-borns, 20 only children (also considered as first-borns), and 20 later-borns. They were given two sessions of puzzles to solve, with a rest period between sessions. Their mothers waited in an adjoining room. At the intermission, half of the mothers were told that their children were performing below average on the puzzles; the other half were told that their children were performing above average. Both the mothers and their children had been instructed to remain in separate rooms during the puzzle-solving sessions and during the break between the sessions. It was made clear that the children's efforts at puzzle solving were to be independently conducted. But the whole point of the procedure was to see by whom and how these rules would be broken. Two unseen judges observed the children who, contrary to instructions, joined their mothers during the breaks.

Their observations revealed that the child's and mother's behavior were related to the child's birth order. The first-borns most frequently sought out their mothers at the intermission and they most frequently solicited their mothers' advice about solving the puzzles. The mothers of the first-borns most frequently gave advice or directly interfered in the problem-solving task. Also, the belief that her child was doing well or poorly seemed to affect the reaction of a "first-born" mother toward her child more than the mothers of later-born children. The latter mothers displayed fairly constant affection no matter how well or poorly their children were supposedly doing. But the mothers of first-born children seemed to approach or withdraw from their children on the basis of

their alleged performance: if a child was supposedly doing well, affection was strongly evident; if a child was reported below par, much less affection was shown. The results indicate two things: first-born (and only) children are more dependent than later-borns on parental approval and assistance, and their mothers make affection contingent on their perception of the children's performance. For the first-born, success — or, more precisely, the parent's belief in the child's success — is often the price of love. This experience may explain why first-borns are not only high achievers as adults but are also conformists.

SELF-CONCEPT

A baby chimpanzee seated in its cage gazing at a full-length mirror just beyond the bars seems an unlikely agent for crumbling a revered belief — that a concept of "self" belongs to humans alone. After all, the chimp is doing nothing so impressive as, say, reading a volume by Darwin. It is just standing before a looking glass and touching with a hairy hand first its nose, then an ear. The chimp moves its hand from body part to body part very slowly — very *deliberately,* you might be tempted to say — while still gazing at the mirror. Still, nothing too impressive. But an investigation conducted by Gordon G. Gallup of Tulane University does indicate something extraordinary. Just as chimpanzees may be capable of rudimentary linguistic skills, they may, under the proper conditions, be able to learn the sort of conception that in a human being would be called a self-image.

Self-Image

In this experiment, Gallup simply put two four-year-old chimpanzees in separate cages. For eight hours each day he placed full-length mirrors outside the cages. For the first few days the animals responded to the mirror-images as though they were other chimpanzees. But by the third day, their attitude had changed. They spent long periods making faces in the mirrors or examining areas of their bodies they could not see directly. Apparently, the chimps had discovered their mirror images.

Gallup was not content with these observations, so he anesthetized the animals and on each painted one eye ridge and one ear with a nontoxic red dye that could not be felt when dry. The chimpanzees were then returned to their cages. For the first 30 minutes they had no view of the mirrors; Gallup wanted to see if they could discover the marks without the mirrors. Only once in that time did either chimp touch a marked area, apparently by accident. But when the mirrors were returned, the chimps repeatedly touched the marks while gazing at their reflections. One even rubbed her dyed brow, then examined the hand carefully, smelling the fingers. Clearly, the marks on the mirror-monkeys meant marks on *the self* for the two chimpanzees. Thus, the chimps were apparently capable of developing a rudimentary image of self.

Self-Esteem

In human beings, the self-concept is more than a self-image in the sense of a visual representation of the body. The mirrors that reflect an individual's self-concept are most often the evaluations of the person expressed by others—especially parents, peers, and teachers. In a very real sense, we are what others say we are. After all, the reactions of others represent the infant's sole source of information about what sort of person he or she is.

How is the self-concept influenced by socialization? Stanley Coopersmith of the University of California at Davis has examined the relationship of child-rearing practices and one important aspect of the self-concept, self-esteem.

Self-Esteem and Behavior. Coopersmith and his associates estimated the relative degree of self-esteem, ranked as low, medium, or high, for each of a group of normal boys, whose lives they followed from preadolescence to early adulthood. Rankings of self-esteem were made on the combined basis of the Thematic Apperception Test, the Rohrschach Test, self-evaluations by the boys, and reports by the boys' teachers. The high-self-esteem group tended to be socially and physically active, and generally successful, both academically and socially. Also, they were significantly less prone to ailments, such as fatigue, headaches, or insomnia, and other psychosomatic ailments (see Chapter 4C). The high-self-esteem children were realistic about their skills and abilities. Indeed, the self-evaluations of the boys with high self-esteem generally agreed with the results of aptitude and intelligence tests. These boys tended to be judged as more expressive and creative than their peers with lower self-esteem. More successful in social relationships than the others, they were also more self-assertive and more frequently took part in discussions, quite often expressing disagreement with the others.

What differences in parental practices account for differences in self-esteem and, indirectly, for differences in behavior among children? Coopersmith found that children with high self-esteem generally had a positive attitude toward their parents. They reported that their parents were fair to them, not overly punitive but not permissive either. Interviews revealed that the parents of boys with high self-esteem were, indeed, strict and fair. They also tended to use rewards for good behavior as much as possible. When punishments, such as withdrawal of privileges or criticism, were administered, they were consistent and prompt. Rarely did the punishment take the form of isolation of the child or withdrawal of affection. These parents were genuinely interested in the interests and activities of their children. In general, they were supportive and accepting. Still, they clearly held high hopes for the children's achievements.

The parents themselves generally had a high degree of self-esteem. The typical family structure could be described as democratic. It was obviously one in which the needs, desires, and wishes of all members, including the children, were important enough to be taken into consideration in making decisions. This respect apparently allowed and encouraged the children to explore their capabilities, led to the willingness to set high goals, and fostered the capacity to achieve them. Surprisingly, the parents' occupations and income level had little relationship to the boys' self-esteem; the proportion of individuals with high self-esteem is just as high in the lower socioeconomic classes as it is in the higher classes.

By contrast, the mothers of the children with low self-esteem tended to be more emotionally distant from their children, either punitive or permissive in their dealings with them (see Chapter 6C for a discussion of punishment). Democratic family structure (involving a sharing of responsibilities and parental consideration of the child's point of view) was less evident with these children; perhaps more significantly, *consistency* in dealing with the children was absent. In general, the parents of children with low self-esteem had little respect for and interest in their children. In return, their children were either indifferent to or hostile to them. And, of course, the child reaped the unsatisfactory harvest of paltry self-esteem.

It seems clear, then, that the roles people play and the esteem experienced in playing them are determined to a large extent by parental child-rearing practices.

C. STAGES OF MORAL DEVELOPMENT

"The Drug Robbery"

In Europe, a woman was near death from a special kind of cancer. There was one drug that the doctors thought might save her. It was a form of radium that a druggist in the same town had recently discovered. The druggist was charging ten times what the drug cost him to make. He paid two hundred dollars for the radium and charged two thousand dollars for a small dose of the drug. The sick woman's husband, Heinz, went to everyone he knew to borrow the money, but he could get together only about one thousand dollars. He told the druggist that his wife was dying and asked him to sell cheaper or let him pay later. The druggist said, "No, I discovered the drug and I'm going to make money from it." So Heinz got desperate and broke into the man's store to steal the drug for his wife. (Kohlberg, 1969)

Should the husband have stolen the drug? Why or why not?

The above situation and question have been selected from research concerned with the growth and development of morality. The point of this material and other questions involving moral issues will be explored in this section.

THE CHILD
AS A MORAL PHILOSOPHER

One of the pioneers in the study of moral development has been Lawrence Kohlberg of Harvard University. He has spent many years studying the role of the child as a moral philosopher. As you might imagine, one's own personal values make it difficult to study morality scientifically. The trick is to avoid allowing those values to bias the examination of values expressed by others. Kohlberg has strenuously wrestled with this problem and has devised a solution. The method he devised is a good example of how research procedures can be developed to answer difficult and controversial questions.

Kohlberg's basic procedure was as follows. He presented each child in his research group with nine stories, such as the one that opened this section. Each story involved a moral dilemma, a problem or a situation that required a moral judgment or decision. After a story was presented, each child was asked a number of questions designed to elicit the moral reasoning that lay behind the child's judgment. Each child's verbal responses were carefully recorded. Originally, Kohlberg selected for study 25 boys ranging in age from 10 to 16, and the question and interview procedures were administered periodically over a 12-year period. As his studies progressed, he added boys from Canada, Great Britain, Mexico, Taiwan, and Turkey in the hope of generalizing his findings on moral judgments across cultures.

The Classification of Moral Judgment. Over a period of years, Kohlberg tried to develop a classification scheme that would organize the responses of the boys to the stories into some simple and meaningful

patterns. Noticing that as the boys grew older their responses changed, Kohlberg was able to trace out the pattern in this change. It seemed to him that younger boys supported their judgments by an appeal to the potential punishments and rewards of someone with authority. As they grew older, they tended to abandon this reason and develop new ones (see Table 12.1). Kohlberg examined the responses of the boys by age to find out if certain kinds of moral judgments are common to certain age groups; he found enough common qualities to make him feel justified in grouping them under different categories. Table 12.1 summarizes the six-step classification scheme he developed. Notice that the categories show a fixed sequence of changing responses with increasing age.

An advantage of Kohlberg's categories and moral-dilemma questions is the relative ease in spotting different kinds of moral reasoning. The actual decisions ("Yes, the husband should have stolen the drug") are not as important to the classification as the reasons the individual gives to justify the decision. Are social standards and attitudes the reason? Or does the individual rely on personal convictions about the general value of human life or honesty?

An example used by Kohlberg illustrates the stages of moral development. Tommy, age ten, was asked the question, "Is it better to save the life of one important person or a lot of unimportant people?" He justified the latter policy by appealing to their greater total material worth: ". . . because one man just has one house, maybe a lot of furniture, but a whole lot of people have an awful lot of furniture." His equation of personal value with material worth marks Tommy as being in Stage One. Three years later, Tommy was asked, "Should a medical doctor mercy kill a fatally ill woman requesting death because

TABLE 12.1 Classification of moral judgment into levels and stages of development

LEVEL	BASIS OF MORAL JUDGMENT	STAGE OF DEVELOPMENT	SAMPLE RESPONSES TO MORAL DILEMMA, "THE DRUG ROBBERY"
I Precon- ventional Morality	Moral value resides in awareness of rules of "good" and "bad" but is interpreted in terms of physical actions and re- ward and punishment.	Stage 1: Obedience and Pun- ishment. Obedience and punishment orientation. Ego- centric deference to superior power or authority, or avoid- ing trouble.	"He was sad to steal be- cause he will get caught and punished."
		Stage 2: Naive Instrumental Hedonism. Naively egoistic orientation. Right action is that instrumentally satisfy- ing the self's needs and oc- casionally others'. Aware- ness of relativism of value to each actor's needs and per- spective. Naive egalitarian- ism and orientation to ex- change and reciprocity.	"He should steal the drug because he needs his wife to live so she could take care of his house for him."
II Conven- tional Morality	Moral value resides in per- forming good or right roles, in maintaining the conven- tional order by conforming to the expectancies of others and social standards.	Stage 3: Approval Seeking, Good-boy Orientation. Ori- entation to approval and to pleasing and helping others. Conformity to stereotypical images of majority.	"If he truly loves his wife he will and should steal the drug for her."
		Stage 4: Maintenence of Authority. Orientation to "doing duty" and to show- ing respect for authority and maintaining the given social order for its own sake. Re- gard for learned expecta- tions of others.	"He shouldn't steal be- cause it's against the law. If people lived by their private rules there would be chaos."
III Postcon- ventional Morality	Moral value resides in con- formity to shared standards, rights or duties. However, this includes a recognition that disobedience of con- ventional standards may, under certain circumstances, be moral and ethical.	Stage 5: Social Contract. Contractual, legalistic orien- tation. Recognition of an ar- bitrary element or starting point in rules or expecta- tions for the sake of agree- ment. Duty defined in terms of contract, general avoid- ance of violation of the will or rights of others, and ma- jority will and welfare.	"As a general rule, the law should be obeyed. How- ever, under certain circum- stances, stealing is justified as in this case, since saving a life is more important than property rights."
		Stage 6: Principles of Con- science. Conscience or prin- ciple orientation. Orienta- tion not only to actually ordained social rules but to principles of choice involv- ing appeal to logical uni- versality and consistency. Orientation to conscience as a directing agent and to mu- tual respect and trust.	"Justice, love, and the right to life are the highest hu- man values and must be satisfied before all other values."

(Kohlberg, 1969, and Buss, 1973)

of her pain?" His response shows his changing view of the value of human life: "Maybe it would be good to put her out of her pain, she'd be better off that way. But the husband wouldn't want it. . . . Well, you can get a new wife, but it's not really the same." To Tommy, at Stage Two now, a wife was of value because she would be hard for the husband to replace. The wife is seen as instrumental in satisfying the husband's need, while life for the wife is based on its hedonistic value for her, which is now impaired by pain. Answering the same question at the age of 16, Tommy said, "It might be best for her, but her husband— It's a human life . . . you can become attached to a dog, but nothing like a human, you know." His answer indicates Stage Three where human life is special because of the empathy that is possible with other people, not because of some intrinsic value. At Stage Four Tommy appeals to some authority or deity who establishes the value of human life. At Stage Five, the moralist appeals to the "rights" and "obligations" of social contract to justify decisions. At Stage Six, self-selected, abstract, ethical principles justify the decision and characterize the reasoning. Examples of the kinds of responses that correspond to each stage of development are presented in Table 12.1.

Developmental Stages. The term "stage" is appropriate because the sequence is invariable—Stage Four follows Stage Three follows Stage Two and so forth. An individual always "moves," in the forward direction and one stage at a time. Although the sequence is invariable, the *rate* of development is readily affected by environmental circumstances such as culture. For example, Kohlberg found that Western urban middle-class children move through the stages faster than rural children or children from less technologically developed cultures. Each step in the Moral Judgment Scale (Table 12.1) is the equivalent of a "philosophical revolution;" that is, the child develops a new moral scheme that permits decisions in a wider range of circumstances and that integrates earlier experience with new experiences.

Like all good research, Kohlberg's work leads to more questions and follow-up research. For instance, what methods can be used to help a person move from one stage of moral development to the next? If the moral stage of prison and reform school inmates is changed, will it result in a decrease of recidivism (return to crime after they are released)? How do various parental child-rearing practices affect the rate of movement from stage to stage? What is the relationship between the stage of an individual's moral reasoning and actual behavior in a crisis requiring a moral decision? For instance, at which stage of moral development is a child less likely to cheat on a test? At which stage is a person more likely to help an accident victim?

SUMMARY

A. The Biological Basis of Development

1. The development of the **embryo** and **fetus** (page 407) from conception to birth follows a sequence that is determined by chromosomes with their DNA codebook of biological instructions.

2. The survival of an individual, as well as many physical and behavioral characteristics, is influenced by the uterine environment, which, in turn, is affected by the mother's diet, health, and prenatal care.

3. The development of many of a child's behaviors, such as crawling, walking, and talking, is a genetically controlled process called **maturation** (page 413), given adequate environmental opportunity and support.

4. The maturation sequence of development can be described in terms of **proximaldistal and cephalocaudal** sequences, **differentiation** and **integration** (page 414).

5. Developmental psychologists use a variety of methods to study maturation and growth, including **longitudinal** and **cross-sectional** (page 411) procedures. These methods indicate that there are wide variations in the rates of maturation and growth between individuals.

B. Socialization

6. **Roles** (page 418) refer to a set of attitudes and behaviors expected of a person in a particular social position.

7. Like other roles, male and female roles are selectively shaped by parents and society through the process of socialization.

8. Birth order influences the parent-child relationship and the role the child learns to play.

9. The self-esteem of an individual is determined by the parent's child-rearing practices.

10. Research on the impact of social deprivation of infant monkeys indicates that peer contact during early development is essential for psychological health and normal development.

C. Stages of Moral Development

11. Moral development can be studied by presenting individuals with moral dilemmas as problems requiring a moral decision. Kohlberg has analyzed responses to such problems and developed a six-stage classification scheme.

12. Moral development follows an invariable sequence from one stage to the next. The rate of development is affected by the culture.

Chapter Thirteen
Attitudes and Prejudice

You ought to try to integrate those schools like we did in Greenwood, Mississippi. Spent the whole summer talking to colored folk trying to get them to commit their kids. Had to lie to them, tell them the government was going to protect them, but we knew damn good and well we were all going to get killed. And you finally get 12 black kids committed. But the morning school is opened you only got eight. Maybe you got to feel what it feels like to be walking down that street with that little black kid's hand in the palm of your hand and your hand soaking wet — from *your* sweat because you know what's going to happen but the kid don't. And as you approach those steps to that school, not only are you attacked by the white mob but also by the sheriff and the police.

Next thing you know you're knocked down in the gutter with that cracker's foot in your chest and a double barrel shot-gun in your throat saying "move, nigger, and I'll blow your brains out" — which is interesting 'cause the only time that a cracker ever admits we got brains is when he says what he's going to do to them.

Maybe you have to lay in that gutter, knowing it's *your* time now, baby, and then you look across the street, laying down in the gutter, from the gutter position, and see the FBI standing across the street taking pictures. . . . And then as you lay there in that gutter, man, it finally dawns on you that that little five-year-old kid's hand is not in the palm of your hand anymore. And that really scares you . . . and you look around trying to find the kid and you find him just in time to see a brick hit him right in the mouth. Man, you wouldn't believe it until you see a brick hit a five-year-old kid in the mouth. (Dick Gregory)

An **attitude** *is a predisposition to act in a certain way toward some aspect of one's environment, including other people.* **Prejudice,** *for example, is an attitude; it is a predisposition to act in a discriminatory manner toward a certain person or group*

of people. Later in this chapter we will return to prejudice. First we will discuss how attitudes are formed, changed, and made resistant to change. In reading the following discussion remember that attitudes are *predispositions* to action; there is not necessarily a one-to-one correspondence between attitude and behavior. For example, a person who is prejudiced may not behave in a discriminatory fashion because of legal counterpressures.

A. ATTITUDE FORMATION

There are three factors involved in the formation of attitudes:
1. Social influences, such as cultural norms.
2. Personality characteristics, such as needs.
3. Information.
The three factors usually interact in varying degrees to form any given attitude. Discussion of social influences and personality characteristics will be deferred until the section on prejudice; for now we will turn our attention to the third factor: information.

Exposure and Repetition. What is the effect on attitude formation of exposure to and repetition of information? Robert Zajonc of the University of Michigan was struck by an interesting phenomenon concerning language that bears on this question. Examine Table 13.1, and perhaps you will notice it too. The first and second columns of the table contain, obviously enough, words. The third column contains the ratio of the frequency with which the first-column word occurs in the written language over the frequency of the second-column word. Zajonc observes:

TABLE 13.1 **Ratio of frequency of occurrence for paired words**

MORE FREQUENT WORD	LESS FREQUENT WORD	RATIO OF FREQUENCY OF OCCURRENCE
Abundance	Scarcity	3 to 1
Affluence	Deprivation	6 to 1
Beauty	Ugliness	41 to 1
Find	Lose	4 to 1
Good	Bad	5 to 1
Happy	Sad	7 to 1
Happiness	Unhappiness	16 to 1
In	Out	5 to 1
Laugh	Cry	2 to 1
Love	Hate	7 to 1
Lucky	Unlucky	13 to 1
Possible	Impossible	3 to 1
Profitable	Unprofitable	5 to 1
Up	Down	2 to 1

(Zajonc, 1968)

Catering to our corporeal sensibilities, things are 3 times more often "fragrant" than they are "foul," 12 times more often "fresh" than "stale," and almost 7 times more often "sweet" than "sour," and everything that can be filled is three times as often "full" as it is "empty." If we have anything, we have "more" of it 6 times more often than we have "less" of it, and 3 times more often "most" of it than "least" of it. And those things that we have so frequently more of are 5 times more often "better" than they are "worse," 6 times more often "best" than "worst," and 4 times more often "superior" than "inferior." Still, they "improve" at least 25 times as often as they "deteriorate." (Zajonc, 1968)

Zajonc's point is that there is an intimate relationship between word frequency (exposure) and meaning: the more frequently a word appears, the more likely it is to have a "good" or "positive" meaning. And the same relationship holds when people are asked to voice their preferences for countries, cities, trees, fruits, flowers, and even vegetables—the more frequently an item appears in the language, the more it is liked. However, all these data, as impressive as they may be, still leave unsolved the chicken-or-the-egg problem; namely, is attitude the result of frequency, or is frequency the result of attitude? In more concrete terms, we can argue that people like roses (attitude) because there are many roses growing (frequency). But we can also argue, with equal plausibility, that many roses are grown (frequency) because people like roses (attitude). In order to resolve this problem we must turn to Zajonc's experimental evidence.

Some Experiments. Zajonc presented his subjects with a number of Turkish words. The subjects viewed these words a varying number of times, ranging from 25 exposures to only a single exposure. The subjects were then told that they had just seen a list of Turkish adjectives and their job was to guess whether each word meant something good or bad. The results: the more often a word had been exposed, the more often it was evaluated as good. The same experiment was repeated with Chinese-like characters, with the same result: increased exposure led to more favorable attitudes. Similarly, pictures of graduating male seniors taken from the Michigan State University Yearbook were exposed with varying frequency to University of Michigan students, who were subsequently asked how much they "liked" each man on the basis of his photograph. And again, the more frequently exposed his picture, the better liked the man. (As Zajonc puts it: "Familiarity breeds comfort.") *Before going further,* please read Focus 13.1: Attitudes toward Words, page 430.

If you read and participated in Focus 13.1, you have just conducted a somewhat truncated version of the final Zajonc experiment to be described. Zajonc and his associate, D. W. Rajecki planted Turkish words such as KADIRGA and IKTITAF in the University of Michigan and Michigan State University student newspapers. These words appeared every day for several weeks without explanation; the "word-of-the-day" was simply set in a rectangle one column wide and one inch deep. The number of times a word was "advertised" varied. It should come as no surprise to you by now that, when Zajonc and Rajecki gave a questionnaire to students on these campuses after the ad campaign, those words that had appeared more frequently were most likely to be rated "good." (Parenthetically, it is of interest to note the response to Rajecki's name, which was printed on the questionnaire the subjects were given to rate the Turkish words. Like the Turkish words used, RAJECKI is a seven-letter three-syllable word, and some of the subjects could not resist rating it as well. These ratings were lower than those of the words seen in the papers—further confirmation of the exposure effect on attitude formation, since the subjects had seen the name only once.)

Some Implications. Now let's translate these findings into pragmatic, everyday terms. They suggest a formula, for instance, for election to public office. You make no speeches. You take no stand on any issue. In fact, you make no public appearances or utterances whatever. All you do is keep your name before the public, saturating the media with its repeated exposure. Such an "exposure" campaign was mounted on behalf of one Pat Milligan. For months the city of San Bernardino, California was flooded with billboards, newspaper ads, and leaflets proclaiming: *"Three Cheers for Pat Milligan."* That was all. Pat Milligan was elected.

B. ATTITUDE CHANGE AND MANIPULATION

There appear to be three basic ways in which attitudes can be changed:
1. The use of positive reinforcement.
2. The use of negative reinforcement.
3. Changing the behavior triggered by the attitude.

Each of these will be examined in this section.

REINFORCEMENT AND ATTITUDE CHANGE

Positive Reinforcement

Irving Janis and his associates at Yale University initially determined the attitudes of subjects (Yale undergraduates) on various issues, including the likelihood of a cure for cancer (the subjects were optimistic) and the success of three-dimensional movies (they were pessimistic). The subjects were then required to read persuasive communi-

Focus 13.1
Attitudes toward Words

Listed below are five Turkish words. We would like you to give us your impression of each of the words. Of course, we realize that (unless you are familiar with the Turkish language) you could not reasonably guess the exact meanings. Simply estimate whether a particular word means something "good" or something "bad." Just circle the number on the scales below which you feel best describes the word in question:

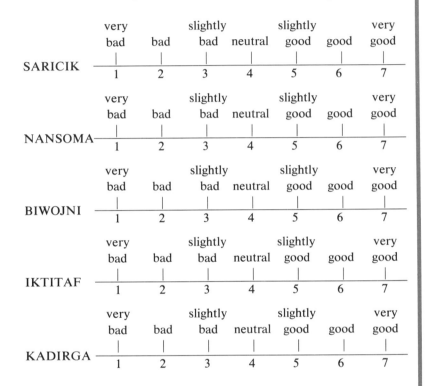

If some (or all) of the words seemed familiar to you, that's understandable. The words have been presented throughout the text at varying frequencies; the words KADIRGA, SARICIK, BIWOJNI, NANSOMA, and IKTITAF appeared at the top of text pages 1, 2, 5, 10, and 25 times, respectively. If you will get together with a group of classmates (preferably, the entire class) and add your circled numbers for each Turkish word, thereby obtaining a group "score" for each word, you will observe an interesting phenomenon. Although you are completely unfamiliar with the actual meanings of the words, you will find that the more times you have been exposed to a word, the "gooder" you, as a group, will have rated it. Thus, IKTITAF (presented 25 times) will be rated as a "better" word than KADIRGA (presented only once), merely because you, and your colleagues, have seen IKTITAF more often than KADIRGA.

cations designed to change their attitudes toward these issues. The conclusions of these communications were:

It will be more than 25 years before satisfactory progress can be expected in the search for a cure for cancer (pessimistic).

Within the next three years, three-dimensional films will replace two-dimensional films in practically all movie theaters (optimistic).

Eating while Reading

Half the students simply sat and read the arguments. The other half, however, were ushered into a room in which the experimenter was eating peanuts and sipping a soft drink; they were offered these refreshments with the simple explanation that "I brought some along for you too." It is important to note a few details of the situation. First, the person who administered the positive reinforcement (food and drink) was not the source of the persuasive communications; they were attributed to fictitious authors who were described as journalists or news commentators. Second, the person who administered the positive reinforcement did not endorse the communications (as a matter of fact, he explicitly stated that he did not necessarily endorse them). And third, the positive reinforcement had nothing to do with the content of the communications or the issues.

Nevertheless, when the subjects' attitudes were reassessed after reading the persuasive statements, those who had eaten while reading had shifted their attitudes in the direction of the opinions expressed to a greater degree than those who had not received any food. Apparently, the food reinforced attitude change in the direction of the arguments with which it was paired, even though it was entirely independent of the source, endorsement, or content of those arguments.

It thus seems that the salesman's ploy of inviting a customer to discuss a deal over drinks, the politician's "free lunch," and taking one's date to dinner have in common a sound psychological basis. Things do, indeed, go better with Coke.

Negative Reinforcement

If attitudes can be changed by positive reinforcement or reward, can they also be changed by negative reinforcement? One way to "negatively reinforce" an attitude would be to associate it with a negative stimulus, such as fear. Numerous studies of this question indicate that fear is generally effective in altering attitudes, but the relationship between fear and attitude change is complex. An experiment conducted by Irving Janis and Robert Terwilliger illustrates this point.

Degrees of Fear. Subjects were initially assessed for their attitudes toward smoking. Then they were asked to read a so-called "scientific digest prepared by members of the faculty of Yale University" arguing that smoking causes lung cancer. In reality, two such "digests" had been prepared by the experimenters. One, given to half the subjects, was designed to elicit *mild fear* concerning smoking. It simply called attention, in highly objective and abstract language, to the dangerous consequences involved, for example:

Since cancer of the lungs is more likely to develop from moderate smoking than is cancer of the lips, some experts have advised all smokers to take account of the symptoms and prognosis of lung cancer. In contrast to cancer of the lips, cancer of the lung is described by medical authorities as a highly malignant disease which is extremely difficult to diagnose before it is too late for effective treatment. (Janis and Terwilliger, 1962)

The second report, received by the other half of the subjects, evoked *strong fear* by elaborating upon the seriousness of lung cancer and emphasizing the pain, tissue damage, and fatalities, and, in general, conveying a more dramatic, frightening picture of the consequences. For example:

Anywhere along the respiratory tract, a single cancerous cell can start the growth of a malignant tumor that eventually may kill. Such a tumor can prove fatal either by causing suffocation or by sending deadly cells into other vital parts of the body. . . . Lung cancer necessitates drastic surgery. In only one out of three victims brought to the hospital will the cancer be localized sufficiently so that the cancerous lung can be removed. Of these, 85 percent will be dead within five years, most of them within two.

Following exposure to these different communications, the subjects' smoking attitudes were remeasured. Strikingly, it was found that the statement employing *mild* fear was more effective in changing attitudes than the one using strong fear. Whereas two-thirds of the subjects exposed to the mild-fear message changed their attitude in an antismoking direction, only half of the strong-fear subjects changed toward antismoking; 18 percent actually became more prosmoking!

The Boomerang Effect. Thus, a mild or moderate amount of fear is effective in changing attitudes, but there seems to be some optimal level of fear beyond which not only is effectiveness reduced, but also a "boomerang" effect is produced. Why is this so? Probably because many people cannot cope realistically with strong or intense fear. Rather, extreme fear simply arouses their psychological defenses so that they tend to distort, minimize, deny, ignore, or reject the information presented. In any event, the results of the Janis and

Terwilliger experiment suggest that while fear is an effective means of changing attitudes, strong fear should be avoided. A little fear is a good thing. Thus, the American Cancer Society ad on the left in Figure 13.1 is probably less effective than the one on the right.

(For a discussion of rewards and punishments in brainwashing and interrogation as a method of attitude change, see Focus 13.2, page 434.)

BEHAVIOR

Thus far we have been concentrating on attempts to change attitudes through attack on the attitude itself. What if the behavior triggered by the attitude were changed? Would this result in a change of the underlying attitude?

Leon Festinger of the New School for Social Research (New York) and Merrill Carlsmith of Stanford University had their subjects perform "the most boring and tedious task we could devise" under the guise of "an experiment on motor performance." For half an hour a subject sat at a table and placed a dozen spools on a tray, emptied the tray, refilled it with spools, and so on. Then, for another half hour the subject was presented with a board containing 48 square pegs, and required to turn each peg a quarter turn clockwise, then another quarter turn, and so on. At the end of the hour of this incredibly dull, monotonous activity, the subject was stopped by the experimenter, thanked, and told that the experiment was over. The experimenter went on to say, however, that he was conducting a similar experiment, using the same boring task, in which the subject was led to believe beforehand that the task was to be pleasant and exciting. Unfortunately, his regular assistant, who conveyed this information

Mark Waters was a chain smoker. Wonder who'll get his office?

Too bad about Mark. Kept hearing the same thing everyone does about lung cancer. But, like so many people, he kept right on smoking cigarettes. Must have thought, "been smoking all my life... what good'll it do to stop now?" Fact is, once you've stopped smoking, no matter how long you've smoked, the body begins to reverse the damage done by cigarettes, provided cancer or emphysema have not developed. Next time you reach for a cigarette, think of Mark. Then think of your office—and your home.

American Cancer Society

"We'll miss ya, baby"

FEMME FATALE.
Cigarettes are part of the costume. Next week she learns how to inhale.

MAN OF DESTINY.
Smokes because he thinks it's good for his "image." Coughs a lot, too

WISE GUY.
Likes to keep a cigarette in his mouth when he talks. Very hard to understand.

ME-TOO.
Smokes because his friends do. Doesn't know whether he likes it or not.

Cigarettes can kill you. Keep smoking 'em and they may. We'll miss ya, baby.
american cancer society

FIGURE 13.1 Antismoking advertisements from the American Cancer Society.

to the subjects, had not shown up today. Would the subject (who had just completed the task) be willing to help out? All the subject had to do was to go into the next room where the next subject was waiting, and tell the person that the task is fun, interesting, enjoyable, intriguing, and so on. In addition, the experimenter was willing to pay for the services.

The Situation. Let's analyze the situation. The subject has just undergone a tedious experience, a dull, repetitive task, and has a negative attitude toward it. Now the subject is being asked to lie about the task, to tell another person that the task is really pleasant and enjoyable. And the subject is being paid to lie—but here Festinger and Carlsmith introduced an important experi-

Focus 13.2

Brain-washing

The technology of changing people's attitudes is obviously a powerful tool for administrators, political candidates, and advertisers—in fact, for anyone who depends on the attitudes of other people. Usually, the change of attitude must be accomplished with the tacit consent of the people we are trying to change. Those we are reaching for have the choice of turning off the TV, closing the magazine, or putting down the newspaper. But in recent years the American public has become increasingly aware of certain techniques of altering opinion that are intended for a *captive* audience. One of these techniques is the "thought reform" or "brainwashing" practiced by Chinese captors on American military prisoners during the Korean War. Through the methods employed a basically loyal American soldier could be "convinced" that he and the United States government were guilty of heinous "crimes against the people." (Unlike the Vietnam War, the Korean undertaking was fully backed by American public opinion.)

In the brainwashing process the prisoner was *informed* that he was guilty, that he had committed "crimes against the people," and that his refusal to cooperate and confess would result in his punishment by fellow captives who had already "advanced" considerably in the reform of their thinking. One former prisoner of the Communist Chinese during the Korean War described the abuse he suffered at the hands of his cell-mates: "They would put me in the middle of a cell and walk around me. Each one as he passed would spit in my face and hit me in the stomach." It was implied to the prisoner that he would receive better treatment if he confessed to his crimes. The abuse he suffered included lack of rest and being made physically helpless with bonds so that for his most basic needs he was at the mercy of his captors.

When exhaustion, pressure, and physical abuse were pressed far enough, a breaking point was reached where the prisoner made a false confession for the sake of some relief from the treatment he could no longer endure. Suddenly, cell-mates and interrogators became friendlier—they were now "fellow students" and "instructors" of the prisoner. But there was a continuing pressure for greater and greater conformity to communist ideology, more vehement denunciation of self and country. Days would be spent confessing "imperialist attitudes" and the jargon of Marxism would become the fabric of everyday speech. Originally, the prisoner knew what part of his "confession" was a fabrication, but the borders between truth and fiction gradually became blurred. After a while ". . . you begin to believe all this, *but it is a special kind of belief. You are not absolutely convinced, but you accept it. . .*" With greater compliance came better treatment and the friendliness of those around. Finally, the prisoner would make a public confession of his crimes that was useful propaganda for his captors. After this he was usually released. Upon release the "reformed" prisoner often felt alienated from his own countrymen, feeling more "communist" than "Western." But as dramatic as the results of the brainwashing process were, they were usually temporary. Eventually, the released prisoner's attitudes reverted to their original form and he often expressed enormous hostility toward those interrogators who, he felt, had manipulated him.

The Korean War brainwashing occurred in a very special situation: the captors had complete control over the physical and, more importantly, the social environments of their captives. Under such conditions a number of psychological manipulations become possible that would be difficult, if not impossible, to bring to bear in a less controlled setting. James McConnell of the University of Michigan has noted a number of these conditions: (1) It is possible to isolate the "target" of attitude change from other people or groups who would support his old attitudes. (2) Since the "target" is completely dependent on the "source" for satisfaction of his needs and his safety, persuasive communications that couple hope with fear have exceptional impact. (3) The "source" is in a position where he can reinforce or reward the "target" for attitude change.

Brainwashing received much publicity after the Korean War, and many Americans are at least familiar with the process, but it is surprising to many to realize that "thought reform" may not be the exclusive domain of foreign powers. Philip Zimbardo of Stanford University has suggested that an even more sophisticated form of thought control is commonly practiced by the American police in their attempt to secure confessions from suspects — techniques so powerful that innocent suspects are known to have confessed to capital offenses.

When Zimbardo examined police interrogation procedures, he found that they bore much in common with those employed in brainwashing. In the first place, the suspect is isolated from any form of psychological and social support, beginning with the physical environment of the interrogation room itself. The room is bare, usually windowless, with two chairs and perhaps a desk. The suspect is placed in an armless, straight-backed chair so that he cannot become comfortable and can be easily observed. There are no pictures, no ashtrays, not even a paper clip that might serve as a form of psychological support. As for the social-psychological characteristics of the situation, the suspect is not interrogated in the presence of anyone he knows. Even a request for a lawyer may be countered with the argument that a lawyer is a "stranger" who will interfere with the "man-to-man" conversation between the suspect and his "friends" in the station. Such manipulations ensure that the suspect is under the complete control and domination of the interrogator. Thus the suspect is placed in a position of vulnerability.

Now, as Zimbardo points out, the situation is ripe for the subtle, and sometimes not-so-subtle, manipulation of the suspect by fear and hope. One very effective method is the "Mutt and Jeff" technique, in which two interrogators enact a well-rehearsed routine. First Jeff, who is big, cruel, and relentless, threatens and badgers the suspect. Then Mutt intervenes and asks Jeff to leave the room. Alone with the suspect, Mutt confides that he detests Jeff's tactics (at the same time implying that they can get worse). He may go on to say that the offense being charged was not so serious, that he understands how these things happen, that there were extenuating circumstances, and so on. He may put his arm around the suspect's shoulder, grip his hand, and offer to get him a drink of water. In short, he is protective, supportive, and sympathetic. Once he has gained the suspect's confidence, he delivers the punch line: if the suspect wishes to avoid further and intensified unpleasantries with Jeff (fear), he must cooperate quickly and confess to Mutt (hope).

The interrogator is also in a position to promise rewards. He may imply that a confession will bring mercy or a reduced or suspended sentence. All the suspect has to do is confess, to sign a simple statement, to go along in this small thing; once he has done that, it will be all over, he will be forgiven, even praised. It is hardly surprising, then, Zimbardo notes, that people subjected to such pressures not only confess to crimes they have not committed, but even come to believe in their own false confessions.

---

mental manipulation. In half the cases they didn't pay the subject very much, only $1.00. In the other half of the cases they paid the subject rather handsomely, $20.00. So the stage was set: the subject entered the next room, prepared to lie, having been paid $1.00 or $20.00 to do it. The "next subject" (a young woman who was actually a confederate of the experimenter) simply sat quietly, letting the real subject say a few nice things about the task. Then she interrupted with: "Oh, I'm surprised, because a friend of mine took the experiment last week and told me I ought to try to get out of it." The subject then responded with something like "Oh,

no, it's really very interesting. I'm sure you'll enjoy it," and went on to convince the girl of the pleasures that awaited her.

A Paradox. Afterwards, each subject was interviewed privately and asked such questions as, "Were the tasks interesting and enjoyable?" and "Would you have any desire to participate in another similar experiment?" Did anybody's attitude change toward the task and experiment and, if so, who changed more, the $1.00 or the $20.00 liars? The subjects who were paid $1.00 to lie shifted their attitude in the direction of the lie. In contradiction to common sense, the $20.00 subjects did not show any attitude change.

A more critical analysis, however, reveals that this paradox is more apparent than real. Festinger and Carlsmith point out that the students who were paid $20.00 for lying had a justification for their behavior—namely, 20 dollars—and thus felt no real discrepancy between their private attitude toward the task and their public portrayal of the task. The subjects who were paid only a dollar had no such justification or rationalization to fall back upon —after all, there are few people whose self-esteem is so low that they can be bought for a dollar. They were forced to face the uncomfortable fact of *a discrepancy between their attitude and their behavior, what they believed and what they did (Festinger calls this* **cognitive dissonance**). They could not change or retract their behavior—they lied, and they knew that they lied. But they *could* change their attitude to bring it into line with their behavior. And they did so.

Such findings have widespread implications for the solution of social problems, from gun control to the energy crisis: if you can change people's attitude-related behaviors, their attitudes may also change. In the section on prejudice we will illustrate an application of this principle. In Focus 13.3 the principle of cognitive dissonance is also applied to understanding the behavior of "true believers" whose prophecies of world destruction have failed.

There is a corollary lesson to be learned from the Festinger-Carlsmith study. Although you can change a person's attitude by inducing behavior that conflicts with that attitude, the inducement must be just sufficient to elicit that behavior, and no more—otherwise you are providing the person with a ready-made justification for

the behavior, and the attitude will be unlikely to change.

RESISTANCE TO ATTITUDE CHANGE

Once formed or changed, how can attitudes be made *resistant* to change? The "inoculation" technique proposed by William McGuire of Yale University affords an answer.

Inoculation

McGuire views an attempt to change a person's attitude as analogous to the attack on an organism by a virus. The person's resistance to a disease can be increased by inoculation with a small dose of the virus, not large enough to cause the disease, but large enough to stimulate the production of antibodies that will serve as defenses in the event of future exposure to the disease itself. So, too, it should be possible to strengthen an attitude's resistance to change by "inoculating" the individual with weak attacking arguments ("virus") and requiring the person to develop refuting arguments ("antibodies") in defense of the attitude.

An Example. Let's take an example. A group of subjects strongly endorses the following attitude (almost everyone does):

Everyone should brush the teeth after every meal if at all possible.

Then they receive the "inoculation," a weak one-line argument against regular tooth-brushing:

Too frequent brushing tends to damage the gums and expose the vulnerable parts of the teeth to decay.

Focus 13.3
When Prophecies Fail

In the Judeo-Christian tradition that dominates our culture, belief in prophecy in the sense of specific predictions concerning crucial future events is an integral part of the religious convictions of many people. The prophecy, when verified, shows that God has spoken through his prophet. But what happens when prophecies fail? Do the believers and the uncommitted perceive the failure as evidence that the prophet has "flunked"? This was precisely the question that Leon Festinger, Henry Riecken, and Stanley Schachter set out to investigate a few years ago when they read that a certain Mrs. Marian Keach had received word "from outer space" that America would be destroyed by flood and submerged "like Atlantis and Mu" by December 31. Further, the faithful who gathered around Mrs. Keach were to be rescued by a spaceship.

Festinger, Riecken, and Schachter were interested in observing carefully what happens when prophecy fails. To do so, they needed to have a current, and therefore *observable,* instance of a group whose members held a belief that was relevant to their actions and who had committed themselves to that belief by actions that were difficult or impossible to undo. Many members of Mrs. Keach's group had exposed themselves to ridicule by publicly identifying themselves with the group. They had even disposed of their worldly possessions in order to join her. It was also important that the belief to which the group was committed was specific enough to be confirmed or disconfirmed by events: the occurrence or nonoccurrence of the flood and the spaceship rescue certainly met this requirement. To study the group carefully, the investigators infiltrated Mrs. Keach's group and became members in good standing. They secretly kept careful notes of their observations.

When December 31 came and passed how would the "faithful" respond? Did they simply leave in anger and embarrassment? When the rendezvous time with flood and spaceship arrived—and nothing happened— Mrs. Keach received a message that the faith of her group had resulted in the sparing of America. The flood had been averted. The faithful received this news with elation and, indeed, began recruiting new converts as they had not done before.

Festinger, Riecken, and Schachter had hypothesized that having committed themselves strongly to the belief in Mrs. Keach's "revelation," the fact of its disconfirmation would represent a stressful cognitive dissonance. Further, they predicted that the group would seek to reduce the dissonant elements. (Dissonant elements are any facts or observations that tend to discredit the commitment.) By reinterpreting the prophecy, the group would reduce the dissonance of its failure. By converting new members to the faith, the group would increase consonant elements—in this case, people who agreed with the original members. Unlike the flood and the spaceship, these predictions both came to pass.

Then they are required to write a brief essay refuting this attack on their attitude. Now comes the critical part of the experiment. The subjects are exposed to a full-scale, strong attack upon their attitude toward tooth-brushing:

SOME DANGERS OF EXCESSIVE
TOOTH BRUSHING

Many people brush their teeth more or less automatically after each meal without paying any attention to medical reports that call this procedure into question. Recent medical and biological studies indicate that the beneficial effects of constant tooth brushing have been exaggerated. Furthermore, it has been demonstrated that a number of bad effects can result from brushing teeth so often. Tooth pastes and powders by necessity contain harsh abrasives that pit the protective enamel of the teeth and open them to infection. Also biochemical studies indicate that most tooth decay occurs while the food is still in one's mouth, so that the brushing comes too late to do much good. Hence, medical authorities are beginning to urge that instead of brushing our teeth so frequently, we take other measures to improve dental health, such as a better diet. Let us review some of this recent evidence demonstrating that constant tooth brushing does not do any great amount of good and can do much harm.

Many tooth pastes and powders have been found to contain harsh abrasives which tend to wear down the enamel sheath that covers our teeth. The enamel sheath is a protective covering over our teeth which also gives them their characteristic whiteness. The abrasives found in dentifrices wear and pit the enamel and throw open a path through which the decay-causing bacteria can invade and destroy our teeth. The presence of some harsh abrasives is required in both tooth pastes and powders in order for these dentifrices to do an adequate job of making our teeth look clean. It is, therefore, inevitable that some harm is done to the enamel whenever we brush our teeth. While the abrasive

effect of each brushing is very slight, the accumulated effects of constant brushing can be disastrous. Hence, brushing after every meal can well cause more harm than good.

Furthermore, it has been conclusively shown (Columbia Dental School, 1957) that almost all tooth decay occurs while the food is still in the mouth. By the time the meal is over and one has a chance to brush his teeth it is already too late for the brushing to do much good. The decay-producing activity of the bacteria depends on certain digestive enzymes which are liberated only while the food is actually in the mouth. Hence, when we stop eating and these enzymes are no longer secreted, the bacteria can no longer produce decay. Since we do not, of course, brush our teeth until after we have finished eating, this measure is, so to speak, like closing the barn door after the horse has already escaped. It would be wiser to utilize safer and more effective ways of preventing dental disease, such as a better diet or more frequent visits to the dentist. Since tooth brushing after every meal can do so little good and, as we have just seen, has serious harmful effects, it seems unwise to recommend this constant brushing as a general health measure. (Papageorgis and McGuire, 1961)

Effectiveness of Inoculation. Although the subjects have not been inoculated against these specific arguments (note that the weak point used in the inoculation is not present in the strong argument), their attitude toward tooth-brushing nevertheless shows remarkable resistance to change! And they are not only more resistant than people who have *not* been inoculated before being attacked, but they are also more resistant than people who have received arguments *supportive* of their attitude prior to attack. As a matter of fact, people who have received only supportive arguments are little more resistant to attack than people who have received no arguments at all. Please re-read this paragraph, because it is important for grasping the impact of McGuire's research.

Relevance of Inoculation

These findings are pertinent to situations beyond the laboratory walls. For example, most children develop their political attitudes in a "germ-free" environment in which they receive only supportive arguments concerning the virtues of our political system. Robert Hess, examining the political attitudes of some 12,000 school children, found that the schools emphasize the wisdom, benevolence, and infallibility of leaders, the power of the individual vote, and the desirability of consensus and unity. There is little classroom discussion of the role of debate, disagreement, and dissent, much less of such topics as lobbies and special interest groups, political patronage and "deals," slush funds and Watergates. As a result, children develop idealized, unrealistic attitudes about government and politics that are open to attack. For instance, eighth-graders believe that the "average person" has more influence on government than "rich people," "big companies," or "newspapers."

If we are interested in strengthening democratic attitudes, it might be desirable to inoculate children with some of the facts of political life. So inoculated, as adults they might be less vulnerable to attacks on the democratic system and counterproductive proposals. They might also be less susceptible to cynical disillusionment and become more sophisticated, aware, and politically active citizens.

ATTITUDES AND THE MEDIA: VIOLENCE

A serious social issue involving attitudes is the effect of the mass media, especially television, on attitudes. More than 95 per cent of homes in the United States have television sets, more than have telephones or bathtubs. A book is considered to be a "best seller" if it reaches a million people. A magazine is doing very well indeed if it has a circulation of five or ten million. But every hour of every night, seven nights a week, year in and year out, any one of the three major networks has the attention of 30 million people! In the average home the television set is on almost six hours a day, day after day, week after week. At this rate the average person will watch television nine full *years* in a lifetime. The average adolescent spends as much time watching television as at school—or even more. The average child entering kindergarten has already spent more hours camped in front of a television set than he or she will spend in a college classroom earning a degree. And here, in the words of Nicholas Johnson, former Commissioner of the Federal Communications Commission, is what the child is being taught:

. . . that conflicts are resolved by force, violence, or 'destroying the enemy,' and not by listening, thinking or understanding; that troubles are dissolved by the 'fast, fast, fast relief' that comes from pills (vitamins, headache pills, sleeping pills, stomach pills, tranquilizers, pep pills, or 'the pill'), and not from dedication, training, or discipline; that personal satisfaction comes from the passivity of possession and consumption (conspicuous whenever possible) of cars, appliances, and toys, cigarettes, soft drinks, and beer, and not from the activity of commitment.

To make this discussion of the possible effects of the media on attitudes more concrete, let's focus on attitudes toward violence. In one city alone, the television stations carried 7887 acts of violence in

FIGURE 13.2 Viewing television violence plays an important role in forming children's attitudes toward violent behavior.

one week. Christmas was celebrated with a traditional Western containing 13 homicides. And this steady diet of violence is cumulative: between the ages of five and 14 the average child viewer witnesses the annihilation of 12 *thousand* human beings. It was in part statistics such as these that led the National Commission on the Causes and Prevention of Violence to conclude:

Violence on television encourages violent forms of behavior, and fosters moral and social values about violence in daily life which are unacceptable in a civilized society. We believe it is reasonable to conclude that a constant diet of violent behavior on television has an adverse effect on human character and attitudes.

Evidence. While these statistics on the incidence and intensity of violence on television are impressive, they do not,

of course, constitute evidence that the mass media do, in fact, affect attitudes toward violence. In recent years psychologists have devoted a good deal of attention to this problem, and numerous studies have been conducted. A good example is an experiment by Richard Walters of the University of Waterloo (Ontario).

Walters had half his subjects watch a knife fight scene from the movie "Rebel without a Cause." The other half of his subjects watched an innocuous film entitled "Picture Making by Teenagers." With the exception of viewing these different film sequences, all subjects were treated exactly alike. They were introduced to another "subject" (a confederate of the experimenter) and told that they were to serve as "teachers" in a learning task. The other "subject" would be the "learner," to whom they were to deliver a shock whenever he made an error. The "teachers" had at their disposal a switch with 11 levels of shock intensity; they were simply told to "punish him by selecting one of the shock intensities and depressing the lever."

The experimental situation was thoroughly realistic and the subjects firmly believed that they were inflicting pain upon another individual. Before beginning the "learning task" the subjects were given a few shocks in order to demonstrate the different levels of pain intensity from which they could choose to punish the "learner." (In reality, of course, the confederate didn't receive any shocks, since the experimenter surreptitiously removed the electrode just before the "learning task" began.) As for the results: The subjects who had seen the violent scene delivered more intense shocks than those who had viewed the nonviolent scene.

Characteristics of the Hero. Albert Bandura and his associates have demonstrated, in a series of experiments, that the effect of observed violence on a predisposition to actual violence is enhanced when the observed model is prestigious, successful, and rewarded for violence. These characteristics are frequently present in the town tamer, the private detective, or even the glamorous gangster. And the University of Wisconsin's Leonard Berkowitz has found that the effect of observed violence on viewer violence is enhanced when the viewer is led to believe that the observed violence is justified. This finding has rather grave implications for the pleadings of the television industry, which often defends itself on the grounds that it portrays violence in the context of "crime doesn't pay" or "the bad guy gets his." Such portrayals apparently not only encourage expression of violence by the members of the audience, but also legitimize a model for solving interpersonal problems, namely, violence. If the TV folkhero repeatedly gains his ends through violence, then the implication is clear: violence is a good thing.

C. AN ATTITUDE: PREJUDICE

Prejudice is an attitude, a predisposition to act in a discriminatory manner toward certain people. How are prejudicial attitudes formed and maintained? The same factors that enter into the formation and maintenance of attitudes in general also play a role in prejudice. We will now examine two of these sources—social influences and personality characteristics—as they apply to prejudice.

SOCIAL INFLUENCES

Social influences include economic factors as well as cultural norms. Consider the economic payoff involved for an advantaged, privileged group that is free to exclude or exploit a disadvantaged, underprivileged group. Economic decline can also exacerbate prejudice. For example, when cotton was a vital staple there was a strong relationship between cotton prices and lynching of blacks—when cotton prices fell, the number of lynchings rose. Further, people tend to believe that the economically deprived "get what they deserve," that is, that they are somehow responsible for their condition or, if not responsible, are inherently worthless and undeserving. There is also a parallel tendency for members of the exploitative group to justify themselves on the grounds that the exploited group is undesirable and unworthy, and therefore deserves its fate.

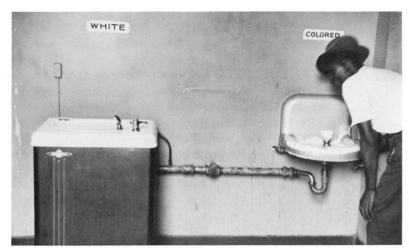

FIGURE 13.3 The once widespread separate facilities for blacks and whites had a detrimental effect on the self-image of black Americans.

Cultural Norms. Although economic factors certainly play a role in prejudice, cultural norms are a more pervasive influence. Consider the following study conducted by Thomas Pettigrew of Harvard University. Pettigrew selected eight small towns, four in the North (New England) and four in the South (Georgia and North Carolina). He went into these towns and polled whites on their antiblack prejudice. In order to disguise the purpose of the investigation and encourage honest answers, Pettigrew told the respondents that the poll was "concerned with the effects of the mass media upon public opinion." The poll contained such antiblack statements as the following, and the respondents were asked whether they agreed or disagreed:

Most Negroes would become officious, overbearing, and disagreeable if not kept in their place.

Laws which would force equal employment opportunities for both Negroes and whites would not be fair to white employers.

Negroes have their rights, but it is best to keep them in their own districts and schools and to prevent too much contact with whites.

Negroes do not deserve the right to vote.

Seldom, if ever, is a Negro superior to most whites intellectually.

The granting of wide educational opportunities to Negroes is a dangerous thing.

In spite of what some claim, Negroes do have a different and more pronounced body odor than whites. (Pettigrew, 1958)

After obtaining a gauge of antiblack sentiments, Pettigrew then gave the respondents a personality test designed to identify people with a high potential for prejudice (see Focus 13.4: The Prejudiced Personality).

Reprise and Results. To review, Pettigrew had three sorts of information concerning his respondents: (1) their area of residence in the country, (2) their personality predisposition to prejudice, and (3) their frequency of endorsement of antiblack statements. When he compared these three pieces of information he found two things:

Focus 13.4

The Prejudiced Personality

Is there such a thing as a prejudiced personality? For the answer to this question we turn to a monumental and classic study in psychology, *The Authoritarian Personality*. Although this study is over 20 years old and has been the center of considerable controversy, it remains the single most important piece of research ever conducted on this subject. The study was conducted at the University of California at Berkeley under the direction of Theodor W. Adorno, Else Frenkel-Brunswik, Daniel Levinson, and Nevitt Sanford, and took over two years to complete. Although it is not possible to summarize the 990 pages of the study here, we would like to present some of its techniques and findings to you.

The investigation was prompted by the events of World War II, particularly those that transpired inside Nazi Germany, and thus was initially directed at understanding the psychological bases of anti-Semitism. As work progressed, however, it became evident that the same personality characteristics that underlay anti-Semitism also underlay prejudice in general. After many trial runs, revisions, and revisions of revisions, the investigators succeeded in developing a personality inventory that could identify prejudiced people or, more accurately, people with a high potential for prejudice. This inventory is the widely used F-scale ("F" stands for "fascism"). Sample items from the F-scale appear in Table 13.2. Agreement with the statements is scored in the direction of prejudice; the higher the score, the more prejudiced the person.

By studying people who scored high on the F-scale with personality tests and clinical interviews, the researchers developed this composite of the prejudiced personality: People with a prejudiced personality place great stock in conventional morality, values, and behavior. They tend to be extremely inhibited in expression of impulses, overcontrolled, and rigid. This rigidity is also characteristic of their thought processes; they tend to view events and make judgments in simplistic, "black-white," "either-or" terms. They exhibit a minimum of self-criticism or insight. They are greatly concerned with authority and power, deferring to those above themselves in the power structure and exploiting those below. In general, their relationships with others are impersonal and manipulative, being more means to ends rather than ends in themselves.

The family backgrounds of the prejudiced have common characteristics. For example, they had parents who were harsh and punitive, who demanded absolute and unquestioning obedience to arbitrary rules and standards, and who, at the same time, were intolerant of any expression of resentment or rebellion on the child's part. Further, the parents tended to employ disciplinary techniques that overwhelmed the child. For example: "I was kind of temperamental when I was little. I had temper tantrums if I didn't get my way. My mother cured them—she dunked me under the water faucet until I stopped screaming." "Father picked up on things and threatened to put me in an orphanage . . . mother had a way of punishing me—locked me in a closet—or threatened to give me to a neighborhood woman, who she said was a witch . . . I think that's why I was afraid of the dark." (Adorno *et al.*, 1950)

TABLE 13.2   **Sample items from the F-scale**

1. Obedience and respect for authority are the most important virtues children should learn.
2. A person who has bad manners, habits, and breeding can hardly expect to get along with decent people.
3. If people would talk less and work more, everybody would be better off.
4. The businessman and the manufacturer are much more important to society than the artist and the professor.
5. Science has its place, but there are many important things that can never possibly be understood by the human mind.
6. Young people sometimes get rebellious ideas, but as they grow up they ought to get over them and settle down.
7. What this country needs most, more than laws and political programs, is a few courageous, tireless, devoted leaders in whom the people can put their faith.
8. No sane, normal, decent person could ever think of hurting a close friend or relative.
9. Nobody every learned anything really important except through suffering.
10. What the youth needs is strict discipline, rugged determination, and the will to work and fight for family and country.

(1) the Southerners were considerably more prejudiced than the Northerners as revealed by their responses to antiblack statements; (2) the Southerners did *not* have more prejudice-prone personalities than the Northerners as indicated by personality test scores. In other words, although there was no difference between Southerners and Northerners in *potential* for prejudice in terms of their personality make-up, the degree of prejudice did vary by region.

This is not to say that personality factors do not play a role in prejudice (we shall soon see that they do), but rather that social factors also operate. Although the South is changing, the region, especially the small towns, has long had cultural norms that explicitly sanction prejudice toward blacks. A more refined analysis of Pettigrew's findings lends added support to the notion that social forces can, and do, work to foster prejudice. For example, in the conventional family, the mother is the prime agent of transmission of cultural norms. Thus, it is pertinent to note that the women in Pettigrew's sample were more prejudiced than men in the South, but *not* in the North. Further, people who are socially ambitious and upwardly mobile must be carefully in tune with established norms to insure their rise in the social structure. Again, upwardly mobile members of the Southern sample tended to be more prejudiced than others, but this was *not* true of the upwardly mobile Northerners. Conformity to Northern norms—unlike conformity to Southern norms—does not imply antiblack attitudes. Similarly, political independents (that is, nonconformists) in the Southern sample were less prejudiced than others, while this is *not* so in the Northern sample. It is clear, then, that social factors play a significant role in prejudice.

PERSONALITY CHARACTERISTICS

Personality factors are also an important source of prejudice. For example, sometimes wishes and needs that are unacceptable to an individual are at the root of prejudice, as when the individual projects such needs onto others. Thus, a white may see blacks as irresponsible, happy-go-lucky, lazy, primitive, sexually potent, promiscuous, and so on—in short, all those things the white fears (or secretly longs) to be. Prejudice can also serve to bolster self-esteem and satisfy security needs. You may be poor and ignorant, but as long as you have that white skin you are better than any black. It was this sort of psychological mechanism that drew the attention of Robert Brannon of the University of Michigan.

Security Needs. Brannon was on hand when a church in a small town split over a racial issue. The national office of the church had come out in favor of desegregation. About half the members of the congregation in question were in favor of desegregation or at least were willing to comply with the national office's proclamation. The other half of the membership

were staunch segregationists, however, and withdrew to form their own church; the first canon of the new church was "Membership shall be reserved only to Christians of the white race."

Brannon hypothesized that if security needs were involved in the race prejudice of the church members, then these needs would be reflected in their religious involvement. Brannon reasoned this way: If someone feels threatened and insecure, that person would view church membership primarily as a means to an end; they would see it as a guarantee of salvation and an emotional crutch to lean on in time of trouble. A person with a secure self-image, on the other hand, would view religion as an end in itself and would live by its teachings, including tolerance and humanity.

The Study. In order to test this hypothesis, Brannon approached the members of the integrationist and segregationist factions with a questionnaire designed to assess the nature of their religious involvement. As predicted, members of the segregationist faction were much more likely to agree with such "means-to-an-end" sentiments as:

What religion offers me most is comfort when sorrows and misfortune strike.

The purpose of prayer is to secure a happy and peaceful life.

In contrast, the integrationist faction more strongly endorsed such "end-in-itself" statements as:

My religious beliefs are what really lie behind my whole approach to life.

Religion is especially meaningful to me because it answers my questions about the meaning of life. (Brannon, 1970)

Hence, the segregationist, prejudiced group demonstrated greater security needs than the intergrationist group. Thus it does appear that personality factors, such as security needs, can contribute to prejudice.

Review. Brannon had three sorts of information on his subjects. First, he had a measure of personality needs, as reflected in the questionnaire on the meaning of religion. Second, he had information on general social and cultural influences; that is, the original church membership was quite homogenous, consisting mainly of small businessmen and professionals living in the same geographical area. Third, he had an index of antiblack prejudice, as revealed by the segregationist-integrationist split. In Pettigrew's investigation, personality factors (prejudice-proneness) were constant, while social factors (area of residence) varied. In Brannon's study, social factors (area, income, etc.) were relatively constant, while personality factors (security needs) varied. This "mirror-image" contrast of the Pettigrew and Brannon studies is depicted in Figure 13.4. Different as they are, both studies clearly demonstrate the effects of the varied factors in prejudice.

We cannot conclude from these studies that one set of factors—social or personality—is more important in accounting for prejudice, but we *can* conclude that they both contribute to the problem. We can further conclude that, when social and personality factors work together, prejudice will be especially virulent. •

AN EXPERIMENT
IN PREJUDICE

It is difficult, if not impossible, for a member of a majority group to comprehend

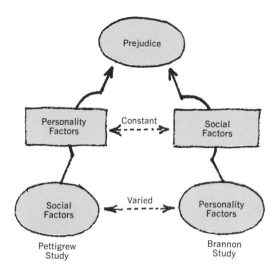

FIGURE 13.4 Schematic representation of the designs of the Pettigrew and Brannon studies.

what it is like to suffer the discrimination felt by a member of a minority. However, a simple experiment with children proved highly successful in enhancing this comprehension. The experiment was designed and conducted by Jane Elliot, a third-grade teacher in the Riceville (Iowa) Community Elementary School. Riceville is all white and all Christian. On Tuesday morning of National Brotherhood Week, right after the Pledge of Allegiance and "God Bless America," Elliot proposed the following "game." For the rest of the day, certain distinctions would be made between students on the basis of eye color. Brown-eyed children would have to sit at the back of the classroom and could not use the drinking fountain. Blue-eyed children would receive five extra minutes of recess and would go first for lunch. Further, brown-eyed children would not be permitted seconds at lunch, on the grounds that "they might take too much."

The segregation of the classroom would

also be strictly enforced on the playground; no mixing of blue-eyes and brown-eyes would be permitted. The blue-eyed children were told that they were smarter than the brown-eyed children, that they were cleaner, that their parents were less violent, that they were more civilized ("After all, George Washington had blue eyes"). The brown-eyed children were told that they were stupid and they had to wear black cardboard collars so that they could be spotted at a distance.

Throughout the day Elliot systematically praised the blue-eyed children and directed caustic comments at the brown-eyed, singling them out and criticizing them for behaviors that were, in reality, quite common among all the children. For example, Elliot would see a brown-eyed child slouching slightly in his seat, berate the child, and comment to the class that "brown-eyed people don't know how to sit on chairs." Or, a brown-eyed child would be caught not paying attention; Elliot would explain that "people with brown eyes are poor listeners."

First-day Results. Initially the children resisted, and even mildly protested, this discriminatory treatment of the brown-eyed class members. As the day progressed, however, the blue-eyes began to join Elliot with enthusiasm. They rapidly outstripped her in the viciousness of their prejudiced remarks and discriminatory behavior. In the space of a single morning, these children were earnestly recommending beatings for other children who just a few hours before had been friends.

The change was both dramatic and frightening. As one blue-eyed boy put it, "I felt like I was a king, like I ruled them brown-eyes, like I was better than them." At recess fights broke out between blue-eyed and brown-eyed children. Blue-eyed children consistently called brown-eyed children "brown-eyes." When Elliot asked a blue-eyed child why he did this, since the other children had brown eyes all their lives and he had never called them "brown-eyes" before, the boy replied, "To be mean. Just the same as other people call black people niggers." The brown-eyed children had their own perception of the situation, of course: "Everything bad happened to us." "When we were treated badly, we didn't even feel like trying."

Although such anecdotes are rather convincing evidence of the "success" of the experiment, Elliot also noted the time required for the blue-eyed and brown-eyed children to work through a deck of vocabulary cards. The blue-eyed children took three minutes, while the brown-eyed children required five minutes.

Roles Reversed. On Wednesday the roles were reversed (brown-eyes became the privileged group and blue-eyes the discriminated group), and the vocabulary card times were reversed: brown-eyes took two-and-one-half minutes while blue-eyes took over four minutes (Figure 13.5). And the subjective experiences of the children were also reversed; as a blue-eyed child remarked at the end of Wednesday, "I know what they felt like yesterday, like you're locking them up in prison and throwing the key away." Another blue-eyed child said that he felt "like a dog on a leash." But perhaps the most eloquent testimony was that of one little boy who, at the end of the experiment, tore his cardboard collar to pieces with his teeth.

A Question Raised. Many implications can be drawn from this little experiment in

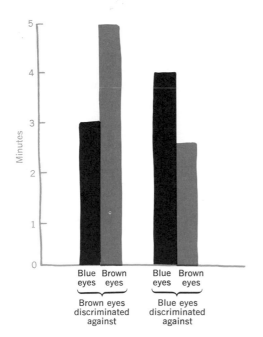

FIGURE 13.5 *Time for blue-eyed versus brown-eyed children to sort through vocabulary cards as a function of discrimination.*

prejudice, but one inescapable conclusion is the fact that *in less than one day,* with the sanction of proper social agents, it is quite possible to teach children to hate for no better reason than some arbitrary and meaningless distinction such as eye color. Of perhaps greater moment, Elliot's experiment demonstrates that, with equal rapidity, it is possible to shake children's feelings of self-worth and self-confidence, and to impair their educational performance. If such results can be obtained in a few hours, what can be the result of a lifetime of exposure to prejudice?

We will make an attempt to provide a partial answer to this question in the final section of this chapter, but first we would like to describe an "experiment" with a more positive outcome, a study in changing prejudiced attitudes.

D. COMBATING PREJUDICE

The major obstacle to overcoming prejudice is that this very attitude prevents a person from having experiences that would challenge those prejudices. For example, a white suburbanite never sees blacks as workers, bosses, mothers, fathers, school children—in short, as humans. The net result is that, in the absence of any direct experience with blacks, whites tend to mutually reinforce one another's prejudices toward blacks. One way to break this vicious circle would be to "force" whites to have extended and intimate contacts with blacks on an equal-status basis. This is, of course, well-nigh impossible under ordinary conditions. But Morton Deutsch of Columbia University and Mary Collins of the Postgraduate Center of Mental Health (New York) took advantage of fortuitous circumstances to conduct a natural experiment in breaking down prejudice.

EQUAL-STATUS CONTACT

It so happened that public housing projects in New York City were, by state law, completely desegregated, that is, families were assigned to apartments irrespective of race or personal preference. Just across the river, in Newark, New Jersey, however, blacks and whites inhabited the same project but were assigned to different buildings on the basis of race. In order to test the hypothesis that more frequent and intimate equal-status contacts between blacks and whites would decrease prejudice, the investigators interviewed white housewives in the integrated and segregated projects. They asked such questions as:

Can you remember what you thought colored people were like before you moved into the project? How much have your ideas about colored people changed since you have lived in the project? In what ways have they changed? What do you think made you change your ideas? (Deutsch and Collins, 1951)

Changes in Attitude. Most white women in both projects were initially quite prejudiced. Those in the integrated project did not like the prospect of living in the same building with black families but had moved into the project because it was the only way they could obtain adequate housing at a low rental. The interview revealed, however, that the women in the integrated project were now much less prejudiced than those in the segregated project; in fact, there was some suggestion that the women in the segregated project were even more prejudiced than when they had moved in. In contrast, the more prejudiced the integrated-project woman was at the outset, the greater was her favorable shift in attitude toward blacks.

The attitude shift was not only more favorable, it was also more realistic. For example, when asked to name the chief faults of blacks, the integrated women mentioned such personal problems as oversensitivity. The segregated women clung to their stereotypes, giving such responses as rowdy, troublemaking, and dangerous. Here are excerpts from interviews that illustrate the changes in attitude so commonly found in the integrated project:

I thought I was moving into the heart of Africa. . . . I had always heard things about how they were . . . they were dirty, drink a lot . . . were like savages. Living with them my ideas have changed altogether. They're just people . . . they're not any different.

I started to cry when my husband told me we were coming to live here. I cried for three weeks. . . . I didn't want to come and live here where there are so many colored people. I didn't want to bring my children up with colored children, but we had to come; there was no place else to go. . . . Well, all that's changed. I've really come to like it. I see they're just as human as we are. They have nice apartments; they keep their children clean, and they're very friendly. I've come to like them a great deal. I'n no longer scared of them. . . . I'd just as soon live near a colored person as a white; it makes no difference to me.

I was prejudiced when I moved in here but not any more. . . . I find there is no such thing as "my kind". . . . I was under the impression that every colored man that looked at you wanted to rape you or was going to pull out a razor. . . . I don't feel that way any more. . . . I know the people. I have been in their homes . . . . been to church with them. . . . I know they're not dirty.

Here is a typical comment from a segregated project interview:

I don't have anything to do with the colored people . . . they don't bother me . . . I don't mingle with them. I guess I don't like them because they're colored . . . the Bible says "God created them equal" so I guess they're equal, but I don't like them. I don't like living so close to them. I think they ought to be in separate projects. Let them live their lives and let us live ours. . . . My ideas haven't changed any since I've lived here. . . . They're colored and I'm white. They don't like us and we don't like them."

Changes in Behavior. These attitudes were not mere verbalizations; they were expressed in behavior. In the integrated project, most of the white women visited back and forth with black neighbors, went shopping or to the movies together, were members of the same social clubs, and helped out by doing the shopping or taking

Focus 13.5

Values and Behavior Changes

_____ freedom	_____ a world at peace
_____ happiness	_____ equality
_____ wisdom	_____ an exciting life
_____ self-respect	_____ a comfortable life
_____ mature love	_____ salvation
_____ a sense of accomplishment	_____ social recognition
_____ true friendship	_____ national security
_____ inner harmony	_____ a world of beauty
_____ family security	_____ pleasure

Rank each of the values listed above, according to their relative personal value for you, on a scale from 1 for the most important to 18 for the least important.

This list was used by Milton Rokeach, now at Washington State University, not merely to survey the ethical attitudes of subjects, but also to determine how values may be changed so as to alter behavior and persist over a long period of time. By **values**, *Rokeach means either an end-state (such as "family security") or a mode of behavior (such as "wisdom") that the individual regards as desirable.*

The average rankings of Rokeach's subjects followed the order of the listing of the values given above. After the values were ranked, half of the subjects were dismissed. The other half were shown the average rankings. They were also told that previous studies revealed a significant relationship between relative rankings of the values "freedom" and "equality" and degree of sympathy toward the civil rights movement. The implication was drawn that those who were unsympathetic to the civil rights movement were concerned only with their *own* freedom, but were relatively indifferent to the freedom of others—an inference designed to arouse cognitive dissonance among those who had given the typical ranking of "freedom" far over "equality." These students were then asked to rate their satisfaction or dissatisfaction with the ranking they had given to each specific value as well as with the general overall ranking.

Rokeach hypothesized that those who expressed the greatest dissatisfaction with their rankings of the values "freedom" and "equality" were providing evidence of significant cognitive dissonance between their values and their sense of fairness, their regard for the freedom of others as well as their own. According to the cognitive dissonance explanation of value change, these were the subjects who would show a significant and enduring change. Rokeach tested his hypothesis by having invitations to join the National Association for the Advancement of Colored People mailed to all of the subjects three to five months after the experimental session and again a year later. To join, students were required to mail in an application form and one dollar, indicating at least a minimal commitment. Of the 366 students approached, 53 joined the NAACP after the initial invitation. Of the 53, 39 were experimental subjects and only 14 were the dismissed subjects.

Rokeach also found that the dissatisfaction with the ranking of "equality" after the experimental session was an extremely accurate predictor of those who would respond to the NAACP invitation. General dissatisfaction with one's ranking seemed also to predict value changes, but not nearly so accurately as dissatisfaction with the specific value.

All in all, the results confirmed what Rokeach had suspected: dissonance between one's expressed values and one's estimate of the "rightness" of those values predicted a significant change in behavior. Further, this dissonance could be produced by nonauthoritarian means, by simply demonstrating the significance of expressed values.

care of the children when they were sick. This was true of less than five percent of the women in the segregated project.

It has often been said that "you can't legislate against prejudice." This may be true in the obvious sense that you are not legislating against prejudice, but against discrimination. Yet the Deutsch and Collins study, and others like it, demonstrate that legislation, fairly enforced, can and does result in a reduction of prejudice.

THE VICTIMS OF PREJUDICE

A great deal of psychological research has focused on the phenomenon of prejudice — what are its sources and how can it be changed — but comparatively little attention has been paid to the objects of prejudiced attitudes. What of the victims?

Kenneth Clark of the City University of New York and Mamie Clark of the Northside Center for Child Development (New York) presented preschool, kindergarten, and first- and second-grade black children with black and white dolls. Then they gave them the following instructions:

1. "Give me the doll that looks like you."
2. "Give me the doll that you like to play with."
3. "Give me the doll that is a nice doll."
4. "Give me the doll that is a nice color."
5. "Give me the doll that looks bad."

The Children Choose.   In response to the first request, most of the children handed the experimenter the black doll, indicating that their self-identity was black. To the second, third, and fourth requests, however, the children selected the white doll, indicating a preference for white. For the fifth and final request, the children chose the black doll. That is, they evaluated the black doll negatively. This rejection of the black doll occurred regularly among even three-year-old children. Here we have a situation, then, in which children of a given skin color, while basing their identity on that color, prefer a different color and reject their own. This study was conducted before the "black is beautiful" movement; it might be hoped that the degree to which this movement was successful would alter these findings if the study were conducted today.

Subjective Reactions.   What this attitude *does* to these children psychologically cannot be fully grasped from the bare results of the study. It does find expression in their spontaneous behavior when they were forced to explain their preferences between the black and white dolls. Most explanations were in rather simple, concrete (yet poignant) terms: " 'cause he's pretty," " 'cause he's white," or " 'cause he's ugly," "got black on him." Some children, however, attempted strained justifications for their choices: the black doll "looks bad because he hasn't got a eyelash," or the white doll's "feet, hands, ears, elbows, knees and hair are clean." One child explained his identification with the black doll with "I burned my face and made it spoil." Others simply broke down and cried, and ran out of the room sobbing.

What sorts of experiences could possibly promote such self-degradation and shame in young children? Obviously traumatic ones, but of such magnitude as to be beyond the understanding of most, if not all, whites. Read this event in the early life of James Farmer, the founder of the Congress of Racial Equality:

The earliest memory of my life is of an incident which occurred when I was three-and-a-half years old in Holly Springs, Mississippi. My father was registrar and professor of religion and philosophy at Rust College, a Negro Methodist institution there.

One hot summer day, my mother and I walked from the college campus to the town square, a distance of maybe half a mile. I remember it as clearly as though it were a few weeks ago. I held her finger tightly and we kicked up the red dust on the unpaved streets leading to the downtown area. When we reached the square she did her shopping and we headed for home. Like any other three-and-a-half-year-old on a hot day, I got thirsty.

"Mother," I said, "I want a Coke." She replied that we could not get Cokes there and I would

have to wait until we got home where there was lots of Coke in the icebox.

"But I want my Coke now," I insisted. She was just as insistent that we could not get a Coke now. "Do as I tell you," she said, "wait 'til we get home; you can have a Coke with plenty of ice."

"There's a little boy going into a store!" I exclaimed as I spied another child who was a little bigger than I. "I bet he's going to get a Coke." So I pulled my mother by the finger until we stood in front of what I recall as a drugstore looking through the closed screen doors. Surely enough, the other lad had climbed upon a stool at the counter and was already sipping a soft drink.

"But I told you you can't get a Coke in there," she said. "Why can't I?" I asked again. Her answer was the same, "You just can't." I then inquired with complete puzzlement, "Well, why can *he*?" Her quiet answer thundered in my ears. "He's white."

We walked home in silence under the pitiless glare of the Mississippi sun. Once we were home she threw herself across the bed and wept. I walked out on the front porch and sat on the steps alone with my three-and-a-half-year-old thoughts. (Farmer, 1969)

Now, go back and read Farmer's first six words again.

Science is supposedly a cold, impersonal, and thoroughly objective enterprise, yet one cannot read the Clark study without being moved. The self-images of these children, the basic element of "humanness," are being systematically and brutally destroyed. What must it mean for a five-year-old child to account for the color of his skin with the words "I burned my face and made it spoil?" As psychologist Erik Erikson has suggested, "Some day, maybe, there will exist a well-informed, well-considered, and yet fervent public conviction that the most deadly of all possible sins is the mutilation of a child's spirit.'' Kenneth Clark himself has summed it up well:

It is now generally understood that chronic and remediable social injustices corrode and damage the human personality, thereby robbing it of its effectiveness, of its creativity, if not its actual humanity. . . . Racial segregation, like all other forms of cruelty and tyranny, debases all human beings—those who are its victims, those who victimize, and in quite subtle ways those who are merely accessories.

SUMMARY

1. An **attitude** (page 427) is a predisposition to act in a certain way toward some aspect of one's environment, including other people. **Prejudice** (page 427) for example, is an attitude: it is a predisposition to act in a discriminatory manner toward a certain person or group of people.

A. Attitude Formation

2. Repeated exposure to an object or person, all things being equal, will result in a more favorable attitude toward that object or person.

3. Three factors are involved in the formation of attitudes: (1) Social influences, (2) personality characteristics, and (3) information.

B. Attitude Change and Manipulation

4. Attitudes can be changed by either positive or negative reinforcement. However, the negative reinforcement must not be too intense, or a boomerang effect occurs.

5. Attitudes can also be changed by changing the behavior triggered by the attitude, creating **cognitive dissonance** (page 437), or a discrepancy between attitude and behavior, which can only be resolved by attitude change.

6. Attitudes can be made resistant to change by "inoculating" an individual by means of weak arguments attacking the attitude. Upon subsequently being exposed to strong attacking arguments, such inoculated people are more resistant to change than people who have received only supportive arguments.

7. Laboratory research suggests that exposure to media representations of violence results in an increased predisposition to violent behavior if the person is instigated to violence.

C. An Attitude: Prejudice

8. Social factors (such as economic advantages or cultural norms) and personality factors (such as unconscious wishes, self-esteem, and security needs) both contribute to prejudice.

9. Prejudiced attitudes can, apparently, be fostered in children by a few hours of intensive training.

D. Combating Prejudice

10. Prejudice can be overcome if the groups involved have extended and intimate contacts with each other on an equal-status basis.

11. Prejudice can have devastating effects on the self-images of its victims, particularly children.

Chapter
Fourteen
Conformity
and
Involvement

At first blush the two components of this chapter—conformity and involvement—may appear to be strange bedfellows. In one sense, conformity and involvement do represent opposite and opposed forms of behavior, for as we shall see, conformity often leads to noninvolvement, while involvement often entails nonconformity. In another sense, though, conformity and involvement are characterized by many of the same social-psychological variables. These include the presence or absence of others, the behavior of others, and the perceived attributes of others. But we are getting far ahead of our story. The purpose of this chapter is to show you how psychologists have attacked such thorny social problems as conformity and involvement. **Conformity** *is defined as the adherence by an individual to social norms or group pressure.* **Involvement** *refers to an individual's taking action in an emergency situation that requires helping others.* To accomplish this purpose we are going to draw on two highly ingenious and sophisticated programs of research. One on conformity was conducted at Yale by Stanley Milgram, now of the City University of New York. The other, on involvement, was carried out jointly by Bibb Latané of Ohio State University and John Darley of Princeton University.

A. CONFORMITY

MILGRAM'S EXPERIMENT

You have responded to a newspaper advertisement soliciting subjects for "participation in a study of memory and learning" at a local university. When you arrive at the laboratory you are greeted by the experimenter, who gives you $4.50 and informs you that the payment is for showing up, and that the money is yours regardless of what happens during the experiment. The experimenter, dressed in a gray lab coat, is middle-aged, and his manner is impassive and somewhat stern. You are introduced to a fellow subject, a mild-mannered and likable man in his late forties. The experimenter gives you both a brief lecture on the presumed relationship between punishment and learning, and then continues:

But actually, we know *very little* about the effect of punishment on learning, because almost no truly scientific studies have been made of it in human beings.

For instance, we don't know how *much* punishment is best for learning—and we don't know how much difference it makes as to who is giving the punishment, whether an adult learns best from a younger or an older person than himself—or many things of that sort.

So in this study we are bringing together a number of adults of different occupations and ages. And we're asking some of them to be teachers and some of them to be learners.

We want to find out just what effect different people have on each other as teachers and learners, and also what effect *punishment* will have on learning in this situation.

Therefore, I'm going to ask one of you to be the teacher here tonight and the other one to be the learner. (Milgram, 1963)

The Task

You and the other subject then draw slips of paper from a hat to determine who will be "teacher" and who will be "learner." You draw "teacher." The experimenter then escorts you both to an adjacent room where the other subject, the "learner," is strapped into an electric chair "to prevent excessive movement" during shocks. Electrode paste is then applied to his wrist "to avoid blisters and burns," and an electrode is attached. The experimenter explains that the electrode is attached to a shock generator in the next room, and says, "Although the shocks can be extremely painful, they cause no permanent tissue damage." Somewhat apprehensive at this point, the learner confides that he has a history of heart trouble but is reassured by the experimenter.

You and the experimenter than leave the learner, strapped in his chair and hooked up to the shock generator, and you are escorted to the next room and seated before an impressive instrument panel. The panel consists of 30 lever switches arranged in a horizontal row. Each switch is labeled with the amount of voltage that it can deliver to the learner. The voltages range from 15 to 450 volts, with a 15-volt increment between each switch. In addition, groups of these switches bear the following labels: "Slight Shock," "Moderate Shock," "Strong Shock," "Very Strong Shock," "Intense Shock," "Extreme Intensity Shock," "Danger: Severe Shock." The last two switches are rather ominously marked "XXX."

The experimenter then proceeds to tell you that the material you are to "teach" the learner consists of a series of word pairs. First, you are to read the word pairs through an intercom to the learner in the next room. Then, you are to read the first word of a pair and four other words. The learner's task is to identify which of the four words was originally paired with the first word, and he will indicate his answer by pressing one of four switches in his room, which in turn will light one of four lamps in an answer box located on top of your panel. You are told to give a shock to the learner every time he is wrong, and to "move one level higher on the shock generator each time the learner flashes a wrong answer." You are also instructed to call out each voltage level before giving the

shock. Your final instructions are to "start from 15 volts and increase the shock level one step each time the learner gives a wrong answer."

Learning Begins. You begin the learning task. The learner is frequently wrong, and, as instructed, you proceed to deliver shocks following wrong answers, working up the shock scale. At 75 volts, you hear the learner give a grunt after the shock. Grunts also follow 90- and 105-volt shocks, and after the 120-volt shock the learner shouts, "Experimenter, the shocks are beginning to hurt!" You are somewhat concerned at this point, and look over at the experimenter and ask, "You want me to keep going?" The experimenter replies, "Please continue."

After the 135-volt shock you hear painful groans, and at the 150-volt level the learner cries out, "Experimenter, get me out of here! I won't be in the experiment any more! I refuse to go on!" At 165 volts you again turn to the experimenter, this time very agitated: "That guy is hollering in there. There's a lot of them [test words] here. He's liable to have a heart condition. You want me to go on?" The experimenter nods and says, "Please go on."

At 180 volts the learner screams, "I can't stand the pain!" Again you confront the experimenter: "He can't stand it! I'm not going to kill that man in there! You hear him hollering? He's hollering. He can't stand it. What if something happens to him? I'm not going to get that man sick in there. He's hollering in there. You know what I mean? I mean I refuse to take responsibility. He's getting hurt in there. He's in there hollering. Too many left here. Geez, if he gets them wrong. There's too many of them left. I mean who is going to take responsibility if anything happens to

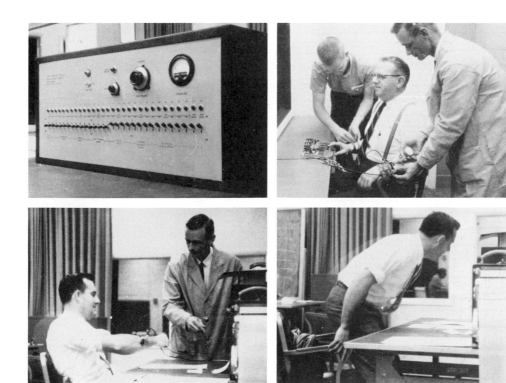

FIGURE 14.1 Shock apparatus and subjects used in Milgram's study. The shock generator is shown at upper left. In the next picture a "learner" is strapped into the electric chair. At lower left a "teacher" gets a sample shock. Lower right, the subject rises, refusing to continue with the experiment.

that gentleman?" Experimenter: "I will take responsibility." You: "All right."

At 195 volts, more agonized screams, and you again protest, "You see, he's hollering. Hear that. Gee, I don't know." Experimenter: "The experiment requires that you go on." You: "I know it does, sir, but I mean—he don't know what he's in for. He's up to 195 volts." At 240 volts you balk again: "Aw, no. You mean I've got to keep going up with the scale? No sir, I'm not going to kill that man! I'm not going to give him 450 volts!" Experimenter: "The experiment requires that you go on." You: "I know it does but that man is hollering in there sir . . ." At 315 volts there are only shrieks of agony whenever you deliver a shock. Shortly thereafter, even these cease.

What Do You Do? Do you indeed go on to deliver the 450-volt XXX maximum? Before you decide, it may be instructive to note that when people are asked what they would do in such a situation, almost all state that they would defy the experimenter and refuse to continue giving shocks. When senior psychology majors were asked to estimate how many subjects would continue to conform to the experimenter's instructions, the most pessimistic predicted three people in a hundred (the average prediction was 1–2 percent). When the same question was put to 40 psychiatrists at a leading medical school, they estimated that only one-tenth of 1 percent would go to 450 volts. In actuality, of all subjects, drawn from diverse occupational, educational, and age groups, *65 percent* comply completely with the experimenter's commands (Figure 14.2). In fact, the "teacher-experimenter" interaction we just portrayed for you is an actual transcript from the experimental situation and, despite this teacher's numerous and agitated objections, he unfailingly obeyed the experimenter and proceeded to the 450-volt level.

The Setup

In reality, of course, the "learner" was a confederate of the experimenter, he was never shocked, and his protestations and cries of distress were prerecorded. How did the experimenter arrange it so the naive subject was always the "teacher"? Both slips of paper drawn from the hat were marked "teacher."

The Subjects. The six out of ten people who did go along with the experimenter's demands did not do so with equanimity. Their distress is readily apparent from the transcripts, as it was at the time from one-way window observation. Indeed, they were in an extreme state of tension, as evidenced by sweating, trembling, stuttering, lip-biting, groaning, and nervous laughter, in addition to what they said. As one observer noted:

I observed a mature and initially poised businessman enter the laboratory smiling and con-

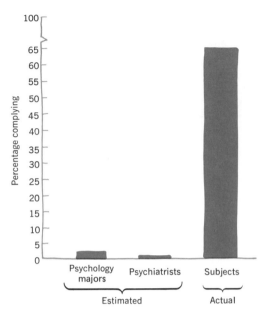

FIGURE 14.2 *Estimated and actual percentage of subjects complying with the experimenter's commands.*

fident. Within 20 minutes he was reduced to a twitching, stuttering wreck, who was rapidly approaching a point of nervous collapse. He constantly pulled on his earlobe, and twisted his hands. At one point he pushed his fist into his forehead and muttered: Oh God, let's stop it. And yet he continued to respond to every word of the experimenter, and obeyed to the end.

And this postexperimental interview with another obedient subject:

I'd like to ask you a few questions. How do you feel? I feel all right, but I don't like what happened to that fellow in there [the victim]. He's been hollering and we had to keep giving him shocks. I didn't like that one bit. I mean he wanted to get out but he [the experimenter] just kept going, he kept throwing 450 volts. I didn't like that.

Who was actually pushing the switch? I was,

but he kept insisting. I told him "No," but he said you got to keep going. I told him it's time we stopped when we get up to 195 or 210 volts.

Why didn't you just stop? He wouldn't let me. I wanted to stop. I kept insisting to stop, but he said "No.". . . I figured the voltage we were giving him was quite a bit. I wanted to stop but he [the experimenter] kept insisting not to stop. I mean the fellow in there is hollering "I don't want to do it. I want to get out of here. I want to get out of here!"

Why didn't you just disregard what the experimenter said? He says it's got to go on, the experiment.

Do you feel a little upset? Well, I mean I feel concerned about the gentleman in there, I do sir . . . I was getting ready to walk out . . . I couldn't see the point of going on when the guy is suffering in there. I figured he was having a heart attack or something. That's the reason I wanted to stop. . . . (*op. cit.*)

It is evident that the emotional strain these subjects were under was a result of their being caught in an approach-avoidance conflict of the type discussed in Focus 11.8. On one hand, the subject was faced with the experimenter's orders to shock the learner. On the other hand, the subject had aversions to hurting a fellow human being. The subject was, obviously, under considerable pressure. Although the majority of subjects resolved this conflict by succumbing to the experimenter, at some point the remainder defied him. Here is an excerpt from the transcript of a defiant one:

The man is banging. He wants to get out . . . I'm sorry. If the man wants to get out I'd just as soon stop . . . I don't want to administer any more (extremely excited) . . . I will gladly refund the check, but I will not harm this man . . . I'm sorry, I will not give him any more if he obviously wants to get out. There is no money in the world that will make me hurt another individual. (*op. cit.*)

Variations

Milgram has conducted a number of similar experiments designed to shed light on the conditions of conformity to the command of authority. For one, the closeness of the "learner" appears to affect whether the "teacher" obeys or defies the experimenter. In one experiment the learner was placed in the same room with the teacher, clearly visible and seated only one-and-one-half feet away. In this setting, 60 percent of the subjects defied the experimenter at some point, refusing to continue shocking the learner to the 450-volt maximum.

In another experiment the learner apparently received a shock only when his hand rested on a shockplate. At the 150-volt level the learner demanded to be released and refused to put his hand on the shockplate. The experimenter then ordered the teacher to force the learner's hand onto the shockplate. Seventy percent of the subjects in this experiment refused to go to the 450-volt level, but 30 percent *did* conform. That is to say, three out of ten people will, on command from a man in a lab coat, get up from a chair, walk over to a helpless victim who has been screaming in anguish, and physically force the person to take a XXX shock. But, of course, the fact remains that when the victim is physically near, conformity does drop off. Why this is so is not immediately clear. A number of factors could be responsible. One of these may be that the visual cues associated with the victim's suffering evoke empathic responses in the subject that provide a more concrete appreciation of what the victim may be going through. When the victim is not visible, however, the situation is analogous to that of a bombardier. That is, a bombardier is intellectually aware of the suffering and death he is causing but, because of distance and the anonymity of his victims, does not experience a strong emotional reaction—they are merely the "faceless enemy."

Proximity and Locus of Authority. The proximity of authority also appears to be a significant variable in conformity. For example, if the experimenter delivers commands by telephone or by tape recording, conformity drops sharply. If the experimenter re-enters the room when the subject refuses to deliver further shocks, however, continued obedience can frequently be reestablished. It is as if both the experimenter and the victim exert fields of force on the subject; these diminish in effectiveness with increasing psychological distance.

Another question that concerned Milgram was the issue of the locus of authority. Is it in the experimenter or in the institution of which the experimenter is a representative? After all, universities are pretty impressive places (at least to some people), and they are often held in respect and occasionally awe. Too, they have the aura of legitimacy, integrity, competence, and good intentions. Indeed, in Milgram's initial studies many of the subjects confided that they would never have shocked the learner had the experiment been conducted elsewhere. To check this out, Milgram moved the scene of the experiment to an office building in the downtown area of an industrial city. The whole setup was marginally respectable: a slightly run-down building, little furniture, with the fictitious title "Research Associates of Bridgeport" listed in the building directory. Subjects were told only that it was "a private firm conducting research for industry." And some subjects displayed skepticism:

. . . Should I quit this damn test? Maybe he passed out? What dopes we were not to check up on this deal. How do we know that these

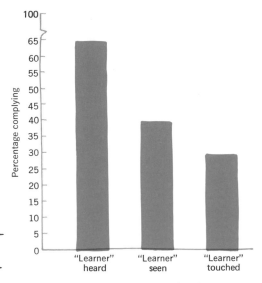

FIGURE 14.3 Percentage of subjects complying with the experimenter's commands as a function of the proximity of the "learner."

guys are legit? No furniture, bare walls, no telephone. We could of called the Police up or the Better Business Bureau. I learned a lesson tonight. How do I know Mr. Williams [the experimenter] is telling the truth . . . I wish I knew how many volts a person could take before lapsing into unconsciousness . . .

Nevertheless, the conformity of the subjects to the experimenter's demands was not appreciably reduced. Apparently the tendency to conform is primarily a function of the perceived authority of the individual rather than the institution.

Allies. What would happen if subjects were tested in groups, so that potential allies were available to defy the experimenter? If a naive subject was tested in the presence of two other "subjects" (actually, trained confederates of the experimenter) who defied the experimenter, then 90 percent of the subjects also defied the experimenter. If the confederates simply complied with the experimenter's commands, there was no increase in the number of naive subjects who obeyed. If, however, the confederates actively encouraged the subjects to give more and intense shocks, the tendency to do so rose dramatically. Finally, and perhaps most frighteningly, if the subject was relieved of direct responsibility for delivering the shocks by being assigned some subsidiary task such as reading the word pairs, while one of the confederates actually threw the switch, less than 10 percent defied the experimenter!

IMPLICATIONS
OF MILGRAM'S STUDIES

One rather grim theme that runs through the Milgram studies is the astonishingly high level of conformity. This result is even more astonishing when you consider the moral pressures involved. The subjects decidedly did not want to shock the learner; they found it an extremely unpleasant task. Some subjects often expressed deep convictions against shocking the learner and viewed it as immoral and reprehensible; others became angry and denounced the experiment as senseless and stupid. Yet, even while they were vigorously protesting, these same people were throwing the switches of the electric chair. And remember, these subjects were no different from you and us. As Milgram points out:

With numbing regularity good people were seen to knuckle under the demands of authority and perform actions that were callous and severe. Men who are in everyday life responsible and decent were seduced by the trappings of authority, by the control of their perceptions, and by the uncritical acceptance of the experimenter's definition of the situation, into performing harsh acts. (*op. cit.*)

Although authority is but one force in initiating and maintaining conformity, it is a pervasive force in our society. As Milgram puts it:

The results, as seen and felt in the laboratory, are to this author disturbing. They raise the possibility that human nature, or—more specifically—the kind of character produced in American democratic society, cannot be counted on to insulate its citizens from brutality and inhumane treatment at the direction of malevolent authority. A substantial proportion of people do what they are told to do, irrespective of the content of the act and without limitations of conscience, so long as they perceive that the command comes from a legitimate authority. If in this study an anonymous experimenter could successfully command adults to subdue a 50-year-old man, and force on him painful electric shocks against his protests, one can only wonder what government, with its vastly greater authority and prestige, can command of its subjects.

Postscript

And we all huddled them up. We made them squat down, and Lieutenant Calley came over and said, you know what to do with them, don't you? And I said Yes. So I took it for granted that he just wanted us to watch them. And he left and came back about 10 or 15 minutes later, and said, how come you ain't killed them yet? And I told him that I didn't think you wanted us to kill them, that you just wanted us to guard them. He said, no, I want them dead. . . . And he told me to start shooting. So I started shooting. I poured about four clips into the group. . . .

Q. Men, women and children?

A. Men, women and children.

Q. And babies?

A. And babies.

A. Okay, then what?

A. So we started to gather them up, more people. . . . And somebody holed up in the ravine, and told us to bring them over to the ravine, so we took them back out, and led them over to—and by that time, we already had them over there, and they had about 70–75 people all gathered up. So we threw ours in with them and Lieutenant Calley told me, he said, Meadlo, we got another job to do. And so we started pushing them off and we started shooting them, so altogether we just pushed them all off, and just started using automatics on them. And then—

Q. Again—men, women, children?

A. Men, women and children.

Q. And babies?

A. And babies. And so we started shooting them, and somebody told us to switch off to single shot so that we could save ammo. So we switched off to single shot, and shot a few more rounds. . . .

Q. Why did you do it?

A. Why did I do it? Because I felt like I was ordered to do it. . . . (*The New York Times*)

B. INVOLVEMENT

AN EXPERIMENT
BY LATANÉ AND DARLEY

You have been invited to an interview to discuss "some of the problems involved in life at a university." When you appear for your appointment, you are ushered into a small waiting room and asked to fill out a preliminary questionnaire before being called to the interview. Two other students have arrived before you, and are busily filling out their questionnaires. You take your seat and begin working on yours. You suddenly notice a stream of whitish smoke puffing into the room through a wall vent. You glance at the other students. They, too, have noticed the smoke, but they merely look at it briefly, and, without saying anything, simply shrug their shoulders and return to their questionnaires. The smoke continues to pour into the room, to the point where visibility is obscured and you begin to cough and rub your eyes. The other students are obviously bothered by the smoke because they wave it away. Even so, they continue to work on without comment. What do you do?

What Actually Happens. It may (or may not) surprise you to know that only one subject out of ten in your position will get up and leave the room to report the presence of smoke. The other nine stay in the smoke-filled room, doggedly filling out questionnaires. If, however, the subject is in the room alone, more than seven out of ten leave their chairs, walk over to the vent, investigate it, sniff the smoke, wave their hands in it, feel its temperature, and then walk out of the room and calmly report the presence of smoke: "There's something strange going on in there, there seems to be some sort of smoke coming through the wall . . ."

The reason, you may conjecture, that so many subjects fail to take positive action in this potentially threatening situation is the presence of the passive, apathetic fellow-students (these are, of course, confederates of the experimenter; they have been instructed to remain unresponsive in the situation). This would be a reasonable assumption on your part, but the fact is that when three genuinely naive subjects are tested together, the report rate is not much better than when confederates are present.

Subjects' Reactions. What is going on here? Perhaps a look at subjects' reactions may provide us with some clues. The subjects who reported the smoke were quite consistent in their reactions. They thought the smoke was "strange," were not sure whether it was dangerous, but thought it was unusual enough to justify some sort of action: "I wasn't sure whether it was a fire, but it looked like something was wrong." "I thought it might be steam, but it seemed like a good idea to check it out." All in all, eminently reasonable behavior.

Subjects who did not report the smoke were also unsure about exactly what it was, but all rejected the notion that it was a fire. Instead, they hit upon an astonishing variety of alternative explanations. All had the common feature of interpreting the smoke as not dangerous. Many perceived the smoke as steam or air conditioning vapors, others thought it was smog that had been purposely injected into the room to simulate an urban environment, and a couple even thought that the smoke was "truth gas" filtered into the room to make them answer the questionnaire honestly! (What is really disturbing is that these last subjects were not particularly concerned about having been "gassed.") In other words, the subjects who failed to report the smoke also behaved in a reasonable fashion—given their interpretation (even if somewhat bizarre) of the situation. They saw no reason to act because they did not perceive the situation to be critical. The question then becomes: Why do the subjects who are alone interpret the smoke as dangerous, while the subjects who are in the presence of others interpret it as nondangerous, sometimes going to rather extreme lengths to do so?

Mutual Observation. It is instructive to note that the subjects who failed to report the smoke were almost universally adamant in denying that they had paid any attention to the reactions of the other students in the room. Yet the presence of others was the *only* difference in the situation for those subjects who did and those who did not report the smoke. Clearly, the presence of other people does have an effect. There are a number of possible explanations.

Most emergency situations are ambiguous. For example, a man who staggers and falls down on the sidewalk may be having a heart attack or he may be drunk. Before you can act in an emergency, you must first interpret or define a situation as a true emergency. And how do we define social situations? On the basis of consensual validation, that is, we look around and see how other people are reacting. After all, no one wants to behave inappropriately. At best you could look like a fool, and at worst you could be sued or suffer physical injury. Each of us not only watches others who are present for cues to the situation (emergency versus nonemergency), but we are also aware that everybody else is similarly watching us. We all know that we must remain calm, cool, and collected in times of crisis—the person who fails to adhere to this stereotype is often open to ridicule and embarrassment. So, everybody is watching everybody else, and everybody is acutely aware of being watched by everybody else. As a result everybody strives hard to keep calm, which means that everybody seems unconcerned. If everybody (else) is unconcerned, then there cannot be a crisis situation. Thus, the presence of other people can lead an individual to interpret a situation as less serious and less demanding of action than it would seem to the person if alone.

An Alternative Explanation. The explanation may not be this complicated, however.

FIGURE 4.4 In every-day life, situations are unclear. Is there an emergency or isn't there? Is the man on the sidewalk having a heart attack or is he a drunk?

As you may have already reasoned, it might just be simple reluctance to show fear in the presence of others that prevented the subjects from leaving the room to report the smoke. So let's look at another Latané-Darley experiment. In this one there was no danger to the subject, and consequently, fear for personal safety and feelings about expressing this concern in the presence of others cannot be a factor.

AN ACCIDENT VICTIM

Here is the scenario. The subject is telephoned and offered two dollars to participate in "a survey of game and puzzle preferences" conducted by a local Consumer Testing Bureau, a market research organization. Appearing for the appointment, the subject is met by the "market research representative," an attractive young woman, shown to a room that contains a table and chairs and a variety of games, and provided with a "game preference questionnaire" to fill out. The basic variation is the same as the "smoke" experiment: the subject works alone or in the company of another subject. The other is either a confederate of the experimenter, a genuine subject who is a stranger, or a genuine subject who is a friend.

The "market researcher" informs the subject(s) that she will be working next door in her office and leaves through a curtain that separates the testing room from her "office." After a few minutes she switches on a prerecorded tape, and the subject(s) hear the following: first, the sound of someone climbing up on a chair, then a loud crash and scream, and the cry, "Oh, my God, my foot . . . I . . . can't move . . . it. Oh . . . my ankle." Then moaning, and "I . . . can't get this . . . thing . . . off me," finally more crying and moaning, which gradually becomes more subdued.

Helping Behavior. Fully seven out of ten subjects who hear the simulated accident while working alone offer to help the victim, either by entering her office or calling out to see if she needs help. If the subject is working in the presence of a confederate who has been instructed to be nonresponsive, however, fewer than one in ten attempt to help in any way. And the response rate for pairs of strangers is not much better than in the subject-confederate condition. The response for pairs of friends is somewhat better, but still not as good as when the subject is alone.

Why? Again, the difference in helping response seems to stem from the subjects' interpretations of the situation. Those who offer assistance usually do so because they think the fall sounds serious or because they aren't sure what has happened and think they should at least investigate. Many of the subjects who fail to offer help also say that they were unsure of what had happened but had decided that it was not serious. A few even went so far as to explain their noninvolvement on the grounds that to intervene would only have embarrassed the victim! But, as in the "smoke" experiment, inaction was consistent with interpretation of the situation—the nonhelpers felt there was no real emergency. Indeed, almost all claimed that in a "real" emergency they would be among the first to act.

What accounts for the differences in interpretation of the situation between helpers and nonhelpers? Again, as in the "smoke" experiment, the only difference in the situation itself was the presence or absence of another person. Yet these subjects also maintained that they were uninfluenced by their coworkers. Observation through a one-way window revealed that when pairs of strangers overhear the accident, they show mutual concern and confusion. In an attempt to interpret the situation, they glance furtively at one another, attempting to discover the other's reaction; yet each is unwilling to meet the other's eyes and betray concern. Thus, each sees an apparently unconcerned partner, and the nonemergency interpretation is made. Why are friends somewhat less susceptible to this phenomenon of "pluralistic ignorance"? Probably because friends are better able to interpret one another's nonverbal behavior (such as a glance of alarm) and, perhaps more importantly, are less concerned about appearing foolish in each other's eyes.

Focus 14.1
Population Density and Behavior

The modern city represents the greatest density of human beings in history. Is it possible that increased population density is accompanied by a kind of "behavior pollution," including bystander apathy, unquestioning conformity to authority, neurosis, crime, and violence, such as murder and rape? Since it is difficult (and in some circumstances, even unethical) to manipulate real human populations for experimental research on this question, John Calhoun of the National Institute of Mental Health employed "overpopulated" rat colonies to explore the effects of population density on behavior.

Calhoun constructed three quarter-acre colonies of rats, each of which was divided into four quadrants. The populations of the colonies could be controlled by removing newborn rat pups as soon as they were weaned. This allowed Calhoun to compare densely populated colonies with those of lower-density populations.

Differences between the populations emerged quickly. In high-density groups, infant mortality rose to over 80 percent (as compared to less than 10 percent in lower-density populations). This mortality was chiefly due to neglect on the part of the mother rats, who failed to provide protection, care, or proper nourishment for their offspring. The pups became the object of cannibalism by adults of both sexes. Social pathology reached incredible proportions in both males and females of the high-density group. Dominant males "corralled" a harem of females, which they protected from less dominant males who, in turn, became homosexual. Rape of the females, unknown in normal, low-density populations, became a common thing. The high density of population resulted in what Calhoun called a "behavior sink" of extreme and varied social pathologies.

Many critics have objected to the generalized application of Calhoun's experimental results to human populations. Some have suggested that the behavior sink response may be a peculiarity of the breed of rat Calhoun employed—a response not even typical of all *rats,* let alone of men. Some theorists have suggested that the critical factor is not the density of population but the absolute number of persons (or rats, or whatever) that the individual must interact with that affects behavior.

Jonathan Freedman and Paul Ehrlich placed groups of four to nine people at Stanford University in crowded or noncrowded situations for varying lengths of time and compared their performance on various tasks.

The subjects in the crowded rooms were seated in such a way that they were not actually touching each other, but there was no room for any additional occupants. There were only about four square feet per person in the crowded situations, while the uncrowded subjects enjoyed a luxurious 15 to 20 square feet apiece. The subjects were given a series of standard tests measuring their ability to carry out routine clerical tasks, memorization, and thought problems. No differences were found in the performances of the crowded and uncrowded groups. In other experiments, Freedman and Ehrlich tested for changes in interpersonal relationships and found that crowding did make a difference in this respect.

In fact, they discovered sex differences in the response to crowding. In a crowded versus noncrowded experiment with high school students, boys in crowded situations tended to become more competitive in a series of games where either a competitive or a cooperative strategy was possible. On the other hand, girls did just the opposite; in crowded situations, they became more cooperative, courteous, and friendly. When adult subjects were put into mock trial situations, where they listened to tape recordings of trials and then acted out the role of the jury, similar responses were observed. All-male "juries" in crowded situations tended to hand out harsher penalties than uncrowded all-male "juries." All-female crowded "juries" became more lenient than usual. Apparently males crowded by other males become more aggressive, perhaps "defending their territory." But, perhaps, the most surprising result is that these response changes in crowded situations only occurred in groups segregated by sex—all-male or all-female groups. When the sexes were integrated, no response to crowding was observed.

These results show at once that crowding in certain instances *does* affect behavior, and at the same time shows that such effects are not simple—nor are they necessarily the danger to society that Calhoun's experiment might make us suspect. Nonetheless, we have only a few studies on the effects of crowding, and even fewer of these have been done with human subjects, so that the results are not safely generalized. The effects of the modern city on the population is not yet settled. Certainly, it has been in urban settings that the major aspects of human culture, including art and science, have developed. But the question, still unanswered, is: has humanity carried a "good thing" too far and overextended human tolerance for the concentrated presence of our kind, endangering the future of the species?

A CRIME

These "emergencies" lack one ingredient that is common to a great many emergencies, namely, a villain. This was the next question to which Latané and Darley addressed themselves: What will happen if more than one person witnesses an emergency in which there is a clear villain? Will the presence of someone else, who might potentially share the risk, sufficiently embolden people to the point where they will become involved?

The scene shifts to the Nu-Way Beverage Center in Suffern, New York, a discount beer store. One or two customers are in the store. A young man enters the store and asks the cashier at the checkout counter, "What is the most expensive imported beer that you carry?" The cashier replies "Löwenbräu. I'll go back and check how much we have," and disappears into the rear of the store. At this point the young man picks up a case of beer stacked near the front, remarks "They'll never miss this," walks out with the case, puts it in his car, and drives off. The cashier returns to the checkout counter and resumes waiting on the customers. After a minute, if nobody has spontaneously mentioned the theft, the cashier asks, "Hey, what happened to the man who was in here? Did you see him leave?"

Reporting Rates. The "robber" and the cashier were, of course, in cahoots. Of customers who were alone, 65 percent mention the theft, either spontaneously or following the cashier's question (although far more had to be prompted than acted spontaneously). If two customers were present, however, in only 56 percent of the cases did even one person report the theft. This figure is much lower than it appears when you consider that two people are free to report the theft. The stunning fact is that the inhibiting influence of the presence of another person is so strong that a theft is, if anything, less likely to be reported when two people are witness to it than when only one is.

Summary.   In short, the cumulative weight of these three experiments—"smoke," "fallen woman," and "theft"—strongly and clearly indicates that people are less likely to take socially responsible action if other people are present than if they are alone. People are less likely to report a possible fire when together than when alone, are less likely to go to the aid of a victim when together than when alone, and are less likely to report a robbery when together than when alone. Contrary to what might be expected, the presence of other people decreases the likelihood of involvement. When faced with an emergency situation, people are far more likely to act if they are alone.

These experiments were conducted in settings wherein the participants could see each other. The thesis was that mutual observation may lead to an interpretation of a situation as being less serious than would result if each participant were alone. The results of these experiments lend strong support to this hypothesis. It occurred to Latané and Darley, however, that in failure to act in a crisis other factors may be operating as well. Interpreting a situation as an emergency is only the first step. Suppose that a person has come to the conclusion that a real emergency exists. A decision still must be made about what, if anything, to do about it. This is the question posed by the next experiment.

A SICK MAN

The subject arrives at the laboratory and is ushered into a small room. After being seated, the subject is told that the experiment is concerned with "the kinds of personal problems faced by normal college students in a high-pressure environment," and that the experimental task is to participate in a discussion about these problems with other students. However, because these problems are personal, and because they might prove embarrassing in face-to-face discussion, all the participants in the discussion will remain out of sight in individual rooms.

The discussion then begins with each participant speaking in turn through an intercom system. The first participant begins by saying how difficult he has found it to become adjusted to the environment and the demands of his studies. Then, with hesitation and embarrassment, he reveals that he is prone to seizures, especially when studying hard or taking exams. Then the other participants take their turns, until it is the first participant's turn to talk again. He makes a few comments and then, growing increasingly loud and incoherent, says: "I er um I think I I need er if if could er er somebody er er er er er er er give me a little or give me a little help here because er I er I'm er er h-h-having a a a a real problem er right now and I er if somebody could help me out it would it would er er s-s-sure be sure be good . . . because er there er er a cause I er I uh I've got a one of the er sei— —er er things coming on and and and I could really er use some help so if somebody would er give me a little h-help uh er-er—er-er-er-c-could somebody er er help er uh uh uh (choking sounds) . . . I'm gonna die er er I'm . . . gonna die er help er er seizure er." Then there is the sound of choking, followed by quiet.

The Setup

There was only one real subject in this situation, and the subject always spoke last. All the other "subjects," including the seizure-prone victim, were figments of the experimenter's imagination. All their statements were on tape and were fed into the subject's room by the intercom to create various illusions of what the "discussion group" consisted of: the subject and the victim; or the subject, the victim, and one other person (who in some cases was a friend—in which case the voice was not simulated); or the subject, the victim, and four other persons. In some cases the subject had a brief "accidental" encounter with the future "victim" prior to the experiment, meeting in the hall and chatting for a minute just before the experiment.

Who Helps? Again, the effect of group size is striking. All subjects who believed that they alone knew of the victim's plight left the room and reported the seizure. Eight of ten subjects who thought that one other person also knew reported the seizure. Only six of ten subjects who thought that four other people also knew reported the seizure (Figure 14.5, page 474).

There are two exceptions to this rule. One occurred when the subjects believed that a friend was in the group. They reported as quickly as subjects who believed themselves to be alone with the victim. But how many emergencies are witnessed by friends? Especially in the anonymity of our large urban centers, if a crisis is encountered in a crowd, the members of the crowd are usually strangers.

The other exception arose when subjects had met the victim before the experiment, even for less than a minute. These subjects often reported that they had actually *pic-*

Focus 14.2

The Bystander's Attitude Toward the Victim

Melvin J. Lerner and Carolyn Simmons of the University of Waterloo (Ontario) have found that a "victim," a person suffering pain or harm from an external agency, is in a very ambivalent position in the eyes of those nearby. If a bystander is helpless to save the victim or for some reason chooses not to help, the bystander is likely to make a low estimation of the victim's character so that the suffering of the victim is seen as somehow justified. Lerner and Simmons believe that this downgrading reflects the bystander's need to see the world as just, as a place where only the "bad guys" and people of "unworthy character" suffer and where the "good" people win, escape suffering, and live happily-ever-after. Awareness of the victim's plight throws the justness of the bystander's world into doubt, a crisis that can be resolved either by assisting the victim or by deciding that the victim *deserves* to suffer. These hypotheses were tested in a series of experiments.

The victim was a young man shown in a ten-minute videotape. He was supposedly a subject in an experiment on learning, during which he received a painful electric shock every time he answered a question incorrectly. The tape was shown to several groups of students. They were asked to vote on whether the young man should be required to go through another session with electric shocks, through a session with monetary rewards, or through a session with neither rewards nor punishments. Some of the groups voted on the question by a show of hands, others by secret ballot. After the voting, the subjects filled out a questionnaire reflecting their attitude toward the victim and the experiment.

Although almost all voted to give the young man the opportunity to receive money, there was a distinct difference in attitudes toward the victim depending on the voting method. Those who had voted on the victim's fate publicly, and who thus *knew* that he had been "rescued" by the vote, rated him more *positively* (more intelligent, friendly, attrac-

tured the victim in the throes of seizure. Apparently, the ability to visualize a known individual in distress increases to some extent the likelihood of helping that individual. But, again, how many emergencies involve acquaintances?

Who Cares? It is noteworthy that the subjects in this "seizure" experiment, whether or not they intervened to help, perceived the fit to be genuine and serious. In other

words, there is no question of their *interpretation* of the event as a crisis situation. Over the intercom came gasps and curses and cries such as "My God, he's having a fit!" One subject exclaimed, "It's just my kind of luck, something has to happen to me." They were frequently confused about what course of action to take: "Oh, God, what should I do?" Those subjects who reported the fit did so with relative calm, saying something like, "Hey, I think Number 1 is very sick. He's having a fit or something."

tive, etc.) than did those who had voted by secret ballot—and consequently did not know the outcome of the vote. Apparently they downgraded the victim to accommodate their uncertainty about his fate.

In other experiments Lerner and Simmons found that downgrading is apparently carried out unconsciously. They informed some groups that the young man in the videotape was simply *acting,* that no real shocks were being delivered, and then asked these students to rate the experiment and the victim and to try to *predict* how naive students would react to the victim. It was apparently unnecessary for the informed students to downgrade the victim, but they were also unable to predict the downgrading effect that their naive classmates would display; this result suggests that the downgrading happens in a way that we are unaware of and that we do not expect.

In another study Lerner and Simmons suggested to the subjects that the victim was genuinely frightened by the shocks he was receiving but had been persuaded to go on in order to provide experimental data that would allow the audience—the very students observing the tape—to receive academic credit by participating in the experiment. In this case, the "martyr" situation, the evaluations of the victim's character plummeted even lower than in the initial experiment.

The implications of Lerner's and Simmons' findings are far-reaching. There are many groups in our society that might be seen as victims: minorities, who are the victims of prejudice; the poor, who are the victims of circumstance; the elderly, who are the victims of the aging process; and so on. The more fortunate seem to show the same downgrading tendency toward these victims as did Lerner's and Simmons' students toward the young man. In the effort to conserve an artificial sense that only the bad guys suffer, we may play the regrettable role of unmerciful bystanders.

Those subjects who failed to report were hardly apathetic or unconcerned, however. When the experimenter finally entered the room to terminate the session, they asked, "Is he being taken care of?" "He's all right, isn't he?" Many were extremely anxious, with trembling hands and sweating palms. If anything, they were more agitated than those subjects who reported the emergency. If they perceived the situation to be an emergency, and reacted at an emotional level, then why didn't they do something about it?

Conflict

The emotional turmoil of the nonhelping subjects is a sign of conflict on their part, a state of indecision about whether to help or not to help, a conflict that the other subjects resolved by *doing* something. Actually, they find themselves in an approach-avoidance conflict (see Focus 11.8). The conditions for this conflict are created by the (believed) presence of other people. On the one hand, there are pressures to help, pressures that operate alike on sub-

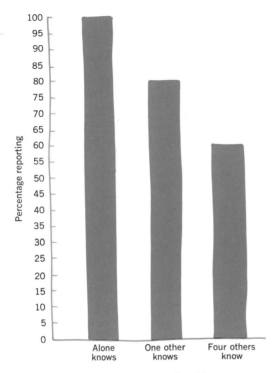

FIGURE 14.5 Percentage of subjects reporting seizure as a function of the number of others believed to know of the victim's plight.

jects who believe they are alone with the victim and subjects who believe others to be present. On the other hand, peculiar to the subjects who believe others to be present, there are pressures *not* to help, such as concern with overreacting, duplicating the actions of others, embarrassment and so forth.

Once again, however, whether asked subtly, directly, tactfully, or bluntly, these subjects did not feel they had been influenced in any way by the presence of others. As in the previous studies, however, the results are clear: the presence of others does decrease the likelihood of helping and, from a victim's point of view, of being helped.

Diffusion of Responsibility

Why is this so, since the subjects of the "seizure" experiment interpreted the situation as a genuine emergency? A person alone is alone responsible for what happens, for better or worse, in the situation. If others are present, however, the responsibility can be diffused. That is to say, the pressures to act are no longer focused on one person alone but are now shared by others. Not only are the pressures to act diluted, but so is the blame for failing to act. Whenever a group is responsible for some punishable act, the blame that accrues to any single individual within that group is likely to be considerably less than what that individual standing alone would bear. Indeed, blame is often nonexistent.

What holds for external sources of blame, such as society or acquaintances, is equally true for internal sources of blame (that is, guilt). It is the rare individual who has the moral fortitude of self-condemnation while seeing others also failing to act; quite to the contrary, noninvolvement on the part of others is used as a salve to the conscience: "No one else tried to help, so why should I?"

Finally, if others are present it can easily be assumed that "Somebody else will do something." The presence of other people, then, even when the situation has been interpreted and identified as an emergency, may still serve to decrease the likelihood of involvement.

Implications

The social-psychological forces of mutual observation and diffusion of responsibility are but two factors that determine whether and to what extent a person will become involved in an emergency. For example,

Focus 14.3

The Not-So-Good Samaritan

In another study of involvement, this one conducted by John Darley and Daniel Batson, the subjects were two groups of Princeton Theological Seminary students. Those in one group were told that they were to give a talk on the parable of the Good Samaritan and were given the following material to read.

" 'And who is my neighbor?' Jesus replied, 'A man was going down from Jerusalem to Jericho, and he fell among robbers, who stripped him and beat him, and departed, leaving him half dead. Now by chance a priest was going down the road; and when he saw him he passed by on the other side. So likewise a Levite, when he came to the place and saw him, passed by on the other side. But a Samaritan, as he journeyed, came to where he was; and when he saw him, he had compassion, and went to him and bound his wounds, pouring on oil and wine; then he set him on his own beast and brought him to an inn, and took care of him. And the next day he took two dennarii and gave them to the innkeeper, saying, "Take care of him; and whatever more you spend, I will repay you when I come back." Which of these three, do you think, proved neighbor to him who fell among the robbers?' He said, 'The one who showed mercy on him.' And Jesus said to him, 'Go and do likewise.' ' (Luke 10: 29–37 RSV)

The members of the second group were told that they were to give a talk on "the jobs in which seminary students would be most effective" and were given a pertinent passage to read.

Both groups were then informed: "Since they're rather tight on space in this building, we're using a free office in the building next door for . . . the talks." With that, each subject was sent to the next building through an alley. As he passed through the alley, he came upon a man "sitting slumped in a doorway, head down, eyes closed, not moving. As the subject went by, the victim coughed twice and groaned, keeping his head down."

Which subjects more frequently stopped to help the man by the side of the road: those who were rehearsing their speech on the Good Samaritan or those who were going to talk on the possible vocational roles of ministers? There was no difference in helping behavior. "Indeed, on several occasions, a seminary student going to give his talk on the parable of the Good Samaritan literally stepped over the victim as he hurried on his way!"

Why? Again, not necessarily because these seminary students were indifferent. Possibly they felt they were already committed to help the experimenter by continuing on their way, possibly they feared an embarrassing scene, or, even, possibly they feared physical attack by the "victim." Thus, the subjects were caught in a conflict produced by the immediate social environment, once again demonstrating the power of social-psychological factors in determining behavior and experience.

Focus 14.4

Ethical Standards for Psychological Research

"The psychologist believes in the dignity and worth of the individual human being. He is committed to increasing man's understanding of himself and others. While pursuing this endeavor, he protects the welfare of any person who may seek his service or of any subject, human or animal, that may be the object of his study."

This excerpt is drawn from the American Psychological Association's *Ethical Standards of Psychologists.* Although the vast majority of psychological experiments cause the subject neither physical nor emotional distress, some phenomena of significance to the psychologist, by their very nature, can be investigated only by exposing the subject to such discomfort. This problem is particularly bothersome in social psychological research, for that deals with the relationships between the individual and others. In order to gain maximum control over experimental variables, as well as to create a realistic setting, it is frequently necessary to employ deception of one sort or another. Two frequently used forms of deception, seen in the Milgram and Latané-Darley work, involve disguising the true purpose of the experiment and using confederates who are passed off on the naive subject as other subjects.

Obviously there is a very real question of whether the risk of distress on the part of the subject is offset by the potential benefit to humanity. More succinctly, do the ends justify the means? This is a particularly sticky question to answer: the concrete benefits to humanity are difficult to ascertain because such benefits may (or may not) be apparent until some time after the research has been completed—sometimes decades. There are rarely dramatic breakthroughs in research; rather, the social significance and weight of research tend to be cumulative, if only for

even if you are convinced that a true emergency exists, and feel personally responsible to help, you may not feel that you have sufficient skill, strength, or knowledge to intervene. In any event, the experiments we have just reviewed cast some suspicion on the old adage "There's safety in numbers." In fact, the opposite seems to be true. Help is more likely to be forthcoming the *fewer* people there are available to become involved—preferably, no more than one.

Postscript

A crowd of 40 persons ignored the screams of an 18-year-old officeworker as she tried to escape from a rapist, a patrolman charged yesterday.

The incident took place in broad daylight, shortly after 4 P.M. on Monday, on one of the busiest streets in the Bronx.

It recalled the fatal stabbing of Miss Catherine Genovese. . . . Detectives found later that 38 persons had seen the attack on Miss Genovese, the reason that the results often call into question social values and norms that, by their very nature, are highly resistant to change.

As the statement on ethics at the beginning of this focus implies, the psychologist has twin obligations: to society and to subjects. There is the obligation to apply talents and skills to the understanding of human behavior for the ultimate betterment of humanity. At the same time, there is the obligation to protect subjects from harm. The psychologist also must never forget that subjects are owed a very great debt; without their cooperation and trust it would not be possible to advance knowledge and understanding. One way in which that debt can partially be repaid is to debrief the subject extensively following an experiment: the psychologist carefully explains the purpose and importance of the research, the subject's role in it, and the necessity for any deception or otherwise potentially stressful manipulation that might have been employed. It is important to make clear in the course of the debriefing that the subjects are no more gullible than anyone else; if deception is deemed necessary to study a certain phenomenon and if the experiment is well designed, then virtually everyone will be deceived. Finally, the psychologist should provide the subject with the results of the experiment when they become available. In this way the subject's participation in psychological research can become a meaningful learning experience, at both an intellectual and emotional level.

The American Psychological Association holds its members accountable for their behavior. Members who violate the Association's *Ethical Standards* are expelled from the Association. However, the burden of ethical decision finally rests squarely on the shoulders of the individual investigator, not only as a professional but also as a member of society and as a human being.

which took place over a 30-minute period, without going to her aid or calling the police. . . .

The girl was naked except for a jacket that the man had wrapped around her. Her eyes were blackened, her mouth was bleeding and there were livid bruises on her neck. . . . The man the policemen seized was George Coughlin, 26 years old . . . who is married and the father of two children. . . . He allegedly entered the office at about 3:40 P.M. finding the switchboard operator alone. She told the police he struck her and she fainted. Coughlin then tore off her clothes, she said, tightened his belt around her neck and raped her.

When she regained consciousness, she said, he held a razor at her throat and warned her he would kill her if she told the police of the attack.

The girl finally broke away and half ran, half fell, down the stairway to the street doorway, screaming, "Help me, help me! He raped me!" Coughlin pursued her down the stairs, the police said. At the doorway, clearly visible from the street, they added, he seized the woman, who screamed repeatedly.

A crowd gathered quickly, but no one moved to interfere as he began to pull her up the stairs. (*The New York Times*)

C. COMPARISONS AND CONTRASTS

At the outset of the chapter we suggested that conformity and involvement, although representing diametrically opposed forms of behavior, share many determinants in common. The Milgram and Latané-Darley studies provide several illustrations of this principle.

In the first place, the presence or absence of other people, and what they do or do not do, has an influence on both types of behavior. If others behave as if the situation were "not serious"—for example, by calling for greater intensities of shock or acting as if an emergency does not exist—the likelihood of conformity increases and the likelihood of involvement decreases. If others behave as if the situation were serious, for instance, by refusing to give further shocks or by indicating that they believe an emergency exists—then conformity decreases and involvement increases. Thus, the phenomenon of mutual observation plays a role in both conformity and involvement.

So, too, does the phenomenon of dif-fusion of responsibility. Whenever others are present to share potential responsibility—another who delivers the shock or who witnesses the plight of a victim—conformity appears to rise and involvement declines. And once the serious import of a situation is recognized, approach-avoidance conflicts, with their attendant emotional stresses, come into play. The individual is caught between the costs of becoming involved and nonconforming, and the implicit rewards for conforming and remaining uninvolved. Visibility of the victim also seems to be important, whether actual physical proximity of another human being in pain or the visualization of the suffering of an acquaintance.

But perhaps the most important common element of the studies reviewed in this chapter is that they provide a common ground for understanding such disparate-appearing phenomena as the massacre and rape cases cited and many, many more incidents like them. For these studies strongly suggest that people who conform to authority are not "sadistic monsters," nor are people who fail to become involved necessarily "dehumanized" or "callous." Rather, the Milgram and Latané-Darley studies indicate that social-psychological factors, particularly those in the immediate environment, determine whether a person will conform or become involved.

SUMMARY

1. **Conformity** and **involvement** (page 457) are determined by many of the same social-psychological variables: the presence or absence of others, the behavior of others, and the perceived attributes of others.

A. **Conformity**

2. When ordered by an experimenter to deliver 450-volt electric shocks to a helpless person in another room, 65 percent of the subjects

complied, even though they were visibly distressed and concerned with the victim's welfare.

3. If the victim is visible, compliance with the experimenter's commands drops to 40 percent. If the subject is required to force the victim's hand onto a shockplate, 30 percent conform.

4. If, however, the subject is relieved of direct responsibility for delivering the shocks, over 90 percent comply.

5. The power of the experimenter to elicit conformity is apparently vested in him as an individual, rather than in the organization or institution of which he is a member.

6. Overcrowding leads to abnormal behavior in rat colonies, but it is not safe to generalize these results to human populations.

B. Involvement

7. A dangerous situation (such as smoke in a room) is less likely to be reported, the more people that are present.

8. An accident victim (such as a woman falling and hurting herself) is less likely to receive help, the more people that are present.

9. A crime (such as a robbery) is less likely to be reported as a crime, the more people that witness it.

10. An acutely ill person (such as a man having a seizure) is less likely to be helped, the more people that are present.

11. These findings indicate that people are less likely to take socially responsible action if other people are present. Contrary to what might be expected, the presence of other people decreases the likelihood of involvement.

12. A bystander who is unable or unwilling to come to the aid of a person in a crisis tends to downgrade the character of the victim so that the suffering of the victim is seen as somehow justified.

13. Psychological research is guided by ethical standards, set up by the American Psychological Association, that protect the rights, dignity, and safety of human subjects.

Chapter Fifteen
Groups

No man is an Iland, intire of itselfe. . . . (Donne)

The propensity of people to form groups is both obvious and ubiquitous. But why do people form groups? An obvious answer is: to fulfill certain needs and to achieve certain goals that they could not accomplish in isolation. For example, one primary function of the group is mutual protection in the face of danger. Prehistoric peoples banded together to ward off larger predators, just as their present-day descendants form armed camps to protect themselves against enemies, both real and imagined. Fear, then, would seem to be a factor in group formation. It is easy enough to provide reasons for affiliation into groups. But how do you test such a proposition experimentally? Here is an experiment conducted and described by Stanley Schachter of Columbia University which does just that.

There are two experimental conditions, one of high anxiety and one of low anxiety. Anxiety was manipulated in the following fashion. In the high-anxiety condition, the subjects, all college girls, strangers to one another, entered a room to find facing them a gentleman of serious mien, horn-rimmed glasses, dressed in a white laboratory coat, stethoscope dribbling out of his pocket, behind him an array of formidable electrical junk. After a few preliminaries, the experimenter began: Allow me to introduce myself, I am Dr. Gregor Zilstein of the Medical School's Department of Neurology and Psychiatry. I have asked you all to come today in order to serve as subjects in an experiment concerned with the effects of electrical shock.

Zilstein paused ominously, then continued with a seven- or eight-minute recital of the importance of research in this area, citing electroshock therapy, the increasing number of accidents due to electricity, and so on. He concluded in this vein: What we will ask each of you to do is very simple. We would like to give each of you a series of electric shocks.

Now, I feel I must be completely honest with you and tell you exactly what you are in for. These shocks will hurt, they will be painful. As you can guess, if, in research of this sort, we're to learn anything at all that will really help humanity, it is necessary that our shocks be intense. What we will do is put an electrode on your hand, hook you into apparatus such as this (Zilstein points to the electrical-looking gadgetry behind him), give you a series of electric shocks, and take various measures such as your pulse rate, blood pressure, and so on. Again, I do want to be honest with you and tell you that these shocks will be quite painful but, of course, they will do no permanent damage.

In the low-anxiety condition, the setting and costume were precisely the same except that there was no electrical apparatus in the room. After introducing himself, Zilstein proceeded:

I have asked you all to come today in order to serve as subjects in an experiment concerned with the effects of electric shock. I hasten to add, do not let the word "shock" trouble you; I am sure that you will enjoy the experiment.

Then precisely the same recital on the importance of the research, concluding with:

What we will ask each one of you to do is very simple. We would like to give each of you a series of very mild electric shocks. I assure you that what you will feel will not in any way be painful. It will resemble more a tickle or a tingle than anything unpleasant. We will put an electrode on your hand, give you a series of very mild shocks and measure such things as your pulse rate and blood pressure, measures with which I'm sure you all are familiar from visits to your family doctor.

From this point on the experimental procedures in the two conditions were identical. . . . Before we begin with the shocking proper there will be about a ten-minute delay while we get this room in order. We have several pieces of equipment to bring in and get set up. With this many people in the room, this would be very difficult to do, so we will have to ask you to be kind enough to leave the room.

Here is what we will ask you to do for this ten-minute period of waiting. We have on this floor a number of additional rooms, so that each of you, if you would like, can wait alone in your own room. These rooms are comfortable and spacious; they all have armchairs, and there are books and magazines in each room. It did occur to us, however, that some of you might want to wait for these ten minutes together with some of the other girls here. If you would prefer this, of course, just let us know. We'll take one of the empty classrooms on this floor and you can wait together with some of the other girls there. (Schachter, 1959)

The results: 63 percent of the subjects in the high-anxiety condition wanted to be with other subjects; only 33 percent of the low-anxiety subjects wished to be together. Thus, it does appear that fear can foster affiliation. But the point of presenting Schachter's study was not just to demonstrate the potential role of fear in group formation, but also to show how psychologists investigate group processes. In this chapter we will discuss psychological research into a number of group phenomena. First, we will treat some characteristics of groups, such as group structure, group "atmosphere," and group cohesiveness, and the effects of these characteristics on the group members. Then we will turn to a discussion of group roles, such as leaders, followers, and deviant group members. Finally, we will examine an instance of group behavior—group decision-making.

A. GROUP STRUCTURE AND ATMOSPHERE

GROUP STRUCTURE

There are certain characteristics that are common to all groups, be they sales groups or sensitivity groups. One of these characteristics is **structure,** *which refers to the regular patterns of behavior among members including status, roles, norms, and a communication network.* There are basically two types of communication network, as shown in Figure 15.1. One permits "free" communication among members, one restricts communication. In the free-communication example every member can communicate with every other member. In the restricted-communication example, however, only member "B" can communicate with all the other members, and they can communicate only with "B."

Performance and Morale. Marvin Shaw of the University of Florida has reviewed a number of experiments in which the structure of laboratory groups was systematically varied and the consequences for group performance and morale were observed. It turns out that when the problem facing a group is simple, requiring, say, only the transmission of available information for its solution, then the highly centralized, restricted-communication structure is more efficient than the free-communication group. If the problem requires any sort of insight or cognitive restructuring, however, then the more flexible free-communication structure is superior. And, regardless of the level of performance, group members are more satisfied within a free- than within a restricted-communication structure.

Communication and Power. Member "B" in the restricted-communication structure is in an enviable position, in that "B" controls all the communication channels, even to the member at the "top" (member "A"). As a matter of fact, the restricted-communication example in Figure 15.1 looks suspiciously like the organization

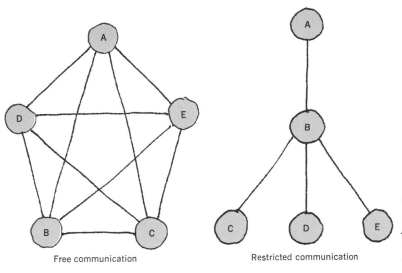

FIGURE 15.1. Basic group structures (lines joining circles represent channels of communication among members).

Free communication

Restricted communication

chart of a typical business (or academic department). Perhaps this is why persons who occupy position "B" in many organizations (such as secretaries) wield tremendous power in spite of their relatively low official status. Every communication must be relayed through this person, who controls both what "A" hears from "C," "D," and "E," and what "C," "D," and "E" hear from "A." Frequently a person in "B" position is the only one who knows what's going on in the organization and in effect runs it. When the trusted secretary decides to leave, the whole organization falls apart. Indirect evidence of the power of these people may be seen in the attempt of the members of the organization, from "A" on down, to ingratiate themselves with "B."

GROUP "ATMOSPHERE"

Closely related to the concept of group structure is, for want of a better term, group "atmosphere." At the University of Iowa, Kurt Lewin, Ronald Lippitt, and Ralph White set up boys' hobby clubs with con-

trasting autocratic and democratic atmospheres. The tone, or atmosphere, of the clubs was established by the behavior of a trained adult supervisor. In the autocratic club the supervisor determined the policy of the group, dictating which activities were to be undertaken and by whom. In the democratic club the supervisor left matters of policy up to the group, with activities and work assignments discussed and decided by the group. What effect did these two different group atmospheres—autocratic versus democratic—have on the boys' behavior? The autocratic club produced a greater quantity of work. Although the output of the democratic club was less, it showed more creativity. Further, when the adult supervisor left the room, the boys in the autocratic club stopped working; those in the democratic club continued. As for the morale of the group members, the boys in the autocratic club showed one of two reactions: either they were sullenly submissive to the adult authority or they were overtly aggressive. This aggression was not, however, directed at the source of irritation, the adult supervisor, but toward other group members. The democratic club, on the other hand, was characterized by friendly, confiding, enthusiastic interaction and a "group-mindedness." For example, these boys made many more statements involving the pronoun "we."

B. GROUP COHESIVENESS

Cohesiveness *refers to whatever it is about a group that draws its members to it and makes them want to remain members of it.* If individuals are highly attracted to a group and value their membership in it, the group may have considerable impact on their behavior. The following experiment by Leonard Berkowitz was designed to test this proposition.

Subjects were approached and told that on the basis of "recent findings" it is possible "to tell what kinds of people would probably like each other and what kinds of people would probably not get along well with each other." Then, before being introduced to two "coworkers" (actually two confederates of the experimenter), the subject was told one of two things about the "work group." In the high-cohesiveness condition, the subject was told that the group was "extremely congenial" and "there was every reason to believe" that the subject and the coworkers would like each other. In the low-cohesiveness condition the subject was told that "due to scheduling difficulties it has been impossible to bring together a congenial group" and that "there is no reason to think that you will like the people working with you or that they will like you. As a matter of fact, you may get to dislike them over time—there isn't enough in common in your personalities."

The Task. The task confronting each three-member "group" was the construction of ashtrays. The labor was divided so that one member cut circular bottom discs from blotter paper; the second member painted designs on the circular pieces of paper; the third member sandwiched the design between the blotter and a glass tray, pasting the whole thing together. After their initial meeting, members worked in separate rooms and could communicate only via written notes that were periodically picked up and delivered by a "messenger," who also collected the finished products.

Although the jobs were ostensibly assigned "at random," the subject was always given the job of "cutter," while the two confederates did nothing (other than wait for the next subject). As the subject sat in a room cutting circles from blotters for nonexistent ashtrays, the "messenger" would show up from time to time to collect the discs for the "painter," and to deliver "messages" for the subject from the "coworkers." These messages were, of course, prewritten and the subject received one of two sets, as shown in Table 15.1. One set of messages exhorted the subject to greater productivity, while the other set urged the subject to slow down.

To recapitulate, there were four groups of subjects, two working under conditions of high cohesiveness, and two working under conditions of low cohesiveness. In each pair of groups, one experienced group pressures to increase output, while the other experienced group pressures to decrease output.

Effectiveness. The effect of cohesiveness in a group is readily apparent in Berkowitz' results (Figure 15.2). The performance of the low-cohesiveness subjects

TABLE 15.1   **Messages communicated to subject**

MESSAGES REQUESTING INCREASED PERFORMANCE	MESSAGES REQUESTING DECREASED PERFORMANCE
"Let's try to set a record" (painter)	"You're getting ahead of me—relax" (assembler)
"The assembler says he is twiddling his thumbs. Let's give him plenty of work" (painter)	"We don't have to wear ourselves out making these ashtrays" (painter)
"I'm running a little short of material" (assembler)	"Take it easy. I'm tired" (assembler)
"Let's keep up a fast, steady clip" (assembler)	"We've done a lot of these things. Let's take it easy now" (assembler)
"This is the last note, so don't slow down" (painter)	"Painting these things takes more time than you think—let's slow down" (painter)

(Berkowitz, 1954)

was virtually unaffected by group pressures to alter output. However, the performance of the high-cohesiveness subjects was dramatically responsive to such pressures, whether greater or lesser output was demanded. If the messages requested in-creased output, then more discs were cut; if, on the other hand, the messages requested reduced output, then fewer discs were produced.

Thus, a cohesive group is able to exert considerable influence on its members. It must be borne in mind, however, that for a group to retain its cohesiveness, and thus its power to influence its members, it must continue to offer adequate attractions and benefits to its membership.

All groups have roles, or "slots," that members fill. Perhaps the role which has been given the most attention by psychologists is that of "leader." What determines who becomes the leader of a group?

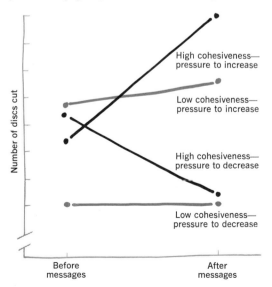

FIGURE 15.2 *Performance of subjects as a function of group cohesiveness and pressures.*

C.   LEADERS, FOLLOWERS, AND DEVIANTS

Leadership is dependent on a number of obvious factors, such as the personal characteristics of the leader and the nature and goals of the group. What is so frequently overlooked, however, is that leadership is a two-way relationship: the leader not only influences the group, but the group also influences the leader's behavior. Indeed, a person's ability to lead is determined to a large extent by the degree to which the group is willing to confer the leadership role upon him or her.

THE LEADERSHIP ROLE

One of the factors determining this "legitimization" of the leader by the group is illustrated in the following experiment conducted by Alex Bavelas and his colleagues at Stanford University. Four-person groups were formed and given human relations problems to discuss. While they discussed the first problem, Bavelas recorded the amount of time each member talked and, immediately following the problem, the members were asked to privately rank each other as to leadership.

Reinforcement for Talking. Now for the crucial part of the experiment. Bavelas next told the subjects that their group dis-

cussions might be more effective "if the participants are given an occasional sign that they are doing the kinds of things that will help the group arrive at intelligent solutions while at the same time yielding the maximum educational benefit to the group." Their attention was now directed to a small box containing a red light and green light in front of each member: the box was shielded so that only one's own lights could be seen. They were further told that "whenever you make a contribution to the discussion which is helpful or functional in facilitating the group process, your green light will go on. . . . Whenever you behave in a way which will eventually hamper or hinder the group process, your red light will go on. . . ."

Then Bavelas selected the member who had talked little during the first problem and was ranked low on leadership by the others after the first problem—this member was the "target." The group was given a second problem to discuss; during this discussion the target member received a green light whenever making a statement or of-

FIGURE 15.3 Groups tend to confer leadership status on the member who does the most talking—at least in the early stages of group formation.

fering an opinion; if other members engaged in such behaviors, however, their red lights were flashed.

Perceived Leadership. Following this second discussion the group members were again requested to rank each other for leadership. The results may be seen in Figure 15.4. Note how the two graphs parallel each other. Clearly the target member more than doubled verbal output (now talking 37 percent of the time); further, the target member's leadership capacity, as perceived by the other members of the group, has risen dramatically. In other words, a group tends to confer leadership status on whoever does the most talking — at least in the early stages of group formation.

THE FOLLOWER AND THE GROUP

Groups exert pressure on their members, sometimes to a profound degree. Recall the Crutchfield conformity situation described in the chapter on creativity. There subjects were asked to make judgments in a "group," but they were isolated from one another rather than in face-to-face contact. The enhanced power of a real group to produce conformity among its rank and file is demonstrated in studies by Solomon Asch.

Procedure. A naive subject and confederates of the experimenter (three seem to be enough) were assembled in a classroom for an "experiment in visual judgment." They were told:

This is a task which involves the discrimination of lengths of lines. You see the pair of white cards in front. On the left is a single line; on the right are three lines differing in length; they are numbered 1, 2, and 3 in order. One of the three

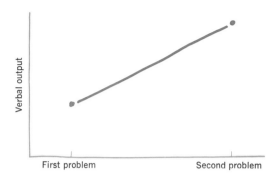

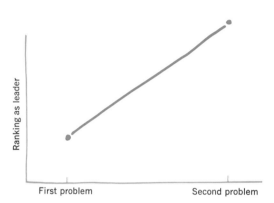

FIGURE 15.4 *Increases by target person, from the first to the second discussion problem, in verbal output (top) and ranking as leader (bottom).*

lines at the right is equal to the standard line at the left — you will decide in each case which is the equal line. You will state your judgment in terms of the corresponding number. There will be 12 such comparisons. As the number of lines is few and the group small, I shall call upon each of you in turn to announce your judgment, which I shall record here on a prepared form. Please be as accurate as possible. Suppose we start at the right and proceed to the left. (Asch, 1956)

A sample comparison appears in Figure 15.5, page 490. As you can see, the lines are quite clearly different in length, and the

Focus 15.1
Leadership: Personality and Situation

What is the "natural-born leader" like? Words like "charismatic" and "commanding" are sometimes tossed around in this connection. Others think of the "natural-born leader" as someone empathetic, someone closely in touch with the thoughts and feelings of his subordinates. The search for the "leader type" is an old one; every military academy attempts to turn out people who will be effective leaders in almost any situation. No less urgent is the attempt of many industrial corporations to identify and develop the "leader type" for the purpose of increasing production. But Fred Fiedler of the University of Washington believes that all of this searching and training has been largely in vain, because there is no "leader type" who is effective in all situations.

Fiedler and his associates conducted an experiment at a Belgian Naval Training Center where, in different military tasks, teams of recruits led by seasoned petty officers were compared to similar teams led by raw recruits. In a wide variety of tasks the teams led by the trained officers did no better than the teams led by recruits. Experience, even very costly military leadership training, seems to be a very poor teacher of leadership. Sensitivity groups, which attempt to foster better rapport between leaders and their subordinates, do not effectively increase production as it was once hoped they would. Neither experience nor empathy alone can make generally effective leaders, Fiedler says, because the "generally effective leader" is a myth.

According to Fiedler, there are essentially two types of leader personalities. One is the *task-oriented* leader whose inclination is to be concerned with the mechanics of the task for which he has responsibility. The other type is the *relationship-oriented* leader who is primarily concerned with his or her personal relationships with subordinates and superiors. Of course, there are relative degrees of talent in either the task-oriented or the relationship-oriented activities which vary from person to person. But even an extreme facility in either style of leadership is not enough to insure successful executive decisions. It is the *situation* combined with the leader's personality, Fiedler asserts, which makes or breaks "leadership." Because *effective* leadership occurs *if* and *only if* the situation and the personality are properly combined. Fiedler calls his view the **contingency model** *of leadership, because success is contingent upon the right combination of leadership type and situation.*

Situations may be favorable, unfavorable, or moderately unfavorable to a leader's strong control. What determines how favorable the situation is? Essentially, three factors: (1) *Leader-member relations.* Good feelings, liking, and respect between leaders and their subordinates are a plus factor. (2) *The task structure.* If the task is highly organized rather than a free-wheeling and spontaneous and ever-changing procedure, this is also a plus factor for the leader's control. (3) *Power position*. The power to hire and fire or to reward and punish entrusted to the leader increases control over the job. Situations such as Civil Service posts, where discharging an unwanted employee is almost impossible, are examples of an unfavorable power position where the leader's control is weakened.

It might seem logical to expect that the more favorable the situation for leader control, the more effective *any* leader would be. Not so. Fiedler finds that the task-oriented leader is likely to be effective at either extreme, when the situation is favorable or unfavorable, but ineffective in the *moderate* situation. It is in the moderately favorable situation that the relationship-oriented leader has his day. When there are interpersonal problems or an unstructured task, this leader is highly effective in repairing the leader-member relations or in soliciting from his subordinates relevant information and suggestions that help in making effective decisions or in motivating subordinates to make responsible decisions in the unstructured task. So the task of the corporation or the army or of any institution that requires effective executive decisions is not merely to *train* leaders intelligently to analyze task mechanics or effectively to relate to subordinates, but to determine what kind of situation is involved and who is the kind of leader most likely to succeed. Only if the person is matched to the situation is effective leadership the result.

Of course, the situation may change, making a once-effective leader ineffective or vice versa. For instance, consider a relationship-oriented leader placed in charge of a moderate situation where the task structure is high and the power position is strong but where leader-member relations are bad; such a person will be more effective than a task-oriented leader in the same situation. But once the relationship-oriented leader's skill has succeeded in repairing the leader-member relations, that person is no longer the best possible leader; the situation has become "favorable," and a task-oriented person would now be the more effective leader.

Fiedler draws two conclusions from his research. First, we should lay to rest the myth of the "leader type," recognizing that effective leadership is as dependent on situation as it is on personality. Second, having recognized this, government agencies and corporations should concentrate on diagnosing situations as well as leaders and matching individuals to situations in which they have the best chance of being effective. This matching should include reassignment in light of changes in the situations that alter the effectiveness of the leader. If we do this, Fiedler concludes, we will be making better use of the leadership potential that is so valuable.

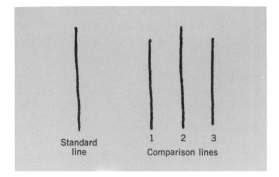

FIGURE 15.5 A sample judgment from the Asch studies.

judgment is evidently an easy one to make.

The seating arrangement was such that the naive subject always judged last, after hearing the "judgments" of the confederates who, of course, were giving prearranged responses. The first couple of comparisons proceeded without incident, as all the group members agreed. On the third comparison, however, the confederates selected a comparison line (say, line 1 in Figure 15.5) that is at odds with objective reality. Putting yourself in the place of the naive subject, you are faced with the choice of expressing what your senses so plainly attest is the correct answer (line 2) or of concurring in the erroneous observation of the group.

Acquiescence. It may (or may not) surprise you to know that three out of four people acquiesce and agree with the group on at least some of the comparisons; some subjects even agree with the group on *all* comparisons. And even when the difference between the lines is as much as seven inches (for example, a ten-inch line versus a three-inch line) there is still appreciable yielding to the group "consensus" that the two lines are of equal length. How can it be explained that healthy, normal, sane people can say that a three-inch line is ten inches long simply because other people say so?

Qualitative observations of the subjects and their comments provide insight into the intensity of group pressure. To begin with, subjects are neither oblivious nor indifferent to the group's judgments vis-à-vis their own. They become concerned, puzzled, and finally confused. Self-doubt is expressed in such statements as "To me it seems I'm right, but my reason tells me I'm wrong, because I doubt that so many people could be wrong and I alone right" or "What I said appeared to me to be right, but I don't know who is right."

Subjects often fidget, shifting in their chairs and showing other signs of nervousness and discomfort. Some consult with their neighbors. Others merely smile sheepishly. A few jump up to get a closer look at the lines. But whatever the reaction, "Most subjects see a disturbance created, not by the majority, but by themselves. They do not call upon the majority to justify its judgments; most simply try to defend the validity of their own reactions. The subject assumes the burden of proof. He, not the majority, becomes the center of the trouble; it is he who is disrupting the consistent trend . . . It is noteworthy that the experimenter, too, despite full knowledge of the situation, at times perceives things in the same way, with the subject as the creator and center of disturbance."

Subjects Who Yield. The reactions of subjects who yield to the group "judgment" are revealing. In a few cases the group pressure was so powerful that the subjects actually *saw* the lines as being equal. As one such subject replied when asked if

FIGURE 15.6 Subjects participating in the Asch study. Person number 6 is the naive subject who is faced with the choice of expressing his own correct answers or conforming to the erroneous observations of the group. This subject held to his own judgment, though not without strain, as the second and third photos show. In the fourth photo he is declaring that he has to call them as he sees them.

he ever responded contrary to what he saw: "No, that would have defeated the purpose of the experiment. . . . If I am asked to give an honest answer, I'll give an honest answer. . . . I never gave an answer that wasn't right. . . . I didn't give any answer that I knew was wrong." Other subjects clearly knew that they were right and the group wrong but were so concerned with appearing "different" that they went along with the group anyway: "I did not want to be apart from the group; I did not want to look like a fool." As one young man put it: "I am not a particularly successful individual—I am rather a mediocre individual. I have a horror of being a solitary individual socially—a horror of being an outcast. I have a basic feeling of insecurity."

Even subjects who ultimately stood fast by their own judgments were not immune to such feelings: "Despite everything was a lurking fear that in some way I did not understand I might be wrong; fear of exposing myself as inferior in some way. It is more pleasant if one is really in agreement." The majority of yielding subjects, however, simply reached the conclusion that "I am wrong, they are right." They viewed their disagreement with the group as a personal deficiency, that they were judging incorrectly. In the words of one such subject, "you just tend to follow."

FIGURE 15.7 A crowd situation, in which group pressures to conform prevail, can easily become a mob scene under appropriate circumstances.

Such tendencies operate in groups at all times, but may be particularly potent in such group-inspired endeavors as lynch mobs and riots, where the effect can snowball. Such phenomena develop in situations much less clear-cut than Asch's experimental setting in which a group of equals were dispassionately making judgments concerning a matter of simple physical relationships. The typical crowd situation is usually fraught with ambiguity and complexity; rumors abound and tensions are high. A few in the crowd who are convinced of the rightness and righteousness of their perceptions convince a few others, who in turn convince a few more, until everybody is convinced. The danger of such consensus, whether springing from mass reactions or fostered by authority, has been duly noted by Asch:

Life in society requires consensus as an indispensable condition. But consensus, to be productive, requires that each individual contribute independently out of his experience and insight. When consensus comes under the dominance of conformity, the social process is polluted and the individual at the same time surrenders the powers on which his functioning as a feeling and thinking being depends. That we have found the tendency to conformity in our society so strong that reasonably intelligent and well-meaning young people are willing to call white black is a matter of concern. It raises questions about our ways of education and about the values that guide our conduct.

THE DEVIATE AND THE GROUP

So far we have talked about the leader and the follower, which leaves us with the deviate or nonconformist. How does the group influence or attempt to influence such an individual? Schachter set up a number of "clubs," and had the members read the following case history of "Johnny Rocco," a juvenile delinquent.

Johnny Rocco was born in a large midwestern industrial city. There were nine other Rocco children, when Johnny was born. One more child, David, came after Johnny. The neighborhood where the Roccos lived was one of the worst slums in the city. It was known for its high rate of crime and juvenile delinquency. It was a neighborhood of factories, junk yards, pool rooms, cheap liquor joints, and broken homes.

Johnny's father worked irregularly, but two things he did regularly — he drank and gambled. In his drunken rages he often attacked the children and their mother. The little ones learned to scramble across the floor, finding shelter under tables or beds where his kicking feet couldn't reach them. Johnny's . . . mother was always sick and complaining. The children fought. They were noisy and destructive. There was seldom enough food in the house. The rent was never paid and Mrs. Rocco lived in constant terror of landlords and evictions.

By the time Johnny's father died four of the older Rocco children had married and moved away. What was left of the Rocco family continued in its dismal course, the children getting into one difficulty after another and Mrs. Rocco, sick and confused, trudging from school to police station to court, listening to complaints about them. Of the remaining children only one boy, Giorgio, the oldest, assumed any responsibility toward the others. When the rest of the children got so out of hand that Mrs. Rocco implored him to do something, he beat them brutally. . . .

Before he was twelve, Johnny's attitudes toward society had crystallized in a bitter core of rancor. He had always been treated badly. He felt no one had ever loved him. Everyone was his enemy — his mother, his brothers, his teachers, the cops — all were against him. Okay, he was at war with them. . . . (Schachter, 1951)

Schachter then asked the group members, "What should be done with this kid?" He had each member publicly select a position from among the seven alternatives running from extreme "love" (position 1) to extreme "punishment" (position 7) which appear in Table 15.2. As you can imagine, the sympathetically written case history

TABLE 15.2 The "love-punishment" scale

1. Love, kindness, and friendship are all that are necessary to make Johnny a better kid. If he can be placed in a more agreeable environment, a warm, friendly foster home, for example, his troubles will clear up.
2. Johnny should be put into surroundings where most emphasis will be placed on providing him with warmth and affection but he will be punished if he really gets out of hand.
3. He should be sent into an environment where providing Johnny with warmth and affection will be emphasized slightly more than punishing him, but discipline and punishment will be frequent if his behavior warrants it.
4. Johnny needs an equal measure of both love and discipline. Thus, he should be placed in an atmosphere where he will be disciplined and punished if he does wrong, but rewarded and given affection if he behaves himself, and where equal emphasis will be placed on both love and discipline.
5. Though they shouldn't be too strong and frequent, punishment and discipline should be more emphasized than kindness and affection. Thus, Johnny should be placed in an atmosphere where he will be seriously disciplined, but which will allow opportunities for warmth and kindness to him.
6. He should be sent into surroundings where most emphasis will be placed on discipline and punishment of Johnny, but there should be possibility for praise and kindness if he really behaves himself.
7. There's very little you can do with a kid like this, but put him in a very severe disciplinary environment. Only by punishing him strongly can we change his behavior.

(Schachter, 1951)

consistently led almost all members to choose a position emphasizing love and kindness (positions 2–4). Unbeknownst to the group, however, Schachter had inserted a confederate who chose the position of extreme discipline (position 7). Thus, a clear deviate was present.

Rejection. The group now entered into discussion of the case. By far the greatest amount of communication was directed at the deviate, as the other group members argued, pleaded, and cajoled in an effort to change his position toward greater conformity with that of the majority of the group. If the deviate withstood this group pressure and held firm, and if the group was cohesive and considered the issue under discussion to be important, a curious thing happened: communications to the deviate from other group members dropped off. The deviate was apparently excluded or ostracized from the group by severed communications.

This interpretation is supported by the results of a poll Schachter held immediately after the discussion. He told the groups that it might be necessary in the future to reduce the size of the clubs, and asked each member to privately rank the other members in terms of preference for continuing membership. The deviate was rejected, the more strongly so the more cohesive the group.

Thus we can see that the deviate's lot in group life is a harsh one. If an individual has certain convictions that are at odds with those of the group, he or she must not only face strong attacks on those convictions but must also run the risk of ultimately being ignored and rejected.

The Deviate Who Yields. But what of the deviate who relents, the deviate who is swayed and eventually converted to the group's position? Schachter also had confederates adopt such a "prodigal child" role. He found that they were accepted by the group just as if they had always been loyal members. Apparently group membership can be regained by the deviate, but only at the price of conformity.

D. GROUP DECISIONS

Thus far we have discussed the internal organization and functioning of groups. Groups act *as* groups, however, and groups frequently make decisions that their individual members would not have made if they had acted alone.

It is generally assumed that a group is less likely to make a rash decision or to take hasty action than an individual. Thus, important decisions are referred to a committee where they will receive due and deliberate consideration, and where the final decision will represent a reasoned and reasonable consensus. How does this axiom fare in the psychologist's crucible? For the answer to this question we turn to a study conducted by Nathan Kogan of the New School for Social Research (New York) and Michael Wallach of Duke University.

The Problem. A half-dozen male university students were presented with the following problem, and asked to make their decisions *independently* and *privately:*

Mr. E is president of a light metals corporation in the United States. The corporation is quite prosperous, and has strongly considered the possibilities of business expansion by building an additional plant in a new location. The choice is between building another plant in the U.S., where there would be a moderate return on the initial investment, or building a plant in a foreign country. Lower labor costs and easy access to raw materials in that country would mean a much higher return on the initial in-

Focus 15.2

Groupthink and International Relations

In modern U.S. history, there have been at least three decisions in international policy that were made by groups, the outcome of which proved costly both in lives and dollars: the lack of defense against attack at Pearl Harbor, the Bay of Pigs Invasion of Cuba, and the continuous and futile escalation of the bombing of North Vietnam. One common characteristic of the decisions involved in each of these situations is that the groups responsible were composed of highly intelligent individuals. "How could we have been so stupid?" asked President Kennedy after the Bay of Pigs fiasco.

Irving Janis of Yale University believes that a large part of the "credit" for this "stupidity" is due to a phenomenon he has termed "groupthink," a process peculiar to decision-making groups where, for the sake of amiability, esprit de corps, and a sense of unanimity, there is a deterioration in critical thinking, reality-testing, and moral judgment that is likely to result in irrational and inhumane decisions.

The symptoms of groupthink generally include a tendency to make a "snap decision" about commitment to a strategy after a very superficial examination of the alternatives. There is, then, an acceptance of the values and assumptions of the group policy, a striving for unanimity, and overconfidence, with a suppression of feedback of evidence critical to the group plans. The specific symptoms of the "groupthink syndrome" are:

1. *Illusions of invulnerability,* the feeling that "our side" cannot lose or even be attacked. When Admiral H. E. Kimmel and his in-group of officers were informed that radio contact with Japanese aircraft carriers had been lost, he joked about the possibility that the reason might be that the Japanese were on their way to Hawaii to attack—which they were! The possibility of "Pearl Harbor" was thought laughable within Kimmel's in-group; as a result, adequate defense procedures were neglected.

2. *Rationale* is also developed to justify persistence in the agreed-on group plan even in the face of setbacks. It was reported that during the Johnson Administration's continued bombing of North Vietnam, a very valuable skill for any member of the President's in-group was the ability to come up with convincing rationalizations for hoping that the continued bombing, if escalated just a little more, would result in the surrender of the enemy.

3. *Morality* quickly comes to mean the morality of the in-group, unquestionably; outsiders, other nations, other points of view are not examined, and individuals become dehumanized, as in the case of the large numbers of North Vietnamese civilians killed in the bombing of their country.

4. *Stereotypes* play a prominent role in groupthink. "We" are the guys

in the white hats and, of course, we always win in the end! "They" are the bad guys; immoral, weak, and stupid. Arthur M. Schlesinger, historian and assistant to President Kennedy, gave an account of the groupthink that preceded the Bay of Pigs Invasion; he portrays exactly this stereotyping in the group's thinking about Fidel Castro, who was assumed to be too weak and incompetent a leader to resist the invasion effectively: a rather serious error.

5. *Pressure* from the group on dissenting individuals to conform becomes very strong. This is the sort of conformity pressure studied by Asch and illustrated in the "Johnny Rocco" study.

6. *Self-censorship,* an unwillingness to express dissenting opinions or critical thoughts, also becomes noticeable in groupthink situations.

7. *Illusions of unanimity* exist within the group, no doubt fostered by the suppression of dissent. This sort of illusion gives the impression of "correctness" to the often rather shady plan—after all, everyone can't be wrong, can they?

8. *Mindguards* are the most extreme form of suppression of critical feedback, individuals who make it their task to silence opposition to the group proposals. During discussions, Schlesinger had voiced his opposition to the plans for the invasion of Cuba. At a social event, Attorney General Robert Kennedy, acting as a "mindguard," privately told Schlesinger, "You may be right or you may be wrong, but the President has made his mind up. Don't push it any further. Now is the time for everyone to help him all they can."

The products of groupthink are not always as dramatic and disastrous as in the instances mentioned above, nor are all errors in group decision the result of groupthink: misinformation and accidents may enter into the picture, and fallibility is a part of the human condition. But the fact that groups of men as individually competent as Kennedy's advisors can be so deluded by the influence of the groupthink process is good reason to ask how often the same thing must occur in countless governmental and industrial decision-making groups. And considering the awesome responsibility that technology has placed in the hands of these groups, the burden borne by a single decision can sometimes be staggering.

vestment. On the other hand, there is a history of political instability and revolution in the foreign country under consideration. In fact, the leader of a small minority party is committed to nationalizing . . . foreign investments.

Imagine that you are advising Mr. E. Listed below are several probabilities or odds of con-

tinued political stability in the foreign country under consideration. Please check the LOWEST probability that you would consider acceptable for Mr. E's corporation to build in that country.

_____ The chances are 1 in 10 that the foreign country will remain politically stable.

_____ The chances are 3 in 10 that the foreign country will remain politically stable.

_____ The chances are 5 in 10 that the foreign country will remain politically stable.

_____ The chances are 7 in 10 that the foreign country will remain politically stable.

_____ The chances are 9 in 10 that the foreign country will remain politically stable.

_____ Place a check here if you think Mr. E's corporation should not build a plant in the foreign country, no matter what the probabilities. (Kogan and Wallach, 1967)

Two of these subjects checked "9 in 10," two checked "7 in 10," and two checked "5 in 10." Following these individual decisions, the subjects were brought together and told that they were to discuss the situation as a group and arrive at a group decision.

The Risky Shift. The group decision was "5 in 10." This is clearly a decision that is more "risky" than the average of individual decisions ("7 in 10"). In fact, it is as risky as the judgment of the most risky individuals in the group. This phenomenon — that *group decisions involve greater risk than the average individual decision* — is quite striking. Known as the **risky shift,** it appears across a wide spectrum of situations, hypothetical or actual, involving positive or negative consequences. Indeed, it crops up in by far the vast majority of situations studied. Why the risky shift occurs is not completely clear at this point, but diffusion of responsibility, as discussed in the last chapter, probably has something to do with it.

Focus 15.3

Lost on the Moon: Effective Group Decisions

You are in charge of a spaceship that has just crashed on the moon, 200 miles from the nearest base. Your task is to rate 15 items in order of their importance to your crew's survival as you all make the 200-mile trek across the moon's surface. The 15 items are:

_____ One case of dehydrated milk
_____ Two 100-pound tanks of oxygen
_____ Stellar map (of the moon's constellation)
_____ Self-inflating life raft
_____ Magnetic compass
_____ Five gallons of water
_____ Signal flares
_____ First-aid kit containing injection needles
_____ Solar-powered FM receiver-transmitter
_____ Box of matches
_____ Food concentrate
_____ Fifty feet of nylon rope
_____ Parachute silk
_____ Solar-powered portable heating unit
_____ Two .45-caliber pistols

Although you can play this game alone, it was designed to study group decision-making. To play this game with a group, you and four to seven other people must first individually rate the items from 1 (most essential) to 15 (least essential) without consulting one another. When you have all independently rated the 15 items, then retake the test as a group, discussing the logical reasons for different ratings until your group comes up with a satisfactory solution, a ranking of the items that all the members find agreeable. Take as much time as needed to come to an agreement, then, turn to page 501 and compare both your own individual ranking and your group decision with the answers provided by experts at NASA. For every point different from NASA's ranking for each item, give yourself (or your group) one point. The sum of the points, which indicates divergence from the technically best solution, is your score.

The object is, of course, to have as *low* a score as possible; a score of zero would mean total agreement with the NASA answer.

Jay Hall, a management training consultant who developed this game and conducted research with it, has developed a list of suggestions for effective group interaction likely to produce the best answers.

As pointed out in Focus 15.2, there is a common syndrome, known as groupthink, resulting from pressure for agreement, which often makes group decisions the worst of decision-making processes. As a reflection of this distrust of group decisions, a camel was once facetiously defined as a horse put together by a committee. But Hall believes that there is nothing inherent in the group situation that makes effective decision-making impossible. There are simply "good" ways and "bad" ways to interact in the group decision-making process. To prove his point, Hall and his associate, Fred Watson, compared groups in a seminar they conducted, all of which were playing the "lost on the moon" game. Some groups had been given five suggestions for group interaction. The other groups were not given the benefit of these suggestions. Results showed that the suggestions on how to manage conflict in group interactions enabled the experimental groups to evolve consensuses that were not only better than the control groups', but better than *any* of the group member's individual rankings.

What are these instructions which work so well? In seeking consensus, it is important to remember that consensus is not merely a matter of a majority overruling a minority; rather, the goal is a jury-type situation where what is sought is a solution acceptable to all members. Even one lone dissenter can block a proposal, although that power should certainly be used responsibly. Bearing this in mind, the most important things to remember are these:

1. Present your own position clearly and seek to hear and understand the alternative views of your fellow group members. Avoid arguing for

its own sake. You are not seeking conflict, but a decision to which all members—including yourself—can commit themselves.

2. Again, don't play winner-and-loser games in a conflict. If there is a stalemate, seek a third solution that is roughly acceptable to all involved.

3. Don't *avoid* conflict for the sake of harmony; conflict is one of your most valuable assets in finding an acceptable solution. A too-quick agreement is to be suspected.

4. Don't cop out of conflicts by flipping a coin or a majority vote or some other method that simply lets you out of the responsibility for the confrontation and conflict.

5. Remember that conflicts are not only natural but valuable; they bring to light broad ranges of information and viewpoint. Seek out the genuine conflicts and try to bring them to some kind of honest understanding. And don't be in too much of a hurry to resolve them, too quick to establish harmony at the expense of examining the pros and cons of all the possible viewpoints. (Hall, 1971)

And now we take you to the war room of a major power.

Mysterious blips have been spotted on the radar screens; they may well be enemy missiles approaching. On the other hand, they may be a flight of migrating geese. A group of decision-makers consult together about whether to retaliate before it is too late, at the risk of beginning a nuclear war. It is presumed that the group members will have a conservative, check-and-balance influence on one another. . . .

FIGURE 15.8 Blips on the radar screen: the group decision is. . . ?

SUMMARY

1. Among the many reasons that people band together into groups, laboratory experiments suggest that fear seems to be one factor — fear fosters affiliation.

A. Group Structure and Atmosphere

2. A "restricted-communication" group **structure** (page 482) is highly efficient in the solution of simple problems. A "free-communication" group structure is more efficient if the problem is complex, requiring cognitive restructuring — and it promotes greater morale among its members.

3. Autocratic groups excel in sheer production. Democratic groups are more creative, self-sustaining, and group-minded.

B. Group Cohesiveness

4. A cohesive group is able to exert considerable influence on its members. For a group to retain its **cohesiveness** (page 484), however, it must offer adequate attractions and benefits to its members.

C. Leaders, Followers, and Deviants

5. Groups tend to confer leadership status on whoever does the most talking — at least in the early stages of group formation.

6. Groups can exert tremendous pressure on their members, sometimes to the point of altering perception of physical events.

7. An individual who resists the pressure of a cohesive group on an important issue is subject to intense attack. If that person yields, group acceptance results. If the person stands firm, however, the outcome is group ostracism.

8. Effective leadership is a function of both the personality of the leader and the characteristics of the group and the problem the group faces.

D. Group Decisions

9. The finding that group decisions involve greater risk than the average individual decision — the **risky shift** (page 497) — occurs across a wide variety of situations.

10. Groups tend to make snap decisions after very superficial examination of alternatives.

11. Group decision-making can be improved by instructing the group to deliberate slowly and to accept and resolve conflict and differences of opinion.

Table 15-3   Lost on the moon: NASA's answers

ITEMS	NASA'S REASONING	NASA's RANKS	YOUR RANKS	ERROR POINTS	GROUP RANKS	ERROR POINTS
Box of matches	No oxygen on moon to sustain flame; virtually worthless	15				
Food concentrate	Efficient means of supplying energy requirements	4				
Fifty feet of nylon rope	Useful in scaling cliffs, tying injured together	6				
Parachute silk	Protection from sun's rays	8				
Solar-powered portable heating unit	Not needed unless on dark side	13				
Two .45 caliber pistols	Possible means of self-propulsion	11				
One case of dehydrated Pet milk	Bulkier duplication of food concentrate	12				
Two 100-pound tanks of oxygen	Most pressing survival need	1				
Stellar map (of the moon's constellation)	Primary means of navigation	3				
Self-inflating life raft	CO_2 bottle in military raft may be used for propulsion	9				
Magnetic compass	Magnetic field on moon is not polarized; worthless for navigation	14				
Signal flares	Distress signal when mother ship is sighted	10				
Five gallons of water	Replacement for tremendous liquid loss on lighted side	2				
First-aid kit containing injection needles	Needles for vitamins, medicines, etc., will fit special aperture in NASA space suits	7				
Solar-powered FM receiver-transmitter	For communication with mother ship; but FM requires line-of-sight transmission and short ranges	5				

Total ————   ————

Error points are the absolute difference between your ranks and NASA's (disregard plus or minus signs).

Scoring for individuals:
0-25 = excellent
26-32 = good
33-45 = average
46-55 = fair
56-70 = poor
71-112 = very poor, suggests possible faking or use of earth-bound logic

Chapter Sixteen

International Conflict

502

A. IS WAR INEVITABLE?

During one of my lectures a Latin-American student, Caesare Innocente, said, "Professor Peter, I'm afraid that what I want to know is not answered by all my studying. I don't know whether the world is run by smart men who are, how you Americans say, putting us on, or by imbeciles who really mean it." Innocente's question summarizes the thoughts and feelings that many have expressed. (Peter and Hull, 1969)

Much has been made in the popular media of purported relationships between territoriality in some species of animals and aggressiveness in humans. Territorial defense is common among vertebrates, occurring widely among fish, reptiles, birds, and mammals (including primates). A good example is provided by the iguanas that live on the rocky Galápagos Islands in the Pacific. Each male stakes out his own territory, where he lives with several females. If a rival approaches his territory the male will begin making threatening gestures (Figure 16.1 top, page 504). He opens his mouth, nods his head, and walks stiff-leggedly up and down in front of his rival. If the rival continues to advance, fighting breaks out. The opponents lower their heads and rush each other, heads clashing; the horn-like scales on top of their heads interlock, and they engage in a shoving contest, each trying to push the other away (Figure 16.1 bottom).

ANALOGY VERSUS IDENTITY

Although analogies between animal and human behavior are provocative, analogies are not identities; uncritical extrapolation from animal to human behavior is unwarranted. A human being is neither a marine iguana nor a naked ape, and the existence of certain behavioral resemblances (often in the eyes of the observer, we might add) in no way guarantees that the same, or even similar, mechanisms are operating.

In the words of S. A. Barnett of the Australian National University in Canberra: "Choose the right animal species, and you can 'prove' anything you like: that it is natural for us to be polygamous or monogamous, aggressive or pacific, acquisitive or altruistic. This is how medieval moralists used animal stories, but it has nothing to do with science."

The available evidence strongly suggests that aggressive behavior is *learned*. The tremendous variation between groups in the expression of aggression suggests that *warfare* is not rooted in a biological urge, but is the outcome of interactions within and between groups (nations). To some groups, such as the Hopi, the Arunta, and the Eskimo, war is unknown. Others, such as the Swedes and the Swiss, have enjoyed prolonged periods of peace. Even within a given society, such as our own, there is considerable variation in the willingness to engage in war—witness "doves" versus "hawks" during the Vietnam war. This variation suggests to us that war is a group product, and group processes can be altered, as we shall show at the conclusion of the chapter.

If the "biological argument" for the inevitability of war is found wanting, so, too, is the "historical argument." The historical argument usually takes some form of the general statement that "since there have always been wars, there always will be." Granted that the fact of approximately one war for every two-and-a-half years of recorded history is not particularly encouraging, the future need not necessarily be cast in the mold of the past. Other social institutions have been equally ingrained and enduring but are now dead or dying—

FIGURE 16.1 A Galá-pagos Islands iguana stakes out a territory; when challenged by a rival, it makes threatening gestures (top) and fights to defend the territory (bottom).

slavery, child labor, oppression of women, and human sacrifice, for notable examples.

One more point. The very belief that war is inevitable prevents people from taking steps to avoid it. After all, if war truly cannot be avoided, then there's nothing you or we or anyone can do to prevent it. Thus, the belief that war is inevitable makes it that much more probable—a prophecy of doom that is self-fulfilling.

THE FACE OF THE ENEMY

To claim that war may not be inevitable is not to say that it is unlikely. Many social,

cultural, economic, even geographic, forces combine to produce war. Psychological factors also contribute to international tension.

One of these psychological factors is the tendency of nations to develop "mirror images" of each other. Each attributes the same virtues to itself and the same vices to the other. Evidence from the mass media and from personal interviews in the United States and the Soviet Union reveals that both view themselves as peace-seeking and trustworthy and the other as aggressive and treacherous. Both feel that every move by the other is hostile in intent while their own moves are strictly defensive in nature. Attempts at negotiation or conciliation on the part of one are viewed as deceit or trickery by the other. The other cannot be trusted to bargain in good faith and understands only force. The citizens of the other country have been duped and exploited by ruthless, power-hungry leaders who are virtually agents of the Devil. Further, the masses in the other are discontented and would overthrow their oppressive leaders if given the opportunity. The aims of each are seen by the other as international expansion and domination, whereas the goal of mere self-preservation is discounted.

Some Examples. But let's take some concrete examples. When the Soviet Union attempted to install some missiles in Cuba, they claimed that the missiles were defensive. The United States, however, did not see it that way, and reacted as if the missiles were for offensive purposes. On the other hand, the United States maintains that its missile bases ringing the Soviet Union are purely defensive. The Soviets do not seem to share this view; they regard these bases as a clear confirmation of aggressive intentions on the part of the United States.

When the Russians invaded Czechoslovakia, the United States saw it as a brutal assault on a small country struggling for autonomy; the Russians saw it as a necessary intervention to prevent a takeover by forces that would imperil their security and that of allied countries. Precisely the same arguments were invoked when the United States invaded the Dominican Republic, although this time the shoe was on the other foot.

A similar situation prevailed in the Vietnam war. Both sides were fighting for

freedom from "foreign domination," although the question of "domination-by-whom" remained in disagreement. So, too, the people of the United States regarded the Viet Cong's practice of beheading and disemboweling their opponents as an outrageous atrocity, while the Viet Cong referred to the widespread napalming and crop poisoning by Americans as the "most cruel and barbaric means of annihilating people," although these fine distinctions were probably lost on the victims (see Figure 16.2, page 506).

Bertrand Russell, commenting on letters written by U.S. and U.S.S.R. statesmen, wrote:

The gist of what both of them say is as follows. "There are two powerful nations in the world which we will call A and B. A is and always has been wholly virtuous; B is and always has been wholly wicked. A seeks freedom; B enforces slavery. A believes in peace; B believes in imperialistic war. A stands for justice to the weak; B stands for the tyranny of the powerful." So far, both these eminent statesmen are in agreement. There is, however, one small point of difference: namely, which is A and which is B.

Self-fulfilling Prophecies. The trouble with such mirror images lies not so much in their relative truth or untruth, but in the fact that they tend to *become* true. A good example of this is the arms race (about which we shall have more to say later) in which each side expects the other to build up its armaments. The response to this perception is, of course, to increase one's own armaments, *thereby fulfilling the expectations of the other side.* Thus, each side's image of the other as an armed camp preparing for war is confirmed and, indeed, approaches reality.

FIGURE 16.2 These Vietnamese children were victims of (top) American napalm bombing and (bottom) a Vietcong attack. To those who are maimed, mutilated, or murdered, the source of violence, as well as the justification offered for it, makes little difference.

B. CONFLICT, COOPERATION, AND POWER

Two men have been charged with the same crime. They can be convicted only if one or the other confesses. The district attorney orders them held in separate rooms and pays each of them a visit in turn. He tells them that if they both confess they will each receive a light prison sentence. If one of them holds out and one confesses, however, the man who refused to confess will receive a stiff prison term, and the man who confessed will not only be set free for turning state's evidence but will also be paid a reward. The bind in which these men find themselves is depicted in Figure 16.3. This situation has been named the "Prisoner's Dilemma." The dilemma lies in the choice confronting each prisoner.

CONFLICT VERSUS COOPERATION

In one sense, confession is the better choice. Let's say prisoner A chooses to confess. If prisoner B remains silent, then A gains his freedom plus the reward; if B also confesses, then A is at least spared a heavy sentence. In another sense, not confessing is the better choice. If A refuses to confess, and B also refuses to confess, they both go free. If, however, A refuses to confess and B does confess, then A is severely punished. It is clear that refusal to confess is the "cooperative" choice in this situation. Only if both refuse to confess can both prisoners *mutually* benefit, that is, both win their freedom. Confessing represents a "competitive" choice, since it is obviously an attempt to take advantage of the other at his expense. The only trouble (other than a moral one) with this choice is that if the other is similarly inclined, then *both lose*.

Laboratory Studies. What happens if this "game" is given to people to play in the laboratory, with "points" or money representing numbers of years in jail or amount of reward? The results are far from encouraging. Only about a third of the subjects make the cooperative choice; the other two-thirds play competitively. If the game is played a number of times, the percentage of cooperative choices drops.

Why does cooperation decline? Put yourself in the position of a player who has made a cooperative choice only to have the opponent make a competitive choice. On the next play of the game the previously

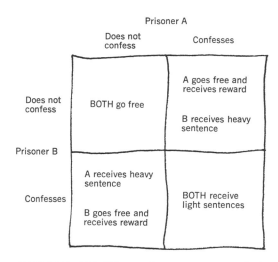

FIGURE 16.3 *The various outcomes of the "Prisoner's Dilemma."*

cooperative player really has no alternative. To preclude suffering another massive loss at the hands of an unscrupulous opponent, the first player opts for the competitive choice too. Both players then become trapped in a competitive struggle in which both suffer consistent losses. Both players may fully realize that they are engaged in a futile struggle that neither can win, and they may wish to turn to the mutually profitable cooperative strategy. Yet each is afraid to make the first move for fear the other will fail to do so. Instead, they become locked into a mutually devastating competitive struggle, continuing to absorb mounting losses—despite the fact that they know they could both win by cooperating.

If a moral can be drawn from this sorry game, it is that conflict, once begun, is difficult to avoid, and cooperation, once lost, is difficult to regain. This state of affairs can be reached by players who are initially cooperative; all that is required is that one of the players succumb to the temptation of the greater temporary advantage yielded by competition, or to the thought that the *other* player might be so tempted.

The Motive To Compete

The motive to compete is very strong, indeed. Look at the situation depicted in Figure 16.4. There is no "dilemma." The greatest gain possible comes from cooperating (choosing choice X), in which case each player will win $4. The only *possible* reason for choosing strategy Y would be to win more than the other person, that is, to compete, since you will actually win less ($3). Even if you fear that the other player is going to play competitively (choice Y), the cooperative choice (choice X) is still your best choice, since you will make at least $1. If you play competitively (choice Y) and the other player also plays competitively, then you wind up with nothing. Nevertheless, despite all of these built-in inducements toward cooperative behavior, 47 percent of subjects' choices were competitive, and this tendency increased with successive plays of the game.

Communication. "Ah," you may object, "these situations are hardly representative of the real world of international affairs. What if the parties were able to communicate with each other? Surely then they would arrive at a reasonable, mutually satisfactory position!" Such conditions have been established experimentally, wherein the players are able to communicate their intentions and expectations prior to making their choices. Communication does increase the percentage of cooperative choices when the players *initially* have a cooperative or at least neutral orientation toward each other. If the players begin the game with a competitive orientation, how-

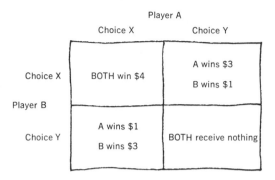

FIGURE 16.4 *A situation conducive to cooperation.*

ever, communication is *ineffective* in promoting cooperation. Now, bearing this point in mind, let's attempt to apply some of these psychological findings to the international scene.

War or Peace?

Suppose that two nations, A and B, are at war. They meet for "peace talks." The choices confronting them appear in Figure 16.5. Or suppose, as in Figure 16.6, that two nations have signed a nuclear test-ban treaty. A number of international situations are, in fact, "prisoner's dilemmas" such as those in Figures 16.5 and 16.6. As we have seen, any attempt by one "player" to gain an advantage over another "player" is self-defeating, leading as it does to a vicious cycle of competitive moves that no one can win and all must lose. We have further seen that communication is of little avail in preventing this cycle when the "players" have adopted a competitive stance. Nations typically enter into negotiations with a competitive attitude. (As a former Chairman of the Armed Services Committee said: "If we have to start over again with another Adam and Eve, then I want them to be Americans and not Rus-

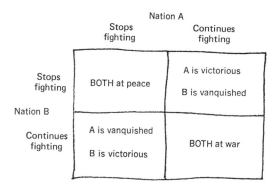

FIGURE 16.5 Choices confronting nations at war.

	Nation A	
	Stops fighting	Continues fighting
Nation B — Stops fighting	BOTH at peace	A is victorious / B is vanquished
Nation B — Continues fighting	A is vanquished / B is victorious	BOTH at war

FIGURE 16.6 Possible outcomes of a test-ban treaty.

	Nation A	
	Keeps treaty	Breaks treaty
Nation B — Keeps treaty	Arms race halted	A at advantage / B at disadvantage
Nation B — Breaks treaty	A at disadvantage / B at advantage	Arms race escalated

sians, and I want them on this continent and not in Europe.") Part of the competitive inclination, at least, is probably fostered by their mirror images of each other as basically malevolent and untrustworthy. In this atmosphere, even the most sincere communications of a desire to cooperate are likely to be viewed with suspicion. One State Department official put it this way: "For Moscow to propose what we can accept seems to us even more sinister and dangerous than for it to propose what we cannot accept." Of course, each nation is also interested in maintaining (or attaining) an advantage over the other for reasons of "security."

Going back to Figures 16.5 and 16.6, it is obvious what the likely outcome of such situations under such conditions will be—the war drags on and the arms race spirals upward. While this is a rather bleak picture, and seems probable in the light of current world conditions, it is not inevitable. Psychologists have suggested and studied ways to interrupt and reverse this cycle. We will look at these strategies later, but suffice it to say for the present that nations have more to gain by cooperating than by competing.

SAVING FACE AND FACING CRISIS

By now you probably have the idea that many psychologists think that intergroup behavior can be likened to a "game" played by "players." We are not claiming that infallible inferences about the behavior of nations in the real world can be made from the behavior of individuals or small groups of individuals engaged in games in a psychological laboratory. We do submit to you the proposition that certain similarities exist. A number of games have been developed that are designed to simulate a variety of conditions in which interacting nation-states might (and do) find themselves. These games are frequently quite complex and defy brief description, but it might be instructive to examine the basic design and results of two games focusing on face-saving and crisis (or pride and panic).

Saving Face

The first study, conducted by Bert Brown of Cornell University, asked the question: Will people suffer losses merely to bolster their self-esteem and preserve their image? Brown had his subjects play a game against a confederate of the experimenter who played in a highly competitive and exploitative manner. The situation was so structured that, for the first part of the game, the subject was at a disadvantage and could not respond effectively to the confederate's exploitations and, consequently, incurred considerable monetary losses.

Then the situation was changed so that the subject was in the driver's seat. The subject now had two options: either play to maximize gains or play to retaliate against the confederate, *but only at considerable cost*. Now, two further conditions were added to the experimental setup: the subject was led to believe that the confederate had (or had not) made the subject look foolish by the exploitative behavior, and the subject was led to believe that the confederate knew (or did not know) how much it would cost the subject to retaliate.

The results: When the subjects believed that the confederate had *not* made them look foolish and *knew* what it would cost them to retaliate, they retaliated less than 10 percent of the time. When, however, the subjects believed that the confederate *had* made them look foolish and did *not* know what it would cost them to retaliate, the subjects retaliated 70 percent of the time. In other words, knowledge that one has been publicly humiliated and that one can keep private the costs of retaliation leads to face-saving behavior. The only purpose of such behavior is to convince others (and, perhaps more importantly, oneself) that one is strong and capable. But the behavior is self-defeating inasmuch as it is costly and requires sacrifice of one's own gains.

An Example. As a war drags on, the combatants may continue to fight primarily to protect their image—to save face. The original purpose of the war is lost sight of, and proving that one is bigger, better, or stronger becomes an end in itself. As Senator William Fulbright ruefully observed, ". . . when a nation shows that it has the stronger army, it is also proving that it has . . . a better civilization."

The Vietnam war provides a good example. Originally the United States justified its entrance into the war on the grounds of keeping its commitments to the Diem regime and preventing the spread of "worldwide Communism." After years of fruitless fighting, however, these goals were largely abandoned. Instead, the country was assured by the then Vice President that "this nation will not go down in humiliating defeat on the battlefields of Southeast Asia —I promise you that." And the Chairman of the Armed Services Committee exhorted: "Let us not leave Vietnam dragging Old Glory in the mud."

Facing Crisis

Another study that carries possible implications for international behavior examined decision-making under conditions of crisis. Charles Hermann of Princeton University used petty officers from the Great Lakes Naval Training Center to simulate six different nations, each consisting of a five-man team, over a ten-hour playing session. From time to time during the session, the "nations" would receive messages indicating that an international crisis was imminent; for example, the country of Enuk might receive the communiqué:

Amra demands Enuk's renouncement of nuclear development or face military steps.

or

Major attack from unidentified source will hit in 10–15 minutes.

What would happen to the decision-making processes in these nations during such crises? First, there is a commitment to action among the decision-makers; there is the general feeling that "we can't just sit here, we must do something." Any action becomes preferable to sustained tension. Second, action is more likely if the decision-makers perceive national goals of high priority (such as survival) to be deliberately endangered by a hostile nation. However, this perception is colored less by information relevant to the immediate situation than by past hostilities and friendships. Third, the more ambiguous the situation, the more likely it is that action will be taken. In other words, although the best policy in an ambiguous situation would seem to be to withhold action until the picture becomes clearer, the opposite tendency appears to operate: "When in doubt, act."

Finally, in a crisis decision-makers do not seek and consider alternative solutions to the crisis. In other words, their perception of possible courses of action becomes narrowed and rigid. For example, Arthur Schlesinger, Jr. reported of the Cuban missile crisis that

On the first Tuesday morning the choice for a moment seemed to lie between an air strike or acquiescence—and the President had made clear that acquiescence was impossible. Listening to the discussion the Attorney General . . . said aloud that the group needed more alternatives: surely there was some course in between bombing and doing nothing. . . .

THE BALANCE OF POWER

For some time the doctrine of balance of power between nations (or, since the advent of nuclear weapons, "balance of terror") has been invoked as justification for massive arms buildups in the name of "deterrence." This policy, of course, has led to the arms race ("mutual deterrence").

Each side develops weapons at an accelerated rate in a frantic effort to keep up with (if not surpass) the other side and thereby maintain the "balance of power" (with a little "margin of superiorty" thrown in for good measure). Aside from the logical absurdity of striving to maintain some sort of balance in weaponry when each side already has more than enough power to destroy the other (if not the world) several times over, the theory of balance of power deserves to be subjected to empirical test.

Acme and Bolt. Here is the experimental situation. Each subject is asked to imagine that he or she is operating a trucking company, either the Acme Company or the Bolt Company (see Figure 16.7). The object is for each player to get the company truck from "Start" to "Destination" as quickly as possible (time is money). There are two routes available to each player, a direct route and an alternative route. The direct route is, as you can see, much quicker; however, the direct route is a one-lane road. If both Acme and Bolt are to use the direct route, they must alternate, with one going first (while the other waits) and then the other. Failure to adopt such a mutually beneficial cooperative strategy results in a costly detour via the alternative route, or an even more costly confrontation and stalemate on the direct route. In order to provide the players with every opportunity to coordinate their movements, they are able to communicate with each other by intercom.

A Gate. This *trucking game,* developed by Morton Deutsch of Columbia University, was played under two conditions. In one condition, the game was just as it has been described. In the other condition,

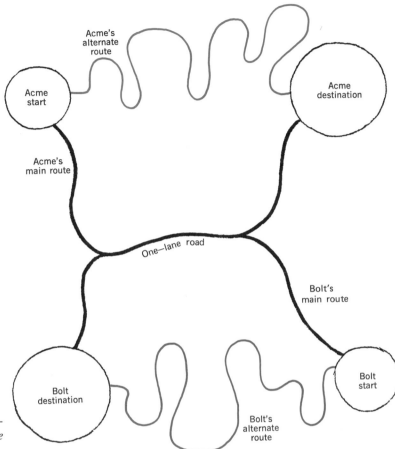

FIGURE 16.7 The subject's road map for the trucking game.

however, each of the players was provided with a "gate" that could, if desired, be closed on the direct route as shown in Figure 16.8, thereby preventing the other player from reaching the destination by means of the direct route. However, the players did not *have* to use their gates; they could, if they wished, simply forget about the gates and take turns using the direct route.

What happened?

In a nutshell, when the game was played without gates, both Acme and Bolt made money. When the game was played with gates, both Acme and Bolt typically used their gates, and they both lost money. And communication (via the "hot line" that was available) was used primarily to exchange threats, insults, and sarcastic remarks.

Implications? It's a long way from Acme and Bolt armed with gates to the United States and the Soviet Union armed with H-bombs. In a laboratory, the higher the

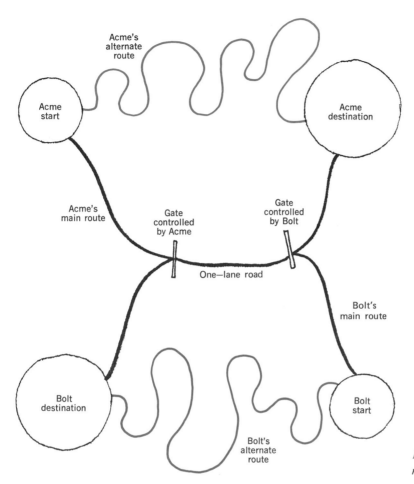

FIGURE 16.8 The road map with gates in place.

stakes involved (substantial sums of money), the more likely the players are to adopt competitive rather than cooperative strategies; however, the consequences are obviously not as severe as those facing two superpowers. Perhaps when the stakes get high enough—perhaps higher than can be successfully simulated in the laboratory—cooperation prevails (when nuclear weapons are involved, of course, the competitive strategy need only be played once, and the game is over.)

Notwithstanding the limitations of labo-

ratory research, however, the possible implications of Deutsch's experiment should not be overlooked: If people have a weapon, they are likely to use it—possession of a threat or a deterrent may precipitate the very situation it was designed to prevent! What this may mean in terms of the arms race, then, is that both sides find that as their military strength increases, their national security must *necessarily* decrease. There may be no technological solution, such as bigger and better missiles (or antimissiles), to this dilemma.

C. REDUCING CONFLICT AND PROMOTING COOPERATION

A way to reverse the arms race — and to reduce international tensions in general — has been proposed by Charles Osgood of the University of Illinois and past president of the American Psychological Association. The essence of Osgood's proposal is embodied in its name: Graduated Reciprocation in Tension Reduction, or GRIT for short, a quality, Osgood says, that would be needed to carry through on the program. Briefly, the principles of GRIT are these:

1. One country unilaterally decreases its threat in some *significant but nonessential* way. For example, the United States could close down a military base that the Soviets perceive as threatening but that is not vital to U.S. national security.

2. That country invites the other to reciprocate.

3. *Whether or not* the other country reciprocates — and this is the core of the proposal — another concession is made. And another. And another. And another — until eventually the other side reciprocates.

4. The unilateral concessions are carefully planned in sequence to produce a visible, verifiable pattern of de-escalation. The program is deliberately pursued on schedule over a considerable period of time, and each step is publicly announced prior to execution and widely publicized after.

5. The unilateral concessions are (at least until the other side begins reciprocating) limited in scope so as to avoid creating serious weaknesses in current defenses.

6. As the other side reciprocates, greater and greater concessions are made, with the result that each side gradually approaches a state of reduced tension.

CONFLICT RESOLUTION

But will GRIT work? Let's turn for an answer to an international simulation study conducted by Wayman Crow of the Western Behavioral Sciences Institute in La Jolla, California. Crow created a miniature world of fictitious nations (see Figure 16.9), in which the subjects took the roles of national decision-makers. The subjects ran their countries over several sessions; at the end of each session they reported the degree of international tension as determined by their perception of the likelihood of war, the amount of mutual trust, and so forth.

The two principal "powers" in this small world were Omne and Utro; they had fought a previous war and were presently in a state of continued tension, or cold war. Omne and Utro were balanced in terms of basic resources, and each had sufficient nuclear capacity to annihilate the other.

Enter GRIT. Unbeknownst to the other subjects, Crow secured the cooperation of the key decision-maker in Omne, so that midway through the game the government of Omne introduced the GRIT strategy. The opening move was for Omne to invite Ingo, an ally of Utro, to attend meetings of the International Organization (from which it had been systematically excluded) as a nonvoting member. Next, Omne volunteered some of its basic resources to a special research and development project whose payoff would go to the three weaker nations. Then Omne announced that it was curtailing its arms build-up and would stand pat with its current nuclear capability as sufficient protection. And so on. Such moves were initially met with suspicion and hostility by Utro, but were eventually reciprocated. The results in terms of international tension may be seen in Figure 16.10.

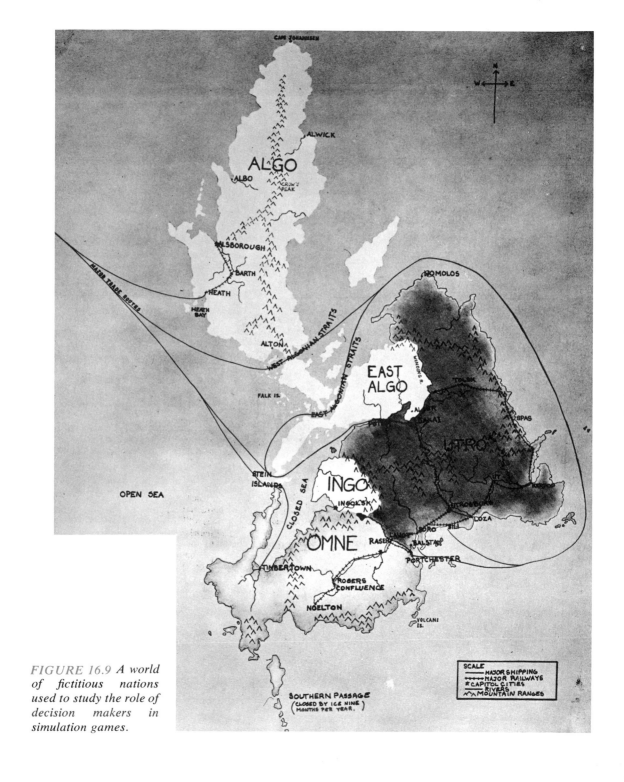

FIGURE 16.9 A world of fictitious nations used to study the role of decision makers in simulation games.

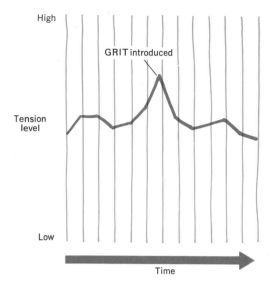

FIGURE 16.10 International tension in a simulation game, before and after the introduction of GRIT.

PROMOTING COOPERATION

Although reducing the probability of international conflict is certainly a worthwhile goal, it is not enough. Accelerated advances in mass communication, mass transportation, and mass destruction have made nations more and more interdependent, to the point where they depend on each other for their very survival. It is clear that some way must be found not merely to reduce conflict, but to promote active international cooperation. In order to explore this question, let's turn to the now-classic work of Muzafer Sherif of Pennsylvania State University. Sherif conducted a series of studies on intergroup behavior, using as subjects 11- and 12-year-old boys. It may seem risky to generalize from the behavior of adolescent boys to the behavior of nations, yet there are, as we shall see, certain obvious parallels.

Green Apples. Sherif studied the boys in a natural setting, a summer camp. The boys were divided into two groups. After an initial period of acquaintance and interaction, the groups were presented with a series of competitive goals, that is, one group could achieve its goal only at the expense of the other. For example, a tournament of games was arranged, consisting of baseball, touch football, a tug-of-war, and so on. It was not long before the two groups became hostile toward each other. Like nations, they developed mirror images, in which one's own group was glorified and the other vilified. Like nations, they began stockpiling ammunition "just in case" (in this situation, green apples). Like nations, they indulged in name-calling. And like nations, they began to fight.

Attempts at Intervention. A number of attempts were made to intervene and bring the groups into some degree of harmony. The camp counselors appealed to fair play, justice, and brotherhood, but to no avail. If a representative of one group approached the other in an attempt to establish peaceful relations, he was greeted with distrust and derision (and a hail of green apples); further, his *own* group rejected him for even making the attempt. Bringing the groups together for some pleasant activity, such as a movie, was not much help. Far from promoting harmony and good will, such situations only served as opportunities for further hostilities; the groups sat apart and hurled insults and spitballs. In short, communication, conferences of leaders, and programs of person-to-person contact all failed to improve the situation — and sometimes made matters worse.

Superordinate Goals. Then Sherif introduced a series of what he calls superordinate goals. *A* **superordinate goal** *is one with compelling appeal for both groups that neither can achieve without the other.* For instance, the groups were camping. When lunch time arrived, the truck that was supposed to go to town for food "wouldn't start." There was a rope available to pull the truck to start it up (as a matter of fact, it was the same rope that had been used in the tug-of-war), but neither group alone would have been able to get the truck moving. The only way anybody could eat was for both groups to pull together. Which they did. Other superordinate goals were a movie that could be rented only if the two groups combined their treasuries and a "disrupted" camp water supply that could be repaired only by cooperative action.

Such joint efforts did not immediately dispel hostilities. But a series of such experiences wrought some dramatic reversals. For example, during the period of intergroup conflict, less than 10 percent of the boys chose members of the other group as "best friend"; after cooperation toward superordinate goals this figure rose to 30 percent. Similarly, the negative mirror images changed. During conflict, 66 percent of the boys viewed all members of the other group as "sneaks," "cheaters," and

other undesirables; following superordinate efforts this figure fell to 15 percent. Other signs of harmony were also evident. The groups now sat together at meals; they actively sought friendly contact; they conducted joint projects; they even requested to go home on the same bus together.

The lesson to be learned from Sherif's study is that cooperation breeds peace, and intergroup cooperation can be accomplished by means of a series of superordinate goals. In this way the basic orientations of groups toward each other may be changed from mutal suspicion to mutual trust. In this atmosphere such steps as summit meetings and cultural exchanges could not help but be more fruitful.

But what sorts of superordinate goals are feasible? Space and undersea exploration, population control, weather prediction and control, control of environmental pollution, eradication of poverty, elimination of communicable disease, not to mention survival, strike us as common and compelling goals. Some encouraging moves have been made in this direction already, such as cooperation in space. As Jerome Frank says: "The psychological problem is how to make all people aware that whether they like it or not, the earth is becoming a single community."

SUMMARY

A. **Is War Inevitable?**
1. Both the "biological" and "historical" arguments for the inevitability of war are found wanting. War appears to be a group product, and group processes can be altered.
2. One psychological factor that contributes to international tension is the tendency of nations to develop "mirror images" of each other; each attributes the same virtues to itself and the same vices to the other.

B. Conflict, Cooperation, and Power

3. Many international situations have the form of "Prisoner's Dilemma" games; any attempt by one nation to take advantage over another nation leads to a vicious cycle of competitive moves that none can win and all must lose.

4. When exploited subjects believe that they have been made to look foolish, and that they can keep private the costs of retaliation, they retaliate even though it means sacrificing their own gains—behavior designed only to save face.

5. According to international simulation studies, when faced with a national crisis the following tendencies arise among the leaders: a commitment to action, a reliance on past (rather than present) hostilities and friendships, a reduced tolerance for ambiguity, a narrowed perception of alternatives.

6. Laboratory games indicate that possession of a threat or a "deterrent" may increase the likelihood of its being used and precipitate the situation it was designed to prevent.

C. Reducing Conflict and Promoting Cooperation

7. Charles Osgood has proposed a method for reducing international tension—GRIT—which involves graduated reciprocation of disarmament. Laboratory studies suggest that this strategy is feasible and viable.

8. Field research suggests that **superordinate goals** (page 517)—goals with a compelling appeal for both groups that neither can achieve without the other—can promote intergroup cooperation that, in turn, breeds peace.

Appendix
The
Scientific
Basis
of
Psychology

There are several characteristics of science that have led observers to compare it to a game. Behavior related to games has the following characteristics:

1. Diversion
2. Competition
3. Socialization
4. Taking a chance
5. Strategy
6. Intellectual challenge
7. Curiosity
8. Excitement and pleasure
9. Social recognition
10. Problem solving (McCann and Segal, 1973.)

These characteristics are also part of the motivations of scientists and of the attractions scientific activity holds for them. Hence the analogy between science and games.

Scientists are *curious;* they constantly ask questions about the aspects of nature that interest them. The questions they ask are posed as a problem that *challenges* their ingenuity in finding *strategies* and methods and instruments to *solve the problem.* The solution to the problem is often dependent on collecting data. The data are often disorganized and incomplete and, like a puzzle, must be put together to make sense. The whole enterprise is *intellectually challenging,* and solving a scientific problem often requires months or years of effort and sacrifice with the *chance* of failure. A successful scientific finding provides a great deal of *excitement* and *pleasure* as well as *social recognition* and prestige.

A comparison of this sort is called an analogy. Like all analogies, the comparison is useful only to the degree it helps our understanding. However, there is a danger in using analogies, for if the comparison goes too far it becomes misleading. For example, some people object to the "game of science" analogy on the grounds that science, unlike game playing, involves a very serious professional effort with outcomes that have large impacts on human lives and the fate of nations. Considering that life-saving drugs and atomic weapons had their origins in the quest to solve the riddles of nature, this objection seems warranted. Comparison of science with a game does tend to obscure the seriousness of science. As long as we are aware of the limitations of an analogy, however, we can still use it to help give us insights. Analogies have played an important role in the history of science and can continue to help us in our understanding of scientific behavior. In this chapter, we will use the analogy to direct our examination of the goals, rules, methods, and strategies of science.

A. THE GOALS OF SCIENCE

The goals of science are the accurate description, prediction, explanation, and control of events. Although description is involved in all stages of research, it is of particular importance in early stages when the area to be studied is identified. **Descriptive statements** *require the observer to specify the characteristics of an object or event.* The descriptive characteristics of a person might include any one or more of the following: age, sex, height, weight, occupation, residence, marital status, education, intelligence, n Ach level, MMPI profile, and so on. There is, indeed, an infinite number of dimensions to describe a person; therefore, no descriptive list related to people can be complete. Since scientists are human beings and have limits to how much they can attend to at one time,

TABLE A.1 **Sample of relationship statements (these statements may or may not be valid)**

1. The bigger they are, the harder they fall.
2. Every time I open the refrigerator, my dog runs up to me and begs for food.
3. $E = MC^2$
4. The rate of speed multiplied by the time equals distance traveled ($R \times T = D$).
5. Whenever a crisis occurs, like getting fired, failing an exam, breaking up with a girl, Tom goes out and gets drunk.
6. The higher the gas flame under a pot, the faster the water will boil away.
7. If you treat people kindly, they will treat you kindly.
8. Haste makes waste.
9. People do those things which lead to success, reward, and approval.
10. The harder you push on the accelerator, the faster the car goes.
11. Antacid medication decreases the pain of heartburn.
12. Fat people act jolly and friendly, and skinny people act sad and unfriendly.
13. Tall people can sink more basketballs than short people.
14. Behavior that only gets rewarded occasionally is harder to extinguish (get rid of) than behavior that is continuously rewarded.
15. Psychological stress is a causal factor in many nervous disorders.

a researcher must restrict descriptions to a few dimensions of concern.

Descriptive statements can be either qualitative or quantitative. *Qualitative* statements classify the object on the basis of some quality, such as shape (round, square), color (blue, orange), sex (male, female), marital status (single, married), age (old, young), and so on. *Quantitative* statements answer questions—such as how many? how much?—that require some form of measurement. For example, "How much does that person weigh?" "What is his WAIS IQ score?" "How many dreams did she have last night?" and so on.

It is possible to make a prediction without being able to explain or understand the causes of an event. For example, the rising of the sun each morning and its setting each evening can be predicted without an understanding of the principles of astrophysics. *Scientific* **prediction** *is based on accurate observation and measurement of how*

events regularly vary together. When stated in words or other symbols, this regular variation is called a relationship statement.

Relationship statements *specify how objects and events regularly go together or indicate how changes in one object or event accompany, precede, or follow changes in another object or event.* There is a wide variety of ways of expressing relationships, as illustrated in Table A.1. Some statements are expressed as equations; others are expressed with precise verbal and quantitative magnitudes and directions of change; yet others are imprecise, vague "rules of thumb" or proverbs of limited or doubtful generality or validity. A major goal of science is to discover regularly recurring relationships in nature and describe them precisely. *"Guessed at," tentative statements of relationships between variables are called* **hypotheses:** "If people are assembled in large groups, then they will not give aid to someone in trouble as often as people who are alone or in very small groups." If the hypothesis is confirmed by repeated research, it may be called a *principle* or even a *scientific law*. The search for relationships among environmental events, the biological characteristics of an organism, and behavior is the main objective of psychology.

When one of the events specified in a relationship statement can be directly changed so as to produce a predicted change in the other event, we say that we can *control* the relationship. For example, when we know the relationship between the speed of a car and the pressure on the accelerator, we can change the speed of the car by pressing on the accelerator, that is, we have control over the speed. Control, as used here, is synonymous with manipulation. There are, of course, many events in nature that can be predicted but not controlled, such as the shifting of the tides and the rising and setting of the sun.

One type of *explanation* consists of describing the manipulations or circumstances that preceded an event. For example, an explanation of the eating behavior of a person (see Chapter 4A) might be based on any one or more of such preceding events as these: The individual has been deprived of food for eight hours; the individual's blood sugar level is falling and contractions of an empty stomach are increasing; people in the immediate environment are eating; a particular center of the brain that has been linked to eating behavior is now sending out neural impulses.

Another type of explanation is to show logically how relationship statements and the events they refer to can be derived from a theory or a set of assumptions. A number of such explanations have been presented in this book: for example, Schachter and Singer's cognitive appraisal theory of emo-

tion, Block's two-factor theory of psychosomatic disorder, and Bandura and Walters' social learning theory of personality development.

Now that we have examined some of the goals of science, let us look at some rules scientists follow in working toward these goals.

B. FOUR BASIC RULES OF THE SCIENCE GAME

What are the rules for the game of science? Ask a dozen scientists and you will probably get a dozen answers. If you examine all the responses carefully, however, you will find at least four common themes. These themes are the importance of supporting evidence, operational definitions, controlled observation, and representative sampling.

Rule One: **Supporting Evidence.** *Statements must be supported by evidence based on observations that can be shared with others.*

This rule means that the final test of the truth or falsity of any scientific descriptive or relationship statement must be based on observation, experience, or experiment. Scientific statements describing or relating objects or events must correspond to observed reality. Furthermore, the observations and experiences must be based on sense data (what we can see, hear, touch, and so on) on which different observers can agree. This definition rules out intuition or divine revelation as well as hallucination, all of which are personal experiences that can't be observed by others. The requirement that the observations must be shared by other observers means that scientific activities are both public and communicable.

To meet the public, communicable aspect of scientific activity, scientists must make written and oral reports of their research available to one another and the interested public. The reports must contain detailed descriptions of the research procedure and findings so that other competent scientists can follow each step of the study and, if desired, carry it out themselves to check on the accuracy of the report. Today there are over four dozen scientific journals that carry the bulk of research carried out by psychologists.

Is seeing believing? Can we always trust our senses to provide us with accurate representations of objects and events? We have all seen the tricks stage magicians play as well as optical illusions (see Chapter 5B); these should make us aware of the fallibility of our senses used alone. Texts of the past often contained statements of "fact" and "evidence" that did not stand up to later observations. No doubt this book, like any modern book, contains statements that may not stand up to future observations. Rule One does not guarantee that truth will always be found, but it opens up every statement to continuous testing and new observation. Just as the skeptic in the audience looks for the trick behind the illusion and checks his hunches by carefully observing the magician, a scientist constantly checks and rechecks observations of his own and others to avoid being fooled. By making the process open and public, science increases the chances of assuring the accuracy of observation and detecting errors in observation. The rule of supporting evidence is often considered to be the most important one for scientific activity. The rest of the rules, which we will turn to now, help specify how observational evidence is to be collected to assure us that

descriptive and relationship statements correspond to "real" objects and events.

Rule Two: **Operational Definition.** *All terms in a statement that refers to objects or events must be carefully defined in terms of the operations involved in observing, measuring, and manipulating the objects or the events.*

Let a songwriter say, "Love makes the world go round," and some scientist will ask, "What do you mean by love?" The scientist, as a lover, knows very well what the songwriter means. The scientist, as a scientist, needs to know the precise meanings of terms. Science requires that scientists be able to communicate with one another clearly and unambiguously. The hallmark of science is its openness. Any scientist with the necessary training should be able to repeat the work of another scientist from the research report. The repeatability of scientific experiments ensures that the findings of science will be checked enough times by enough people so that their accuracy can be accepted and further work can be built on these findings and the work that preceded them. In order to be sure they are communicating clearly and unambiguously, scientists try, as much as they are able, to define their terms operationally.

As we have previously noted, *an operational definition of a term specifies the operations (or procedures) that must be carried out in order to point to or in order to observe, measure, or manipulate an object or event referred to by the term.* An operational definition, therefore, is always given in terms of observables. Here are some operational definitions as they might be used in psychology:

Intelligence is the score attained on an intelligence test.

Memory is the number of names a person can recall from a list of 25 names studied for a five-minute period exactly one hour before the attempt to recollect them.

Hunger is the state of the organism (animal or human) after being deprived of food for 24 hours.

Although some of the richness of ordinary speech is lost in such definitions, many benefits follow. Talking in terms of "observables," such as scores on a test, number of items recalled from a list, or hours of deprivation, ensures that events, behaviors, and objects can be made unmistakably clear and explicit.

To define love operationally, one scientist might refer to the number of times two people kiss without prompting during a two-hour period when they do not know they are being observed. Another scientist might define it as the distance a man would swim through swiftly moving 50-degree water to get to the girl he says he loves when he hasn't seen her for three months.

The two scientists might not be dealing with the same emotion, but they would never be confused into thinking they were just because they both used the word *love* to refer to what they were observing in their studies. Each scientist has given love a distinctive operational definition. They might be surprised if the results of their separate investigations did not match, but they would not be confused, since their operational definitions make it clear that they are using different behaviors to "define" or indicate the emotion.

You might think of the operational definition as a kind of recipe or a set of instructions. The instructions tell us what we must do in order to observe, measure, or manipulate the objects or events to which a term refers.

Rule Three: **Controlled Observation.** *In order to state that changes in Event A "cause" changes in Event B, Event B must be observed when different values of Event A occur and when all other events can be discounted as a "cause" of any changes observed in Event B.*

Imagine this scene taking place some time in the Old West. A traveling salesman is making his pitch to a crowd of onlookers about how his "snake oil elixir" can cure headache, backache, cramps, toothache, heart pain, rheumatism, Monday morning blues, among other things. Suddenly, a man crawls through the crowd and cries, "Help me! I've just been bitten by a rattlesnake!" His leg shows fang marks. In a dramatic flourish, the pitchman offers the stricken man a drink of his cure as a humanitarian gesture. The man drinks the medication and the next day walks around . . . cured. "See," says the pitchman, "My elixir is also a snake bite cure. It will cure diseases and ailments that doctors haven't discovered yet." Would you have bought some? Appeals, claims, and evidence of this kind have sold billions of dollars of worthless medicine over the years, and still do. The purchasers would be quick to tell you that "seeing is believing."

Rule Three tells us that the conditions under which we see are as important as what we see. The conditions under which the "snake oil" was administered do not satisfy the rule of controlled observation. First of all, we can't be sure that the victim was bitten by a snake and, if bitten by a snake, that the snake was a rattlesnake. Even if it were a rattlesnake, it might not have had enough venom left from its last strike to be dangerous. Second, there is the possibility that the victim was an actor hired by the pitchman to put on a performance to help sell the medication—like the actors in TV commercials who help sell billions of dollars of questionable medication every year. Third, even if the man had really been bitten by the snake, he might have had a natural immunity or already been treated by a medical doctor or a friend; he might have been on the way to recovery and only suffering from the effect of shock.

Can you think of any other reasonable explanations for the man's supposed recovery? If you can, and if the observed data can reasonably be accounted for by any of these explanations, the conditions required by Rule Three, controlled observation, have not been met. Controlled observation requires all of the factors that could account for the victim's recovery other than the administration of the medication to have been discounted. Since this has not been done, the pitchman's conclusions are not justified.

Controlled observation also requires systematic variations in the manipulation of Event A, the medication. This is best accomplished in an experiment. (Experiments will be discussed more fully later.) For this example, one group of men bitten by rattlesnakes should be given the "snake oil" and another group of bitten men deprived of the snake oil. If the members of the treated group survive and those in the nontreated group die, then supporting evidence is provided for the pitchman's claims.

Rule Four: **Sampling and Generalization.** *Generalization of descriptive and relationship statements to objects and events other than those observed can be made only if the objects and events are adequate representative samples from the set of objects and events to which you wish to generalize.*

David McClelland of Harvard University and his colleagues have been studying the "need for achievement" over many years. Need for achievement, as we saw in Chapter 4B, is broadly defined in terms of working toward success in a competitive setting. The operational definition of need for achievement (abbreviated n Ach) requires the counting of success words and themes in a subject's imaginative stories made up to a set of ambiguous pictures. The greater the number of achievement-related words and themes, the greater the need for achievement. McClelland has found that subjects with high n Ach scores are more successful in business in terms of income and leadership, get higher grades in college, and gamble less than low n Ach subjects. However, this finding holds up for men only, not for women. For predictions using n Ach, samples of men are not "representative" samples of all human beings. When selecting a representative sample of any group of people, gender has often been found to be a very important factor to consider. For example, if a researcher wanted to generalize findings to a population containing 40 percent males and 60 percent females, then a representative sample should contain the same ratio of men to women.

McClelland began his studies using only American college students. Over the years, he has expanded his sample to include students in European and Asian colleges, as well as businessmen in various countries. His findings have held up so well for the several hundred subjects of diverse ages, occupations, and cultures he has studied over the years, he feels safe in concluding that they can be generalized to most males.

This example illustrates several major applications and implications of the sampling and generalization rule. It is obviously too costly in time, money, and resources to observe every object or event in the universe in order to get the evidence needed to support a descriptive or relationship statement. Practically, representative samples have to be taken from the population of objects or events we wish to study. If the samples are "truly" representative, then our findings from the sample can be generalized to the population of objects or events from which we took our samples. We can't study all men, so we study a representative sample of men and assume that what we find can also be found for men in general. When we apply what we have learned from a sample to the population from which the sample was drawn, we have made a generalization. A representative sample, representative of the major characteristics of the population—such as age distribution, occupational levels, and cultural background—enables us to make valid generalizations. Psychologists constantly make generalizations about the effects of environment, heredity, and biological factors as they relate to behavior.

C. ASKING QUESTIONS ABOUT BEHAVIOR AND EXPERIENCE

An important skill needed in playing the game of science is the asking of questions that can lead to research that achieves the goals of science. The kind of question directs not only what is studied, but also the strategies that may be used in the study. In this section, we will examine some of the characteristics of the questions scientists ask.

ASKING "SIGNIFICANT" QUESTIONS

Here are some frequently asked questions about behavior and experience.

How much influence does the environment have on the development of intelligence?

Why don't bystanders help people who are faced with an emergency or crisis?

Why do societies go to war periodically?

Why are many people prejudiced toward other people?

How can we ever be sure that people are honest when they tell about their experiences?

Why do some people conform to society and others rebel?

Why does a person's behavior change when he is under stress?

What happens in the brain when a person learns or memorizes something?

Why does a supposedly comical event produce laughter in some people and not in others?

What factors cause mental illness?

How is hereditary information coded in the gene?

Can one person "really" ever know how another feels?

If you expect to get answers to these questions as they are stated, you are headed for a great disappointment. No one can answer these questions, as they are stated, in a manner that meets the rigorous standards acceptable to science. The questions are so comprehensive, so big, that they can't be answered. Before "big" questions like these can be answered scientifically, they must be broken down into several manageable, smaller questions. Each question must be phrased in terms that lead to observation, measurement, and testing.

SCIENTIFICALLY ANSWERABLE QUESTIONS

To give you a sense of why and how the "big" question is broken down, let us take one of the questions presented in the open-

Focus A.1
The Naming Fallacy and Circular Reasoning

In our daily life, we often assume that motivation and intelligence are in the person, that gravity reaches out and pulls things down, that energy pushes things around, and that culture is in the members of a society. In these instances, we have taken a concept, a label for a set of observed events, and acted as if the label gave us knowledge of invisible, unobserved, nonmeasurable internal causes, processes, or mechanisms. *To use the name of an event as an explanation of the event is faulty reasoning and is called the* **naming fallacy**, *sometimes evident in* **circular reasoning.** For example, if in answer to the question, "Why does Mary get good grades?" we answer, "Because she is intelligent," the next question is, "What do you mean by intelligence?" The answer: "Intelligence is getting good grades." Or, "why does Myron act that way?" Answer: "Because he's schizophrenic." Question: "What is schizophrenic?" Answer: "Behavior we don't understand." Question: "What is this behavior we don't understand?" Answer: "Schizophrenia." You can see by these examples that using the name of the event to explain it leads in circles and adds nothing to our original knowledge.

ing of this section and try to "answer" it.

How much influence does the environment have on the development of intelligence? There can be no doubt that this is a significant question with profound implications for education from nursery school to college. We know that intelligence is rewarded by society in the form of "good" jobs, money, prestige, and access to the "finer" things in life. But before we go any further, we need to define the key words in the question. What do we mean when we say intelligence and environment? These words are ambiguous; you will probably find as many definitions for them as there are people to ask. When a word has many different referents, you must pin down and share one of its referents in order to communicate accurately and answer the question asked.

Concepts. Intelligence has no odor, color, texture, or taste. It's not an object or event that is observable. It's not an "it." Intelligence is a concept, and like all concepts, it is a word that is used to name a category of events that share common characteristics. Concepts, like other ideas, are not observable but are useful in helping us bring order and simplicity into the complexity of the events that bombard us through our senses. Intelligence is a concept that is of particular research interest to psychologists (see Chapter 8).

Like any other concept, it was invented to describe certain characteristics regularly observed in human behavior. The concept became popular when people felt that the idea represented by the concept helped make sense out of their own behavior and the behavior of others. Words like energy, force, and gravity in physics or valence in chemistry are used in similar ways.

Reducing Big Questions to Manageable Size. The concept of intelligence involves a wide variety of behaviors and the concept of environment involves a host of events—more behaviors and events than any one investigation can focus on. This

TABLE A.2   A small sample of behaviors used by researchers to define intelligence

Number of words in a person's vocabulary
Number of digits a person can recall
Number of arithmetic problems a person can solve in a fixed time limit
Number of words a person can associate to the letter S
Time it takes to assemble a puzzle
Time it takes to copy a complex pattern
Number of letters decoded in a decoding task
Number of facts recalled from common experience
Correct identification and matching of three-dimensional figures
Procedure used to put a puzzle together
Correct identification of errors in complex diagrams or pictures
Correct completion of a complex number series or an abstract sequence of patterns
Complexity of problem solutions
Strategy used to solve a problem
The time it takes for a person to unscramble five scrambled words or sentences
The number of correct inferences a person can make from logical arguments

TABLE A.3   A small sample of events used by researchers to define environment

Number of minutes of oxygen deprivation at birth or during surgery
Number of children in the family
Family position of the individual, i.e., eldest child, younger child
Income of parents
Schooling experience, such as rural or urban
Age of weaning
Number of books or magazines in the home
Frequency with which parents read to child
Number and kind of toys available at home
Attendance at preschool, kindergarten, etc.
Age schooling began
Instructional methods used by teachers
Discipline pattern of parents
Opportunities to explore household during early childhood
Opportunity to manipulate objects during early childhood
Frequency of parent-child conversation
Complexity of parent-child conversation

means that no one investigator can study all the various meanings of and relationships between intelligence and environment. What every researcher must do, then, is to *narrow down* and select no more than a few specific observations and meas- urements to study. The process of operationally defining the concepts in a question, in effect, helps to reduce the big, significant question to manageable size. Tables A.2 and A.3 provide a partial list of behaviors used as operational definitions of intelligence and different operationally defined environmental events.

Putting Questions Together. The process of breaking down any concept into its component parts is called *analysis*. One of the results of analysis is a list of potential operational definitions for the key concepts in the big question. Examine the following scientifically answerable questions that deal with small but observable and hence testable aspects of the big question. The parentheses contain an operational definition of the preceding variable.

What is the relationship between the income (yearly income before taxes) of the parents and the size (number of words) of a child's vocabulary?

What is the relationship between the opportunity a person has had to explore the environment during childhood (the number of hours per day an infant is allowed to crawl around the house) and logical reasoning (number of correct inferences)?

What effect do different degrees of oxygen deprivation (minutes and seconds of deprivation) have on memory (number of digits recalled)?

Different researchers would select different measures and observations for their studies of the relationship between environment and intelligence. A researcher's choice reflects personal hypotheses and training. Regardless of the choice, when the original question is stated in a form ready for answering, something happens to the questions.

Obviously, the small answerable question does not have the profundity and grandeur of the big question. Rather than ask about the complex forces of nature and environment or the inner workings of the "mind," we are forced to look at simple, everyday behaviors. All the rich connotations of the words "environment" and "intelligence" that occur in everyday speech have been purged and stripped away. We are left with questions that refer to raw, observable behavior or environmental events. This is the price we pay for the precision and objectivity of science.

BEHAVIOR AS THE PRODUCT OF ENVIRONMENT AND PERSON

As we have noted, psychologists spend much of their time in the attempt to learn how behavior is related to events in the environment and the characteristics of the organism. Environmental events and organismic characteristics act together to produce behavior. In order to pursue this goal, psychologists break down questions about the environment and the organism into factors that they think affect behavior (*variables*).

The Environment. Any number of classifications could be used to categorize environmental events. Table A.4 provides a few examples psychologists have found useful. The particular categories used

TABLE A.4 **Classification of environment**

SOCIAL ENVIRONMENT
Socioeconomic class, status and role, parental or peer expectancies, experimenter's instructions to the subject.

PHYSICAL ENVIRONMENT
Type, intensity, pattern, and duration of a stimulus such as sound, light, temperature, humidity; physical setting such as indoors, outdoors, small room, large room.

TABLE A.5 Organismic variables

Age	Bodily Changes Due to
Sex	Drugs
Height	Damage to Nervous
Weight	Tissues
Blood Pressure	Loss of Limb or Organ
Perspiration	Impaired Organ or Limb
Genotype	Functioning
Phenotype	Physical Illness
Amount of Sleep	Hormone Flow
Metabolic Rate	Past Experience

would, of course, depend on the point of view and research purpose of the psychologist.

Organismic Variables and Subject Characteristics. The environment and the stimuli that relate to behavior and experience do not operate in a vacuum. There is an organism (an animal or person) that must behave and react to the stimuli. There are innumerable characteristics of an organism that interact with the environmental stimuli to produce behavior. These characteristics are often referred to as *organismic variables* (or subject characteristics or person variables). Table A.5 lists some common organismic variables that are considered important in the study of behavior.

The classification and labeling of the objects and events of interest to psychologists will vary from text to text and person to person, depending on point of view, purpose, and experience. This is true for the objects and events of interest to any scientific discipline as well as to people in daily life.

Criteria for Identifying Scientific Questions. What are the rules for asking good,

scientifically answerable questions? Unfortunately, a simple set of infallible "how to" rules for asking scientific questions cannot be presented. Asking significant scientific questions is a creative act. However, the major points we have discussed will provide you with some criteria for identifying scientific questions and asking some of your own.

D. A CASE STUDY IN EXPERIMENTAL METHODS

The most powerful research tool used by any science to study the relationships between variables is the experiment. Experiments provide the means to determine more precisely how variables relate and are causally linked than is possible with the other principal tools—naturalistic observation, surveys, and case study methods.

We will examine those methods later. In this section we will examine the procedures and logic involved in the experimental method. The work of Bibb Latané and John Darley on bystander apathy covered in Chapter 14B will serve as an illustrative case.

BREAKING DOWN THE BIG QUESTION

Why do people fail to come to the aid of another person who is in an emergency? Before Latané and Darley could answer this question, they had to recognize it as a "big" question. The "big" question contains many abstract and vague terms. Each term can potentially refer to a wide variety of people, events, and circumstances. Before we can answer the "big" question, we must examine the possible

Focus A.2
"Why?" Questions Can Be Troublesome

"Daddy, why do children cry?"

"Because they are spanked."

"Why are children spanked?"

"Because they are naughty."

"Why are children naughty?"

"Well, because . . . they just are, that's all. Stop asking why."

Many children constantly ask their parents "why" questions until the parents are driven to distraction. The answers to such questions are often disappointing to a child, and each answer tends to lead to another "why" question. "Why" questions tend toward ultimate causality, which cannot be determined scientifically. A scientist, as a person, may grapple with such questions but not while playing the role of scientist.

If "why" is shorthand for a relationship question such as, "What is the relationship between . . . ?" or "Under what conditions . . . ?" and if the events involved are operationally defined, then, and only then, can the word be used scientifically. In this book, the word "why" is used in this sense.

operational definitions of each term and then focus on smaller questions that can be answered. Here are a few questions about the meaning of each key term and some possible definitions.

The first question you might ask is, "Who is being called on to help?" Men, women, old people, young people? Brother, sister, or friend? Medical doctor, policeman, or passerby? The second question might be, "Who is calling for help?" Man, woman, child, brother, sister, friend, stranger? A third question, "What kind of aid or help is needed?" Calling the police, applying first aid, being a witness at a trial, lending money? The fourth question, "In what kind of emergency situation or environmental context is the help required?" A burning building, a holdup on a lonely street, an automobile accident on a busy street corner, a friend telephoning to say that she is going to commit suicide, a man collapsing on a busy street? You can see

that the answer to a "big" question cannot be given unless you define in specific terms what is meant by the abstract and vague terms: people, aid, and emergency. Notice how Latané and Darley break up the "big" question and define their terms operationally.

Are Bystanders Really Apathetic? When Latané and Darley examined news reports of bystander apathy carefully, they noticed a few things that others had ignored or dismissed. First, the bystanders were not in fact apathetic. True, they didn't lift a finger to help, but they were not indifferent. During the crisis they watched with fascination and horror, and in interviews after the crime, they expressed their sympathy and concern for the victim.

Second, they noticed that the reported crimes were witnessed by crowds of people. Nearly everyone has seen or been part of the passive, uninvolved crowds that swarm around highway accidents, drownings, fires, and suicide attempts. This observation led them to the following question: "Is there something about crowds that inhibits bystanders from helping in a crisis?" The researchers had a hunch that the answer to the question was affirmative. They examined the research literature and carefully worked out the following explanation of apathy, which they tested in their experiment.

Most emergencies, they reasoned, begin as ambiguous events. For example, a man staggering on the street may be drunk, suffering from a heart attack, or experiencing the onset of diabetes. Before taking action, a person must first notice the event, decide whether or not it is an emergency, and then decide what action to take. Decision-making is determined by many factors, including the words and actions of others. If other bystanders take no action or say nothing, they are likely to inhibit a potential Good Samaritan. Latané and Darley's argument would lead to the following hypothesis: Individuals are less likely to help in an emergency if they witness it in the presence of other people than if they witness it alone.

Their next step was to devise an experiment to test their hypothesis.

THE PSYCHOLOGICAL EXPERIMENT

Psychological experiments *consist of the manipulation of some environmental event in order to observe the effects of the manipulation on the behavior of subjects under controlled conditions.* In one experiment, described in Chapter 14B, Latané and Darley presented their male college student subjects with an "emergency." The subjects were led into an office, where they were asked to fill out a questionnaire; while they were doing so, smoke was blown through a ventilation duct into the office. Each subject's behavior in response to the smoke was observed and recorded through a one-way mirror. In order to determine the effects of bystanders on the subjects' behavior, the experimenters compared three different conditions. In the first condition, the subjects answered the questionnaire alone as the smoke filled the room. In the second condition, each subject was placed in the room with two confederates of the experimenter who were instructed to remain unresponsive as the smoke filled the room. The third group consisted of three naive subjects.

Independent and Dependent Variables. Any event that yields measurable changes is called a **variable.** *The event manipulated by the experimenter is called an* **independent variable.** It is "independent" because it is manipulated by the experimenter independently of anything the subject says or does. In this experiment the type of group the subjects were in was manipulated. Subjects were placed in a room alone, or with two other naive subjects, or with two unresponsive confederates. The group type was the independent variable. The behavior of the subject, that is, whether or not he left the room and went for help, was the **dependent variable.** *It is called dependent because its value is dependent on manipulation of another variable, the independent variable.* Notice that whether or not the subject left the room for help is behavior that was *dependent* on whether or not bystanders were present. In experiments the dependent variable is the behavior selected for observation. Dependent variables in psychology usually are behaviors or some product of behavior.

What effect did the manipulation of group type (the independent variable) have on the subjects' response to the smoke (the dependent variable)?

This study supports the hypothesis that when people witness an emergency in a group, they are less likely to respond than people who witness an emergency alone.

Experimental and Control Groups. The experimenters found that, of the subjects who waited in the room with the two unresponsive confederates, only one in ten took action. Can any conclusions be drawn from this bit of data alone? If this were all the information you had about the study, you would no doubt ask: "What would have happened if the subjects had waited alone?" As you probably realize by now, every experiment requires *at least* two different values of the independent variables so the effects of one can be compared with the effects of the other.

In this experiment, the behavior of subjects who were in the room alone was compared to the behavior of those who were in the room with two unresponsive confederates and those who were in the room with other naive subjects. When groups are used in this way for contrast, one group is usually referred to as the "control" group, and the other group(s) as the "experimental" group(s). The experimental groups are subjected to the values of the independent variable that the investigator hypothesizes as important. Thus, for the Latané and Darley experiment, the *experimental* groups were those in which people other than the subject were present, since the hypothesis was that the presence of others somehow inhibited action. The group of subjects who worked alone, that is, in the absence of others, is then the *control* group. *It is*

customary to call the group that receives the experimental manipulation the "**experimental**" *group, while the contrasting group that is not manipulated is called the* "**control**" *group.*

Experimental Control. Can we be sure from this study that it was in fact the manipulation of the independent variable—that is, the number of people in the room—that caused the different responses of the subjects? After all, most human environments bombard each person with innumerable stimuli that can potentially affect behavior. How can we ever be certain that the behavior observed actually is a result of the variable manipulated? The subjects in this or in any experiment may differ in their feelings, moods, expectancies, motivations, or intelligence. Any one of these factors may have accounted for the behavior observed. In order to isolate the effects of the independent variable under study, an experimenter tries to keep constant any and all other variables that could influence the dependent variable. One way to do so is to make the environment of the subjects as identical as possible, such as testing all subjects in the same room and giving them the same instructions. Another way is to make sure that the subjects in the experimental and control groups are as equivalent as possible in such organismic factors as intelligence, sex, age, maturation, and so on. *Experimental control* is a matter of holding constant all characteristics of the environment and subjects, except the independent variable. Any change in the behavior of the subjects related to the dependent variable can then be attributed to changes in the independent variable. Experimental control was essential in the "Smoke-Filled Room" study because the experimenters wanted to determine whether the manipulation of the independent variable—the number of witnesses—was responsible for the subjects' behavior in each group and not age, sex, intelligence, education, and so on. Had the groups differed on these or other important variables, the experimenters could not claim that differences in behavior were necessarily attributable to the number of witnesses.

SINGLE- AND DOUBLE-BLIND CONTROL

What would the outcome of the "Smoke-Filled Room" study have been if each subject was aware of the purpose of the study and whether or not he was in the experimental group?

The Single-Blind Study. Latané and Darley believed that, if their subjects knew the purpose of the study and which groups they were in, the outcome of the experiment would have been affected. In order to prevent this from happening, they had to keep their subjects uninformed, or "blind." This can be a problem, because people do not volunteer for most experiments unless they know what they are for, or at least think they do. In such cases, it is necessary to provide a "cover story" that may involve deception and incomplete information. *This procedure—in which the subjects are uninformed about the real purpose of the study or which treatment group they are in—is called a* **single-blind control.**

Without single-blind controls, an experimenter may not be able to determine whether the experimental outcome is the result of the *manipulation* of the independent variable or the subject's *knowl-edge* of the experimental purpose and manipulation.

Single-Blind Drug Studies and Placebos. A person's belief and expectancy can have a very profound effect on behavior and experience. For example, people in pain will often experience and report dramatic reduction in the pain if they are given a sugar pill or an injection of salt water and told that it is a "pain killer." In order to study the effects of a drug, the experimenter must be able to separate the effects of the drug from the effects of suggestions and the subject's expectancy. Therefore, subjects in both experimental (drug) and control (sugar pill) groups are told they have been given the drug.

The sugar pill treatment is called a **placebo.** *The term also refers to any treatment whose effects are due to suggestion and expectation.*

Double-Blind Controls. The uncontrolled bias and expectancies of the experimenter can have as distorting an effect on the experimental outcome as the uncontrolled expectancies of the subjects. Experimenters are human; they carry out research to serve many of their own human "needs,"—for challenge, for fame, for humanitarian reasons, to prove their theory correct, and so on. The experimenter's expectancies can be communicated unconsciously to subjects by gestures, tone of voice, and subtle changes in instructions. All or any of these factors unwittingly provide suggestions to the subjects, influence their behavior, and alter the experimental outcome. To minimize this, experimenters often hire lab technicians or assistants who are kept uninformed about the purpose of the study and the distribution of subjects in experimental and control groups. The assistants, not the experimenter, meet subjects, give instructions, carry out the manipulation of the independent variable, and collect data. *This procedure—in which both the experimenter's assistants and the subjects are kept uninformed about the purpose of the study and which group is which—is called a* **double-blind control.**

THE VIRTUES AND LIMITATIONS OF EXPERIMENTS

Controlled experiments, when carried out with care and precision, constitute the most powerful tool of science, for they permit the isolation of precise cause-and-effect relationships. Experiments can also be repeated by others to check on the reliability and generalizability of the findings. Still, there are a number of problems that seriously limit the usefulness of experiments in the social and behavioral sciences.

The first limitation is the problem of generalizing from the experimental situation to real life. In any experiment that involves humans we must ask, "Are the manipulated situations sufficiently realistic?" Are they close enough to the events in real life to allow us to generalize from experimental to real-life events? As an affirmative example, Latané and Darley present evidence in reports of their research to convince the most critical reviewer that their subjects believed that the situation was real.

The second limitation is a moral one. It stems from the need to make many experimental manipulations believable to the subjects. How far should a researcher go in creating an artificial and sometimes stressful condition and then deceiving a subject into believing that it is real? What

responsibility does the researcher have to his subjects after the experiment in informing them about the manipulation and in handling any emotional upset or disturbance the experiment may have elicited? We have touched on these issues before in Focus 14.4: Ethical Standards for Psychological Research.

The third limitation is also a moral one. Regardless of any "scientific" value, certain possible experimental manipulations, by their very nature, would not be moral or legal and would not be acceptable to society or the subjects involved or to the vast majority of scientists. For example, few mothers would permit their babies to be isolated from love and care in order to permit a researcher to study the effects of isolation on human development. Similarly, few people would permit a part of the brain to be removed to determine its effect on memory or personality.

Psychologists are dependent on the cooperation of human subjects who, for the most part, are volunteers. Therefore, every effort is extended to prevent a credibility gap or loss of confidence. Psychologists are first of all human beings who are, for the most part, compassionate and honest, and who feel a strong responsibility to safeguard the rights and dignity of their research subjects. As we pointed out in Focus 14.4, this concern for the rights and dignity of subjects is reflected in the American Psychological Association Ethical Standards, which holds all of its members accountable for their ethical behavior as researchers. The code covers such topics as the civil rights, confidentiality, and the health and safety of subjects. Deviant members can be dropped from Association membership, and this can impair their professional advancement and the future acceptance of their research findings.

E. NATURALISTIC OBSERVATION, SAMPLE SURVEYS, AND CASE STUDIES

Although the experimental method can potentially provide the most rigorous information about the relationship between variables, it is not always possible to use for a variety of reasons, as noted in the previous section. In this section we will examine several nonexperimental methods used by psychologists—naturalistic observation, sample surveys, and case studies.

NATURALISTIC OBSERVATION

Naturalistic observation *involves watching and noting behavior in a natural, real-life setting.* With this approach psychologists have studied children at play, the nest-building of birds, the social behavior of chimpanzees in the wild, the behavior of people in crowds. Jean Piaget made use of naturalistic observation of the development of his own children and took the resulting data as a basis for his theories of cognitive development (see Chapter 8B).

Naturalistic observation provides a researcher with several distinct advantages over the experiment:
1. Natural events that cannot be duplicated in a laboratory can be studied.
2. The subject is usually unaware of the observation so the subject's awareness does not alter the behavior being observed.
3. The subject's cooperation is not needed.

Naturalistic observation requires the observer to keep any bias or interpretation out of the record. Careful descriptions of the behavior being observed as well as special training of observers ensure the collection of undistorted data.

SAMPLE SURVEYS

*A **sample survey** is a research procedure in which the investigator defines a group, or "population," of interest (e.g., college students, voters, married women), then selects a sample from the population and collects some measurable or descriptive data for each subject in the sample (e.g., attitude toward drugs, educational goals, smoking habits, age) in order to describe the population.*

Public attitude and opinion polls are one common type of sample survey, but a sample survey can focus on any aspect of behavior or experience that may be of interest to the investigator.

Sample surveys enable researchers to ask and answer questions that are difficult, and sometimes impossible, to answer by any other method. Here are some examples. What are the stages of moral development among children? To what extent do American married men and women approve of abortion? Does acceptance of minority groups (blacks, Chicanos, Indians) increase as white Anglo-Saxon Protestant Americans get older? Is there a relationship between parental education (number of years and level of schooling) and the kinds of punishment (spanking, scolding, removal of privileges) used to discipline their children? Notice that the sample survey can deal with the descriptive characteristics of a sample as well as with changes in behavior over time and relationships between different measured characteristics.

Selecting a Sample. In almost all research studies, regardless of the method, the researcher is interested in generalizing the findings beyond the sample of objects or events studied to some population of objects or events. As we have already seen, justification of such generalizations must be based on the representativeness of the sample. You can see now why researchers spend a great deal of thought and effort in selecting samples that are representative of the population of objects or events to which they want to generalize. For example, it would be very costly, indeed, and very impractical to survey every voter one month before an election to find out voters' preferences. In fact, it would probably cost as much as the election itself. In this case, pollsters select a representative cross section of the voting population for their sample. A carefully selected sample of 2000 people across the nation can provide a very accurate picture of how millions of Americans will vote.

The Survey. Once the sample is selected, the researcher must then collect some measure of some characteristic of each subject under study. The measure can be a **verbal report** (*a statement made by a person about what was or is experienced, felt, perceived, believed, etc.*) based on an interview or questionnaire, a test of some kind, such as intelligence or personality tests, or an observation, such as the number of children in the home, kinds of books on the shelf, or mannerisms of the subject. Of course, whatever the measure, it must be very carefully defined and described.

Sample surveys are important in many sciences. Biologists might be interested in sampling fish from a lake in a study of the average size or health of the species inhabiting the lake. A Department of Health may take a survey of a group of smokers over time to determine the relationship between smoking, heart disease, and cancer. A political candidate may hire a professional poll taker to determine the

political issues of interest to the voters. Psychologists who focus on attitudes, opinions, beliefs, and child-rearing practices, make extensive use of survey research procedures.

THE CASE STUDY

In the **case study (or clinical) method** *information is gathered about the life history of a person or of a group.* The information can be obtained through interviewing the individual under study as well as friends, parents, teachers, and so on. Other sources of data can also be included, such as public records, psychological tests, and naturalistic observation.

One of the most famous and extensive uses of the case study method is found in the work of Sigmund Freud, who based most of his theory on his observations and interpretations of his patients' behavior (see Chapter 10A).

As with naturalistic observation, caution must be taken to minimize the bias of the observer in recording the data.

A RESEARCH TECHNIQUE: THE INTERVIEW

There are many kinds of individual and group behaviors and experiences that are beyond the practical limits of direct observation, such as private behavior (sexual activity, husband-wife arguments), or antisocial behavior ("immoral" or illegal acts) or behavior protected by custom or law (religious confession, doctor-patient conversation), as well as all the events a person may have witnessed in a lifetime or events that are not observable to others (ideas, feelings, attitudes, moral beliefs, opinions). In order to gain access to this vast potential source of data, psychologists, as do other social and behavioral scientists, often make use of a variety of verbal report methods. The verbal report is often obtained with a technique called the **interview.** *During the* **interview,** *which usually takes the form of a conversation, the interviewer asks questions and the interviewee answers them.* There are essentially two forms of the interview: the structured interview and the unstructured interview.

In the **structured interview,** *the interviewer entirely controls the wording and sequence of the questions and the responses are confined to a pre-specified set of answers presented in a multiple choice format.*

For example, consider the question, "When do you think the UN will get the power to prevent war?"
Answers: (1) within 5 years
          (2) within 10 years
          (3) within 20 years
          (4) over 20 years
          (5) never
or, "How strongly do you agree with the following statement: 'College tuition should be used to support the full cost of a college education.' "
Answers: (1) strongly agree
          (2) mildly agree
          (3) unsure
          (4) mildly disagree
          (5) strongly disagree
or, simply, "Have you been on a date with a companion of the opposite sex in the last month?"
Answers: (1) Yes   (2) No

During the **unstructured interview,** *both the interviewer and the interviewee are given very wide freedom in their questions and responses, but the interviewer is constrained to focus on the topic or area that is defined by the purpose of the interview.* The interviewer might have an outline of questions or topics but would be free to word and place them in any sequence. The interviewer may also use a variety of general questions designed to help the interviewee elaborate on the topic, but with minimal interviewer influence. For example, "Would you tell me more about that?" "I don't understand. Could you explain?" To encourage the interviewee to continue the interviewer may nod, smile, shake his or her head, or simply say, "Mmmmm."

Although the unstructured interview is more time-consuming than the structured interview and yields information that is more difficult to quantify, it has certain advantages. Because of the greater detail and richness of responses obtained and because of the interviewer's freedom to probe or require elaboration, the unstructured interview is often superior in determining the interviewee's "true" perceptions, opinions, and attitudes (see Table A.6).

F. QUANTIFICATION AND STATISTICS

If you were asked to bring back a "lot of milk" from the store, it would be very unlikely you would know what quantity to buy. How much is a "lot of milk"? If quantity were added to the request—"Bring back four quarts of milk"—you would be able to bring back the exact amount requested. Quantification adds to the precision of description. Requests for descriptive information (how much, how many, how big, how far, how fast) are ambiguous unless some quantitative dimension or measure is specified. For example, the question, "How big?" should be rephrased as, "How many feet tall?" "How smart?" should be rephrased as, "What was the person's score on the Stanford-Binet IQ test?"

TABLE A.6   **Comparison of interview methods**

	CONTROL OVER INVESTI-GATOR'S QUESTIONS	CONTROL OVER RESPONDENT'S ANSWERS	DEGREE OF PRECISION AND REPRODUCI-BILITY	BREADTH AND DEPTH OF POTENTIAL RESPONSES
Unstructured Interview	Low	Low	Low	High
Semistructured Interview				
Structured Interview: e.g., Multiple Choice, Checklist, Questionnaire				
Formal Tests: e.g., Attitude, IQ, Aptitude	High	High	High	Low

(Based on Berelson and Steiner, 1964.)

Remember that accurate and precise description and reporting of observations is an important aspect of a scientific study.

Quantification is also an essential part of making relationship statements. The greatest precision and accuracy in reporting relationships is achieved by stating relationships in numerical or quantitative terms. This section will explore some of the issues and methods involved in quantification and measurement in psychology.

MEASUREMENT

The **measurement procedure** *consists of applying numbers or labels to objects or events (or their characteristics) in accordance with systematic rules.* When you observe a group of people and count the number of men and women, according to implicit rules of gender labeling, you are carrying out a measurement at a very basic level. When you use a ruler to find out and report the length of a room, you are measuring at a much "higher" level. Each of these measurement procedures requires you to follow some very careful rules so that if others check up on you, they will come up with similar results. Scientific measurement procedures must have the rules or operations very carefully defined and described so that a trained observer can carry them out. The measurement process involves four basic elements:

1. An object or event or some characteristic of the object or event that is to be measured (e.g., intelligence).
2. A specified standard unit of comparison

or classification (e.g., a correct response to a Stanford-Binet test item).

3. An explicit set of rules and procedures that is to be followed when using the unit or classification for measurement (e.g., standardized administration and scoring procedures).
4. A descriptive statement that assigns a category, label or number to the object or event (or its characteristic) (e.g., an IQ of 120).

Some measurement actually includes the scientist as part of the rule. For example, chemists insert a piece of litmus paper into a solution, and, if the paper turns "pink," the solution is classified as an acid. If the paper turns "blue," the solution is classified as a base. The chemist must look at the paper and report what is seen. Both the chemist and the litmus paper are part of the measurement operation. What happens if the chemist is color blind? Obviously, such a person might not classify the solutions in the same way as his fellow chemists. However, scientific reporting, careful specification of the measurement rule, and the replication and check by other scientists would certainly detect and correct for the error.

In describing and analyzing their data, psychologists often use descriptive and inferential statistics, which we shall examine next.

DESCRIPTIVE STATISTICS

Descriptive statistics *is used to organize, summarize, and compare data collected* from a research study. The "raw scores" listed in Table A.7 correspond to the retention scores subjects obtained in a hypothetical memory study. Raw scores are difficult to study so they are placed in a

frequency distribution. A *frequency distribution lists the scores from the lowest to the highest, and a tally is made of the frequency of each score.* Examination of the frequency distribution quickly reveals the outcome of the memory study. These data can also be displayed in a **histogram,** (a bar graph), or a **frequency polygon,** as shown in Figure A.1.

Central Tendency

In a frequency distribution the score around which most other scores cluster is called the central tendency. Three com-

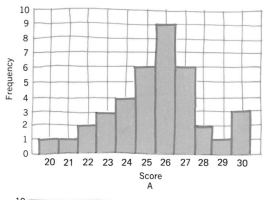

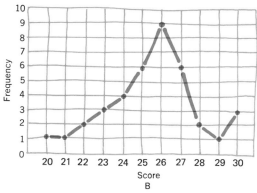

FIGURE A.1 Statistical refinement of raw scores. (A) A histogram. (B) A frequency polygon.

TABLE A.7   **Statistical refinement of raw scores**

FREQUENCY DISTRIBUTION

RAW SCORES		SCORE	FREQUENCY	CENTRAL TENDENCY
30	25	30	3	$\text{mean} = \dfrac{\text{sum of scores}}{\text{number of scores}}$
30	25	29	1	
30	25	28	2	
29	25	27	6	
28	25	26	9	$= \dfrac{971}{38} = 25.55$
28	25	25	6	
27	24	24	4	
27	24	23	3	median $= 26$
27	24	22	2	
27	24	21	1	mode $= 26$
27	23	20	1	
27	23			
26	23			
26	22			
26	22			
26	21			
26	20			
26				
26				
26				
26				

mon measures of central tendency are the **mean, median,** and **mode.** Each describes an average score, but they may not always be identical, depending on the distribution of the scores.

Mean. To compute the mean you add up all the scores and divide the sum by the number of scores (see Table A.7). Since all scores contribute to the mean, a few extreme scores can raise or lower it. For example, an exceptional subject in a memory study may receive very high scores and raise the mean for the group. Whenever there are a few extremely high or low scores that can raise or lower the mean, the median may be called for.

Median. The median is a measure of central tendency that corresponds to the score above which and below which lie 50 percent of the cases. If there is an odd number of scores, the median is simply the middle score. If there is an even number of scores, the median is an average of the two scores in the middle of the distribution. The median is not affected by extremely high or low scores.

Mode. The mode is simply the most frequently occurring score in a distribution. It is not affected by extreme score variations. The mode does not have many useful mathematical properties and is seldom used by psychologists.

INFERENTIAL STATISTICS

As we saw in Sections B and E, sampling and inferring the characteristics of a sampled population make up a powerful research tool. **Inferential statistics** *consists of a wide variety of methods that enable a researcher to infer the descriptive characteristics of a larger population on the basis of a representative sample.* If, for example, a representative sample of 100 female students in your college is selected and given an IQ test, inferential statistical methods would enable the researcher to predict the average IQ of the women in the college along with a statement of how accurate, in terms of probability, the prediction would be.

Inferential statistics *is also used to determine whether or not differences between experimental and control groups in a study can be attributed to the manipulation of the independent variable or to chance factors.*

CORRELATION

Tall people tend to weigh more than short people. This relationship between height and weight is not a perfect one, however, since some very tall people are very skinny and weigh less than some short people who are very fat. The relationship between height and weight can be expressed quantitatively with a statistic called a **correlation coefficient.** Figure A.2A, which contains the paired height-weight scores of 15 men, expresses the relationship visually. Each dot in the diagram represents one man. For each dot, you can read the weight of the subject on the vertical scale and you can read the subject's height from the horizontal scale. *A diagram like this, which displays the relationship between two measures for each subject, is called a*

scatter plot *or* **scatter diagram.** A mathematical formula applied to these data indicates that the correlation (symbolized by the letter *r*) between height and weight of these men is .61. If the taller men were always heavier than the shorter men, the

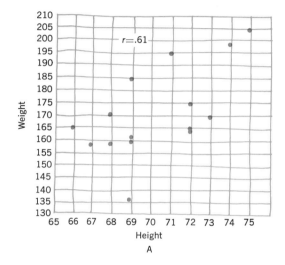

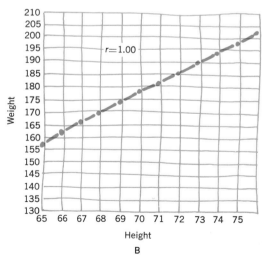

FIGURE A.2 Height-weight scatter plots. (A) Correlation between height and weight of 15 men selected from a psychology class. (B) A hypothetical perfect correlation between height and weight.

correlation would be $r = 1.00$. This is a perfect positive correlation. If the correlation were perfect, you could predict a person's exact weight by knowing his height. Figure A.2B illustrates a perfect correlation between height and weight with hypothetical data.

Notice in Figure A.3 that both height and weight scores are ordered in rank from highest to lowest. The lines connecting the pairs of scores link each man's height score with his weight score. In the "real" data for height and weight (Figure A.3A), where $r = .61$, the lines do cross. In the case of the hypothetical data (Figure A.3B), where $r = 1$, the lines do not cross.

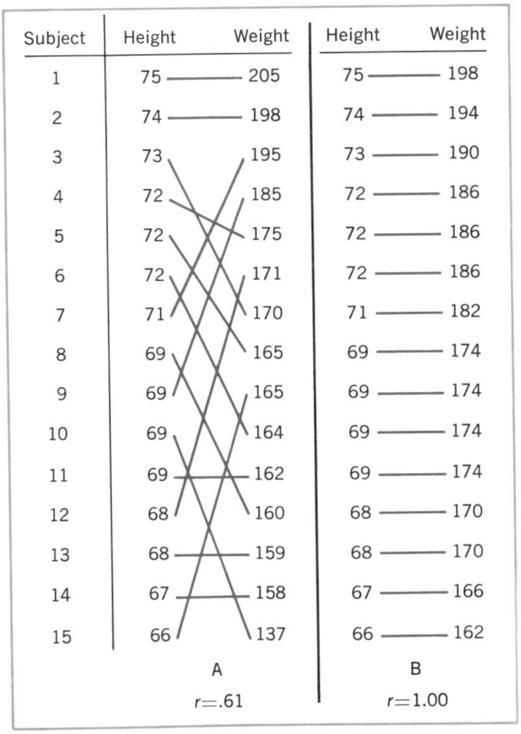

Subject	Height	Weight	Height	Weight
1	75	205	75	198
2	74	198	74	194
3	73	195	73	190
4	72	185	72	186
5	72	175	72	186
6	72	171	72	186
7	71	170	71	182
8	69	165	69	174
9	69	165	69	174
10	69	164	69	174
11	69	162	69	174
12	68	160	68	170
13	68	159	68	170
14	67	158	67	166
15	66	137	66	162
	A		B	
	$r = .61$		$r = 1.00$	

FIGURE A.3
Height-weight correlation. (A) Fifteen men from a psychology class. (B) A hypothetical perfect case.

As the correlation approaches zero, there will be more crossing-over of the lines.

A negative correlation indicates an inverse relationship; in this case, the high scores on one measure are associated with low scores on the other measure. For example, the price of a used car usually decreases with its age; the older the car, the less it is worth. As one variable — age — increases, the other — price — decreases. Negative correlations range from -1.00 to zero just as positive correlations range from $+1.00$ to zero. Negative and positive correlations of the same size indicate the same degree of relationship, although in a different direction.

A correlation of .00 indicates that there is no relationship between the two variables. You would expect zero correlation between the length of a people's noses and intelligence, between the number of freckles on a person's face and income. When $r = .00$ or is close to zero, knowledge of the value of one variable in no way helps you predict the value of the other variable.

Despite the decimal point in the correlation coefficient, correlations cannot be interpreted as a proportion or as a percentage. A correlation of .50 is not twice as large as one of .25. In order to be able to compare correlations in terms of size and percentage, they must be squared: $.70^2 = .49$. A relationship expressed by $r = .70$ is nearly two times greater than the relationship expressed by $r = .50$ ($.50^2 = .25$). The correlation squared tells us the percentage of change or variation in one variable that can be accounted for by knowing the other variable. For example, the $r = .61$ for the weight-height data above indicates that 37 percent ($r^2 = .37$) of the variation in the weight scores can be attributed to height and the remainder, $1 - r^2$, to other factors, such as diet, exercise, and so on.

Correlation coefficients of .80 and above are considered high. If your IQ were measured on two different days of the same week, the correlation between the two scores would be very high, above $r = .90$.

Correlations between .60 and .79 are considered moderate. The correlation between first- and second-term grades of a freshman class is about .75.

Correlations between .40 and .59 are considered low. The correlation between freshman grades in college and scholastic aptitude test scores is about .40.

Correlation and Causality. Correlation coefficients represent the degree of association of two variables but *not* the extent of their causal relationships. Since 1900 women's skirts have had rises and falls that have corresponded to the rises and dips in the American economy, but it is unlikely that any one of them caused the other. There is a very high correlation between the time indicated on your watch and the time on the watches of the other students in your psychology class, but your watch didn't cause the other students' watches to register the same time. Some third factor, a human effort to synchronize time, accounts for the correspondence of the watches.

As another example, there is a positive correlation between the incidence of lung cancer and the installation of air conditioners. Do air conditioners cause lung cancer? Does lung cancer cause people to buy air conditioners? Both hypotheses are rather unlikely. What is likely is that a third factor—namely, air pollution—is responsible for the increase in both air conditioning and lung cancer. Thus whenever two variables, A and B, correlate, we cannot immediately assume that one causes the other.

STATISTICS AND LIFE

A basic knowledge of statistics is useful not only in pyschology, but also in daily life. For instance, automobile manufacturers frequently advertise that their products obtain an "average" of so many miles per gallon of gasoline. But what sort of "average" are they employing? If they are using the mean, it may be wise to keep in mind that the mean is affected by extreme scores. Thus, if a few of the cars in their test sample achieved extremely high mpg scores, the mean would be pulled up disproportionately. But when you go to the showroom to purchase a car, the chances of your receiving one of these exceptional cars are, obviously, against you. Thus, a more useful measure of "average" from your point of view would be the median number of miles per gallon obtained. This figure would tell you how the "middle" car in the test sample performed—50 percent of the test cars did better and 50 percent did worse. The median car is far more likely to represent the one you are likely to be sold—should you still wish to purchase.

Further, sample size is important. The accuracy of generalization from sample to population increases with sample size. For instance, what if you learned that the "average" miles per gallon quoted by the manufacturer was based on a sample of only two test cars, and that one car recorded 50 mpg and the other 10 mpg, for an "average" of 30 mpg? Would you still be interested in buying a car from this manufacturer?

Advertising often makes use of correlation to imply causation. For instance, the correlation between eating a certain breakfast food and athletic prowess may be very real indeed, but it is unlikely that the cereal produced the athletes or that being an athlete leads to eating vast quantities of cereal. Rather, another explanation seems probable, that the correlation results from the practice of the breakfast food company to pay athletes large sums to endorse the product and maybe even eat some. This is a rather blatant example, but if you examine advertising claims carefully, you will discover that such correlation-equals-causation assumptions are frequently, and often subtly, made.

SUMMARY

1. There are numerous characteristics of scientific behavior that have led observers to compare it to a game. Comparisons like this, called analogies, can be helpful in understanding science as long as you keep the limitations of such comparisons in mind.

A. **The Goals of Science**
2. The goals of science are accurate description, prediction, explanation, and control of events.
3. Scientific **prediction** (page 522) is based on accurate observations and measurement of how events regularly vary together. When stated in words or other symbols, this regular variation is called a **relationship statement** (page 522).
4. The main objective of psychology is the search for relationship among environmental events, the biological characteristics of an organism, and behavior.

B. **Four Basic Rules of the Scientific Game**
5. The four basic rules of science deal with **supporting evidence (page 523), operational definitions (page 524), controlled observations (page 525), and sampling** and **generalization (page 526).**

C. **Asking Questions about Behavior and Experience**
6. Scientifically answerable questions must be stated in terms that lead to observation, measurement, and testing of relationships.
7. Relationship statements studied by psychologists deal with how behavior is related to environmental events and organismic characteristics.

D. A Case Study in Experimental Methods

8. **Psychological experiments** (page 533) consist of the manipulation of some environmental event — the **independent variable** (page 533) — in order to observe the effect of the manipulation on the behavior of subjects — **dependent variable** (page 533) — under controlled conditions.

9. **Experimental control** (page 534) can be achieved by a variety of techniques, depending on the design of the experiment, including **single-blind control** (page 535) and **double-blind control** (page 536).

E. Naturalistic Observation, Sample Surveys, and Case Studies

10. Although experimental methods provide rigorous information about the relationship between variables, it is not always possible to use them, for a variety of reasons. Nonexperimental methods used by psychologists include **naturalistic observation (page 537)**, **surveys** (page 537), and **case studies** (page 538). A common research technique for obtaining information through verbal reports is the **interview,** either **structured** or **unstructured** (page 539).

F. Quantification and Statistics

11. Quantification, which involves **measurement** (page 540), is an essential part of making scientific relationship statements and achieving precision in science.

12. **Descriptive statistics** (page 541) is used to organize, summarize and compare data collected from a research study.

13. **Inferential statistics** (page 543) enables a researcher to infer the descriptive characteristics of a population from a sample and determine whether or not differences between experimental and control groups can be attributed to the manipulation of the independent variable or to chance factors.

14. A **correlation coefficient** (page 543) is a number that indicates the degree to which two measures vary together.

REFERENCES

Adamson, R.E. (1952) Functional fixedness as related to problem solving. *Journal of Experimental Psychology,* 44, 288–291.

Adjutants General's Office, War Department (1951) *Army general classification test.* Chicago: Stoelting.

Adorno, T.W., Frenkel-Brunswik, E., Levinson, D.J., & Sanford, R.N. (1950) *The authoritarian personality.* New York: Harper.

Alexander, F. (1950) *Psychosomatic medicine: Its principles and application.* New York: Norton

Altus, W.D. (1965) Birth order and achievement—paper read under the auspices of the Arts and Lectures Committee, University of California, Santa Barbara (Feb., 1966).

Altus, W.D. (1966) Birth order and its sequelae. *Science,* 151, 44–49.

American Psychological Association (1963) Ethical standards of psychologists. *American Psychologist,* 18, 56–100.

Asch, S.E. (1955) Opinions and social pressure. *Scientific American,* 193(5), 31–35.

Asch, S.E. (1956) Studies of independence and submission to group pressure: I. A minority of one against a unanimous majority. *Psychological Monographs.* 7 NO416.

Aserinsky, E. & Kleitman, N. (1953) Regularly occuring periods of eye motility and concomitant phenomena during sleep. *Science,* 118, 273–274.

Atkinson, R.C. & Shiffrin, R.M. (1968) Human memory: A proposed system and its control processes. In K.W. Spence & J.T. Spence, eds., *The psychology of learning and motivation: Advances in research and theory, Vol. II,* 89–195. New York: Academic Press.

Azrin, N. & Holz, W.C. (1966) Punishment. W.K. Honig, ed., *Operant behavior: Areas of research and application.* New York: Appleton-Century-Crofts, 380–441.

Bach, G. (1954) *Intensive group psychotherapy.* New York: Ronald Press.

Baddeley, A.D. (1966) Short-term memory for word sequences as a function of acoustic, semantic, and formal similarity. *Quarterly Journal of Experimental Psychology,* 18, 362–365.

Bandura, A., Ross, D., & Ross, S.A. (1961) Transmission of aggression through imitation of aggressive models. *Journal of Abnormal and Social Psychology,* 63, 575–582.

Bandura, A., Ross, D., & Ross, S.A. (1963) Imitation of film mediated aggressive models. *Journal of Abnormal and Social Psychology,* 66, 3–11.

Bandura, A. & Walters, R. (1963) *Social learning and personality development.* New York: Holt, Rinehart and Winston.

Barron, F. (1958) The psychology of imagination. *Scientific American,* 199, 151–166.

Barron, F. (1968) *Creativity and personal freedom.* Princeton, N.J.: Van Nostrand.

Barron, F., Jarvik, M.E., & Bunnell, S. (1971) (originally published 1964) The hallucinogenic drugs. In *Contemporary Psychology.* San Francisco: W.H. Freeman.

Bass, M.J. & Hull, C.L. (1934) The irradiation of a tactile conditioned reflex in man. *Journal of Comparative Psychology,* 17, 47–65.

Beach, F. (1964) It's all in your mind. *Psychology Today,* 3(2), 33–35.

Beach, F., ed. (1965) *Sex and behavior.* New York: Wiley.

Belmont, L., and Marolla, F.A. (1973) Birth order, family size, and intelligence. *Science,* 182, 1096–1101.

Berkowitz, L. (1954) Group standards, cohesiveness, and productivity. *Human Relations,* 7, 509–519.

Berkowitz, L. (1964) The effects of observing violence. *Scientific American,* 210(2), 35–41.

Bernal, M.E., Duryee, J.S., & Pruett, H.L. (1968) Behavior modification and the brat syndrome. *Journal of Consulting and Clinical Psychology,* 32, 447–455.

Berne, Eric (1961) *Transactional analysis in psychotherapy.* New York: Grove Press.

Berne, E. (1964) *Games people play.* New York: Grove Press.

Binet, A. & Simon, T. (1916) *The development of intelligence in children.* Baltimore: Williams & Wilkins.

Block, J.H., Jennings, P.H., Harvey, E., & Simpson, E. (1964) The interaction between allergic predisposition and psychopathology in childhood asthma. *Psychosomatic Medicine, 26,* 307–326.

Blum, G. & Miller, D. (1952) Exploring the psychoanalytic theory of the "Oral character." *Journal of Personality, 20,* 287–304.

Bower, G.H. Organizational factors in memory. *Journal of Cognitive Psychology,* 1, 18–46.

Brady, J. (1958) Ulcers in "executive" monkeys. *Scientific American* Reprints, No. 425. San Francisco: W.H. Freeman.

Brannon, R.C.L. (1970) Gimme that old-time racism. *Psychology Today,* 3(11), 42–44.

Brever, J. & Freud, S. (1936) *Studies on hysteria.* New York: Nervous and Mental Disease Publishing Co.

Briggs, K.C. & Myers, I.B. (1968) *Myers-Briggs type indicator.* Princeton, N.J.: Educational Testing Service.

Bronfenbrenner, U. (1961) The mirror image in Soviet-American relations: A social psychologist's report. *Journal of Social Issues,* 17, 45–46.

Brown, B.R. (1968) Face-saving in a two-person bargaining game. *Journal of Experimental Social Psychology,* 4, 107–122.

Brown, R. & McNeill, D. (1966) The "tip-of-the-tongue" phenomenon. *Journal of Verbal Learning and Verbal Behavior,* 5, 325–337.

Bruner, J.S. & Goodman, C.C. (1947) Value and need as organizing factors in perception. *Journal of Abnormal and Social Psychology,* 42, 33–44.

Burnstein, E. (1969) An analysis of group decisions involving risk ("the risky shift"). *Human Relations,* 22, 381–395.

Burtt, H.E. (1941) An experimental study of early childhood memory: Final report. *Journal of Genetics and Psychology,* 58, 435–439.

Buss, A.H. (1973) *Psychology—Man in perspective.* New York: Wiley.

Calhoun, J.B. (1962) Population density and social pathology. *Scientific American,* 206, 134–150.

Cameron, N. (1963) *Personality development and psychotherapy.* Houghton Mifflin.

Carmichael, L., Hogan, H.P., & Walter, A.A. (1932) An experimental study of the effect of language on the reproduction of visually perceived forms. *Journal of Experimental Psychology,* 15, 73–86.

Cattell, R.B. (1971) *Abilities: Their structure, growth, and action.* Houghton Mifflin.

Cattell, R.B. (1973) Personality pinned down. *Psychology Today,* 7(2), 40–46.

Chapin, K. (1967) A rewarding race in Detroit. *Sports Illustrated,* 27(2), 22–23.

Chomsky, N. (1968) *Language and mind.* New York: Harcourt Brace Jovanovich.

Clark, K.B. (1965) *Dark ghetto.* New York: Harper & Row.

Clark, K.B. & Clark, M.P. (1958) Racial identification and preference in Negro children. In E.E. Maccoby, T.M. Newcomb, & E.L. Hartley, eds., *Readings in social psychology* (3rd ed.), 602–611. New York: Holt, Rinehart and Winston.

Cohen, B.H. (1966) Some-or-nothing characteristics of coding behavior. *Journal of Verbal Learning and Verbal Behavior,* 5, 182–187.

Coleman, J.C. (1972) *Abnormal psychology and modern life* (4th ed.). Chicago: Scott, Foresman.

Conrad, R. (1964) Acoustic confusion and immediate memory. *British Journal of Psychology,* 55, 75–84.

Coopersmith, S. (1967) *The antecedents of self-esteem.* San Francisco: W.H. Freeman.

Covington, M.V., Crutchfield, R.S., Davis, L.B., & Olton, R.M. *The productive thinking program.* Columbus, Ohio: Charles E. Merrill.

Crick, F.H.C. (1962) The genetic code. *Scientific American,* 207, 66–74.

Crow, W.J. (1963) A study of strategic doctrines using the inter-nation simulation. *Journal of Conflict Resolution,* 7, 580–589.

Crutchfield, R.S. (1955) Conformity and character. *American Psychologist,* 10, 191–198.

Daley, E.A. (1969) Is T.V. brutalizing your child? *Look,* 33(24), 99–100.

Dastur, D.K., Mann, J.D., & Pollin, W. (1963) Hippuric acid secretion, coffee, and schizophrenia. *Archives of General Psychiatry.*

de Charms, R. & Moeller, G.H. (1962) Values expressed in American children's readers: 1800–1950. *Journal of Abnormal and Social Psychology.*

Delaney, L.T. (1970) Racism and strategies for change. In *Readings in social psychology today,* 53–57. Del Mar, Ca.: CRM Books.

Delgado, J.M.R. (1970) *Physical control of the mind.* New York: Harper & Row.

Dement, W. (1960) The effect of dream deprivation. *Science,* 131, 1705–1707.

Dement, W. (1965) An essay on dreams: The role of physiology in understanding their nature. In F. Barron, ed., *New directions in psychology,* Vol. II., 135–257. New York: Holt, Rinehart and Winston.

Dement, W. & Wolpert, E.A. (1958) The relation of eye movements, body motility, and external stimuli to dream content. *Journal of Experimental Psychology,* 55, 543–553.

Deutsch, M. (1960) The effect of motivational orientation upon trust and suspicion. *Human Relations,* 13, 123–139.

Deutsch, M. & Collins, M.E. (1951) *Interracial housing.* Minneapolis: University of Minnesota Press.

Deutsch, M. & Collins, M.E. (1958) The effect of public policy in housing projects upon interracial attitudes. In E.E. Maccoby, T.M. Newcomb, & E.G. Hartley, eds., *Readings in social psychology* (3rd ed.), 612–623. New York: Holt, Rinehart and Winston.

Deutsch, M. & Krauss, R.M. (1962) Studies of interpersonal bargaining. *Journal of Conflict Resolution,* 6, 52–76.

DiCara, L.V. & Miller, N.E. (1968) Changes in heartrate instrumentally learned by curarized rats as avoidance responses. *Journal of Comparative and Physiological Psychology,* 65, 8–12.

Dollard, J., & Miller, N.E. (1950) *Personality and psychotherapy.* New York: McGraw-Hill.

Duncker, Karl (1945) On problem solving. *Psychological Monographs,* 58, No. 5, Whole No. 270.

Durkin, H. (1937) Trial-and-error, gradual analysis, and sudden re-organization. *Archives of Psychology,* 30, No. 210.

Eibl-Eibensfeldt, I. (1967) Ontogenetic and maturational studies of aggressive behavior. In C.D. Clemente & D.B. Lindsley, eds., *Brain Functions,* 57–71. California: University of California Press.

Elliot, J. (1970) Subject of *The eye of the storm.* ABC-T.V., May 11, 1970, produced and directed by William and Muriel Peters.

Erikson, E.H. (1963) *Childhood and society* (2nd ed.). New York: Norton.

Erlenmeyer-Kimling, L. & Jarvik, L.F. (1963) Genetics and intelligence: A review. *Science,* 142, 1477–8.

Fantz, R.L. (1963) Pattern vision in newborn infants. *Science,* 140, 296–297.

Farmer, J., (1969) The shock of black recognition. *Esquire,* 71(5), 139.

Festinger, L. & Carlsmith, J.M. (1959) Cognitive consequences of forced compliance. *Journal of Abnormal and Social Psychology,* 58, 203–210.

Festinger, L., Riedken, H.W., & Schachter, S. (1956) *When prophecy fails.* Minneapolis: University of Minnesota Press.

Fiedler, F.E. (1971) *Leadership.* New York: General Learning Press.

Flavell, J.H. (1963) *The developmental psychology of Jean Piaget.* Princeton, N.J.: Van Nostrand.

Fleming, J.D. (1974) Field report: The state of the apes. *Psychology Today, 7*(8), 31–36.

Fouts, R.S. (1972) Use of guidance in teaching sign language to a chimpanzee. *Journal of Comparative and Physiological Psychology, 80*(3), 515–522.

Frankenburg, W.K. & Dodds, J.B. (1967) The Denver development screening test. *Journal of Pediatrics, 71,* 181–191.

Freedman, A.M., Kaplan, H.I., & Sadock, B. (1972) *Modern synopsis of psychiatry.* Baltimore: Williams & Wilkins.

Freedman, J.L. (1971) The crowd—Maybe not so maddening after all. *Psychology Today, 5*(4), 58–61.

Freedman, J.L., Klavansky, S., & Ehrlich, P. (1971) The effect of crowding on human task performance. *Journal of Applied Social Psychology, 1,* 7–25.

Freud, S. (Originally published in 1900.) *The interpretation of dreams.* New York: Basic Books.

Freud, S. (1949) *An outline of psychoanalysis.* New York: Norton.

Fuller, J.L. & Thompson, W.R. (1960) *Behavior genetics.* New York: Wiley.

Gallup, G.G. (1971) It's done with mirrors— Chimps and self-concept. *Psychology Today, 4*(10), 58–61.

Gardner, B.T. & Gardner, R.A. (1969) Two-way communication with an infant chimpanzee. In A. Schrier and F. Stollnitz, eds., *Behavior of non-human primates, Vol. III.* New York: Academic Press.

Gardner, R.A. & Gardner, B.T. (1969) Teaching sign language to a chimpanzee. *Science, 165,* 664–672.

Gates, A.I. (1917) Recitation as a factor in memorizing. *Archives of Psychology,* No. 40. New York: The Science Press.

Gibson, E.J. & Walk, R.D. (1956) The "visual cliff." *Scientific American, 202*(4), 67–71.

Gluksberg, S, & R.W. Weisberg (1966) Verbal behavior and problem solving: Some effects of labeling in a functional fixedness problem. *Journal of Experimental Psychology, 71,* 659–664.

Greenfield, P.M. & Bruner, J.S. (1971) Learning and language. *Psychology Today, 5*(2), 40–43.

Greenfield, P.M., Reich, L.C., & Olver, R.R. (1966) On culture and equivalence: II. In J.S. Bruner, et al., *Studies in cognitive growth.* New York: Wiley.

Gregory, R.L. (1966) *Eye and brain: The psychology of seeing.* New York: McGraw-Hill.

Grinspoon, L. Marijuana (1969) *Scientific American,* Reprint No. 524. San Francisco: W.H. Freeman.

Grossman, S.P. (1973) *Essentials of physiological psychology.* New York: Wiley.

Guilford, J.P. (1967) *The nature of human intelligence.* New York: McGraw-Hill.

Guilford, J.P., Wilson, R.C., Christiansen, P.R., & Lewis, D.J. (1951) A factor-analytic study of creative thinking: I. Hypothesis and descriptions of tests. Los Angeles: University of Southern California Report from the Psychology Laboratory No. 3.

Gumpert, P., Deutsch, M. & Epstein, Y. (1969) Effects of incentive magnitude on cooperation in the prisoner's dilemma game. *Journal of Personality and Social Psychology, 11,* 66–69.

Gazzaniga, S. (1967) The split brain in man. *Scientific American, 217*(2), 221–229.

Hall, C.S. (1953) A cognitive theory of dreams. *Journal of General Psychology, 49,* 273–282.

Hall, C.S. & Lindzey, G. (1970) *Theories of personality* (2nd ed.). New York: Wiley.

Hall, J. (1971) Decisions. *Psychology Today, 5*(6), 51–54.

Hall, S. & van de Castle, R.L. (1966) *The content analysis of dreams.* New York: Appleton-Century-Crofts.

Hardych, C.D., Petrinovich, L., & Ellsworth, D.W. (1966) Feedback of speech muscle activity during silent reading: Rapid extinction. *Science, 154,* 1467–1468.

Harlow, H.F. (1949) The formation of learning sets. *Psychological Review,* 56, 51–65.

Harlow, H.F. (1958) The nature of love. *American Psychologist,* 13, 673–685.

Harlow, H.F. (1966) Learning to love. *American Scientist,* 54, 244–272.

Harris, T.A. (1967) *I'm O.K. – You're O.K.* New York: Harper & Row.

Hathaway, S.R. & McKinley, J.C. (1940) A multiphasic personality schedule (Minnesota): 1. Construction of the schedule. *Journal of Psychology,* 10, 249–254.

Hathaway, S.R. & McKinley, J.C. (1951) *Minnesota multiphasic personality inventory.* New York: The Psychological Corporation.

Hathaway, S.R. & Meehl, P.E. (1951) *An atlas for the clinical use of the MMPI.* Minneapolis: University of Minnesota Press.

Hatstorf, A. & Cantril, H. (1954) They saw a game: A case study. *Journal of Abnormal and Social Psychology,* 49, 129–134.

Hebb, D.O. (1961), Distinctive features of learning in the higher animal. In J.F. DelaFresnaye, ed., *Brain Mechanisms and Learning.* London: Oxford University Press.

Held, R. & Hein, A. (1963) Movement-produced stimulation in the development of visually guided behavior. *Journal of Comparative Physiology and Psychology,* 56, 872–876.

Hermann, C.F. (1969) *Crises in foreign policy.* Indianapolis: Bobbs-Merrill.

Hess, R.D. & Torney, J.V. (1967) *The development of political attitudes in children.* Chicago: Aldine.

Heston, L.L. (1966) Psychiatric disorders in foster home reared children and schizophrenic mothers. *British Journal of Psychiatry,* 112, 819–825.

Heston, L.L. (1970) The genetics of schizophrenic and schizoid disease. *Science,* 167, 249–256.

Higgins, J. (1967) Creativity in comic strip authors. *Journal of Creative Behavior,* 1, 366–369.

Hilgard, E.R. (1965) *Hypnotic susceptibility.* New York: Harcourt Brace Jovanovich.

Hillton, I. (1967) Differences in the behavior of mothers toward first and later born children. *Journal of Personality and Social Psychology,* 7, 282–290.

Hoffman, M. (1968) *The gay world: Male homosexuality and the social creation of evil.* New York: Basic Books.

Hoffman, M. (1969) Homosexual. *Psychology Today,* 3(2), 43–45.

Horner, M. (1969) Fail: Bright women. *Psychology Today,* 3(6), 36–38.

House, T.T. (1974) The electric ear. Described in *Newsweek,* April 1, 1974, p. 50.

Houston, J.P. & Mednick, S.A. (1963) Creativity and the need for novelty. *Journal of Abnormal and Social Psychology,* 66, 137–141.

Hubel, D.H. & Wiesel, T.N. (1962) Receptive fields, binocular interaction, and functional architecture in the cat's visual cortex. *Journal of Physiology,* 160, 106–154.

Hull, C. (1952) *A behavior system: An introduction to behavior theory concerning the individual organism.* New Haven: Yale University Press.

James, W. (1890) *Psychology.* New York: Holt.

Janis, I.L. (1971) Groupthink among policy makers. In N. Sanford, ed., *Sanctions for evil.* San Francisco: Jossey-Bass.

Janis, I.L., Kaye, D., & Kirschner, P. (1965) Facilitating effects of "eating-while-reading" on responsiveness to persuasive communications. *Journal of Personality and Social Psychology,* 1, 181–186.

Janis, I.L. & Terwilliger, R.F. (1962) An experimental study of psychological resistances to fear arousing communications. *Journal of Abnormal and Social Psychology,* 65, 403–410.

Jenkins, J.G. & Dallenbach, K.M. (1924) Obliviscence during sleep and waking. *American Journal of Psychology,* 35, 605–612.

Jensen, A. (1969) How much can we boost IQ and scholastic achievement? *Harvard Educational Review,* 39, 1–223.

Johnson, N. (1970) Big brother is watching you. *The Key Reporter,* 26(3), 3–4.

Jones, E. (1961) *The life and works of Sigmund Freud.* New York: Basic Books.

Jones, M.C. (1924) The elimination of children's fear. *Journal of Experimental Psychology,* 1, 382–390.

Kagan, J. (1964) Acquisition and significance of sex typing and sex role identity. In M.L. Hoffman and L. W. Hoffman, eds., *Review of child development research,* 137–167. New York: Russell Sage.

Kagan, J. (1969) Check one: Male – Female. *Psychology Today,* 3(2), 39–41.

Kamiya, J. (1969) Operant control of the EEG alpha rhythm and some of its reported effects on consciousness. In C. Tart, ed., *Altered states of consciousness,* 507–517. New York: Wiley.

Kisker, G.W. (1964) *The disorganized personality.* New York: McGraw-Hill.

Koestler, A. (1964) *The act of creation.* London: Hutchinson.

Kogan, N. & Wallach, M.A. (1967) Risk taking as a function of the situation, the person, and the group. *New Directions in Psychology,* 3, 111–278.

Kohlberg, L. (1964) Development of moral character and ideology. In M.L. Hoffman, ed., *Review of Child Development Research.* New York: Russell Sage.

Kohlberg, L. (1968) The child as a moral philosopher. *Psychology Today,* 2(4), 24–30.

Kohlberg, L. & Turiel, E. (1971) *Research in moral development: The cognitive-developmental approach.* New York: Holt, Rinehart and Winston.

Kohler, W. (1925) *The mentality of apes.* New York: Harcourt.

Korner, A.F. (1969) Neonatal startles, smiles, erections, and reflex sucks as related to state, sex, and individuality. *Child Development,* 40, 1039–1053.

Kozol, J. (1970) *Death at an early age.* Boston: Houghton Mifflin.

Krueger, W.C.F. (1929) The effect of overlearning on retention. *Journal of Experimental Psychology,* 12, 71–78.

Lang, P.J. & Lazovik, A.D. (1963) Experimental desensitization of aphobia. *Journal of Abnormal and Social Psychology,* 66, 519–525.

Lang, P.J., Melamed, B.G., & Hart, J. (1970) A psychophysiological analysis of fear modification using an automated desensitization procedure. *Journal of Abnormal and Social Psychology,* 76, 220–234.

Latané, B. & Darley, J.M. (1969) Bystander "apathy." *American Scientist,* 57, 244–268.

Latané, B. & Darley, J.M. (1970) *The unresponsive bystander: Why doesn't he help?* New York: Appleton-Century-Crofts.

Leckart, B.T. & Bennett, K.S. (1968) Reinforcement effects of food and stimulus novelty. *Psychological Record,* 18, 253–260.

Lerner, M.I. (1968) *Heredity, evolution, and society.* San Francisco: W.H. Freeman Co.

Lerner, M.J. (1970) The desire for justice and reactions to victims. In J. Macaulay and L. Berkowitz, eds., *Altruism and helping behavior,* 205–229. New York: Academic Press.

Leventhal, A.M. (1968) Use of a behavioral approach within a traditional psychotherapeutic context. *Journal of Abnormal Psychology,* 73, 178–182.

Lewis, D.J. & Duncan, C.P. (1958) Expectation and resistance to extinction of a lever-pulling response as a function of percentage of reinforcement and number of acquisition trials. *Journal of Experimental Psychology,* 55, 121–128.

Lidz, T. et al. (1962) Differentiation and schizophrenic symptom formation in identical twins. *Journal of The American Psychoanalytic Association,* 10, 74–90.

Lidz, T., Fleck, S., & Cornelison, A.R. (1963)

Schizophrenia and the family. New York: International Universities Press.

Lindsley, D. (1951) Emotion. In S.S. Stevens, ed., *Handbook of experimental psychology,* 473–516. New York: Wiley.

Lindzey, G. & Winston, H. (1962) Maze learning and effects of pre-training in inbred strains of mice. *Journal of Physiological Psychology,* 55, 748–752.

Lovaas, O.I., Berberich, J.P., Perloff, B.F., & Schaeffer, B. (1966) Acquisition of imitative speech by schizophrenic children. *Science,* 151, 705–707.

Lovaas, O.I., Freitag, G., Gold, V.J., & Kassorla, I.T. (1965) Experimental studies in childhood schizophrenia: Analysis of self-destructive behavior. *Journal of Experimental Child Psychology,* 2, 67–84.

Luchins, A.S. (1942) Mechanization in problem-solving. *Psychological Monographs,* Vol. 54, No. 6.

Luria, A.R. (1968) *The mind of a mnemonist.* New York: Basic Books.

MacKinnon, D.W. (1962) The nature and nurture of creative talent. *American Psychologist,* 17, 484–495.

Mahoney, M. & Thorsen, C. (1974) *Self-control: Power to the person.* Monterey, Ca.: Brooks/Cole Publishing Co.

Maltzman, I. (1960) On the training of originality. *Psychological Review,* 67, 224–242.

Mandler, G. (1962) Emotions. In R. Brown et al., eds., *New directions in psychology.* New York: Holt, Rinehart and Winston.

Marcia, J.E., Rubin, M.M., & Efran, J.S. (1969) Systematic desensitization. *Journal of Abnormal Psychology,* 74, 383–387.

Maslow, A.H. (1970) *Motivation and personality* (2nd ed.). New York: Harper & Row.

Masters, W. & Johnson, V. (1966) *Human Sexual Response.* Boston: Little, Brown.

McClelland, D.C. (1961) *The achieving society.* Princeton, N.J.: Van Nostrand.

McClelland, D.C. & Atkinson, J.W. (1948) The projective expression of needs. I: The effect of different intensities of the hunger drive on perception. *Journal of Psychology,* 25, 205–222.

McClelland, D.C., Atkinson, J.W., Clark, R.A., & Lowell, E.L. (1953) *The achievement motive.* New York: Appleton-Century-Crofts.

McClelland, D.C. & Winter, D.G. (1969) *Motivating economic achievement.* New York: Free Press.

McConnell, J.V. (1970) Criminals can be brainwashed. *Psychology Today,* 3 (11), 14.

McGraw, M.B. (1935) *Growth: A study of Johnny and Jimmy.* New York: Appleton-Century-Crofts.

McGuire, W.J. (1964) Inducing resistance to persuasion. In L. Berkowitz, ed., *Advances in Experimental Social Psychology,* Vol. I., 191–224. New York: Academic Press.

McKinley, J.C. & Hathaway, S.R. (1940) A multiphasic personality schedule (Minnesota): II: A differential study of hypochondriasis. *Journal of Psychology,* 10, 255–268.

McLeoch, J.A. (1942) *The psychology of human learning.* New York: Longmans.

McNeil, E.B. (1967) *The quiet furies: Man and disorder.* Englewood Cliffs, N.J.: Prentice-Hall.

Mead, M. (1935) *Sex and temperament in three primitive societies.* New York: Morrow.

Mednick, S.A. (1962) The associative basis of the creative process. *Psychological Review,* 69, 220–232.

Mednick, S.A. (1967) *Remote associates test.* Boston: Houghton Mifflin.

Mednick, S.A. (1971) Birth defects and schizophrenia. *Psychology Today,* 4(11), 49–50.

Mednick, S.A. & Higgins, J., eds. (1960) *Current research in schizophrenia.* Ann Arbor, Michigan: Edwards.

Mednick, S.A. & McNeil, T.F. (1968) Current methodology in research on the etiology of schizophrenia. *Psychological Bulletin,* 70, 681–693.

Melton, A.W. & Irwin, J.M. (1940) The influence of degree of interpolated learning on retroactive inhibition and the overt transfer of specific responses. *American Journal of Psychology,* 53, 173–203.

Milgram, S. (1963) Behavioral study of obedience. *Journal of Abnormal and Social Psychology,* 67, 371–378.

Milgram, S. (1964) Group pressure and action against a person. *Journal of Abnormal and Social Psychology,* 69, 137–143.

Milgram, S. (1964) Issues in the study of obedience. *American Psychologist,* 19, 848–852.

Milgram, S. (1965) Liberating effects of group pressure. *Journal of Personality and Social Psychology,* 1, 127–134.

Milgram, S. (1965) Some conditions of obedience and disobedience to authority. *Human Relations,* 18, 56-57.

Miller, G.A. (1956) The magical number seven, plus or minus two: Some limits on our capacity for processing information. *Psychological Review,* 63, 81–97.

Miller, G.A. (1962) Some psychological studies of grammar. *American Psychologist,* 17, 784–792.

Miller, N.E. (1959) Liberalization of basic S-R concepts: Extensions to conflict behavior, motivation, and social learning. In S. Koch, ed., *Psychology: A study of a science.* Vol. II., 196–292. New York: McGraw-Hill.

Miller, N.E. & Banuazizi, A. (1968) Instrumental learning by curarized rats of a specific, visceral response, intestinal or cardiac. *Journal of Comparative and Physiological Psychology,* 65, 1–7.

Miller, N.E. & DiCara, L.V. (1967) Instrumental learning of heartrate changes in curarized rats: Shaping and specificity to discriminative stimulus. *Journal of Comparative and Physiological Psychology,* 63, 12–14.

Milner, B. (1959) The memory defect in bilateral hippocampal lesions. *Psychiatric Research Reports,* 11, 43–52.

Minas, J.S., Scodel, A., & Marlow, D. (1960) Some descriptive aspects of two-person non-zero-sum games. II. *Journal of Conflict Resolution,* 4, 193–197.

Money, J. & Ehrhardt, A.A. (1973) *Man and woman, boy and girl: The differentiation and dimorphism of gender identity from conception to maturity.* Baltimore: Johns Hopkins University Press.

Morgenstern, J. (1972) The new violence. *Newsweek,* 71(7), 66–69.

Murray, H.A. (1943) *Thematic apperception test.* Cambridge, Massachusetts: Harvard University Press.

Olds, J. Pleasure centers in the brain. *Scientific American,* Reprint No. 30. San Francisco: W.H. Freeman.

Olds, J. & Milner, P. (1965) Drives, rewards, and the brain. In F. Barron, et al., *New Directions in Psychology, Vol. II.,* 322–410. New York: Holt, Rinehart and Winston.

Olton, R.M. & Crutchfield, R.S. (1969) Developing the skills of productive thinking. In P. Mussen et al., eds., *Trends and issues in developmental psychology.* New York: Holt, Rinehart and Winston.

Orne, M.T. (1959) The nature of hypnosis: Artifact and essence. *Journal of Abnormal and Social Psychology,* 58, 277–299.

Osgood, C.F. (1962) *An alternative to war or surrender.* Urbana, Illinois: University of Illinois Press.

Paige, K.E. (1973) Women learn to sing the menstrual blues. *Psychology Today,* 7(4), 41–46.

Papageorgis, D. & McGuire, W.J. (1961) The generality of immunity to persuasion produced by pre-exposure to weakened counterarguments. *Journal of Abnormal and Social Psychology,* 62, 475–481.

Pavlov, I.P. (1927) *Conditioned reflex.* London: Oxford University Press.

Penfield, W. & Roberts, L. (1959) *Speech and brain mechanisms.* Princeton, N.J.: Princeton University Press.

Peter, L.J. & Hull, R. (1969) *The peter principle*. New York: Morrow.

Peterson, M.J. & Peterson, L.R. (1959) Short-term retention of individual items. *Journal of Experimental Psychology,* 58, 193–198.

Pettigrew, T.F. (1958) Personality and socio-cultural factors in intergroup attitudes. *Journal of Conflict Resolution,* 2, 29–42.

Piaget, J. (1954) *The construction of reality in the child.* New York: Basic Books.

Pinard, A. & Sharp, E. (1972) IQ and point of view. *Psychology Today,* 6(1), 65–68.

Premack, A.J. & Premack, D. (1972) Teaching language to an ape. *Scientific American,* 222(4), 92–99.

Premack, D. (1965) Reinforcement theory. In D. Levine, ed., *Nebraska Symposium on Motivation.* Lincoln: University of Nebraska Press.

Premack, D. (1970) The education of Sara. *Psychology Today,* 4(4), 54–58.

Pryor, K. (1969) The porpoise caper. *Psychology Today,* 3(7), 46–49.

Public Health Service (1970) *The community mental health center.* Washington, D.C.: U.S. Government Printing Office (PHS Pub. No. 1643).

Ratliff, F. & Hartline, H.R. (1959) The responses of limulus optic nerve fibers to patterns of illumination on the receptor mosaic. *General Psychology,* 42, 1241–1255.

Ratliff, F., Hartline, H.K. & Miller, W.H. (1959) Spatial and temporal aspects of retinal inhibitory interaction. *Journal of the Optical Society of America,* 53, 110–121.

Razran, G. (1949) Stimulus generalization of conditioned responses. *Psychological Bulletin,* 46, 337–365.

Resource book for drug abuse education. (1969) Drug Abuse Education Project. National Science Teachers Association (NTA).

Reynolds, S.S. (1968) *A primer of operant conditioning.* Glenview, Ill.: Scott, Foresman.

Rogers, C.R. (1951) *Client-centered therapy.* Boston: Houghton Mifflin.

Rokeach, M. (1971) Long-range experimental modification of values, attitudes, and behavior. *American Psychologist,* 26(5), 455–459.

Rorschach, H. (1942) *Psychodiagnostics.* Berne, Switzerland: Verlag Hans Huber.

Rosenzwieg, M.R. (1966) Environmental complexity, cerebral change, and behavior, *American Psychologist,* 21, 321–332.

Rosenzwieg, M.R., Krech, D., Bennett, E.L., & Diamond, M.C. (1968) Modifying brain chemistry and anatomy by enrichment or improvement of experience. In G. Newton and S. Levine, eds., *Early experience and behavior.* Springfield, Ill.: Charles C. Thomas.

Ross, S. & Lockman, R.F. (1965) *A career in psychology.* Washington, D.C.: American Psychological Association.

Rumbaugh, D.M., Gill, T.V., & von Glasersfeld, E.C. (1973) Reading and sentence completion by a chimpanzee. *Science,* 182 (4113), 731–733.

Russell, R.B. (1968) *U.S. News and World Report,* 65(23), 13.

Sachs, J.S. (1967) Recognition memory for syntactic and semantic aspects of connected discourse. *Perception and Psychophysics,* 2, 437–442.

Salinger, J.D. (1951) *Catcher in the rye.* Boston: Little, Brown.

Sargent, J., Green, E., & Walters, E. (1971) Preliminary report on the use of autogenic feedback techniques in the treatment of migraine and tension headaches. Unpublished manuscript, Menniger Foundation.

Scarr-Salapatek, S. (1971) Race, social class, and IQ. *Science,* 174, 1285–95.

Scarr-Salapatek, S. (1971) Unknowns in the IQ Equation. *Science,* 174, 1223–28.

Schachter, S. (1951) Deviation, rejection, and communication. *Journal of Abnormal and Social Psychology,* 46, 190–207.

Schachter, S. (1959) *The psychology of affiliation.* Stanford, Cal.: Stanford University Press.

Schachter, S. (1968) Obesity and eating. *Science,* 161, 751–756.

Schachter, S. & Gross, L. (1968) Manipulated time and eating behavior. *Journal of Personality and Social Psychology,* 10, 98–106.

Schachter, S. & Singer, J. (1962) Cognitive, social, and physiological determinants of emotional state. *Psychological Review,* 69, 379–399.

Scheerer, M. (1971) (Originally published in 1963) Problem solving. In *Contemporary Psychology: Readings from Scientific American,* 241–248. San Francisco: W.H. Freeman.

Schlesinger, A.M., Jr., (1965) *A thousand days.* Boston: Houghton Mifflin.

Segal, M.H., Campbell, D.T., & Herskovits, M.J. (1966) *The influence of culture on perception.* New York: Bobbs-Merrill.

Seligman, M.E.P. (1973) Fall into helplessness. *Psychology Today,* 7(1), 43–48.

Seligman, M.E.P., Maier, S.F., & Greer, J.H. (1968) Alleviation of learned helplessness in the dog. *Journal of Abnormal Psychology,* 73, 256–262.

Selye, H. (1956) *The stress of life.* New York: McGraw-Hill.

Shaw, M.E. (1964) Communication networks. In L. Berkowitz, ed., *Advances in experimental social psychology, Vol. I.,* 111–147. New York: Academic Press.

Sherif, M. & Sherif, C.W. (1953) *Groups in harmony and tension.* New York: Harper.

Shields, J. (1962) *Monozygotic twins.* London: Oxford University Press.

Silverman, J. (1967) Personality trait and "perceptual style": Studies of psychotherapists of schizophrenic patients. *Journal of Nervous and Mental Diseases,* 145, 5–17.

Skinner, B.F. (1953) *Science and human behavior.* New York: Macmillan.

Skinner, B.F. (1957) *Verbal behavior.* New York: Appleton-Century-Crofts.

Skinner, B.F. (1971) *Beyond freedom and dignity.* New York: Knopf.

Smith, B. (1967) The polygraph. *Scientific American,* Reprint No. 503. San Francisco: W.H. Freeman.

Smock, C.D. & Holt, B.G. (1962) Childrens' reactions to novelty: An experimental study of "Curiosity Motivation." *Child Development,* 33, 631–642.

Sperling, G. (1960) The information available in brief visual presentations. *Psychological Monographs,* 74(11, Whole No. 498).

Sperry, R.W. (1964) The great cerebral commissure. *Scientific American,* 210(1), 42–52.

Spooner A. & Kellogg, M. (1947) The backward conditioning curve. *American Journal of Psychology,* 60, 327–334.

Stuart, R.B. & Davis, B. (1972) *Slim chance in a fat world.* Champaign, Ill.: Research Press.

Terman, L.M. & Merrill, M.A. (1960) *Stanford-Binet intelligence scale.* Boston: Houghton Mifflin.

Transcripts of interview of Vietnam war veteran on his role of alleged massacre of civilians at Songmy. (1969) *The New York Times,* 119(40), 16.

Trowill, J.A. (1967) Instrumental conditioning of the heartrate in the curarized rat. *Journal of Comparative and Physiological Psychology,* 63, 7–11.

Tryon, R.C. (1942) Individual differences. In F.A. Moss, ed., *Comparative psychology.* Englewood Cliffs, N.J.: Prentice-Hall.

Tulvig, E. & Pearlstone, Z. (1966) Availability versus accessibility of information in memory for words. *Journal of Verbal Learning and Verbal Behavior,* 5, 381–391.

Turnbull, C.M. (1961) Some observations regarding the experiences and behavior of BaMbuti pygmies. *American Journal of Psychology,* 74, 304–308.

Ullman, M. & Krippner, S. (1970) ESP in the night. *Psychology Today,* 4(1), 46–50.

Underwood, B.J. (1957) Interference and forgetting. *Psychological Review,* 64, 49–60.

Underwood, B.J. (1971) (originally published in 1964) Forgetting. In *Contemporary Psychol-*

ogy: *Readings from Scientific American,* 219–233. San Francisco: W.H. Freeman.

U.S. National Commission on the causes and prevention of violence. (Final report, 1970) New York: Praeger.

Van de Castle, R.L. (1971) *The psychology of dreaming.* New York: General Learning Press.

Very, P.S. & Zannini, J.A. (1969) Relation between birth order and being a beautician. *Journal of Applied Psychology,* 53, 149–151.

Wallach, M.A., Kogan, N., & Blum, D.J. (1964) Diffusion of responsibility and level of risk taking in groups. *Journal of Abnormal and Social Psychology,* 68, 263–274.

Walters, R.H., Thomas, E.L., & Acker, C.W. (1962) Enhancement of punitive behavior by audio-visual displays. *Science,* 136, 872–873.

Warren, J.R. & Heist, P.A. (1966) Personality attributes of gifted college students. *Science,* 132, 330–337.

Watson, J.B. & Rayner, R. (1920) Conditioned emotional reactions. *Journal of Experimental Psychology,* 3, 1–14.

Wechsler, D. (1958) *The measurement and appraisal of adult intelligence.* Baltimore: Williams & Wilkins.

Weil, A. (1972) *The natural mind.* Boston: Houghton Mifflin.

Weil, A., Zinberg, N.E., & Nelsen, J.M. (1968) Clinical and psychological effects of marijuana in man. *Science,* 162, 1234–1242.

Welsh, G.S. (1959) *Welsh figure preference test.* Palo Alto, Ca.: Consulting Psychologists Press.

Wernick, R. (1966) Close-up: Hal Evry will elect you to office if you have $60,000, an IQ of at least 120, and can keep your mouth shut. *Life,* 60(22), 41–46.

White, R. & Lippitt, R. (1968) Leader behavior and member reaction in three "social climates." In D. Cartwright and A. Zander, eds., *Group dynamics* (3rd ed.). New York: Harper & Row.

Winterbottom, M.R. (1953) The sources of achievement motivation in mothers' attitudes toward independence training. In D.C. McClelland, et al., eds., *The achievement motive.* New York: Appleton-Century-Crofts.

Wolpe, J. (1958) *Psychotherapy by reciprocal inhibition.* Stanford, Ca.: Stanford University Press.

Young, W.C., Goy, R.W., & Phoenix, C.H. (1964) Hormones and sexual behavior. *Science,* 143, 212–218.

Zajonc, R.B. (1968) Attitudinal effects of mere exposure. *Journal of Personality and Social Psychology Monograph Supplement,* No. 2, Part 2.

Zajonc, R.B. (1970) Brainwash: Familiarity breeds comfort. *Psychology Today,* 3(9), 32–35.

Zajonc, R.B. & Rajecki, D.W. (1967) Exposure and affect: A field experiment. *Psychonomic Science,* 17, 216–217.

Zax, M. & Stricker, S. (1963) *Patterns of psychopathology.* New York: Macmillan.

Zeigler, H.P. & Leibowitz, H. (1957) Apparent visual size as a function of distance for children and adults. *American Journal of Psychology,* 70, 106–109.

Zeller, A.F. (1950) An experimental analogue of repression. II. The effects of individual failure and success on memory measured by relearning. *Journal of Experimental Psychology,* 40, 411–422.

Zimbardo, P.G., and Ebbsen, E.B. (1969) *Influencing attitudes and changing behavior* Reading, Mass.: Addison-Wesley.

CREDITS

CHAPTER ONE

Photo page 2 (top): Chromosomes courtesy T. T. Puck and J. H. Tijio, Eleanor Roosevelt Institute for Cancer Research, Denver. **Photo page 2 (bottom):** Courtesy Willard R. Centerwall, Loma Linda University School of Medicine. **Photos page 3:** Courtesy José M. R. Delgado, Facultad de Medicina Universidad Autonoma, Madrid. **Photo page 4 (top):** Esais Baitel/Rapho Guillumette. **Photo page 4 (bottom):** Courtesy Philip Teitelbaum, University of Illinois, Urbana. **Photo page 5:** From D. C. McClelland, et al., *The achievement motive.* Copyright 1953 by Naiburg Publishing Company. Used by permission. **Photo page 6:** William Vandivert. **Photos page 7:** Courtesy A. J. Bachrach, Naval Medical Research Institute. **Photo page 8:** Courtesy National Institutes of Health, Gerontology Research Center. **Photo page 9:** Ron Sherman/Nancy Palmer. **Photo page 10:** Burk Uzzle/Magnum. **Photo page 11:** Nina Leen. Copyright © Time, Inc. **Quotations page 12:** (1) from G. W. Kisker, *The disorganized personality,* 2nd Ed. Copyright 1972 by McGraw Hill Book Company. Reprinted by permission. (2) From J. C. Coleman, *Abnormal psychology and modern life,* 4th Ed. Copyright 1972 by Scott, Foresman and Company. Reprinted by permission. (3) From N. Cameron, *Personality development and psychopathology.* Copyright 1963 by Houghton Mifflin Company. Reprinted by permission. **Photo page 14:** Harry F. Harlow, University of Wisconsin Primate Laboratory. **Photo page 15:** Copyright 1965 by Stanley Milgram. From the film "Obedience," distributed by the New York University Film Library. **Photo page 17 (top):** Hugh Rogers/Monkmeyer. **Photo page 17 (center):** Mimi Forsyth/Monkmeyer. **Photo page 17 (bottom):** Burk Uzzle/Magnum. **Drawing page 20:** Courtesy Prints Division, The New York Public Library, Astor, Lenox and Tilden Foundations. From J. A. Michener, *The Hokusai sketchbooks.* Copyright Charles E. Tuttle Company.

CHAPTER TWO

Figure 2.1: Courtesy Dr. John Philip, Chromosome Laboratory, Rigshospitalet, Copenhagen, Denmark. **Figure 2.2:** Landrum B. Shettles. **Figure 2.3:** Courtesy Hafner Press. From E. J. Farris, and J. Q. Griffiths, *The rat in laboratory investigation.* Copyright 1967 Hafner Press. By permission of J. B. Lippincott Company, original publishers, 1942 edition. **Figure 2.4:** Wisconsin Primate Center. **Figure 2.7:** Photo courtesy Willard R. Centerwall, Loma Linda University School of Medicine. **Figure 2.9:** Courtesy W. Roy Breg, M.D., Southbury Training School, Southbury, Connecticut. **Figure 2.13:** Wide World Photos. **Figure 2.14:** From G. Lindzey and H. Winston, "Maze learning and effects of pretraining in inbred strains of mice." *Journal of physiological psychology,* 55, 748–752. Copyright 1962 by the American Psychological Association. Used with permission.

CHAPTER THREE

Figure 3.8: From G. C. Simpson and W. S. Beck, *Life: An introduction to biology.* Copyright 1965 by Harcourt Brace Jovanovich. **Figure 3.9 and 3.10:** Adapted from P. Mussen, et al., *Psychology: An introduction.* Copyright 1973 by D. C. Heath and Company Lexington, Mass. Used with permission. **Figure 3.11:** Adapted from W. Penfield and T. Rasmussen, *The cerebral cortex of man.* Copyright 1950 by Macmillan Company. Used with permission. **Figure 3.12:** Courtesy J. Olds, Division of Biology, California Institute of Technology. **Figure 3.13:** Courtesy David Kopf Instruments. **Figure 3.14:** Adapted from A. H. Buss, *Psychology—man in perspective.* Copyright 1973 by John Wiley & Sons. Used with permission. **Figure 3.16:** Courtesy Wilder Penfield. From W. Penfield, *The excitable cortex in conscious man.* Copyright 1958 by C. C. Thomas. **Tables 3.3 and 3.4:** Adapted from D. K. Dastur, J. D. Mann, and W. Pollin, "Hippuric acid secretion, coffee, and schizophrenia," *Archives of General Psychiatry* 1963.

CHAPTER FOUR

Figure 4.1: Courtesy Philip Teitelbaum, University of Illinois, Urbana. **Quotation pages 98 and 99:** From M. J. Mahoney and C. E. Thoresen, *Self-control: Power to the Person.* Copyright 1974 by Wadsworth Publishing Company, Inc., Belmont, California. Reprinted by permission. **Figure 4.4:** Adapted from D. C. McClelland, et al., *The achievement motive.* Copyright 1953 by Naiburg Publishing Company. **Figure 4.5:** Adapted from D. C. McClelland, *The achieving society.* Copyright 1961 by Van Nostrand. **Figure 4.7:** Data from S. Schachter and J. Singer, 1962. "Cognitive, social, and physiological determinants of emotion." *Psychological Review,* 69, 379–399. Drawing adapted from Chapter 4, "Emotion" by G. Mandler, from *New directions in psychology* by R. Brown, E. Galanter, E. H. Hess, and G. Mandler. Copyright 1962 by Holt, Rinehart and Winston, Inc. Used with permission. **Figure 4.10:** Courtesy Joseph V. Brady, Johns Hopkins University School of Medicine. **Figure 4.11:** Courtesy C. H. Stoelting Company. **Figure 4.12:** Harry F. Harlow, University of Wisconsin Primate Laboratory. **Figure 4.13:** Mimi Forsyth/Monkmeyer. **Figure 4.14:** Sybil Shelton/Monkmeyer.

CHAPTER FIVE

Figure 5.1: Adapted from F. B. McMahon, *Psychology, the hybrid science,* p. 149. Copyright 1972 by Prentice-Hall, Inc., Englewood Cliffs, N.J. Used with permission. **Figure 5.2:** Adapted from H. C. Lindgren and O. Byrne, *Psychology — an introduction.* Copyright 1971 by John Wiley & Sons. Used with permission. **Figure 5.3:** Adapted from E. Hilgard, et al., *Introduction to psychology,* 5th edition. Copyright 1971 by Harcourt Brace Jovanovich, Inc. Used with permission. **Figure 5.5:** Adapted from J. E. Hochberg, *Perception.* Copyright 1964 by Prentice-Hall, Inc., Englewood Cliffs, N.J. Used with permission. **Figure 5.6:** Adapted from F. L. Ruch and P. G. Zimbardo, *Psychology and life,* 8th edition. Copyright 1971 by Scott, Foresman and Company. Used with permission. **Figure 5.7:** Adapted from A. H. Buss *Psychology — man in perspective.* Copyright 1973 by John Wiley & Sons. Used with permission. **Demonstration 2:** George Roos. **Demonstration 9:** George Roos. **Figure 5.11:** From H. P. Zeigler and H. Leibowitz, "Apparent visual size as a function of distance for children and adults." *American Journal of Psychology,* 70, 106–109. Copyright 1957. Reprinted by permission of University of Illinois Press. **Demonstration 11:** Bell Telephone Laboratories. **Demonstration 22:** Escher Foundation Collection, Haags Gementemuseum, The Hague. **Figure 5.14:** Adapted from F. Ratliff, H. K. Hartline, and W. H. Miller "Spatial and temporal aspects of retinal inhibitory interaction." *Journal of the Optical Society of America,* 53, 110–121. Copyright 1959 by the American Institute of Physics. Used with permission. **Figure 5.20:** Photo by William Vandivert. **Figure 5.21:** David Linton. **Figure 5.22:** From R. L. Gregory, *Eye and brain: The psychology of seeing.* Copyright 1973 by George Weidenfeld & Nicolson Ltd., London. Used with permission. **Table 5.2:** Adapted from A. M. Weitenhoffer and E. R. Hilgard, "Stanford Hypnotic Susceptibility Scale." Copyright 1962 by Stanford University Press, Stanford, California Distributed by Consulting Psychologists Press. **Figure 5.24:** Don Hunstein/Photo Trends. **Figure 5.25:** Adapted from A. H. Buss, *Psychology — man in perspective.* Copyright 1973 by John Wiley & Sons. Used with permission. **Figure 5.26:** The National Gallery of Art, Washington, D.C., Chester Dale Collection, 1962. **Figure 5.27:** Courtesy the Institute for Parapsychology, Durham, North Carolina.

CHAPTER SIX

Figure 6.1: The Bettmann Archive. **Figure 6.5:** Adapted from M. Bass and C. L. Hull, "The irradiation of a tactile conditioned reflex in man." *Jounral of Comparative and Physiological Psychology.* Copyright by the American Psychological Association. Used with permission. **Figure 6.7:** Composite curve from research of Wolfle and of Spooner and Kellogg. Adapted from A. Spooner and M. Kellogg, "The backward conditioning curve." *American Journal of*

lanti Press. **Figure 8.9:** Courtesy Noel Schwartz. **Figure 8.11:** Adapted from J. Shields, *Monozygotic twins.* Copyright 1962 by Oxford University Press. Used with permission. **Figure 8.12:** Courtesy J. R. Rosenzweig, University of California, Berkeley. From E. L. Bennett, et al. *Science 146:* 610–619, 1964. Copyright 1964 by the American Association for the Advancement of Science.

CHAPTER NINE

Figure 9.1 A: Brown Brothers. **Figure 9.1 B:** The Bettmann Archive. **Figure 9.1 C:** United Press International. **Figure 9.1 D:** Historical Pictures. **Figure 9.2 A:** Hans Namuth. **Figure 9.2 B:** Martha Swope. **Figure 9.2 C:** Collection of American Literature, Beinecke Rare Book and Manuscript Library, Yale University. **Figure 9.2 C:** Barrington Brown/Camera Press-Transworld Feature Syndicate. **Figure 9.4:** Adapted from J. P. Houston and S. A. Mednick, "Creativity and the need for novelty." *Journal of Abnormal and Social Psychology,* 66, 137–141. Copyright 1963 by the American Psychological Association. Used with permission. **Figure 9.5:** Reproduced by special permission from Welsh Figure Preference Test by George S. Welsh, Ph.D. Copyright 1949 by Consulting Psychologists Press, Inc. **Quotation pages 303–304:** From K. C. Briggs and I. B. Myers, *Myers-Briggs type indicator.* Copyright 1968 by Educational Testing Service, Princeton, N.J. **Figure 9.6:** Courtesy Richard A. Crutchfield, Institute of Personality Assessment and Research, University of California, Berkeley. **Figure 9.7 A:** The Tate Gallery, London. **Figure 9.7 B:** Courtesy The Brooklyn Museum, Frank C. Babbott & A. Augustus Healy Funds. **Figure 9.10:** Adapted from Karl Duncker, "On problem solving," *Psychological Monographs,* 58, No. 5. Whole No. 270. Copyright 1945 by American Psychological Association. Used with permission. **Figure 9.11:** Courtesy Deafness Research & Training Center, New York University School of Education. **Figure 9.12:** Courtesy Beatrice T. Gardner, University of Nevada, Reno. **Table 9.4 and Figure 9.13:** Adapted from G. A. Miller, "Some psychological studies of grammar." *American Psychologist,* 17, 748–762. Copyright 1962 by American Psychological Association. Used with permission.

CHAPTER TEN

Figure 10.1 A: Historical Pictures Service. **Figure 10.1 B:** Courtesy Albert Bandura, Stanford University. **Figure 10.1 C:** Courtesy University of Waterloo, Ontario, Canada. **Quotation page 344:** From G. Blum and D. Miller, "Exploring the psychoanalytic theory of oral character." *Journal of Personality,* 20, 287–304. **Figure 10.2:** Courtesy Albert Bandura, Stanford University. **Figure 10.3:** Courtesy Starke R. Hathaway. **Figure 10.4:** Reproduced by permission. Copyright 1943, renewed 1970 by the University of Minnesota. Published by The Psychological Corporation, New York, N.Y. All rights reserved. **Quotation pages 352–353:** From S. Hathaway and P. Meehl, *An atlas for the clinical use of the MMPI.* Copyright 1951 by the University of Minnesota Press, Minneapolis. **Figure 10.6:** Harvard University News Office. **Figure 10.7:** Copyright 1943 by the President and Fellows of Harvard College; 1971 by Henry A. Murray.

CHAPTER ELEVEN

Quotation page 363: From T. S. Lewinson, "Dynamic disturbances in the handwriting of psychotics." *American Journal of Psychiatry,* 97, 102–135. Copyright 1940 by the American Psychiatric Association. Reprinted by permission. **Figure 11.1:** A. E. Woolley. **Quotation pages 368–370, and 372:** From N. Cameron, *Personality development and psychopathology.* Copyright 1963 by Houghton Mifflin Company. Reprinted by permission. **Figure 11.2:** John Launois/Black Star. **Quotation pages 373–374:** From M. Zax and G. Stricker, *Patterns of psychopathology.* Copyright 1963 by the Macmillan Company. Reprinted by permission. **Quotation pages 375–377:** From E. B. McNeil, *The quiet furies: Man and disorder,* 85–85. Copyright 1967 by Prentice-Hall, Englewood Cliffs, N.J. Reprinted by permission. **Quotation page 379:** From T. Lidz, et al., "Differentiation and schizophrenic symptom formation in identical twins." *Journal of the American Psychoanalytic Association,* 10, 74–90. **Figure 11.3:** Charles Gatewood/Magnum. **Quotation pages 382–383:** From J. C. Coleman, *Abnormal psychology and modern life,* 4th Ed. Copyright 1972 by Scott, Foresman and Company. Reprinted by permission. **Quotation page 384:** From G. W. Kisker, *The disorganized personality,* 2nd Ed. Copyright 1972 by McGraw-Hill Book Company. Reprinted by permission. **Figure 11.4:** Bill Bridges/Globe Photos. **Figure 11.6:** Alan Grant. **Figure 11.7:** The Bettmann Archive. **Figure 11.8:** Ken Heyman. **Quotation pages 398–399:** From G. Bach, *Intensive group psychotherapy.* Copyright 1954 by Ronald Press.

CHAPTER TWELVE

Figure 12.1: Courtesy of The American Museum of Natural History. **Figure 12.2:** Courtesy Carnegie Institution of Washington. **Figure 12.3:** Wayne Miller/Magnum. **Figure 12.5:** Adapted from W. K. Frankenberg and J. B. Dodds, "The Denver development screening text." *Journal of Pediatrics,* 1967, 71, 181–191. **Figure 12.6:** Harry F. Harlow, University of Wisconsin Primate Laboratory. **Table 12.1:** Based on L. Kohlberg, "The child as moral philosopher." *Psychology Today,* September 1968. Copyright 1968 by Ziff-Davis Publishing Company. Table adapted from A. H. Buss, *Psychology—man in perspective.* Copyright 1973 by John Wiley & Sons. Used with permission.

CHAPTER THIRTEEN

Table 13.1 and quotation page 428: From R. B. Zajonc, "Attitudinal effects of mere exposure." *Journal of Personality and Social Psychology Monograph Supplement,* No. 2, Part 2. Copyright 1968 by the American Psychological Association. Reprinted by permission. **Focus 13.1:** Use of experiment courtesy R. B. Zajonc. **Quotation page 439:** From D. Papageorgis and W. J. McGuire, "The generality of immunity to persuasion produced by pre-exposure to weakened counter-argument." *Journal of Abnormal and Social* Psychology, 62, 475–481. Copyright 1961 by American Psychological Association. Reprinted by permission. **Figure 13.2:** George Roos. **Figure 13.3:** Elliot Erwitt/Magnum. **Table 13.2:** From T. W. Adorno, E. Frenkel-Brunswik, D. J. Levinson, and R. N. Sanford, The authoritarian personality. Copyright 1950 by Harper & Row. **Quotation page 450:** From M. Deutsch and M. E. Collins, *Interracial housing.* Copyright 1951 by the University of Minnesota Press, Minneapolis. Reprinted by permission. **Quotation page 453:** From J. Farmer, "The shock of black recognition." *Esquire,* 71 (5), 139.

CHAPTER FOURTEEN

Quotation pages 457, 460–461, 462, 463: From S. Milgram "Behavioral study of obedience. *Journal of Abnormal and Social Psychology,* 67, 371–378. Copyright 1963 by American Psychological Association. Reprinted by permission. **Figure 14.1:** Copyright 1965 by Stanley Milgram. From the film "Obedience," distributed by the New York University Film Library. **Figure 14.4:** Jim Jowers/Nancy Palmer. **Figure 14.5:** From J. M. Darley and B. Latané, "Bystander intervention in emergencies: Defusion of responsibility." *Journal of Personality and Social Psychology,* 8, 377–383. Copyright 1968 by the American Psychological Association. Reprinted by permission.

CHAPTER FIFTEEN

Quotation pages 481–482: From S. Schachter, *The psychology of affiliation.* Copyright 1959 by Stanford University Press, Stanford, California. **Table 5.1 and Figure 15.2:** Adapted from L. Berkowitz "Group standards, cohesiveness, and productivity." *Human Relations,* 7, 509–519. Copyright 1954 by Plenum Publishing Corporation. Used with permission. **Figure 15.3:** Marion Faller/Monkmeyer. **Figure 15.4:** From A. Bavelas, A. H. Hastorf, A. E.

Gross, and W. R. Kite, "Experiments on the alteration of group structure." *Journal of Experimental Social Psychology,* 1965, 1, 55–70. Copyright 1965 by American Psychological Association. Reprinted by permission. **Figure 15.6:** William Vandivert. **Figure 15.7:** Charles Moore/Black Star. **Quotation page 493 and Table 15.2:** From S. Schachter, "Deviation, rejection, and communication." *Journal of Abnormal and Social Psychology,* 46, 190–207. Copyright 1951 by American Psychological Association. Reprinted by permission. **Quotation pages 494–497:** N. Kogan and M. A. Wallach, "Risk taking as a function of the situation, the person, and the group." *New Directions in Psychology,* 3, 111–278. **Figure 15.8:** Philip Jones Griffiths/Magnum.

CHAPTER SIXTEEN

Figure 16.1 (top): Eugene Gordon/Nancy Palmer. **Figure 16.1 (bottom):** Francisco Erize/ Bruce Coleman. **Figure 16.2 (top):** Wide World Photos. **Figure 16.2 (bottom):** United Press International. **Figures 16.7 and 16.8:** From M. Deutsch and R. M. Krauss, "The effect of threat upon interpersonal bargaining." *Journal of Abnormal and Social Psychology,* 61, 181–189. Copyright 1960 by The American Psychological Association. Reprinted by permission. **Figure 16.9:** Courtesy Robert Noel, University of California, Santa Barbara, and Wayman J. Crow, Western Behavioral Sciences Institute. From "The valid use of simulation results," Western Behavioral Sciences Institute Study. **Figure 16.10:** From W. J. Crow, "A study of strategic doctrines using the inter-nation simulation." *Journal of Conflict Resolution,* 1963, 7, 580–589.

COLOR PLATES

Figure 5.16: Courtesy Eastman Kodak Company, "The Gift of Color" Exhibition. **Figure 5.19:** Courtesy Dr. Henry Crawford and Eastman Kodak Company, "The Gift of Color" Exhibition. **Figure 9.16:** Courtesy Eastman Kodak Company, "Gift of Color" Exhibition. **Figure 10.8:** Hans Huber, Berne, Switzerland. **Figure 11.5:** Guttmann Maclay Collection, Institute of Psychiatry, London.

Glossary and Index

electrical stimulation, 73, 75
evolution of, 67
localization of, 71
pain center, 74
research methods, 75
speech center, 72
Brain stem, 68, 69
Brainwashing, 434–436
Bystander apathy, 464, 472–473

Cannon-Bard theory of emotion, 114
Case study (or clinical method): Method of gathering information about the life history of a person or of a group, 538–539
Causality, 525–526, 545
Cell division, 40
Central nervous system (CNS), 68–69
Central tendency: The score around which most other scores cluster in a frequency distribution, such as the mean or median, 541–542
Cephalocaudal sequence of maturation: Refers to the progression of the infant's development from head to foot (*cephalo* meaning "head" and *caudal* meaning "tail"), 414
Cerebellum: A part of the brain that coordinates voluntary movements, body balance, and muscle tone, 68
Cerebral cortex: The surface layers of the cerebrum which are involved with higher mental processes such as speech, learning, problem solving, perception, and movement, 67, 138, 142–144
Cerebral dominance, 58
Cerebrum: Main portion of the brain consisting of a left and right hemisphere, 67–69
Childhood (*see* also Development):
autism, 386
birth order, 418–419
birth process, 410–415
creativity training, 306–307
dependency, 344–345

language, 328–329
motor development, 412–415
rewards and punishment (*see* Socialization)
self-concept, 57
sex role development, 127–129
Chlorpromazine, 65
Chomsky's theory of language, 326
Chromosomes: Structures that contain hereditary information and that are found in the nucleus of every cell, half of which are contributed by each parent to the offspring, 29, 37, 39, 40, 44, 407
Chronological age, 261
Chunking: An active process of organizing information into meaningful units, or "chunks," that are easily remembered, 234
Circular reasoning, 528
Clairvoyance, 182
Classical conditioning: Can be described as learning through stimulus substitution so that the functions of the original unconditioned stimulus (UCS) are acquired by the new, conditioned stimulus (CS) by repeated associations (*see also* Conditioning; Discrimination; Extinction; Generalization; Spontaneous recovery), 189–200
adaptive significance, 200
of emotional responses, 197
experimental neurosis, 199
Client-centered therapy, 390–392
Clinical method (*see* Case study)
Clinical psychologist: A psychologist who has been specially trained to treat emotional and behavioral disorders, 23, 386
Closure: A principle of perception that states that figures with gaps in them tend to be filled in and perceived as a whole, 158
Cocaine, 86
Cochlea, 145, 147
Codeine, 86

Name Index

Sarnoff A. Mednick received his B.S. from The City College of New York, his M.A. from Columbia University, and his Ph.D. from Northwestern University. He has published widely in the areas of stimulus generalization, schizophrenia, and thinking. He is Director of the Psykologisk Institut, Kommunehospitalet, Copenhagen, and concurrently Professor of Psychology at the New School for Social Research. In 1972 he was the recipient of the Stanley R. Dean Award.

Jerry Higgins is Associate Professor of Psychology at the University of California, Santa Barbara. From 1973 to 1975 he was on leave as Director of the University of California Tokyo Study Center. He received his B.A. from the University of Toronto and his M.A. and Ph.D. degrees from the University of Michigan. His major areas of research and publication include schizophrenia, creativity, and memory.

Jack Kirschenbaum has a B.A. from the University of California at Los Angeles, an M.A. from California State University, Los Angeles, and a Ph.D. from the Claremont Graduate School. At Fullerton College, where he teaches psychology, his interest in innovative methods of teaching has led him to develop a computerized testing service and test data bank. Outside the college he has been a consultant on the development of computer programs in education and testing.